Civilian Protection in Armed Conflict

This is not an official publication of the United States Military Academy, Department of the Army, or Department of Defense. The views expressed in this volume represent the authors' personal views and do not necessarily reflect those of the Department of Defense, the United States Army, the United States Military Academy, or any other department or agency of the United States Government. The analysis presented stems from their academic research of publicly available sources, not from protected operational information.

The Lieber Studies is the flagship publication of the Lieber Institute for Law and Warfare. It is designed to provide scholars, practitioners, and students with in-depth and critical analysis of the most challenging legal issues related to warfare in the 21st Century. Established by the Department of Law of the United States Military Academy at West Point, the mission of the Lieber Institute is to foster a deeper understanding of the complex and evolving relationship between law and land warfare in order to educate and empower current and future combat leaders. It does so through global academic engagement and advanced interdisciplinary research. As such, it lies at the crossroads of scholarship and practice by bringing together scholars, military officers, government legal advisers, and members of civil society from around the world to collaboratively examine the role and application of the law of armed conflict in current and future armed conflicts, as well as that of other regimes of international law in situations threatening international peace and security.

Lieber Institute for Law and Warfare

The Lieber Studies

VOLUME 11

Civilian Protection in Armed Conflict

Select Issues

General Editors

PROFESSOR MICHAEL N. SCHMITT

PROFESSOR SEAN WATTS

Managing Editor

PROFESSOR ROBERT LAWLESS

Volume Editors

JELENA PEJIC

CAPTAIN MARGARET KOTLIK

OXFORD
UNIVERSITY PRESS

OXFORD
UNIVERSITY PRESS

Oxford University Press is a department of the University of Oxford.
It furthers the University's objective of excellence in research, scholarship,
and education by publishing worldwide. Oxford is a registered trade mark of
Oxford University Press in the UK and certain other countries.

Published in the United States of America by Oxford University Press
198 Madison Avenue, New York, NY 10016, United States of America.

Library of Congress Cataloging-in-Publication Data
Names: Pejic, Jelena, editor. | Kotlik, Margaret, editor.
Title: Civilian protection in armed conflict : select issues /
[edited by] Jelena Pejic, Margaret Kotlik.
Description: New York : Oxford University Press, 2025. |
Series: Lieber studies series | Includes bibliographical references and index.
Identifiers: LCCN 2024056758 | ISBN 9780197793176 (hardback) |
ISBN 9780197793183 (epub) | ISBN 9780197793190 (updf) | ISBN 9780197793206 (online)
Subjects: LCSH: Combatants and noncombatants (International law) |
War—Protection of civilians. | Civilians in war. | Humanitarian law.
Classification: LCC KZ6515 .C597 2025 | DDC 341.6/7—dc23/eng/20241125
LC record available at https://lccn.loc.gov/2024056758

DOI: 10.1093/oso/9780197793176.001.0001

Printed by Marquis Book Printing, Canada

Note to Readers
This publication is designed to provide accurate and authoritative information in regard to the subject matter covered. It is based upon sources believed to be accurate and reliable and is intended to be current as of the time it was written. It is sold with the understanding that the publisher is not engaged in rendering legal, accounting, or other professional services. If legal advice or other expert assistance is required, the services of a competent professional person should be sought. Also, to confirm that the information has not been affected or changed by recent developments, traditional legal research techniques should be used, including checking primary sources where appropriate.

(Based on the Declaration of Principles jointly adopted by a Committee of the American Bar Association and a Committee of Publishers and Associations.)

CONTENTS

FOREWORD[1]

This volume in the *Lieber Studies* series is the next step in fostering a "deeper understanding of the complex and evolving relationship between law and war" central to the Lieber Institute's mission. Such an understanding could not be of greater importance than as applied to the protection of civilians, the subject of this volume, "Civilian Protection in Armed Conflict: Select Issues." History and temporal experiences graphically illustrate the unfortunate reality when actors on the battlefield have failed to understand the requirement of civilian protection. And without that understanding, the future looks equally bleak.

No responsible nation seeks armed conflict, in urban areas or anywhere else. While we stand ready to fight and win our Nation's wars when necessary, the goal of the United States Department of Defense is to provide the military forces to *deter* war. That deterrence necessitates organizing, equipping, and training the military. It also entails planning for the conduct of hostilities, including the protection of civilians. This volume and the larger series are critical to succeeding at that.

The business of predictions, especially about warfare, is always a fraught enterprise. We know, however, with certainty, that destruction of the enemy's army on an insular battlefield is no longer the sole objective, and thus geography and demographics must inform our planning and training. In short, where people will live and where militaries are likely to operate—in highly and densely populated, urban environments—reflect the need for increased consideration of protection of civilians.

Through the Civilian Harm Mitigation and Response Action Plan, the United States is in the process of creating new institutions and processes to enhance the ability to mitigate civilian harm during military operations. Through continued learning, this approach will enhance our assessments of future battlespaces to minimize civilian harm and our ability to effectively respond and more fulsomely investigate when allegations of civilian harm arise.

1. At the time of writing, Major General Joseph B. Berger III was the Deputy Judge Advocate General of the United States Army.

Protecting civilians is a core component of the law of war, which, in regulating the conduct of hostilities seeks to limit its effects toward, among others, those not taking part in the conflict and safeguard civilians in enemy hands. The protection of civilians during armed conflict remains a moral, political, and legal priority for the United States. As an Army technical publication explains, "[c]ommunities on the ground and around the world expect Army units and Soldiers to protect the population. Failure to do so jeopardizes the credibility and legitimacy of the operation and undermines other objectives."[2]

The topics in this volume, which comprises eighteen chapters covering a range of diverse issues, all help facilitate reflection and planning necessary to meet such expectations by responsible nations. The authors provide, inter alia, perspectives on the protection of unprivileged belligerents and of civilians in the invasion phase of international armed conflict. They deal with humanitarian corridors, the "screening" of civilians on the move, and civilian data protection as an evolving area of research and reflection. The unique challenges of those forcibly conscripted are addressed, as is the prohibition of deportation in the law of armed conflict. The effects of extraterritorial data migration on civilian protection are examined, helping the reader better understand, and thus better plan for, minimizing the impact of cyber operations on an inextricably digitally connected population and their infrastructure. And the authors help the reader think through investigations when that detailed planning fails, while managing the dead and preventing the missing. Gender-related and environmental concerns that may arise in war are likewise discussed.

Interpreting the law of war plays a significant role, both in the conduct of military operations and in this volume of the *Studies*. It remains fundamentally necessary to recognize that those interpretations can and do vary based on facts and context, with results which often defy responsible, detailed planning. That's not meant in evaluative terms, that is, *what* to think of a given chapter, but rather as a suggestion that readers differentiate in *how* they think about a given chapter.

In the conduct of military operations, military lawyers rely on *lex lata*, the law as it exists. In this volume, some authors challenge the reader to consider *lex ferenda*, the law as it could be.

Similarly, military lawyers are generally focused on identifying a "workable" interpretation of a given law of armed conflict provision, sometimes under time-compressed circumstances, and in support of military decision-making that yields consistent answers regardless of the type or characterization of the battlefield. In comparison, some chapters engage in the impressive, methodical research needed to try and identify the "perfect" interpretation divorced from other factors.

I am confident that readers will find the chapters thought and discussion provoking, and I strongly urge both.

This volume of the *Lieber Series* is particularly well timed. It will not only help foster a deeper understanding of the relationship between law and war, it will also

2. ATP 3-07.6 Army Techniques Publication (*ATP*) 3-07.6, Protection of Civilians.

serve as an important academic contribution to continued learning on protection of civilians.

I congratulate the Lieber Institute, the volume editors, and the chapter authors for this powerful intellectual contribution to a broader understanding of protection of civilians.

Major General Joseph B. Berger III
Judge Advocate General
United States Army

PREFACE

Civilian protection in armed conflict is a vast area in both legal and practical terms. The phrase evokes images of civilians and/or civilian infrastructure damaged in the conduct of hostilities. The scenarios less seen in the public eye are ones in which the need for civilian protection nevertheless equally arises—when civilians have fallen or are likely to fall into enemy hands. *Some* of these protections and the legal issues they generate (hence the qualifier "select" in the title) are the focus of this book.

The topics were chosen with two considerations in mind. First, to explore certain subjects along the possible timeline of a civilian's real-life contact with the adverse party. This can happen already in the invasion phase of an international armed conflict; when civilians are screened at a checkpoint; when a house is searched; or when they are detained. The book's timeline thus spans the duration of an armed conflict and runs through to military investigations into possible violations, war crimes prosecutions, and redress to civilians.

The second consideration was to provide analyses of a few longstanding, current, or emerging issues of civilian protection. The aim was to reflect on certain legal and practical challenges resulting from a lack of agreement by the relevant actors on how the law is to be interpreted, with, it must be acknowledged, nefarious consequences for the protection of civilians. In other cases, the goal was to provide a reminder of certain legal issues that have arisen against the backdrop of ongoing armed conflicts, both international and non-international. In still others, the purpose was to shed light on the impact of new technologies on civilians, and to likewise expand the legal horizon to encompass environmental concerns, gender considerations, and forensic science as areas essential to comprehensive civilian protection.

It should be stressed that the topics of the separate chapters were identified based on legal challenges experienced or observed by the editors of the volume, and the authors, in military operations on the ground. It is thus hoped that the book may be of interest to not only academics and students of the law but also to military legal advisors, practitioners, commanders, and policymakers alike.

This volume is the outcome of discussions among the contributors gathered for the Annual Workshop of the Lieber Institute for Law and Warfare held at the United States Military Academy at West Point in November 2023. The authors submitted their chapters in advance, which enabled an exchange of views on each of the topics and served as guidance for subsequent revisions of the texts. While the book is a collection of submissions, it does not and may not be taken to reflect collective agreement on the views expressed in each chapter, which remains the responsibility of the individual contributor.

The editors would like to most warmly thank all the authors represented in the book, whose expertise, time, dedication, and goodwill enabled the production of the book. Their collaboration at the November 2023 Workshop and later, with the editors, was marked by a spirit of friendliness, thus greatly reducing the inevitable stress involved in the preparation of such a volume.

The editors would also like to sincerely thank Brigadier General Shane Reeves, Dean of the United States Military Academy, for his unfailing support to the Lieber Institute and the annual workshops, as well as to Colonel Winston Williams, Professor and Head of the Department of Law at the Academy, for keeping a watchful eye on the process.

The book could not have been completed without the gentle guidance of the General Editors of the *Lieber Studies*, Professors Sean Watts and Michael N. Schmitt, and to them a huge debt of gratitude is owed as well. Last but not least, the editors of this volume would like to thank Professor Robert Lawless who, as Managing Editor of the *Lieber Studies*, helped bring it across the finish line.

Jelena Pejic
Nonresident Senior Fellow at the Lieber Institute
for Law and Warfare at the United States Military Academy
and the Institute's Lieber Scholar for 2023. Former Senior
Legal Advisor with the International Committee
of the Red Cross (ICRC) in Geneva

Margaret Kotlik
Captain, United States Army, Judge Advocate
Assistant Professor in the Department of Law and
Philosophy at the United States Military Academy

TABLE OF CASES

INTERNATIONAL COURTS

African Commission on Human and Peoples' Rights

Court of Justice of the European Union

Eritrea-Ethiopia Claims Commission

European Court of Human Rights

European Court of Justice

Extraordinary Chambers in the Courts of Cambodia

Human Rights Committee

Inter-American Commission on Human Rights

Inter-American Court of Human Rights

International Arbitration Awards

International Court of Justice

International Criminal Court

International Criminal Tribunal for the former Yugoslavia

International Criminal Tribunal for Rwanda

Iran–United States Claims Tribunal

Permanent Court of International Justice

Special Court for Sierra Leone

United Nations War Crimes Commission

U.S. Military Tribunal

National Courts

Columbia

Germany

Israel

Japan

Kosovo

Nepal

Netherlands

New Zealand

United Kingdom

United States

TABLE OF TREATIES

AFRICAN UNION

COUNCIL OF EUROPE

EUROPEAN UNION

GENEVA CONVENTIONS AND ADDITIONAL PROTOCOLS

HAGUE CONVENTIONS AND REGULATIONS

ORGANIZATION OF AMERICAN STATES

UN GENERAL ASSEMBLY (UNGA)

UN SECURITY COUNCIL (UNSC)

OTHER TREATIES

OTHER INSTRUMENTS

CONTRIBUTORS*

Lieutenant General Joseph B. Berger III is the Judge Advocate General of the U.S. Army.

Lieutenant Colonel W. Casey Biggerstaff is an Academy Professor in the Department of Law and Philosophy at the United States Military Academy.

Russell Buchan is a Professor of International Law at the University of Reading, United Kingdom.

Tom Dannenbaum is an Associate Professor of International Law at the Fletcher School of Law & Diplomacy, where he is also Co-Director of the Center for International Law & Governance.

Colonel Nathalie Durhin is a French Air Force Legal Advisor, and a Faculty Advisor within the French War College (Ecole de Guerre) in Paris, France.

Julia Grignon is the Research Director of the Institute for Strategic Research of the French Military Academy, a Member of the Paris Human Rights Center at Assas University, and a Visiting Professor of the Faculty of Law at Laval University (Canada).

Jann K. Kleffner is a Professor of International Law at the Swedish Defence University, Extraordinary Professor at the Faculty of Law of the University of Pretoria, South Africa, and Senior Fellow at Melbourne Law School, Australia.

Captain Margaret Kotlik is an Assistant Professor in the Department of Law and Philosophy at the United States Military Academy and a Judge Advocate in the U.S. Army.

David Kretzmer is a Professor Emeritus of International Law at the Hebrew University of Jerusalem.

Kubo Mačák is a Professor of International Law at the University of Exeter, United Kingdom.

* The Contributors' affiliations are listed as of the time of writing.

Jennifer Maddocks is an Assistant Professor in the Department of Law and Philosophy at the United States Military Academy.

Michael W. Meier is an adjunct Professor of Law at Georgetown University School of Law and the former Senior Civilian Adviser for the U.S. Army Judge Advocate General.

Fionnuala Ní Aoláin is University Regents Professor; holder of the Robina Chair in Law, Public Policy, and Society; and faculty director of the Human Rights Center at Minnesota Law School. She is concurrently a Professor of Law at the Queen's University of Belfast, School of Law and a K.C. (Hons).

Kosuke Onishi is a Legal Adviser at the ICRC Regional Delegation for the United States & Canada.

Valerie Oosterveld is a Professor at Western University's Faculty of Law, Canada, and the Western Research Chair in International Criminal Justice.

Jelena Pejic is a nonresident Senior Fellow at the Lieber Institute for Law and Warfare at the United States Military Academy and was the Institute's Lieber Scholar for 2023. She is a former Senior Legal Advisor with the ICRC in Geneva.

Ellen Policinski is a Legal Adviser on the Commentaries Update Project with the ICRC.

Marco Sassòli is a Professor of International Law at the University of Geneva, Switzerland.

Michael N. Schmitt is the G. Norman Lieber Distinguished Scholar at West Point's Lieber Institute; Professor of Public International Law at the University of Reading (UK); Professor Emeritus and Charles H. Stockton Distinguished Scholar-in-Residence at the United States Naval War College; and Strauss Center Distinguished Scholar and Visiting Professor of Law at the University of Texas.

Lakmini Seneviratne is the Legal Adviser and Head of the Legal Department at the ICRC Regional Delegation for the United States & Canada, based in Washington, D.C.

Morris Tidball-Binz is the UN Special Rapporteur on Extrajudicial, Summary or Arbitrary Executions.

Leah West is an Associate Professor of International Affairs at the Norman Paterson School of International Affairs at Carleton University.

Marten Zwanenburg is a Professor of Military Law at the University of Amsterdam and at the Faculty of Military Sciences of the Netherlands Defence Academy.

PART ONE

Foundational Issues

1

The Protection of Civilians During the Invasion Phase of an International Armed Conflict

MICHAEL W. MEIER*

1. INTRODUCTION

In February 2022, Russia unlawfully invaded Ukraine, and Europe found itself embroiled in the largest armed conflict on its soil since World War II.[1] Some Russian forces entered Ukraine through Belarus and began to push their way toward the Ukrainian capital, Kyiv. On February 27, Russian forces entered the city of Bucha, an outlying area of Kyiv, and remained there until driven out by Ukrainian forces on April 1, 2022.

Although the town's mayor alleged that war crimes were being committed in Bucha, it was not until after the Russian withdrawal that video footage showed the full extent of potential war crimes.[2] There were reports of civilians left dead on the road and the discovery of an apparent "execution chamber" in the basement of a

* Michael W. Meier is an adjunct Professor of Law at Georgetown University School of Law and the former Senior Civilian Adviser for the U.S. Army Judge Advocate General.

1. *Russia's War in Ukraine: Insights from RAND*, RAND, https://www.rand.org/latest/russia-ukraine.html.

2. Simon Gardner, *Ukrainian Mayor Shows Dead Bodies Amid Battle-Scarred City of Bucha*, REUTERS (Apr. 3, 2022), https://www.reuters.com/world/europe/ukrainian-mayor-shows-dead-bodies-liberated-city-bucha-2022-04-03/.

Michael W. Meier, *The Protection of Civilians During the Invasion Phase of an International Armed Conflict*
In: *Civilian Protection in Armed Conflict*. Edited by: Jelena Pejic and Captain Margaret Kotlik,
Oxford University Press. © Michael W. Meier 2025. DOI: 10.1093/oso/9780197793176.003.0001

house.[3] Footage showed dead bodies with their hands bound, victims seemingly executed summarily by gunshots, and allegations of torture and rape. The death toll in Bucha was estimated to be over 300 civilians.[4]

Reports of Russian atrocities were not limited to the town of Bucha. In April 2022, Human Rights Watch (HRW) documented cases of possible war crimes in Chernihiv, Kharkiv, and the Kyiv regions of Ukraine, which included allegations of rape, torture, summary executions, enforced disappearances, unlawful killing of civilians, violence and threats against civilians, as well as the looting of civilian property.[5] According to Hugh Williamson, HRW's Europe and Central Asia Director, "the cases we documented amount to unspeakable, deliberate cruelty and violence against Ukrainian civilians. Rape, murder, and other violent acts against people in the Russian forces' custody should be investigated as war crimes."[6]

The U.S. Department of State assessed there were credible reports that Russia engaged in indiscriminate attacks and attacks that deliberately targeted civilians. There were documented reports that Russian forces destroyed apartment buildings, schools, hospitals, and other civilian infrastructure across Ukraine. The State Department estimated that over 2,400 civilians were killed in Mariupol, including in strikes against a maternity hospital and theater that had clearly been marked with the word "children" visible from the air.[7] This led U.S. Secretary of State, Antony J. Blinken, to announce that the U.S. government assessed Russian forces had committed war crimes in Ukraine and that it would continue to track reports of further war crimes in Ukraine.[8]

The most appropriate starting point for analyzing the protections civilians will receive in the invasion phase of an international armed conflict is the 1949 Geneva Convention relative to the Protection of Civilian Persons in Time of War (GC IV).[9] However, the treaty does not provide protections for all civilians, so one must look to Article 4 to determine which civilians are considered "protected persons."

3. Cara Anna, *War Crimes Watch: A Devastating Walk Through Bucha's Horror*, AP News (Apr. 10, 2022), https://apnews.com/article/russia-ukraine-europe-war-crimes-7791e247ce7087ddd f64a2bbdcc5b888.

4. *Id.*

5. Human Rights Watch, *Ukraine: Russian Forces' Trail of Death in Bucha*, Human Rights Watch (Apr. 21, 2022), https://www.hrw.org/news/2022/04/21/ukraine-russian-for ces-trail-death-bucha.

6. Human Rights Watch, *Ukraine: Apparent War Crimes in Russia-Controlled Areas*, Human Rights Watch (Apr. 3, 2022), https://www.hrw.org/news/2022/04/03/ukraine-apparent-war-crimes-russia-controlled-areas.

7. Antony J. Blinken, *War Crimes by Russia's Forces in Ukraine*, U.S. Department of State (Mar. 23, 2022), https://www.state.gov/war-crimes-by-russias-forces-in-ukraine/.

8. *Id.*

9. Convention (IV) Relative to the Protection of Civilian Persons in Time of War, Aug. 12, 1949, 6 U.S.T. 3516, 75 U.N.T.S. 287 [hereinafter GC IV].

Article 4 of GC IV defines persons protected by the Convention as "those who at a given moment and in any manner whatsoever, find themselves, in case of a conflict or occupation, in the hands of a Party to the conflict or Occupying Power of which they are not nationals."[10] Although Article 4 may appear on its face to be broad in application, it also specifically excludes from the Convention's personal scope certain categories of individuals, essentially based on their nationality. According to the International Committee of the Red Cross (ICRC) 1958 Commentary to GC IV, there are two main classes of protected persons under the Convention: "(1) enemy nationals within the national territory of each of the Parties to the conflict and (2) the whole population of occupied territories (excluding nationals of the Occupying Power). The other distinctions and exceptions extend or restrict these limits, but not to any appreciable extent."[11]

Certain States, including the United States, have taken a restrictive view of Article 4. The *Department of Defense Law of War Manual* (DoD LOWM), in Section 10.3.2.2, states that "[t]o be entitled to the protections provided under [GC IV] for 'protected persons,' a person must be located in either (1) occupied territory or (2) the home territory of a party to the conflict."[12] Under this narrow interpretation, in the scenario discussed previously, outside of Crimea and other territories currently occupied by Russia, only Ukrainian civilians in Russia or Russian civilians in Ukraine would be "protected persons" under GC IV and receive the protections of the Convention.

Why is being considered a "protected person" important? Apart from the obvious—which is that such status entitles persons to the considerable safeguards of GC IV—it is because only individuals who commit unlawful acts against "protected persons" constituting "grave breaches" of the Convention can be held criminally responsible under the principle of universal jurisdiction. Parties to the Conventions are obligated to search for persons alleged to have ordered or committed "grave breaches" under Article 147[13] and to bring them, regardless of nationality, before their own courts or extradite them to another State.[14]

10. *Id.*, art. 4.

11. Oscar M. Uhler et al., Commentary to Geneva Convention Relative to the Protections of Civilian Persons in Time of War 46 (1958) [hereinafter GC IV Commentary].

12. Office of the General Counsel, U.S. Department of Defense, Law of War Manual § 10.3.2.2. (rev. ed., July 2023) [hereinafter DoD LOWM].

13. GC IV, *supra* note 9, art. 147. Article 147 defines a grave breach as follows: "Grave breaches [] shall be those involving any of the following acts, if committed against persons or property protected by the present Convention: wilful killing, torture or inhuman treatment, including biological experiments, wilfully causing great suffering or serious injury to body or health, unlawful deportation or transfer or unlawful confinement of a protected person, compelling a protected person to serve in the forces of a hostile Power, or wilfully depriving a protected person of the rights of fair and regular trial prescribed in the present Convention, taking of hostages and extensive destruction and appropriation of property, not justified by military necessity and carried out unlawfully and wantonly."

14. GC IV, *supra* note 9, art. 146.

This chapter will consider which civilians are considered "protected persons" under GC IV. If the definition of "protected persons" is as restrictive as found in the DoD LOWM, then Ukrainian civilians who did not take a direct part in hostilities and were killed in Bucha and other parts of Ukraine during the invasion phase would not be considered protected persons, and certain unlawful acts against them would not be considered "grave breaches" of the Fourth Convention. This chapter will: (1) provide an overview of GC IV and its protections; (2) consider the "nationality" component of Article 4; (3) analyze whether the United States' narrow interpretation is the correct one; and (4) discuss the protection of civilians since the adoption of GC IV.

2. OVERVIEW OF GC IV AND ITS PROTECTIONS

The 1949 Geneva Conventions are considered a milestone in the development of the law of armed conflict (LOAC), also known as international humanitarian law (IHL). These Conventions, which were adopted after the widespread suffering of civilians and other war victims in World War II, marked a shift from instruments such as the Hague Regulations[15] dealing mainly with the belligerent relations between States to agreements focused on humanitarian protections for the victims of armed conflict.[16] Noted scholar Richard Baxter explained that GC IV, which contains 159 articles, provides different protections for different groups of people. For example, there are general protections covering the entire populations of the countries in conflict against certain consequences of war. Other protections are contained in provisions common to the territories of the parties to the conflict. Additional rules relate to aliens in the territory of a party to the conflict and to persons in occupied territories, respectively.[17]

There are four parts of GC IV. Part I, titled "General Provisions," includes some of the articles common to the Geneva Conventions (Articles 1–3), the definition of protected persons (Article 4), derogations from the definition of protected persons (Article 5), as well as other general articles covering special arrangements,[18]

15. Regulations Respecting the Laws and Customs of War on Land, annexed to Convention No. IV Respecting the Laws and Customs of War on Land, Oct. 18, 1907, 36 Stat. 2227, T.S. 539 [hereinafter Hague Regulations].

16. Sarina Landefeld, *The Changing Significance of Nationality for the Protection of Civilians in the Hands of a Party to an International Armed Conflict*, 28 Journal of Conflict & Security Law 501 (2023).

17. Richard R. Baxter, *The Geneva Conventions of 1949*, 62 International Law Studies Ser. U.S. Naval War College 220, 228 (1980).

18. GC IV, *supra* note 9, art. 7.

non-renunciation of rights,[19] protecting powers and the activities of the ICRC,[20] as well as conciliation procedures.[21]

Part II is titled "General Protection of Populations Against Certain Consequences of War." Article 13 specifies that its provisions cover "the whole of the populations of the countries in conflict, without any adverse distinction based, in particular, on race, nationality, religion or political opinion, and are intended to alleviate the sufferings caused by war."[22] It contains provisions related to the protection of hospitals and hospital staff, the wounded and sick, neutralized zones, medical transports and medical supplies, as well as measures related to child welfare, family news, and dispersed families.[23]

Part III of GC IV, titled "Status and Treatment of Protected Persons," contains the bulk of protections for "protected persons." Section I applies both to the "Territories of the Parties to the Conflict and to Occupied Territories." Baxter describes these provisions as "a bill of rights for enemy civilians in time of war."[24] Article 27 makes clear that protected persons are entitled "in all circumstances, to respect for their persons."[25] They must be treated humanely and protected against all acts or threats of violence. Women are protected against rape, indecent assault, and enforced prostitution. Article 33 prohibits collective punishments, pillage, and reprisals, and the taking of hostages is also forbidden.[26] Section I likewise makes clear that the presence of protected persons does not "render certain points or areas immune from military operations."[27]

Part III, Section II, applies to "Aliens in the Territory of a Party to the Conflict."[28] Although this section does not use the term "home territory," it is generally accepted that it relates to enemy aliens who might be the territory of a party to the conflict, such as an enemy alien in the United States during an international armed conflict or a Russian alien in the territory of Ukraine. It includes certain obligations that a party to the conflict could only comply with in its home territory, such as the right of a protected person to leave the territory,[29] repatriation,[30]

19. *Id.*, art. 8.

20. *Id.*, arts. 9–11.

21. *Id.*, art. 12.

22. *Id.*, art. 13.

23. *Id.*, arts. 14–26.

24. Baxter, *supra* note 17, at 228.

25. GC IV, *supra* note 9, art. 27.

26. *Id.*, art. 33.

27. *Id.*, art. 28.

28. *Id.* at § II.

29. *Id.*, art. 35.

30. *Id.*, art. 36.

employment,[31] internment,[32] and the transfer of protected persons to another power.[33]

Part III, Section III, contains the provisions applicable in occupied territory and provides certain obligations and rights of an occupying power. Section III is designed to fill in the gaps from Articles 42 to 56 of the Hague Regulations based on the comprehensive nature of the German occupation of several countries in Europe during World War II.[34] Joyce A.C. Gutteridge has noted that the provisions in Section III go "very far beyond" what is found in the Hague Regulations and wondered whether "they go too far" as regards the occupying power's rights in the administration of occupied territory.[35] Some of the protections of persons in occupied territory include prohibitions on forcible transfers or deportations,[36] compelling inhabitants to engage in military operations against their own country, or to perform work that is not necessary for the needs of the occupying power.[37]

Section IV covers the "Regulations for the Treatment of Internees," which are detailed provisions on civilian internment, whether in a party's own or in occupied territory. Covering twelve chapters (Articles 79–135), Section IV deals with places of internment, food and clothing, religious and physical activities, internee property, camp administration and discipline, relations with the exterior, transfers, death, and release from internment.[38] Section V, titled "Information Bureaux and Central Agency," establishes the official Information Bureaus responsible for receiving and transmitting information about protected persons in the power of parties to the conflict. It also requires the creation of a Central Information Agency for protected persons, in practice known as the Central Tracing Agency, which is part of the ICRC.[39]

Finally, Part IV, on the "Execution of the Convention," importantly contains the "grave breaches" provisions. Article 146 requires the High Contracting Parties to undertake to enact legislation necessary to provide effective penal sanctions for persons committing, or ordering to be committed, any grave breaches of GC IV, to search for such persons, and to bring such persons, regardless of their nationality, before their own courts. Article 146 also permits a High Contracting Party,

31. *Id.*, art. 40.

32. *Id.*, arts. 41–43.

33. *Id.*, art. 45.

34. Joyce A.C. Gutteridge, *The Geneva Conventions of 1949*, 26 British Yearbook of International Law 294, 322 (1949).

35. *Id.* at 325.

36. GC IV, *supra* note 9, art. 49.

37. *Id.*, art. 51.

38. *Id.* at § IV.

39. *Id.* at § V. *See also* ICRC Central Tracing Agency, *available at* https://missingpersons.icrc.org/directory/icrc-central-tracing-agency.

if it prefers, to hand such persons over for trial to another High Contracting Party concerned if such party has made out a prima facie case.[40]

2.1 The Nationality Component of Article 4

The adoption of the Fourth Geneva Convention was a defining moment in the development of LOAC because it was the first international instrument to expand on the very rudimentary protections for civilians that existed prior to 1949.[41] However, as Gutteridge has correctly pointed out, the "full title of [GC IV] is misleading. It is not, as might seem implied, a Convention for the protection of *all* civilians in *all* circumstances in time of war."[42] As already noted previously, Article 4 establishes nationality as an essential requirement for the Convention's personal scope of application. The treaty covers enemy nationals who find themselves in the adverse party's home territory or in occupied territory,[43] but expressly excludes (1) nationals of a State which is not bound by GC IV;[44] (2) nationals of a neutral State who find themselves in the territory of a belligerent State; (3) nationals of a co-belligerent State, while the State of which they are nationals has normal diplomatic representation with the State in whose hands they are; and (4) persons protected by the First, Second, or Third Geneva Convention.[45]

In this context it should be recalled for the sake of completeness that Article 5 of GC IV ("Derogations") provides for the possible loss of certain protections of GC IV if an individual is (1) definitely suspected of or engaged in activities hostile to the security of the State in its own territory; or (2) is detained in occupied territory as a spy or saboteur or under definite suspicion of activity hostile to the security of the occupying power.[46]

It is understandable that States were primarily concerned with enemy nationals in their home territory as part of the negotiations of GC IV. H.F. van Panhuys noted that "nationality acts as a presumption (rebuttable or not) of a disposition directed against the interest of the state; *enemy* nationality supposes *hostile* disposition."[47] During the negotiations of GC IV, it was emphasized that "[m]odern warfare does not take place on the battlefields alone; it also filters into the domestic life of the

40. GC IV, *supra* note 9, art. 146.

41. Landefeld, *supra* note 16, at 1.

42. Gutteridge, *supra* note 34, at 319.

43. *Id.* at 502.

44. This is no longer relevant as all States have ratified GC IV.

45. GC IV, *supra* note 9, art. 4.

46. *Id.*, art. 5.

47. H.F. van Panhuys, The Role of Nationality in International Law 115 (Leyden A.W. Sythoff ed., 1959) (emphasis in original).

belligerent."[48] Given that enemy nationals were perceived as security concerns for a State, GC IV regulated the possible security and control measures that could be applied to them because they were at risk for arbitrary acts and abuses of power.[49] In other words, GC IV was drafted, at least in part, to "prevent such people from becoming victims."[50]

But why make further distinctions based on nationality? To recall, under Article 4 the nationals of neutral and co-belligerent States are generally excluded from GC IV protections, while enjoying protected person status if normal diplomatic relations are disrupted. The exclusion derives from an understanding that such individuals retain the protection of their home State as long as it has continued relations with the State in which they find themselves.[51] At the Diplomatic Conference, this led some to argue that the text of GC IV offered "greater protections for enemy nationals than neutrals."[52] Sarina Landefeld interpreted the language of Article 4 regarding "normal diplomatic representation" as an indication that the drafters were more concerned with the relations between States than with whether a State can provide actual protections to the nationals in question.[53]

What about the exclusion of a State's own citizens from the protections of GC IV? This can be explained, at least in part, by the drafters not viewing these individuals as a security threat or in need of protection. Landefeld suggests that at the time the Convention was adopted, States generally assumed international legal obligations only with respect to aliens, while their own citizens were protected as part of a State's domestic law. The drafters felt that any attempt to do otherwise would be "contrary to international law and [that it would] indeed [be] difficult to conceive of a power assuming obligations towards its own nationals by treaty with a foreign Power."[54]

Although, as just explained, certain categories of persons were specifically excluded from the coverage of GC IV, an unresolved issue is what safeguards apply under GC IV to civilians in invaded territory. There are two main frameworks of protection. The first, mentioned previously, is set forth in Article 4(3) and "covers the whole of the populations" of the States in conflict. The second, which is the focus of this chapter, is who is a "protected person" under GC IV entitled to protection under some or all of the articles in Part III of the Convention. Certain States, including the United States, have taken a narrow view of "protected persons."

48. GC IV Commentary, *supra* note 11, at 232.

49. Landefeld, *supra* note 16, at 9.

50. *Id.*; GC IV Commentary, *supra* note 11, at 5.

51. Landefeld, *supra* note 16, at 14.

52. Final Record of the Diplomatic Conference of Geneva of 1949 (Vol. II (A), Federal Political Department 1950) 794.

53. Landefeld, *supra* note 16, at 14–15.

54. *Id.* at 12–13, *quoting* A. Krafft, *The Present Position of the Red Cross Geneva Convention*, 37 Trans Grotius Society 131, 141 (1951).

Therefore, for an individual to receive protected person status, they must be "either (1) foreign civilians who are in the territory of a party to the conflict when hostilities break out, or (2) civilians who are in occupied territory."[55] Under this interpretation, civilians who find themselves in invaded territory that is not yet occupied would not be considered "protected persons."

2.2 U.S. Interpretation of Article 4

The United States, at least since 2004, has taken a restrictive interpretation of "protected persons." The DoD LOWM states in Section 10.3.2.2:

> To be entitled to the protections provided under the GC for "protected persons," a person must be located in either (1) occupied territory or (2) the home territory of a party to the conflict. The references in the GC that limit the scope of protections for protected persons to those "in the territory of a Party to the conflict" refer to the home territory of the party to the conflict in whose hands the protected person finds himself or herself. For example, Section II of Part III of the GC, which applies to "Aliens in the Territory of a Party to the Conflict," addresses the protection of aliens present on the home territory of a party to the conflict in relation to that State.[56]

However, the United States has not always had such a narrow approach. *Army Field Manual* (FM) 27-10, published in 1956, appeared to take a broader view of protected persons, stating that, subject to the limitations in Article 5, "those protected by [GC IV] also include all persons who have engaged in hostile or belligerent conduct but who are not entitled to treatment as prisoners of war."[57] This was further explained in DA Pam. 27-161-2, which provides:

> The 1949 Convention manages to circumvent, in part, a reliance on the fact of occupation in order to afford protection to civilian persons. Civilian persons are protected who "at a given moment and any manner whatsoever, find themselves, in cases of a conflict or occupation, in the hands of a Party to the conflict or occupying Power of which they are not nationals." Therefore, in regard to the protection of persons, the narrow time and space requirements (during occupation) of the Hague Regulations are not applicable. An area need not be occupied. For general protection the person need only be "in the hands of a party to the conflict."[58]

55. *Id.*, *citing* ALLAN ROSAS, THE LEGAL STATUS OF PRISONERS OF WAR: A STUDY IN INTERNATIONAL LAW APPLICABLE IN ARMED CONFLICTS (1976).

56. DoD LOWM, *supra* note 12, at § 10.3.2.2.

57. Department of the Army, FM 27-10, The Law of Land Warfare, ¶ 247b (1956).

58. Department of the Army, DA PAM 27-161-2, at 161 (1962).

AR 27-161-2 also notes that Articles 27–34 (provisions common to the territories of the parties to the conflict) "apply to any area in which a protected person finds himself in the power of a party to the conflict, principally an enemy power."[59]

A primary reason for the narrow interpretation in the DoD LOWM is two Department of Justice Office of Legal Counsel (OLC) opinions issued in 2004 and 2005 that examined who were "protected persons" under GC IV in Iraq and Afghanistan. The first, authored in March 2004 by Professor Jack Goldsmith, titled "'Protected Person' Status in Occupied Iraq Under the Fourth Geneva Convention,"[60] established that the United States did not have treaty obligations under GC III for Al Qaeda members or operatives captured by U.S. forces in occupied Iraq as they did not meet the qualifications for enemy prisoners of war.[61] OLC also addressed whether those individuals would be entitled to protections under GC IV. It concluded that the "protections afforded to 'protected persons' by [GC IV] apply only to persons who 'find themselves' in occupied territory or in the home territory of party to the conflict."[62] This conclusion looked primarily at the narrower scope of application found in Part III of GC IV, especially Section II and Section III.

The Goldsmith opinion conceded that certain unprivileged belligerents (including Iraqi nationals) could be protected persons if they "find themselves" in Iraqi occupied territory.[63] However, any non-Iraqi Al Qaeda forces who decided to travel to Iraq to fight against U.S. forces did not "passively find themselves" in that country and would not be considered "protected persons."[64]

The second OLC memorandum, written in August 2005 (and only made public due to litigation), considered whether persons captured or detained in Afghanistan were "protected persons" under GC IV.[65] Authored by Howard C. Nielson, Jr., this memorandum focused on whether persons captured or detained by the United States in Afghanistan may be considered protected persons. As noted by

59. *Id.* at 133–34.

60. Memorandum from Assistant Attorney General Jack L. Goldsmith III to Alberto R. Gonzales, Counsel to the President, "Protected Person" Status in Occupied Iraq Under the Fourth Geneva Convention (Mar. 18, 2004), https://www.justice.gov/d9/olc/opinions/2004/03/31/op-olc-v028-p0035_0.pdf.

61. *Id.* at 35–36; *see* Beth Van Schaack, *Animating the U.S. War Crimes Act*, 97 International Law Studies 1565 (2021).

62. Memorandum from Assistant Attorney General Jack L. Goldsmith III, *supra* note 60, at 41–42.

63. *Id.* at 49; *see* Van Schaack, *supra* note 61, at 1566.

64. Memorandum from Assistant Attorney General Jack L. Goldsmith III, *supra* note 60, at 60.

65. Memorandum for the Files from Howard C. Nielson, Jr., Deputy Assistant Attorney General, Whether Persons Captured and Detained in Afghanistan are "Protected Persons" under the Fourth Geneva Convention (Aug. 5, 2005), *available at* https://www.justice.gov/sites/default/files/olc/legacy/2009/12/30/aclu-ii-080505.pdf.

Ambassador Beth Van Schaack, it is not clear why OLC issued this memorandum given that it was drafted more than three years after the international armed conflict in Afghanistan had ended.[66] She asserts it was less about Afghanistan, but rather "geared toward subsequent [international armed conflicts] while also laying the argumentative groundwork for a set of defenses against future accountability efforts."[67]

Like the Goldsmith memo, Nielson concluded that the text, structure, and negotiating record led to the following conclusion:

> (A) that "protected person" status is subject to territorial limits, and applies only to persons in the hands of an occupying power in occupied territory or to persons in the hands of a party to the conflict in "the territory of a Party to the conflict"; and (B) that for purposes of [GC IV], "territory of a Party to the conflict" means the *home* territory of the party to the conflict in whose hands a person finds himself but does not include territory belonging to its enemies. We then turn to the negotiating record (C), which confirms that "protected person" status is available only to persons in the hands of an occupying power in occupied territory or to persons in the hands of a party to a conflict in that party's home territory.[68]

3. IS THIS NARROW INTERPRETATION OF GC IV CORRECT IN LIGHT OF THE INTERPRETATION OF THE VIENNA CONVENTION ON THE LAW OF TREATIES?

Section 2 of this chapter has demonstrated that there are two main classes of protected persons under GC IV: (1) enemy nationals in the home territory of each of the parties to the conflict; and (2) the population of occupied territories (excluding nationals of the occupying power). As noted in the GC IV Commentary: "The other distinctions and exceptions extend or restrict these limits, but not to any appreciable extent."[69] If this interpretation is correct, it would mean that outside of Crimea and the territories in Eastern Ukraine currently occupied by Russia, "protected persons" would only be Ukrainian civilians in Russia or Russian civilians in Ukraine. Is that really what the drafters intended? Were Ukrainian civilians located in places such as Bucha and Mariupol not covered by GC IV until there was an occupation?

66. Van Schaack, *supra* note 61, at 1566.

67. *Id.*

68. Nielson, *supra* note 65, at 3.

69. GC IV Commentary, *supra* note 11, at 46.

This section will analyze, through the lens of the Vienna Convention on the Law of Treaties (VCLT), whether this narrow nationality-focused interpretation is the proper one considering the relevant provisions of the treaty, the context of the Convention, and its object and purpose.

3.1 Vienna Convention on the Law of Treaties

The 1969 Vienna Convention on the Law of Treaties[70] provides the general rules for treaty interpretation in Articles 31 and 32, which have been recognized as customary international law by the United States.[71]

Article 31, which is entitled the "general rule" of interpretation, consists of a single rule with several elements. It requires good faith interpretation of a treaty, based on the ordinary meaning to be given to its terms, in their context, and in light of the treaty's object and purpose. Although the paragraphs may appear to create a hierarchy of interpretation, Article 31 represents a logical progression in the way one should interpret a treaty. Accordingly, one would first look at the text of the treaty, followed by context, and then look to other matters, in particular, subsequent material, in order to determine the parties' intention.[72]

Interpreting a treaty in good faith means, among other things, that even when the words of the treaty are clear, they must be interpreted in a way that does not defeat its object and purpose, or render its meaning manifestly absurd or unreasonable. Giving a term its ordinary meaning is the most likely reflection of the intention of the treaty parties, absent some evidence to the contrary.

Article 31(2) deals with context and is a key component for treaty interpretation. The ICRC correctly notes that in addition to the text of a treaty, consideration must be given to its preamble and any annexes.[73] It also includes consideration of any agreement between all the parties in connection to the conclusion of the treaty, or an instrument made by one or more of the parties in connection with the conclusion of the treaty accepted by the others.

Finally, Article 31(3)(a) provides that, together with the context, any subsequent agreement between the parties regarding interpretation of the treaty or application of its provisions should be considered. Reference to an "agreement"

70. Vienna Convention on the Law of Treaties, May 23, 1969, 1155 U.N.T.S. 331, 341 [hereinafter VCLT].

71. *See* William P. Rogers, Letter of Submittal, Oct. 18, 1971, *in Message of the President of the United States Transmitting the Vienna Convention on the Law of Treaties Signed for the United States on April 24, 1970*, 92 Congress, Executive L, at 1 (1971) ("Although not yet in force, the Convention is already generally recognized as the authoritative guide to current treaty law and practice.").

72. Anthony Aust, Modern Treaty Law and Practice 208 (3d ed. 2013).

73. International Committee of the Red Cross, Updated Commentary to Geneva Convention III, ¶¶ 83–85 (2020).

indicates there is no requirement that such agreement itself be a treaty, but it must exist "between the parties."[74] The most important aspect of Article 31(3) for treaty interpretation is Subparagraph (b) related to consideration of subsequent practice in the application of a treaty by the parties. As Anthony Aust notes, "however precise a text appears to be, the way in which it is actually applied by the parties is usually a good indication of what they understand it to mean, provided the practice is consistent and common to, or accepted, expressly or tacitly, by both or all the parties."[75] Article 31(4) also provides that other relevant rules of international law applicable in the relations between the parties should be considered. Therefore, a treaty must be interpreted within the wider context of international law. This means that an interpretation may require regard to not only international law in 1949 when the Geneva Conventions were adopted, but may look to contemporary norms as well.

Article 32 of the VCLT addresses supplementary means of interpretation, such as the *travaux préparatoires* of a treaty,[76] when this may be necessary in order to confirm the meaning of its terms resulting from the application of Article 31.[77] The second part of Article 32 provides recourse to supplementary means of interpretation when the primary source leaves the meaning "ambiguous or obscure" or leads to a "manifestly absurd or unreasonable" result. Here, unlike in the first part of Article 32, the aim of reliance on preparatory materials is not to "confirm," but rather to determine the meaning of a treaty's terms.[78]

3.2 Ordinary Meaning of the Treaty Terms

GC IV Article 4(1) establishes the definition of "protected persons," who are "those who, at a given moment and in any manner whatsoever, find themselves, in case of a conflict or occupation, in the hands of a Party to the conflict or Occupying Power of which they are not nationals."[79] There is nothing in the plain language of this paragraph that sets forth any restriction of territorial application only to the "home" territory of a party to the conflict. The GC IV Commentary to Article 4 states that "[t]he definition has been put in a negative form; as it is intended to cover anyone who is *not* a national of the Party to the conflict or Occupying Power

74. VCLT, *supra* note 70, at art. 31(3).

75. Aust, *supra* note 72, at 215.

76. *Id.* at 218 (a *travaux préparatoires* is "generally understood to include written materials, such a successive drafts of the treaty, conference records, explanatory statements by an expert consultant at a codification conference, uncontested interpretative statements by the chairman of a drafting committee").

77. *Id.* at 217.

78. *Id.* at 218.

79. GC IV, *supra* note 9, art. 4.

in whose hands he is."[80] It goes on to note that it was phrased in this way to remain faithful to international law and to not interfere in a State's relations with its own nationals. This interpretation would remain valid in a situation of invasion, as it would also be limited to individuals who are in the hands of a party to the conflict of which they are not nationals.

The ordinary meaning of the terms "at a given moment and in any manner whatsoever" and "in the hands of" would appear to reflect the drafters' intention of providing broad protections to those encompassed. The Commentary states that "at a given moment and in any manner whatsoever" was "intended to ensure that all situations and cases were covered."[81] Similarly, the term "in the hands of" was intended to be used in an "extremely general sense" and was not limited to mean "in the hands of" in a physical sense, but rather that the "person is in territory which is under control of the Power in question."[82]

Both the Goldsmith and Nielson memoranda acknowledge the "broad" scope of the definition of Article 4. Goldsmith argues that the limitation of protected persons to situations of occupation or the home territory of a party to the conflict "does not emerge from article 4 itself, but rather from other provisions in GC4, notably Part III of GC4, which governs the 'Status and Treatment of Protected Persons.' "[83] The Nielson memo reiterates this point by noting that "[c]onsidered in isolation," Article 4, subject to its specific exclusions, would confer protected person status on "any person anywhere" who finds themselves under the control of a party to the conflict.[84]

Thus, the ordinary meaning of Article 4, read in conjunction with the exclusions set forth in Articles 4 and 5, is that in an international armed conflict, civilians who find themselves in the hands of an enemy party of which they are not nationals would be considered protected persons under GC IV.

3.3 Context of Relevant Provisions of GC IV

As reflected in the VCLT, the ordinary meaning of treaty terms must be interpreted in their context and in conjunction with the entire agreement, not in isolation. The Nielson memo made the argument that Article 4(1), when read in light of other provisions of GC IV, particularly Part III ("Status and Treatment of Protected Persons"), narrowed down "protected person" status and made it available only in occupied territory or in the home territory of a party to the conflict.[85]

80. GC IV Commentary, *supra* note 11, at 46.

81. *Id.* at 47.

82. *Id.*

83. Memorandum from Assistant Attorney General Jack L. Goldsmith III, *supra* note 60, at 41.

84. Nielson, *supra* note 65, at 4.

85. *Id.*

There are certainly different scopes of protection within GC IV, depending on the stage of a military campaign.[86] The LOAC distinguishes between an invasion and occupation. The primary distinction between the two, as codified in the Hague Regulations, is that occupation occurs when enemy territory is placed under the control and authority of the invading army, while during the invasion phase, the military is focused on subduing the enemy's forces.[87] GC IV supplements the Hague Regulations pertaining to occupation by specifying certain protections for civilians who find themselves in occupied territory.

Looking at the definition of Article 4 in the context of the rest of the Convention, it is important to discern what protections apply to which civilians at a particular stage of the conflict. Part II of the Convention by its terms has a scope of application beyond protected persons. Article 13 sets forth that Part II applies to the "the whole of the populations of the countries in conflict."[88] It is broader than just "protected persons" and includes even individuals who are exempt by its terms, such as nationals of neutral states and a State's own nationals.[89]

Part III of the Convention contains the bulk of the treaty's protective provisions and is most relevant to this analysis as it offers various scopes of application depending on the territory in question. For purposes of this chapter, we can set aside Section II as it specifically addresses protections for aliens in a belligerent States' home territory.[90] Those articles contain certain obligations that a party to the conflict could only reasonably apply in its own territory, such as repatriation or employment.

Section III applies to protected persons in occupied territory and elaborates the obligations of an occupying power. The meaning of "occupied territory" is relatively clear, given that there is nothing to indicate that GC IV was intended to expand the definition of occupation laid down in the traditional Hague Law sense.[91]

86. John Embry Parkerson, Jr., *United States Compliance with Humanitarian Law Respecting Civilians During Operation Just Cause*, 133 Military Law Review 31, 71 (1991).

87. *Id.*

88. GC IV, *supra* note 9, art. 13.

89. Parkerson, *supra* note 86, at 73.

90. *Id.*

91. *Id.* at 74. *But see* Marten Zwanenburg, Michael Bothe, & Marco Sassòli, *Is the Law of Occupation Applicable to the Invasion Phase?*, 94 International Review of the Red Cross 29 (2012). Zwanenburg, Bothe, and Sassòli discuss whether, based on the ICRC's 1958 Pictet Commentary on GC IV, that "occupied territory" under GC IV is broader than occupied territory as defined by the 1907 Hague Regulations, such that GC IV rules governing occupation would also apply during the invasion stage before territory is considered occupied. The *DoD Law of War Manual*, *supra* note 12, at § 11.1.3.1, notes that "mere physical presence of a belligerent's military forces in the territory of the enemy alone does not constitute military occupation." However, guidance to U.S. forces has sought to apply the rules of occupation as a matter of policy when passing through an area during the invasion phase.

What is less clear and most relevant is the scope of application of Section I of Part III, comprising "Provisions Common to the Territories of the Parties to the Conflict and to Occupied Territories." The conclusion of the Goldsmith and Nielson memos is that all of Part III of GC IV is limited to protected persons in the home territory of a party or in occupied territory. However, there is nothing in the text of GC IV that supports their conclusion that the limited scope of application of Section II or III was intended to apply to Section I.

Article 27 of Section I requires parties to the conflict and occupying powers to, inter alia, ensure that protected persons are treated humanely and are protected against all acts or threats of violence. It also proscribes rape, enforced prostitution, and other acts of sexual violence against women. There is no indication in Section I that a geographical restriction to the "home" territory of a party to the conflict was intended. The first part of the title refers to "Provisions Common to the Territories of the Parties to the Conflict," which logically means all the parties to the conflict. With respect to the Russia-Ukraine conflict, this would include the territories of both Russia and Ukraine.

The GC IV Commentary suggests that Article 27 is a key provision and the "basis of the Convention, proclaiming as it does the principles on which the whole of 'Geneva Law' is founded. It proclaims the principle of respect for the human person and the inviolable character of the basic rights of individual men and women."[92] The Commentary further discusses the importance of Article 27(2) on the treatment of women:

> Paragraph 2 denounces certain practices which occurred, for example, during the last World War, when innumerable women of all ages, and even children, were subjected to outrages of the worst kind: rape committed in occupied territories, brutal treatment of every sort, mutilations, etc. In areas where troops were stationed, or through which they passed, thousands of women were made to enter brothels against their will or were contaminated with venereal diseases. . . . These facts revolt the conscience of all mankind and recall the worst memories of the great barbarian invasions.[93]

Additionally, there are provisions that would lead to an absurd result if they were limited to the home territory of a party to the conflict. Article 31, which prohibits "physical or moral coercion" against protected persons, while certainly applicable in occupied territory, would be a practice more likely to occur in invaded than in home territory. The Commentary provides that "coercion is forbidden for any purpose or reason. [...] Thus, the custom [. . .] that an invasion army may force the inhabitants of an occupied territory to serve as 'guides' is now forbidden. Furthermore, the prohibition is no longer limited in scope to the population of an

92. GC IV Commentary, *supra* note 11, at 199–200.

93. *Id.* at 205.

occupied territory, but covers all protected persons [. . .]"[94] There would be no reason for an invading army to need "guides" in its "home" territory, but rather when it is in the territory of its enemy short of occupation.

Finally, Article 32 provides the following:

> The High Contracting Parties specifically agree that each of them is prohibited from taking any measure of such a character as to cause the physical suffering or extermination of protected persons in their hands. This prohibition applies not only to murder, torture, corporal punishment, mutilation and medical or scientific experiments not necessitated by the medical treatment of a protected person, but also to any other measures of brutality whether applied by civilian or military agents.[95]

According to the GC IV Commentary, "Article 32 states a principle common to the four Geneva Conventions of 1949."[96] The Commentary also specifies that "those who benefit under Article 32 *are alien or enemy civilians in the hands of a Party to the conflict*"[97] (emphasis added). It recalls that some delegations who took part in the treaty negotiations remarked that bombardments or long-range weapons could cause death or suffering to individuals who were "not in the hands" of a party to the conflict in the same way as direct cruelty. They therefore wanted to extend it to the entire civilian population. However, the Diplomatic Conference determined this would encroach upon the sphere of the Hague Regulations and was beyond the intended scope of the Geneva Conventions. The Commentary notes that "the problems of the laws and customs of war are of a quite different nature and the words 'in their hands' define exactly the purpose of this Article."[98]

Richard Baxter, in an already mentioned lecture at the Naval War College on the Geneva Conventions, described Part II of GC IV as "deal[ing] with the general protection of populations against certain consequences of war" and called it "a Wounded and Sick Convention within the Civilians Convention."[99] Baxter stated that Part III, Section I, "which has application to the territory of parties to the conflict and to occupied territory, is basically a bill of rights for enemy civilians in time of war." It seems clear that Baxter did not think the notion of "protected persons" was so narrowly defined as to be limited in application only to enemy aliens in the home territory of the party to a conflict or occupation.

94. *Id.* at 220.

95. GC IV, *supra* note 9, art. 32.

96. GC IV Commentary, *supra* note 11, at 221.

97. *Id.* at 220.

98. *Id.* at 222.

99. Baxter, *supra* note 17, at 228.

4. OBJECT AND PURPOSE OF GC IV

GC IV must also be considered in light of its object and purpose. According to the GC IV Commentary, the main object of the treaty "is to protect a strictly defined category of civilians from arbitrary action on the part of the enemy, and not from the dangers due to the military operations themselves."[100]

John Embry Parkerson, Jr., considered the object and purpose of GC IV when he analyzed whether Panamanian civilians were protected persons under GC IV during Operation Just Cause in 1989. He argued that if the narrow interpretation of protected persons was accurate, as suggested by the DoD LOWM and the OLC memos, it would render the definition of "protected persons" "essentially meaningless" for the Panama invasion.[101] A gap would exist in the protections of civilians who found themselves "in the hands" of U.S forces during the invasion and fighting short of occupation.[102] The gap has also been acknowledged by Baxter with respect to Article 5 and unprivileged belligerents, and, indeed, some of the provisions found in Additional Protocol I were drafted in response to it.[103]

Noting that there is some ambiguity in the scope of protection of Part III, Section I, Parkerson concludes that a major gap in the Convention's protections for civilians who find themselves in the power of the enemy in their home state "would appear contrary to the 'object and purpose' of the Convention" as expressed in Article 2 (which makes GC IV's provisions applicable to any armed conflict between party States), and to Article 4, "which does not appear to possess the geographical imitation in defining protected civilians."[104] Parkerson concludes that when reading the treaty as a whole, in light of its object and purpose, the drafters must have intended for the protections found in Section I to also apply to civilians in the country in which the conflict is occurring, even before such territory is considered occupied.[105] He states:

> A construction that found an absolute gap in the Convention's protections, however, would appear contrary to the "object and purpose" of the Convention . . . . Reading the treaty as a whole, the drafters must have intended that *some* protections be afforded the category of civilians that appear to fall in the gap created by a literal reading of several of its provisions.[106]

100. GC IV Commentary, *supra* note 11, at 10.

101. Parkerson, *supra* note 86, at 75.

102. *Id.*

103. *Id.* at 76. *See* Michael Bothe, Karl Joseph Partach, & Waldemar Solf, New Rules for Victims of Armed Conflict 440, 442, 443 (1982).

104. Parkerson, *supra* note 86, at 76.

105. *Id.* at 77.

106. *Id.* at 76.

Although GC IV does not protect all civilians, the exceptions are specifically set forth within its text. As the GC IV Commentary to Article 4 concludes:

> In short, all the particular cases we have just been considering confirm a general principle which is embodied in all four Geneva Conventions of 1949. Every person in enemy hands must have some status under international law: he is either a prisoner of war and, as such, covered by the Third Convention, a civilian covered by the Fourth Convention, or again, a member of the medical personnel of the armed forces who is covered by the First Convention. There is no intermediate status; nobody in enemy hands can be outside the law.[107]

It is unfathomable that the drafters of GC IV, which was negotiated right after the horrors of World War II, intended an interpretation of its defining provision so narrow that it categorically excludes from protection, apart from the provisions of Part II, civilians in the territory in which a conflict is occurring. Construing GC IV as narrowly as the DoD LOWM and OLC memoranda do, would thus go against the rules of treaty interpretation based on the text of the treaty, the relationship between Article 4 and the other provisions, and run counter to its object and purpose.

5. PROTECTION OF CIVILIANS SINCE THE ADOPTION OF GC IV

5.1 Additional Protocol I

It is obvious there are recognized gaps in the protections afforded certain civilians under GC IV. These shortcomings were recognized by the Diplomatic Conference on Additional Protocol I, which expanded the coverage of civilians in several of its provisions. Article 75 of Additional Protocol I provides fundamental guarantees of humane treatment for all individuals who do not benefit from more favorable safeguards under the Geneva Conventions or the Protocol itself.[108] Article 73 also explicitly stipulates that individuals who were considered refugees or stateless persons prior to the conflict are protected persons within the meaning of Parts I and III of GC IV. If an individual became a refugee or stateless person after the conflict started, they would receive protection under Article 75. Its guarantees likewise apply to nationals of neutral and co-belligerent states even if they have diplomatic representation in a party to the conflict.

107. GC IV Commentary, *supra* note 11, at 51.

108. Protocol Additional to the Geneva Conventions of 12 August 1949, and Relating to the Protection of Victims of International Armed Conflicts art. 75, June 8, 1977, 1124 U.N.T.S. 609; Landefeld, *supra* note 16, at 21.

Article 75 is an important advancement that provides a consistent minimum standard of humane treatment in international armed conflicts. It does away with the distinction found in GC IV regarding whether the party to the conflict is a friend or foe and covers those who are in "the power of a Party to the conflict," without the restrictor of nationality.[109] Landefeld argues that Article 75 moves away from the reciprocal regulation of inter-State relations as the safeguards apply irrespective of nationality.[110] Theodor Meron has said that Article 75 is a shift away from reciprocity to the principle of humanity.[111]

The United States has accepted that "Article 75 reflects fundamental guarantees for the persons detained during an international armed conflict" and chooses "out of a sense of legal obligation" to treat the principles contained in Article 75 as applicable to any individual it detains in an international armed conflict and expects other States to do so as well.[112] This statement by the United States is aimed at "the crystallization of the principles in Article 75 as rules of customary international law in international armed conflict."[113]

5.2 International Jurisprudence

International jurisprudence has also adopted an expansive reading of Article 4 to broaden its scope of application. In the *Tadić* case, the International Criminal Tribunal for the former Yugoslavia (ICTY) considered the scope of Article 4 in circumstances involving alleged grave breaches by Bosnian Serb forces (acting on behalf of another State) against Bosnian Muslim victims in Bosnia. The ICTY Appeals Chamber held:

> Article 4(1) of Geneva Convention IV (protection of civilians), applicable to the case at issue, defines "protected persons"—hence possible victims of grave breaches—as those "in the hands of a Party to the conflict or Occupying Power of which they are not nationals". In other words, subject to the provisions of Article 4(2), the Convention intends to protect civilians (in enemy territory, occupied territory or the combat zone) who do not have the nationality of the belligerent in whose hands they find themselves, or who are stateless persons.[114]

109. Landefeld, *supra* note 16, at 25.

110. *Id.* at 24. She notes that the AP I Commentary admits this is a theoretical question since all States have ratified AP I, but Article 75 expressly covers nationals of non-contracting parties.

111. Theodor Meron, The Humanization of International Law (Martinus Nijhoff ed., 2006).

112. DoD LOWM, *supra* note 12, § 8.1.4.2.

113. *Id.*

114. Prosecutor v. Tadić, Case No. IT-94-1-A, Appeals Chamber Judgment, ¶ 164 (Int'l Crim. Trib. for the former Yugoslavia July 15, 1999).

One author argued that "rigid adherence" to the traditional definition of protected persons would have "absurd results" in the Bosnian conflict.[115] The *Tadić* opinion recognized that a national may lack "both allegiance to a State and diplomatic protection" because of their ethnicity or religion. This evolution, as well as the goal of Article 4 to "protect[] civilians to the maximum extent possible," means that protected person status could no longer be determined based solely on legal relations between an individual and a State. Accordingly, in *Tadić*, the ICTY determined that Article 4 and the corresponding protections for protected persons may also apply to those possessing the same nationality as the perpetrators of war crimes.[116]

In 2017, the U.K. Court of Justice examined who could receive "protected person" status. The Court held that whether one was a "protected person" hinged on that individual being "in the hands of" a party of opposing nationality, regardless of on which party's territory the individual is located. The Court further emphasized that "[i]t is not necessary to interpret this description as restricted to actions done by parties to the conflict within their own territories and in occupied territories."[117]

6. CONCLUSION

This chapter has explored which civilians are considered "protected persons" under GC IV. The United States, as reflected in the DoD LOWM, which in turn relies on two OLC memoranda, has determined that to be entitled to the protections provided by GC IV to a "protected person," a civilian must be located in either (1) occupied territory or (2) the home territory of a party to the conflict. Russian forces in Ukraine who have willfully killed, raped, and tortured Ukrainian civilians would thus not be committing a "grave breach" of the Geneva Conventions and be subject to universal jurisdiction for such acts.

Consider if the same set of circumstances occurred in the United States. Under this restrictive interpretation, U.S. citizens in the United States would not be considered protected persons during an invasion by foreign forces even if willfully killed, raped, or tortured by them. Such an outcome could not have been the intention of the States parties to the Convention who were coming out of the horrors of World War II. The United States should not rely on two flawed OLC opinions that were specifically focused on Al Qaeda and counterterrorism

115. Shane Reeves, *The Expansive Definition of "Protected Persons" in War Crimes Jurisprudence*, Army Lawyer 23, 25 (May 2009).

116. *Id.* at 26, *citing* Prosecutor v. Tadić, Case No. IT-94-1-I, Decision on the Defence Motion for Interlocutory Appeal on Jurisdiction (Int'l Crim. Trib. for the former Yugoslavia Oct. 2, 1995), *in* International Committee of the Red Cross, How Does Law Protect in War? 1859 (Marco Sassòli & Antoine Bouvier eds., 1999).

117. Alseran & Ors. v. MOD [2017] EWCH 3289 (QB) ¶ 273.

operations to restrict the protections of its citizens. Accordingly, the United States should withdraw both of those legal opinions.

A narrow interpretation entails ignoring the plain text of GC IV and requires a tortuous conclusion grafted onto the structure of GC IV. It also sidesteps the GC IV Commentary, relevant jurisprudence, and scholarship in this area. The result is that an *invading* military would be less constrained under GC IV than the invaded state's military because only the invaded state would have obligations with respect to the protection of civilians in the State in which war is taking place.

Although GC IV does not protect *all* civilians in *all* circumstances in time of war, the most appropriate interpretation is one that provides protections to civilians in invaded territory under Part III, Section I. To read it any other way would go against the object and purpose of GC IV and lead to an absurd result.

2

Are "Unprivileged Belligerents" Protected by the Civilians Convention and, If So, How?

MARTEN ZWANENBURG*

1. INTRODUCTION

During the diplomatic conference which drafted and adopted the four Geneva Conventions of 1949, one of the Dutch representatives stated:

> That persons who do not fall under Article 3 [now Article 4 GC III] are automatically protected by other Conventions is certainly untrue. The Civilians Convention, for instance, deals only with civilians under certain circumstances; such as civilians in an occupied country or civilians who are living in a belligerent country, but it certainly does not protect civilians who are in the battlefield, taking up arms against the adverse party. These people, if they do not belong to Article 3, and if they fall into the hands of the adverse party, might be shot and that is a decision which we do not want to leave in the hands of one man.[1]

* Marten Zwanenburg is a Professor of Military Law at the University of Amsterdam and at the Faculty of Military Sciences of the Netherlands Defence Academy.

1. Final Record of the Diplomatic Conference of Geneva of 1949, vol. II-B (1949), 271, 13th Plenary Meeting, July 26, 1949 (Captain Mouton).

Marten Zwanenburg, *Are "Unprivileged Belligerents" Protected by the Civilians Convention and, If So, How?*
In: *Civilian Protection in Armed Conflict*. Edited by: Jelena Pejic and Captain Margaret Kotlik,
Oxford University Press. © Marten Zwanenburg 2025. DOI: 10.1093/oso/9780197793176.003.0002

This prompted a representative of the Soviet Union to reply that "[i]f a person is not recognized as a prisoner of war . . . , such a person would then be a civilian and would enjoy the full protection afforded by the Civilians Convention."[2]

These statements reflect the fact that the personal scope of application of the Fourth Geneva Convention (GC IV) was a highly contentious issue at the conference. Unfortunately, this has remained the case, from the adoption of the final text of GC IV to the present day. The bulk of the protections in the treaty apply only to "protected persons." Article 4 of the Convention defines who is and who is not a "protected person." Under the first paragraph of the article, protected persons are "those who, at a given moment and in any manner whatsoever, find themselves, in case of a conflict or occupation, in the hands of a Party to the conflict or Occupying Power of which they are not nationals." The rest of the article excludes certain categories of persons from the definition, including persons protected by one of the three other Geneva Conventions. This seems to suggest that, under the Geneva Conventions, persons are either combatants protected by Geneva Conventions I–III, or, as long as they meet the nationality criteria in Article 4 GC IV, "protected persons" covered by GC IV.

On closer inspection, however, the issue is not so clear. There are some who submit that there is a third category of persons, often referred to as "unlawful combatants" or "unprivileged belligerents," who are neither lawful combatants nor civilians to whom GC IV applies.[3] Although different definitions of the term "unprivileged belligerent" are used, it essentially denotes persons who directly participate in hostilities against the adversary in an international armed conflict without being entitled to combatant and therefore prisoner of war (POW) status upon capture.[4] This has been referred to as the "restrictive interpretation" of GC IV or the "total exclusionary theory."[5] Others do not go so far as to argue that there is a third class of persons who are neither combatants nor civilians, but contend that certain categories of civilians are either not protected by GC IV as a whole,

2. *Id.* (Mr. Morosov).

3. *See, e.g.*, Ingrid Detter, *The Law of War and Illegal Combatants*, 75 George Washington Law Review 1049, 1064 (2007); Robert K. Goldmann & Brian D. Tittemore, *Unprivileged Combatants and the Hostilities in Afghanistan: Their Status and Rights under International Humanitarian and Human Rights Law*, American Society of International Law 38 (2002).

4. *See, inter alia*, Jelena Pejic, *"Unlawful/Enemy Combatants": Interpretations and Consequences*, *in* International Law and Armed Conflicts: Exploring the Faultlines 335, 337–38 (Michael N. Schmitt & Jelena Pejic eds., 2007). The U.S. Department of Defense *Law of War Manual* states: "'Unlawful combatants' or 'unprivileged belligerents' are persons who, by engaging in hostilities, have incurred one or more of the corresponding liabilities of combatant status (*e.g.*, being made the object of attack and subject to detention), but who are not entitled to any of the distinct privileges of combatant status (*e.g.*, combatant immunity and POW status)." U.S. Office of the General Counsel, Department of Defense Law of War Manual § 102 (2015) [hereinafter U.S. DoD Law of War Manual].

5. Yutaka Arai-Takahashi, *Unprivileged (Unlawful) Belligerents Captured on a Battlefield and the Geneva Conventions*, 48 Israel Yearbook on Human Rights 63, 74 (2018).

or not protected by parts thereof. This interpretation has been referred to as the "intermediate theory" regarding the scope of application of GC IV. It does not per se exclude the possibility that "unprivileged belligerents" could be protected persons. It will be referred to as the "intermediate theory" in this chapter. Within this theory, different interpretations can be distinguished. One interpretation is that GC IV only covers "unprivileged belligerents" in occupied territory or if they are aliens in enemy territory. Under this view, "unprivileged belligerents" in the territory of their own State which is not occupied are excluded from the entire framework of GC IV.[6]

A second interpretation under the "intermediate theory" is that "unprivileged belligerents" in the territory of their own State which is not occupied are not fully excluded from protection under GC IV. Rather, they are only excluded from the protection of Part III of GC IV, while still benefiting from the provisions in Part II.[7] This appears to be the interpretation adopted in the U.S. Department of Defense (DoD) *Law of War Manual*. The manual states in Paragraph 10.3.2.2:

> To be entitled to the protections provided under the GC for "protected persons," a person must be located in either (1) occupied territory or (2) the home territory of a party to the conflict. The references in the GC that limit the scope of protections for protected persons to those "in the territory of a Party to the conflict" refer to the home territory of the party to the conflict in whose hands the protected person finds himself or herself.[8]

It may be noted that this text refers to exclusion from protections afforded to "protected persons," and not to the protections which are granted to a wider group of persons in Part II of GC IV.

The question of the personal scope of application of GC IV gained particular prominence due to the decision by the United States in the early 2000s to

6. Richard Baxter, *So-Called "Unprivileged Belligerency": Spies, Guerrillas, and Saboteurs*, 28 British Yearbook of International Law 323, 329 (1951); Jason Callen, *Unlawful Combatants and the Geneva Conventions*, 44 Virginia Journal of International Law 1025, 1038–39 (2004).

7. Arai-Takahashi, *supra* note 5, at 76; Derek Jinks, *The Declining Significance of POW Status*, 45 Harvard International Law Journal 367, 381 (2004).

8. U.S. DoD Law of War Manual, *supra* note 4, at §§ 670–71. The manual also explains that "unprivileged belligerents" are not per se excluded from "protected person" status, from which it may be concluded that it does not follow the "restrictive interpretation." *Id.* at § 671, ¶ 10.3.2.4. The manual is somewhat confusing in that it could also be read as suggesting that there is a third category of persons, who are neither combatants nor civilians: "Although seldom explicitly recognized as a class in law of war treaties, the category of unprivileged belligerent may be understood as an implicit consequence of creating the classes of lawful combatants and peaceful civilians. The concept of unprivileged belligerency, i.e., the set of legal liabilities associated with unprivileged belligerents, may be understood in opposition to the rights, duties, and liabilities of lawful combatants and peaceful civilians." *Id.* at § 102, ¶ 4.3.1.

deny the protection of GC IV to detainees in Afghanistan and Iraq, which it initially referred to as "unlawful combatants" and subsequently as "unprivileged belligerents." It has remained topical since.

A considerable amount of ink has been spilled in academic literature on the issue of the personal scope of application of GC IV and, in particular, the status under international humanitarian law (IHL) of "unprivileged belligerents." This chapter does not intend to recapitulate the ground already covered.[9] Rather, it aims to provide an overview and appreciation of the main salient issues in the debate, focusing on the issue of "unprivileged belligerents." It will do so taking the rules of treaty interpretation as a starting point. After all, determining the meaning of the terms of Article 4 GC IV in its context is essentially a question of treaty interpretation. The established rules of interpretation set out in the Vienna Convention on the Law of Treaties (VCLT) will be relied on.

This chapter is structured as follows: after the introduction, the main rules of treaty interpretation are discussed in section 2. The next section (section 3) will focus on the textual interpretation of Article 4 GC IV in the context of the treaty as a whole. Section 4 will look at whether the *travaux préparatoires* of GCs IV and III shed further light on the scope of application of GC IV. Sections 3 and 4 will argue that there are strong reasons to conclude that civilians, including but not limited to civilians who qualify as unprivileged belligerents, who find themselves in the hands of a party to the conflict in territory of their home State that is not occupied, do not benefit from the protections of an important part of GC IV. Section 5 will clarify that this does not mean that they enjoy no IHL protection at all, by setting out the minimum safeguards that do apply to them. A "protection gap" is still left, however. Section 6 discusses an approach that has been put forward to close it, by using a broad interpretation of the notion of "occupation" for the purposes of GC IV. It will conclude that such an approach, while laudable, is not convincing. The chapter concludes with a few final remarks (section 7).

2. THE RULES OF TREATY INTERPRETATION

The main source for the rules of treaty interpretation is the VCLT. The rules on treaty interpretation in the VCLT, specifically Articles 31–32, are widely used by States and international and national courts and tribunals. It has been stated that they can now be identified as generally applicable to all treaties.[10] Article 31 VCLT sets out the general rule of treaty interpretation:

9. This chapter will not, for example, discuss issues surrounding nationality and the role it plays in determining who is protected.

10. Richard Gardiner, Treaty Interpretation 6 (2015).

1. A treaty shall be interpreted in good faith in accordance with the ordinary meaning to be given to the terms of the treaty in their context and in the light of its object and purpose.
2. The context for the purpose of the interpretation of a treaty shall comprise, in addition to the text, including its preamble and annexes:
   (a) any agreement relating to the treaty which was made between all the parties in connection with the conclusion of the treaty;
   (b) any instrument which was made by one or more parties in connection with the conclusion of the treaty and accepted by the other parties as an instrument related to the treaty.
3. There shall be taken into account, together with the context:
   (a) any subsequent agreement between the parties regarding the interpretation of the treaty or the application of its provisions;
   (b) any subsequent practice in the application of the treaty which establishes the agreement of the parties regarding its interpretation;
   (c) any relevant rules of international law applicable in the relations between the parties.
4. A special meaning shall be given to a term if it is established that the parties so intended.

Article 31 does not provide a hierarchy between the various means of interpretation that are part of the general rule. As a consequence, the various means set forth in Article 31 must be considered to be of equal value. They are to be considered in one (and the same) process of application: they are part of one "single combined operation."[11]

Article 32 VCLT provides for supplementary means of interpretation. These may be used to confirm the meaning resulting from the application of Article 31 or to determine the meaning when the interpretation according to Article 31: (a) leaves the meaning ambiguous or obscure, or (b) leads to a result that is manifestly absurd or unreasonable. Article 32 does not contain an exhaustive list of supplementary means of interpretation. It only provides that such means include the preparatory work of the treaty and the circumstances of its conclusion. What supplementary means may be considered along with those mentioned in the text has not yet been established conclusively in practice or doctrine.[12] There is no doubt, however, that the subsequent practice of States not meeting the criteria of Article 31 qualifies as another supplementary means of interpretation.[13]

11. Mark Villiger, Commentary on the Vienna Convention on the Law of Treaties 435 (2009).

12. Oliver Dörr & Kirsten Schmalenbach, *Article 32: Supplementary Means of Interpretation*, *in* The Vienna Convention on the Law of Treaties 617, 626 (Oliver Dörr & Kirsten Schmalenbach eds., 2012).

13. *See* Villiger, *supra* note 11, at 446.

Although the VCLT was adopted decades after the Geneva Conventions, it is legitimate to apply the former treaty's rules of treaty interpretation to the latter. This is because it is now broadly accepted that the provisions on interpretation of treaties contained in Articles 31 and 32 of the VCLT reflect preexisting customary international law.[14] This conclusion is buttressed by the fact that the International Court of Justice, as well as many other international courts and tribunals, have applied the VCLT's rules to treaties concluded before the entry into force of the VCLT. It is therefore common for States, courts, and commentators to use the VCLT's rules to interpret the Geneva Conventions.[15]

3. ARTICLE 4 GC IV IN ITS CONTEXT

As set out in the preceding, the "general rule" of treaty interpretation is that a treaty shall be interpreted in good faith in accordance with the ordinary meaning to be given to its terms in their context and in the light of the treaty's object and purpose. The main provision that needs to be interpreted to determine the scope of application of GC IV is Article 4(1), which was reproduced in section 1 above. The text of the paragraph seems all embracing:[16] all persons would be protected as long as they find themselves in the hands of a party to the conflict or occupying power. It is important to point out that, pursuant to the prevailing interpretation, the expression "in the hands of" in Article 4(1) GC IV should be understood in a very general sense. It refers not (only) to a person physically held by the enemy. It is sufficient for a person to be in the territory of a party to the conflict or in occupied territory for them to be deemed in the hands of the power concerned.[17] It has been suggested, including in the U.S. DoD *Law of War Manual*, that the words "find themselves" imply an element of happenstance or coincidence. For example, persons who deliberately travel to an occupied State to fight against the occupying power would not "find themselves" in the hands of the occupying power. On this view, the words "find themselves in the hands of" and "are in the hands of" should not be equated because if the drafters had intended to mean "are" they could have

14. Gardiner, *supra* note 10, at 13.

15. *See, e.g.*, Kubo Mačák, *The Role of International Human Rights Law in the Interpretation of the Fourth Geneva Convention*, 52 Israel Yearbook on Human Rights 219, 222 (2022).

16. Knut Dörmann, *The Legal Situation of "Unlawful Combatants/Unprivileged Belligerents,"* 85 International Review of the Red Cross 45, 48 (2003).

17. Oscar M. Uhler et al., Commentary to Geneva Convention IV Relative to the Protection of Civilian Persons in Time of War (1958) [hereinafter 1958 Commentary]; United Kingdom Ministry of Defence, Ministry of Defence Law of War Manual 224 (2004) [hereinafter U.K. Law of War Manual].

simply used that word.[18] It seems more likely that if the drafters had wanted to exclude a category of persons from Article 4 GC IV by assigning a specific meaning to the term "find themselves in the hands of," they would have done so explicitly. The words "at a given moment and in any manner whatsoever" also suggest that the term "find themselves in the hands of" was not intended to be interpreted restrictively. In conformity with this reasoning, a broad understanding of the latter term is the majority view today.[19]

The rest of Article 4 expressly excludes certain categories of persons from the definition of "protected person." Paragraph 2 excludes nationals of a State which is not bound by GC IV. It also excludes nationals of a neutral State who find themselves in the territory of a belligerent State, and nationals of a co-belligerent State, while the State of which they are nationals has normal diplomatic representation in the State in whose hands they are. Finally, Article 4(4) provides that persons protected by Geneva Conventions I–III shall not be considered protected persons within the meaning of GC IV. These exclusions from the "protected persons" definition are not contentious.

This is not the case for other purported exclusions, however. It may be recalled that supporters of the "total exclusionary theory" argue that "unprivileged belligerents" are excluded from the protection of GC IV as a whole. This would apply regardless of where "unprivileged belligerents" are found. In other words, they would not be protected by the treaty whether found in enemy territory, occupied territory, or on the battlefield. It may be noted that the text of Article 4 does not exclude "unprivileged belligerents" as such from the definition of "protected person." Thus, it does not provide any support for the "total exclusionary theory." According to arguments put forward in support of this theory, belligerents must distinguish themselves from the civilian population, failing which they lose protection under IHL. Ingrid Detter states in rather sweeping terms:

> [T]hroughout the history of warfare there has been a rule that those who do not openly show that they are belligerents, especially by wearing a uniform, are excluded from protective rules of the law of war.[20]

Proponents of this theory also frequently refer to the judgment of the U.S. Supreme Court in *Ex parte Quirin*, which states:

18. United States Department of Justice, "Protected Person" Status in Occupied Iraq under the Fourth Geneva Convention, Memorandum for the Counsel to the President 51 (Mar. 18, 2004).

19. William H. Boothby & Wolff Heintschel von Heinegg, The Law of War: A Detailed Assessment of the US Department of Defense Law of War Manual 248–49 (2018); U.K. Law of War Manual, *supra* note 17, at 224.

20. Detter, *supra* note 3, at 1064.

> By universal agreement and practice, the law of war draws a distinction between the armed forces and the peaceful populations of belligerent nations and also between those who are lawful and unlawful combatants. Lawful combatants are subject to capture and detention as prisoners of war by opposing military forces. Unlawful combatants are likewise subject to capture and detention, but in addition they are subject to trial and punishment by military tribunals for acts which render their belligerency unlawful.[21]

Neither argument is very persuasive. As regards *Ex parte Quirin*, the judgment predates the Geneva Conventions. Therefore, it has no obvious role to play in the interpretation of these treaties. The situation would perhaps be different if the judgment had played a role in the drafting of the conventions, but there is no indication that this was the case.

As regards Article 4 GC IV itself, there is nothing in the text of GC IV that supports the theory. On the contrary, the existence of a derogation clause in Article 5 GC IV points in the opposite direction.[22] The clause limits the rights of precisely the class of persons who would be excluded from GC IV protection based on the total exclusionary theory.[23] If such persons were indeed excluded, why would Article 5 be needed?[24] Another counterindication is Article 45(3) of Additional Protocol I (AP I). This provision contains an implicit confirmation of the interpretation according to which at least certain "unprivileged belligerents" are protected persons as long as they fulfill the nationality criteria of Article 4 GC IV.[25] Moreover, the total exclusionary theory is also difficult to reconcile with the humanitarian object and purpose

21. *Ex parte Quirin*, 317 U.S. 1, 30–31 (1942). Detter refers to this judgment, as does Dinstein. Detter, *supra* note 3, at 1049; Yoram Dinstein, *Unlawful Combatancy*, 32 ISRAEL YEARBOOK ON HUMAN RIGHTS 247, 249 (2002).

22. The first two paragraphs of Article 5, which are the most relevant here, read:

> Where, in the territory of a Party to the conflict, the latter is satisfied that an individual protected person is definitely suspected of or engaged in activities hostile to the security of the State, such individual person shall not be entitled to claim such rights and privileges under the present Convention as would, if exercised in the favour of such individual person, be prejudicial to the security of such State.
>
> Where in occupied territory an individual protected person is detained as a spy or saboteur, or as a person under definite suspicion of activity hostile to the security of the Occupying Power, such person shall, in those cases where absolute military security so requires, be regarded as having forfeited rights of communication under the present Convention.

23. Pejic, *supra* note 4, at 340.

24. Dörmann, *supra* note 16, at 50.

25. *Id.* at 50–51.

of GC IV, and does not find support in the *travaux préparatoires* (as discussed further in section 4).[26]

There is also little State practice supporting the theory. This author has been able to identify only one possible example. The Russian law of war manual states that a "civilian is any person present in the area of combat operations, who is not a member of armed forces and refrains from any act of hostility."[27] The implication is that an unprivileged belligerent is not a civilian, and *a fortiori* cannot be a "protected person." Other State practice rejects this view. Israel argued for recognition by the Israeli Supreme Court of a third category of person, neither civilian nor combatant, in the so-called *Targeted Killings Case*. It was denied by the Court, which held that "[i]n our opinion, as far as existing law goes, the data before us are not sufficient to recognize this third category. That is the case according to the current state of international law, both international treaty law and customary international law."[28] Other State practice also rejects the view that there is a third category between civilian and combatant. This includes practice from the Netherlands, as well as other States.[29] The German law of war manual states:

> Any person without combatant status who has directly taken part in hostilities and is not entitled to prisoner-of-war status, will, if he or she fulfils the nationality criteria . . . , generally be treated as a protected person in accordance with the Fourth Geneva Convention.[30]

The Danish military manual also excludes the existence of a third category, stating that "IHL does not recognise any intermediate categories; a person is either a civilian or a combatant."[31] The same goes for the French and New Zealand manuals on the law of war.[32] Based on the preceding, it is concluded that the "total exclusionary theory" must be rejected.[33]

26. Arai-Takahashi, *supra* note 5, at 75.

27. Russian Ministry of Defense, Manual on International Humanitarian Law for Armed Forces of the Russian Federation (2001), unofficial English translation, *reproduced in* 99 International Law Studies 773, 779 (2022).

28. HCJ 769/02 Public Committee against Torture in Israel v. Government of Israel, 62(1) PD 507, ¶ 28 (2006) (Isr.), *reprinted in* 46 International Legal Materials 373.

29. Handelingen II (Parliamentary papers) 2005–2006, nr. 59, at 3826.

30. Federal Ministry of Defence (Germany), ZDV 15/2, Law of Armed Conflict Manual ¶ 48 (2013

31. Ministry of Defence, Military Manual on International Law Relevant to Danish Armed Forces in International Operations 166 (2016).

32. French Ministry of Defence, Manuel de droit des opérations militaires 110 (2022); New Zealand Defence Force, Manual of Armed Forces, Vol. 4, Law of Armed Conflict 6–7 (2017).

33. Dörmann, *supra* note 16, at 50–52; Pejic, *supra* note 4, at 342.

As noted in the introduction, the "intermediate" interpretation of the scope of application of GC IV does not go so far as to suggest that there is a third category of persons who are neither (lawful) combatants nor civilians. It was explained that two different interpretations can be distinguished within this theory. One interpretation is that GC IV only covers "unprivileged belligerents" in occupied territory or if they are aliens in enemy territory. Under this view, "unprivileged belligerents" in the territory of a non-occupied home State are excluded from the entire framework of GC IV.[34] This interpretation will be referred to as the "narrow intermediate theory." It may be noted that in contrast to the "total exclusionary theory," unprivileged belligerents do fall within the personal scope of GC IV, but only if they are found in certain territories. The second interpretation under the "intermediate theory" is that "unprivileged belligerents" in the non-occupied territory of their own State are only excluded from the protection of Part III of GC IV, but benefit from the provisions in Part II.[35] This interpretation will be referred to as the "broad intermediate theory."

Proponents of the "narrow intermediate theory" stress that Article 4 GC should be read together with Article 5 GC IV. This accords, in principle, with the rules of treaty interpretation, pursuant to which the totality of a treaty should be taken into account when interpreting a specific provision. Proponents of the "narrow intermediate theory" argue that persons participating in hostilities who fail to qualify for POW status are covered by GC IV depending on where they are found. They recall that the scope of protection is governed principally by Articles 4 and 5. The authority to derogate in Article 5, however, only extends to two types of territory: (a) the home territory of the detaining power; and (b) occupied territory. Because Article 5 does not address non-occupied, enemy territory, the argument goes, GC IV does not apply in this context. As Richard Baxter states:

> [T]he failure of Article 5 to refer to areas where fighting is in progress outside occupied territory or the territory of the detaining state suggests that both Articles 4 and 5 were directed to the protection of inhabitants of occupied areas and of the mass of enemy aliens on enemy territory and that unlawful belligerents in the zone of operations were not taken into account in connexion with the two articles.[36]

Proponents of the "narrow intermediate theory" thus argue that the absence of an option to derogate under Article 5 of the Convention in respect of persons in non-occupied territory of their home State suggests that they are excluded from the ambit

34. Baxter, *supra* note 6, at 329 and following; Jason Callen, *Unlawful Combatants and the Geneva Conventions*, 44 Virginia Journal of International Law 1025, 1038–39 (2004).

35. Arai-Takahashi, *supra* note 5, at 76; Jinks, *supra* note 7, at 381.

36. Baxter, *supra* note 6.

of "protected persons." If the term "protected person" was meant to include them, the derogation clause would have been drafted accordingly.[37]

The reasoning for the "narrow intermediate theory" is, however, not convincing. First, the suggestion that persons in the non-occupied territory of their home State are not "protected persons" goes against the plain reading of Article 4, the scope of which is not limited to that effect.[38] It does not automatically follow from the more restricted territorial scope of application of Article 5 that Article 4 must have the same scope of application, that is, that it excludes persons not covered by Article 5 from being "protected persons" as such. The question of whether an individual is a "protected person" is separate from the issue of the substantive protections that may apply to them. As will be submitted in the following, the answer to the latter question does depend on where the person concerned is found.

Second, as Derek Jinks states, proponents of the "narrow intermediate theory," such as Baxter, assume that the territorial limitations in Article 5 are not explicable if the Convention is read to protect civilians on the battlefield in enemy territory. The underlying claim by Baxter and others is that a justification for derogation would be as compelling (if not more so) on the battlefield in enemy territory, as it is in occupied territory or the home territory of the belligerent State but is missing from the text. That claim is not correct, however. As Jinks explains, "Article 5 was designed to address problems of internal security and order maintenance. That the provision authorizes no derogation in zones of active operations is therefore unsurprising."[39]

Third and finally, Article 4(3) explicitly provides that Part II of GC IV has a broader scope of application, as it is not limited to "protected persons" but applies to all persons referred to in Article 13. There is nothing in the text of Article 13 that excludes unprivileged belligerents as such, or unprivileged belligerents specifically in non-occupied home territory, from the protection of Part II. It must therefore be considered to also include persons, including unprivileged belligerents, in the non-occupied territory of their home State.[40]

Under the "broad intermediate theory," it is argued that persons meeting the criteria of Article 4 GC IV are all "protected persons." This comprises persons in non-occupied territory of their home State, including those who participate directly in hostilities (and are thus "unprivileged belligerents"). However, the extent of protection of any protected person will vary depending on where they find themselves, because different parts of GC IV provide different levels of protection.[41]

37. Callen, *supra* note 34, at 1038–39.

38. Jinks, *supra* note 7, at 397.

39. *Id.* at 395.

40. Arai-Takahashi, *supra* note 5, at 77.

41. *See, e.g.*, Marco Sassòli, International Humanitarian Law: Rules, Controversies and Solutions to Problems Arising in Warfare 273–75 (2019).

This interpretation acknowledges that Part II of GC IV applies also to protected persons found in non-occupied territory of their home State, including unprivileged belligerents. Its particular focus is on Part III of GC IV, which contains the bulk of the treaty's protections. Section II of Part III covers all protected persons in the territory of the party in whose hands they find themselves. In other words, all protected persons in the territory of the enemy. This follows from the title of the section, which is "Aliens in the territory of a party to the conflict." The use of the word "aliens" excludes protected persons who are in the territory of their home State. Section III of Part III covers protected persons who "fall into the hands" of the enemy in occupied territory. This follows from the title of the section ("Occupied Territories"). It also follows from the content of its provisions. Section IV of Part III governs the treatment of interned persons. The first article in the section, Article 79, provides that parties to the conflict shall not intern protected persons, except in accordance with the provisions of Articles 41, 42, 43, 68, and 78. As the latter articles are contained in Sections II and III, respectively, of Part III, Section IV tracks the limited scope of application of those sections.

Finally, the provisions of Section I of Part III are, according to the title of that section, common to the territories of the parties to the conflict and to occupied territories. This can be understood as referring (only) to enemy territory and occupied territory, thus reflecting the scope of application of Sections II and III.[42] It is also possible to come to a different interpretation. This will be discussed in more detail later in section 5.

From this overview of the different sections of Part III, it can be concluded that the textual structure of Part III supports the "broad intermediate theory."

4. THE *TRAVAUX PRÉPARATOIRES*

This section will explore whether the *travaux préparatoires* of GC IV confirm the hypothesis that the drafters of the convention intended to exclude unprivileged belligerents in their home territory from the full ambit of protections provided for in the convention. Much of the literature on the scope of application of GC IV refers to the treaty's preparatory work. A particularly in-depth analysis has been conducted by Yutaka Arai-Takahashi, who consulted not only the Final Records of the Diplomatic Conference of Geneva in 1949 but also many other published and unpublished materials as well.[43] His analysis will be regularly referred to in the following.

42. Arai-Takahashi, *supra* note 5, at 95, n. 96, states that this is the "conventional understanding."

43. Yutaka Arai-Takahashi, *Teasingly Inconclusive?—Teasing Out from the Travaux Préparatoires the Drafters' Intentions on the So-called "Homeland Battlefield Unprivileged Belligerents" under the 1949 Geneva Conventions*, Israel Yearbook on Human Rights 1 (2003–2004).

As a starting point, in view of the close relationship between GC III and GC IV, it is necessary to look at the *travaux* of both conventions. The drafters of GC III extensively discussed the legal consequences for persons not benefiting from POW status.[44] GC IV was adopted by Committee III of the 1949 Diplomatic Conference, which did not discuss the personal scope of application of GC IV, or what would become its Article 4, in any detail. Draft Article 3 of the "Stockholm draft" of GC IV, which was the text submitted to the diplomatic conference, did not contain a territorial limitation. What would become Article 5 of GC IV was not part of the Stockholm draft, but was introduced during the Geneva Conference.

What can be gleaned from the discussions on these articles is that several delegates in Committee III considered that draft Article 3 was too broad. Some delegates seemed to be of the view that unprivileged belligerents should be excluded from the scope of GC IV, or at least from the protections granted to "protected persons." They considered that the Stockholm draft did not provide for such an exclusion. Thus, the U.K. delegate in Committee III stated that "[i]f Article 3 remained unchanged . . . [this] would also cover individuals participating in hostilities in violation of the laws of war."[45] A similar position seems to have been taken by the delegates of Switzerland and Norway.[46] Other delegations disagreed.[47] Ultimately, a compromise was found in what is now Article 5.[48] This provision treats unprivileged belligerents as "protected persons," but allows States to derogate from certain protections in certain circumstances.

The rest of the discussions in Committee III suggest that the representatives generally understood that the scope of Part III of GC IV was limited to protected persons in enemy territory and occupied territory only. It seems that they considered that civilians, including but not limited to unprivileged belligerents, in non-occupied home territory were not covered.[49] One particularly clear indication is that the report of Committee III to the Plenary expressly mentioned that Section I of Part III would apply to "aliens in the territory of a belligerent State" in addition to "the population–national or alien–resident in a country occupied by the enemy."[50] The report did not refer to persons in non-occupied home territory. It is submitted that this indicates that the drafters considered that Section I also did not apply to the latter category of persons.[51]

44. Arai-Takahashi, *supra* note 5, at 68.

45. Final Records, *supra* note 1, at 621, Committee III, 2nd Meeting, Apr. 26, 1949 (Brigadier Page, UK).

46. *Id.*

47. Dörmann, *supra* note 16, at 57.

48. *Id.*

49. Arai-Takahashi, *supra* note 43, at 23–24.

50. Final Record, *supra* note 1, at vol. II-A, at 821.

51. For additional indications, *see* Arai-Takahashi, *supra* note 43, at 13–24.

Of interest in the *travaux préparatoires* of GC III are the discussions concerning draft Article 3 of the Stockholm draft, which was to become Article 4A and 4B in the final text. Particularly relevant are the discussions concerning Article 3(3) of the Stockholm draft of GC III. This provision, which had been introduced by the United States, provided a "safety net" for persons captured or detained. It read:

> The present Convention shall also provide a minimum standard of protection for any other category of persons who are captured or detained as the result of an armed conflict and whose protection is not specifically provided for in any other Convention.[52]

This provision would have provided minimum protections for persons who did not meet the criteria for POW status. The third paragraph of draft Article 3 was ultimately not adopted. It appears from the discussions on this paragraph that both supporters and opponents of its adoption considered that the scope of application of GC IV was not comprehensive and did not include civilians in unoccupied home territory.[53] Supporters seem to have considered that the paragraph was important for protecting unprivileged belligerents in their home territory, implying that this gap was not already filled by GC IV. Denmark, for example, emphasized the gap-filling role of the third paragraph for all participants in hostilities who would not qualify for POW status.[54] Opponents of the paragraph, on the other hand, appear to have objected to the third paragraph because they considered that providing protection to unprivileged belligerents would disincentivize them to comply with POW conditions.[55]

The question of whether GC IV serves as a gap-filler for battlefield unprivileged belligerents also led to a debate in the context of Article 4 of the Stockholm draft of GC III, which became Article 5 of that treaty. Draft Article 4 provided for a tribunal to determine the status of captured persons whose status was unclear. In the debate on this provision, the Netherlands delegate made the statement cited at the beginning of this chapter. The statement excluded civilians who took up arms against the adverse party on the battlefield from GC IV. Thus, the delegate rejected the "safety net" role of GC IV for persons excluded from the ambit of GC III.[56] Arguably, the Dutch delegate only meant to exclude persons participating in

52. Final Record, *supra* note 1, at vol. I, at 73–74.

53. Arai-Takahashi, *supra* note 43, at 44.

54. Final Record, *supra* note 1, at vol. II-A, at 242–43.

55. Arai-Takahashi, *supra* note 43, at 38.

56. Arai-Takahashi notes that the statement may also be interpreted as recognizing a third category of persons, between civilians and combatants. Arai-Takahashi, *supra* note 43, at 42. It may be noted that the existence of such a category was later rejected by the Dutch government. *See* Parliamentary papers, *supra* note 29.

hostilities and not "peaceful" civilians found on the battlefield. This could be said to follow from his use of the words "civilians who are in the battlefield, taking up arms against the adverse party." As was already pointed out in the introduction, the Russian delegate did not agree. He stated that "[i]f a person is not recognized as a prisoner of war . . . , such a person would then be a civilian and would enjoy the full protection afforded by the Civilians Convention."[57] The United States may have shared the USSR's view. Arai-Takahashi infers this from a U.S. proposal in relation to the first subparagraph of Article 3(2) of the Stockholm POW draft.[58] The suggestion was to delete text in the draft article that provided rights to ex-members of the regular armed forces of an occupied State under GC III. The U.S. delegate explained that the reason for the proposed deletion was that the United States believed that persons to whom the text referred ought to be covered by the Civilians Convention and not by the Prisoners of War Convention.[59]

It appears that most of the drafters of GC III considered that the personal scope of protection of Part III of GC IV was not comprehensive in nature. They believed that Article 3(3) of the Stockholm POW draft would be the only gap-filler for persons who did not enjoy the protection of GC III. The *travaux préparatoires* thus seem to confirm that the majority of negotiators were of the view that Part III of GC IV only applied to protected persons in occupied territory or enemy territory.[60] This comports with the conclusion based on the text of Article 4 GC in its context, outlined in section 3.

5. NO COMPLETE EXCLUSION FROM GC IV PROTECTION OF CIVILIANS IN NON-OCCUPIED HOME TERRITORY

The interpretation of Article 4 GC IV advocated previously would exclude a potentially large group from the protection of Part III of GC IV. This does not, however, mean that they enjoy no protection whatsoever.

First, as already mentioned, Part II of the convention still covers them, as its scope of application is wider than that of Part III. Article 4(3) GC IV explicitly states that the provisions of Part II apply not only to "protected persons" as defined in Article 4, but are wider in application, as laid out in Article 13. The latter article provides that Part II covers "the whole of the populations of the countries in conflict, without any adverse distinction based, in particular, on race, nationality, religion or political opinion." This means that, as the original International

57. Final Record, *supra* note 1, at vol. II-B, at 271; 13th Plenary Meeting (Mr. Morosov), *supra* note 1.

58. Arai-Takahashi, *supra* note 43, at 45.

59. Final record, *supra* note 1, at vol. II-A, at 431.

60. *Id.* at 45–46.

Committee of the Red Cross (ICRC) commentary to Article 13 states, "the mere fact of a person residing in a territory belonging to or occupied by a party to the conflict, is sufficient to make Part II of the Convention applicable to him."[61] This includes both so-called "peaceful civilians" as well as "unprivileged belligerents" in non-occupied home territory, regardless of nationality.

Second, it can be argued that not all of Part III of GC IV is excluded in all cases. Section II of Part III only applies to aliens in the territory of an armed conflict and Section III only to persons in occupied territory. Section IV of Part III tracks the scope of application of Sections II and III, as discussed previously. Section I of Part III, however, has been understood to have a broader scope of application. This section is entitled "Provisions common to the territories of the parties to the conflict and to occupied territories." The fact that the title does not include the word "adverse" or "enemy" before the word "parties" has been interpreted as implying it has a broader scope of application than the rest of Part III.[62] This interpretation is reinforced by the fact that the title of this section uses the plural "territories" of the parties to the conflict, rather than the singular "territory."[63] It can thus encompass both the territory of the invading State and that of the invaded State. As was seen earlier in section 4, this does not seem to have been intended by the drafters of GC IV. However, if the general rule of treaty interpretation in Article 31 VCLT can lead to the conclusion that Section I has a broader scope of application, then in principle there is no need to consult the *travaux préparatoires* as a subsidiary source of treaty interpretation.

Civilians in non-occupied home territory also benefit from minimum standards that apply under customary IHL and are reflected in Common Article 3 and Article 75 AP I.[64] Under customary IHL, for example, arbitrary deprivation of liberty is not allowed.[65] The implementation of this rule would arguably encompass certain procedural requirements. Article 75 AP I provides fundamental guarantees for persons affected by an armed conflict who are in the power of a party to the conflict and who do not benefit from more favorable treatment under the Geneva Conventions or AP I. This includes individuals who are not "protected persons" in the sense of Article 4 GC IV because of their nationality. It is submitted that it also includes unprivileged belligerents on their own territory

61. 1958 Commentary, *supra* note 17, at 119–20.

62. Arai-Takahashi, *supra* note 5, at 95.

63. Arai-Takahashi, *supra* note 5, at 94–95.

64. *See, e.g.*, William H. Taft IV, *The Law of Armed Conflict after 9/11: Some Salient Features*, 28 Yale Journal of International Law 319, 321–22 (2003); Pejic, *supra* note 4, at 341; Dörmann, *supra* note 16, at 67–68.

65. 1 Jean-Marie Henckaerts & Louise Doswald-Beck, Customary International Humanitarian law 344 r. 99 (2005).

which is not occupied. They are "other persons denied prisoner-of-war status," which is one of the categories mentioned in the ICRC commentary to Article 75 AP I as being covered by its provisions.[66]

Finally, international human rights law will in principle continue to apply during an armed conflict.[67] As such, it may provide additional protection. This is the case in particular for persons, including unprivileged belligerents, who are detained. There is little doubt that detainees fall within the "jurisdiction" of a detaining power, and thus enjoy the protections provided for by applicable human rights treaties.[68] Of particular relevance, at least for States parties to the European Convention in Human Rights (ECHR), is the judgment of the Grand Chamber of the European Court of Human Rights in *Hassan v. United Kingdom*.[69] The case concerned a person detained by British forces in Iraq, who had reason to believe that he might be:

> either a person who should be detained as a prisoner of war or whose internment was necessary for imperative reasons of security, both of which provided a legitimate ground for capture and detention under the Third and Fourth Geneva Conventions.[70]

The Court found that Article 5 of the ECHR applied, albeit interpreted in a manner which took into account the context and the rules of IHL. It then went on to apply adapted procedural safeguards to the situation of the victim, who may have been an unprivileged belligerent. In other words, it did not suggest that unprivileged belligerents would be excluded from procedural safeguards.

Still, accepting the "intermediate theory" as the correct interpretation of the personal scope of application of GC IV entails the exclusion of civilians, both "peaceful" and unprivileged belligerents, from important protections in Sections

66. Claude Pilloud, Jean de Preux, Yves Sandoz & Bruno Zimmermann, Commentary on the Additional Protocols of 8 June 1977 to the Geneva Conventions of 12 August 1949, at 854 (1987).

67. Regarding the application of the International Covenant on Civil and Political Rights during armed conflict, *see* UN Human Rights Committee (HRC), *General Comment No. 31*, The nature of the general legal obligation imposed on States Parties to the Covenant, CCPR/C/21/Rev.1/Add.13, 5, ¶ 11 (May 26, 2004).

68. *See* Walter Kälin & Jörg Künzli, *Human Rights Bodies: A Comparative Approach*, *in* Research Handbook on Human Rights and Humanitarian Law 188, 198–99 (Robert Kolb, Gloria Gaggioli, & Pavle Kilibarda eds., 2022).

69. Hassan v. United Kingdom, 2014-VI Eur. Ct. H.R. 1, https://www.echr.coe.int/Documents/Reports_Recueil_2014-VI.pdf.

70. *Id.* at ¶ 109.

II, III, and IV of Part III of GC IV, thus creating a significant normative gap.[71] This merits thinking about how the lacuna can be mitigated, which is explored in the following.

6. ENLARGING THE PERSONAL SCOPE OF APPLICATION OF GC IV: DEFINING OCCUPATION

As was discussed in the preceding sections, there are strong arguments for concluding that GC IV should be interpreted as not protecting civilians in non-occupied territory of their home State under Part III, while covering those in occupied territory. In consequence, the question of what constitutes an occupation is of great importance.[72] More precisely, the issue is at which point an invasion turns into an occupation. The sooner this is the case, the sooner the protections of Part III will apply to civilians in their home territory.

The traditional understanding of when there is an occupation is based on Article 42 of the 1907 Hague Regulation, which reads:

> Territory is considered occupied when it is actually placed under the authority of the hostile army. The occupation extends only to the territory where such authority has been established and can be exercised.

Based on these provisions, a clear distinction has been made in the literature between the phases of occupation and invasion.[73] At least until the adoption of the Geneva Conventions, it was generally accepted that the law of occupation starts to apply only after a minimum level of stability has been reached in an invaded area.

The provisions on occupation in the Hague Regulations were complemented by Section III of Part III of GC IV. The convention broadened the scope of application of occupation law by providing in Article 2(2) that an occupation meeting no armed resistance is also covered. GC IV is silent on when an invasion turns into an occupation. In his commentary to the Geneva Conventions, Jean Pictet[74] argued that the term "occupation" as used in GC IV must be construed more widely than the same term used in Article 42 of the Hague Regulations. According to Pictet,

71. Jelena Pejic, *The Other Side of Civilian Protection: The 1949 Fourth Geneva Convention*, Articles of War (Mar. 7, 2022), https://lieber.westpoint.edu/other-side-civilian-protection-fourth-geneva-convention/.

72. Kenneth Watkin, *Warriors Without Rights? Combatants, Unprivileged Belligerents, and the Struggle over Legitimacy*, Harvard University Program on Humanitarian Policy and Conflict Research Occasional Paper 54 (2005).

73. *See, e.g.*, Yoram Dinstein, The International Law of Belligerent Occupation 38 (2009).

74. *See* 1958 Commentary, *supra* note 17, at 60.

the provisions of GC IV are triggered as soon as enemy forces exercise control over a person. The test to be applied is based on control over persons, rather than over territory as required under the Hague Regulations. Consequently, according to Pictet:

> There is no intermediate period between what might be termed the invasion phase and the inauguration of a stable regime of occupation. Even a patrol which penetrates into enemy territory without any intention of staying there must respect the Conventions in its dealings with the civilians it meets.[75]

Such an understanding would leave no loophole in the protection provided by GC IV as "all persons who find themselves in the hands of a Party to the conflict or an Occupying Power of which they are not nationals are protected persons."[76] Because this interpretation would increase the number of persons protected by GC IV, it has also been referred to as the "maximalist protection theory" on the scope of application of that treaty.[77]

The theory finds some support in the literature.[78] It also appears to have been embraced by a Trial Chamber of the International Criminal Tribunal for the former Yugoslavia in the *Naletilić and Martinović* case.[79] There are serious arguments, however, for questioning the "Pictet theory." This author has discussed them elsewhere in detail[80] and only a brief summary is therefore provided in this chapter. The first concerns the wording of Article 4 GC IV. It refers to persons who find themselves in the hands of, inter alia, an occupying power. The article thus appears to require a preexisting occupation, in the context of which persons find themselves in its hands. In other words, an occupation does not come about through the fact that persons find themselves in the hands of an adverse party, without more.

A second argument is that accepting the "Pictet theory" would lead to a situation in which the determination of whether a person is a "protected person" is conflated with the test for determining whether there is an occupation.[81] This

75. *Id.*

76. *Id.*

77. Arai-Takahashi, *supra* note 5, at 83.

78. *See, e.g.*, MICHAEL SIEGRIST, THE FUNCTIONAL BEGINNING OF BELLIGERENT OCCUPATION (2011); D. Thürer, *Current Challenges to the Law of Occupation*, PROCEEDINGS OF THE BRUGES COLLOQUIUM 9, 20–21 (2005).

79. Prosecutor v. Naletilić and Martinović, Case No. IT-98-34-T, Judgment, ¶¶ 219–21 (Int'l Crim. Trib. for the former Yugoslavia Mar. 31, 2003).

80. Marten Zwanenburg, *Challenging the Pictet Theory*, 94 INTERNATIONAL REVIEW OF THE RED CROSS 30 (2012).

81. VAIOS KOUTROULIS, LE DEBUT ET LA FIN DE L'APPLICATION DU DROIT DE L'OCCUPATION 69 (2010).

is difficult to reconcile with the existence of a section in the Fourth Geneva Convention that is specifically devoted to situations of occupation. Third, nothing in the *travaux préparatoires* of the Geneva Conventions suggests that the drafters intended to depart from the previously accepted notion of occupation.[82] If they had intended to introduce such a radical departure in the Fourth Geneva Convention, one would at the very least expect such an intent to have been mentioned during the debates. Finally, the theory can be criticized for its practical viability. It must be questioned whether an occupying power can fulfill many of the obligations imposed by GC IV on occupying powers unless it has effective territorial control.[83] It has been suggested by proponents that there is no obligation for an occupying power to respect all the provisions of the law of occupation from the beginning.[84] Commentators have proposed particular standards for determining which rules would apply and which not.[85] It may be questioned, however, whether these standards provide sufficient guidance. It is thus submitted that the "Pictet theory" must be rejected,[86] as it does not offer a possibility to "close the gap" in the protection offered by GC IV.

7. CONCLUSION

This chapter focused on the personal scope of application of GC IV, in particular on the protection of "unprivileged belligerents." The issue is important, because whether or not a person falls within the scope of GC IV determines whether or not they enjoy important protections during international armed conflict. A case in point is the armed conflict between Russia and Ukraine in which there have been reports of a range of serious violations of GC IV against civilians, including those who may be deemed "unprivileged belligerents." The apparent resurgence of armed conflicts between States[87] indicates that the unresolved questions related to their protection are likely to remain on the legal (and operational) agenda. Another development that underlines the importance of the scope of application

82. Marten Zwanenburg, *The Law of Occupation Revisited: The Beginning of an Occupation*, 10 Yearbook of International Humanitarian Law 99, 108 (2007).

83. Arai-Takahashi, *supra* note 5, at 90.

84. *See, e.g.*, Robert Kolb & Sylvain Vité, Le Droit de l'Occupation Militaire: Perspectives Historiques et Enjeux Juridiques Actuels 145–46 (2009).

85. Julia Grignon, *The Beginning of Application of International Humanitarian Law: A Discussion of a Few Challenges*, 96 International Review of the Red Cross 139, 154 (2014).

86. For a similar conclusion, *see* Arai-Takahashi, *supra* note 5, at 92; Watkin, *supra* note 72, at 55.

87. *See, e.g.*, ICRC, Twelve Issues for 2022: What States Can Do to Ensure Respect for International Humanitarian Law 2 (2022).

of GC IV is the "civilianization" of warfighting.[88] This refers to the increasing role that civilians play in armed conflicts.

Interpretations of the scope of application of GC IV range from a "maximalist protection" view to the "total exclusionary theory." Between these two extremes lies the "intermediate theory," which itself has a narrow and a broad variant. This chapter analyzed the different interpretations, taking the rules of treaty interpretation as a starting point. The main provision examined was Article 4 GC IV, which includes a definition of the term "protected person." The chapter also analyzed other treaty provisions which must be read in conjunction with Article 4, including in, particular, Article 5 GC IV. It found that arguments for the "total exclusionary theory" and the "narrow intermediate theory" are problematic. Support for the "broad intermediate theory," on the other hand, can be found in the textual structure of GC IV, as well as in the *travaux préparatoires* of the Geneva Conventions. Although this interpretation excludes a potentially large group of persons from the ambit of Part III of GC IV, it does not result in a complete lack of protection. Such persons are covered by rules in Part II of GC IV, rules of customary law in common Article 3 and Article 75 AP I, as well as, arguably, Section I of Part III of GC IV. The chapter also analyzed the arguments of those who have attempted to further increase protection by suggesting that the term "occupation" in GC IV has a different meaning than in the 1907 Hague Regulations. It was found that the "maximalist protection" theory, although appealing, must be rejected.

88. *See, e.g.*, Charles Garraway, *The Changing Character of the Participants in War: Civilianization of Warfighting and the Concept of "Direct Participation in Hostilities,"* 87 International Law Studies 177 (2011); Andreas Wenger & Simon Mason, *The Civilianization of Armed Conflict: Trends and Implications*, 90 International Review of the Red Cross 835 (2008).

3

The Object and Purpose of the Fourth Geneva Convention

KUBO MAČÁK* AND ELLEN POLICINSKI**

1. INTRODUCTION

The 1949 Geneva Convention Relative to the Protection of Civilian Persons in Time of War (Fourth Convention) provides a practical and effective framework for the protection of civilians in international armed conflicts that retains its relevance 75 years after adoption. As is the case with all treaties, the Convention's object and purpose has[1] a concrete impact on how its terms are interpreted, giving insights into the ordinary meaning of the text and allowing the aim of the Convention to be fully grasped.

This chapter aims to identify the object and purpose of the Fourth Convention. It starts by expanding on certain specificities relevant to determining the object

* Professor of International Law, University of Exeter, United Kingdom.

** Legal Adviser, Commentaries Update Project, International Committee of the Red Cross. The following is an extract of a longer text initially published as: Kubo Mačák & Ellen Policinski, *In Pursuit of a Treaty's Soul: A Study of the Object and Purpose of the Fourth Geneva Convention*, 73(2) INTERNATIONAL AND COMPARATIVE LAW QUARTERLY 385 (2024). It has been edited for length and readability. Previous versions were presented at Temple University's Beasley School of Law on Oct. 30, 2023 and at the Lieber Workshop on Civilian Protection in Armed Conflict: Select Issues on Nov. 7, 2023 at West Point. The authors gratefully acknowledge the engagement and insights of all participants, as well as the research support of Elias Alhihi, Elina Hammarström, Thibaud de la Bourdonnaye, and Stella Nasirumbi. The opinions expressed do not necessarily reflect those of the ICRC or its Legal Division.

1. The authors submit that the formulation "object and purpose" is a singular concept, which is why it is referred to in this chapter in the grammatically singular form.

Kubo Mačák and Ellen Policinski, *The Object and Purpose of the Fourth Geneva Convention* In: *Civilian Protection in Armed Conflict*. Edited by: Jelena Pejic and Captain Margaret Kotlik, Oxford University Press.
 DOI: 10.1093/oso/9780197793176.003.0003

and purpose of international humanitarian law (IHL) treaties, including the Fourth Convention. It then outlines elements key to discerning the object and purpose of IHL treaties and applies them to establish the object and purpose of the Convention. The chapter concludes by demonstrating how the object and purpose of the Fourth Convention may help resolve specific interpretive dilemmas.

2. WHAT ARE THE SPECIFICITIES OF HUMANITARIAN LAW TREATIES?

International humanitarian law, though designed to apply in the most extreme of circumstances, is subject to the same principles of public international law as other bodies of international law. Its sources correspond to those provided for in Article 38 of the Statute of the International Court of Justice (ICJ), and it is adjudicated by international and domestic tribunals. This has been confirmed time and again by the practice of States,[2] international bodies[3] and courts,[4] and legal scholarship.[5] IHL treaties are also subject to the same basic rules of interpretation as other

2. *See, e.g.*, Comprehensive Agreement on Respect for Human Rights and International Humanitarian Law between the Government of the Republic of the Philippines and the National Democratic Front of the Philippines, The Hague (Mar. 16, 1998); Arrangement between the Government of the United Kingdom and the Government of the United States of America concerning U.S. support for the transfer of UK-held detainees from UK detention to the Afghan authorities, Parwan (May 2, 2013). *See also* the ICRC's study on customary international humanitarian law: 2 Customary International Humanitarian Law (Jean-Marie Henckaerts & Louise Doswald-Beck eds., 2005).

3. *See, e.g.*, U.N. Secretary-General, Bulletin: Observance by United Nations Forces of International Humanitarian Law, U.N. Doc. ST/SGB/1999/13 (Aug. 6, 1999); Official Journal of the European Union, 2009/C327/04 (2005).

4. Tribunals have been established specifically to address violations of international law, including IHL. In addition, the International Criminal Court (ICC), established by the Rome Statute in 1998, has jurisdiction over certain serious violations of the Geneva Conventions, and the ICJ has also rendered decisions related to IHL, for example, the *Wall* Advisory Opinion and the *Nuclear Weapons* Advisory Opinion: Legal Consequences of the Construction of a Wall in the Occupied Palestinian Territory, Advisory Opinion, 2004 I.C.J. Rep. 136 (July 9); Legality of the Threat or Use of Nuclear Weapons, Advisory Opinion, 1996 I.C.J. Rep. 226 (July 8), respectively.

5. *See, e.g.*, Mary Ellen O'Connell, *Historical Development and Legal Basis*, *in* The Handbook of International Humanitarian Law 10 (Dieter Fleck eds., 4th ed. 2021); Ellen Policinski, *Treaty Interpretation in the Fog of War: The Evolution of ICRC's Methodology*, *in* Practice of Interpretation (Panos Merkouris and Sotirios-Ioannis Lekkas eds., forthcoming). *But see* Lisa Hajjar, *The Counterterrorism War Paradigm versus International Humanitarian Law: The Legal Contradictions and Global Consequences of the US "War on Terror,"* 44(4) Law & Social Inquiry 922 (2019).

treaties.[6] There are, however, three specificities of IHL treaties that are relevant for their interpretation in general and for the determination of their object and purpose in particular.

2.1 *Jus Cogens* Nature of Norms Contained in Humanitarian Law Treaties

First, many IHL norms have the character of *jus cogens*, or peremptory norms. The Vienna Convention on the Law of Treaties (VCLT) defines a peremptory norm of general international law as "a norm accepted and recognized by the international community of States as a whole as a norm from which no derogation is permitted and which can be modified only by a subsequent norm of general international law having the same character."[7] The ICJ has held that "a great many rules of humanitarian law" constitute "intransgressible principles of international customary law."[8] For its part, the International Law Commission (ILC) has observed that it is "generally accepted" that these rules are peremptory in nature.[9]

The Geneva Conventions expressly prohibit any agreement that would diminish the protections individuals are entitled to under the Conventions.[10] This bolsters the argument that numerous norms in the Conventions are non-derogable and, therefore, of a peremptory nature. Certain scholars even contend that *all* rules

6. Robert Kolb & Katherine Del Mar, *Treaties for Armed Conflict*, *in* The Oxford Handbook of International Law in Armed Conflict 50, 79 (Andrew Clapham & Paola Gaeta eds., 2014); Marco Sassòli, International Humanitarian Law: Rules, Controversies and Solutions to Problems Arising in Warfare (2019).

7. Vienna Convention on the Law of Treaties art. 53, adopted May 23,1969, entered into force Jan. 27, 1980, 1155 U.N.T.S. 331 [hereinafter VCLT].

8. *Nuclear Weapons* Advisory Opinion, *supra* note 4; *Wall* Advisory Opinion, *supra* note 4.

9. Commentary on art. 40, Articles on State Responsibility ILC, A/56/10, ¶ 5 (2001).

10. Geneva Convention (I) for the Amelioration of the Condition of the Wounded and Sick in Armed Forces in the Field, Aug. 12, 1949, 75 U.N.T.S. 31 [hereinafter GC I]; Geneva Convention (II) for the Amelioration of the Condition of the Wounded, Sick and Shipwrecked Members of the Armed Forces at Sea, Aug. 12, 1949, 75 U.N.T.S. 85 [hereinafter GC II]; Geneva Convention (III) Relative to the Treatment of Prisoners of War, Aug.12, 1949, U.N.T.S. 135 [hereinafter GC III]; Geneva Convention (IV) Relative to the Protection of Civilian Persons in Time of War, Aug. 12, 1949, 75 U.N.T.S. 287 [hereinafter GC IV], common arts. 6/6/6/7 and 7/7/7/8; and GC IV art. 47. *See also* Georges Abi-Saab, *The Specificities of Humanitarian Law*, *in* Studies and Essays on International Humanitarian Law and Red Cross Principles in Honour of Jean Pictet 273 (Christophe Swinarski ed., 1984).

in the Geneva Conventions should be considered *jus cogens*,[11] a contention that probably goes too far.[12]

Given the peremptory character of many of the rules contained in IHL treaties, Georges Abi-Saab has advocated for their interpretation "towards perfecting the content and expanding the ambit of humanitarian protection."[13] Echoing this, Robert Kolb and Katherine Del Mar have suggested that "if it is held that IHL contains a great number of public order, public policy or *jus cogens* norms, it seems quite understandable that the interpretation of such texts has to be expansive rather than narrow."[14] These statements should not be misunderstood as endorsing unbridled, expansive approaches to the interpretation of treaties containing peremptory norms. Rather, the fact that no derogation is permitted from certain rules means that their interpretation must closely align with the community interest they reflect.

When interpreting IHL treaties containing peremptory norms, like the Geneva Conventions, emphasis should be placed on strengthening the humanitarian protection they aim to provide. Kolb and Del Mar speak in this connection of a "human-centred" approach to IHL.[15] This is also how Abi-Saab's goal of "perfecting the content and expanding the ambit" should be understood.[16] Accordingly, the *jus cogens* nature of many IHL rules supports adopting a protective approach to interpreting the object and purpose of the treaties in which they are contained.

2.2 *Erga Omnes* Character of Humanitarian Law Treaties

The second specificity is the *erga omnes partes* character of IHL treaties, which differ from many other international treaties in that they are not transactional. This feature is, of course, not unique to IHL treaties. For instance, the 1948 Genocide Convention is also not designed to serve the interests of individual

11. *See, e.g.*, Egon Schwelb, *Some Aspects of International Jus Cogens as Formulated by the International Law Commission* 61(4) AJIL 946, 956–57 (1967); ALEXANDER ORAKHELASHVILI, PEREMPTORY NORMS IN INTERNATIONAL LAW 90 (2006).

12. *See* Iain Scobbie, *The Invocation of Responsibility for the Breach of "Obligations under Peremptory Norms of General International Law,"* 13 EUROPEAN JOURNAL OF INTERNATIONAL LAW 1201, 1211(2002); Asif Hameed, *Unravelling the Mystery of Jus Cogens in International Law*, 84(1) BRITISH YEARBOOK OF INTERNATIONAL LAW 52, 70 (2014).

13. Abi-Saab, *supra* note 10, at 273.

14. Kolb & Del Mar, *supra* note 6, at 80 (internal footnote omitted).

15. *Id.*

16. Abi-Saab, *supra* note 10, at 273.

States, but rather "a common interest, namely the accomplishment of those high purposes which are the *raison d'être* of the convention."[17]

Similarly, the object and purpose of the 1984 Convention against Torture (CAT) is "to make more effective the struggle against torture . . . throughout the world."[18] On that basis, the ICJ held in *Belgium v. Senegal* that "[t]he States parties to the Convention have a *common interest* to ensure, in view of their shared values, that acts of torture are prevented and that, if they occur, their authors do not enjoy impunity." The ICJ went on to describe States' obligations under the CAT as *erga omnes* in nature and made a link to the Genocide Convention.[19] In 2023, Canada and the Netherlands instituted proceedings against Syria before the ICJ citing the *Belgium v. Senegal* case in seeking compliance with Syria's obligations under the CAT and describing them as "of an erga omnes partes nature, and . . . thus owed to the Applicants."[20]

The Geneva Conventions likewise create *erga omnes partes* obligations for the High Contracting Parties, which, given the universal ratification of the Conventions, means all States.[21] For example, under Common Article 1 of the Conventions, States must not only apply their provisions, but must also do everything reasonably in their power to ensure respect for the provisions by others. In doing so, the Conventions reaffirm the legal interest of the entire international community in their observance, demonstrating the *erga omnes* nature of the obligations created by these core IHL treaties.[22]

To sum up, if the effect of a treaty is *erga omnes*, this logically means that its object and purpose cannot be to merely establish a reciprocal exchange of rights and duties between the State parties for their mutual benefit.[23] There must, instead, be some "high ideal"[24] that the parties aspire to. For IHL treaties, such a high ideal is greater

17. Reservations to the Genocide Convention on the Prevention and Punishment of the Crime of Genocide, Advisory Opinion, 1951 I.C.J. Rep. 15, 23 (May 28).

18. Convention Against Torture and Other Cruel, Inhuman or Degrading Treatment or Punishment Preamble, Dec. 10, 1984, 1465 U.N.T.S. 85.

19. Questions Relating to the Obligation to Prosecute or Extradite (Belgium v. Senegal), Judgment, 2012 I.C.J. Rep. 422, 449 (July 20).

20. Joint Application Instituting Proceedings Concerning a Dispute under the Convention Against Torture and Other Cruel, Inhuman or Degrading Treatment or Punishment (Canada and the Kingdom of the Netherlands v. The Syrian Arab Republic), 2023 I.C.J., ¶ 7 (June 8).

21. International Committee of the Red Cross, Commentary on the Third Geneva Convention: Convention (III) Relative to the Treatment of Prisoners of War, at 48 ¶ 152 (2021) [hereinafter Commentary on GC III]; *Wall* Advisory Opinion, *supra* note 4, at 199 ¶ 157; Prosecutor v. Kupreškić et al. (Judgment) 2000 IT-95-16-T ¶ 519 (Jan. 14, 2000).

22. Commentary on GC III, *supra* note 21, at 48–49 ¶¶ 152–53.

23. *See, e.g.*, *The Effect of Reservations on the Entry into Force of American Convention on Human Rights (Arts. 74 and 75)*, Advisory Opinion, 8 Inter-Amer. Comm'n H.R. (1982).

24. *Reservations to the Genocide Convention*, *supra* note 17, at 23.

protection of persons affected by and amelioration of suffering in armed conflict.[25] These treaties, including their object and purpose, should be interpreted in light of that overarching approach.

2.3 Balance Between Humanity and Military Necessity

A balance between humanitarian considerations and military necessity is a hallmark of IHL,[26] reflecting and informing the entire normative framework of this body of norms. It shapes the context in which its rules and other principles must be interpreted. At first glance, these two pillars of IHL may seem diametrically opposed. However, the true picture is more nuanced. IHL is not based on a balance between pacifism and militarism, or between the rights of civilians/persons *hors de combat* and military practicality. It reflects a balance between humanity, a principle that "impose[s] certain limits on the means and methods of warfare, and require[s] that those who have fallen into enemy hands be treated humanely at all times,"[27] and military necessity, "the necessity for measures which are essential to attain the goals of war, and which are lawful in accordance with the laws and customs of war."[28]

These IHL tenets therefore both contribute to the overall center of gravity of IHL as a legal framework, which is the protection of those affected by armed conflict.[29] In other words, military necessity is not only permissive. It also limits military action to what is *necessary*, thereby delivering protection in its own right.[30] For example, once a combatant is captured, it is no longer necessary to kill them to gain any military advantage as they have already been taken out of the fight.

25. *See, e.g.*, Application of the Convention on the Prevention and Punishment of the Crime of Genocide (Croatia v. Serbia) 2015 I.C.J. Rep. 3, 68 (Feb. 3); War and International Humanitarian Law, International Committee of the Red Cross (Oct. 29, 2010), https://www.icrc.org/en/article/war-and-international-humanitarian-law.

26. Commentary on GC III, *supra* note 21, at 26 ¶ 91.

27. Nils Melzer, International Humanitarian Law: A Comprehensive Introduction 19 (2022).

28. Commentary on the Additional Protocols of 8 June 1977 to the Geneva Conventions of 12 August 1949, at 393 (Yves Sandoz, Christophe Swinarski, & Bruno Zimmerman eds., 1987).

29. Commentary on GC III, *supra* note 21, at 183 ¶ 497, note 181. At the time of writing, this is not a universally shared view. For a different approach, *see, e.g.*, Michael N. Schmitt, *Military Necessity and Humanity in International Humanitarian Law: Preserving the Delicate Balance*, 50(4) Virginia Journal of International Law 795, 798–801 (2010). For discussion of the normative effect of these principles, *see, e.g.*, *Forum: The ICRC Interpretive Guidance on the Notion of Direct Participation in Hostilities Under International Humanitarian Law*, 42(3) New York University Journal of International Law and Politics 637–916 (2010).

30. *See, e.g.*, Office of the General Counsel, U.S. Department of Defense, Law of War Manual, § 1035 (rev. ed., 2023). *See also* Yishai Beer, *Humanity Considerations Cannot Reduce*

Similarly, the use of a weapon that causes unnecessary suffering to neutralize a combatant fails the test of military necessity by definition.

Whenever new IHL treaties are made, both "States' military interest and realpolitik on the one hand, and concerns for humanity on the other" animate the negotiating and drafting process.[31] The balance between these principles must therefore also underlie the interpretive process, including in the determination of a treaty's object and purpose.

3. WHAT INTERPRETIVE ELEMENTS MUST BE CONSIDERED?

The VCLT does not establish a methodology for the determination of the object and purpose of international treaties, and there is no other binding international instrument that provides it. Relevant scholarship is in agreement about the importance of evaluating the entire text of a treaty in order to determine its object and purpose.[32] Richard Gardiner considers that while "the preamble may be used as the source of a convenient summary of the object and purpose of a treaty, both the Vienna Convention (Article 31(2)) and practice make it clear that *an interpreter needs to read the whole treaty*."[33] Similarly, Mustapha Yasseen observes that "the object and purpose emerge from the text of the treaty; typically, they are stated in the preamble, but it is possible that the treaty doesn't expressly state them; the object and purpose can then be identified by examination of the text, *the entire text*, in light of the context for the purpose of interpreting the treaty."[34]

War's Hazards Alone: Revitalizing the Concept of Military Necessity 26(4) European Journal of International Law 801, 828 (2015).

31. Cordula Droege & Eirini Giorgou, *How International Humanitarian Law* Develops, 104 International Review of the Red Cross 1798, 1802 (2022). *See also* Schmitt, *supra* note 29, at 796; Kolb & Del Mar, *supra* note 6, at 50; Chris af Jochnick & Roger Normand, *The Legitimation of Violence: A Critical History of the Laws of War*, 35 Harvard International Law Journal 49, 50 (1994); Louise Arimatsu, *Territory, Boundaries and the Law of Armed Conflict*, 12 Yearbook of International Humanitarian Law 157, 161 (2009).

32. Alexander Orakhelashvili, The Interpretation of Acts and Rules in Public International Law 343 (2008); Katayoun Hosseinnejad, *Interpretation in Light of Which "Object and Purpose"?*, 61 German Yearbook of International Law 377, 388 (2018); Ulf Linderfalk, *On the Meaning of the "Object and Purpose" Criterion, in the Context of the Vienna Convention on the Law of Treaties, Article 19*, 72(4) Nordic Journal of International Law 429, 441–42 (2003); Vesna Crnić-Grotić, *Object and Purpose of Treaties in the Vienna Convention on the Law of Treaties*, 7 Asian Yearbook of International Law 141, 174 (1997).

33. Richard Gardiner, Treaty Interpretation 218 (2d ed. 2015) (emphasis added).

34. Mustapha Yasseen, *L'interprétation des traités d'après la Convention de Vienne sur le droit des traités*, 151 Recueil des Cours 1, 57 (1976) (authors' translation) (emphasis added).

The entire text of a treaty encapsulates its title, preamble, and all of its provisions, as well as any annexes.[35] Some of the provisions may be "programmatic" in nature in that they fix "an objective, in the light of which the other [t]reaty provisions are to be interpreted and applied."[36] Given that such provisions articulate the goals for which a given treaty was concluded, they should (if they exist) be given particular weight in the determination of that treaty's object and purpose.[37] Article 1 of the UN Charter, which lists the purposes of the United Nations, is a good example.[38]

The most authoritative text concerning the determination of the object and purpose of international treaties is the ILC's 2011 Guide to Practice on Reservations to Treaties.[39] Given that a reservation incompatible with the object and purpose of a treaty is impermissible under international law,[40] the ILC discussed at some length how the object and purpose should be determined.[41]

The Guide notes that in order to determine the object and purpose of a treaty, "a fairly general approach is required: it is not a question of 'dissecting' the treaty in minute detail and examining its provisions one by one, but of extracting the 'essence,' the overall 'mission' of the treaty."[42] It proposes a specific methodology for extracting this essence in succinctly formulated guideline 3.1.5.1:

35. *See, e.g.*, Oliver Dörr, *Article 31*, *in* VIENNA CONVENTION ON THE LAW OF TREATIES: A COMMENTARY 543 (Oliver Dörr & Kirsten Schmalenbach eds., 2012).

36. Oil Platforms Case (Islamic Republic of Iran v. United States of America), Preliminary Objection, Judgment, 1996 I.C.J. Rep. 803, 814 (Dec. 12).

37. *See, e.g.*, Isabelle Buffard & Karl Zemanek, *The "Object and Purpose" of a Treaty: An Enigma?*, 3 AUSTRIAN REVIEW OF INTERNATIONAL AND EUROPEAN LAW 311, 333 (1998).

38. These goals include "to maintain international peace and security [;] to develop friendly relations among nations [;] to achieve international co-operation in solving international problems of an economic, social, cultural, or humanitarian character, and in promoting and encouraging respect for human rights and for fundamental freedoms for all [;] and to be a centre for harmonizing the actions of nations in the attainment of these common ends." UN Charter art. 1.

39. Guide to Practice on Reservations to Treaties, *Report of the ILC*, 63rd session (April 26 to June 3 and July 4 to Aug. 12, 2011) U.N. Doc. A/66/10/Add.1 [hereinafter ILC Guide].

40. VCLT, *supra* note 6, art. 19; Vienna Convention on the Law of Treaties between States and International Organizations or between International Organizations art. 19, U.N. Doc. A/CONF.129/15 (1986).

41. It should be noted that there is some controversy as to whether the term "object and purpose" has the same meaning in, on the one hand, the context of assessing the compatibility of reservations and in, on the other hand, the context of treaty interpretation. The present text proceeds on the assumption that their meaning is indeed identical or at least sufficiently similar to allow for reliance on the ILC's analysis. *See* ILC Guide, *supra* note 39, commentary to guideline 3.1.5, ¶ 3.

42. ILC Guide, *supra* note 39, commentary to guideline 3.1.5, ¶ 2.

> The object and purpose of the treaty is to be determined in good faith, taking account of the terms of the treaty in their context, in particular the title and the preamble of the treaty. Recourse may also be had to the preparatory work of the treaty and the circumstances of its conclusion and, where appropriate, the subsequent practice of the parties.

The centrality of the text of a treaty is immediately evident, including "in particular" its title and preamble. The ILC also ascribes a certain weight to the preparatory work and the circumstances of the conclusion of the treaty. Its reference to the subsequent practice of the parties was motivated by "the view that the object and purpose of a treaty was likely to evolve over time,"[43] although, as will be seen, such subsequent practice has been fairly limited in relation to the Fourth Convention.

Overall, the process of identifying the object and purpose of a treaty is by necessity inductive. The individual elements listed in Paragraph 3.1.5.1 must be weighed and a good faith attempt made to derive the object and purpose from them. The process may even appear circular to some extent, because the VCLT formula for treaty interpretation already contains all of these elements *and* the object and purpose.[44]

4. HOW ARE THE INTERPRETIVE ELEMENTS APPLIED TO THE FOURTH GENEVA CONVENTION?

4.1 Title

The title of the Convention is "Geneva Convention *relative to* the Protection of Civilian Persons in Time of War of 12 August 1949" (emphasis added). The first two of the four Geneva Conventions use a different construction: Their titles use the preposition "for" to link the words "Geneva Convention" with the rest of the title ("for the Amelioration of the Condition of the Wounded and Sick in Armed Forces in the Field" and "for the Amelioration of the Condition of Wounded, Sick and Shipwrecked Members of Armed Forces at Sea," respectively).

The difference is not unintentional. The Fourth Convention was also originally drafted with the preposition "for." However, at the very end of the negotiating process, the delegation of Canada convinced the participants of the Diplomatic Conference to replace the word "for" with the phrase "relative to."[45] This phrase

43. ILC Guide, *supra* note 39, commentary to guideline 3.1.5.1, ¶ 7.

44. See William Schabas, *Reservations to Human Rights Treaties: Time for Innovation and Reform*, 32 Canadian Yearbook of International Law 39, 48 (1994).

45. *See* Final Record of the Diplomatic Conference of Geneva of 1949 (Federal Political Department, Bern) (Final Record) vol. II-B, at 456–58.

was modeled on the title of the 1929 Prisoners of War Convention and was reused in the title of the corresponding 1949 Third Geneva Convention.

Though intentional, this last-minute change was, however, unrelated to the overall goal of the Fourth Convention. It was motivated by a desire to ensure that the title accurately reflected the treaty's content. According to the delegation of Canada, the original formulation gave the inaccurate impression that the Convention dealt with "all aspects of the treatment of civilians in time of war."[46] As underscored by the Canadian and other delegations, this new convention would not regulate the conduct of hostilities,[47] a type of wartime conduct that profoundly affects civilians, but which would continue to be regulated by the 1899 and 1907 Hague Conventions and their accompanying regulations.[48]

Seconding the Canadian proposal, the Danish delegate noted that "we have drafted a text concerning only certain rights of the civilian population in time of war and under occupation, but the population has many other rights and privileges which are not provided for in this Convention."[49] It was for these reasons—to avoid an impression that the Convention was comprehensive in scope—that the change was adopted at the Conference. Thus, the title of the Fourth Convention does not determinately establish a clear object and purpose.

4.2 Preamble

The preamble of each of the four 1949 Geneva Conventions is a single sentence simply stating that the negotiators had agreed to the relevant treaty.[50] The reasons for the brevity of the preambles are well known and will not be repeated here.[51] Suffice it to say that although a detailed preamble for inclusion in all four draft conventions had been proposed, delegations could not agree on several aspects of it, such as whether and how to refer to a divine authority, and as a result they settled for the lowest common denominator, which was to remove all the substantive content from the drafts.[52]

46. *Id.* at 456.

47. *Id.* at vol. II-A, at 805 (United States); vol. II-B, at 407–09 (United States, Canada, Switzerland); 498 (Australia); 504 (Switzerland).

48. *See* GC IV, *supra* note 10, art. 154.

49. Final Record, *supra* note 45, at vol. II-B, at 457.

50. GC I, *supra* note 10, Preamble; GC II, *supra* note 10, Preamble; GC III, *supra* note 10, Preamble; GC IV, *supra* note 10, Preamble.

51. *See* Commentary on GC III, *supra* note 21, at 40–42 ¶¶ 135–39.

52. Final Record, *supra* note 45, vol. II-A, at 813.

Hence, the adopted preamble to the Fourth Convention consists merely of an introductory formula that links the title of the Convention with its substantive parts, but does not elaborate on the motivations behind the substantive text. It reads: "The undersigned Plenipotentiaries of the Governments represented at the Diplomatic Conference held at Geneva from April 21 to August 12, 1949, for the purpose of establishing a Convention for the Protection of Civilian Persons in Time of War, have agreed as follows[.]"

Discerning readers will notice that the preamble uses the "for" formulation instead of the "relative to" formulation that was included in the revised title. As noted in the original 1958 commentary, "this was no doubt an oversight"—the drafters apparently forgot to fix the preamble after they had agreed to amend the title.[53] One should thus not read more into this difference in wording.

Each of the first three Conventions of 1949 had a predecessor which did contain a specific preamble.[54] To some extent, those prior treaties' preambles can help cast light on the object and purpose of the successor treaties.[55] In the case of the Fourth Convention, no such source is available given that the Convention did not succeed any preexisting treaty on the same subject matter.[56] Thus, like the title, the preamble is of limited use when it comes to identifying the object and purpose of the Fourth Convention.

4.3 Substantive Text of the Treaty

In contrast to the elements of the Fourth Convention analyzed thus far, its substantive text gives a very clear indication of the treaty's underlying aims. This is the case despite the absence of programmatic articles that would establish an overarching objective in light of which the rest of the Convention's provisions are to be interpreted and applied. Instead, it is necessary to review the entirety of the text to extract its overall essence or mission.

53. Commentary on the Fourth Geneva Convention 10 note 1 (J. Pictet ed., 1958).

54. Preamble, Convention for the Amelioration of the Condition of the Wounded in Armies in the Field, 22 August 1864, 22 Stat. 940, 129 Consol. T.S. 361; Preamble, Convention for the Amelioration of the Condition of the Wounded and Sick in Armies in the Field, 6 July 1906, 35 Stat. 1885, 202 Consol. T.S. 144; Preamble, Convention No. X for the Adaptation to Maritime Warfare of the Principles of the Geneva Convention, 18 October 1907, 36 Stat. 2371, T.S. No. 543; Preamble, Convention Relative to the Treatment of Prisoners of War, 27 July 1929, 47 Stat. 2021, 118 L.N.T.S. 343.

55. *See* Jean-Marie Henckaerts, Kubo Mačák, Mikhail Orkin, & Ellen Policinski, *ICRC Perspectives on the Interpretation of the Third Geneva Convention More Than Seventy Years after Its Adoption, in* Prisoners of War in Contemporary Conflict 386–87 (Michael N. Schmitt & Christopher J. Koschnitzky eds., 2023).

56. On the relationship between the Fourth Convention and the 1899 and 1907 Hague Regulations, *see, e.g.*, Paolo Benvenuti, *Relationship with Prior and Subsequent Treaties and*

The text of the Convention, comprising 159 articles, is of considerable length. It is impossible to analyze each provision here, but certain overarching patterns and trends can nonetheless be identified. The vast majority of the treaty's substantive provisions lend protection to individuals who find themselves in the power of a party to the conflict. Only a few go in the direction of authorizing certain forms of conduct that can be seen as restrictive of individual rights. And even these provisions in fact set limits on the conduct that parties to an armed conflict may engage in, effectively precluding them from taking action that goes beyond a circumscribed sphere of permissible conduct.

For example, Article 5 authorizes parties to an international armed conflict to restrict the rights provided to persons protected by the Convention. It also underscores that such persons must nevertheless be treated humanely and must not be deprived of the rights of a fair and regular trial, thus setting clear and absolute limits on permissible derogations under the Convention.[57]

The ratio of protective/restrictive versus permissive/enabling provisions in the Convention is overwhelmingly in favor of the former. This is clear from the structure of the Convention: Aside from the general opening provisions and the closing provisions on the execution of the treaty, the core of the Convention (Articles 13–141 representing more than 80 percent of the text) is found in two parts expressly directed to the protection of the whole of the populations of the countries in conflict (Part II) and to the protection of a certain category of civilians designated as protected persons (Part III). The specific geographic and personal scope of application of these parts differs,[58] but common to them is the aim of enhancing the protection of individuals falling within their respective scope.[59]

This is also clear from the language used across the Convention. When it speaks of individuals or their property, it uses almost exclusively adjectives indicative of protection such as "respected,"[60] "protected,"[61] or entitled."[62] Conversely, when it refers to the parties to the conflict, it typically uses modal verbs characteristic of

Conventions, *in* THE 1949 GENEVA CONVENTIONS: A COMMENTARY 689 (Andrew Clapham, Paola Gaeta, & Marco Sassòli eds., 2015).

57. *See also* COMMENTARY ON THE FOURTH GENEVA CONVENTION, commentary on Article 5 (ICRC, forthcoming).

58. *See, e.g.*, Nishat Nishat, *The Structure of Geneva Convention IV and the Resulting Gaps in that Convention*, *in* THE GENEVA CONVENTIONS, A COMMENTARY 1069 (Andrew Clapham, Paola Gaeta, & Marco Sassòli eds., 2015).

59. For Part II specifically, *see* GC IV, *supra* note 10, art. 13, which expressly states that provisions in the said Part of the Convention are "intended to alleviate the sufferings caused by war."

60. *See, e.g.*, GC IV, *supra* note 10, arts. 18, 20, 21, 22, 130.

61. *See, e.g.*, GC IV, *supra* note 10, arts. 18, 20, 21, 27(1), 27(2), 85. This list does not include the numerous provisions that use the adjective in the phrase "protected persons."

62. *See, e.g.*, GC IV, *supra* note 10, arts. 19(1), 20(3), 27(1), 35(1), 35(2), 43(1).

assigning obligations such as "shall" or "must."[63] This reflects a global post–World War II trend in IHL to grant rights directly to individuals, which correspond to obligations incumbent on States (and in some cases on non-State armed groups).[64]

Provisions that authorize States to take certain measures, such as the already mentioned Article 5, or, to give other examples, rules authorizing the establishment of measures of control and security (including assigned residence and internment),[65] or the requisition or destruction of property by the occupying power,[66] are subject to strict conditions. The Convention makes it clear that they are exceptional in nature, while their role is to clarify and calibrate the necessary balance between humanity and military necessity.

Thus, for example, the regime of civilian internment elaborated in the Convention was meant to protect against the excesses of previous wars, during which civilians could be rounded up indiscriminately and detained without regard to their living conditions or ability to communicate with the outside world and thus be at risk, inter alia, of disappearance.[67] Far from undermining the protective tenor of the Fourth Convention, the legal regime governing security measures was developed to enhance the protection of civilians.

This understanding is also reflected in the scholarly literature.[68] For example, Yoram Dinstein observes that "the bulk of the instrument *lends protection*—either exclusively or *inter alia*—to the civilian population of occupied territories."[69] Similarly, Eyal Benvenisti highlights that "the focus of attention" in the Convention is on "the

63. *See, e.g.*, GC IV, *supra* note 10, arts. 9(2), 12(2), 15(2), 17, 18(4), 24(1), 24(2), 79, 81, 121(2), 132(2), 136(1), 136(2), 149(3).

64. *See generally* Lawrence Hill-Cawthorne, *Rights under International Humanitarian Law*, 28(4) European Journal of International Law 1187 (2017).

65. GC IV, *supra* note 10, arts. 27(4), 41–42, and 78. *See also* Anne Quintin, The Nature of International Humanitarian Law: A Permissive or Restrictive Regime? (2020).

66. GC IV, *supra* note 10, art. 53.

67. *See, e.g.*, Preliminary conference of the National Red Cross Societies for the study of the Conventions and of various problems relative to the Red Cross), Documents furnished by the ICRC, vol. III, 5–8 (Geneva, July 26–Aug. 3, 1946.

68. *See, e.g.*, Els Debuf, Captured in War: Lawful Internment in Armed Conflict 341–42 (2013),; Françoise Hampson, *Administrative Detention in Non-International Armed Conflicts*, *in* The Grey Zone: Civilian Protection Between Human Rights and the Laws of War 161 (Mark Lattimer & Philippe Sands eds., 2018); Marco Sassòli, *Legislation and Maintenance of Public Order and Civil Life by Occupying Powers*, 16 European Journal of International Law 661, 664–65 (2005). This view has also been adopted by some courts at international and domestic level. *See* Hassan v. the United Kingdom, Appl. no. 29750/09, ¶ 102, Eur. Ct. H.R., Judgment of Sept. 16, 2014; Abd Ali Hameed Al-Waheed et al. v. Ministry of Defence [2017] UKSC 2, 58.

69. Yoram Dinstein, The Law of Belligerent Occupation 6, 186 (2d ed. 2019).

protection of the population in the enemy's hands."[70] The substantive core of the Convention is indeed strongly protective in nature, with certain carefully calibrated adjustments to reflect the legitimate security needs of the belligerents.

4.4 The Other Three Geneva Conventions

The context of a treaty includes "any instrument which was made by one or more parties in connection with the conclusion of the treaty and accepted by the other parties as an instrument related to the treaty."[71] This means that the context for each Geneva Convention comprises the other three Conventions adopted simultaneously at the same Diplomatic Conference.[72] Examining each of their object and purpose thus informs the object and purpose of the Fourth Convention.

The overall object and purpose of the First Geneva Convention is to ensure respect for and protection of the wounded and sick, as well as the dead, in international armed conflict,[73] and of the Second Convention to ensure respect for and protection of the wounded, sick, and shipwrecked, as well as the dead, in international armed conflict at sea or other waters.[74] The Third Convention's overall object and purpose is to ensure that prisoners of war are humanely treated at all times, while allowing belligerents to intern captured enemy combatants to prevent them from returning to the battlefield.[75]

The object and purpose of the Fourth Convention must be consistent with the object and purpose of the other three Geneva Conventions of 1949. They all share a strong protective aim designed to improve respect for and the protection of the categories of persons they cover. Together they form a protective whole, encompassing all categories of individuals *hors de combat*. A recognition that belligerents are allowed to impose certain measures of control and security is part of the object and purpose of the Third Convention, reflecting the fact that

70. Eyal Benvenisti, The International Law of Occupation 11–12 (2d ed. 2012).

71. VCLT, *supra* note 7, art. 31(2)(b).

72. *See* Commentary on GC III, *supra* note 21, at 24–25 ¶ 85. Other such instruments made in connection with the Convention include the Final Act of the 1949 Diplomatic Conference and the resolutions adopted at the conference.

73. International Committee of the Red Cross, Commentary on the First Geneva Convention: Convention (I) for the Amelioration of the Condition of the Wounded and Sick in the Armed Forces in the Field ¶¶ 31, 30 (2016) [hereinafter Commentary on GC I].

74. International Committee of the Red Cross, Commentary on the Second Geneva Convention: Convention (II) for the Amelioration of the Condition of the Wounded, Sick and Shipwrecked Members of Armed Forces at Sea ¶¶ 31, 30 (2017) [hereinafter Commentary on GC II].

75. Commentary on GC III, *supra* note 21, at 26 ¶ 89.

the treaty contains strong permissions for belligerents to intern captured enemy combatants in order to prevent them from returning to the battlefield.[76] The Fourth Convention similarly establishes a regime of measures of control and security, such as internment if a civilian's activity poses a serious security threat, designed to circumscribe these measures within permissible limits to prevent abuses like those seen in World War II.[77] Thus, the object and purpose of the Fourth Convention, as outlined in this chapter, is similar to the object and purpose of the Third Convention. By contrast, the same cannot be said about the object and purpose of the First or Second Conventions, which do not establish measures of security and control.

4.5 Supplementary Means of Interpretation

Supplementary means of interpretation under Article 32 of the VCLT include the preparatory work of the treaty, the circumstances of its conclusion, and the subsequent practice of the parties. Early in the drafting process, the drafters agreed that they had an "obligation to come to an agreement in order to protect civilian populations from the horrors of war."[78] That formulation was built into the draft preamble of the future Civilians' Convention, which, as explained previously, was ultimately significantly shortened and stripped of all substantive content. Nonetheless, enhancing the protection of civilians in time of armed conflict was the motivation of the entire drafting and negotiation process, as evidenced by numerous expressions of the drafters attending the 1949 Diplomatic Conference in Geneva, whether in relation to the work of the conference as such or specifically in regard to the future Fourth Convention.

In alphabetical order: Australia referred to "the purpose of this Conference" as being "concerned with the alleviation of the sufferings of the victims of war."[79] Bulgaria stated that "the purpose of the Convention" was to defend "elementary human rights."[80] Czechoslovakia stated that the purpose of the Conference was "to draw up a new Convention for the protection of civilians in time of war."[81] According to Denmark, "[the Conventions'] object is to protect wounded,

76. *Id.*; *see also* Quintin, *supra* note 65, at ch. 7.

77. Preliminary conference of the National Red Cross Societies for the study of the Conventions and of various problems relative to the Red Cross Documents furnished by the ICRC, vol. III, at 1–2 (of the English document) (Geneva, July 26–Aug. 3, 1946).

78. Preamble, Revised and New Draft Conventions for the Protection of War Victims: Texts Approved and Amended by the XVIIth International Red Cross Conference (Stockholm, Aug. 1948).

79. Final Record, *supra* note 45, at vol. II-B, at 498.

80. *Id.* at vol. II-A, at 797.

81. *Id.* at vol. II-B, at 508.

sick and shipwrecked persons, prisoners of war and civil populations, in all circumstances."[82] France stated that "the object of the Convention was to provide for the protection of persons, and not to safeguard the rights of States."[83] The Holy See described "the main purpose of the Civilians' Convention [as] to protect civilian populations against the horrors of war."[84] Lebanon noted that "the object of [the Civilians Convention] was to humanize the rules of war."[85] Mexico stated that "the principal aim of the Convention was the protection of the civilian population."[86] Monaco described "[t]he purpose of the Civilians' Convention [as] to carry peace on into war."[87] The Soviet Union considered that "the humanitarian interests . . . were the object of the Convention"[88] and added that this was "a Convention whose purpose was the protection of the civilian population."[89] Switzerland said that "the purpose of our Conventions is to protect persons."[90] And the United States noted that "the present Conference had not been convened to revise the laws and customs of war; its purpose was to ensure the protection of war victims."[91]

The present authors have not been able to locate any statements that would negate these declarations of the Convention's protective aims. Two nonetheless deserve to be mentioned for the sake of completeness. First, in response to the French statement quoted earlier, the Australian delegate cautioned that "the rights, duties and obligations of States had to be taken into account no less than those of individuals."[92] However, viewed in the light of Australia's later express description of the purpose of the Convention as being "concerned with the alleviation of the sufferings of the victims of war,"[93] it seems that Australia's considered view did not actually differ from that taken by the other delegations.

Secondly, the United Kingdom stated that "[t]he object of the laws and customs of war was to establish a reasonable balance between the interests of the

82. *Id.* at 268, at 426.

83. *Id.* at vol. II-A, at 622.

84. *Id.* at 692.

85. *Id.* at 695.

86. *Id.* at 671.

87. *Id.* at 693.

88. *Id.* at 648.

89. *Id.* at 766.

90. *Id.* at vol. II-B, at 229, 415.

91. *Id.* at vol. II-A, at 650.

92. *Id.* at 622.

93. *Id.* at vol. II-B, at 498.

civilian population and those of the occupying forces."[94] This would appear to be a more cautious statement than that of other delegations, as it placed the interests of the individuals on a par with those of the States. However, a careful reading reveals that the U.K. delegate spoke of the entirety of IHL, and not of the draft Convention specifically. This baseline description of IHL is compatible with a normative approach designed to strengthen the protective/humanitarian side of the equation.[95] In fact, the United Kingdom considered the protective approach as the preferred purpose of the Convention, as is now known from an internal memorandum written at the time, which stated expressly:

> It is the view of the Government of the United Kingdom that *it should be the purpose of the Civilian Convention to protect, in time of war, those persons who have, by reason of the war, ceased to enjoy the diplomatic protection which would be theirs in peace time.*[96]

Agreement among delegations as to the essence of the Convention that was being drafted is confirmed by a contemporary report of Colonel Du Pasquier who represented Switzerland,[97] and also served as the rapporteur of Committee III tasked with the drafting of the Civilians' Convention. He reported:

> [A]ll the Delegations [were] fully convinced that the essential object of our Convention is effectively to prohibit the inhuman behaviour, one might say ferocity, with which the authorities of certain countries treated the civilians whom they had in their power' during the Second World War.[98]

Little more needs to be said of the circumstances of the Fourth Convention's conclusion. In general terms, the phrase "circumstances of its conclusion" from Article 32 of the VCLT is understood to refer to the political, social, cultural, and other

94. *Id.* at vol. II-A, at 767.

95. *See* § 2.3.

96. Government of the United Kingdom, Propositions and Observations of the Governments and other bodies on the 1948 Stockholm Draft, Memorandum by the Government of the United Kingdom 4 (emphasis added).

97. *See* Final Record, *supra* note 45, at vol. III, at 183–85.

98. *Id.* at 184. *See also* Final Record, *supra* note 45, at vol. II-A, at 806–07; Diplomatic conference of 1949, Minutes of Meetings, Commission III, Session 51, 11–12; Claude Du Pasquier, *Observations générales sur l'élaboration de la Convention relative à la protection des civils, à la Conférence diplomatique de Genève, in* 368 Revue internationale de la Croix Rouge 631 (1949).

factors surrounding a treaty's adoption.[99] The Fourth Convention was drafted and agreed on against the fallout of World War II and was designed to protect civilians against the recurrence of the horrors experienced. The circumstances of its conclusion thus further confirm the protective purpose behind it.

By contrast to the richness of the preparatory work, the relevant subsequent practice of the parties to the Convention related specifically to its object and purpose has been fairly scarce. The research for this chapter did not reveal any express statements by States parties on this topic.[100] A possible avenue for such expressions is the submission by States of reservations to international treaties or their reactions to reservations submitted by other States,[101] as illustrated by examples from the context of other IHL treaties.[102] A few reservations have been deposited in relation to the Fourth Convention,[103] but on none of these occasions did the acting States (whether those submitting a reservation or those reacting to one) expressly elaborate on what they considered the Convention's object and purpose to be.[104]

Many States have incorporated the Geneva Conventions into their military manuals.[105] However, such incorporations have avoided specifying a given State's view on the object and purpose of the Conventions. For example, the 2004

99. Mark E. Villiger, Commentary on the 1969 Vienna Convention on the Law of Treaties 445 (2009); Gardiner, *supra* note 33, at 398–400; The Vienna Convention on the Law of Treaties: A Commentary vol. I, 860 (Olivier Corten & Pierre Klein eds., 2011).

100. Some statements related to the "spirit" and "ideals" of the Convention(s) can be found in the preparatory work for the Additional Protocols to the Geneva Conventions. All of them are in line with the argument of the present chapter. *See, e.g.*, Conference of Government Experts on the Reaffirmation and Development of International Humanitarian Law Applicable in Armed Conflicts (Geneva, May 24–June 12, 1971) vol. I, Annex III Resolution XIII of the XXIst International Conference of the Red Cross (Istanbul, Sept. 1969); Official Records of The Diplomatic Conference on the Reaffirmation and Development of International Humanitarian Law Applicable in Armed Conflicts Geneva (1974–1977), vol. IV, 177–78, vol. IX, 47 and 452, vol. XII, 124.

101. *ILC Guide*, *supra* note 32.

102. *See, e.g.*, Harold Koh, Legal Adviser, US Department of State, Letter to Paul Seger, Legal Adviser of Switzerland regarding Switzerland's Position on the U.S. Reservation to Protocol III of the Convention on Certain Conventional Weapons, Dec. 30, 2009.

103. For the full list, *see* ICRC IHL Databases, Treaties and State Parties, *available at* https://ihl-databases.icrc.org/en/ihl-treaties/gciv-1949/state-parties.

104. The closest document in this regard the present authors could identify was Israel's Declaration relating to the Declaration Made upon Accession by Democratic Yemen, 1080 U.N.T.S. 370 (1978), stating that certain political pronouncements made in Yemen's declaration were "in flagrant contradiction to the principles, objects and purposes of the [Geneva] Conventions." The statement by Israel did not, however, express a view on what those "principles, objects and purposes" were.

105. For a list of military manuals consulted by the ICRC up until 2020 in the process of updating the Commentaries on Geneva Conventions, *see* Commentary on GC III, *supra* note 21, at 2079–93.

U.K. military manual contains a sizable chapter on the "Protection of Civilians in the Hands of a Party to the Conflict," which so closely mirrors the Fourth Convention that its introduction says that the treaty will be referred to only as *the Convention*.[106] And yet, the manual does not attempt to delineate the treaty's object and purpose. To the best of the authors' knowledge, no other military manual does so either.[107]

States had a particular opportunity to enunciate a modern understanding of the goals underpinning the Convention at one of the three conferences of High Contracting Parties to the Fourth Geneva Convention convened by Switzerland as the depositary of the Convention in 1999,[108] 2001,[109] and 2014.[110] However, the outcome declarations of these conferences did not (for the most part) contain general pronouncements regarding the Convention.[111]

106. United Kingdom, UK Ministry of Defence, The Manual of the Law of Armed Conflict 215 (2004).

107. Many military manuals include more general statements on the aims and purposes of IHL, also called the law of armed conflict (LOAC), highlighting the protective nature of IHL. *See, e.g.*, Australia, Australian Defence Force, Law of Armed Conflict, Australian Defence Doctrine Publication, Executive Series ADDP 06.4 (May 11, 2006); Canada, Office of the Judge Advocate General, Department of National Defence, The Law of Armed Conflict at the Operational and Tactical Levels, Joint Doctrine Manual, B-GJ-005-104/FP-021 (Aug. 13, 2001); Germany, Federal Ministry of Defence, Law of Armed Conflict—Manual, Joint Service Regulation (ZDv) 15/2, DSK AV230100262, official English translation of Humanitäres Völkerrecht in bewaffneten Konflikten—Handbuch, Berlin (May 2013); the Netherlands, Humanitair Oorlogsrecht: Handleiding (The Humanitarian Law of War: A Manual), Voorschift No. 27-412, Section 5, Koninklijke Landmacht, Militair Juridische Dienst (Sept. 2005); Philippines, Armed Forces of the Philippines, The Law of Armed Conflict, Teaching File for Instructors (2006); Peru, Centro del Derecho Internacional Humanitario de las Fuerzas Armadas, Manual de Derecho Internacional Humanitario para las Fuerzas Armadas (Manual of International Humanitarian Law for the Armed Forces), Resolución Ministerial N° 1394-2004-DE/CCFFAA/CDIH-FFAA (Dec. 1, 2004) published in 8 Diario Oficial El Peruano 8 December 2004; Sierra Leone, IHL Code of Conduct (2006); United Kingdom, UK Ministry of Defence, The Manual of the Law of Armed Conflict (2004).

108. Conference of the High Contracting Parties to the Fourth Geneva Convention, *Statement*, July 19, 1999, *available at* https://www.un.org/unispal/document/auto-insert-194091/.

109. Pierre-Yves Fux & Mirko Zambelli, *Mise en oeuvre de la Quatrième Convention de Genève dans les territoires palestiniens occupés: Historique d'un processus multilateral (1997–2001)*, 661 International Review of the Red Cross 84, 87 (2002).

110. Swiss Federal Council, *Switzerland Hosts Conference of High Contracting Parties to the Fourth Geneva Convention*, Press Release, *available at* https://www.admin.ch/gov/en/start/documentation/media-releases.msg-id-55724.html.

111. *See* Matthias Lanz, Emilie Max, & Oliver Hoehne, *The Conference of High Contracting Parties to the Fourth Geneva Convention of 17 December 2014 and the Duty to Ensure Respect for International Humanitarian Law*, 96 International Review of the Red Cross 895–96, 1115 (2014).

An exception in this regard was the 2001 declaration, which noted the agreement of the participating States that the Fourth Convention "takes fully into account imperative military necessity."[112] Although not specifically expressing the Convention's object and purpose, the formulation confirms that the Convention, like the rest of IHL, reflects a balance between humanity and military necessity. The States participating in the 2001 conference thus reaffirmed that they viewed the protective aim of the Convention as realistic given that it was constructed by taking "fully into account" the relevant military considerations.[113]

Overall, the supplementary means of interpretation confirm the interim conclusion of the previous sections. There is no doubt that the drafters intended to endow the Convention with a strong protective core, which radiates throughout the entirety of the text. The subsequent practice of States does not cast doubt on this center of gravity; rather, it confirms that the Convention's overwhelmingly protective approach reflects a pragmatic balance between humanitarian considerations and military necessity.

5. CONCLUSION

Although it is only one element of interpreting the terms of a treaty, identifying a treaty's object and purpose is an indispensable interpretive step, one of the items on "a set menu of which no course may be skipped."[114] Its weight relative to the other elements (including good faith interpretation, the ordinary meaning of the relevant terms, and their context) should not be overstated, but, equally, should not be ignored.

The interpretive process of IHL treaties like the Fourth Geneva Convention has certain specific features. Identifying their object and purpose is in some respects easier, as these instruments are generally designed to enhance protection and reduce suffering in times of armed conflict. However, it is also complicated by the fact that every IHL instrument reflects a careful balance between humanity and military necessity.

On the basis of the preceding analysis, this chapter establishes that the overall object and purpose of the Fourth Convention is to protect civilians during armed conflict, including in circumstances where they are subject to permissible measures of control and security. This conclusion, based on a rigorous application of

112. Conference of High Contracting Parties to the Fourth Geneva Convention, *Declaration*, Dec. 5, 2001, at ¶ 5, *available at* https://www.un.org/unispal/document/auto-insert-199888/.

113. *Id.*

114. Henckaerts et al., *supra* note 55, at 382.

the methodology described previously, is consistent with a long line of scholarship[115] and international case law.[116]

Where dilemmas arise in determining the ordinary meaning of individual provisions of the Fourth Convention, resort to its object and purpose may prove helpful. One of the best-known examples arose in the context of the conflict in the former Yugoslavia in the 1990s. The question was whether allegiance can in certain cases constitute a sufficient legal basis for protected status under Article 4 of the Convention in addition to the nationality criterion.[117] There is broad (though not universal) agreement that if a particular conflict takes place along ethnic, religious, or similar lines, and such distinctive features become more important than nationality, counting allegiance toward identifying protected persons is consistent with the Convention's object and purpose.[118] In these circumstances, individuals may exceptionally qualify for protected status even if they share the formal nationality of the State in whose hands they find themselves.[119]

115. *See, e.g.*, Michael Siegrist, The Functional Beginning of Occupation 14 (2011); Ardi Imseis, *On the Fourth Geneva Convention and the Occupied Palestinian Territory*, 44 Harvard International Law Journal 65, 137 (2003); International Commission of Jurists, *Israel's Separation Barrier: Challenges to the Rule of Law and Human Rights*, ¶ 17 (2012), *available at* https://www.icj.org/israels-separation-barrier-challenges-to-the-rule-of-law-and-human-rights/; Michael A. Newton, *The Iraqi High Criminal Court: Controversy and Contributions*, 88 862 *IRRC* 399, at 419–20 (2006); Dinstein, *supra* note 69, at 6; Nishat, *supra* note 58, at 1078 .

116. Judgment, *Delalić* (IT-96-21-T), Trial Chamber, Nov. 16, 1998, at 265–66; Judgment, *Tadić* (IT-94-1-A), Appeals Chamber, July 15, 1999, at 166, 168; Judgment, *Delalić* (IT-96-21-A), Appeals Chamber, Feb. 20, 2001, at 113; *Wall* Advisory Opinion, *supra* note 4, at 175. *See also* general statements on the purpose of the four Geneva Conventions, *e.g.*, IACommHR, *Tablada*, Report No. 55/97, Case No. 11.137, Argentina, OEA/Ser/L/V/II.98, Doc. 38, December 1997, at 159; *Hassan v. the United Kingdom*, *supra* note 68, at 102.

117. *See Tadić*, *supra* note 116, at 166; *see also* Prosecutor v. Prlić et al., Case No. IT-04-74, Appeals Chamber Judgment, ¶ 355 (Int'l Crim. Trib. for the former Yugoslavia Nov. 29, 2017).

118. *See, e.g.*, Theodor Meron, *The Humanization of Humanitarian Law*, 94 American Journal of International Law 239, 260 (2000); Kriangsak Kittichaisaree, International Criminal Law 140–41 (2001); Natalie Wagner, *The Development of the Grave Breaches Regime and of Individual Criminal Responsibility by the International Criminal Tribunal for the former Yugoslavia*, 85 International Review of the Red Cross 351, 375–76 (2003); Kubo MAčáK, Internationalized Armed Conflicts in International Law 233–37 (2018); *But see, e.g.*, Marco Sassòli & Laura Olson, *The Judgment of the ICTY Appeals Chamber on the Merits in the Tadić Case*, 82 International Review of the Red Cross 733, 743–44 (2000); Tamás Hoffmann, *The Perils of Judicial Construction of Identity—A Critical Analysis of the International Criminal Tribunal for the Former Yugoslavia's Jurisprudence on Protected Persons*, *in* Allegiance and Identity in a Globalised World 497–521 (Fiona Jenkins, Mark Nolan, & Kim Rubinstein eds., 2014).

119. *See also* Commentary on the Fourth Geneva Convention, commentary on Article 4 (forthcoming).

To give another example, the fact that very few Protecting Powers have been appointed in international armed conflicts since 1949 presents a challenge to the application of Convention provisions that are premised on the existence of such a Power.[120] The requirement in Article 61 that the distribution of relief in occupied territory must be carried out with the cooperation and under the supervision of the Protecting Power is a case in point. The absence of a State performing that role does not mean that the distribution cannot take place, as this would deprive the population of an occupied territory of humanitarian relief contrary to the object and purpose of the Convention. To address this issue, the occupying power should, subject to security considerations, permit a neutral State or an impartial humanitarian body, such as the ICRC, to undertake the functions envisaged in Article 61.[121] In practice, relief in occupied territory is indeed frequently distributed under the supervision of the ICRC and National Red Cross or Red Crescent Societies, confirming that this interpretation, which draws on the object and purpose of the Convention, also reflects a pragmatic and realistic solution.[122]

As these examples show, the object and purpose of the Fourth Convention has a concrete impact on how its terms are interpreted by providing insights into the ordinary meaning of the text and allowing the protective intent of the Convention to be fully realized.

120. Since the adoption of the 1949 Conventions, Protecting Powers have only been appointed in five international armed conflicts. *See* Commentary on GC III, *supra* note 21, at 15–16 ¶¶ 49–51 and 471–73 ¶¶ 1296–1302.

121. *See also* Commentary on the Fourth Geneva Convention, Article 61 (forthcoming).

122. *See, e.g.*, ICRC, *Israel and the Occupied Territories: Facts and Figures January to June 2023*, at 148 (Oct. 1, 2023), *available at* https://www.icrc.org/en/document/israel-and-occupied-territories-facts-and-figures-january-june-2023; ICRC, Annual Report 2003 (2004) 264–67, and Annual Report 2002 (2003) 148.

PART TWO

Law and Reality

4

Measures of Control for Security Reasons Other Than Civilian Internment in Armed Conflict: A Military Perspective

NATHALIE DURHIN*

1. INTRODUCTION

The protection of civilians in high-intensity conflicts is mostly viewed through the angle of the conduct of hostilities. The main challenges relate to targeting and combat engagement issues such as implementation of the principles of distinction and proportionality, the protection of objects necessary to the survival of the population, or of installations containing dangerous forces. In lower-intensity confrontations, but even high intensity ones, threats to the safety of civilians are nevertheless not limited to "attacks" in the conduct of hostilities.[1] Civilians also remain at enormous risk of harm and mistreatment when belligerents place them under their control.

* Colonel Nathalie Durhin is a French Air Force Legal Advisor, and at the time of this writing, was a Faculty Advisor within the French War College (Ecole de Guerre) in Paris, France.

1. Protocol Additional to the Geneva Conventions of 12 August 1949, and Relating to the Protection of Victims of International Armed Conflicts art. 49, ¶ 1, June 8, 1977, 1125 U.N.T.S. 3 [hereinafter AP I].

Nathalie Durhin, *Measures of Control for Security Reasons Other Than Civilian Internment in Armed Conflict: A Military Perspective* In: *Civilian Protection in Armed Conflict*. Edited by: Jelena Pejic and Captain Margaret Kotlik, Oxford University Press. © Nathalie Durhin 2025. DOI: 10.1093/oso/9780197793176.003.0004

One such measure of control is internment.[2] This type of noncriminal detention for security reasons is extensively regulated in international humanitarian law (IHL) including, for civilians, in the Fourth Geneva Convention (GC IV).[3] The Convention specifies that, along with assigned residence, civilian internment is the severest measure of control that a State party may take.[4] This begs the question of what other measures of control and security may be applied pursuant to Article 27(4). The provision authorizes parties to an international armed conflict to "take such measures of control and security in regard to protected persons as may be necessary as a result of the war."[5]

Unlike internment, the content and possible limits of these other measures are not precisely defined in the treaty, but are widely applied by armed forces in practice to fulfill their mandate or reach their strategic, political, and/or military goals. Measures of control and security can range from checkpoints and search and seizure operations to biometric data collection, intelligence collection, and the jamming of communications. They constitute an infringement of basic human rights such as liberty, property, privacy, and so forth, but are acceptable under IHL.

It can be argued that due to a lack of detailed IHL provisions, there is a "gap to fill" by resort, for example, to international human rights law (IHRL) in order to provide a better framework for the protection of civilians. Given that measures of control may constitute a use of force[6] to varying degrees, a main challenge for the military is to find a balance between military necessity and the protection of civilians. This chapter will present some military practice and possible precautionary measures, grounded either in IHRL or based on policy considerations, that could mitigate the very real risks.

2. Internment is a security measure and cannot be used as a form of punishment. This means that each interned person must be released as soon as the reasons which necessitated his or her internment no longer exist. Furthermore, while combatants may be subject to internment on account of their membership in the armed forces of the enemy, the internment of civilians must be undertaken on an individual basis, and entire groups of civilians may not be collectively interned.

3. Convention (IV) Relative to the Protection of Civilian Persons in Time of War, Aug. 12, 1949, 6 U.S.T. 3516, 75 U.N.T.S. 287 [hereinafter GC IV].

4. *Id.*, art. 41(1). *See also* Jelena Pejic, *The Other Side of Civilian Protection: The 1949 Fourth Geneva Convention*, Articles of War (Mar. 7, 2022), https://lieber.westpoint.edu/other-side-civilian-protection-fourth-geneva-convention/.

5. GC IV, *supra* note 3, art. 27(4).

6. For the military, the use of force may be largely defined as "actions which are likely to cause death or injury, or to damage or destroy material or immaterial property" but may encompass, for the forces on the ground, a diverse array of actions". *See* NATO Rules of Engagement, MC 0362/2 (Final) (INV), Sept. 18, 2019, ¶¶ 22–23 (not available to the public) [hereinafter NATO Rules of Engagement].

2. MEASURES OF CONTROL OTHER THAN DEPRIVATION OF LIBERTY

2.1 IHL Provisions Pertaining to Other Measures of Control Are Insufficiently Detailed

GC IV is silent on measures of control over civilians other than internment and assigned residence. Older treaties that do provide certain generic authorizations also lack detail. For instance, Article 43 of the 1907 Hague Convention IV Regulations[7] relates to the duty of the occupying power to restore and ensure, as far as possible, *public order and safety*. This article is rather broad, and the term "all steps in his power" could encompass a variety of measures of control that are, unfortunately, not specified. However, the article includes a major limitation, that is, respect for the laws of the occupied territory, which can be viewed as allowing the incorporation of an IHRL standard into IHL. Analyzed in relation to subsequent legal frameworks and contemporary conflicts, Article 43 is indeed recognized as permitting certain measures of control derived from law enforcement, for instance, restrictions of freedom of movement such as limitations on demonstrations, the establishment of curfews, and so forth.

Another indirect way of understanding measures of control is to focus on the exceptions to generic prohibitive provisions. For instance, under IHL, many provisions deal with the prohibition of the destruction and seizure of property of an adversary.[8] But almost all mention the exception of the "necessities of war" (Article 23(g) of the 1907 Hague Regulations[9]) or "military necessity" (Articles 50 of GC I[10], 51 of GC II,[11] and 147 GC IV[12]). It can be inferred from these exceptions that a belligerent or an occupying power can use force and impose measures of control on the private property of civilians, including search and seizure, if deemed necessary.

7. Regulations Respecting the Laws and Customs of War on Land, annexed to Convention No. IV Respecting the Laws and Customs of War on Land art. 43, Oct. 18, 1907, 36 Stat. 2227 ("The authority of the legitimate power having actually passed into the hands of the occupant, the latter shall take all the measures in his power to restore, and ensure, as far as possible, public order and safety, while respecting, unless absolutely prevented, the laws in force in the country") [hereinafter 1907 Hague Regulations].

8. *See* 2 Customary International Humanitarian Law 50 (Jean-Marie Henckaerts & Louise Doswald-Beck eds., 2005).

9. 1907 Hague Regulations, *supra* note 7, art. 23(g).

10. Convention (I) for the Amelioration of the Condition of the Wounded and Sick in the Armed Forces in the Field art. 50, Aug. 12, 1949, 6 U.S.T. 3114, 75 U.N.T.S. 31 [hereinafter GC I].

11. Convention (II) for the Amelioration of the Condition of the Wounded, Sick, and Shipwrecked Members of Armed Forces at Sea art. 51, Aug. 12, 1949, 6 U.S.T. 3217, 75 U.N.T.S. 85 [hereinafter GC II].

12. GC IV, *supra* note 3, art. 147.

As already mentioned, the only provision referring to the term "measures of control" is found in the last paragraph of Article 27 of GC IV. According to the International Committee of the Red Cross's (ICRC's) 1958 Commentary:[13]

> [T]he various security measures which States might take are not specified; the Article merely lays down a general provision. There are a great many measures, ranging from comparatively mild restrictions such as the duty of registering with and reporting periodically to the police authorities, the carrying of identity cards or special papers, or a ban on the carrying of arms, to harsher provisions such as a prohibition on any change in place of residence without permission, prohibition of access to certain areas, restrictions of movement, or even assigned residence and internment (which, according to Article 41, are the two most severe measures a belligerent may inflict on protected persons).

Obviously, to be subjected to measures of control, civilians must pose a threat based on their activity, but this assertion needs to be further examined.

2.2 Measures of Control for Security Reasons May Be Implied Under IHL

It can be argued, firstly, that there is in practice a kind of "operational continuum" between certain security measures and the possible future internment of civilians. Some military measures restraining freedom of movement or imposing constraints on civilians can be aimed at facilitating or enabling internment if it transpires that certain civilians actually pose a major threat to the security of the force. The establishment of checkpoints, the collection of biometric data, or operations of search and seizure in civilian compounds can fall within this category. The application of these specific measures of control may indeed be a way of preempting civilians from becoming "lawful targets" by temporarily depriving them of liberty for security reasons.

Secondly, it may be argued that measures of control are naturally linked to the notion of military necessity.[14] This principle permits measures that are actually essential to accomplish a legitimate military purpose and are not otherwise prohibited by IHL. As emphasized by scholars who have referred to the work of the International Law Commission

13. Oscar M. Uhler et al., Commentary to Geneva Convention IV Relative to the Protection of Civilian Persons in Time of War (1958) [hereinafter 1958 Commentary on GC IV].

14. *See, e.g.*, International Committee of the Red Cross, *How Does Law Protect in War, Military Necessity*, https://casebook.icrc.org/a_to_z/glossary/military-necessity (last accessed June 3, 2024).

(ILC),[15] "military necessity is the justifying factor inherent in all rules of IHL which, in derogation from the rules applicable in peacetime, permit the resort to measures meeting the needs of the extreme circumstances prevailing in situations of armed conflict."[16] It is clear that military necessity does not justify violations of positive IHL obligations. However, as Michael Schmitt has explained, "although carte blanche deviation from established legal norms based on military necessity is impermissible, the balancing of necessity and humanity pervades contemporary international law in both a general and a specific sense."[17]

According to Nobuo Hayashi, the definition of military necessity "gives rise to four requirements: that the measure be taken primarily for some specific military purpose, that the measure be required for the attainment of that purpose, that the purpose be in conformity with international humanitarian law, and that the measure itself be otherwise in conformity with that law."[18] Hayashi incidentally sheds an interesting light on examples of military necessity outside the context of combat or attack, such as property destruction or forcible evacuation.[19]

As regards the destruction of property, the absence of active combat does not per se indicate the absence of military necessity. In the *Hardman* case,[20] an occupation force's destruction of a house and its contents for the maintenance of sanitary conditions among its members was held to constitute military necessity. Pursuant to Article 53 GC IV, the destruction of certain categories of property in occupied territory may be justified where this is "rendered absolutely necessary by military operations."[21] When an International Criminal Tribunal for the former Yugoslavia (ICTY) chamber made a finding of militarily unnecessary property destruction, it did not do so on the basis of

15. International Law Commission, Report on the Work of its thirty-second session (May 5–July 25, 1980), 2 Yearbook of the International Law Commission, 45, ¶ 27 (Part 2) (1980) [hereinafter ILC Report].

16. Nils Melzer, *Targeted Killing or Less Harmful Means? Israel's High Court Judgment on Targeted Killing and the Restrictive Function of Military Necessity*, 9 Yearbook of International Humanitarian Law 104 (2006).

17. Michael Schmitt, *Military Necessity and Humanity in International Humanitarian Law: Preserving the Delicate Balance*, 50 Virginia Journal of International Law 4, 795–839 (2010).

18. Nobuo Hayashi, *Requirements of Military Necessity in International Humanitarian Law and International Criminal Law*, 28 Boston University International Law Journal 1, 123 (2010).

19. *Id.* at 123–30.

20. Hardman v. U.S. (commonly cited as U.K. v. U.S.), 6 R. Int'l Arb. Awards 25, 26 (Arb. Trib. 1913).

21. GC IV, *supra* note 3, art. 53.

little or no fighting, but on the ground that the destruction was ethnically driven.[22]

As regards forced movement, Article 49 GC IV prohibits deportation and transfer of protected persons from occupied territory, except in situations of temporary evacuation where "the security of the population or imperative military reasons so demand." According to the ICRC, "imperative military reasons" exist "when the presence of protected persons in an area hampers military operations."[23]

The notion of imperative military reasons can thus justify the use of force and the implementation of measures of control outside of scenarios of attack or detention operations. However, due to lack of extensive analysis of this notion by tribunals and scholars, we cannot agree more with the ICRC's 1958 Commentary on Article 27 GC IV when it states that "a great deal is thus left to the discretion of the Parties to the conflict as regards the choice of means. What is essential is that the measures of constraint they adopt should not affect the fundamental rights of the persons concerned."[24] The possible impacts on these fundamental rights will be discussed later in this chapter, as well as the question of whether this "grey zone" in IHL needs to be clarified or not.

To recapitulate, while Article 27(4) GC IV explicitly provides a generic authorization for the application of measures of control, IHL contains no further guidance on what they may be. But the possibility of exerting control over civilians is also implied in IHL, either through capture and detention, or more generally, under the paradigm of military necessity. This permits the military to use force (often nonlethal but possibly up to deadly force) to put civilians under their control where necessary to reach the desired military end state and fulfill their mandate. When a particular mandate is broad, it is a means of "diversifying" military operations allowing avoidance of resort mainly to attacks and detention, which would otherwise be allowed. When the mandate is more restrictive, for instance, in a peacekeeping mission, or when the scope of the mission is limited by a UN Security Council Resolution,[25] recourse to military measures of control and security can be the only available way of operating.

22. Prosecutor v. Kordić & Čerkez, Case No. IT-95-14/2-A, Appeal Judgment, ¶¶ 484–85, 583–86 (Int'l Crim. Trib. for the former Yugoslavia Dec. 17, 2004).

23. 1958 Commentary on GC IV, *supra* note 13 at ¶ 280. The commentary continues: "Evacuation is only permitted in such cases, however, when overriding military considerations make it imperative; if it is not imperative, evacuation ceases to be legitimate."

24. *Id.*

25. *See, e.g.*, S.C. Res. 1244, ¶ 9 (June 10, 1999) (detailing the responsibilities of the international security presence to be deployed and acting in Kosovo).

3. THE MITIGATION OF RISKS POSED TO BASIC RIGHTS WHEN APPLYING MEASURES OF CONTROL

3.1 Checkpoints: How to Find a Balance Between the Necessary Restriction of Freedom of Movement and the Security of Civilians

One of the most habitual ways of restricting the freedom of movement[26] (FoM) of civilians is by establishing and operating checkpoints. As defined by the United Nations, checkpoints are any staffed physical impediments to travel within a territory.[27] They are a common feature of armed conflicts in countries such as Israel,[28] the Democratic Republic of Congo,[29] Central African Republic,[30] Syria and Iraq, and, more recently in Ukraine, both before the 2022 invasion[31] and during the ongoing war.[32] Checkpoints may be imposed for security reasons, more specifically, to control a territory, interdict access to certain areas, disarm combatants/insurgents, prevent them from establishing foreign sanctuaries, prevent civilians from sharing information with the enemy, to gather intelligence and possibly capture persons posing a threat to the force, and so forth.[33]

26. *See, e.g.*, International Covenant on Civil and Political Rights art. 12, Dec. 16, 1966, 999 U.N.T.S. 171 ("1. Everyone lawfully within the territory of a State shall, within that territory, have the right to liberty of movement and freedom to choose his residence. 2. Everyone shall be free to leave any country, including his own").

27. Matthew Longo, Daphna Canetti, & Nancy Hite-Rubin, *A Checkpoint Effect? Evidence from a Natural Experiment on Travel Restrictions in the West Bank*, 58 American Journal of Political Science 4, 1006–23 (2014).

28. UN Office for the Coordination of Humanitarian Affairs (OCHA), *Longstanding Access Restrictions Continue to Undermine the Living Conditions of West Bank Palestinians*, The Humanitarian Bulletin (Mar.–May 2020), https://ochaopt.org/content/longstanding-access-restrictions-continue-undermine-living-conditions-west-bank–palestinians.

29. Oxfam Briefing Paper, *Secure Insecurity, The Continuing Abuse of Civilians in Eastern DRC as the State Extends Its Control* (Mar. 6, 2015), https://www.oxfam.org/en/research/secure-insecurity.

30. Louisa Lombard, *Navigational Tools for Central African Roadblocks*, 36 Political and Legal Anthropology Review 157–73 (2013).

31. OSCE Thematic Report, Checkpoints Along the Contact Line: Challenges Civilians Face when Crossing, SEC.FR/876/20 (Dec. 29, 2020).

32. OSCE, Report on Violations of International Humanitarian Law and Human Rights Law, War Crimes and Crimes Against Humanity (July 14, 2022), https://reliefweb.int/report/ukraine/report-violations-international-humanitarian-and-human-rights-law-war-crimes-and-crimes-against-humanity-committed-ukraine-1-april-25-june-2022.

33. One of the risks associated with checkpoints is that they may become de facto illegal detention centers. The other main risk for civilians at checkpoints is violence. The current war in Ukraine is but one example, with reports of kidnapping at checkpoints, application of the "filtration" policy, illegal detention, and other abuses. In some States the risk is high because

Restricting FoM at a checkpoint must be distinguished from detention. In an international armed conflict (IAC) situation, one of the questions to ponder in relation to GC IV is when the internment of detained protected persons begins.[34] According to the 2022 French manual for military operations,[35] detention is preceded by capture, which is an action leading to the temporary deprivation of (or restriction on) the FoM of an individual. However, not every deprivation of liberty constitutes internment, the threshold between immobilization for reasons of security and capture for the purpose of internment being when the forces involved know that the person at issue poses an imperative threat to the security of the force or of the civilian population.[36] Temporarily holding a civilian to carry out a control at a checkpoint is thus different from capture and, a fortiori, from detention.

The FoM of civilians may be restricted in armed conflict situations, even severely, if circumstances so require. As explained by the ICTY:

> [T]here is no absolute right in the Geneva Conventions to freedom of movement. However, this does not mean that there is a general suspension of this right during armed conflict either. To the contrary, the regulations concerning civilians in the territory of a party to an armed conflict are based

many soldiers who manage checkpoints are poorly trained and equipped. Checkpoints can be a cause of great uncertainty for civilians; sometimes armed groups deliberately create uncertainty through violent actions undertaken in order to intimidate civilians. Checkpoint violence can thus deter displacement and lead to what Stephen Lubkemann calls "involuntary immobility." Stephen C. Lubkemann, *Involuntary Immobility: On a Theoretical Invisibility in Forced Migration Studies*, 21 Journal of Refugee Studies 4, 454–75 (2008).

34. *See* Pejic, *supra* note 4.

35. Ministère des Armées, Manuel de Droit des Opérations Militaires (2022).

36. *Id.* at 170:

> Toute privation de liberté incidente à la conduite des opérations militaires ne constitue pas un internement. Les mesures de sécurité qui visent à vérifier le statut d'un individu, son identité et le degré de menace qu'il peut éventuellement représenter pour la sécurité des forces et de la population civile, tels que les arrêts à des postes de contrôle ou des restrictions temporaires à la liberté de mouvement durant les fouilles ne sont pas assimilables à un internement. Le point de basculement entre l'immobilisation pour des raisons de sécurité et la capture en vue d'un internement intervient lorsque les forces armées françaises ont la connaissance que la personne en cause représente une menace impérieuse pour la sécurité de la force ou de la population. Lorsque la décision de détenir un individu est arrêtée, la clarté des motifs de l'internement et les procédures garantissant certains droits à l'individu détenu constituent les conditions nécessaires pour éviter toute privation arbitraire de liberté.

> on the concept that the individual freedom of civilians should remain unimpaired. The right in question is therefore a relative one, which may be restricted.[37]

The establishment of checkpoints must obviously be grounded in security reasons. When this is the case, measures should be taken to avoid uncertainty, violence, and unnecessary suffering that may be caused to the civilian population. First, checkpoints may only be temporary, and should be dismantled when there is no longer a threat (to the force and/or to the civilian population). Ideally, information should be provided to civilians regarding the setting up of checkpoints, their location, and the procedures to be followed when crossing them. Second, if security screening is conducted, the relevant procedures are to be applied consistently and without discrimination, as civilians should be presumed not to pose a threat until the contrary is proven. Special provisions should be designed to identify, prioritize, and expedite the security screening of any vulnerable individuals, and information should be given about the nature and application of the procedures, including in relation to the location of those undergoing screening and the timeline for the process.

Third, special attention should be given to vulnerable persons coming to/crossing checkpoints,[38] for instance, pregnant women,[39] elderly persons, children, persons with serious medical conditions, persons with disabilities, traumatized persons, and so forth. Gender considerations and vulnerability assessments should be combined to allow the prioritization of cases and expedite screening. It should be kept in mind, however, that the question of the military's duty to provide for the basic needs of civilians at checkpoints[40] is complex, and has to be addressed on a case-by-case basis, based on the relevant security context and operational constraints.

37. *See* Prosecutor v. Mucić et al. ("Čelebići"), Case No. IT-96-21, Judgment, ¶ 565 (Int'l Crim. Trib. for the former Yugoslavia Nov. 16, 1998).

38. In particular, this means applying a gender perspective to the planning and conduct of this kind of military operation.

39. Laura Wick, *Birth at the Checkpoint, the Home or the Hospital? Adapting to the Changing Reality in Palestine*, Relief Web (2002), https://reliefweb.int/report/israel/birth-checkpoint-home-or-hospital-adapting-changing-reality-palestine; UN Human rights Comm., Annual Report, *The Issue of Palestinian Pregnant Women Giving Birth at Israeli Checkpoints*, A/HRC/7/44 (Feb. 8, 2008).

40. The authorities must provide for the physical safety and basic needs of all persons waiting at checkpoints or in transit facilities, based on the circumstances. In practice, this means that the checkpoint/transit facility should be at a safe distance from the front lines and military installations and cleared of mines or other explosive devices. To protect life and avoid suffering, basic needs such as food, water, shelter, and medical aid should also be provided if possible.

Moreover, "unimpeded" access for humanitarian aid and health care must be granted.[41] Additional Protocol I (AP I) provides that "only in case of imperative military necessity may the activities of the relief personnel be limited or their movements temporarily restricted."[42] The exception of imperative military necessity is justified on the basis that relief operations may not interfere with military operations, lest the safety of humanitarian relief personnel be endangered. However, the restrictions may only be limited and temporary. It is widely acknowledged, for example, that delays in or denials of passage for medical transport due to checkpoint controls can be seriously detrimental to the evacuation of the sick and wounded on the ground.[43]

Granting unimpeded access for humanitarian aid and health care may pose a challenge for military personnel guarding or operating checkpoints, especially if they are insufficiently experienced and/or there is a lack of communication on this issue. Consequently, procedures must be established and be known and implemented by the soldiers, for instance, lighter controls for medical vehicles and prioritization of their passage. Soldiers also must be trained in IHL in general, and on the protection of civilians in particular, and on how to operate a specific checkpoint: knowledge of the risk environment and awareness of vulnerable persons, gender issues and/or biases in the area, the routines of the civilians versus tactics of the enemy, and so forth. Cooperation also needs to be established with the humanitarian actors present, even before checkpoints are set up. In its 2014 handbook,[44] the ICRC specifically suggested measures militaries may take to enhance their understanding of the operational environment. These include mapping health care providers, nongovernmental organizations, and other relevant actors, as well as coordination with them in order to minimize delays, enable prioritization measures, and find solutions when transit is denied.

These efforts must be balanced with force protection, as attacks can be conducted at checkpoints, or improvised explosive device (IED) may laid at or near checkpoints, especially in counterinsurgency situations. Armed forces also have to deal more and more with the misuse of medical transports for nonmedical

41. *See* International Committee of the Red Cross, Customary International Humanitarian Law Database, ch. 2, r. 55, *available at* https://ihl-databases.icrc.org/en/customary-ihl/v1.ICRC: "[T]he parties to the conflict must allow and facilitate rapid and unimpeded passage of humanitarian relief for civilians in need, which is impartial in character and conducted without any adverse distinction, subject to their right of control"; and Rule 56: "[T]he parties to the conflict must ensure the freedom of movement of authorized humanitarian relief personnel essential to the exercise of their functions."

42. AP I, *supra* note 1, art. 71(3).

43. International Committee of the Red Cross, Promoting Military Operational Practice that Ensures Safe Access to and Delivery of Health Care (2014), https://www.icrc.org/en/publication/4208-promoting-military-operational-practice-ensures-safe-access-and-delivery-health.

44. *Id.* at Annex 1.

purposes, including military, and with the improper use of distinctive emblems with the specific intent to deceive the adversary in order to kill or injure. In addition, for many years now, certain warring parties have used humanitarian access as a bargaining chip, with devastating consequences for the populations in need. It is thus a real challenge for militaries to find the right balance at checkpoints between security requirements and the necessary protection of civilians.

3.2 Infringement of Property Rights: For Security Reasons and Subject to Strict Procedures

IHL prohibits the destruction of public or private property, but mainly in relation to the conduct of hostilities. Thus, the 1907 Hague Regulations proscribe the destruction or seizure of enemy property, unless imperatively demanded by the necessities of war.[45]

Contrary to the broad scope of the 1907 Hague Regulations, Article 53 of GC IV is more limited and focuses on the destruction of property during occupation: "Any destruction by the Occupying Power of real or personal property belonging individually or collectively to private persons, or to the State, or to other public authorities, or to social or co-operative organizations, is prohibited, except where such destruction is rendered absolutely necessary by military operations." Article 147 of GC IV defines as a grave breach of the Convention "the extensive destruction and appropriation of property, not justified by military necessity and carried out unlawfully and wantonly."

There are, however, other cases in which there may be a need to search and possibly seize private property not included in the aforementioned provisions that can be assessed as measures of control. For instance, armed forces may need to search for enemy forces, especially if they are hiding among the civilian population, or to collect evidence of the presence of combatants, or of civilians directly participating in hostilities. In other words, such operations may be necessary to reduce the level of threat to one's forces through the collection of intelligence, the removal of weapons, or the capture of individuals.

Seizure is the temporary taking of private or State property. In the non-international armed conflicts (NIACs) in Afghanistan or Mali, for example, NATO and/or French armed forces often conducted operations to search for combatants during which they were authorized to seize goods and material of intelligence value facilitating the future capture or neutralization of combatants. Examples of seizable property included arms and ammunition, radios, computers, and other communications equipment, as well as construction equipment, vehicles, and so forth.

45. 1907 Hague Regulations, *supra* note 7, art. 23: "In addition to the prohibitions provided by special Conventions, it is especially forbidden . . . (g) To destroy or seize the enemy's property, unless such destruction or seizure be imperatively demanded by the necessities of war."

Similar to the establishment of checkpoints, the requirement of a lawful purpose must be met before conducting search and seizure operations. Such operations have to be justified by security reasons and based on a strict threat assessment, not conducted in a blanket or indiscriminate manner. Additionally, and especially in extraterritorial NIAC situations when armed forces operate with the consent of the host nation, mitigation of the infringement of property rights should be based on cooperation with the relevant authorities. There is always a legal/political requirement to act in accordance with host nation law, but also a political/moral requirement to respect the local culture. This is essential in order to generate the support of the population, or at least to avoid massive rejection.

The use of force to search and seize property will generally be authorized under rules of engagement (ROE) for a temporary period, and only when the mission is conducted jointly with host nation security forces. The latter are a priori best placed to know and respect local customs, including gender considerations, and mitigate harm to the local population. However, when engaged in partnered operations, armed forces must be ready to remind the relevant host nation authorities of their international obligations and the need to protect the civilian population, up to interfering to prevent violations or abuse when necessary. The level of force authorized under ROE is generally limited to nonlethal force. Even though entry by military force into a private property may not always be authorized under the proper domestic legal framework, certain procedures may be adopted to mitigate risks such as invasion of privacy, fear, violence, or damage to property. Precautionary measures can include generic warnings about possible search and seizure operations (aimed at preventing the civilian population from supporting belligerents, from keeping weapons at home,[46] or directly participating in hostilities); the conduct of such operations only in daytime so as not to heighten perceptions of threat when entering homes; warnings before entering (knock on the door at a minimum) followed by a proper explanation; use of translators; inclusion of females in military teams to facilitate better engagement with the civilian population, and so forth.

Detailed standard operating procedures (SOP) dealing with entry into civilian homes and taking possession of private property will likewise need to be drawn up and implemented. In addition to the aforementioned precautionary measures related to the act of intrusion itself, any goods seized have to be properly registered, and the condition of the property and the circumstances of the seizure have to be recorded. If security conditions allow, a receipt should be given for the property seized. Units likely to seize property (typically airborne and light units with a few specialized vehicles) should train in seizure, registration/documentation, and reporting procedures. Finally, it should be acknowledged that despite

46. It should be noted that in some countries the holding of weapons at home is a cultural fact. Consequently, intelligence collection must be properly conducted to distinguish between arms that are used by combatants (or civilians directly participating in hostilities) and arms held with no hostile motive.

legal obligations[47] the issue of returning of property to its owners at the end of the hostilities is complicated, but that is beyond the scope of this chapter.

3.3 The Risks to Privacy Rights Posed by Biometric Data Collection

Militaries have been using biometrics for more than twenty years now. The aim of biometrics is to collect information to enable the recognition of individuals mainly for force protection reasons. The use of biometrics generally allows the verification of the identity of enemy personnel and of other enemy threats with a high degree of confidence.[48]

In an armed conflict situation, biometrics thus permits militaries to check identity (e.g., at a checkpoint or during a patrol), to identify captured persons before deciding to detain them,[49] to complement intelligence on individuals under surveillance with a view to targeting them (if they are members of organized armed groups, for instance), or even to participate in fact-finding during investigations of IHL violations. Consequently, the use of biometrics cannot be limited just to combatants or fighters, as one of its purposes is their identification. Biometrics is thus a tool applied also to the civilian population.

Even if not a weapon or means of warfare,[50] biometrics can be qualified as a measure of control because it implies the use of a certain level of military force, either in support of other weapons or because the collection process may require

47. According to Article 53 of the 1907 Hague Regulations, *supra* note 7, private personal property, if taken, must be returned when no longer required, or else the user must compensate the owner.

48. *See* Marten Zwanenburg, *Know Thy Enemy: The Use of Biometrics in Military Operations and International Humanitarian Law*, 97 International Law Studies 1404 (2021).

49. Collecting biometric data may contribute to the purpose underlying Article 122 of GC III as regards prisoners of war. Convention (III) Relative to the Treatment of Prisoners of War art. 122, Aug. 12, 1949, 6 U.S.T. 3316, 75 U.N.T.S. 135 [hereinafter GC III]. Nevertheless, the ICRC's 2020 Commentary to GC III states that "Article 122 does not provide a basis to collect biological samples and the resulting DNA profiles from all prisoners of war; there must be a specific purpose for doing so." International Committee of the Red Cross, Commentary on Geneva Convention III Relative to the Treatment of Prisoners of War ¶ 4975 (https://ihl-databases.icrc.org/en/ihl-treaties/gciii-1949/article-122/commentary/2020).

50. *See* Zwanenburg, *supra* note 49, at 1415:

> Biometrics is not a weapon or other means of warfare. Biometrics in itself is not capable of causing injury, death, damage, or destruction. Biometrics is also not a weapons system or platform and is not employed for the purposes of attack as a means in itself but only in support of attacks by other means. Arguably, biometrics also does not constitute a method of warfare. It is not a manner of using a weapon or otherwise conducting hostilities, although its use can, if applied in particular ways, support the use of weapons.

a certain level of coercion. Hence, the right to use biometrics should be specified in SOP and ROE, along with details on the conditions under which these specific operations can be conducted and the appropriate level of use of force that may be applied.

The legal framework for the use of biometrics in armed conflicts is not, however, sufficiently settled. Its use can be limited because of constraints on the collection process, the storage of data, and the sharing of this sensitive information. Furthermore, IHRL and data protection law, which continue to apply during armed conflicts, may impose certain restrictions additional to those imposed by IHL.

When it comes to the collection of biometric data among civilians, it must first be recalled that according to Article 27 of GC IV, "protected persons are entitled, in all circumstances, to respect for their persons."[51] Pursuant to the ICRC's 1958 Commentary, this covers "in particular the right to physical, moral and intellectual integrity."[52] However, most scholars[53] consider that even if this right includes a right to privacy, there is no generic limitation on biometric enrollment as such. In addition, the prohibition in Article 31 of GC IV of "physical or moral coercion"[54] against protected persons, "in particular to obtain information from them or from third parties" is not absolute. The 1958 Commentary to this Article indeed states:

> [T]he prohibition only applies in so far as the other provisions of the Convention do not implicitly or explicitly authorize a resort to coercion. Thus, Article 31 is subject to the unspoken reservation that force is permitted whenever it is necessary to use it in the application of measures taken under the Convention.[55]

When planning and conducting the collection of biometrics, the military must, first, precisely define the aim of the operation and limit its duration. The IHL principle of necessity must be observed, but similar IHRL requirements may also serve as guidance. Some countries, like France, have incorporated into their national law authorizations necessary for the military to collect biometric data abroad and have listed its relevant, limited objectives (the identification of individuals killed in action, of captured persons, and of persons who are believed to pose a threat

51. GC IV, *supra* note 3, art. 27.

52. 1958 Commentary on GC IV, *supra* note 13, at ¶ 201.

53. *See, e.g.*, Asaf Lubin, *The Rights to Privacy and Data Protection under International Humanitarian Law and Human Rights Law*, *in* RESEARCH HANDBOOK ON HUMAN RIGHTS AND HUMANITARIAN LAW: FURTHER REFLECTIONS AND PERSPECTIVES 463–92 (Robert Kolb, Gloria Gaggioli, Pavle Kilibarda, & Edward Elgar eds., 2022).

54. GC IV, *supra* note 3, art. 31.

55. 1958 Commentary, *supra* note 13, at 220.

to the security of the force or to civilian populations based on specific and serious reasons).[56] Too broad a purpose, as was the case with one of the United States' biometrics programs in Iraq some 20 years ago, would be more than questionable as it would obviously trample human rights[57] at the time of the collection or later. The mass collection of biometric data by the United States, referred as "identity dominance,"[58] aimed to obtain information about the entire Iraqi population, including biographical details, ethnical or religious affiliations, and other sensitive features. Moreover, there was no deadline for keeping the collected data, and the United States even intended to transfer the database to the Iraqi authorities without any safeguards, which could have led to its further misuse and instrumentalization.

Second, armed forces have to deal with the issue of consent. For example, the updated ICRC Commentary to GC I specifically states in respect to DNA samples that these "may not be taken without the person's consent, unless there is a legal justification, such as in the case of a criminal investigation, or to identify

56. Code de la Défense [C. Def.], Article L2381-1 (Fra.) (modifié par la loi n° 2018-607 du 13 juillet 2018), Article 39:

> I. Dans le cadre d'une opération mobilisant des capacités militaires se déroulant à l'extérieur du territoire français, les membres des forces armées et des formations rattachées peuvent procéder à des opérations de relevés signalétiques, aux fins d'établir l'identité, lorsqu'elle est inconnue ou incertaine, ainsi que la participation antérieure aux hostilités:
>
> 1° Des personnes décédées lors d'actions de combat;
>
> 2° Des personnes capturées par les forces armées;
>
> 3° Des personnes dont il existe des raisons précises et sérieuses de penser qu'elles présentent une menace pour la sécurité des forces ou des populations civiles.
>
> Dans les mêmes conditions et aux mêmes fins, des membres des forces armées et des formations rattachées peuvent procéder à des prélèvements biologiques destinés à permettre l'analyse d'identification de l'empreinte génétique de ces personnes. Les prélèvements biologiques opérés sur les personnes mentionnées au 3° ne peuvent être que salivaires.
>
> *Les personnes mentionnées au même 3° sont informées, préalablement à tout relevé signalétique ou prélèvement biologique, des motifs et des finalités de ces opérations* [emphasis added].
>
> II.—Dans le même cadre, des membres des forces armées et des formations rattachées peuvent procéder à des opérations de relevés signalétiques et à des prélèvements biologiques sur les personnels civils recrutés localement et sur les personnes accédant à une zone protégée ou placée sous le contrôle de l'autorité militaire française, aux fins de vérification de leur identité et de leurs antécédents."

57. *See* Avi Asher-Schapiro & Nazih Osseiran, *Why Does the US Still Retain the Biometrics of Millions of Iraqis?*, Context (Mar. 16, 2023), https://www.context.news/digital-rights/why-does-the-us-still-retain-the-biometrics-of-millions-of-iraqis.

58. John Woodward, *Using Biometrics to Achieve Identity Dominance in the Global War on Terrorism*, Military Review 30–34 (2005), https://www.rand.org/pubs/reprints/RP1194.html. John Woodward was the director of the Department of Defense's Biometrics Management Office from 2003 to 2005.

remains."[59] But the consent issue is also an IHRL concern, and the question arises as to whether the military should take it into account. In some cases, such as controlling the entry of persons into military compounds, biometric data will not be collected from civilians without their consent because the consequences of refusal are not dramatic: access to the compound will simply be denied. This will not, however, preclude the possible use of a certain level of force against such persons, that is, control at gun point, where deemed necessary for reasons of force protection. If a civilian refuses to consent to the collection of his or her biometric data in this scenario and also adopts a threatening attitude, they could be subject to warnings and other measures according to criteria detailed in the ROE.

The military can also decide to make the collection of biometric data dependent on consent when controlling people at checkpoints, for instance. The reason is twofold: either because a legal risk assessment would be necessary based on the extraterritorial application of human rights law,[60] or because seeking consent from individuals, when possible, can help to not alienate the civilian population. Whether consent is given or not, it is always unacceptable to bargain for the collection of biometric data against the provision of humanitarian aid, as some armed forces were sometimes tempted to do as a means of ensuring "biometric coverage" of the largest part of a host nation's population.

However, implementing a requirement of consent, and even more so the IHRL notion of "informed consent," is unworkable in combat engagement situations because it would pose a threat to the military and contradict the main objective, which is to compare data collected with that already in a database so as to correlate it with existing intelligence assessments on a combatant and his/her possible characterization as "hostile."[61] The concern in this context relates more to the conditions and length of time for which data can be stored in specific databases, especially if the scanned individual(s) had not been considered hostile at the time

59. International Committee of the Red Cross, Commentary on the First Geneva Convention: Convention (I) for the Amelioration of the Condition of the Wounded and Sick in the Armed Forces in the Field ¶ 1584 (2016), https://ihl-databases.icrc.org/en/ihl-treaties/gci-1949?activeTab=1949GCs-APs-and-commentaries.

60. This would be the case, for instance, for States party to the 1950 European Convention on Human Rights, Convention for the Protection of Human Rights and Fundamental Freedoms, Nov. 4, 1950, 213 U.N.T.S. 222 [hereinafter ECHR].

61. In combat situations, the question of consent is also challenged by new biometrics technologies, especially remote collection, as there is an increasing move towards systems that provide better standoff distance between sensor and target. *See* William C. Buhrow, *Biometrics in Support of Military Operations: Lessons from the Battlefield*, CRC Press (2017). Zwanenburg, *supra* note 49, also reports that "the Turkish armed forces have unmanned aerial vehicles capable of facial recognition," and that some recent U.S. programs "aim to cultivate new algorithm-based software systems capable of performing whole body biometric identification from drones and other platforms."

of the initial data collection.[62] That is why procedures should be put in place to secure the preservation of biometric data and to deal with the sharing of information, either with the host nation authorities or between allies. Within NATO, for instance, many member States consider themselves bound by the European Regulations pertaining to biometrics[63] even in armed conflict, and have caveats and conditions when it comes to the implementation of the NATO policy[64] and the merging of thousands of data points in a single allied database.

3.4 Even Traditional Means of Military Action (Intelligence Collection, Jamming) Can Jeopardize Certain Basic Human Rights

IHL does not directly address how intelligence gathering may interfere with individual privacy. For instance, unmanned aerial vehicles (UAVs) are able to hover over an area for hours and transmit video footage of events on the ground. They are equipped with specialized equipment to help an operator identify military targets. Their continuous flights over civilian facilities can be rightly perceived as a permanent measure of control and can have an adverse psychological effect on the civilian population. Yet protection of privacy and mental health will often be seen by the military as subordinate to the interest of distinguishing combatants from civilians not directly participating in hostilities.

In addition to surveillance and intelligence collection, many other technologies can be used in armed conflict, such as signals generated by telephone communications for mapping networks of contact, or the planting of locator chips in houses or private communication devices detectable by night vision equipment or UAVs thanks to infrared light. IHL's primary focus on accurate target identification reflects the fact that the international community treats any deliberate attack against civilians as a serious violation of this body of norms, which is not the case

62. IHRL norms may be taken into consideration in this scenario to frame and secure the future use (possibly after the duration of active hostilities) of biometric data. This could explain why some States consider that they should abide by IHRL provisions from the very beginning of a conflict, to protect themselves in the long term.

63. ECHR, *supra* note 61, art. 8 discusses the right to respect for private and family life, home, and correspondence. *See also* European Union (EU) General Data Protection Regulation 2016/679 (2016); EU Directive on the protection of natural persons with regard to the processing of personal data by competent authorities for the purposes of the prevention, investigation, detection or prosecution of criminal offences or the execution of criminal penalties, and on the free movement of such data 2016/680 (2016).

64. NATO Concept for Biometrics in Support of Operations (Mar. 21, 2012) (not available to the public). *See also* Mark Lunan, *New Doctrinal Concepts: Biometrics*, The Three Swords Magazine (2018), *available at* https://www.jwc.nato.int/images/stories/threeswords/Biometrics_2018.pdf.

with accompanying intrusions on privacy[65] that may be necessary to prevent such a violation.

Certain military measures of control can also have a direct impact on data protection,[66] and, as mentioned by the ICRC in 2015, military operations affecting data "could cause more harm to civilians than the destruction of physical objects."[67] For instance, the interception of communications and other surveillance operations are conducted without judicial supervision in armed conflict, with precautionary measures—if any—voluntarily undertaken by the military to protect from possible criticism of overreach. These oversight measures are much less stringent and detailed than the ones required in peacetime for law enforcement and intelligence agencies. It is submitted that the regulation of such quasi-permanent measures of control over the civilian population should be better taken into consideration by the armed forces, especially by States concerned about violating IHRL.

Still other military measures that cannot be strictly qualified as measures of control may nevertheless have the same impact on the civilian population and should be applied with precaution. By way of example, an electronic warfare (EW) device may be installed to prevent interference with communications in order to protect a military compound. Military EW technologies include countermeasures such as radio frequency weapons, signal jamming, spoofing, and lasers. They enable armed forces to disrupt, deny, degrade, destroy, or deceive enemy communications and personnel using offensive options such as electromagnetic energy, anti-radiation weapons, and directed energy against radar-equipped defense systems.

The jamming of enemy communications has assumed a substantial role in modern warfare, even though radio frequency signals, while interfering with enemy communications by saturating them with false information, may severely impact civilian means of communication. When used in defense, EW solutions conceal the location of troops and provide protection to the armed forces and their infrastructure against the effects of electronic attacks by enemy forces. But they can also disrupt or even neutralize local communications, with the risk of endangering the provision of basic needs to the population, for instance, humanitarian relief and emergency assistance.

Jamming operations are often deemed an essential routine wartime activity. According to Theresa Hitchens, "when employed outside a theater of conflict, the

65. *See* United Nations Office on Drugs and Crime (UNODC), Module for lecturers, Privacy and Intelligence Gathering in Situations of Armed Conflict (July 2018), https://www.unodc.org/e4j/en/terrorism/module-12/key-issues/privacy-intelligence-gathering-in-armed-conflict.html.

66. *See* Robin Geiß & Henning Lahmann, *Protection of Data in Armed Conflict*, 97 International Law Studies 556 (2021).

67. International Committee of the Red Cross, *International Humanitarian Law and the Challenges of Contemporary Armed Conflicts* (Oct. 31, 2015), https://www.icrc.org/en/document/international-humanitarian-law-and-challenges-contemporary-armed-conflicts.

US considers satellite interference to be 'irresponsible' and potentially dangerous,"[68] but when used in an armed conflict situation, the United States (like many other States) considers these actions as part of any basic military engagement.

Russian forces have actively been jamming GPS signals in Ukraine since February 2022[69] and have conducted several cyberattacks on commercial communications providers with significant effects on civilian communications. As pointed out by Stuart Eves and Gilles Doucet, "essential civilian services including humanitarian relief are at risk of being disrupted or significantly degraded due to military operations against satellites and space infrastructure."[70] Indeed, "the increasing reliance of military operations on both military and commercial space systems in current and future armed conflicts will certainly increase the risk of these systems being targeted, resulting in significant risk of harm on civilians and humanitarian actors relying on the services provided by these systems."[71]

EW operations that do not amount to an attack are nevertheless considered to be a use of force and are consequently dealt by ROE. In order to reduce potential harm and lessen control exercised over civilians, ROE series[72] dealing with electronic countermeasures often contain amplifications focusing on precautionary measures to mitigate the impact on civilian broadcast or communication means.

In summary, intelligence collection and jamming may, depending on the circumstances, be considered semipermanent measures of control that can impose constraints on civilians, intrude on their privacy, and/or reduce their right to access basic needs. These issues should be addressed through an IHL lens with the aim of minimizing possible incidental damage (physical, mental, psychological) caused to the population, but possibly also through an IHRL lens so as to broaden the scope of civilian protection.

4. CONCLUDING REMARKS

Militaries are, for security reasons and within the paradigm of military necessity, often led to use force in situations different from "attack" or "detention" and

68. *See* Theresa Hitchens, *Satellite Jamming "Normal" by Militaries During Conflict, not Peacetime: State Dept. Official*, Breaking Defense (Mar. 21, 2022), https://breakingdefense.com/2022/03/satellite-jamming-normal-by-militaries-during-conflict-not-peacetime-state-dept-official/.

69. *See, e.g.*, Vitaly Shevchenko, *Russia Blamed for GPS Interference Affecting Flights in Europe*, BBC (May 2, 2024), https://www.bbc.com/news/articles/cne900k4wvjo.

70. Stuart Eves & Gilles Doucet, *Reducing the Civilian Cost of Military Counterspace Operations*, Humanitarian Law and Policy (Aug. 17, 2023), https://blogs.icrc.org/law-and-policy/2023/08/17/reducing-civilian-cost-of-military-counterspace-operations/.

71. *Id.*

72. In NATO doctrine, ROE are listed in a compendium and numbered in "series," each series dealing with a specific type of use of force. *See* NATO Rules of Engagement, *supra* note 6.

regularly plan and implement measures of control as diverse as checkpoints, the search and seizure of civilian property, biometrics and intelligence collection, or communications jamming. This may result in restrictions of certain human rights such as freedom of movement, the right to property, the right to liberty and security, or privacy. Consequently, the notion of military necessity must be interpreted in a cautious and responsible manner, balancing the realities of war which demand effective military operations[73] with the immediate protection of civilians and possible impacts on their security and basic rights.[74]

The main challenge posed by measures of control applied by the military is how to monitor them, minimize impact on the civilian population, and prevent excesses. The absence of precise IHL guidance on how to mitigate the effect of control measures does not necessarily mean that there is a "void" to be filled by IHRL norms. As regards checkpoints, for instance, mitigation measures can be inferred from IHL (no detention, procedures to protect civilians and especially the most vulnerable, and allowing access to humanitarian aid and health care). As regards measures of control contravening property rights (where the only IHL limit is the prohibition of destruction), mitigation measures must be based on cooperation with the host nation and respectful of the local culture and/or on the establishment of procedural safeguards. With respect to biometrics, there is a tendency to have recourse to IHRL norms, especially because biometric enrollment can often shift from strict military necessity to broader, including more political, objectives.

Given that measures of control automatically impact human rights, armed forces may tend to draw upon IHRL law by default, analogy, partially and/or imperfectly. They can thus interpret, incorporate, or integrate the relevant norms in a systemic manner, that is, take into account the applicable IHL and IHRL rules in light of each other.[75] However, systematically turning to IHRL norms can also

73. Raphaël van Steenberghe, *The Impacts of Human Rights Law on the Regulation of Armed Conflict: A Coherency-Based Approach to Dealing with Both the "Interpretation" and "Application" Processes*, 104 International Review of the Red Cross 919, 1372 (2022): the considerations of effectiveness "may be context dependent" and "assessed on a case-by-case basis, notably in light of the capacities of the parties, especially armed groups in NIACs, and the particular circumstances ruling at the time, like the degree of territorial control exercised by the concerned party."

74. *Id.* at 1372: the "failure to duly take account of the realities of war in any regulation of armed conflict is likely to result in a loss of credibility of that regulation and ultimately to lead to its non-respect or even rejection. This would considerably lessen or even entirely annihilate the protection afforded to individuals in armed conflict."

75. Marco Sassòli, *The Interplay between International Humanitarian Law (IHL) and International Human Rights Law (IHRL)*, *in* San Remo Workshop, Application of IHL and IHRL in an Armed Conflict (2019). Sassòli argues for the application of the *lex specialis* principle as requiring priority to be given to the rule having the "larger 'common contact surface area' with the situation" at stake. However, another factor might be taken into account, namely, a "less formal (and less objective) factor, [which] is the extent to which the solution conforms to the systemic objectives of the law."

lead to overregulation and, consequently, to the inhibition of military action. This could likewise create overly high expectations among the civilian population, especially if armed forces are not actually able to implement the standards they are trying to promote.

The military should leave aside theoretical debates about the IHL/IHRL interplay and adopt a pragmatic approach, finding ways of balancing respect for basic human rights with the necessary protection of their own forces in the extreme circumstances of armed conflict. The key to success lies in the anticipation of the risks posed to the civilian population and the incorporation of "precaution" into the military's planning of measures of control, even if this does not strictly equate with the implementation of IHRL standards. However, the application of human rights norms can also be decided on in order to avoid discrepancies in the status/treatment of protected persons, for political or policy reasons, or to strengthen a strategic narrative.

Finally, the scant literature that exists on measures of control for security reasons[76] sometimes misrepresents them by implying that such measures are either exceptional, restricted, or strictly legally framed. My view is that, because they are generally implied under IHL (more specifically by the principle of military necessity), it would be of greater importance and utility to try to understand military practice rather than seek to minimize the role of measures of control, or even deny that they should exist. At the same time, and whatever the legal basis of diverse mitigation measures, these have to be grounded in the need to protect civilians.

76. *See, e.g.*, Andrew Clapham, Paola Gaeta & Marco Sassòli, *The 1949 Geneva Conventions: A Commentary*, Oxford Public International Law (2015). In the part dealing with GC IV, there are large sections addressing issues related to civilians in enemy hands, internment, and occupation law (lawmaking and judicial guarantees, economic, social and cultural rights, protection of private property, etc.), but no attention is given to how the military can ensure security through measures of control even though they can have a great impact on civilians.

5

The Law Applicable to the "Screening" of Civilians

JANN K. KLEFFNER*

1. INTRODUCTION

Parties to international and non-international armed conflicts regularly take measures that aim to ascertain the facts surrounding the identity, conduct, status, and condition of individuals whom they encounter in the course of their operations (hereafter generically and interchangeably referred to as "screening," "screening operations," or "screening processes"). In the context of screening operations, parties typically restrict—presumably temporarily—the movement of the individuals concerned and take various measures, such as identity checks, searches, interviews, interrogations, registration and recording of personal data, and transfer. While these practices of parties to armed conflicts and the frequency of their occurrence clearly suggest that screening operations are an integral part of today's operational reality, the legal framework governing them is not readily discernible.

The conventional and customary law of armed conflict (LOAC) and international human rights law (IHRL) set forth at times quite detailed rules that govern situations such as detention, internment, evacuation, deportation, and displacement, as well as setting out standards of treatment of individuals who find themselves in these situations. In contrast, the legal regulation of the phase immediately preceding these situations, that is, the phase during which parties to an

* Dr. Kleffner is a Professor of International Law at the Swedish Defence University, Extraordinary Professor at the Faculty of Law of the University of Pretoria, South Africa, and Senior Fellow at Melbourne Law School, Australia. The author wishes to thank Helmer Jonelid and Marisa Giustiniani for their invaluable research assistance.

Jann K. Kleffner, *The Law Applicable to the "Screening" of Civilians* In: *Civilian Protection in Armed Conflict*. Edited by: Jelena Pejic and Captain Margaret Kotlik, Oxford University Press.
DOI: 10.1093/oso/9780197793176.003.0005

armed conflict seek to ascertain the factual basis for a decision to detain, intern, evacuate, deport, displace and so forth, is unclear. Does that mean that parties to an armed conflict are free to act as they see fit? If not, what are the outer legal bounds for screening processes? When, if at all, do screening processes amount to any of the more directly regulated measures, such as detention, internment, and confinement? And if outer legal bounds cannot readily be discerned from the positive LOAC, as complemented by applicable human rights law, or the latter leave specific aspects of screening operations unanswered, how *should* that void be filled *de lege ferenda*?

In addressing the aforementioned questions, I will proceed as follows. First, I will present some factual scenarios in which screening processes occur to illustrate their operational reality. Second, I will examine where screening processes sit in the broader context of operations that involve a restriction of movement of individuals to ascertain if and when screening operations trigger the regulatory frameworks that govern persons "in the hands of"/"in the power of" a party to an armed conflict, detention, internment, evacuation, deportation, displacement, and so forth. Third, I will offer the hypothesis that the lawfulness of screening operations is contingent on the fulfillment of a number of conditions, followed by conclusions.

Before proceeding, a few caveats are in order to further circumscribe the inquiry.

First, screening processes that occur in the context of the conduct of hostilities, such as the determination of a person's status or conduct for purposes of targeting fall outside the purview of the present analysis. Second, I will limit myself to screening processes that involve a restriction of the movement of the individual subjected to it. While this may seem obvious, one can contemplate screening processes where that is not the case, for instance, those conducted through means such as drone operations, cyber, or other forms of technology to ascertain the facts surrounding the identity, conduct, status, and condition of individuals without that coinciding with a restriction of movement. Third, the following analysis will focus on "presumed" civilians to the exclusion of individuals who are *clearly* (as opposed to *presumably*) members of armed forces.[1] Screening processes that pertain to such members, for example, the questioning of (presumed) prisoners of war (POWs) at the beginning of their captivity as regulated in the Third Geneva Convention relative to the Treatment of Prisoners of War (GC III)[2] are beyond

1. On the different presumptions of status in case of doubt, contrast Article 5(2) of GC III regarding persons who have committed belligerent acts and have fallen into the hands of the enemy and who shall enjoy the protection of GC III, with the second sentence of Article 50(1) of AP I, which obliges States to presume civilian status in case of doubt. Convention (III) Relative to the Treatment of Prisoners of War art. 5(2), Aug. 12, 1949, 6 U.S.T. 3316, 75 U.N.T.S. 135 [hereinafter Third Geneva Convention or GC III]; Protocol Additional to the Geneva Conventions of 12 August 1949, and Relating to the Protection of Victims of International Armed Conflicts art. 50(1)2, June 8, 1977, 1125 U.N.T.S. 3 [hereinafter Additional Protocol I or AP I].

2. *Cf.* Third Geneva Convention, *supra* note 1, art. 17.

the purview of the present contribution. By contrast, screening processes that also serve the purpose of ascertaining the status of an individual in case of doubt[3] fall into the ambit of the present contribution. For that reason, I will refer to persons who are subjected to screening operations generically as "individuals." Another caveat is that the present analysis aims to capture screening processes that occur in the context of both international armed conflicts (IACs) and non-international armed conflicts NIACs), despite the regulation of restrictions of movement differing, both in the degree of detail and actual content, between these two types of armed conflicts.[4] These differences manifest themselves, inter alia, in what may constitute a specific lawful purpose of a screening process (see section 4, later). The primary aim of the current inquiry is thus to focus on guiding principles rather than detailed rules. Accordingly, the regulatory framework is painted with a somewhat broad brush.

2. EXAMPLES OF FACTUAL SCENARIOS

The working definition of screening processes as those that aim to ascertain the facts surrounding the identity, conduct, status, and condition of individuals encountered by parties to an armed conflict in the course of their operations is meant to capture a broad set of factual occurrences. These range from transient restrictions of the movement of individuals, for instance, at checkpoints or roadblocks when individuals are crossing from one security perimeter to the next, or spontaneous stops to check identity documents, travel permits, and the like, to those that involve longer-lasting confinement en masse. Examples of the latter include "filtration camps" used to register, interrogate, and detain Ukrainian citizens in regions under Russian occupation during the ongoing Russian-Ukrainian IAC,[5] or the screening processes in "welfare centers" in Sri Lanka at the end of the NIAC between the Sri Lankan government and the Liberation Tigers of Tamil Eelam (LTTE) in 2009, where large numbers of internally displaced persons (IDPs) were screened for LTTE affiliation.[6] Other instances of screening operations range from security sweeps by armed forces in their search for members of armed groups, to the boarding of enemy merchant vessels to ascertain who may and who may not be detained. Still other factual scenarios are the screening of individuals in refugee and IDP camps for a wide array of purposes, ranging from initial identity checks and registration, family

3. *Cf. id.*, art. 5(2), which refers to such a screening process by a competent tribunal.

4. An example is the far more detailed regulation of security detention/internment in IACs (including periodic reviews, for instance), as compared to the fairly generic regulation under the law of NIAC, leaving more room for human rights law to supply the relevant legal parameters.

5. *See, e.g., Russian Filtration Camps for Ukrainians*, United Nations Press Release (Sept. 7, 2022), https://press.un.org/en/2022/sc15023.doc.htm.

6. World Report 2010, Sri Lanka, Human Rights Watch, https://www.hrw.org/world-report/2010/country-chapters/sri-lanka (last visited Feb. 29, 2024).

reunion, and the search for missing persons, to the search for individuals alleged to having committed international (or domestic) crimes. A last set of examples of screening processes are those that may occur in the context of evacuations and safe passage for civilians from areas under siege and the coincidental screening of relief personnel, including to ensure that the latter respect the security requirements of the party in whose territory they are carrying out their duties.

3. SCREENING IN THE LEGAL CONTEXT OF RESTRICTIONS OF MOVEMENT

The foregoing examples illustrate that screening operations span a broad range of measures that differ significantly as far as their purpose, degree of intrusiveness, and duration are concerned. Common to all of these screening operations, however, is that they regularly involve at least a temporary restriction of the movement of individuals subjected to them. In consequence, screening operations have to be considered in the context of other measures that involve such restrictions of movement. The LOAC and IHRL employ partially overlapping legal terms of art to denote restrictions of movement, most pertinently deprivations and restrictions of liberty, arrest, detention, internment/administrative detention, confinement, and the notion of a person being "in the hands of" and "in the power of" a party to an armed conflict. It is therefore necessary to clarify the aforementioned notions and to determine if and when screening may amount to any of them, thus triggering the respective regulatory framework.

The notions of "deprivation of liberty" and "restriction of liberty" feature in the LOAC.[7] It is not immediately obvious where the distinguishing line is to be drawn between the two. However, the ordinary meaning of the two terms would seem to suggest that the former refers to measures that would negate the possibility of one's exercising the right to liberty in its entirety, whereas the latter would negate that possibility only to some extent. In other words, the distinction between the two lies in the degree to which the measure in question impacts the (physical) liberty of the person in question.[8] This finds support in the pertinent human

7. *See, e.g.*, Additional Protocol I, *supra* note 1, arts. 11(1), 75(5); Protocol Additional to the Geneva Conventions of August 12, 1949, and Relating to the Protection of Victims of Non-international Armed Conflicts art. 2(2), June 8, 1977, 1125 U.N.T.S. 609 [hereinafter Additional Protocol II or AP II].

8. In this vein, *see* The Copenhagen Process on the Handling of Detainees in International Military Operations, the Copenhagen Process: Principles and Guidelines 5, ¶¶ 1.1 and 1.4 (2012), https://iihl.org/wp-content/uploads/2018/04/Copenhagen-Process-Principles-and-Guidelines.pdf. *See also* Michael Bothe, Karl Josef Partsch, & Waldemar A. Solf, New Rules for Victims of Armed Conflicts, Commentary on the Two 1977 Protocols Additional to the Geneva Conventions of 1949, at 740 (1982) (persons under a curfew "prohibiting them to leave their local community at all or during certain hours" belong to the category of persons restricted in their liberty).

rights jurisprudence of the European Court of Human Rights and the UN Human Rights Committee.[9] Some human rights jurisprudence would seem to suggest that a deprivation (as opposed to a mere restriction) also includes spatial and temporal factors, in the sense that deprivation is predicated on the confinement in a particular restricted space for a not negligible length of time.[10] Thus understood, a deprivation of liberty is largely analogous to "detention," as understood in the LOAC.[11]

Internment, in turn, is a specific form of detention, namely administrative detention, that is, a "deprivation of liberty of a person that has been initiated/ordered by the executive branch—not the judiciary—without criminal charges being brought against the internee/administrative detainee."[12] The notion of internment/administrative detention is hence commonly used in contradistinction to judicial/law-enforcement detention, that is, a deprivation of liberty initiated or ordered by the judiciary for the purpose of judicial proceedings (criminal or other) against the detainee. The International Committee of the Red Cross (ICRC) has also made a distinction between "detention" and internment, the former being understood to cover the period "prior to . . . a decision on internment."[13]

As alluded to, it would seem the notion of "confinement" can also be related to the notion of "deprivation of liberty" ("detention") and "restriction of liberty." If

9. Guzzardi v. Italy, App. No. 7367/76, ¶ 93 (1980) (ECtHR), https://hudoc.echr.coe.int/eng?i=001-57498; De Tommaso v. Italy, App. No. 43395/09, ¶ 80 (2017) (ECtHR), https://hudoc.echr.coe.int/eng?i=001-171804; U.N. Human Rights Comm., *General Comment No. 35: Article 9 (Liberty and security of person)*, ¶¶ 5 and 60, U.N. Doc. CCPR/C/GC/35 (Dec. 4, 2014) [hereinafter Human Rights Comm., *General Comment No. 35*]. *See also* Ilias Bantekas & Oette Lutz, International Human Rights: Law and Practice 340 (2013).

10. Storck v. Germany, App. No. 61603/00, ¶ 74 (2005) (ECtHR), https://hudoc.echr.coe.int/eng?i=001-69374.

11. Commentary on the Additional Protocols of 8 June 1977 to the Geneva Conventions of 12 August 1949, ¶ 3062 (Yves Sandoz, Christophe Swinarski, & Bruno Zimmermann eds., 1987) [hereinafter ICRC APs Commentary]. *See also* Additional Protocol II, *supra* note 7, art. 5(1)3, which refers to "persons deprived of their liberty for reasons related to the armed conflict, whether they are interned or detained," distinguishing them from "persons who are not covered by paragraph 1 but whose liberty has been restricted in any way whatsoever for reasons related to the armed conflict." *See also* Office of the General Counsel, U.S. Department of Defense, Law of War Manual (rev. ed. 2016), which uses the terms "detainee" interchangeably with someone "deprived of [their] liberty," at, *e.g.*, §§ 8.14.2 and 8.14.3.2. *See also* U.N. Working Group on Arbitrary Detention, *Deliberation No. 9: Concerning the Definition and Scope of Arbitrary Deprivation of Liberty under Customary International Law*, ¶ 57, U.N. Doc. A/HRC/45/16 (Dec. 24, 2012), https://documents.un.org/doc/undoc/gen/g12/189/35/pdf/g1218935.pdf?token=Sn4jCU6cS3iAhiNLzY&fe=true ("The Working Group regards as detention all forms of deprivation of liberty . . .").

12. Jelena Pejic, *Procedural Principles and Safeguards for Internment/Administrative Detention in Armed Conflict and Other Situations of Violence*, 94 International Review of the Red Cross 812 (2005).

13. ICRC APs Commentary, *supra* note 11, at ¶ 3062.

and when such confinement occurs "in a particular restricted space for a not negligible length of time,"[14] it amounts to detention. Below that spatial and temporal threshold, confinement amounts to a restriction of liberty. There is some evidence in the literature that such a distinction, and the consequent construction of "confinement" as being broader than "detention," is in line with the criminalization of unlawful confinement as a war crime, which extends to unlawful assigned residence, the latter being distinct from internment.[15] However, it should be noted that it will depend on the specific form that assigned residence takes to determine whether it amounts to confinement above or below the requisite threshold for it to amount to a deprivation of liberty/detention. It will make a difference, for example, whether the person subject to assigned residence retains some freedom to move outside the place of residence (by, for instance, being permitted to move freely in a specified area in which the assigned residence is located) or is placed under house arrest, that is, confined to the actual place of assigned residence such as an apartment or house.

As a distinct notion, "arrest"[16] has been defined by the ICRC for purposes of Article 75 of the First Additional Protocol to the Geneva Conventions (AP I) as "the period that a person is in the hands of the police, preceding the trial stage . . . or prior to internment."[17] That definition partially overlaps with what is considered to amount to "arrest" by different UN and human rights bodies, although these shift the focus to the act of taking into custody and apprehension of a person.[18] The Human Rights Committee considers "arrest" to amount to a deprivation of liberty.[19]

14. Storck v. Germany, *supra* note 10.

15. Knut Dörmann, Elements of War Crimes Under the Rome Statute of the International Criminal Court: Sources and Commentary 112–13 (2003) (The *travaux préparatoires* to the Rome Statute clarify that "confinement" in the context of "unlawful confinement" is a broader term than "detention," since it includes not only detention in prisons or detention camps but also assigned residence). For more detailed discussion of the war crime of unlawful confinement, *see* Marco Sassòli's chapter in the present volume.

16. *Cf.* Additional Protocol I, *supra* note 1, art. 75(3).

17. ICRC APs Commentary, *supra* note 11, at ¶ 3061.

18. *Cf.* U.N. Economic and Social Council, *Study of the Right of Everyone to Be Free From Arbitrary Arrest, Detention and Exile*, ¶ 21, U.N. Doc. E/CN.4/826 (Jan. 5, 1962), https://digitallibrary.un.org/record/642868?ln=fr&v=pdfis, according to which arrest is the "act of taking a person into custody under the authority of the law or by compulsion of another kind and includes the period from the moment he is placed under restraint up to the time he is brought before an authority competent to order his continued custody or to release him." Although dated, the study has been referred to by the Working Group on Arbitrary Detention as "the one and only detailed multilateral study on the issue" as recently as 2012. U.N. Working Group on Arbitrary Detention, *supra* note 11, at ¶ 52. *See also* U.N. Human Rights Comm., *General Comment No. 35*, *supra* note 9, at ¶ 13: "The term 'arrest' refers to any apprehension of a person that commences a deprivation of liberty and the term 'detention' refers to the deprivation of liberty that begins with the arrest and continues in time from apprehension until release."

19. *General Comment No. 35*, *supra* note 9, at ¶ 13.

Last but not least, any restriction of the movement of a person for the purpose of screening renders that person to be legally considered "in the power of" or "in the hands of" the party to the armed conflict that carries out the screening. There is broad consensus that these two interchangeable notions are to be construed broadly to extend beyond deprivations of liberty/detention as previously defined to include situations in which persons find themselves in territory under the control of a party,[20] regardless of whether they do come into actual contact with that party.[21] A fortiori, persons that do by virtue of the fact that they are subjected to a restriction of movement in the course of screening ipso facto find themselves "in the power of" or "in the hands of" the party to the armed conflict that carries out the screening.

Beyond being considered "in the power of" or "in the hands of" a party to an armed conflict, the foregoing suggests that screening amounts in the overwhelming amount of cases at least to a restriction of liberty, for instance, when ascertaining the facts surrounding the identity, conduct, status, or condition of an individual at a military checkpoint or roadblock or during security sweeps, as well as in the context of evacuations and safe passage for civilians from areas under siege and the coincidental screening of relief personnel, provided that such restrictions of liberty are transient, that is, for a "negligible length of time," or do not involve confinement in a particular restricted space. Above that threshold for confinement, other instances of screening will amount to a deprivation of liberty, in the form of an arrest followed by detention. The latter would include the en masse confinement of persons in camps, but also the confinement of individuals or small groups in holding centers, their own homes, or other restricted spaces for longer periods than a "negligible length of time." Except in cases where such confinement above the de minimis threshold occurs for the purpose of judicial proceedings (for instance, in the context of searching for suspected war criminals or in the context of arresting individuals for domestic crimes in a situation of belligerent occupation to ensure public order and safety), deprivations of liberty for screening purposes will amount to administrative detention/internment.

Against this background, it would appear obvious that screening operations are subject to the legal regulations that govern the respective forms of restriction of movement and deprivation of liberty/detention. These include pertinent standards of treatment and procedural safeguards as stipulated by the LOAC and applicable human rights law, including humane treatment without adverse distinction and

20. Marco Sassòli, International Humanitarian Law: Rules, Controversies, and Solutions to Problems Arising in Warfare 289 (2019); Prosecutor v. Rajić, Case No. IT-95-12-S, Review of the Indictment Pursuant to Rule 61 of the Rules of Procedure and Evidence, ¶ 37 (Int'l Crim. Trib. for the former Yugoslavia Sept. 13, 1996).

21. Oscar M. Uhler et al., Commentary to Geneva Convention IV Relative to the Protection of Civilian Persons in Time of War 47 (1958) [hereinafter 1958 GC IV Commentary].

other fundamental guarantees, periodic reviews in case of internment in international armed conflicts, contact with family members during internment, and so forth. However, all of these rules and principles pertain to either the treatment of individuals subject to screening (i.e., *during* the screening process) or to the situation *after* the screening has led to a determination of the identity, conduct, status, and condition of individuals and a subsequent decision to either release or detain the person concerned or to otherwise restrict the person's liberty. In other words, these rules do not speak to the lawfulness of the measure of screening individuals as such. It is to the parameters for that lawfulness to which we now turn.

4. TOWARD A REGULATORY FRAMEWORK FOR SCREENING OPERATIONS

In order to devise a regulatory framework for screening operations, a distinction will be made between such a framework construed under the LOAC (section 4.1) and under human rights law (section 4.2). Section 4.3 offers an attempt at a synthesis of the two fields.

4.1 Permissibility Under the LOAC

As a preliminary point, the question arises whether the absence of specific regulation of the lawfulness of screening operations under the LOAC means that these are ipso facto legally permissible. In other words, we need to address whether the law pertaining to screening is built on a restrictive or a permissive logic.[22] If the former, the absence of a specific prohibition to carry out screening operations would indicate its permissibility and our analysis would end right here.[23] If the latter, the absence of a permission under the LOAC[24] to engage in screening operations would indicate its unlawfulness.

It is submitted that in the realms of deprivation and restriction of liberty of (presumed) civilians, the LOAC proceeds from the latter assumption. In these areas, pertinent provisions are generally couched in terms that suggest respect and protection as a starting point, to which any measures that negatively impact that protection and respect constitute articulated exceptions. For example,

22. *See generally* Anne Quintin, The Nature of International Humanitarian Law—A Permissive or Restrictive Regime? (2020). That debate is an inherent structural feature of international legal argument and not limited to the LOAC, *see* Martti Koskenniemi, From Apology to Utopia: The Structure of International Legal Argument (2006).

23. On this understanding of what is meant when the LOAC is said to be "restrictive," *see* Quintin, *supra* note 22, at 62–66.

24. *Id.* at 69–70. "Permission" is understood here to correspond to the construct of a "strong permission" in the sense of an articulated entitlement in the LOAC to take a given action.

Article 5 of the Fourth Geneva Convention relative to the Protection of Civilian Persons in Times of War (GC IV) is formulated as an exception to the "rights and privileges under the Convention,"[25] stipulating both the reasons for it (being "definitely suspected of or engaged in activities hostile to the security of the State") and some of the required safeguards (humane treatment, fair and regular trial in case of criminal proceedings, etc.). Similarly, Article 17 of the Second Additional Protocol to the Geneva Conventions (AP II) formulates the prohibition of forced movement of civilians in a way that disallows displacement unless the reasons for the exception are satisfied ("the security of the civilians involved or imperative military necessity"). In other words, pertinent rules that regulate what may and what may not be done vis-à-vis (presumed) civilians seem to suggest that they rest on the general assumption that parties to an armed conflict are prohibited from doing what is not permitted.

What does the foregoing mean for the purpose of determining whether and under what conditions screening is lawful or not?

Lawful purpose

As already noted, no positive, specific rule of the LOAC stipulates an express permission to conduct screening operations. Yet it is submitted that that fact alone is insufficient to conclude that such measures are ipso facto impermissible. The requisite permission does not need to take the form of an express and specific rule to the effect that measures that aim to ascertain the facts surrounding the identity, conduct, status, and condition of individuals are allowed. Rather, such a permission can be deduced from those rules of the LOAC that articulate a *lawful purpose* for which screening operations may be conducted. The act of screening needs to serve a purpose that the LOAC recognizes as lawful and can, as such, be construed as logically implied in the quest to pursue that lawful purpose. Simply put, if the LOAC stipulates that a given action vis-à-vis an individual is legally permissible and under what conditions that is the case, then screening for the purpose of ascertaining whether those conditions are met is equally permissible. Any other conclusion would produce the incongruous result that a process to ascertain whether the legal prerequisites for a given action have been met would be deemed unlawful, ultimately undermining the likelihood of that action being carried out in accordance with the legal prerequisites.

A number of rules supply such a lawful purpose, the pursuit of which implies processes that aim to ascertain the facts surrounding the identity, conduct, status, and condition of individuals. The denial of certain rights and privileges of protected persons because they are "definitely suspected of or engaged in activities hostile to the security of the State"[26] under GC IV, for instance, presupposes an individualized screening process to ascertain whether an individual is indeed

25. *Cf.* Convention (IV) Relative to the Protection of Civilian Persons in Time of War art. 5(1), Aug. 12, 1949, 6 U.S.T. 3516, 75 U.N.T.S. 287 [hereinafter Fourth Geneva Convention or GC IV].

26. *Cf. id.*, art. 5(1).

implicated in such activities. Similarly, screening measures can be implied in Article 27(4) GC IV, which allows for "such measures of control and security in regard to protected persons as may be necessary as a result of the war."[27] Here, the express opening in the rule for considerations of military necessity provides a lawful purpose for screening measures.[28] Another example would be the screening of persons in the context of local agreements for the purpose of their removal from besieged or encircled areas, which presupposes determining whether they do indeed belong to the categories of persons who are to be removed (wounded, sick, infirm, elderly, children, maternity cases, etc.).[29] The screening of individuals to ascertain whether they are civilians and whether their security or imperative military reasons warrant their displacement also pursues a lawful purpose, as provided for in GC IV,[30] AP II,[31] and customary law.[32] A last example relates to the lawful purpose for which screening operations may be carried out, provided for in the context of the right to leave under Article 35(1) GC IV. The rule recognizes an exception to the entitlement of protected persons who are aliens in the territory of a party to the conflict to leave the territory if and when "their departure is contrary to the national interests of the State."[33] Measures to establish whether that is indeed the case, which may include an incidental process to determine the facts surrounding matters such as the identity[34] and conduct[35] of a given individual, would hence pursue a purpose that the LOAC recognizes as lawful.

27. *See further* on Article 27 of GC IV Nathalie Durhin's chapter in the present volume.

28. Indeed, on account of the ICRC's 1958 Commentary, belligerent parties are left with a considerable amount of discretion as regards the choice of means, which may include "comparatively mild restrictions such as the duty of registering with and reporting periodically to the police authorities, the carrying of identity cards or special papers, or a ban on the carrying of arms, to harsher provisions such as a prohibition on any change in place of residence without permission, prohibition of access to certain areas, restrictions of movement, or even assigned residence and internment." 1958 GC IV Commentary, *supra* note 21, at 207.

29. *Cf.* Fourth Geneva Convention, *supra* note 25, art. 17.

30. *Id.*, art. 49(2).

31. *Cf.* Additional Protocol II, *supra* note 8, art. 17.

32. *Cf.* 1 Customary International Humanitarian Law, r. 129 (Jean-Marie Henckaerts & Louise Doswald-Beck eds., 2005) [hereinafter ICRC CIHL Study].

33. *Cf.* Fourth Geneva Convention, *supra* note 25, art. 35(1).

34. An example would be to ascertain whether a given individual protected person is of an age to bear arms. *See* 1958 GC IV Commentary, *supra* note 21, at 236.

35. *See id.* The Commentary asserts that the notion of "national interests of the State" is broader than "security considerations" to include situations "when the national economy would suffer as a result . . . in particular . . . where the departure of too large a proportion of aliens might prejudice national interests by creating manpower or economic problems." On this understanding, a screening process to ascertain the economic consequences of the departure of a given (group of) protected person(s) would satisfy the lawful purpose requirement.

The aforementioned examples are not meant to provide an exhaustive list of rules that can be construed as providing a lawful purpose for screening operations. However, they illustrate the process of deducing from the LOAC lawful purposes for which screening processes may be permissible by way of logical implication. Importantly, that process takes as its starting point the specific provision at hand. It does not rely on a purported suspensory effect of the law's generic underlying precepts of military necessity and humanitarian considerations. The argument is not, in other words, that it is sufficient for a permission of screening operations to rely on military necessity or humanitarian considerations as independent bases, divorced from and external to a specific rule. Rather, the permission is a logical consequence of openings in individual rules of the LOAC that can be construed as permitting screening in pursuit of a purpose that that specific rule stipulates. Absent such openings, screening becomes impermissible. Such a construction of the requirement of a lawful purpose also entails that screening is legally impermissible if it is carried out in pursuit of an unlawful purpose. If the purpose is, for instance, to carry out extrajudicial executions of men and boys of a certain age, screening processes to identify such individuals are equally unlawful. Similarly, if screening is carried out for the unlawful purpose of collectively punishing[36] or intimidating[37] the civilian population, it becomes unlawful.

Necessity

In addition to the requirement of a lawful purpose, the permissibility of screening processes is further conditioned by their being necessary, in the sense that a specific screening operation or process is required to achieve the lawful purpose. Necessity also implies that the screening measure is to cease once the lawful purpose has been achieved. In other words, necessity in the present context means that the screening only continues for as long as it is necessary.

The conceptualization of the notion of necessity in the present context is analogous to the notion of military necessity.[38] This is self-evident in cases where the identified lawful purpose is couched in terms of military necessity, such as in the context of control and security measures with regard to protected persons that may be necessary as a result of the war in accordance with Article 27(4) GC IV, and in the context of evacuations of civilians warranted by imperative military reasons as provided for in GC IV,[39] AP II,[40] and customary law.[41] In these cases,

36. As prohibited by: GC IV, *supra* note 25, art. 33; Additional Protocol I, *supra* note 1, art. 75 (2)(d); Additional Protocol II, *supra* note 8, art. 4 (2)(b); ICRC CIHL Study, *supra* note 32, r. 103.

37. As prohibited by Fourth Geneva Convention, *supra* note 25, art. 33, for instance.

38. *See generally* Nobuo Hayashi, Military Necessity—The Art, Morality and Law of war (2020); Sigrid Redse Johansen, the Military Commander's Necessity (2019).

39. Fourth Geneva Convention, *supra* note 25, art. 49(2).

40. *Cf.* Additional Protocol II, *supra* note 8, art. 17(1).

41. *Cf.* ICRC CIHL Study, *supra* note 32, at r. 129.

the requirement that screening be necessary flows directly from the requirement that the lawful purpose for which screening is carried out is itself subject to considerations of military necessity. At the same time, it must be readily acknowledged that not all lawful purposes are couched in terms of *military* necessity. The rule that allows evacuations of civilians if their security so demands provided for in GC IV,[42] AP II,[43] and customary law[44] provides a pertinent example: here, the necessity is not of a military nature in the sense that the evacuation would serve a military purpose, but rather serves the protective purpose of preventing civilians from being exposed to danger. Yet the lawfulness of such an evacuation for that purpose is equally conditioned by its being necessary.[45] So is the lawfulness of a screening process for the purpose of ascertaining whether a given civilian's security demands evacuation. To conceptualize the normative content of "non-military" necessity by analogy to military necessity is justified by the analogous normative function that both fulfill: they condition the lawfulness of exceptions to the main rule stipulated in a given provision. Only if the envisaged measure is "necessary as a result of the war," "warranted by imperative military reasons," demanded by the security of civilians, and so on, may the belligerent parties resort to it. The requirement of military and "non-military" necessity, in turn, can be said to have the following dimensions:

First, in order to be considered necessary, screening and the specific form it takes must be apt to achieve the lawful purpose, that is, they must reasonably be capable of doing so.[46] Screening that is inapt to achieve the lawful purpose is unnecessary. The requirement of aptitude means, for instance, that a screening process for the purpose of identifying whether a specific protected person may be subject to internment, which in turn presupposes that the threat analysis needs to be individualized, must be designed in a way that allows for a determination of whether a given individual poses a security threat. It would follow that screening processes that are not apt to ascertain the facts surrounding the identity, conduct, status, and condition of a given individual, but would only consider those that pertain to a group to which the individual belongs (e.g., an ethnic group presumed to sympathize with the belligerent opponent), would be unnecessary and hence impermissible. Similarly, a screening process that "does not ask the right questions" about whether a given individual poses the requisite security threat to justify internment (such as being involved in insurrectional activities,

42. Fourth Geneva Convention, *supra* note 25, art. 49(2).

43. *Cf.* Additional Protocol II, *supra* note 8, art. 17(1).

44. *Cf.* ICRC CIHL Study, *supra* note 32, at r. 129.

45. In this vein, *see also* the 1958 GC IV Commentary, *supra* note 21, at 283: "Thus, two considerations—the security of the population and "imperative military reasons"—may, according to the circumstances, justify either the evacuation of protected persons (paragraph 2) or their retention (paragraph 5). In each case real necessity must exist."

46. Hayashi, *supra* note 38, at 276–81.

membership in organizations that aim to cause disturbances, direct assistance to the opponent belligerent, acts of sabotage and espionage, and the like) and instead solely considers an individual's age, nationality, or kinship with members of the opponent's armed forces, for example, would be impermissible, as it would be inapt to bring to the fore facts that are needed to determine whether internment can be justified.

Secondly, screening and the specific form it takes must be proportionate in relation to the lawful purpose pursued. If less severe or intrusive forms of screening were available to achieve the lawful purpose, those, rather than the more intrusive form, would have to be adopted.[47] If, for instance, screening is conducted for the purpose of detaining a single known individual engaged in activities hostile to the security of a party to an armed conflict, who is known to be present in a given area under the full control of its armed forces, it would in all likelihood be disproportionate to detain all civilians who attempt to leave that area, if less intrusive means to ascertain their identity, such as identity checks at roadblocks/checkpoints, facial recognition, and biometrics, were reasonably available.

The aforementioned examples readily illustrate that a determination of whether or not a given screening process satisfies the necessity requirement, including its aptitude and proportionality, depends significantly on the circumstances and the means available to the party to the armed conflict concerned. More often than not, several courses of action will be available that can reasonably be expected to be apt and proportionate in pursuit of the lawful purpose for which a screening process is being devised. Indeed, when estimating the aptitude or proportionality of an envisaged course of action or assessing it in hindsight, unforeseen and extraneous factors will often compound the challenge of determining whether such a course was indeed causal to the success or failure of a given screening process. This suggests that parties to an armed conflict possess a significant degree of discretion in appreciating the necessity requirement.

General conformity with LOAC and applicable human rights law

A last requirement for the lawfulness of screening is its general conformity with LOAC and applicable human rights law in the sense that the specific screening measure and the way in which it is carried out is not otherwise prohibited. The specific requirements in that regard will largely be informed by whether or not screening amounts to or coincides with any of the legal terms of art (deprivation or restriction of liberty, detention, internment, confinement, etc.) discussed previously in section 3, which trigger specific subsets of standards of treatment and procedural guarantees.[48] In any event, and beyond these specific requirements,

47. Etienne Henry, Le Principe de la Necessit[é] Militaire: Histoire et Actualit[é] d'une Norme Fondamentale du Droit International Humanitaire 602 (2016).

48. An example would be the requirement for individualized processes and procedural guarantees (periodic reviews) in case of internment in accordance with GC IV, *supra* note 2, if and when screening amounts to internment.

base-line protections will apply in the form of fundamental guarantees that the LOAC and applicable human rights law provide. Accordingly, any screening process needs to be carried out in conformity with the requirement of humane treatment, as manifested in prohibitions such as those relating to murder, ill-treatment, including torture, cruel or inhuman treatment and outrages upon personal dignity, corporal punishment, mutilation, acts of sexual violence, slavery, forced labor, hostage-taking, the use of human shields, and enforced disappearance.[49] In addition, screening processes may not amount to collective punishment.[50] Furthermore, screening operations need to conform with other legally required standards of treatment that pertain to specific categories of persons, such as the wounded, sick and shipwrecked, displaced persons, women, children, the elderly, disabled, and infirm.[51]

4.2 Permissibility Under Human Rights Law

Screening operations also implicate States' obligations under human rights law. An obvious case in this regard is when a State engages in screening processes on its own territory, for example, when a non-international armed conflict takes place between itself and an organized armed group on its territory, or when a State has liberated parts of its own, previously occupied territory in an international armed conflict. Furthermore, the nature of screening operations described for purposes of the present chapter is such that they regularly bring individuals subject to them into the "jurisdiction" of the State carrying them out.[52] Accordingly, even extraterritorially conducted screening operations trigger the human rights obligations of that State.[53]

49. ICRC CIHL Study, *supra* note 32, at rr. 87–98.

50. *Id.* at r. 103.

51. *Id.* at rr. 109–11, 129–33, 134, 135, 138.

52. On the notion of jurisdiction, *see, e.g.*, Human Rights Comm., *General Comment No. 31: Nature of the General Legal Obligation Imposed on States Parties to the Covenant*, ¶ 10, CCPR/C/21/Rev.1/Add.13 (May 26, 2004) [hereinafter Human Rights Comm., *General Comment No. 31*]; Banković and Others v. Belgium, App. No. 52207/99, ¶¶ 59–61, 67, 71 (2001) (ECtHR), https://hudoc.echr.coe.int/eng?i=001-43151; The Environment and Human Rights, Advisory Opinion OC-23/17, ¶ 74 (2017) (IACtHR), https://www.corteidh.or.cr/docs/opiniones/seriea_23_ing.pdf.

53. On extraterritorial application of human rights, *see, e.g.*, Human Rights Comm., *General Comment No. 31, supra* note 52, at ¶ 10; Al-Skeini and Others v. United Kingdom, App. No. 55721/07, ¶ 137 (2011) (ECtHR), http://hudoc.echr.coe.int/eng?i=001-105606; *see also* Georgia v. Russia II, App. No. 38263/08, ¶ 83 (2021) (ECtHR); The Environment and Human Rights, Advisory Opinion OC-23/17, ¶ 74, 101–02 (2017) (IACtHR), https://www.corteidh.or.cr/docs/opiniones/seriea_23_ing.pdf. Note that the United States and Israel have objected to the extraterritorial application of human rights treaties. U.N. Human Rights Comm., *Concluding Observations of the Fourth Periodic Report of the United States of America*, ¶ 4, U.N. Doc.

An exhaustive treatment of all human rights that could possibly be applicable to situations where individuals are subject to screening operations is beyond the purview of the present chapter. Instead, I will focus on those that are most directly implicated: the right to liberty,[54] the right to liberty of movement,[55] and the right to privacy.[56] This is so because screening operations as defined for purposes of the present chapter amount to at least a restriction of movement and in many cases also to a deprivation of liberty. In addition, the operational rationale of ascertaining the facts surrounding the identity, conduct, status, and condition of individuals involves the gathering of information, thus implicating the right to privacy. These three rights are set forth in a number of human rights treaties, but not necessarily in identical terms.[57] It would go beyond the purpose of the present exercise to tease out all such differences in the context being discussed. Instead, these rights and the conditions that screening operations would have to satisfy for them to be permissible will be painted with a broad brush, taking their codification in the International Covenant on Civil and Political Rights (ICCPR) as a starting point.

A first legal parameter for determining whether screening operations are permissible under human rights law is provided by the possibility of derogations.

CCPR/C/USA/CO/4 (Apr. 23, 2014); U.N. Human Rights Comm., *Concluding Observations of the Fourth Periodic Report of Israel*, ¶ 5, U.N. Doc. CCPR/C/ISR/CO/4 (Nov. 21, 2014). *See also* Legal Consequences of the Construction of a Wall in the Occupied Palestinian Territory, Advisory Opinion, 2004 I.C.J. Rep. 136, ¶¶ 109, 111–13 (July 9) (where the International Court of Justice rejects Israel´s position and reaffirms extraterritorial jurisdiction) [hereinafter *Wall* opinion].

54. International Covenant on Civil and Political Rights art. 9, Dec. 16, 1966, 999 U.N.T.S. 171 [hereinafter ICCPR]; Convention for the Protection of Human Rights and Fundamental Freedoms art. 5, Nov. 4, 1950, 213 U.N.T.S. 222 [hereinafter ECHR]; American Convention on Human Rights art. 7, Nov. 22, 1969, 1144 U.N.T.S. 123 [hereinafter ACHR]; African Charter on Human and People's Rights art. 6, June 27, 1981, 1520 U.N.T.S. 363; Convention on the Rights of the Child art. 37(b), Nov. 20, 1989, 1577 U.N.T.S. 3.

55. ICCPR, *supra* note 54, art. 12; ECHR, *supra* note 54, Protocol 4, arts. 2 and 3; ACHR, *supra* note 54, art. 22; African Charter on Human and People's Rights, *supra* note 54, art. 12.

56. ICCPR, *supra* note 54, art. 17, ECHR, *supra* note 54, art. 8; ACHR, *supra* note 54, art. 11.

57. The elements of the right to freedom of movement differ for each treaty, with one key difference concerning the restrictions to entry or exit from a country. Additionally, the grounds for restrictions listed in the treaties may differ. For instance, compared to Article 12 of the ICCPR, *supra* note 54, Article 2 of Protocol 4 to the ECHR, *supra* note 54, includes a longer lists of possible grounds for restriction, adding "public safety, the prevention of crime" and regulating restrictions of movement in certain areas. Another difference is that the text of the ECHR expressly states that restrictions must be "necessary in a democratic society," whereas Article 12 of the ICCPR does not. In practice, the Human Rights Committee has read this condition into Article 12. *See* Human Rights Comm., *General Comment No. 27*: Article 12 *(Freedom of Movement)*, ¶ 11, U.N. Doc. CCPR/C/21/rev.1/Add.9 (Nov. 2, 1999) [hereinafter Human Rights Comm., *General Comment No. 27*]. For a more detailed explanation, *see* Louise Doswald-Beck, Human Rights in Times of Conflict and Terrorism 71–72, 376–77 (2011).

States are allowed to derogate from the right to liberty, to freedom of movement, and to privacy in time of public emergency which threatens the life of the nation,[58] and the existence of an armed conflict may very well qualify as such. Accordingly, provided that screening operations are strictly required by the exigencies of the situation, are implemented in a nondiscriminatory manner, and are otherwise consistent with a State party's other obligations under international law, including those that derive from the LOAC, they may be permissible, subject to certain procedural requirements being met.[59]

A second legal parameter for determining whether screening operations are permissible under human rights law flows from the non-absolute nature of the right to liberty, to freedom of movement, and to privacy. Accordingly, they may be limited when balanced against collective interests.[60] It is to the permissibility of these limitations in respect to the three identified rights to which we now turn.

As far as the right to liberty under the ICCPR is concerned, screening that amounts to a deprivation of liberty must be non-arbitrary, meaning that it must be appropriate, just, reasonable, necessary, proportionate, predictable, and in accordance with a procedure prescribed by law.[61] To avoid arbitrariness, screening amounting to detention must be carried out with "no element of bad faith or deception from the authorities."[62] The measure must further genuinely conform to the ground of detention relied on by the government and the place and conditions of detention need to be appropriate.[63] The notion of arbitrariness may vary depending on the type of detention and may include an assessment of the necessity of the detention.[64] According to the Human Rights Committee, a measure is reasonable when it is "proportional to the end sought and . . . necessary in the circumstances of any given case."[65] Indeed, detention should be a last resort where "less severe measures have

58. *Cf.* ICCPR, *supra* note 54, art. 4(1); ECHR, *supra note* 54, art. 15; ACHR, *supra* note 54, art. 27(1).

59. This includes that the State party must have officially proclaimed a state of emergency and complies with a regime of international notification. The latter includes informing other States parties to the relevant human rights treaty about the start and end of derogation measures, the human rights provision(s) affected by them, and the reasons for taking them. International Covenant on Civil and Political Rights, *supra* note 54, art. 4(3).

60. Doswald-Beck, *supra* note 57, at 68.

61. U.N. Human Rights Comm., *General Comment No. 35*, *supra* note 9, at ¶ 12. *See also* Human Rights Comm., *Gorji-Dinka v. Cameroon*, ¶ 5.1, U.N. Doc. CCPR/C/83/D/1134/2002 (Apr. 1, 2005); Human Rights Comm., *Van Alphen v. Netherlands*, ¶ 5.8. Comm. No. 305/1988 (July 23, 1990).

62. Saadi v. the United Kingdom, App. No. 13229/03, ¶ 69 (2008) (ECtHR), https://hudoc.echr.coe.int/eng?i=001-84709.

63. *Id.*

64. For a detailed outline of the key principles, *see Saadi*, *supra* note 62, at ¶¶ 68–74.

65. Human Rights Comm., *Toonen v. Australia*, ¶ 8.3, U.N. Doc. CCPR/C/50/D/488/1992 (Mar. 31, 1994).

been considered and found insufficient" to achieve the stated aim.[66] The principle of proportionality requires the duration of the deprivation of liberty to be proportionate to its purpose.[67] If and when screening operations amount to administrative detention, the aforementioned requirements of necessity and proportionality have been interpreted to mean that it shall be limited to "the most exceptional circumstances" to counter "a present, direct and imperative threat" which cannot be addressed by alternative measures. Moreover, such detention may not last longer than absolutely necessary and the longer it lasts, the heavier the burden on the State in proving that it is in fact absolutely necessary.[68] Importantly, the aforementioned requirements have not prevented the Human Rights Committee to postulate that "[s]ecurity detention authorized and regulated by and complying with international humanitarian law in principle is not arbitrary."[69]

As to the right to liberty of movement, any restriction in the form of screening operations must be "provided by law, . . . necessary to protect national security, public order (*ordre public*), public health or morals or the rights and freedoms of others, and . . . consistent with the other rights recognized [in the ICCPR]."[70] The national security and public order exceptions, in particular, provide States with a significant margin of appreciation into which screening operations can very well fall provided that the State can make a reasonable case for their being necessary and proportionate to achieve these purposes. Pertinent in the present context, the Human Rights Committee has held in the specific case of screening conducted at checkpoints that they must not prevent religious pilgrimage,[71] urgent medical care, or access to food and water.[72] Neither may they be used as means of extortion.[73] The Committee further held that, generally, access to restricted areas should be made available through several different checkpoints.[74]

66. *Id.* at ¶ 70.

67. *Id.* at ¶¶ 54, 70; A. and Others v. the United Kingdom, App. No. 3455/05, ¶ 164 (2009) (ECtHR); U.N. Human Rights Comm., *General Comment No. 35*, *supra* note 9, at ¶ 15.

68. *Comment No. 35*, *supra* note 9, at ¶ 15.

69. *Id.* at ¶ 64.

70. ICCPR, *supra* note 54, art. 12(3). On these notions, *see* U.N. Human Rights Comm., *General Comment No. 27*, *supra* note 57, at ¶¶ 11 and 14, U.N. Doc. CPR/C/21/Rev.1/Add.9 (Nov. 2, 1999).

71. *Cf.* U.N. Human Rights Comm., *Concluding observations on the fourth periodic report of Cyprus*, ¶ 18, U.N. Doc. CCPR/C/CYP/CO/4 (Apr. 30, 2015).

72. U.N. Human Rights Comm., *Concluding observations on the fourth periodic report of Israel*, ¶ 12, U.N. Doc. CCPR/C/ISR/CO/4 (Nov. 21, 2014).

73. U.N. Human Rights Comm., *Concluding observations on the situation of civil and political rights in Equatorial Guinea*, ¶ 13, U.N. Doc. CCPR/CO/79/GNQ (Aug. 13, 2004).

74. U.N. Human Rights Comm., *Concluding observations on the sixth periodic report of Morocco*, ¶ 9, U.N. Doc. CCPR/C/MAR/CO/6 (Dec. 1, 2016).

The Human Rights Committee's jurisprudence likewise prohibits "arbitrary or unlawful interference" with the right to privacy, requiring that any such interference be in accordance with the law, necessary, and proportionate.[75] Accordingly, interference with the right to privacy in the form of screening operations must be based on domestic law that provides adequate safeguards for protection against arbitrary interference[76] and be "in accordance with the provisions, aims and objectives" of the ICCPR.[77] Screening operations must further be necessary in a democratic society, that is, account for a "pressing social need."[78] Due deference is given to the State in evaluating such need.[79] However, a restriction in the form of screening resulting from a need must be "proportionate to the legitimate aim pursued."[80] Screening must not impair the right's essence[81] and should be the "least intrusive" measure.[82]

75. U.N. Human Rights Comm., *General Comment No. 16: Article 17 (Right to Privacy), The Right to Respect of Privacy, Family, Home and Correspondence, and Protection of Honour and Reputation*, ¶ 4 (Apr. 8, 1988) [hereinafter U.N. Human Rights Comm., *General Comment No. 16*]: "Even interference provided for by law should be in accordance with the provisions, aims and objectives of the Covenant and should be, in any event, reasonable in the particular circumstances." The Human Rights Committee has later clarified that this means that "any interference with privacy must be proportional to the end sought and be necessary in the circumstances of any given case," *see* Human Rights Comm., *Toonen v. Australia*, *supra* note 65, at ¶ 8.3. *See also* United Nations General Assembly, *The right to Privacy in the Digital Age*, ¶ 4, U.N. Doc. A/RES/73/179 (Jan. 21, 2019).

76. Beghal v. the United Kingdom, App. No. 4755/16, ¶ 89 (2019) (ECtHR), https://hudoc.echr.coe.int/eng?i=001-191276; Council of Europe, *Guide to Article 2 of Protocol No. 4 to the European Convention on Human Rights: Freedom of Movement* (Aug. 31, 2022), https://www.echr.coe.int/documents/d/echr/Guide_Art_2_Protocol_4_ENG#:~:text=1.-,Article%202%20of%20Protocol%20No.,out%20in%20the%20second%20paragraph.

77. U.N. Human Rights Comm., *General Comment No. 16*, *supra* note 75, at ¶ 4.

78. Handyside v. United Kingdom, App. No. 5493/72, ¶ 48 (1976) (ECtHR), https://hudoc.echr.coe.int/?i=001-57499.

79. *Id.* at 48–49 (on the ECtHR's doctrine of the "margin of appreciation").

80. Human Rights Comm., *General Comment No. 27*, *supra* note 57, at ¶ 14.

81. *Id.* at ¶ 13. *See also* Constitutional Rights Project, Civil Liberties Organisation and Media Rights Agenda v. Nigeria, African Comm'n H.P.R., Coms. Nos. 140/90, 141/94, and 145/95, ¶ 42 (Nov. 5, 1999).

82. *General Comment No. 27*, *supra* note 57, at ¶ 13. This statement was cited with approval by the ICJ in the *Wall* opinion, *supra* note 53, at ¶ 136. *See also* Advisory Opinion OC-5/85, ¶ 46 (1985) (IACtHR), https://www.corteidh.or.cr/docs/opiniones/seriea_05_ing.pdf.

4.3 Reconciling LOAC and IHRL on the Permissibility of Screening

The foregoing demonstrates that screening operations are oftentimes simultaneously governed by both the LOAC and human rights law. It also follows from the preceding analysis that the legal parameters for the permissibility of screening under the two respective fields of law often align or at least closely resemble one another. For example, if the right to freedom of movement under human rights law allows for restrictions in the form of screening operations for the purpose of protecting national security and public order to the extent that they are necessary and proportionate, the lawful purposes under the LOAC as construed previously (see section 4.1) can easily be aligned with the notions of national security and public order. For its part, the notion of necessity under the LOAC with its subdimensions of aptitude and proportionality captures, at least in generic terms, the requirements of necessity and proportionality under human rights law.

At the same time, notable differences exist between the LOAC and human rights law when it comes to conditions relevant for the permissibility of screening operations. The requirement under human rights law that such operations, which amount to a restriction of the right to privacy, be based on domestic law that provides adequate safeguards against arbitrary interference may serve as an example. No such requirement can be deduced from the LOAC. Differences between the LOAC and human rights law are exacerbated when one considers how the human rights most directly implicated in the context of screening operations are formulated at the regional, more specifically European level. The LOAC accepts screening operations that are conducted for the lawful purpose of security (administrative detention) if and when necessary, as permissible deprivations or restrictions of liberty. The European Convention, however, provides a strictly exhaustive list of purposes for which individuals may be deprived of their liberty,[83] from which administrative detention for security reasons is absent.

How, then, are such differences between the LOAC and human rights law to be reconciled? It is submitted that the dominant view on the simultaneous application of human rights law and the LOAC is that their mutual relationship is governed by complementarity and the *lex specialis* maxim.[84]

By describing the relationship between human rights law and the LOAC as "complementary," the two fields are regarded as mutually reinforcing in as much as they complete and perfect each other.[85] Accordingly, if a given question is

83. European Convention of Human Rights, *supra* note 54, art. 5(1)(a)–(f).

84. Jann K. Kleffner, *Human Rights and International Humanitarian Law: General Issues*, *in* The Handbook of International Law of Military Operations 35, 57–58 (Terry Gill & Dieter Fleck eds., 2d ed. 2015).

85. On the three possible scenarios of mutual reinforcement, *see* the *Wall* opinion, *supra* note 53, at ¶ 106; Armed Activities on the Territory of the Congo (Dem. Rep. Congo v. Uganda), Judgment, 2005 I.C.J. Rep. 168, ¶ 216 (Dec. 19).

regulated exclusively by the LOAC, the mutual reinforcement takes the form of the LOAC filling the gaps left by human rights law. For example, the right of access of protecting powers and ICRC delegates as stipulated by the Fourth Geneva Convention[86] to places where protected persons subject to screening processes are held complement any gap that might exist under human rights law in that respect. If, on the other hand, a given question is regulated exclusively by human rights law, answers to questions that arise in relation to these rights fall into the exclusive province of human rights law. For example, a given screening operation that is conducted without the requisite nexus to an armed conflict because its sole purpose is the prevention of the spread of a pandemic will only be governed by human rights law. Similarly, in a scenario in which the right to freedom of expression of a person or their communication with their family or with the outside world during a screening process is at issue, pertinent human rights law would fill any gap that the LOAC leaves unaddressed. However, where a matter is regulated by both the LOAC and human rights law the applicable law will have to be determined by recourse to the general rule that priority should be given to the norm that is more specific (*lex specialis derogat legi generali*). The *lex specialis* maxim operates as a rule of interpretation and as a rule of conflict resolution.[87]

As a technique of interpretation, the LOAC informs the interpretation of human rights law if and when the former is more specific. This is the approach adopted by the International Court of Justice in its *Nuclear Weapons* Advisory Opinion when discussing the right not arbitrarily to be deprived of one's life in times of armed conflict. In the words of the Court, "[t]he test of what is an arbitrary deprivation of life . . . falls to be determined by the applicable *lex specialis,* namely, the law applicable in armed conflict which is designed to regulate the conduct of hostilities."[88] In the present context of reconciling the LOAC and applicable human rights law in order to conceptualize the permissibility of screening operations, it is noteworthy that the Human Rights Committee seems to have adopted the same approach when interpreting the notion of "arbitrary arrest and detention" enshrined in the ICCPR.

The Committee found that "[s]ecurity detention authorized and regulated by and complying with international humanitarian law in principle is not arbitrary."[89] Accordingly, when screening operations that involve a deprivation or restriction of liberty are conducted in compliance with the LOAC parameters examined in the previous section, this creates a strong presumption in favor of their compatibility with the right to liberty as enshrined in

86. *Cf.* Fourth Geneva Convention, *supra* note 25, art. 143.

87. Kleffner, *supra* note 84, at 58.

88. Legality of the Threat or Use of Nuclear Weapons, Advisory Opinion, 1996 I.C.J. Rep. 226, ¶ 25 (July 8).

89. *General Comment No. 35*, *supra* note 9, at ¶ 64.

the ICCPR. However, and contrary to what seems to have been suggested at times,[90] the maxim of *lex specialis* reaches its limits as an interpretive tool when it is necessary to reconcile clearly incompatible norms. In such a situation, the maxim serves as a tool for conflict of norms resolution, with the consequence that the more specific norm supplants the incompatible general rule. For instance, rules of the LOAC that supply the specific lawful purposes for which screening operations may be conducted will supersede human rights rules that would render screening operations for such purposes impermissible. The regulation of lawful purposes for which individuals can be deprived of their liberty under the European Convention on Human Rights[91] is a case in point. Application of the *lex specialis* rule would suggest that a conflict between the exhaustive list of purposes for which persons can be deprived of liberty under Article 5 of the Convention (from which security reasons are absent), and the LOAC, under which security reasons can be a lawful purpose for deprivation of liberty (including for screening operations that amount to such deprivation), is to be resolved in favor of the rule of the LOAC.

5. CONCLUSION

Whereas screening operations are an integral feature of contemporary military operations, they do not fall into a legal vacuum that leaves the reasons for, and ways in which they are to be conducted unanswered. The LOAC and human rights law supply the legal parameters for their permissibility. As to the former, permissibility hinges on a screening process that pursues a lawful purpose, is necessary to achieve that lawful purpose, and is otherwise carried out in conformity with the LOAC and applicable human rights law. These LOAC parameters align to a significant extent with those provided by human rights law. To the extent that they do not, both areas of law can be reconciled by relying on their complementary relationship and the maxim of *lex specialis*. It is submitted that, thus construed, legal parameters deriving from both the LOAC and human rights law can provide a reasonable balance between operational realities that may necessitate the ascertainment of the facts surrounding the identity, conduct, status, and condition of individuals whom armed forces encounter in the course of their operations, and the need to impose constraints on the actions of belligerents so as to avoid abuse and ensure the legitimacy of military operations.

90. Hassan v. United Kingdom, 2014-VI Eur. Ct. H.R. 1, ¶ 104, https://www.echr.coe.int/Documents/Reports_Recueil_2014-VI.pdf: By reason of the co-existence of the safeguards provided by international humanitarian law and by the Convention in time of armed conflict, the grounds of permitted deprivation of liberty set out in subparagraphs (a) to (f) of that provision should be accommodated, as far as possible, with the taking of prisoners of war and the detention of civilians who pose a risk to security under the Third and Fourth Geneva Conventions.

91. European Convention on Human Rights, *supra* note 54.

6

Setting Up Humanitarian Corridors in Armed Conflict

JULIA GRIGNON*

1. INTRODUCTION

Although the expression "humanitarian corridors" is (overly) commonly used in practice, it is not found in treaty international humanitarian law (IHL) and has mostly not been dealt with in the relevant literature. However, "humanitarian corridors" describes a reality that comes with significant challenges. To address these challenges, be they in law or practice, it is first necessary to agree on a definition, which is no easy task. As underlined by Roz Price, the term "humanitarian corridor" is closely linked to other terms such as "humanitarian pause," "temporary cessation of hostilities," or even "days of tranquility," and "[t]he terminology is often used interchangeably with little consistency in [its] use."[1] Nevertheless, keeping to the law of armed conflict (LOAC), the closest provision to what a "humanitarian corridor" may be is probably found in Article 17 of Geneva Convention IV which reads: "The Parties to the conflict shall endeavour to conclude local agreements for the removal from besieged or encircled areas, of wounded, sick, infirm, and aged persons, children and maternity cases, and for the passage of

* Dr. Julia Grignon is the Research Director of the Institute for Strategic Research of the French Military Academy, a member of the Paris Human Rights Center at Assas University, and a Visiting Professor of the Faculty of Law at Laval University (Canada). She thanks Tara Ibrahim, PhD student at Laval University, for her invaluable research support in the preparation of this chapter. She also thanks Émilie Max for her decisive language revision.

1. Roz Price, *Humanitarian Pauses and Corridors in Contexts of Conflict*, Institute of Development Studies (Sept. 17, 2020).

Julia Grignon, *Setting Up Humanitarian Corridors in Armed Conflict* In: *Civilian Protection in Armed Conflict*.
Edited by: Jelena Pejic and Captain Margaret Kotlik, Oxford University Press. © Julia Grignon 2025.
DOI: 10.1093/oso/9780197793176.003.0006

ministers of all religions, medical personnel and medical equipment on their way to such areas."[2]

This chapter demonstrates that the expression "humanitarian corridors" simultaneously covers more and less than that. For purpose of this contribution the author defines humanitarian corridors as "agreements between parties to [an] armed conflict to allow for safe passage for a limited time in a specific geographic area."[3] A humanitarian corridor may be said to have a dual aim: on the one hand its goal is "to help people trapped in hostilities,"[4] that is, to allow civilians to leave or the evacuation of wounded, sick, or dead, and, on the other, to permit access to victims of armed conflicts.[5]

There have been numerous illustrations of this practice over the last decades. The most cited examples include the "Kindertransport" that occurred during World War II, which allowed the evacuation of children from a Nazi-controlled zone to the United Kingdom; the humanitarian corridor established in relation to the siege of Sarajevo, and the recent evacuation of civilians from Ghouta in Syria.[6] Headlines often present the establishment of such corridors as a crucial gain.[7] Most of the time, however, the establishment of a humanitarian corridor rather

2. Geneva Convention (IV) Relative to the Protection of Civilian Persons in Time of War art. 17, Aug. 12, 1949, 6 U.S.T. 3516, 75 U.N.T.S. 287 [hereinafter Geneva Convention IV or GC IV].

3. *How Humanitarian Corridors Work to Help People in Conflict Zones*, International Committee of the Red Cross (June 3, 2022), https://www.icrc.org/en/document/how-humanitarian-corridors-work. The United Nations Office for the Coordination of Humanitarian Affairs (OCHA) proposed a definition close to this one: "Specific routes and logistical methods agreed upon by all relevant parties to allow the safe passage of humanitarian goods and/or people from one point to another in an area of active fighting." *Glossary of Terms: Pauses During Conflict*, Office for the Coordination of Humanitarian Affairs (June 2011), https://www.unocha.org/sites/unocha/files/dms/Documents/AccessMechanisms.pdf. See also the definition proposed by Nathalie Weizmann: "[D]esignated routes that are demilitarized for a specified period of time, in order to permit humanitarian relief to be delivered and allow civilians and other protected persons to move freely or be evacuated, without being exposed to the dangers of hostilities." Nathalie Weizmann, *Humanitarian Corridors, in* The Companion to International Humanitarian Law, 390, 392 (Dražan Djukić & Niccolò Pons eds., 2018).

4. *How Humanitarian Corridors Work to Help People in Conflict Zones*, *supra* note 3.

5. *Id.*

6. *See* Sophia Hoffmann, *Humanitarian Corridor, in* Humanitarian Keywords 95, 95–96 (Antonio De Lauri ed., 2020). For a comprehensive historical approach, *see* Maelle L'Homme, *Humanitarian Corridors: Negotiated Exceptions at Risk of Manipulation*, 4 Journal of Humanitarian Affairs 48 (2022).

7. For example, Kenneth Chan Yoon Onn describes them as "highly valuable tools." Kenneth Chan Yoon Onn, *The International Law of Protected Spaces and the Collapse of the Humanitarian Corridors in Ukraine*, EJIL: Talk! (Mar. 11, 2022), https://www.ejiltalk.org/the-international-law-of-protected-spaces-and-the-collapse-of-the-humanitarian-corridors-in-ukraine/. *See also* the more tempered appreciation of David Matyas about Russia-Ukraine negotiations who found them a "positive development. Precarious, incomplete, and risky, but positive." David Matyas, *Humanitarian Corridors in Ukraine: Impasse, Ploy or Narrow Passage of Hope?*, Just Security

testifies to a salient *failure* to obtain respect for the law. As exemplified by UN resolutions calling for their implementation,[8] such corridors are indeed necessary when at least one party to the conflict has massively violated IHL, for instance, by targeting civilians, their goods, medical facilities, and food or water supplies. Further, while humanitarian access during armed conflict is neither temporarily nor geographically limited (despite a few exceptions strictly framed by the law), a humanitarian corridor translates to an agreement aimed at obtaining a temporary and restricted right of passage that is additionally contingent on the precarious willingness of the parties involved in the conflict.[9] This alone speaks volumes about the challenges attached to setting up humanitarian corridors.

In short, humanitarian corridors constitute a last resort when there is no alternative way of accessing people affected by armed conflict. This chapter does not deal with humanitarian corridors either in the context of natural disasters or as a means of overcoming bureaucratic impediments posed by States outside situations of armed conflicts. Instead, it starts with a brief reminder of UN action related to the establishment of humanitarian corridors and then situates humanitarian corridors within the law applicable during armed conflict. It subsequently looks at the practical challenges inherent to such corridors.

2. THE LAW

2.1 A Notion That May Be Dealt with Under Distinct Legal Paradigms

It is worth briefly recalling action that has been taken in support of the establishment and operation of humanitarian corridors by various organs of the United Nations, including the UN Security Council (UNSC), occasionally in an enforcement capacity.[10]

UN General Assembly (UNGA) Resolution 45/100 of December 14, 1990,[11] is often quoted as the first iteration of the concept of humanitarian corridors.[12]

9. "A corridor cannot serve as a substitute for the general obligation of all parties to armed conflict to allow and facilitate rapid and unimpeded passage of humanitarian relief for civilians in need, subject to their right of control," Weizmann, *supra* note 3, at 391.

10. International refugee law and international criminal law are two branches of international law that may also be studied when it comes to examine the legal implications of "humanitarian corridors." However, given the context of this contribution, they will not be examined.

11. Humanitarian Assistance to Victims of Natural Disasters and Similar Emergency Situations, G.A. Res. 45/100, U.N. Doc. A/RES/45/100 (Dec. 14, 1990).

12. *See, e.g.*, L'Homme, *supra* note 6, at 49.

(Mar. 8, 2022), https://www.justsecurity.org/80576/humanitarian-corridors-in-ukraine-impasse-ploy-or-narrow-passage-of-hope/.

8. *See* the comprehensive list *infra* section 2.1.

With this text, the UNGA endorsed the UN Secretary General's suggestion to establish "on a temporary basis, where needed, and by means of concerted action . . . relief corridors for the distribution of emergency medical and food aid."[13] The exact term "humanitarian corridor" can be found in at least four later UNSC resolutions: a 1996 resolution on the situation in Burundi, which in the preamble "[e]mphasiz[ed] the urgent need to establish humanitarian corridors to ensure the unimpeded flow of humanitarian goods to all people in Burundi";[14] another 1996 resolution about the situation in the Great Lakes region, in which the Council "[r]equest[ed] the Secretary-General . . . [t]o draw up a concept of operations and framework for a humanitarian task force, with military assistance if necessary . . . with the objectives of: . . . Establishing humanitarian corridors for the delivery of humanitarian assistance and to assist the voluntary repatriation of refugees . . .";[15] a 2009 resolution about the situation in the Gaza strip in which it "[w]elcome[d] the initiatives aimed at creating and opening humanitarian corridors and other mechanisms for the sustained delivery of humanitarian aid";[16] and a 2017 resolution regarding the situation in Sudan and South Sudan that "recogniz[ed] cooperation between Sudan and South Sudan on refugees [and] humanitarian corridors."[17]

Over the years—even when they were not designated as such—humanitarian corridors have continued to be established by the UNSC and/or to be enforced by the United Nations.[18] Resolution 2165 of July 14, 2014, regarding the situation in Syria, constitutes perhaps the most significant example of such practice. The UNSC decided to authorize "the United Nations humanitarian agencies and their implementing partners . . . to use routes across conflict lines and the border crossings of Bab al-Salam, Bab al-Hawa, Al Yarubiyah and Al-Ramtha, in addition to those already in use, in order to ensure that humanitarian assistance, including medical and surgical supplies, reaches people in need throughout Syria."[19] Other resolutions have used the terms "relief corridor,"[20] "security corridor,"[21]

13. G.A. Res. 45/100, *supra* note 11, at ¶ 6.

14. S.C. Res. 1072, Aug. 30, 1996).

15. S.C. Res. 1078, ¶ 10 (Nov. 9, 1996). In the preamble, the UNSC "[t]ak[es] note of the request addressed to the Council by the regional leaders . . . to take urgent measures to ensure the establishment of safe corridors and temporary sanctuaries by deploying a neutral force."

16. S.C. Res. 1860, ¶ 3 (Jan. 8, 2009).

17. S.C. Res. 2386, Preamble (Nov. 15, 2017).

18. *See, e.g.*, S.C. Res. 688, ¶ 3 (Apr. 5, 1991) (Iraq); S.C. Res. 764, ¶¶ 5–6 (July 13, 1992) (Bosnia and Herzegovina); S.C. Res. 767, ¶ 8 (July 27, 1992) (Somalia); S.C. Res. 900, ¶ 2 (Mar. 4, 1994) (Sarajevo).

19. S.C. Res. 2165, ¶ 2 (July 14, 2014).

20. S.C. Res. 834, ¶ 13 (June 1, 1993); S.C. Res. 851, ¶ 19 (July 15, 1993), both appearing as *couloirs humanitaires* in the French versions.

21. S.C. Res. 764, Preamble (July 13, 1992).

"safe corridor,"[22] or solely "corridor." It is worth mentioning that on November 15, 2023, Resolution 2712 called for "urgent and extended humanitarian pauses and *corridors* throughout the Gaza Strip."[23]

The aforementioned examples give rise to legal issues, some of which are mentioned here, but will not be elaborated on. These include queries such as a multilateral organization's motivation for establishing a humanitarian corridor and the lawfulness thereof, the binding effects of the corresponding resolution, as well as its means of enforcement, and the fact that so-called "humanitarian interventions" and the enforcement of the "responsibility to protect" doctrine have sometimes been put under the "umbrella" of a humanitarian corridor (thus making this very notion "part of the interventionist diplomacy lexicon"[24]). While the authorization of a humanitarian corridor through a UNSC resolution may involve aspects of Council's *jus ad bellum* powers, it is crucial to underline that the actual implementation and operation of such a corridor remain exclusively governed by *jus in bello*. In practice, the primary objective of a humanitarian corridor established by a UNSC resolution consists in both addressing humanitarian needs and protecting civilians. In other words, if the establishment of a humanitarian corridor may trigger challenges under *jus ad bellum*, its effects in an armed conflict trigger challenges under *jus in bello*.

2.2 Legal Challenges of Humanitarian Corridors Under International Humanitarian Law

A last resort response to repeated violations of IHL

While it may be misleading, the term "humanitarian corridor" refers to the implementation of measures designed as a last resort in response to the extremely dire situation of a civilian population, which is often the result of a series of violations of the law. As Sophia Hoffman puts it: "The need for humanitarian corridors arises when armed conflict cuts off large numbers of civilians from accessing

22. S.C. Res. 1296, ¶ 15 (Apr. 19, 2000).

23. S.C. Res. 2712, ¶ 2 (Nov. 15, 2023), emphasis added. The full paragraph reads as follows:

> [The Security Council] [c]alls for urgent and extended humanitarian pauses and corridors throughout the Gaza Strip for a sufficient number of days to enable, consistent with international humanitarian law, the full, rapid, safe, and unhindered humanitarian access for United Nations humanitarian agencies and their implementing partners, the International Committee of the Red Cross and other impartial humanitarian organizations, to facilitate the continuous, sufficient and unhindered provision of essential goods and services important to the well-being of civilians, especially children, throughout the Gaza Strip, including water, electricity, fuel, food, and medical supplies, as well as emergency repairs to essential infrastructure, and to enable urgent rescue and recovery efforts, including for missing children in damaged and destroyed buildings, and including the medical evacuation of sick or injured children and their care givers.

24. L'Homme, *supra* note 6, at 49.

basic needs. This may occur incidentally as conflict parties fight without taking the civilian presence into account. But it may also happen deliberately through sieges, in which armed actors purposefully cut off residential areas from water, electricity, food, and health care, and effectively hold civilian populations to ransom."[25] Indeed, sieges—another notion with no definition under IHL—consist of restricting the movement of resources, individuals, and weaponry, intended to either pressure enemy forces into surrender, confine them to a specific area, or establish authority over a particular region. The link with humanitarian corridors is easily made, given the situation that results for the civilian population.

When a humanitarian corridor is called for, certain provisions of international humanitarian law are most likely to have been violated. Among them is Article 51 of Additional Protocol I (AP I), which, as a general rule, establishes that the civilian population "shall enjoy general protection against dangers arising from military operations"[26] and specifies that "the civilian population as such, as well as individual civilians, shall not be the object of attack."[27] AP I likewise prohibits the starvation of civilians as a method of warfare and attacking, destroying, removing, or rendering useless objects indispensable to the survival of the civilian population, whatever the motive.[28] These (and other relevant rules), violation of which would justify the evacuation of affected civilians, are followed by "mirroring" rules on the delivery of humanitarian relief. The relevant provisions foresee that the civilian population in need has the right to receive relief actions, which are both humanitarian and impartial in character and conducted without any adverse distinction.[29] Correspondingly, relief organizations have the right to access civilians in need.[30] Needless to say, these rules are also regularly violated during armed conflicts.

Humanitarian corridors may be envisioned from the perspective of both the military and humanitarian organizations. In either perspective, the following elements must be borne in mind: first, that setting up a humanitarian corridor constitutes a military operation, and second, that the addressees of the LOAC are the parties to the conflict.

25. Hoffmann, *supra* note 6, at 96.

26. Protocol Additional to the Geneva Conventions of 12 August 1949, and Relating to the Protection of Victims of International Armed Conflicts art. 51(1), June 8, 1977, 1125 U.N.T.S. 3 [hereinafter AP I].

27. *Id.*, art. 51(2).

28. *Id.*, art. 54.

29. *Id.*, art. 70(1).

30. AP I, *supra* note 26, art. 70(2).

Humanitarian corridors are not protected zones provided for by IHL

The establishment of humanitarian corridors presupposes an agreement between the warring sides involved. In this context it should be mentioned that humanitarian corridors are not the only option that can be relied on to ensure civilian protection. The relevant IHL treaties expressly provide for protected zones, which under certain circumstances are also subject to the agreement of the parties to the conflict. Geneva Convention IV and AP I, applicable in international armed conflict, envisage four such zones: "hospital and safety zones and localities,"[31] "neutralized zones,"[32] "non-defended localities,"[33] and "demilitarized zones."[34] In non-international armed conflicts, Common Article 3 to the four Geneva Conventions allows for the conclusion of special agreements by parties to the conflict. Such agreements may reflect and therefore trigger the applicability of the rules of the Geneva Conventions otherwise applicable in international armed conflict.

All protected zones are exclusively dedicated to the civilian population. Some, such as hospital and safety zones and localities, are even dedicated to specific (sub)categories of the civilian population such as the wounded and sick, the elderly, children below fifteen, or pregnant women.[35] In addition, all protected zones result from either a written agreement between the parties (hospital and safety zones and localities, neutralized zones, and demilitarized zones), or a unilateral declaration acknowledged by the adverse party or parties (hospital and safety zones and localities and nondefended localities). Furthermore, these zones may be established far from the hostilities (hospital and safety zones and localities), set within a combat zone (neutralized zones, nondefended localities), or neither specifically far nor close to the fighting, but exempt from military operations (demilitarized zones). Finally, protected zones may be temporary (neutralized zones) or perennial (hospital and safety zones and localities, nondefended localities, and demilitarized zones).

However, and this is key, all protected zones must be distinguished from "humanitarian corridors" in that they do not entail "safe passage," be it of the civilian population or of humanitarian personnel.[36] Consequently, an IHL provision (in

31. Geneva Convention IV, *supra* note 2.

32. *Id.*, art. 15.

33. AP I, *supra* note 26, art. 59.

34. *Id.*, art. 60.

35. Geneva Convention IV, *supra* note 2, art. 14.

36. Similarly, *see* Weizmann, *supra* note 3, at 390–91, or Marco Sassòli, according to whom "[t]he aforementioned zones, which are established under *jus in bello*, must be distinguished from the safe areas, humanitarian corridors or safe havens created under Chapter VII of the UN Charter (that is, under *jus ad bellum*)." Marco Sassòli, International Humanitarian Law: Rules, Controversies, and Solutions to Problems Arising in Warfare 378, ¶ 8.360 (2019). For a divergent opinion, *see* Onn, *supra* note 7, according to whom they "fall within the understanding of DMZs described in Article 60 API."

addition to Article 17 of Geneva Convention IV mentioned previously) that echoes the concept of "humanitarian corridors" would be Article 70(2) of AP I on the delivery of humanitarian assistance. This article reads: "The Parties to the conflict and each High Contracting Party shall allow and facilitate rapid and unimpeded *passage* of all relief consignments, equipment and personnel provided in accordance with [the provisions governing relief in favour of the civilian population], even if such assistance is destined for the civilian population of the adverse Party."[37]

An agreement between the warring parties

Because humanitarian corridors depend on an agreement, their establishment presupposes that there will be communication between the warring parties. As indicated in the International Committee of the Red Cross's (ICRC's) Customary IHL Study, "Commanders may enter into non-hostile contact through any means of communication. Such contact must be based on good faith."[38] This rule is rooted in the historical authorization for belligerents to send *parlementaires* in order to communicate with one another; a practice as old as the Brussels Declaration of 1874[39] and the Oxford Manual of 1880,[40] and reflected in the Hague Regulations of 1907.[41] The rule is applicable both in international and non-international armed conflicts, and acknowledges that parties to a conflict may need to speak in order "in particular to conclude local arrangements dealing with such issues as the search for the wounded, sick and dead, the disposal of the dead, exchange of prisoners, evacuation of persons from a besieged area, passage of medical and religious personnel and flights of medical aircraft."[42] In practice, these exact issues are those that may be encompassed by a humanitarian corridor. Thus, even if IHL makes no express reference to the practice, the term acts as an umbrella, reflecting under a single heading a wide range of measures that can be taken under IHL.

It is worth noting that, as a side effect, third parties may be involved as intermediaries in nonhostile contacts between warring parties with their consent. This can be an impartial and neutral humanitarian organization such as

37. AP I, *supra* note 26, art. 70(2) (emphasis added). Today, this provision is recognized as being customary.

38. 1 Customary International Humanitarian Law 6, 227 (Jean-Marie Henckaerts & Louise Doswald-Beck eds., 2005).

39. Project of an International Declaration concerning the Laws and Customs of War, Brussels, Aug. 27, 1874, https://ihl-databases.icrc.org/en/ihl-treaties/brussels-decl-1874.

40. Institute of International Law, The Laws of War on Land, Sept. 9, 1880, https://ihl-databases.icrc.org/en/ihl-treaties/oxford-manual-1880 [hereinafter Oxford Manual].

41. Regulations Respecting the Laws and Customs of War on Land, annexed to Convention No. IV Respecting the Laws and Customs of War on Land art. 32, Oct. 18, 1907, 36 Stat. 2227, T.S. No. 539 [hereinafter Hague Regulations].

42. 1 Customary International Humanitarian Law, *supra* note 38, at 227.

the ICRC, as well as international organizations, or members of peacekeeping forces. Their services should not be perceived as hostile or non-neutral. Finally, as already mentioned, any contact or agreement between the parties must be governed by good faith. With regards to humanitarian corridors this implies that such corridors must be respected as regards both the time and geographical limits agreed upon between the parties. Any failure to do so would contravene the principle of good faith.

The right of the population to leave (or stay) within an unsafe area

Humanitarian corridors aim to help people trapped by hostilities by allowing civilians to leave, permitting the evacuation of the wounded, sick, or deceased, and facilitating access to victims of armed conflict. A civilian population has the right to leave a place that has become unsafe or, conversely, to stay put, and humanitarian agencies have a right to be granted access to those in need. Regarding the former, IHL foresees the right to leave a territory affected by an armed conflict. Article 35 of GC IV states that "[a]ll protected persons who may desire to leave the territory at the outset of, or during a conflict, shall be entitled to do so, unless their departure is contrary to the national interests of the State."[43] Because of the provision's localization in Section II of GC IV, such right is, admittedly, limited to protected persons in the territory of a party to the conflict, thus excluding the territorial State's own nationals.

However, one might argue that the personal scope of the rule has been expanded to apply to all individuals trapped by hostilities. It is submitted that such an enlarged contemporary interpretation may be based on (1) a necessary evolutive interpretation of IHL; (2) Article 17 of AP II dealing with non-international armed conflict, according to which "[c]ivilians shall not be compelled to leave their own territory for reasons connected with the conflict"; and (3) the development of relevant international human rights law (IHRL).[44]

It is also worth noting that in the context of the prohibition of starvation, several military manuals state that the inhabitants of a besieged city must be allowed to leave it. For example, the *U.S. Department of Defense Law of War Manual* underlines that while "[i]n the past, it was permissible, but an extreme measure, to refuse to allow civilians to leave a besieged locality and to use force to drive any who attempted to flee back to the besieged locality . . . such actions would now

43. Convention (IV), *supra* note 2, art. 35. A right to leave the territory also reflected in the provisions applicable to occupied territory in Article 48 of the same Convention "Protected persons who are not nationals of the Power whose territory is occupied, may avail themselves of the right to leave the territory subject to the provisions of Article 35. . . ."

44. Protocol Additional to the Geneva Conventions of August 12, 1949, and Relating to the Protection of Victims of Non-international Armed Conflicts, June 8, 1977, 1125 U.N.T.S. 609 [hereafter AP II]. *See also* G.A. Res. 217 (III) A, Universal Declaration of Human Rights (Dec. 10, 1948); International Covenant on Civil and Political Rights art. 12, Dec. 16, 1966, 999 U.N.T.S. 171, entered into force Mar. 23, 1976.

be prohibited because they would not be consistent with the duty to take feasible precautions for the protection of civilians."[45] According to the French *Manual on the Law of Military Operations*, "both parties shall take all possible measures to protect the civilian population, in particular by allowing civilians to leave the besieged area as far as possible."[46]

As previously mentioned, the right to leave is coupled with a right to stay. If protected persons choose or have no other choice but to remain in a territory in which hostilities are ongoing (for example, persons with disabilities, or hospital staff who will not abandon their patients), they benefit from the "provisions concerning aliens in time of peace. In any case, the following rights shall be granted to them: (1) They shall be enabled to receive the individual or collective relief that may be sent to them. (2) They shall, if their state of health so requires, receive medical attention and hospital treatment to the same extent as the nationals of the State concerned."[47]

At the other end of the spectrum, humanitarian corridors can have the perverse effect of giving the undue impression that persons who do not to seize the opportunity to flee do so because they desire to take part in hostilities. This can lead to a loss of protection for the individuals concerned, who risk not only being targeted but also subjected to ill-treatment or detention.[48] In reality and as a matter of law, a civilian who cannot or does not wish to leave an area remains protected by relevant rules of IHL, including the prohibition of reprisals and collective punishment. In other words, civilians remain fully protected even if they opt against evacuation.

On another hand, while parties to the conflict may *evacuate* civilians from an unsafe area to a safer location, IHL prohibits deportation, as well as the forcible transfer of the civilian population.[49] Such a—sometimes subtle—nuance might explain why humanitarian organizations can be cautious, if not fully reluctant, to

45. Office of the General Counsel, U.S. Department of Defense, Law of War Manual, at 314 (rev. ed. Dec. 2016). Similarly, *see* Israeli Military Manuel, as quoted by 1 Customary International Humanitarian Law, *supra* note 38, at 188.

46. Ministry of the Armed Forces, Manual on the Law of Military Operations, ¶ 161 (2023). Our translation: "*La mise en œuvre de plusieurs règles découlant des principes de distinction et de précaution exige que les deux parties prennent toutes les mesures possibles pour protéger la population civile, notamment en permettant aux civils de quitter la zone assiégée dans toute la mesure du possible*," at 161.

47. GC IV, *supra* note 2, art. 38.

48. *See* Weizmann, *supra* note 3, at 391.

49. Based on Article 49 of Convention (IV), *supra* note 2, this prohibition is today recognized as a customary rule both in international and non-international armed conflicts. *See* 1 Customary International Humanitarian Law, *supra* note 38, at r. 129 (1), at 457. For the transfer of protected persons by a territorial state, *see* art. 45 of Convention (IV), *supra* note 2. For forced displacement in NIAC, *see* art. 17 of AP II, *supra* note 26, and Customary International Humanitarian Law, *supra* note 38, at r. 129(2), at 457.

either call for or participate in humanitarian corridors (see section 3). The recent examples of people fleeing the hostilities in Ukraine or in the Gaza strip perfectly exemplify the risks. The humanitarian corridors allegedly put in place by Russia led directly either to Belarusian or Russian territory, thus obviously not allowing those fleeing to find themselves in safer conditions.[50] Following the adoption of UNSC Resolution 2712 relating to civilians in Gaza, ten humanitarian organizations adopted a press release stating that the resolution "does not outline measures for the Council to monitor or implement these arrangements, and has not been accepted by parties on the ground,"[51] and further underlining that "[t]wo one-way routes were prescribed by Israel . . . to force civilians to relocate from northern Gaza to areas south of Wadi Gaza."[52]

Finally, it must be mentioned that under IHL, any displacement of the civilian population requires that all possible measures be taken to ensure that people are "received under satisfactory conditions of shelter, hygiene, health, safety and nutrition and that members of the same family are not separated."[53]

The right of the civilian population to receive humanitarian assistance

The second category of IHL provisions relevant to understanding humanitarian corridors concerns the right of humanitarian organizations to be granted access to persons in need. This chapter will not delve into the matter because the issues have been examined at length in recent literature.[54] Suffice it to say that Rule 55 of the ICRC's Customary IHL Study may be relied on, as it summarizes all the relevant treaty provisions.[55] It provides that "[t]he parties to the conflict must allow

50. *See* Lionel Beehner & John Spencer, *Russia's Humanitarian Corridors in Ukraine Endanger Human Life*, Wall Street Journal (Mar. 16, 2022), https://www.wsj.com/articles/humanitarian-corridors-in-ukraine-endanger-human-life-russia-kyiv-refugees-supplies-aid-war-11647439369; and John Reed & Guy Chazan, *"People Don't Want to Go to Russia": Putin's "Humanitarian Corridors" Spark Anger* (Mar. 7, 2022), https://www.ft.com/content/36fac8f4-234c-4499-ac68-38e27f0a7f21.

51. Action Against Hunger, Handicap International—Humanity & Inclusion, Médecins du Monde (France, Spain, and Swiss), Nobel Women's Initiative, Norwegian Refugee Council, Oxfam, Refugees International, Save the Children, *Pauses, Corridors, and Safe Zones in Gaza: Rhetoric vs. Reality* (Nov. 22, 2023), *available at* https://reliefweb.int/report/occupied-palestinian-territory/pauses-corridors-and-safe-zones-gaza-rhetoric-vs-reality.

52. *Id.*

53. 1 Customary International Humanitarian Law, *supra* note 38, at r. 131, at 463.

54. *See* Oxford Guidance on the Law Relating to Humanitarian Relief Operations in Situations of Armed Conflict (Dapo Akande & Emanuela-Chiara Gillard eds., 2016), *available at* https://www.law.ox.ac.uk/content/oxford-guidance-law-relating-humanitarian-relief-operations-situations-armed-conflict; Emanuela-Chiara Gillard, *The Law Regulating Cross-Border Relief Operations*, International Review of the Red Cross 351 (2013).

55. Those rules are arts. 23 and 59 of Convention IV, *supra* note 2, art. 70 of AP I, *supra* note 26, and art. 18 of AP II, *supra* note 44. *See* Marco Sass°li, Antoine Bouvier, Anne Quintin, &

and facilitate rapid and unimpeded passage of humanitarian relief for civilians in need, which is impartial in character and conducted without any adverse distinction, subject to their right of control."[56] In other words, parties to an armed conflict—as well as States whose territories must be crossed by (food and medical) relief operations—have an obligation to both permit and actively support the swift and unhindered passage of essential supplies, equipment, and personnel involved in food assistance or medical relief efforts. While States retain the right to prescribe the technical details of such passage, they must do so with utmost good faith. Furthermore, such measures should not impede the prompt and principled delivery of food and medical assistance in any way concerning its character, scope, or consequences.[57] It is worth recalling that there is obviously no need for humanitarian corridors if and when the passage of relief operations is actually facilitated, rapid, and unimpeded.

If one carefully looks at the architecture of the rules governing the protection of civilians against the effects of hostilities under IHL, humanitarian corridors should not even exist. This conclusion further explains why the expression is not found in the LOAC. Not only may civilians not be directly targeted, but they must also be spared the effects of hostilities, even those taking place farthest from them. Civilians must also be allowed to flee an area that has become unsafe, and humanitarian organizations should be granted access wherever their assistance is needed. Nonetheless, humanitarian corridors are in fact sometimes essential for safeguarding a civilian population that is systematically and/or disproportionately affected by armed conflict. Essential or not, they give rise to practical challenges.

3. THE PRACTICE

In addition to the aforementioned legal challenges, humanitarian corridors raise a number of practical issues. The first lies in the wording. Contrary to what the terms suggests, a humanitarian corridor is essentially a *military* operation aimed at enforcing humanitarian obligations. Yet humanitarian assistance is fundamentally *civilian* in character, and the implementing role of civilian organizations is indisputable. The core distinction between civilians and combatants, which lies at the very heart of IHL, causes the many difficulties generated by this misleading, paradoxical wording.

57. Oxford Guidance on the Law Relating to Humanitarian Relief Operations in Situations of Armed Conflict, *supra* note 54, at ¶¶ 91, 94.

Julia Grignon, How Does Law Protect in War? Online Casebook, https://casebook.icrc.org/law/ihl-and-humanitarian-assistance.

56. 1 Customary International Humanitarian Law, *supra* note 38, at r. 55, at 193.

3.1 A Dangerous Blurring of What Is Military and What Is Civilian

To begin with, humanitarian corridors constitute a challenge to principled humanitarian action. Both the name and stated purposes of humanitarian corridors create the false belief that a neutral measure is involved, akin to what humanitarian assistance should be. It is the contrary: humanitarian corridors are in fact military operations enforced by military means, but with a humanitarian label. Even though humanitarian organizations may be involved in their implementation, humanitarian corridors consist, as explained previously, of agreements between parties to the conflict, that is, State entities and/or armed groups. Such an agreement is hardly neutral per se. It challenges the concept of humanitarian action, which, as inter alia specified by Resolution 46/182 of the UNGA,[58] must be principled in nature. This not only means that a humanitarian organization should never be perceived as aligning with political and/or military objectives but that it must also remain both neutral and impartial in carrying out its activities. Neutrality implies refraining from taking sides in hostilities or from engaging in controversies of a political, racial, religious, or ideological nature.[59]

When actively participating in the establishment or operation of humanitarian corridors, humanitarian actors might, because of the very nature of such corridors, be perceived as taking sides in a conflict or aligning themselves with a specific party to the conflict. This holds especially true if an agreement establishing a humanitarian corridor only allows for the evacuation of the wounded and the sick, even though all affected people should be authorized to flee a zone in which they are not safe. Such a perception can undermine the humanitarian organization's reputation, endanger its personnel, and, in the long run, prevent it from participating in future operations. Moreover, humanitarian organizations may face operational constraints or restrictions when working within a humanitarian corridor as they must adhere to the conditions and requirements set by the parties involved in its creation. These constraints may limit their ability to reach all affected populations in need of assistance. This could also lead to the perception of an organization's participation in a humanitarian corridor as favoring certain areas or populations, especially if aid distribution becomes concentrated along the corridor itself. Such a perception risks, in turn, eroding the perceived impartiality of the humanitarian organization. Blurring the lines between civilian and military activities also risks endangering the affected population if/when the parties to the conflict seek to cause a humanitarian corridor to fail, either by impeding it, or worse, by targeting

58. G.A. Res. 46/182, Strengthening of the Coordination of Humanitarian Emergency Assistance of the United Nations (Dec. 19, 1991).

59. *See* International Committee of the Red Cross, The Fundamental Principles of the International Red Cross and Red Crescent Movement, *available at* https://www.icrc.org/sites/default/files/topic/file_plus_list/4046-the_fundamental_principles_of_the_international_red_cross_and_red_crescent_movement.pdf.

it. There are many recent examples of such a situation, including the failed evacuation of Mariupol, which was announced several times before being aborted at the last moment.[60]

Humanitarian organizations' involvement in humanitarian corridors also risks influencing how the latter are perceived by the people who should benefit from them. An organization's active engagement in support of a humanitarian corridor may contribute to conveying a false impression of safety to the people intending to use it. However, despite the parties' consent to a humanitarian corridor, protection is never totally guaranteed. Humanitarian organizations must therefore be cautious not to convey an erroneous impression of safety. In the same vein, all those involved in setting up and enforcing a humanitarian corridor must ensure that no military component is in control of the humanitarian corridor as this increases the risks of being targeted by parties to the conflict. As underlined by Nathalie Weizmann, sometimes "a robust military presence (such as a peacekeeping force mandated by the UNSC) will be required to ensure the protection of those travelling through [a humanitarian corridor]. However, the presence of military forces to protect the corridor can also draw attacks from enemy parties, exposing civilians and other protected persons to hostilities and thereby undermining the very purpose of the corridor."[61]

The blurring of lines between military and civilian roles also means that collaboration for the purpose of establishing a humanitarian corridor may lead to humanitarian organizations' operational dependency on the parties involved, whether governments or armed groups. Such dependence can negatively affect the ability of humanitarian organizations to maintain their independence and impartial decision-making regarding the allocation of aid and resources.

The political implications of humanitarian corridors constitute the last major risk worth examining here. The risk is closely linked to their inherently military character. Humanitarian corridors may first impact the overall dynamic of a conflict.[62] In particular, they may directly affect territorial control, contradict siege strategies, and/or disrupt military operations, thus exposing them to a high risk of instrumentalization by one or all the warring parties. History shows that humanitarian corridors may sometimes be used for the illicit transport of weaponry and ammunition or for returning military personnel to their home country. Moreover, the "[s]heltering of civilian populations has served the strategies of war, either by forcing the population of a rebel zone to return to a government zone,

60. *See, e.g.*, Mstyslav Chernov & Yuras Karmanau, *Russian Force Pressure Mariupol; Authorities Again Fail to Open Evacuation Corridor for Civilians Trapped in Devastated Port City*, Associated Press (Mar. 8, 2022), https://apnews.com/article/russia-ukraine-kyiv-europe-united-nations-evacuations-62fa232dcb9d6260fef0e9c7f5386f9a.

61. *Id.*

62. *See* Claude Bruderlein, *Setting Up Humanitarian Corridors*, and Maëlle L'Homme, *Humanitarian Corridors in the Law*, *in* Negotiating Humanitarian Corridors During Armed Conflicts (Apr. 25, 2022).

or by making an evacuated town a legitimate target, or finally, and in the worst cases, by using civilians as human shields to safeguard a military position."[63] Such corridors may likewise simply be used to falsely reassure public opinion or, worse, to divert public attention from atrocities happening elsewhere. Indeed, "the humanitarian corridors to which they agreed also serve to improve [the] image and sometimes reinforce [the] credibility [of those who set them up] in the eyes of the international community when they are not purely and simply used for political purposes."[64] This tragically happened in Bosnia[65] and, more recently, in Ukraine.[66] In that sense, not only are humanitarian corridors subject to political instrumentalization but they may also be seen as a weapon of war.[67]

3.2 A Paradox and a Misleading Expression

There lies an obvious paradox in asking the parties to a conflict whose unlawful behavior is precisely what led to the establishment a humanitarian corridor to respect the law. The paradox speaks volumes about the practical difficulties encountered in establishing humanitarian corridors. If armed conflicts are extreme situations of violence, humanitarian corridors constitute a response to the most extreme violations happening within such an extreme. Consequently, convincing the civilian population that a humanitarian corridor will lead it to safety may not be easy. As Weizmann puts it, "the dire circumstances that typically prompt the idea of a humanitarian corridor are the exact circumstances that make it difficult to secure the agreement of all parties in order to make it safe and effective. Unless the agreement of all parties and proper safety guarantees are in place, concentrating civilians and other protected persons in a given area can expose them to attack by a party to the conflict."[68] Instead of offering a safe passage,

63. *See* Françoise Duroch & Maelle L'Homme, *Humanitarian Corridors in Ukraine: The Illusion of an Ideal Solution*, GENEVA SOLUTIONS (Mar. 10, 2022, https://genevasolutions.news/peace-humanitarian/humanitarian-corridors-in-ukraine-the-illusion-of-an-ideal-solution.

64. *Id.*

65. *See* United Nations High Commissioner for Refugees, *The Humanitarian Operation in Bosnia, 1992–95: Dilemmas of Negotiating Humanitarian Access* (Working Paper No. 8) (May 1999), https://www.unhcr.org/sites/default/files/legacy-pdf/3ae6a0c58.pdf.

66. *See* Lucian Kim, *The Battle of Ilovaisk: Details of a Massacre Inside Rebel-Held Eastern Ukraine; Reporting from Both Sides of the Makeshift Border in Eastern Ukraine, Newsweek Describes the Bloodshed That Has Occurred Inside Rebel-Held Ukraine*, NEWSWEEK (Apr. 11, 2014).

67. *See* Bette Brown, *The Weaponisation of Aid and Healthcare*, THE MEDICAL INDEPENDENT (Mar. 19, 2023), https://www.medicalindependent.ie/in-the-news/news-features/the-weaponisation-of-aid-and-healthcare/; Lance Davies, *Russia's Invasion of Ukraine and Weaponization of the "Humanitarian Space"* (Policy Memo No. 831), PONERS EURASIA (Feb. 2023), *available at* https://www.ponarseurasia.org/russias-invasion-of-ukraine-and-weaponization-of-the-humanitarian-space/.

68. Weizmann, *supra* note 3, at 391.

a humanitarian corridor might in fact be a trap for the affected population. This explains why humanitarian organizations remain very cautious about the practice and think twice before asking parties to the conflict to establish one. While acknowledging that humanitarian corridors have saved hundreds of thousands of lives, the ICRC, for example, speaks of "hazardous operations" that "encompass major risks for the affected populations, the humanitarian personnel involved, and the belligerents concerned."[69]

As previously explained, even if humanitarian corridors are perceived as a (major) achievement by the general public, they are rather seen as a stopgap by humanitarian organizations. Due to the attendant geographical and temporal limitations involved, they may not be the ideal solution for organizations requiring unrestricted humanitarian access in order to effectively provide relief wherever required.[70] Moreover, "setting up humanitarian corridors usually implies renouncing broader access and potentially leaving other needs unaddressed."[71] Humanitarian corridors may also foster the false idea that rules relating to humanitarian relief do not apply beyond a corridor's delimited area agreed by the concerned parties. In other words, they represent a huge temporally and territorially circumscribed compromise leading to the challenge of what happens beyond such compromise, that is, outside a humanitarian corridor or after it closes. The impression that what is not incorporated into one is not humanitarian must be avoided. From the perspective of humanitarian organizations, humanitarian corridors are "characterized by [their] highly restricted, narrow space, which distinguishes [them] from humanitarian projects carried out within a wider or unrestricted space."[72] As stated by an ICRC delegate in the context of Iraq 20 years ago: "They are not an ideal solution for the ICRC, which wishes to be able to work wherever and whenever necessary."[73]

3.3 Practical Lessons Learned

Controversies and challenges related to humanitarian corridors continue to lie at the heart of long-standing discussions within the humanitarian sphere. By way of example, almost ten years ago, some 40 humanitarian organizations expressed

69. International Committee of the Red Cross, *supra* note 3. For Médecins Sans Frontières (Doctors Without Borders), humanitarian corridors give rise to similar questions as well. *See* L'Homme, *supra* note 6, at 49.

70. *See* Weizmann *supra* note 3, at 391.

71. L'Homme, *supra* note 6, at 51.

72. Hoffmann, *supra* note 6, at 95.

73. *Access to War Victims in Iraq: Humanitarian Corridors and Access to Victims of War—Interview*, International Committee of the Red Cross (Apr. 3, 2003), https://www.icrc.org/en/doc/resources/documents/interview/5l9jzb.htm.

their deep concern about a so-called humanitarian corridor envisioned in August 2016 by Russia and Syria in the context of the siege of Aleppo. In a joint statement,[74] these organizations notably reiterated that neither the individuals' freedom to choose whether to leave, nor their potential decision to stay, should be interpreted as their loss of protection against attack. They recalled instead that the shelling of hospitals must stop and unimpeded and immediate humanitarian access be granted. In other words, they called for respect of the basic rules of IHL. For its part, on a dedicated web page published in June 2022, the ICRC generally stated that "humanitarian corridors" are not its "preferred option" because of the "complexity of the[ir] design and implementation."[75]

Based on its own experience, the Center of Competence on Humanitarian Negotiations listed, through five lessons learned, the practical challenges stemming from humanitarian corridors.[76] First, humanitarian corridors require the involvement of all the stakeholders of the conflict. This includes parties to the conflict or any other armed actor involved in the situation at every level of the chain of command, as well as other relevant stakeholders such as intergovernmental or humanitarian organizations. Second, humanitarian corridors require both military and logistical procedures along a preestablished route, meaning that every aspect of such corridors must be carefully agreed upon and communicated to all stakeholders involved, as well as to people who will hopefully benefit from the humanitarian assistance. Third, one should remember that humanitarian corridors are risky endeavors. A series of preventive measures is therefore essential to minimize those risks. Fourth, entering and/or exiting humanitarian corridors may generate significant protection risks. It requires a strong assessment procedure, as well as the ability to know the needs of the addressee population well. Moreover, humanitarian organizations must also ensure that the dignity of those concerned will not be affected. The potential instrumentalization of humanitarian corridors by parties to the conflict must be assumed. Having that in mind, the humanitarian organizations involved must maintain an open dialogue with the parties throughout the process, so as to forestall diversion of the humanitarian goal or their use as a means to hide further violations. Finally, setting up a humanitarian corridor should not serve as a pretext to not seek the enforcement of all existing implementation and prevention mechanisms by the parties.

74. *Humanitarian Corridor Proposal Deeply Flawed*, Joint Press Release (Aug. 2, 2016), https://www.wvi.org/syria-crisis/pressrelease/%e2%80%9chumanitarian-corridor%e2%80%9d-proposal-deeply-flawed.

75. International Committee of the Red Cross, *supra* note 3.

76. *Setting up Humanitarian Corridors In Zones Of Hostility, Five Essential Lessons*, Center of Competence on Humanitarian Negotiations (Mar. 2022), https://frontline-negotiations.org/wp-content/uploads/2022/04/Policy-brief-March-2022-Humanitarian-corridors.pdf.

4. CONCLUSION

The term "humanitarian corridor" is so misleading that one could argue it should be abandoned. It perpetuates the misconception that the establishment of such a corridor provides solutions to protection issues when, in fact, it may not only put the civilian population at risk but also create the undue impression that the humanitarian efforts being undertaken in a given situation are exhaustive. In reality, a humanitarian corridor is a measure of last resort to be implemented when violations of IHL are so egregious that the only avenue is to set one up. When that is the case, the establishment of a humanitarian corridor should actually be perceived as indicative of significant challenges, or as an acknowledgment of extreme civilian vulnerability, rather than an accomplishment worth celebrating.

7

The Law and Politics of Civilian Protection in the Occupied West Bank

DAVID KRETZMER*

1. INTRODUCTION

Following the murder of two Israeli brothers in the West Bank town of Huwara on February 26, 2023, members of the Israeli settler community carried out what can only be described as a "pogrom" in the town.[1] Even though the settlers had published their intention to carry out a reprisal on social media, the Israel Defence Forces (IDF) did not prevent the attack, and it took time before sufficient forces entered the town and managed to restore order. During the attack, dozens of homes and cars were intentionally set on fire, 387 Palestinians were injured, and one Palestinian man was killed. Some of the few IDF soldiers who were in the village stood by while settlers went on a rampage. Officers from the Israeli Civil Administration in the West Bank were able to save Palestinians from burning

* David Kretzmer is a Professor Emeritus of International Law at the Hebrew University of Jerusalem. This chapter was written in September 2023, before the Hamas attack on Israel on October 7 and the subsequent war in Gaza and before the July 2024 Advisory Opinion of the International Court of Justice on the legality of Israel's policies and practices in the Occupied Territories. The chapter has not been amended to take into account events in the West Bank that have occurred since that war began and the implications of the ICJ Advisory Opinion.

1. *See* David Kretzmer & Limor Yehuda, *Red Alert: Who Will Protect the Palestinians?*, Just Security (Mar. 27, 2023), https://www.justsecurity.org/85693/red-alert-who-will-protect-the-palestinians/.

David Kretzmer, *The Law and Politics of Civilian Protection in the Occupied West Bank* In: *Civilian Protection in Armed Conflict*. Edited by: Jelena Pejic and Captain Margaret Kotlik, Oxford University Press.
© David Kretzmer 2025. DOI: 10.1093/oso/9780197793176.003.0007

houses. Although about 200 people took part in the attack, less than ten people were arrested after it ended.

This failure to protect the civilian population in the West Bank was not unique. On the contrary, it is part of a pattern that started in the West Bank soon after Israel's settlement project gained momentum there in the early eighties of the last century. What was new in the Huwara pogrom and subsequent settler attacks on Palestinians and their property was the *overt* support and encouragement the settlers received from ministers and members of the Knesset who are part of the coalition government of Prime Minister Benjamin Netanyahu that assumed power in December 2022.[2]

Although the failure to protect Palestinians in the occupied West Bank is not necessarily representative of other cases of belligerent occupation, in this chapter I discuss the protection of the civilian population in this particular context. I show that the lack of protection is intimately connected with the establishment of settlements by the occupying power, an issue that has received a great deal of attention in the international community and has led many commentators to question the real (as opposed to formal) status of the West Bank. This concern is reflected in the December 2022 UN General Assembly resolution requesting an Advisory Opinion from the International Court of Justice (ICJ) on two questions, the second of which is how do the policies and practices of the occupying power "affect the legal status of the occupation, and what are the legal consequences that arise for all States and the United Nations from this status?"[3]

The legal obligation of an occupying power to protect the civilian population in occupied territory is beyond dispute. Article 43 of the Hague Regulations[4] obligates the occupying power to maintain public order, while Article 46 demands, inter alia, that the lives and property of persons in occupied territory be respected. Article 27 of the Fourth Geneva Convention[5] provides that protected persons in occupied territory are entitled in all circumstances to respect for their persons and that they "shall be protected especially against all acts of violence or threats thereof." Furthermore, as both the ICJ and the UN Human Rights Committee have held, Israel is bound by its international human rights obligations in the West Bank.[6] As a party to the International Covenant on Civil and Political Rights

2. *Id.*

3. G.A. Res. 77/247 (Dec. 30, 2022).

4. Regulations Respecting the Laws and Customs of War on Land annexed to Convention no IV Respecting the Laws and Customs of War on Land, Oct. 18, 1907, 36 Stat. 2227 [hereinafter Hague Regulations].

5. Convention (IV) Relative to the Protection of Civilian Persons in Time of War, Oct. 21, 1950, 75 U.N.T.S. 287 [hereinafter GC IV].

6. Legal Consequences of the Construction of a Wall in the Occupied Palestinian Territory, Advisory Opinion, 2004, I.C.J. 136 (July 9, 2004) [hereinafter the *Wall* opinion]; U.N. Human Rights Committee, *Concluding Observations on Fourth Periodic Report of Israel*, ¶ 5 (2014) U.N. Doc. CCPR/C/ISR/CO/4 (Nov. 21, 2014), *available at* https://www.ohchr.org/en/documents/concluding-observations/ccprcisrco4-concluding-observations-fourth-periodic-report-israel.

(ICCPR) it is obligated to ensure all the rights of the civilians in the occupied territory, including the rights to life and personal security.[7]

The Israeli authorities have never denied their duty both to respect and protect the lives and personal security of the local population in the West Bank. The problem does not lie in their declared commitment to ensure the security of the civilian population but in the glaring deficiency gap in enforcing it. In examining this gap, we must distinguish between the duty to respect and the duty to protect.

Article 27 makes the clear distinction between the right of civilians in occupied territory to respect for their persons and their right to protection against all acts or threats of violence. Lack of respect by the IDF for the lives of Palestinians in the West Bank has over the years been, and continues to be, a burning issue that relates to the rules of engagement, their enforcement, and the inadequacy of investigations into the use of lethal force.[8] While I do not want to underplay the seriousness of that issue in any way, in this chapter I shall confine myself to the duty to protect, which is connected to the settlement of Israeli civilians in the West Bank.

The chapter is divided into four parts. I first briefly describe the legal position of the Israeli authorities immediately after the territories were captured in the course of the 1967 War, and how it was modified in light of domestic political attitudes. The next part is devoted to judicial review over actions of the military in the occupied territory. In the next part I review Israeli policies in the occupied territory,

7. International Covenant on Civil and Political Rights, Dec. 19, 1966, 999 U.N.T.S. 171 [hereinafter ICCPR].

8. In the last two years, there has been a significant and disturbing rise in the number of Palestinians in the West Bank who have been killed and injured by Israeli forces. According to the figures published by the UN Office for the Coordination of Humanitarian Affairs (OCHA), the following are the figures for the number of Palestinians killed by Israeli forces in the West Bank in the last three years: 2021: 78; 2022: 151; first seven months of 2023: 165. The number of Palestinians injured has been far greater: *Protection of Civilians Report | 25 July–7 August 2023*, OCHA (Aug. 11, 2023), *available at* https://www.ochaopt.org/poc/25-july-7-august-2023. According to information collected by an Israeli NGO, Yesh Din, less than 1 percent of the complaints involving use of force by Israeli forces against Palestinians led to indictments: Data Sheet, December 2022: *Law Enforcement on Israeli Civilians in the West Bank (Settler Violence)* 2005–2022, Yesh-Din (Feb. 1, 2023), https://www.yesh-din.org/en/data-sheet-december-2022-law-enforcement-on-israeli-civilians-in-the-west-bank-settler-violence-2005-2022/. According to press reports, after the Palestinian-American journalist Shireen Abu Akleh was killed, almost definitely by fire from Israeli forces, the Biden administration requested Israel to re-examine the rules of engagement in the West Bank: Ben Samuels, *U.S. to Ask Israel to Reexamine Rules of Engagement in West Bank After Abu Akleh Report*, Ha'aretz (Sept. 6, 2022), https://www.haaretz.com/israel-news/2022-09-06/ty-article/.premium/u-s-to-ask-israel-to-reexamine-rules-of-engagement-in-west-bank-after-abu-akleh-report/00000183-143d-d0bd-a5d7-147d94ae0000. The rules of engagement had been relaxed at the end of 2021 after soldiers complained that they were too restricted in using force against Palestinians who had thrown stones or fire-bombs: *IDF Issues New Rules Of Engagement for West Bank—Report*, The Jerusalem Post (Dec. 19, 2021), https://www.jpost.com/breaking-news/idf-issues-new-rules-of-engagement-for-west-bank-report-689199. The Israeli Prime Minister and Defense Minister rejected the U.S. request.

first and foremost among which is the establishment of Israeli settlements and their influence on the lack of protection of Palestinian inhabitants of the territory. The last part relates to the duty of the international community to ensure that the occupying power meets its legal obligation to protect the local population. I conclude with short remarks on the lessons to be learned from this case study.

2. POLITICS AND THE LAW OF BELLIGERENT OCCUPATION

When the IDF gained control over the West Bank in June 1967, the initial approach of military lawyers was that the legal regime was one of belligerent occupation in which both the Hague Regulations and Convention (IV) relative to the Protection of Civilian Persons in Time of War (GC IV) applied.[9] The first military order promulgated by the military commander of the West Bank stated expressly that the military courts established to try persons charged with security offences would apply the provisions of GC IV and that, in case of a clash between military orders and the Convention, the latter would prevail.[10]

While military lawyers initially had no problem in regarding the territories taken in the war as occupied, politicians and senior foreign office officials had difficulties with such a categorization. In a secret memorandum submitted to the deputy director general of the Ministry of Foreign Affairs dated June 22, 1967, an adviser to the Foreign Minister expressed the opinion that all reference to "occupied" territories should be avoided.[11] The Minister of Defense also told the Cabinet that he had been warned by a senior Foreign Ministry official that the Geneva Convention was "a load of trouble" and that Israel should not even consider "accepting it."[12] He had therefore informed an International Committee of the Red Cross (ICRC) representative that the legal advisers were examining the situation and that in the meantime Israel would be prepared to discuss specific issues without accepting that the Convention applies.

9. David Kretzmer & Yaël Ronen, The Occupation of Justice: The Supreme Court of Israel and the Occupied Territories 55–57 (2d ed. 2021); Hague Regulations, *supra* note 4; GC IV, *supra* note 5.

10. Security Provisions Order (West Bank) (June 7, 1967) sec. 35. English translation *available at* http://www.militarycourtwatch.org/page.php?id=SNHdhRow9Pa30432AKJqGwVetO9.

11. The adviser was worried about the ICRC having formal status in the newly occupied territories, rather than being allowed to operate there on what he termed a "pragmatic basis." He suggested that the territories be termed territories under military rule or "territories under Israel's control" and stated that he preferred the latter term. Akevot Institute, *It Is Necessary to Warn Against the Use of Certain Phrases Specified in the Convention*, Akevot (Sept. 2016), https://www.akevot.org.il/article/comay-memo-terminology/

12. Minutes of Cabinet Meeting 55/5727, 14–15 (July 2, 1967), https://www.archives.gov.il/archives/Archive/0b0717068031be30/File/0b07170680348bd6/Item/09071706897b3668.

Emerging political attitudes had no influence over Theodor Meron, the young legal adviser of the Ministry of Foreign Affairs at the time. As pressure by Israeli citizens on the government to allow settlement in the West Bank began to grow, Prime Minister Levy Eshkol asked for an opinion on the legality of establishing such settlements. In a secret memorandum written in September 1967, Meron opined that the establishment of Israeli settlements in the area would be regarded as a violation of Article 49(6) of GC IV.[13] He added that, given the reference to GC IV in the aforementioned military order, Israel could not deny that the Convention applied to its actions on the West Bank and that in any event the international community was clearly of the opinion that it did.

Soon after Meron sent his memorandum to the Prime Minister, the military order provision mentioning GC IV was deleted and replaced by another that incorporated a specific provision of the Convention.[14] It is unclear whether this was done in response to Meron's memorandum or to the pending article of an Israeli academic who contested application of part of the law of belligerent occupation in the West Bank.[15] Whatever the reason, the official position of the government of Israel became that it was doubtful whether GC IV applied to Israel's actions in the West Bank, but that Israel would nevertheless abide by the "humanitarian provisions" of the Convention.[16] Meron's opinion was ignored and remained secret until discovered in the archives by a historian working on the settlement policy in the first decade of the occupation.[17]

13. Letter from Theodor Meron, Legal Advisor, Ministry of Foreign Affairs, to Adi Yaffe, The Prime Minister's Political Secretary, regarding the Settlement in the Held Territories (Sept. 18, 1967), *available at* https://www.thelawfilm.com/inside/wp-content/uploads/2013/02/meron-memo.pdf.

14. Security Provisions Order (West Bank) (Amendment No. 9) (Order No 144) (Oct. 22, 1967). The new provision incorporated the substance of GC IV, *supra* note 5, art. 69 (that relates to deduction of the period spent in pretrial detention from the period of imprisonment) in the military orders. For details, *see* Yaël Ronen, *Blind in Their Own Cause: The Military Courts in the West Bank*, 2 CAMBRIDGE JOURNAL OF INTERNATIONAL AND COMPARATIVE LAW 738, 746 (2013).

15. Yehuda Z. Blum, *The Missing Reversioner: Reflections on the Status of Judea and Samaria*, 3 ISRAEL LAW REVIEW 279 (1968). In his autobiography, Meir Shamgar, who in September 1967 was still chief of the Israeli Defense Forces Legal Advisors and about to be appointed Attorney General of Israel, refers to Blum's article and mentions that, together with the denial by Israel's representatives to the United Nations that the territories were occupied, Blum's opinion formed the basis for the government's argument that GC IV did not apply to Israel's rule in the West Bank. *See* MEIR SHAMGAR, AN AUTOBIOGRAPHY 107 (2015).

16. Meir Shamgar, *The Observance of International Law in the Administered Territories*, 1 ISRAEL YEARBOOK ON HUMAN RIGHTS 262 (1971).

17. GERSHOM GORENBERG, THE ACCIDENTAL EMPIRE: ISRAEL AND THE BIRTH OF THE SETTLEMENTS, 1967–1977 (2007).

3. ENTER JUDICIAL REVIEW

3.1 Application of the Law of Belligerent Occupation

Soon after the 1967 War ended, Palestinian residents of the newly occupied territories petitioned the Israel Supreme Court, which sits as the High Court of Justice that exercises review of administrative action, in an attempt to challenge the legality of measures adopted by the military authorities in the territories. The authorities did not contest the Court's jurisdiction to consider such petitions,[18] and the Court later ruled that it is based on its statutory power to issue orders against "all persons exercising public functions under law."[19] In the years that have passed, the Court has considered thousands of petitions by Palestinian residents of the West Bank and other territories occupied in 1967.

Having conceded the Court's jurisdiction to consider Palestinian petitions, the authorities were forced to decide on their approach to legal arguments raised by petitioners that relied on the international law of belligerent occupation, as reflected both in the Hague Regulations and GC IV. Initially, they adopted a pragmatic approach. Government counsel informed the Court that, while the government did not concede the military authorities were bound by the provisions of the Hague Regulations and GC IV, the military commander was convinced that his actions were compatible with the provisions cited, and therefore agreed that the Court review his actions accordingly.[20] Most of the judges were willing to play this "game." At the same time, they followed their own jurisprudence on the place of international law in the domestic legal system according to which customary international law is part of the law of the land, but treaties binding on the State are not, unless they have been adopted by parliamentary legislation. They originally assumed that neither the Hague Regulations nor GC IV were part of customary international law and would thus not be enforced.[21] After Professor Yoram Dinstein pointed out that the Nuremburg Tribunal had ruled that the Hague Regulations were part of customary international law,[22] the Court admitted that it had been mistaken. It ruled that the Hague Regulations were indeed part of customary law

18. Eli Nathan, *The Power of Supervision of the High Court of Justice over Military Government*, *in* Military Government in the Territories Administered by Israel 1967–1980, at 109 (Meir Shamgar ed., 1982).

19. HCJ 393/82 Jam'iyat Iskan v. IDF Commander in Judea and Samaria 37(4) PD 785 (1983) (Isr.).

20. The *Wall* opinion, *supra* note 6, at 28–31.

21. HCJ 302/72 Abu Helou v. Government of Israel 27(2) PD 169 (1973) (Isr.).

22. Yoram Dinstein, *The Judgment in the Rafah Approach Case*, 3 Iyunei Mishpat 934 (1974).

that may be enforced by the Court.[23] This became the accepted jurisprudence of the Court.[24]

The pragmatic approach could not, and did not, last long. The 1979 *Elon Moreh* case, which spelled its end, involved the seizure of private land for the establishment of a civilian settlement.[25] The potential settlers argued that international law was irrelevant in assessing the legality of the land seizure, since the West Bank was part of the ancient Jewish homeland. The Court's response was that the only legal basis for seizure of the land was the military commander's power under international law to do so for military needs. The Court explained that if it were to accept the settlers' argument that international law is irrelevant it would have to rule that the commander had acted ultra vires.[26] It proceeded to hold that while under the international law of belligerent occupation the commander does have the power to seize property for military needs, the dominant reason for the land seizure in the case before it had been political, not military, and that the seizure order was therefore null and void.

Since the *Elon Moreh* case, the Court has ruled time and again that the legal regime in the West Bank is one of belligerent occupation.[27] Government counsel regularly rely on it before the Supreme Court when defending infringements on the rights of the Palestinian population. In a case challenging the government and Knesset's decision to withdraw all Israeli settlements from Gaza in the framework of the "Disengagement Plan," the government rested part of its defense on the regime of belligerent occupation being temporary by its very nature.[28]

The Supreme Court has stated that there was never any controversy over the application of the Hague Regulations in the West Bank.[29] It has placed emphasis on Article 43 of the Regulations, which defines the primary obligation of an

23. HCJ 606/78 Ayoub v. Minister of Defense 33(2) PD 113 (1979) (Isr.), *reprinted in* Shamgar, *supra* note 16, at 371 [hereinafter the Beth El case]. As Israel never joined the 1907 Hague Convention, it is not clear why the Hague Regulations should have applied to Israel's actions, unless they had become part of customary international law.

24. The *Wall* opinion, *supra* note 6, at 64.

25. HCJ 390/79 Dweikat v. Government of Israel 34(1) PD 1 (1979) (Isr.), *reprinted in* Shamgar, *supra* note 16, at 404 [hereinafter the Elon Moreh case].

26. One of the first decisions of the Supreme Court after the State of Israel was established laid down a fundamental principle in the public law of Israel: no governmental authority may restrict the rights or liberties of an individual unless it has been given the legal power to do so. HCJ 1/49 Bijerano v. Minister of Police 2 PD 80 (1949) (Isr.). This principle is reflected in Israel's Basic Law: Human Dignity and Liberty, and in the ICCPR that Israel became a party to in 1991. According to the general limitations clause in the Basic Law, and the various limitation clauses in the Covenant, the first condition for the legitimacy of a restriction on a right is that it is prescribed by law.

27. The *Wall* opinion, *supra* note 6, at 64–68.

28. HCJ 1661/05 Gaza Coast Regional Council v. Knesset 59(2) PD 481 (2005) (Isr.).

29. *Id.* at ¶ 41.

occupying power to restore and ensure, as far as possible, public order and public life in the occupied territory.[30] As stressed by the Court, this article is "a quasi-constitutional framework provision that sets out the general framework for the way the duties and powers of the military commander must be exercised in occupied territory."[31]

Despite the Court's jurisprudence, outside the domestic courtroom government lawyers still try to argue that the application of the law of belligerent occupation is based on the pragmatic approach. In December 2019, Israel's Attorney General prepared a memorandum contesting the International Criminal Court's jurisdiction to consider the situation in Palestine.[32] In describing the legal status of the West Bank, he declared:

> Israel's presence in the West Bank is fully in accordance with international law: Israel gained control over the territory in an act of lawful self-defense; it applies the humanitarian provisions of the international law of occupation (despite its principled position that they do not apply *de jure*) . . .[33]

This statement, which is incompatible with the jurisprudence of Israel's Supreme Court reviewed previously, is evidence (if needed) of the dissonance between the formal case law of the Supreme Court and the government's stance outside the domestic courtroom.[34]

30. Kretzmer & Ronen, *supra* note 9, at 133–60. In an early case, Justice Sussman pointed out that the accepted English version of Article 43, which refers to "public order and safety," is an inaccurate translation of the original French text and that a better translation would be "public order and public life." *Id.* at 139.

31. HCJ 2164/09 Yesh Din v. IDF Commander in Judea and Samaria, Nevo, ¶ 8 (2011) (Isr.).

32. *The International Criminal Court's Jurisdiction over the So-Called "Situation in Palestine,"* State of Israel, Office of the Attorney General (Dec. 20, 2019), https://www.gov.il/BlobFolder/reports/20-12-2019/en/Memorandum-Attorney-General.pdf.

33. *Id.* at ¶ 39. In support of this statement, the Attorney General cited a 1971 article written by his predecessor and simply ignored all the decisions of the Supreme Court delivered after it was written in which the Court categorically held that the legal regime in the West Bank is one of belligerent occupation. The Attorney General's memorandum also mentioned that "Israel has a longstanding claim to the West Bank and Gaza Strip." *Id.* at ¶ 41.

34. The term "humanitarian provisions of the international law of occupation" refers to the declaration of Israel that, although GC IV does not formally apply in the West Bank, the IDF would comply with its humanitarian provisions. Use of this term is highly misleading, since the declaration refers to GC IV and not to the Hague Regulations. Agreeing, as it were, to the application of IHL, but not de jure, ignores the fact that the Supreme Court regularly relies on the law of belligerent occupation to justify infringements on the rights of the local population. A glaring example is the Court's reliance on the law of belligerent occupation in cases relating to the construction of the Separation Barrier (Wall) in the West Bank. The Court justified taking and destroying private land and placing severe restrictions on the freedom of movement of Palestinians by citing various provisions in the Hague Regulations and GC IV. Kretzmer & Ronen, *supra* note 9, at 233–72.

3.2 Legal Implications of Belligerent Occupation and Political Reality

The Supreme Court has spelled out the implications of the regime of belligerent occupation in a number of cases over the years. In the leading case of *Jami'yat Iskan* from 1983,[35] Justice Aharon Barak stated as follows:

> The powers and authority of the military commander are derived from the rules of public international law that deal with belligerent occupation . . . The considerations of the military commander are, on the one hand, ensuring his security interests in the [occupied] area, and, on the other hand, ensuring the interests of the civilian population in the area. Both of these considerations are directed towards the [occupied] area itself. The commander is not allowed to consider the national, economic or social interests of his own state, to the extent that they do not have implications for his security interests in the area or the interests of the local population. Even military needs are his military needs in the area, and not national security interests in the wide sense. An area subject to belligerent occupation is not a field open to economic or other exploitation.[36]

This dictum is an exceptionally clear judicial statement of the limits on the legal powers of the military commander in occupied territory. It is, however, divorced from the reality of Israel's rule over the West Bank. According to the Court, the military commander derives his power and authority from international law. But the commander is an official of the executive branch of government in Israel, and as such he is called upon to implement government policy in the occupied territory.[37] There can be no doubt that in setting policy in the West Bank the government is guided by what it perceives to be the national, economic, social, and security interests of Israel itself, and not by the narrow security interests of the military commander in the occupied territory, or the interests of the civilian population in that area. In a later case, the Supreme Court itself relied on the duty of the military commander as an organ of the government to respect the constitutional rights of Israeli citizens in the West Bank, holding that in fulfilling this duty he may curb the rights of Palestinians under the law of belligerent occupation.[38]

35. *Iskan, supra* note 19.

36. *Id.* at ¶ 10. *See also* the Elon Moreh case, *supra* note 25, at ¶ 22, in which Justice Landau declared: "[N]o military government may create in its area facts for its military purposes that are intended from the very start to exist even after the termination of military rule in that area, when the fate of the territory after the termination of the military rule is unknown."

37. On the dual capacity of the military commander in occupied territory, *see* Eliav Lieblich & Eyal Benvenisti, Occupation in International Law 63–64 (2022); David Kretzmer, *The Occupation in the Israeli Constitution, in* The Handbook Of Israeli Constitutional Law) Aharon Barak, Barak Medina, & Yaniv Roznai eds., forthcoming).

38. HCJ 7957/04 Mara'abe v. Government of Israel 60(2) PD 477 (2005) (Isr.).

Justice Barak's dictum has remained in the realm of judicial rhetoric and has not formed the basis for the Court's judgments in cases relating to the Occupied Territories. In a study of the Court's case law, Yaël Ronen and I have shown that the Court has explicitly or implicitly legitimized virtually all government policies and practices in the West Bank, even when these were clearly incompatible with the principles of the law of belligerent occupation spelled out by Justice Barak.[39] The dissonance between the Supreme Court's rhetoric and the law applied in practice is glaring. The Court's refusal to rule on the legality of establishing Israeli settlements in the West Bank is the main manifestation of such incongruence.

3.3 The Legality of Settlements

The international community and most international lawyers have consistently taken the position that Israel violates international law by establishing Israeli settlements in the West Bank.[40] This view rests on Article 49(6) of GC IV prohibiting an occupying power from transferring part of its own civilian population into an occupied territory. There are, however, additional cogent reasons for holding that the establishment of settlements in occupied territory is incompatible with international law.[41] As noted previously, the Supreme Court of Israel has held that in using his powers, the military commander in occupied territory may only consider one or both of two considerations: his military needs in the occupied territory and the benefit of the local population. In two early cases the Supreme Court did indeed hold that the taking of private land for the establishment of a particular settlement could be justified if the military authorities proved that it would fulfil a specific military purpose.[42] However, since the 1979 *Elon Moreh* case,[43] the government has not attempted to justify settlements on security grounds. Hence, even according to the Court's jurisprudence, allowing the establishment of settlements is incompatible with the military commander's powers in occupied territory.

How has the Supreme Court coped with the glaring disparity between the legal regime that applies in the West Bank according to its own jurisprudence and the establishment of settlements? In the first cases, mentioned previously, in which it was argued that establishing a settlement in the West Bank is incompatible with Article 49(6) of GC IV, the Court relied on the distinction between customary and treaty law. It held that Article 49(6) does not reflect customary international law

39. Kretzmer & Ronen, *supra* note 9.

40. *Id.* at 186–87.

41. *Id.*; Eyal Benvenisti, The International Law of Occupation 241 (2d ed. 2012).

42. The Beth El case, *supra* note 23; HCJ 258/79 Amerah v. Minister of Defense 34(1) PD 90 (1979) (Isr.), *reprinted in* Shamgar, *supra* note 18, at 398.

43. The Elon Moreh case, *supra* note 25.

and that it would therefore refrain from addressing the argument.[44] In the *Bargil* case, a petition was submitted challenging the government's settlement policy on a range of grounds, including grounds based on customary international law. The Court held that the dominant nature of the settlements issue is political and that it is therefore nonjusticiable.[45] Since the judgment in the *Bargil* case, it has become the accepted jurisprudence of the Court that the legality of settlements is a political issue on which the Court will not deliver an opinion.[46]

After the *Elon Moreh* case, the government decided that in future all settlements would be established on what it termed "state land."[47] It then adopted a policy of declaring land to be "government property" if it is not private according to a strict interpretation of the Ottoman land laws that were still in force in the West Bank when the IDF took control of the area in 1967.[48] The Court refused to intervene in the system of declaring land to be "government property"[49] and to entertain the argument that using public property for the establishment of settlements is incompatible with Article 55 of the Hague Regulations.[50]

The Supreme Court's refusal to address the legality of settlements and the use of public land for this purpose has led it legitimize acts that result in lack of civilian protection in the West Bank. The Court has also catered to the interests of the settlers at the expense of the rights of Palestinian inhabitants in other ways.[51] Thus, for example, while the Court does not allow the taking of private land for

44. *Id.*; the Beth El case, *supra* note 23.

45. HCJ 4481/91 Bargil v. Government of Israel 47(4) PD 210 (1993) (Isr.). The non-justiciability argument is more or less equivalent to the U.S. "political question" doctrine.

46. The Beth El case, *supra* note 23.

47. Kretzmer & Ronen, *supra* note 9, at 205–10. The term "state land" is not a legal term. Under a military order promulgated in the West Bank, land may be recognized as "government land," which will then be administered by the Custodian of Government Property appointed by the military commander. Use of the term "state land," rather than the legal term "government property," is clearly politically motivated to create the impression that such land belongs to the State of Israel, since the government does not recognize any other State with a legitimate claim to rights in the West Bank.

48. *Id.*

49. HCJ 285/81 Al-Nazer v. IDF Commander in Judea and Samaria 36(1) PD 701 (1982) (Isr.).

50. HCJ 227/84 Ghrayeb v. Appeals Committee 38(4) PD 413 (1986) (Isr.) (holding that the Palestinian petitioner lacked the standing to challenge use of the land for a settlement). According to figures revealed by the Civil Administration in the West Bank, 99.76 percent of the government land allocated for private use has been allocated for use by Israeli civilians: https://www.meida.org.il/8531.

51. Kretzmer & Ronen, *supra* note 9, at 489.

the settlements themselves,[52] it has refused to intervene when such land is taken on the grounds that it is needed in order to protect the settlements.[53] Hence large tracts of private Palestinian land have been seized as part of what may be called "the settlement project."[54] While refusing to rule on the argument that use of public land for settlements is unlawful, the Court has legitimized such use by, inter alia, approving building plans for settlements on public land.[55]

4. ISRAELI SETTLEMENTS AND THE DUTY TO PROTECT THE LOCAL POPULATION

The establishment of settlements for citizens of the occupying power in the occupied West Bank has created a situation in which two groups live side by side: the local population who perceive the military rulers as part of a "hostile army," and have no political rights in Israel, and the Israeli settlers, who have such rights and view the military as "their army." This inherent imbalance has deepened since the introduction of a number of mechanisms aimed at applying Israeli law to the settlers and the settlements.[56] The Supreme Court recognized that different legal regimes apply to Israeli settlers and the local Palestinian population, but did not seem to find it problematic.[57] The existence in the same territory of two populations, distinguished on ethnic/national grounds, but subject to different legal regimes, provides the basis for the claim that the regime in the West Bank constitutes apartheid.[58] Even if one rejects such an assertion, a UN independent fact-finding mission showed that the Israeli settlements in the West Bank have had a disastrous effect on the rights and liberties of the Palestinian inhabitants.[59]

52. *But see* CivFH 6364/20 Minister of Defense v. Salakh, Nevo (2022) (Isr.), in which the Court refused to order evacuation of an unauthorized settlement that had been built on private land by relying on a "good faith" provision introduced into West Bank law by a military order.

53. HCJ 5139/05 Sha'ib v. State of Israel, Nevo ¶ 9 (2007) (Isr.).

54. Kerem Navot, *Seize the Moral Low Ground: Israeli Land Seizure for "Security Needs" in the West Bank* (2018); *For the Common Good: Military Expropriation Orders in the West Bank, 1967–2022* (Dec. 2022), https://www.keremnavot.org/.

55. Kretzmer & Ronen, *supra* note 9, at 210–14, 287–95.

56. Benvenisti, *supra* note 41, at 233–35.

57. HCJ 358/18 Hebron Municipality v. State of Israel, Nevo (June 30, 2019) (Isr.).

58. *See, e.g.*, John Dugard & John Reynolds, *Apartheid, International Law, and the Occupied Palestinian Territory*, 24 EJIL 867 (2013); Oren Yiftachel, *Creeping Apartheid? Regime, Space and Citizenship in Israel/Palestine*, 13 Public Space 139 (2018); Michael Sfard, *The Israeli Occupation of the West Bank and the Crime of Apartheid: Legal Opinion*, Yesh Din (June 2020), https://s3-eu-west-1.amazonaws.com/files.yesh-din.org/Apartheid+2020/Apartheid+ENG.pdf.

59. U.N. Human Rights Council, Report of the Independent international fact-finding mission to investigate the implications of the Israeli settlements on the civil, political, economic, social

The international law of belligerent occupation relies on a balance between the military needs of the occupying power and the benefit of the local population. It places serious limitations on the scope of governmental authority of the occupying power. When the relevant restrictions are ignored, this body of norms may serve the occupying power almost entirely as an instrument to legitimize restrictions on the rights and liberties of the local population in the occupied territory.[60] It thus becomes clear why the government continues to rely on a pretense of adherence to the law of belligerent occupation in the West Bank. Apart from avoiding charges of annexation in violation of the prohibition on acquiring territory through use of force, occupation law is used to exploit the power of an occupant to seize land ostensibly for military purposes, to place heavy restrictions on the rights and liberties of the local population, and to justify long-term rule over Palestinians in the West Bank without their enjoyment of political rights in the State that controls their lives.

The military authorities' failure to protect West Bank Palestinians from the violence of Israeli settlers reached the Supreme Court and Israeli civil authorities in the early eighties of the last century. In an initial case, Palestinian merchants in a building in the center of Hebron, the largest West Bank city, petitioned the Court to order the military commander to take action to evacuate settlers who had taken over the top floor of the building and were harassing them and causing damage to their property. They argued that the settlers in the building were trespassers and that that their complaints to the authorities had not received proper attention. The Court rejected the argument that the settlers were trespassers, and since government counsel assured the Court that the complaints would be investigated, it dismissed the petition. It did, however, mention the duty of the military commander "to maintain law and order" and to do so even if the victims of force or harassment did not lay a complaint.[61] The apparent assumption of the Court was that the authorities would indeed change their conduct and that the harassment would end without forcing evacuation of the settlers. From another case relating to the same building some years later, it was clear that the assumption was false.[62] Nevertheless, when the military commander declared that security measures were needed to protect the settlers in the building, the Court refused to interfere with the commander's decision, despite the serious restrictions it imposed on access to the Palestinian merchants' stores.[63]

and cultural rights of the Palestinian people throughout the Occupied Palestinian Territory, including East Jerusalem, U.N. Doc. A/HRC/22/63 (Jan. 31, 2013), *available at* https://www.ohchr.org/en/hr-bodies/hrc/regular-sessions/session19/israeli-settlements-in-the-opt.

60. David Kretzmer, *The Law of Belligerent Occupation as a System of Control: Dressing Up Exploitation in Respectable Garb*, *in* The Impacts of Lasting Occupation: Lessons from Israeli Society 31 (Daniel Bar-Tal & Izhak Schnell eds., 2013).

61. HCJ 175/81 Al-Natsheh v. Minister of Defense 38(4) PD 293 (1981) (Isr.).

62. HCJ 72/86 Zalloum v. Military Commander in Judea and Samaria 41(1) PD 528 (1987) (Isr.).

63. *Id.*

Soon after the first Hebron case just described, the Attorney General received a letter from Israeli law professors complaining about lack of enforcement of the law against settlers who had used violence against Palestinians.[64] The Attorney General set up a task force, headed by the Deputy Attorney General, to look into the matter. The task force's report painted a bleak picture of the handling of cases of violence against Palestinians. Most had not been investigated; the duty to investigate felonies even in the absence of a complaint had been ignored; the military government had interfered with investigations; settlers refused to cooperate with investigators, and the authorities took no action to arrest and investigate them. Investigations that were carried out were prolonged and often included major deficiencies.[65]

The report had little, if any effect, on the authorities. After a settler massacred 29 Palestinian worshippers in the Hebron Cave of the Patriarchs in February 1994, a Commission of Inquiry headed by the President of the Supreme Court was highly critical of the lack of law enforcement against Israelis in the West Bank who had attacked Palestinians or their property. It cited lack of investigations, prolonged investigations, and a failure to prosecute settlers.[66]

A military order promulgated in 1967 had given Israel Police law enforcement powers in the West Bank. Following the Commission of Inquiry, a new regional Israel Police command was established in the hope that it would improve enforcement of the law against the Israeli settlers. It did not do so. Many years later the State Comptroller examined the situation in the West Bank and found there was no coordination between the various law enforcement authorities.[67]

The mindset of the military was starkly illustrated in the *Murar* case before the Supreme Court in which Palestinians once again complained that the authorities were not protecting them from settler violence and were likewise preventing access to their agricultural lands.[68] Israeli settlements had been established near Palestinian villages and the military commander had placed restrictions on movement in what he deemed were "friction areas." He claimed that he had to limit access to areas close to the Israeli settlements due to fear that "hostile elements" would enter them under the guise of agricultural work and attack the settlers.

64. *See* Letter from Deputy Attorney General Judith Karp to Attorney General regarding investigations against Israelis in Judea and Samaria (May 23, 1983), *available at* https://www.keremnavot.org/_files/ugd/cdb1a7_3342db25459b43ff8dab68d9ee20e32e.pdf. The letter of the law professors is mentioned in this letter.

65. *Id.*

66. *Commission of Inquiry—Massacre at The Tomb of the Patriarchs in Hebron—26-Jun-94*, section 11 (June 26, 1994), *available at* https://embassies.gov.il/MFA/AboutIsrael/state/Law/Pages/COMMISSION%20OF%20INQUIRY-%20MASSACRE%20AT%20THE%20TOMB%20OF%20THE.aspx.

67. State Comptroller, *Report no. 63b*, ch. 3. (2012).

68. HCJ 9593/04 Murar v. IDF Commander in Judea and Samaria 61(1) PD 844 (2006) ¶ 23 (Isr.).

The commander had also imposed restrictions on the movement of Palestinians, the object of which was to protect *them* from settler violence. This was too much for the Court to countenance. While it recognized the duty of the commander to protect the lives of all inhabitants of the area involved, it found that placing restrictions on Palestinians in order to protect *them* from violence by settlers was irrational and failed to meet the proportionality test that the Supreme Court applies to measures restricting individual freedoms.[69]

Ensuring public order by a hostile army in an occupied territory is complicated enough, even if there are no citizens of its own nationality living in it. The military are supposed to apply a law enforcement legal framework in carrying out this duty, not a natural role for soldiers untrained in policing methods.[70] As mentioned in the introduction, the large number of Palestinian casualties in the West Bank, of which many, if not most, did not pose an imminent threat to soldiers (or often no threat at all), shows that the IDF is failing in this duty.

The position of the military becomes even more complicated when it is called upon to enforce the law against its fellow citizens. In a democratic State, the army is not involved in internal policing. From early on in the occupation, Israeli settlers objected to the use of soldiers in removing them from unauthorized settlements.[71] As the number of Israeli settlers in the West Bank grew, the military expressed great reluctance at having to enforce the law against Israeli citizens and delegated this authority to the Israel police. While such delegation does not relieve the IDF of its duty to enforce the law in the West Bank, when soldiers are called upon to intervene in settler attacks on Palestinians they often claim that the police should be called.[72]

Despite official reports, and exhortations of the Supreme Court, the failure to protect the Palestinians from settler violence continues. Credible nongovernmental organization reports criticize this failure time and again.[73] There has been only one change, and not for the better. In the past, decision makers confronted with

69. *Id.*

70. On the legal framework for ensuring order in occupied territory, *see* Marco Longobardo, The Use of Armed Force in Occupied Territory (2018).

71. Eilat Maoz, Living Law: Police and Sovereignty in an Occupation Regime 65 (2020), who reports a case in which the representative of settlers who were about to be evacuated by the military applied to a Supreme Court judge for an injunction to stop the evacuation on the grounds that the police should be dealing with the matter, not the military. The judge rejected the application.

72. According to a press report, in a Cabinet meeting that took place in January 2022, the Minister of Internal Security complained that while soldiers in the West Bank had the same powers as the police to detain Israelis involved in nationalist crimes, they were not using them. The Chief of Staff denied that the soldiers possessed such powers. Barak Ravid, *Confrontation between Minister Bar-Lev and Kochavi over the Authority of Soldiers to Act Against Settlers Who Attack Palestinians*, Walla)Jan. 31, 2022), https://news.walla.co.il/item/3486128.

73. *Law Enforcement on Israeli Civilians in the West Bank (Settler Violence)*, Yesh Din (Dec. 2022), https://s3.eu-west-1.amazonaws.com/files.yesh-din.org/law+data+dec+22/Law+data+22+ENG.pdf; *Settler Violence = State Violence*, B'tselem—The Israeli Information Center

the phenomenon of settler violence would have been ill at ease. Since the establishment in December 2022 of the present government headed by Prime Minister Netanyahu, which includes the most extreme elements in Israeli society, settler violence has received support from politicians, including members of the Cabinet.[74]

In his final judgment before retiring from the Supreme Court, Deputy President of the Court Salim Joubran stated:

> The Palestinian inhabitants of the Area are not like any other group of individuals who are subject to this or that administrative authority. We are speaking of protected persons under international law, who as such are entitled to special protection in a wide range of spheres, including the sphere of private property . . . Notwithstanding these provisions, the protected persons are inherently in an inferior position to that of the Israeli settlers in the Area, who are full citizens with equal rights in the State of Israel.[75]

This is a sad recognition of the reality in the West Bank following the massive introduction of Israeli settlers into the occupied territory. The consistent failure of the IDF to protect Palestinians in the West Bank from settler violence is a reflection of the Palestinians' "inherently inferior position."

5. DUTIES OF THE INTERNATIONAL COMMUNITY

In 1967, Israel somewhat reluctantly and ambiguously conceded that the law of belligerent occupation applied to its rule over the West Bank. In its discourse, at least, the Supreme Court has adopted the position that the legal regime on the West Bank is that of belligerent occupation. However, from the very start of the occupation that view did not reflect the real intentions or planned policies of the occupying power in the West Bank. Israel was not prepared to abide by the limitations on the freedom of action of an occupying power and to refrain from exploiting the resources of the occupied territory for its own benefit. In reality, domestic politics determine the policies and practices of the occupying power, while the law serves as a tool to legitimize restrictions on the rights and liberties of the Palestinians. The failure of the occupying power to fulfill its obligation to protect the Palestinian population from settler violence in the West Bank has been an endemic feature of

for Human Rights in the Occupied Territories, https://www.btselem.org/settler_violence_updates_list. *See also* Maoz, *supra* note 71.

74. Kretzmer & Yehuda, *supra* note 1. *See also* report by TOI Staff, *Ben Gvir Praises Settler Who Killed Palestinian in Clash: "Should Get Medal of Honor,"* The Times of Israel (Aug. 6, 2023), https://www.timesofisrael.com/ben-gvir-praises-settler-who-killed-palestinian-in-clash-should-get-medal-of-honor/ (Minister of National Security praises settler arrested on charge of killing a Palestinian in a recent incident).

75. HCJ 794/17 Ziada v. IDF Commander in the West Bank, Nevo, ¶ 116 (Oct. 31, 2017) (Isr.).

the occupation since the government policy of establishing settlements gained momentum. Representatives of the settler community currently hold major positions in the government of Israel,[76] meaning that the chance of any changes from within the Israeli political or legal system are slimmer than ever.[77] In this context it seems appropriate to examine the legal obligations of the international community to ensure compliance by the occupying power with its legal obligations.

It is the duty of all the States party to the Fourth Geneva Convention to ensure respect for that treaty. As the ICRC has explained in Paragraph 153 of its recent Commentary on the First Geneva Convention:[78]

> The High Contracting Parties also have positive obligations under common Article 1, which means they must take proactive steps to bring violations of the Conventions to an end and to bring an erring Party to a conflict back to an attitude of respect for the Conventions, in particular by using their influence on that Party. . . . This obligation is not limited to stopping ongoing violations but includes an obligation to prevent violations when there is a foreseeable risk that they will be committed and to prevent further violations in case they have already occurred.

In Resolution 681 (1990), adopted unanimously, the UN Security Council called "upon the high contracting parties to the [Fourth Geneva] Convention to ensure

76. The leader of the "Religious Zionist" party, which represents large parts of the settler community, was appointed both as Minister of Finance and as a minister in the Department of Defense in charge of settlements in the West Bank; the head of the "Jewish power" party, which also strongly supports grabbing the land of Palestinians in the West Bank, is no less than Minister of National Security.

77. After the present government assumed office, the Minister of Defense instructed the Chief of Staff not to evacuate a religious academy (*yeshiva*) that had been built illegally, and even to facilitate construction of the *yeshiva* on what was termed "state land." HCJ 2821/19, Fozzi v. IDF Commander in Judea and Samaria, Nevo, Response of the respondents to the petition of Palestinian Landowners, ¶ 7 (Aug. 2, 2023) (Isr.). Relying on the formal grounds that the facts had changed since the petition was submitted, the Supreme Court dismissed the petition. *See further Landowners from Burqa Petitioned the High Court of Justice to Allow Them to Access Their Land Where the Settlement of Homesh Was Located*, Yesh Din (Apr. 18, 2019), https://www.yesh-din.org/en/landowners-from-burka-petitioned-the-high-court-of-justice-to-allow-them-to-access-their-land-where-the-settlement-of-homesh-was-located/; Hagar Shezaf, *Israel's High Court Dismisses Appeal Against West Bank Outpost of Homesh*, Ha'aretz (Aug, 2. 2023), https://www.haaretz.com/israel-news/2023-08-02/ty-article/.premium/israels-high-court-dismisses-appeal-against-west-bank-outpost-of-homesh/00000189-b712-db5d-a5fd-b73b56730000. At the time of writing the government of Israel has proposed radical changes in Israel's constitution and laws. On the connection between these proposals and its plans for the West Bank, *see* David Kretzmer, *The "Constitutional Reform" and the Occupation*, 56 Israel Law Review 3 (2023).

78. International Committee of the Red Cross, Commentary 2016 to Convention (I) for the Amelioration of the Condition of the Wounded and Sick in Armed Forces in the Field of 12 August 1949 (2016), https://ihl-databases.icrc.org/en/ihl-treaties/gci-1949/article-1/commentary/2016?activeTab=undefined#_Toc452378938.

respect by Israel, the occupying Power, for its obligations under the Convention in accordance with article 1 thereof."[79] In considering the consequences of the construction of the separation barrier in the West Bank, the ICJ pointed to the obligation of all States parties to the Geneva Conventions to ensure respect for it by other States parties.[80] There are numerous other resolutions of the UN Security Council declaring that Israel is bound by GC IV, stating that the settlements are unlawful and that it will not recognize changes beyond the lines that existed before the June 1967, except those agreed upon in negotiations between the parties.[81]

In December 2022, the UN General Assembly requested an ICJ Advisory Opinion on "the legal consequences arising from the ongoing violation by Israel of the right of the Palestinian people to self-determination, from its prolonged occupation, settlement and annexation of the occupied territory since 1967, . . . and from its adoption of related discriminatory legislation and measures."[82] The Prosecutor of the International Criminal Court has also opened an investigation of the situation in Palestine.[83]

It remains to be seen whether decisions by these international bodies will encourage third-party States to use their legal and political power to ensure compliance by the occupying power with its obligation to protect the civilian population in the West Bank.

6. CONCLUDING OBSERVATIONS

Most occupying powers since World War II have ignored the law of belligerent occupation or argued that it does not apply to their specific context.[84] The occupation by Israel of the West Bank is an apparent, though highly ambiguous exception, given that in defending its actions before its own courts the occupying power has at least relied on the international law of belligerent occupation. The problem is that it has done so mainly to justify employing the broad powers enjoyed by an occupying army to protect its security and fulfill its military needs, while ignoring those parts of the law of belligerent occupation that place severe restrictions on the occupying power's freedom to pursue its own political interests in the occupied territory. This chapter shows that ignoring these essential parts of the law may have dire consequences. By establishing Israeli settlements in the occupied territory, the occupying power undermined its duty to act for the benefit of the

79. S.C. Res. 681 (Dec. 20, 1990).

80. The *Wall* opinion, *supra* note 6, at ¶ 158.

81. S.C. Res. 2334 (Dec. 23, 2016). This is the latest resolution, adopted by 14 of the 15 members of the Security Council, with the United States abstaining.

82. G.A. Res. 77/247, *supra* note 3.

83. ICC 01/18, *Situation in the State of Palestine* (Mar. 3, 2021), https://www.icc-cpi.int/palestine.

84. For a thorough discussion of these cases, *see* Benvenisti, *supra* note 41, at 167–202.

local population and, most importantly, in consequence, consistently failed in its obligation to protect that population from violence by Israeli citizens who settled in the area.

While there is an assumption that belligerent occupation is a temporary regime and will therefore be short-term, there are no legal limits on its length. However, as occupation continues, and the occupying power starts acting as if it were the sovereign of a territory, it is essential that the legal analysis not be confined to the area's formal status but to the real nature of the existing regime.[85] These questions have recently gained prominence in the legal literature[86] and in reports of UN organs that have looked into the situation in the West Bank.[87] Changing the characterization of the legal regime could have important implications for the obligations of other States to ensure protection of the civilian population in the West Bank.

One of the central issues that arises, and will likely be examined by the ICJ in its pending Advisory Opinion on the legal status of the West Bank, is whether Israel has annexed either the whole territory or at least Area C, comprising 60 percent of the West Bank, in which all the Israeli settlements have been built. As is well known, annexation of occupied territory is unlawful under international law as it violates the prohibition on the acquisition of territory by use of force. But whether territory has in practice been annexed, or this has been achieved by means of a legal act under the domestic law of the occupying power, the annexation has no validity in international law.[88] And, even if invalid under international law, it may have important implications in relation to the duties of third States.[89]

85. *See, e.g.*, *Report of the Special Rapporteur on the Situation of Human Rights in the Palestinian Territories Occupied since 1967*, ¶ 8, U.N. Doc. A/62/275 (Aug. 17, 2007), recommending an ICJ Advisory Opinion on "the legal consequences of a prolonged occupation that has acquired some characteristics of apartheid and colonialism. . . ."

86. *See, e.g.*, Orna Ben-Naftali, Aeyal M. Gross, & Keren Michaeli, *Illegal Occupation: Framing the Occupied Palestinian Territory*, 23 Berkeley Journal of International Law 551 (2005); Ronit Levin-Schnur, Tamar Megiddo, & Yael Berda, *A Theory of Annexation* (Jan. 23, 2023), *available at* https://papers.ssrn.com/sol3/papers.cfm?abstract_id=4330338; Jamil Hilal, *Rethinking Palestine: Settler-Colonialism, Neo-Liberalism and Individualism in the West Bank and Gaza*, Contemporary Arab Affairs 351 (2015); Kretzmer & Ronen, *supra* note 9, at 511; Human Rights Research Council of South Africa, *Occupation, Colonialism, Apartheid? A Re-assessment of Israel's Practices in the Occupied Palestinian Territories Under International Law* (May 2009).

87. U.N. Secretary-General, *Report of the Independent International Commission of Inquiry on the Occupied Palestinian Territory, including East Jerusalem, and Israel*, U.N. Doc. A/77/328 (Sept. 14, 2022); *Report of the Special Rapporteur on the Situation of Human Rights in the Palestinian Territories Occupied since 1967*, *Study on the Mandate*, U.N. Doc. A/77/356 (Sept. 21, 2022).

88. Guilia Pinzauti, *Belligerent Occupation or Creeping Annexation? Identifying the Red Flags*, 61 The Military Law and Law of War Review 86 (2023). *See also* S.C. Res. 478 (Aug. 20, 1980), in which the Security Council declared that all legislative and administrative actions of Israel, the occupying power, changing the status of Jerusalem are null and void.

89. Pinzauti, *supra* note 88; Levin-Schnur et al., *supra* note 86; *Report of the Special Rapporteur*, *supra* note 85.

8

A Reflection on the Cost of Counterterrorism for Civilian Protection in Armed Conflict

FIONNUALA NÍ AOLÁIN*

1. INTRODUCTION

The terrorist of today can be likened to the pirate of old, the "enemy of all mankind."[1] As a legal and political category, terrorism maintains a distinct repugnance. Its unacceptability was reiterated after the attacks of 9/11 by the UN Security Council in Security Council Resolution 1373 and confirmed as a threat to global peace and security.[2] Terrorism has wrought extraordinary harm to individuals, communities,

* Fionnuala Ní Aoláin is Honorary King's Counsel; University Regents Professor; holder of the Robina Chair in Law, Public Policy, and Society; and faculty director of the Human Rights Center at Minnesota Law School. She is concurrently a Professor of Law at the Queen's University of Belfast, School of Law.

1. Jody Green, *Hostis Humani Generis*, 34(4) Critical Inquiry 683, 683 (2008) (*citing* Senator Arlen Specter, who once said that "[t]he threat posed by terrorists is just as universal as that once posed by pirates, and like piracy, terrorism should be prosecuted as a universal crime against humanity"); Nat'l Inst. for Justice, State-Sponsored Terrorism, Report Prepared for the Senate Subcommittee on Security and Terrorism (1985).

2. S.C. Res. 1368 (Sept. 12, 2001). U.N. Secretary-General, *Terrorism and Human Rights*, ¶ 1, U.N. Doc. A/78/269 (Aug. 2, 2023) (affirming the unacceptability of terrorism in "all its forms and manifestations"); S.C. Res. 1373 (Sept. 28, 2001) regrettably contains only a narrow reference to international law, specifically human rights and refugee law in Paragraph 3(f) and (g), while in Paragraph 8 States' obligations are affirmed in line with the Charter (an implicit recognition also of Article 1(3) of the Charter, affirming "human rights and fundamental freedoms for all."

Fionnuala Ní Aoláin, *A Reflection on the Cost of Counterterrorism for Civilian Protection in Armed Conflict* In: *Civilian Protection in Armed Conflict*. Edited by: Jelena Pejic and Captain Margaret Kotlik, Oxford University Press.
 DOI: 10.1093/oso/9780197793176.003.0008

and countries, devastating and upending lives, destroying infrastructure and social cohesion, and upending economies and political functionality.[3] But, despite broad consensus on its objectionable nature, terrorism lacks an agreed international definition even though there is considerable legal clarity on what kinds of acts of violence constitute terrorist acts.[4] So, paradoxically, global repugnance is tacked onto a phenomenon which lacks essential legal clarity. As a result, the attachment of the term to individuals has a complicated set of legal and political consequences. To be named a terrorist is to be placed in a category of "other" that has few comparators. As I explore in this chapter, the category now even appears to have greater negative attachment for individuals and communities than terms like *génocidaire* or war criminal.[5]

As noted elsewhere,[6] in line with an expansionist and securitizing trend, there is an evidenced tendency to consider any act of violence and many nonviolent acts carried out by members of a non-State armed group in a non-international armed conflict as being "terrorist" by definition, sidestepping assessment of lawfulness under international humanitarian law (IHL) and the legal and political significance of non-international armed conflicts on the territories of States.[7] Moreover, the post 9/11 embrace of terrorism discourse and classification, accompanied by rhetoric—including the now maligned terminology of a "war on terror" that deliberately conflates armed conflict and terrorism—has operated as a means to weaken the application of norms of both IHL and international human rights law (IHRL).[8] The "counterterrorism" qualifier, which should be applied to action

3. *See generally* Satya P. Das, *Economic Costs of Terrorism and Counter-Terrorism Measures*, *in* Economics of Terrorism and Counter-Terrorism Measures (2022); *Cf.* Vision of Humanity, *2022 Global Counter-Terrorism Index*, https://www.visionofhumanity.org/maps/global-terrorism-index/#/.

4. *See generally* United Nations 19 Sectoral Counter-Terrorism Conventions and Protocols, *available at* https://www.ohchr.org/en/special-procedures/sr-terrorism/international-standards-promotion-and-protection-human-rights-and-fundamental-freedoms-while.

5. Rep. of the Special Rapporteur on Human Rights While Countering Terrorism, Preliminary findings of the Special Rapporteur on the promotion and protection of human rights and fundamental freedoms while countering terrorism on her visit to Bosnia and Herzegovina from January 13 to January 20, 2023, *available at* https://www.ohchr.org/sites/default/files/documents/issues/terrorism/sr/statements/2023-01-20/SR-Terrorism-EoM-Bosnia-And-Herzevogina-20Jan23.pdf. Here, I observed after visiting prisons that men who had been convicted of crimes against humanity and war crimes serving long sentences were given markedly preferential treatment to men who had returned from conflict zones, serving sentences for crimes such as travel to a conflict zone or membership of a terrorist organization. The contrast was notable.

6. Fionnuala Ní Aoláin (Special Rapporteur on the Promotion and Protection of Human Rights and Fundamental Freedoms while Countering Terrorism), *Rep. of the Special Rapporteur on the Promotion and Protection of Human Rights and Fundamental Freedoms while Countering Terrorism*, ¶ 10, U.N. Doc. A/75/337 (Sept. 3, 2020).

7. *Id.*

8. Richard A. Abel, Law's Wars, The Fate of the Rule of Law in the US "War on Terror" (2018).

against the most serious and violent acts defined by international law, has regrettably been embraced with enthusiasm to legitimize a range of State action, in some contexts precisely, it would appear, to justify the exclusion of the protective norms of both IHL and IHRL.[9] Such weakening includes interconnected degradation of the status of combatant and civilian in favor of the overarching category of "terrorist." This political move has downstream and specific effects on the protection of individual and group rights. Intentionally or not, it can obscure and undermine the specific customary and treaty law obligations of States derived from the application of human rights law and IHL, respectively. It is the power of the rhetorical move, the insidious but effective garnering of outrage that attends to terrorism, which frequently functions to derail questioning of the legitimacy of the terrorist category itself, which underpins my enquiry in this chapter.

To explore these themes, section 2 briefly revisits the principle of distinction, and sets out its pedigree and importance. Section 3 traces the contemporary encroachment of terrorism-related legal and political frameworks, and practices, on the legal category of civilian. Section 4 examines the ways in which masculinity tropes and validations overlay the internalized acceptance of who is (and who is not) a civilian, with distinct consequences for men as civilians in situations of armed conflict. Section 5 uses the ongoing conflict in northeast Syria as a case study to illuminate the pervasive tug toward counterterrorism regulation at the expense of civilian protection and highlights the extreme costs that follow for the boy-child in situations where terrorism threats and the presence of designated terrorist groups determine the legal rights of men and boys, particularly in the context of detention regimes.

2. THE DISTINCTION BETWEEN COMBATANT AND CIVILIAN

I pause to recall why the principle of distinction between combatant and civilian is essential to the protection of persons in armed conflict, and how it plays a broader ordering function in the conduct of hostilities. This formal distinction is found in the law of armed conflict applicable to international armed conflicts (IACs), though as I note later the principle and practice of distinction play a constitutive role in non-international armed conflicts as well. The principle is one of the foundational *grundnorms* of IHL and serves as the foundation from which

9. *See*, e.g., Special Procedures Communications, U.N. Doc. OL IND 6/2023; Special Procedures Communications, U.N. Doc. OL SWE 2/2023; Special Procedures Communications, U.N. Doc. AL EGY 3/2023; Special Procedures Communications, U.N. Doc. AL DZA 3/2023; Special Procedures Communications, U.N. Doc. AL TUR 2/2023; Special Procedures Communications, U.N. Doc. OL BHR 2/2023; Special Procedures Communications, U.N. Doc. OL TJK 5/2022; Special Procedures Communications, U.N. Doc. AL USA 26/2022; Special Procedures Communications, U.N. Doc. AL CHN 12/2022; Special Procedures Communications, U.N. Doc. UA GBR 13/2022.

multiple other core norms follow or intersect.[10] The principle can be described as one of the most significant battlefield principles and its place in the hierarchy of IHL norms is well established.[11] The ICRC's *Study of Customary International Humanitarian Law* opens with Rule 1, which states that "[t]he parties to the conflict must at all times distinguish between civilians and combatants. Attacks may only be directed against combatants. Attacks must not be directed at civilians."[12] In early articulations of legal principle governing the conduct of hostilities,[13] States recognized the particular need to distinguish and privilege persons lawfully engaged in hostilities and protect those who were not. The functional practice of distinction whereby combatants distinguish themselves by wearing a uniform or some other form of distinctive sign recognizable at a distance has been the longstanding basis for lawful targeting in armed conflicts. Even as the terminology of "direct participation in hostilities" has assumed greater rhetorical and practical importance in defining the category of participation, the distinction still holds traction.[14]

It states the obvious to note that the privilege and status of combatant has a distinct political resonance, and that for some groups the importance of self-definition as combatants (as opposed to terrorists or criminals) has had an outsized political value.[15] In tandem, political concerns by many States about the consequences of conflict status recognition on combatant status has led to complex maneuvering to avoid the appearance of donning a combatant or conflict status the veneer of

10. Including proportionality, military necessity, and unnecessary suffering. COMMENTARY ON THE ADDITIONAL PROTOCOLS OF 8 JUNE 1977 TO THE GENEVA CONVENTIONS OF 12 AUGUST 1949 ¶ 598 (Yves Sandoz, Christophe Swinarski, & Bruno Zimmermann eds., 1987), sets out that "[t]he entire system established in The Hague in 1899 and 1907 . . . and in Geneva from 1864 to 1977 is founded on this rule of customary law."

11. Legality of the Threat or Use of Nuclear Weapons, Advisory Opinion, 1996 I.C.J. 226, ¶¶ 78, 92, & 95 (July 8) (specifying distinction as one of the four "cardinal principles").

12. 1 JEAN-MARIE HENCKAERTS & LOUISE DOSWALD-BECK, CUSTOMARY INTERNATIONAL HUMANITARIAN LAW 3 (2005).

13. Hague Convention (IV) Respecting the Laws and Customs of War on Land preamble, Jan. 26, 1910, U.S.T.S. 539 (citing the "Martens Clause"); Declaration Renouncing the Use, in Time of War, of Explosive Projectiles Under 400 Grammes Weight, Saint Petersburg, Nov. 29–Dec. 11, 1868 (otherwise known as the "Saint Petersburg Declaration").

14. INTERNATIONAL COMMITTEE OF THE RED CROSS, INTERPRETATIVE GUIDANCE ON THE NOTION OF DIRECT PARTICIPATION IN HOSTILITIES UNDER INTERNATIONAL HUMANITARIAN LAW (2020).

15. *See, e.g.*, IRA special status protests in Northern Ireland prisons, including and leading to hunger strikes; ANC unilateral deposit of ratification of GC; Kieran McEvoy, *Hunger Strike and Dirty Protest: Resistance as Self-Sacrifice*, *in* PARAMILITARY IMPRISONMENT IN NORTHERN IRELAND 72 (2001); Noelle Higgins, *The Regulation of Armed Non-State Actors: Promoting the Application of the Laws of War to Conflicts Involving National Liberation Movements*, 17 HUMAN RIGHTS BRIEF 12–18 (2009).

legitimacy. It is here, at the interplay between combatant status and terrorist designation, that some of the reflections at the heart of this chapter lie.

Civilian status is a category of presumption and is not triggered by identifiable signs enabling confirmation of status.[16] As early as 1868, the St. Petersburg Declaration focused on targeting enemy forces and not the civilians who supported the enemy, illustrating the longevity of the (albeit imperfect) protective category.[17] The formal treaty crystallization of civilian status is found in the Fourth Geneva Convention of 1949 and in Additional Protocol I to the Conventions.[18] Additional Protocol II contains a more oblique articulation, "the civilian population and individual civilians shall enjoy general protection against the dangers arising from military operations."[19] Thus, as a formal matter, protecting civilians is found in the mainstream of both the ethical and utilitarian value system that has historically maintained the legitimacy of IHL. The virtue signaling of civilian protection has been maintained despite discomfort with the misuse of civilian status and the perceived disadvantages it poses in asymmetrical conflicts.

Precisely because of that discomfort, the tenacity and validity of the bold distinction between the categories of civilian and combatant has been a nodal point of debate and controversy among States, practitioners, and human rights advocates. The articulation and affirmation of the "direct participation in hostilities" continuum and ongoing concerns by States that the civilian category was being misused by certain non-State armed groups to advance their military objectives have been the hallmarks of legal and political disputes. Many of the scholarly debates have concentrated on the adequacy and limits of the civilian category,[20] the (lack of) consequence for a failure to enforce and observe prohibitions on targeting, as well as protracted discussions on how to enhance the protective scope of the civilian category. Relevant to this analysis is the question of whether contestation related to the norm of civilian appurtenance functions to undermine the

16. This protection consolidated from the *jus in bello* practice of sparing civilians, maturing over time as customary international law.

17. Saint Petersburg Declaration, *supra* note 13: "The only legitimate object which states should endeavour to accomplish during the war is to weaken the military forces of the enemy"; *see also* U.S. Department of War, Instructions for the Government of Armies of the United States in the Field, General Orders No. 100, Apr. 24, 1863, art. 22 [hereinafter Lieber Code].

18. Geneva Convention (IV) Relative to the Protection of Civilian Persons in Time of War, art. 49, Aug. 12, 1949, 6 U.S.T. 3516, 75 U.N.T.S. 287 [hereinafter GC IV]. Protocol Additional to the Geneva Conventions of 12 August 1949 and Relating to the Protection of Victims of International Armed Conflicts arts. 48 and 50–51, June 8, 1977 [hereinafter AP I].

19. Protocol Additional to the Geneva Conventions of 12 August 1949 and Relating to the Protection of Victims of Non-International Armed Conflicts art. 13(1), June 8, 1997, 1125 U.N.T.S. 609 [hereinafter AP II].

20. Nils Melzer, *The Principle of Distinction Between Civilians and Combatants*, *in* The Oxford Handbook of International Law in Armed Conflict (Andrew Clapham & Paola Gaeta eds., 2014).

integrity of this norm entirely or in part.[21] In some instances, it is recognized that applicatory contestation can strengthen a norm by bringing clarity to the norm's meaning and requirements,[22] reducing "the pressure for validity contestation"[23] and enhancing the legitimacy of the norm through legal justification, interpretation, and enforcement. However, where applicatory contestation is widespread, comes from a diverse range of actors, and results in a norm being broadened to the extent that it is left "empty and toothless"[24] or narrowed to such a degree that its applicability is substantially reduced, this may weaken a norm. Such, I would argue, is the precarious state of the principle of distinction in contexts defined by States as "counterterrorism" operations and not armed conflicts.

While recognizing the background relevance of these conversations, this chapter now moves to address a different question, namely, the growth and influence of normative and rhetorical counterterrorism on the integrity of the civilian category, particularly for men and boys.

3. CONSEQUENCES OF A SHIFT FROM STATUS PROTECTION TO PEJORATIVE CATEGORY

The question of how conflicts, groups, and individuals are classified is key to understanding the challenges posed by global counterterrorism frameworks to the effective application of IHL and highlights a boiling point in the entanglement between armed conflict and counterterrorism contexts. The labeling of non-State armed groups as "terrorist" or "violent extremist," whether through resolutions and sanctions regimes by the United Nations,[25] or by national governments, has introduced a permissive international framework grounded in legal exceptionalities and a securitization discourse empowering government action in countering terrorism or preventing violent extremism, however defined. Terms widely used by the UN Security Council and key to international counterterrorism

21. Jutta Brunnée & Stephen J. Toope, *Norm Robustness and Contestation in International Law: Self-Defense against Nonstate Actors*, 4 Journal of Global Security Studies 73, 74 (2019).

22. Antje Wiener, *Contested Compliance, Interventions on the Normative Structure of World Politics*, 10 European Journal of International Relations 189 (2004); Holger Niemann & Henrik Schillinger, *Contestation "All the Way Down"? The Grammar of Contestation in Norm Research*, 43 Review of International Studies 29 (2017).

23. Brunnée & Toope, *supra* note 21, at 74.

24. Nicole Deitelhoff & Lisbeth Zimmermann, *Things We Lost in the Fire: How Different Types of Contestation Affect the Robustness of International Norms*, 22 International Studies Review 51, 7 (2020).

25. *See, e.g.*, S.C. Res. 1267 (Oct. 15, 1999); S.C. Res. 1390 (Jan. 16, 2002); S.C. Res. 1988 (June 17, 2011); S.C. Res. 1989 (June 17, 2011); S.C. Res. 2170 (Aug. 15, 2014); S.C. Res. 2178 (Sept. 24, 2014); S.C. Res. 2253 (Dec. 17, 2015); S.C. Res. 2368 (July 20, 2017).

frameworks such as "terrorism," "terrorist," "violent extremism," "foreign terrorist fighter," "radicalization," and "associated with" (designated terrorist groups) are at once symbolic, political, highly context-dependent given the lack of definitions, and have little legal grounding, but are highly stigmatizing and delegitimizing. This nomenclature—sustained and increasingly promoted by the United Nations itself—uncritically legitimizes national political agendas grounded in identifying "terrorists" and "extremists." The consequences of an expansive and legitimized counterterrorism nomenclature, allied with an ever-expanding normative framework, continues to bite at core international law frameworks. I claim that the law of armed conflict's core principles are at particular risk from counterterrorism institutions, norms, and practice, with the diminution of the generic civilian category squarely in the mainframe of counterterrorism expansion.

I note as a general and regulatory matter that IHL, on the one hand, prohibits and regards as war crimes specific acts of terrorism perpetrated in armed conflict[26] and, on the other hand, prohibits and usually regards as war crimes a range of other acts that would commonly be deemed "terrorist" if committed outside an armed conflict.[27] Article 51(2) of Additional Protocol I and Article 4(2) of Additional Protocol II specifically prohibit acts of terrorism in the conduct of hostilities, providing that "acts or threats of violence the primary purpose of which is to spread terror among the civilian population are prohibited."[28] The prohibition has been deemed to be customary international law in a decision of the International Criminal Tribunal for the former Yugoslavia.[29] So, while it is evident that acts of terrorism can be squarely managed within the four corners of the law of armed conflict, we see little meaningful utilization of this subsidiary management capacity in situations of armed conflict. Rather, it is counterterrorism that increasingly shapes and defines the broader legal terrain in which both force is used, and in which States otherwise exercise their coercive power, such as through detention, listing, or other related administrative measures.

When the status of a conflict and the resulting actualization of combatant status are lost to the "terrorist designation," several consequences follow. The move governments increasingly deploy is to consider any act committed by members of a non-State armed group as unlawful ("terrorist"), irrespective of its possible non-prohibition under IHL and irrespective of the broader legal and political significance of a contemporaneous non-international armed conflict. The proposed solution is usually articulated as the military defeat of the terrorist group, as well as both lethal and criminal law action under domestic counterterrorism legislation

26. GC IV, *supra* note 18; AP II, *supra* note 19, art. 4(2)(d).

27. Jelena Pejic, *Armed Conflict and Terrorism: There Is à (Big) Difference*, *in* COUNTERTERRORISM: INTERNATIONAL LAW AND PRACTICE 173 (Ana Maria Salinas de Frias, Katja L.H. Samuel, & Nigel D. White eds., 2012).

28. AP I, *supra* note 18; AP II, *supra* note 19.

29. Prosecutor v. Stanislav Galić, Case No. IT-98-29-A, Judgment, ¶¶ 87, 91 (Int'l Crim. Trib. for the former Yugoslavia Nov. 30, 2006).

against its members. Importantly, this is often accompanied by a legitimization of government action by international counterterrorism frameworks leading, in turn, to increased provision of security assistance to the government both bilaterally and by UN counterterrorism entities.[30]

As both a legal and political matter, this approach limits the capacity to treat conflicts as complex, particularly non-international armed conflicts in which non-State armed groups—regardless of their designation as "terrorist" or otherwise—are parties to a conflict seeking legitimacy within and control over local populations and territory. Such groups exploit dysfunctionalities between the government and parts of its population, communities, ethnic and religious groups, or minorities to obtain support through various means. This can involve the exploitation and leveraging of ideological and religious belief, the provision of basic assistance including security in insecure environments, or the use of sheer force to compel a local population to bend to its will. A mature conflict analysis would generally entail an in-depth examination of the causes, factors, and motives leading individuals and groups to support and engage in violence.[31]

The solution might involve judicial measures against a range of individuals for the commission of human rights violations/abuses and other international crimes, and advance nonjudicial measures such as structural reforms that could sustainably lessen the risk of violence. In this perspective, both IHL and IHRL would be applicable and have primacy over the domestic counterterrorism framework, which means that the IHL principles governing the lawfulness of the use of force would apply, including those related to distinction and the rules on direct participation in hostilities.[32] The loss of both conflict and individual categorization also has significant consequence for the application of the appropriate detention regimes, and for the possibility or availability of amnesty to persons who have directly participated in hostilities.[33] While counterterrorism frameworks and corresponding legal devices may serve governmental agendas, given the dynamics of these highly complex conflict situations in which non-State armed groups also designated as terrorist operate, the "counterterrorism first" approach creates significant challenges to protection, accountability, and humanitarian access, all of which can be observed in multiple contemporary contexts.

30. Promotion and Protection of Human Rights and Fundamental Freedoms while Countering Terrorism, U.N. Doc. A/76/261 (Aug. 3, 2021).

31. UNDP, Journey to Extremism in Africa: Pathways to Recruitment and Disengagement 40 (2023); World Bank, The World Bank Development Report: Conflict, Security and Development (2011).

32. Gary Solis, The Law of Armed Conflict: International Humanitarian Law in War 128 (3d ed. 2022); Fritz Kalshoven & Lisebeth Zegveld, Constraints on the Waging of War 88 (4th ed. 2020).

33. AP II, *supra* note 19, art. 6(5). By way of example, in Iraq, amendments to the amnesty law resulted in no possibility for any member of ISIL to qualify.

In these contexts, it is also the case that the generic category of civilian is being lost to the designation of terrorist. The dangers of such displacement are not merely formalistic but have tangible effects. These include the use of military force, including targeting, against already disenfranchised and marginalized populations. And even where a counterterrorism use of force leads to the elimination of certain key members of the designated armed groups, it states the obvious that the root causes of conflict do not disappear. Violence against certain groups, communities, or areas becomes entrenched, and the cyclical nature of conflict and violence is entrenched.

The current situation in northeast Syria, where thousands of men, women, and children from Iraq, Syria, and third countries are caught in the aftermath of a highly complex decade-long conflict, is a static humanitarian catastrophe, but largely viewed as a counterterrorism problem. These individuals, whether internally displaced or arbitrarily detained in camps such as Al-Hol and Roj, or in one of the numerous other prisons and detentions centers, are held absent any due process or judicial oversight. The broader point remains that counterterrorism framing, conveniently available to States with interests in the territory, excludes the necessary traction to force the application of IHL and the resulting protections that might follow for this large detainee population.

4. CIVILIAN STATUS FOR MEN AND BOYS THROUGH A MASCULINITY LENS

A fairly substantial amount of literature has been generated over the years regarding the forms of masculinity that emerge in times of armed conflict and war.[34] Some of that scholarly writing addresses the legal form and function of categorization as a civilian, and more recently other writing has emerged to address the intersection of the civilian category with masculinity.[35] In recent work I have explored the interplay between being a civilian man living in armed conflict/occupation and the ways in which the ideologies and practices of masculinity shape the experience and performance of life and protection as such a man or boy.[36] I have been drawn to exposition of the meaning and form of the civilian category

34. Nira Yuval-Davis, *Gendered Militaries, Gendered Wars*, 1 Gender & Nation 93–115 (1997); Joshua S. Goldstein, War and Gender: How Gender Shapes the War System and Vice Versa (2001).

35. Charlie Carpenter & Helen M. Kinsella, The Image Before the Weapon: A Critical History of the Distinction between Combatant and Civilian 16 (2011); Alana Foster, *Pulling the Tail of the Cat: An Exploration of Palestinian Peacebuilders' Conceptualisations of Men and Masculinities in the Israeli-Palestinian Conflict* (2011) (Master's Thesis, Victoria University of Wellington), *available at* http://researcharchive.vuw.ac.nz/bitstream/handle/10063/2293/thesis.pdf?sequence=1.

36. Seamus Campbell & Fionnuala Ní Aoláin, *Masculinities and/under Protracted Occupation*, *in* The Masculinities, Conflict Peacebuilding Handbook (Philipp Schulz et al. eds., 2024).

for men and boys because the literature on civilian masculinities is far more limited than the literature on men as combatants or fighters. This chapter extends my thinking by considering how the diminution of the civilian category through the overuse of misuse of terrorist designations shapes the practice and definition of masculinity in conflict/terrorism arenas.

As canvassed in the preceding, the term "civilian" has specific legal meaning within the law of armed conflict, particularly in respect of IACs. "Civilian" is also a term broadly used outside of the legal literature to denote a person who is vulnerable in a situation of conflict, and as such deserves protection and support. While it has been acknowledged that many men do not take up arms during periods of armed conflict,[37] it nevertheless remains the case that civilian men continue to remain largely invisible within IHL scholarship, the media, and indeed within humanitarian policy and practice.[38] Moreover, civilian men remain at high risk in situations of conflict, because their gender as men often means that they are not deemed civilians in practice and are presumed to be combatants or fighters (or potential combatants or fighters) simply because they are men. In this regard, while the category of civilian is perceived by many as gender-neutral, in practice men are often de facto excluded from the protection the law is supposed to provide.

In reality, large numbers of men and boys do not experience armed conflict through the particularity of combatancy or direct participation in hostilities, although, as explored further later, many men and boys are presumed to be combatants or fighters by virtue of their sex, age, ethnicity, religious affiliation, or geography. For many men, armed conflict involves dispossession, subjugation, and military occupation.[39] While combatancy or direct participation in hostilities is employed by or forced upon some as a means to regain or assert manhood,[40] many men will experience conflict as civilians and maintain the well-observed vulnerability of any citizen, but layered by the added supposition of being a

37. Hannah Wright, Masculinities, Conflict, and Peacebuilding: Perspectives on Men through a Gender Lens (2014), *available at* https://www.files.ethz.ch/isn/185845/masculinities-conflict-and-peacebuilding.pdf.

38. Foster, *supra* note 35; Kimberly Hutchings, *Gendered Humanitarianism: Reconsidering the Ethics of War*, *in* Experiencing War 28–41 (Christine Sylvester ed., 2011); Jennifer Allsopp, *The Refugee Crisis: Demilitarising Masculinities*, openDemocracy (May 20, 2017), https://www.opendemocracy.net/en/5050/refugee-crisis-demilitarising-masculinities/; Seamus Campbell, *Civilian Masculinities and Conflict: An Examination of Northern Ireland and the Occupied Palestinian Territories* (July 2020) (Doctoral Thesis, Transitional Justice Institute, Ulster University).

39. Amal Amireh, *Between Complicity and Subversion: Body Politics in Palestinian National Narrative*, 4 South Atlantic Quarterly 102, 747–72 (2003).

40. *Id.*; Gil Z. Hochberg, *"CHECK ME OUT" Queer Encounters in Sharif Waked's Chic Point: Fashion for Israeli Checkpoints*, 16(4) GLQ: Journal of Lesbian & Gay Stud. 577–97 (2010); Joseph Massad, *Conceiving the Masculine: Gender and Palestinian Nationalism*, 49(3) Middle East Journal 467–83 (1995).

combatant or fighter by virtue of sex. I also observe here that there is a significant lack of scholarly and policy attention to the forced, particularly indirect conscription or utilization of men for combat, in contexts where the choice to refrain from hostilities is in practice highly constrained.[41]

Broadly, therefore, it remains the case that there is little acknowledgment that men can be vulnerable to the effects of armed conflict.[42] Men who lose their lives during such periods have often been represented as heroes and warriors, but rarely as victims, and I argue here that a narrowly gendered understanding of conflict has served to downplay male vulnerability to both psychological and physical abuse.[43] Rethinking the gendered nature of warfare, therefore, means acknowledging the toll which violent conflict exerts upon men,[44] and recognizing the extent to which the experience of vulnerability can have a profound effect upon the ways in which masculinities are enacted within conflicted societies.[45] In particular, as the terrain of armed conflict is encroached upon by the terminology and normative rules of counterterrorism, the vulnerability of men is heightened and extended because terrorism and counterterrorism are overtaking the legal and political terrain of armed conflict. Thus, a specific focus on the intersection between terrorist and civilian allows us to ground this assessment of the civilian man in a new way, demonstrating how conflict or the designation of geographies as contexts in which terrorism takes place is experienced by men who are not combatants or fighters, and subject to the vastitudes of the State or military power in all aspects of their lives.

While the civilian protection regime is not gendered per se, it is often associated with "women and children" as opposed to adult men,[46] with the former

41. On the complexity of consent, *see* Austin Choi-Fitzpatrick & Amelia Watkins-Smith, *Agency Continuum? A Non-Binary Approach to Agency Among Human Rights Victims and Violations*, 43 Human Rights Quarterly 714–35 (2001); *see* Prosecutor v. Dražen Erdemović, Case No. IT-96-22-T, Sentencing Judgment (Int'l Crim. Trib. for the former Yugoslavia Nov. 29, 1996), which surfaces some of these complexities.

42. R. Charli Carpenter, *"Women and Children First": Gender, Norms, and Humanitarian Evacuation in the Balkans 1991–1995*, 57(4) International Organization 661–94 (2003); Hutchings, *supra* note 38; Henri Myrttinen, Lana Khattab, & Jana Naujoks, *Re-thinking Hegemonic Masculinities in Conflict-Affected Contexts*, Critical Military Studies 103–19 (2017).

43. Lynne Segal, *Gender, War and Militarism: Making and Questioning the Links*, 88 Feminist Review 21–35 (2008).

44. *Id.*

45. Chris Dolan, *Collapsing Masculinities and Weak States—A Case Study of Northern Uganda*, *in* Masculinities Matter! Men, Gender, and Development 57–83 (Frances Cleaver ed., 2002); Foster, *supra* note 35; Desiree Lwambo, *Before the War, I Was a Man: Men and Masculinities in the Eastern Democratic Republic of Congo*, 21(1) Gender & Development 47–66 (2013); Hannah Wright, Masculinities, Conflict, and Peacebuilding: Perspectives on Men through a Gender Lens (2014), *available at* https://www.files.ethz.ch/isn/185845/masculinities-conflict-and-peacebuilding.pdf.

46. Carpenter, *supra* note 42.

group epitomizing innocent civilians in a way in which the latter group does not.[47] The conflation of "womenandchildren" as a singular category has further fused these two groups, and despite the fact that the melding of these two categories has not functioned to prevent harm in armed conflict, policy and practice have prioritized their collective protection and intermingling. As Hugo Slim[48] and Gabriella Blum note,[49] innocence denotes the inability to threat or cause harm, and thus presumed male ability to participate effectively in conflict seemingly renders civilian men less innocent and vulnerable, and thus less worthy of protection. Hence, while men are often those most vulnerable to the direct effects of conflict-related violence, including "battlefield" deaths and injuries,[50] they are also those most likely to struggle to credibly assert their civilian identities to either enemy forces or international protectors.[51] There is thus a need to look beyond women, children, or other "ideal"[52] or "paradigmatic"[53] civilians and recognize the potential vulnerability and protection requirements of battle-age men.

The consequences of the extent to which civilian men represent something of a blind spot in both military and humanitarian thinking is evident when one examines death and injury within a particular conflict site. I will refer to the Occupied Palestinian Territory as an example of the broader point. Ninety-four percent of the 4,228 Palestinians who lost their lives as a result of the conflict between September 2000 and July 2007 were male, and of those killed by the Israeli Security Forces during that period, 59 percent were believed to be civilian.[54] Similarly, 67 percent of the 6,128 Palestinians who lost their lives between January 1, 2008, and October 10, 2022, were male, 59 percent of whom were believed to be civilian.[55]

47. *Id.*; CYNTHIA ENLOE, THE MORNING AFTER: SEXUAL POLITICS AT THE END OF THE COLD WAR (1993).

48. HUGO SLIM, KILLING CIVILIANS: METHOD, MADNESS, AND MORALITY IN WAR (2008).

49. Gabriella Blum, *The Dispensable Lives of Soldiers*, 2 JOURNAL OF LEGAL ANALYSIS 69 (2010).

50. GENDERCIDE AND GENOCIDE 1–38 (Adam Jones ed., 2004).

51. Susan F. Hirsch, *Civilians under the Law: Inequality, Universalisms and Intersectionality as Intervention, in* CIVILIANS AND MODERN WAR: ARMED CONFLICT AND THE IDEOLOGY OF VIOLENCE 251–71 (Daniel Rothbart, Karina Korostelina, & Mohammed Cherkaoui eds., 2012).

52. *Id.* at 254.

53. HELEN M. KINSELLA, THE IMAGE BEFORE THE WEAPON: A CRITICAL HISTORY OF THE DISTINCTION BETWEEN COMBATANT AND CIVILIAN 16 (2011).

54. OCHA, *Israeli-Palestinian Fatalities Since 2000—Key Trends* (Aug. 2007), https://www.un.org/unispal/document/auto-insert-208380/.

55. OCHA, *Data on Casualties*, https://www.ochaopt.org/data/casualties (last visited Feb. 13, 2024). These figures have been created using the cross-tabulations function on the Data on Casualties page of the United Nations Office for the Coordination of Humanitarian Affairs website. They include deaths resulting from the context of occupation and conflict between January 1, 2008, and October 14, 2022. Figures for 2022 are provisional.

Some high-profile efforts are being made to mitigate against the perceived weakening of civilian protection in armed conflict situations. In August 2022, the U.S. Department of Defense issued the Civilian Harm Mitigation and Response Action Plan (CHMR-AP),[56] "to improve how the Department of Defense (DoD) mitigates and responds to civilian harm resulting from military operations." Its issuance was accompanied by the recognition that "the protection of civilians is a strategic priority as well as a moral imperative,"[57] and a response to sustained pressure about the scale of and transparency related to civilian causalities in the so-called "war on terror."[58] That pressure had already produced effects, including the issuance every year of a report on civilian casualties by the DoD.[59] More ambitious in scope, the Action Plan envisages substantial institutional changes.[60] Reflection on the adequacy and strength of those changes is not my objective here. Rather, I ponder how the stated focus on "comprehensive perspectives . . . including second and third-order effects in the operational environment during planning and joint targeting processes,"[61] can engage the vulnerability and civilian categorization of men in conflict zones. It is welcome to see the terminology of misidentification, cognitive bias, and confirmation bias articulated in the Action Plan and a clear commitment to address these specific challenges by "training and education, red teaming procedures, specific positive identification (PID) policies for targeting, [and] use of structural analytic techniques."[62] But it is not clear to me that the focus on data collection, integration, and expanding information sources[63] gets at the more fundamental psychological and social barriers I identify here, namely, the fundamental inability to view certain men in certain cultures and settings as civilian, per se.

56. U.S. Dept. of Defense, Civilian Harm Mitigation and Response Action Plan (2022), *available at* https://media.defense.gov/2022/Aug/25/2003064740/-1/-1/1/CIVILIAN-HARM-MITIGATION-AND-RESPONSE-ACTION-PLAN.PDF [hereinafter CHMR-AP].

57. *Id.* at 1.

58. *See, e.g.*, Azmet Kahn, *Hidden Pentagon Records Reveal Patterns of Failure in Deadly Airstrikes*, N.Y. Times (Dec. 18, 2021), https://www.nytimes.com/interactive/2021/12/18/us/airstrikes-pentagon-records-civilian-deaths.html; Miriam Berger, *Post-9/11 Wars Have Contributed to Some 4.5 Million Death, Report Suggests*, Wash. Post (May 15, 2023), https://www.washingtonpost.com/world/2023/05/15/war-on-terror-911-deaths-afghanistan-iraq/.

59. National Defense Authorization Act for Fiscal Year 2018, H.R. 2810, 115th Cong. (2017); John S. McCain National Defense Authorization Act for Fiscal Year 2019, H.R. 5515, 115th Cong. (2018); National Defense Authorization Act for Fiscal Year 2020, S. 1790, 116th Cong. (2019)

60. CHMR-AP, *supra* note 56.

61. *Id.* at 13.

62. *Id.*

63. *Id.* at 17.

5. THE BOY AS A CIVILIAN

While boys should presumptively be thought of as civilians, they may also, depending on their age, be thought of as men,[64] and thus be liable to the forms of repression and harm often inflicted on males of "battle age."[65] The boy-child occupies a particularly precarious space in armed conflict contexts. His theoretical status both as a civilian and as a child should offer elevated protection from the vastitudes of harm in conflict. In practice, his sex operates as a constraint on what protection he receives, undermining simultaneously both the requirements of civilian protection and the special protections owed to children in armed conflict.

International law provides robust protections for children.[66] Several international human rights treaties—namely, the Convention on the Rights of the Child (CRC), the most widely adopted international human rights treaty, and its Optional Protocols, as well as the International Covenant on Civil and Political Rights[67] and the International Covenant on Economic, Social and Cultural Rights,[68] provide for a wide range of children's rights. These fully apply in contexts in which counterterrorism, security, or emergency measures are in force, including settings where non-State armed groups designated by the United Nations as terrorist organizations control territory or institutions. The treaties are supplemented by several nonbinding human rights law instruments, including the UN Rules for the Protection of Juveniles Deprived of their Liberty,[69] the UN Standard Minimum Rules for the Administration of Juvenile Justice[70] (Beijing Rules), and the Principles and Guidelines on Children Associated with Armed Forces or Armed Groups[71] (Paris Principles), each of which provides further guidance on the requisite protections of children with relevance to counterterrorism and related contexts. Despite further normative development to protect, inter alia,

64. *See* U.N. Special Procedures, Position of the United Nations Special Rapporteur on the promotion and protection of human rights and fundamental freedoms while countering terrorism on the human rights of adolescents/juveniles being detained in North-East Syria, at 6–7 (May 2021), *available at* https://www.ohchr.org/sites/default/files/Documents/Issues/Terrorism/SR/UNSRCT_Position_human-rights-of-boys-adolescents-2021_final.pdf.

65. Gendercide, *supra* note 50.

66. G.A. Res. 44/25, Convention on the Rights of the Child, art. 1 (Nov. 20, 1989) [hereinafter CRC].

67. International Covenant on Civil and Political Rights, Dec. 16, 1966, 999 U.N.T.S. 171.

68. International Covenant on Economic, Social and Cultural Rights, Dec. 16, 1966, 993 U.N.T.S. 3.

69. G.A. Res. 45/113 (Dec. 14, 1990).

70. Standard Minimum Rules for the Administration of Juvenile Justice, U.N. Doc. A/RES/40/33 (Nov. 29, 1985).

71. February 2007, *available at* https://childrenandarmedconflict.un.org/wp-content/uploads/2016/04/The-Paris-Principles-En-1.pdf.

the boy-child in armed conflict, such as the Vancouver Principles,[72] the application of both hard and soft law standards remains peripatetic and inconsistent.

The encroachment of counterterrorism discourse, standards, and practice has played an instrumental part in an increasingly ragged protection picture. A 2023 joint statement of the Special Representatives of the UN Secretary-General for Children and Armed Conflict and on Violence against Children, respectively, and of the UN Committee on the Rights of the Child recognized this by expressing alarm at "[i]ncreasing practices of arresting and detaining children identified as associated with armed groups," including UN-designated terrorist groups, and by underscoring the importance and urgency of respecting, protecting, and fulfilling child rights in the context of counterterrorism measures.[73]

The situation of boys in northeast Syria intensely illustrates the vulnerability of the boy-child,[74] which starts from the location of his birth. By virtue of being in a territory where designated terrorist groups are operative,[75] geography becomes destiny and functions as the first of a set of factors that makes for presumptive terrorist or "affiliated" status. The second is religious identity, as Muslim boys carry the burden that their religious affiliation justifies a perception of their presumptive dangerousness.[76] The third factor are paternal links to men who were/are members of ISIS as fathers, brothers, uncles, grandfathers that add to cumulative presumptions about the inherent "extremism" of the boy child. The fourth factor pulling a boy away from presumptive civilian status is his mother being presumed to be a family member of an ISIS adherent, regardless of possible coercion, grooming, trafficking, resistance, or patriarchal control.

In northeast Syria, the language of exceptionalism pervades the ways in which certain actors and institutions identify and define the boy-child. Media reporting, as well as some scholarly writing on the boy-child, is replete with inflammatory language, including terms like "cubs of the caliphate," "extremists," or "terrorists"

72. The Vancouver Principles on Peacekeeping and the Prevention of the Recruitment and Use of Child Soldiers (Nov. 15, 2017), *available at* https://www.international.gc.ca/world-monde/issues_development-enjeux_developpement/human_rights-droits_homme/principles-vancouver-principes-pledge-engageons.aspx?lang=eng.

73. Press Statement, UN Office of the Special Representative of the Secretary-General for Children and Armed Conflict, *UN Experts Stress Urgent Need to Ensure Child Rights while Implementing Counter-terrorism and National Security Measures* (Mar. 14, 2023), https://childrenandarmedconflict.un.org/2023/03/un-experts-stress-urgent-need-to-ensure-child-rights-while-implementing-counter-terrorism-and-national-security-measures/#:~:text=*%20The%20Special%20Representative%20of%20the,its%20current%20Chair%2C%20Mikiko%20Otani.

74. *See* Martha Fineman, *The Vulnerable Subject: Anchoring Equality in the Human Condition*, 20 Yale Journal of Law & Feminism 8–40 (2008).

75. S.C. Res. 2253 (Dec. 17, 2015).

76. *See generally* Maha Hilal, Innocent Until Proven Muslim: Islamophobia, The War on Terror, and the Muslim Experience Since 9/11 (2022).

to describe two-year-olds, three-, four-, and five-year-olds born in that territory by no choice of their own.[77] There is a harmful obliqueness to the depictions of these boys, whereby their extreme youth (under ten, as an example) precludes directly naming them as terrorists, but terms like "children associated with ISIL" and "children of ISIS" have the effect of displacing their child status with a de facto terrorist designation. This juxtaposition produces a sleight of hand because their potentiality as terrorists justifies their treatment as security threats, namely, "terrorists in waiting." The logic is inescapable. The boy-child is excluded from the boxes of required protection, both as an actual or potential terrorist, in a kind of Schrodinger's cat exercise on the life of the child who cannot escape the inevitability of being in the "terrorism" box by virtue of geography, gender, and religious identity. Thus, in an unexpected way, brutal intersectionality operates to undermine the child's status and protection rather than to elevate it.

As of this writing, the scale of detention of children in general, and of the boy-child in particular, in northeast Syria is astounding. Over 60 percent of the population in Al-Hol camp alone is under the age of twelve, facilitated by the rhetoric of counterterrorism displacing civilian protection norms under the law of armed conflict. The range of rights violations is extensive and systematic, and is imbued with discrimination based on national, religious, and ethnic grounds. Child rights violations are ingrained, including disregard for the right to life, freedom from torture, or other cruel, inhuman, or degrading treatment or punishment, and freedom from arbitrary deprivation of liberty. The rule that "arrest, detention or imprisonment of a child . . . shall be used only as a measure of last resort and for the shortest appropriate period of time" and that "[n]either capital punishment nor life imprisonment without possibility of release shall be imposed for offences committed by persons below eighteen years of age"[78] is ignored in the breach.

In tandem, fundamental procedural guarantees are structurally denied to the boy-child. These include a minimum age of criminal responsibility; the right to prompt and direct notification of charges and access to legal and other appropriate assistance; non-retroactivity of charges; the right to be considered innocent until proven guilty; the right to maintain contact with family when in detention and to be treated in a manner that takes into account the needs of persons of their age; and the right to a hearing before a competent, independent, and impartial authority or judicial body without delay.[79] The litany of layered harms likewise includes denial of the right to preserve one's identity, including nationality, name, and family relations as recognized by law without unlawful interference.[80] With the massive incarceration of children as "terrorists," "extremists," or "potential terrorists and extremists," the rights to freedom of expression, to thought,

77. Mia Bloom, *Cubs of the Caliphate: The Children of ISIS*, Foreign Affairs (July 21, 2015), https://www.foreignaffairs.com/middle-east/cubs-caliphate.

78. CRC, *supra* note 66, arts. 6, 37.

79. *Id.*, arts. 37, 40.

80. *Id.*, art. 8.

conscience, and religion, and to association—and ensuring that any child capable of forming his or her own views enjoys the right to express those views freely in all matters affecting the child—are entirely discarded.[81] This array of systematic practices operates in a context where there is no right to legal protection against "arbitrary or unlawful interference" with the child's privacy, family, home, or correspondence, nor is there protection against "unlawful attacks on his or her honour and reputation."[82] The absolute absence of meaningful rights to health care, education, social security, and a standard of living adequate for the child's physical, mental, spiritual, moral, and social development compounds the evisceration of child rights in this territory.[83]

An extraordinary and pervasive harm is the structured practice of forced separation of boys from parents, generally mothers, occurring on a systematic scale against the child's will.[84] In multiple prisons and detention facilities in northeast Syria, hundreds of boys, according to a conservative estimate,[85] have been separated from family members, particularly mothers, based on a presumption that they are "ISIL affiliated." In the vast majority of cases, it is clear that the boys concerned cannot be presumed to be fighters as there is either no evidence or insufficient evidence that they have directly participated in hostilities or had any battlefield exposure at all. Moreover, the age of many of the youngest boys when Baghuz fell, who are now from nine to twelve, makes their participation in hostilities entirely implausible.[86] The inability to classify the boys as fighters, coupled with a clear desire to remove them from the civilian category, has led to the boys being deemed "terrorists."

Northeast Syria provides the most extensive and systematic contemporary example of the application of the badge of "terrorism" as a tool for the wholesale removal of children from the ambit of human rights and humanitarian law protection. Tolerance for mass arbitrary detention of children and their separation from their mothers or other family members speaks to the power of the "terrorist" heuristic and its capacity to draw back the protective mantle of IHL and IHRL.

81. *Id.*, arts. 12–15.

82. *Id.*, art. 6.

83. *Id.*, arts. 24–29.

84. *Id.*, art. 9.

85. Rep. of the Special Rapporteur on Human Rights While Countering Terrorism, Technical Visit to the Northeast of the Syrian Arab Republic: End of Mission Statement, ¶ 9, https://www.ohchr.org/sites/default/files/documents/issues/terrorism/sr/statements/EoM-Visit-to-Syria-20230721.pdf.

86. Notably, under IHRL standards, even if one were to verify such participation they would still be treated as juveniles and victims. *See generally* The United Nations Standard Minimum Rules for the Treatment of Prisoners, G.A. Res. 31 (Aug. 30, 1955); *see also* The United Nations Standard Minimum Rules for Non-custodial Measures, A/RES/45/110 (Dec. 14, 1990). Under IHL, the prohibition on the use of child soldiers is noted.

6. CONCLUSION

In Hartian[87] terms, the notion of "civilian" has a core meaning denoting a formal and defined legal category, lending specific protections to persons who find themselves caught up in the maelstrom of armed conflict. But civilian also has social and political underpinnings which define a penumbra meaning that may be attached to the category. Thus, threats, crisis, and armed conflict shape the social construction of the "civilian," which is increasingly disconnected from the objective legal category of "civilian."

I have argued that the civilian category is facing sustained normative pressure from the expanded application of the term "terrorist." This is primarily because States actively pursue political strategies to avoid or deflect classification of violence as situations of armed conflict. Post 9/11, the terrain of terrorism has both literally and metaphorically exploded at the expense of acknowledgment of the existence of situations of armed conflict that meet the relevant thresholds for the application of international humanitarian law. Simultaneously, and not coincidentally, States rely on the terminology of "contexts"/"situations" of terrorism to advance a hegemonic status for counterterrorism norms and exploit the ambiguous legal status that follows for individuals deemed to be "terrorist." That status allows for promiscuous national security norms to define the course and limits of State action, generally at a cost to both protective categories under international humanitarian law and human rights. The ubiquity and exceptional nature of terrorism regulation has indisputable and evident benefits for States not least that few, if any, other States question the validity or legitimacy of using this terminology. The result has been an erosion of the normative force of both international humanitarian law and human rights in practice. The degradation has generated little pushback, as many States embrace the benefits to their freedom of action that follows from the elevation of counterterrorism norms and institutions, long past the original crisis that enabled these exceptional norms to emerge post 9/11.

Undermining the category of civilian is also not gender-neutral. I argued here that it overwhelmingly attaches to men, who are presumed noncivilian and nonprotected by virtue of intersecting factors including sex, age, religious affiliation (perceived or actual), and geography. This observation has significant consequences for protection and for humanitarian assistance on the ground. It attaches not only to adult men defined as "terrorist" but also increasingly to the boy-child; he is made vulnerable by the same logic of expanded terrorism definitions applied at the expense of IHL protections. Undermining protection for men and boys has broader consequences for the integrity of the civilian category as a whole. This is one fundamental reason why we ought to pay attention to the erosion of protection in practice and continue to assert that discrimination on the basis of sex must not be hardwired into the civilian category under international humanitarian law.

87. H.L.A. Hart, The Concept of Law (1961).

9

Deportation in International Humanitarian and Criminal Law Against the Backdrop of the War in Ukraine

MICHAEL N. SCHMITT*

1. INTRODUCTION

The United Nations estimates that the conflict in Ukraine has displaced well over five million people within Ukraine's borders.[1] At the same time, more than six million Ukrainians who fled the country remain abroad.[2] The plight of such internally displaced persons and refugees, respectively, is an all-too-common feature of international armed conflict.[3]

* Professor Michael N. Schmitt is the G. Norman Lieber Distinguished Scholar at West Point's Lieber Institute; Professor of Public International Law at the University of Reading (UK); Professor Emeritus and Charles H. Stockton Distinguished Scholar-in-Residence at the United States Naval War College; and Strauss Center Distinguished Scholar and Visiting Professor of Law at the University of Texas.

1. United Nations High Commissioner for Refugees, *Ukraine Emergency*, https://www.unrefugees.org/emergencies/ukraine/ (as of May 2023) (last visited Oct. 22, 2023).

2. *Id.*

3. On the law governing internally displaced persons and refugees in the conflict in Ukraine, *see* Julia Grignon, *Law Applicable to Persons Fleeing Conflicts*, ARTICLES OF WAR (Mar. 15, 2022), https://lieber.westpoint.edu/law-applicable-persons-fleeing-armed-conflicts/; Ruvi Ziegler, *Displacement from Conflict: Old Realities, New Protections?*, ARTICLES OF WAR (Mar. 17, 2022), https://lieber.westpoint.edu/displacement-conflict-old-realities-new-protections/. On internal

Michael N. Schmitt, *Deportation in International Humanitarian and Criminal Law Against the Backdrop of the War in Ukraine* In: *Civilian Protection in Armed Conflict*. Edited by: Jelena Pejic and Captain Margaret Kotlik, Oxford University Press. © Michael N. Schmitt 2025. DOI: 10.1093/oso/9780197793176.003.0009

Tragically, the conflict has also witnessed the mass *deportation* of Ukrainian nationals from occupied territory to Russia. Soon after the most recent round of fighting commenced in February 2022 (the armed conflict began in 2014), allegations of Russian forces deporting Ukrainians began to surface. For instance, the next month, an official in the besieged city of Mariupol charged that Russian forces had taken "between 4,000 and 5,000 Mariupol residents forcibly across the border."[4] The Ukrainian Ministry of Foreign Affairs labeled the action "a gross violation of international law."[5] At the same time, the U.S. ambassador to the United Nations observed that, if true, "[i]t is unconscionable for Russia to force Ukrainian citizens into Russia and put them in what will basically be concentration and prisoner camps."[6]

The same month, Ukraine's Prosecutor General accused Russia of "the forcible transfer of 2,389 children from temporarily occupied territories of Ukraine to Russia."[7] Citing a Ukrainian Ministry of Foreign Affairs statement on the matter, the U.S. embassy in Kyiv acknowledged the claim, adding that the children were from "Donetsk and Luhansk oblasts" and stated, "This is not assistance. It is kidnapping."[8]

Expectedly, the Russian embassy to the United States denied the accusations. Instead, Russia's Defense Ministry claimed they were "refugees" from Mariupol.[9] More broadly, Russian officials assert that Ukrainians are fleeing to Russia willingly. For instance, the head of Russia's National Defense Control Center claimed that over 7,800 Ukrainians "expressed their desire to escape to the Russian Federation" on a single day in March.[10] The Russian Ministry of Defense has asserted that 2.6 million people asked to be evacuated to Russia by March 2022.[11]

displacement, *see also* Guiding Principles on Internal Displacement, U.N. Doc. E/CN.4/1998/53/Add.2 (1998).

4. Valarie Hopkins, *A Mariupol Official Accuses Russia of Forcibly Taking Ukrainians Across the Border*, N.Y. Times (Mar. 19, 2022), https://www.nytimes.com/2022/03/20/world/europe/ukraine-russia-war-mariupol.html.

5. Samantha Lock & Martin Belam, *Russian Forces "Kidnapped" 2,389 Children from Donetsk and Luhansk, US Embassy Says*, The Guardian (Mar. 22, 2022), https://theguardian.com/world/live/2022/mar/22/russia-ukraine-war-zelenskiy-urges-talks-with-putin-biden-flags-clear-sign-russia-considering-chemical-weapons-live?page=with:block-623964f18f081efd327711a6.

6. Ted Hesson & Richard Cowan, *U.S. Envoy to U.N. Decries Reports of Ukrainians Deported to Russia*, Reuters (Mar. 20, 2022), https://www.reuters.com/world/us-envoy-un-decries-disturbing-claims-ukrainians-deported-russia-2022-03-20/.

7. Iryna Venediktova, X (Mar. 21, 2022,), https://twitter.com/VenediktovaIV/status/1505988764023377920.

8. U.S. Embassy Kyiv, X (Mar. 22, 2022), https://twitter.com/USEmbassyKyiv/status/1506214727394988032.

9. Reuters, *Mariupol Says Russia Forcefully Deported Thousands of People*, Reuters (Mar. 19, 2022), https://www.reuters.com/world/europe/ukraines-mariupol-says-russia-forcefully-deported-thousands-its-people-2022-03-20/.

10. Hopkins, *supra* note 4.

11. Reuters, *supra* note 9.

The Russian claims appear to be ludicrous. A year and a half later, it is unquestionable that Russia is deporting Ukrainian nationals to its territory. In this regard, the United Kingdom's Secretary of State for Foreign, Commonwealth, and Development Affairs, speaking at the UN Security Council in July 2023, noted that 2.5 million adults had been deported to Russia and 19,000 Ukrainian children remained in Russian camps. He charged Russia with trying to erase Ukrainian identity and culture and with weaponizing children to do so.[12]

Russian deportation of adults usually starts at "filtration camps," where Ukrainian nationals are interrogated to determine whether they pose a perceived threat to Russian control over the occupied territory. The U.S. State Department believes that while individuals deemed nonthreatening are released, Russia detains those considered threatening in eastern Ukraine or Russia. Individuals determined to be less threatening but still hostile are often forcibly deported to Russia.[13] Children moved to Russia "undergo psychological 'rehabilitation' and are forced to complete unspecified educational projects." According to the State Department, "[s]ome of these children have no identity documents or information on the location of their parents."[14]

In March 2023, the International Criminal Court (ICC) issued arrest warrants for Russian President Vladimir Putin and Maria Lvova-Belova, the Russian Commissioner for Children's Rights. The warrants allege that from at least February 2022, they committed the war crimes of "unlawful deportation of population (children) and unlawful transfer of population (children) from occupied areas of Ukraine to the Russian Federation" (under Articles 8(2)(a)(vii) and 8(2)(b)(viii) of the Rome Statute, respectively).[15] The ICC's Prosecutor, Karim Khan, explained:

> Incidents identified by my Office include the deportation of at least hundreds of children taken from orphanages and children's care homes. Many of these children, we allege, have since been given for adoption in the Russian Federation. The law was changed in the Russian Federation, through Presidential decrees issued by President Putin, to expedite the conferral of Russian citizenship, making it easier for them to be adopted by Russian families.

12. United Nations Security Council, *Press Release, 9380th Meeting*, U.N. Doc. SC/15358 (July 17, 2023).

13. U.S. Department of State, *Russia's Filtration Operations and Forced Relocations*, https://www.state.gov/russias-filtration-operations-and-forced-relocations/ (last visited Oct. 22, 2023).

14. *Id.*

15. International Criminal Court, Press Release, *ICC Judges Issue Arrest Warrants Against Vladimir Vladimirovich Putin and Maria Alekseyevna Lvova-Belova* (Mar. 17, 2023), https://www.icc-cpi.int/news/situation-ukraine-icc-judges-issue-arrest-warrants-against-vladimir-vladimirovich-putin-and.

> My Office alleges that these acts, amongst others, demonstrate an intention to permanently remove these children from their own country. At the time of these deportations, the Ukrainian children were protected persons under the Fourth Geneva Convention.[16]

This chapter surveys the international humanitarian law and international criminal law rules governing the deportation of nationals from occupied territory into another country during an international armed conflict. Using the Russia-Ukraine conflict as the backdrop, it discusses applicable prohibitions and offenses, including nuances and exceptions. As will become apparent, the law on the matter is largely unequivocal. So is Russia's responsibility.

2. THE INTERNATIONAL HUMANITARIAN LAW PROHIBITION

The prohibition on deportation in international humanitarian law is longstanding. Article 23 of the 1863 Lieber Code, for example, prohibited "private citizens" from being "carried off to distant parts."[17] Interestingly, the 1899 and 1907 Hague Regulations annexed to Conventions II and IV, respectively, did not address deportation.[18] Lest this absence be interpreted as permitting deportation, the International Committee of the Red Cross (ICRC) has explained that "this was probably because the practice of deporting persons was regarded at the beginning of the century as having fallen into abeyance."[19] And the great international law scholar Georg Schwarzenberger suggested, "To raise the issue of the illegality of deportation of the population of occupied territories was considered unnecessary; the illegality was taken for granted."[20]

16. International Criminal Court, *Statement by Prosecutor Karim A. A. Khan KC on the Issuance of Arrest Warrants Against President Vladimir Putin and Ms Maria Lvova-Belova* (Mar. 17, 2023), https://www.icc-cpi.int/news/statement-prosecutor-karim-khan-kc-issuance-International Criminal Court arrest-warrants-against-president-vladimir-putin.

17. U.S. Department of War, Instructions for the Government of Armies of the United States in the Field, General Orders No. 100, art. 23, Apr. 24, 1863 ("Private citizens are no longer . . . carried off to distant parts").

18. Convention No. II with Respect to the Laws and Customs of War on Land, July 29, 1899, 32 Stat. 1803, T.S. No. 403; Convention No. IV Respecting the Laws and Customs of War on Land, Oct. 18, 1907, 36 Stat. 2227, T.S. No. 539 [hereinafter 1907 Hague Regulations].

19. Commentary to Geneva Convention IV Relative to the Protection of Civilian Persons in Time of War 279 (Jean Pictet ed., 1958) [hereinafter 1958 Geneva Convention IV Commentary].

20. Georg Schwarzenberger, International Law as Applied by International Courts and Tribunals, Vol. II, The Law of Armed Conflict 227 (1968).

In the aftermath of World War I, it became clear that the prohibition had not fallen into desuetude. As early as 1919, the Report of the Commission on Responsibility of the Authors of the War, created at the Versailles Conference, labeled the "deportation of civilians" a "violation of the laws and customs of war."[21] The 1934 Tokyo Draft International Convention on the Condition and Protection of Civilians, adopted by the 25th International Conference of the Red Cross, likewise provided, "[d]eportations outside the territory of the occupied State are forbidden, unless they are evacuations intended, on account of the extension of military operations, to ensure the security of the inhabitants."[22] And in its 2012 *Jurisdictional Immunities* judgment, the International Court of Justice addressed the World War II deportation of an Italian civilian to Germany as a slave laborer, noting "there can be no doubt that this conduct was a serious violation of the international law of armed conflict applicable in 1943–1945."[23]

However, it is Article 49 of the 1949 Convention relative to the Protection of Civilian Persons in Time of War (Geneva Convention IV), which derives from the Tokyo Draft, that sets out the fundamental prohibition applicable in international armed conflict today.[24] When it was adopted in 1949, the need to confirm the illegality of deportation had become tragically evident. As explained in the 1958 ICRC Commentary to the article (which the Diplomatic Conference, despite some discussion on wording, voted for unanimously):

> There is doubtless no need to give an account here of the painful recollections called forth by the "deportations" of the Second World War, for they are still present in everyone's memory. It will suffice to mention that millions of human beings were torn from their homes, separated from their families and deported from their country, usually under inhumane conditions. These mass transfers took place for the greatest possible variety of reasons, mainly as a consequence of the formation of a forced labour service. The thought of the physical and mental suffering endured by these "displaced persons", among whom there were a great many women, children, old people and sick,

21. Commission on the Responsibility of the Authors of the War and on Enforcement of Penalties, *Report Presented to the Preliminary Peace Conference*, 29 March 1919, *reprinted in* 14 American Journal of International Law 95, 114 (1920).

22. Draft International Convention on the Condition and Protection of Civilians of Enemy Nationality Who are on Territory Belonging to or Occupied by a Belligerent, art. 19(b), Tokyo (1934), *available at* https://ihl-databases.icrc.org/pt/ihl-treaties/tokyo-draft-conv-1934?activeTab=historical.

23. Jurisdictional Immunities of the State (Ger. v. It., Greece Intervening), Judgment, 2012 I.C.J. 99, ¶ 52 (Feb. 3).

24. Geneva Convention (IV) Relative to the Protection of Civilian Persons in Time of War, art. 49, Aug. 12, 1949, 6 U.S.T. 3516, 75 U.N.T.S. 287 [hereinafter GC IV]. On the provision's development and substance, *see generally* Jean-Marie Henckaerts, *Deportation and Transfer of Civilians in Time of War*, 26 Vanderbilt Journal of Transnational Law 469 (1993–1994).

can only lead to thankfulness for the prohibition embodied in this paragraph, which is intended to forbid such hateful practices for all time.[25]

Article 49(1) provides: "Individual or mass forcible transfers, as well as deportations of protected persons from occupied territory to the territory of the Occupying Power or to that of any other country, occupied or not, are prohibited, regardless of their motive." Violation is a "grave breach" of the Convention (see section 3).[26] Notably, the prohibition applies to the deportation of both individual persons and groups, distinguishing Geneva Convention IV somewhat from international human rights law treaties.[27]

The reference to "transfer" in Article 49 refers to the involuntary movement of individuals within occupied territory.[28] Deportation, by contrast, denotes the forcible movement of such individuals into the occupying power's territory, as Russia has done, or to any other country. It only encompasses "protected persons," which Article 4 of Geneva Convention IV defines as "those who at a given moment and in any manner whatsoever, find themselves, in case of a conflict or occupation, in the hands of a Party to the conflict or Occupying Power of which they are not nationals." Importantly, Article 4 excludes nationals of the State in whose hands they find themselves; nationals of neutral or co-belligerent States, so long as their State maintains diplomatic relations with the State exercising control over them; the wounded, sick, and shipwrecked; and prisoners of war.[29] Thus, Article 49's prohibition on deportation does not apply to Russian nationals or nationals of

25. 1958 Geneva Convention IV Commentary, *supra* note 19, at 278–79.

26. GC IV, *supra* note 24, art. 147.

27. For instance, the International Covenant on Civil and Political Rights addresses only individual expulsions. International Covenant on Civil and Political Rights, art. 13, Dec. 16, 1966, 999 U.N.T.S. 171.

28. Unlike deportation from occupied territory, transfer into occupied territory is not a grave breach. Additional Protocol I remedied that omission. Protocol Additional (I) to the Geneva Conventions of 12 August 1949, and Relating to the Protection of Victims of International Armed Conflicts art. 85, June 8, 1977, 1125 U.N.T.S. 3 [hereinafter AP I]. As there are few reports indicating this is occurring on any significant scale into occupied Ukrainian territory, the violation shall not be mentioned further.

29. GC IV, *supra* note 24, art. 4. *See also* Office of the General Counsel, U.S. Department of Defense, Law of War Manual § 11.12.3.2 (rev. ed. Dec. 2023). *But see* the allegiance test articulated by the Appeals Chamber in *Tadic*, where the Chamber extended the notion of protected persons to individuals "who, while having the nationality of the Party to the conflict in whose hands they find themselves, are refugees and thus no longer owe allegiance to this Party and no longer enjoy its diplomatic protection." It explained, "not only the text and the drafting history of the Convention but also, and more importantly, the Convention's object and purpose suggest that allegiance to a Party to the conflict and, correspondingly, control by this Party over persons in a given territory, may be regarded as the crucial test." Prosecutor v. Tadić, Case No. IT-94-1-A, Appeals Chamber Judgment, ¶¶ 164–66 (Int'l Crim. Trib. for the former Yugoslavia July 15, 1999).

other States that maintain a diplomatic presence in Moscow. Protection for these individuals may lie in the remaining three 1949 Geneva Conventions, depending on the facts in a given case or other rules of international law.

Article 49 undoubtedly applies in occupied Ukrainian territory, for Russia and Ukraine are party to the 1949 Geneva Conventions. And even if that was not the case, in its *Nuclear Weapons* Advisory Opinion, the International Court of Justice observed that the four Geneva Conventions are "fundamental rules . . . to be observed by all States whether or not they have ratified the conventions that contain them, because they constitute intransgressible principles of international customary law."[30] In my view, therefore, the ICRC 2005 *Customary International Humanitarian Law* study has correctly confirmed the customary law status of the prohibition. Rule 129(A) of that work notes "[p]arties to an international armed conflict may not deport or forcibly transfer the civilian population of an occupied territory, in whole or in part, unless the security of the civilians involved or imperative military reasons so demand."[31]

It must be cautioned that the view that Article 49 in its entirety reflects customary law is not universally held. Most notably, Israel's Supreme Court has expressed a contrary view on multiple occasions, particularly concerning individual transfers.[32] In *Affo*, for example, it argued that the Convention's drafters intended Article 49's prohibition on deportation to address "mass deportations for purposes of extermination, mass population transfers for political or ethnic reasons or for forced labor."[33] To extend the rule further would mean that "from the commencement of military rule over the territory there is a total freeze on the removal of persons, and whosoever is found in a territory under military rule cannot be removed for any reason whatsoever, as long as the military rule continues."[34]

30. Legality of the Threat or Use of Nuclear Weapons, Advisory Opinion, 1996 I.C.J. 226, ¶ 79 (July 8).

31. 1 Customary International Humanitarian Law, r. 129(A) (Jean-Marie Henckaerts & Louise Doswald-Beck eds., 2005). Rule 129(b) deals with displacement during non-international armed conflict: "Parties to a non-international armed conflict may not order the displacement of the civilian population, in whole or in part, for reasons related to the conflict, unless the security of the civilians involved or imperative military reasons so demand." Additionally, Additional Protocol II to the Geneva Conventions prohibits the displacement of the civilian population in non-international armed conflict for parties to that instrument. Protocol Additional (II) to the Geneva Conventions of August 12, 1949, and Relating to the Protection of Victims of Non-international Armed Conflicts art. 17, June 8, 1977, 1125 U.N.T.S. 609 [hereinafter AP II].

32. *See* Yoram Dinstein, The International Law of Belligerent Occupation 174–84 (2d ed. 2019). For early treatment of the subject by Israeli courts, *see* Yoram Dinstein, *The Israeli Supreme Court and the Law of Belligerent Occupation: Deportations*, 23 Israel Yearbook on Human Rights 1 (1993).

33. HCJ 785/87 Affo et al. Commander of IDF Forces in the West Bank et al., Judgement, ¶ 28 (1988) (Isr.), *available at* https://hamoked.org/files/2011/280_eng.pdf https://hamoked.org/files/2011/280_eng.pdf.

34. *Id.*

Given the Vienna Convention on the Law of Treaties' requirement to look to the "ordinary meaning" of the text when interpreting a provision, the court's understanding is difficult to accept.[35] As Yoram Dinstein has observed, it "failed to notice that, in international law, the cardinal rule for any interpretation is the primacy of the text."[36]

Restatement of the rule against deportation is a common feature in the guidance States provide their armed forces. In the United States, for instance, the Department of Defense *Law of War Manual*, Army and Marine Corps *Commander's Handbook on the Law of Land Warfare*, and Navy, Marine Corps, and Coast Guard *Commander's Handbook on the Law of Naval Operations* all paraphrase Article 49.[37] Military manuals of other nations, such as the United Kingdom's *Manual of the Law of Armed Conflict*, do as well.[38] Concerning the current conflict, Ukraine's 2004 *International Humanitarian Law Manual* states "[i]t shall be prohibited to issue orders and instructions regarding forcible movement of civilian persons in connection with the armed conflict unless this is required by the considerations of their security."[39] The 2001 Russian Federation's *Regulations on the Application of International Humanitarian Law* similarly provide "[d]eportation of the civilian population from the occupied territory to the territory of another state shall be prohibited."[40]

The UN General Assembly and Security Council have often addressed displacement.[41] But as to deportation from occupied territory, the former has focused on the situation in areas Israel occupies. As an illustration, in 1981, the General Assembly condemned the "evacuation, deportation, expulsion, displacement and transfer of Arab inhabitants of the occupied territories and denial of

35. Vienna Convention on the Law of Treaties art. 31(1), May 23, 1969, 1155 U.N.T.S. 331.

36. Dinstein, *Belligerent Occupation*, *supra* note 32, at 178.

37. DoD Law of War Manual, *supra* note 29, at § 11.12.3; Department of the Army, FM 27-10, The Law of Land Warfare ¶ 6-52 (rev. ed. 2019); U.S. Navy, U.S. Marine Corps & U.S. Coast Guard, NWP 1-14M/MCTP 11-10B/COMDTPUB P5800.7A, The Commander's Handbook on the Law of Naval Operations ¶ 6.2.6.1 (2022).

38. United Kingdom Ministry of Defence, The Manual of the Law of Armed Conflict ¶ 11.55 (2004).

39. Ukraine Ministry of Defence, Manual on the Application of International Humanitarian Law Rules, § 1.4.16 (2004), *available at* https://ihl-databases.icrc.org/en/customary-ihl/v2/rule129. *See also* §1.8.5 ("Serious violations of international humanitarian law directed against people include . . . deportation . . . or unlawful movement of the population of occupied territory (both within or outside this territory)").

40. Russian Federation Ministry of Defence, Regulations on the Application of International Humanitarian Law by the Armed Forces of the Russian Federation, § 75 (2001), *available at* https://ihl-databases.icrc.org/en/customary-ihl/v2/rule129.

41. *See* compilation practice supporting Customary International Humanitarian Law study, r. 129, *available at* https://ihl-databases.icrc.org/en/customary-ihl/v2/rule129.

their right to return."[42] Similarly, a 2003 emergency special session dealing with East Jerusalem reaffirmed "the illegality of the deportation of any Palestinian by Israel, the occupying Power, and affirm[ed] its opposition to any such deportation." In the resolution, the General Assembly also reiterated "the need for respect, in all circumstances, of international humanitarian law, including the Geneva Convention relative to the Protection of Civilian Persons," and demanded "that Israel, the occupying Power, desist from any act of deportation."[43]

It is evident that Article 49 of Geneva Convention IV and its customary law counterpart apply to the actions of Russia in occupied Ukrainian territory.

2.1 Nuance in the Rule

Several nuances in the prohibition on deportation merit mention. As noted, it applies to protected persons taken from occupied territory, but nationals of the occupying power do not qualify as protected persons. Thus, the prohibition does not reach Russian nationals, many of whom are present in Ukraine. In this regard, the "passportization" (and purported naturalization) of nearly a million Ukrainians, especially from the Donbas region of eastern Ukraine, is highly questionable as a matter of law.[44] As Anne Peters has pointed out, any claim that their deportation does not violate international humanitarian law because of Russia's mass naturalization program would be badly flawed. Instead, the legal issue would be the voluntariness of their removal from occupied territory.[45]

Some of those deported from occupied territory are likely to have been dual Russian-Ukrainian nationals. In my estimation, they would enjoy the protection of the prohibition so long as their Ukrainian nationality is "dominant and effective."[46] This is the case for most of them, especially those who have lived in Ukraine for an extended period.

42. G.A. Res. 36/147C. ¶ 7 (Dec. 16, 1981). *See also* G.A. Res. 37/88 C (Dec. 9, 1982); G.A. Res. 38/79 D (Dec. 15, 1983); G.A. Res. 39/95 D (Dec. 14, 1984; G.A. Res. 40/161 D (Dec. 16, 1985).

43. G.A. Res. ES-10/12, pmbl. and ¶ 2 (Sept. 19, 2003).

44. On the passportization, *see* Fabian Burkhardt, *Russia's Passportization of the Donbas*, Stiftung Wissenschaft und Politik (Aug. 3, 2020), https://www.swp-berlin.org/10.18449/2020C41/.

45. Anne Peters, *Passportisation: Risks for International Law and Stability—Part I*, EJIL:Talk! (May 9, 2019).

46. This for example, was the standard applied by the Iran–United States Claims Tribunal to make the determination of jurisdiction. Dual Nationality, Iran v. United States, Iran–United States Claims Tribunal, Decision, Case No. A/18, Decision No. DEC 32-A18-FT, ¶ 29 (1984), *available at* https://jusmundi.com/en/document/decision/en-islamic-republic-of-iran-v-united-states-of-america-decision-decision-no-dec-32-a18-ft-friday-6th-april-1984. *See also*, *e.g.*, International Law Commission, Draft Articles on Diplomatic Protection, art. 7 (2006).

The other limitation of Article 49 is that the deportation must have been from occupied territory. Article 42 of the 1907 Hague Regulations sets forth the accepted conditions for the existence of occupation: "Territory is considered occupied when it is actually placed under the authority of the hostile army. The occupation extends only to the territory where such authority has been established and can be exercised."[47] This requirement is generally framed in terms of "effective control" over the area concerned. There is no question that the territory from which Ukrainian nationals are being deported is now occupied as a matter of law.[48] However, two points deserve mention in this regard.

First, the precise moment territory becomes occupied can be unclear. Nevertheless, in the case of Russia's actions, the roundup of civilians is evidence of the Russian forces' ability to administer at least the area from which they transported the individuals. This logic applies equally to situations where civilians might have fled from fighting (for instance, in Mariupol) into Russian-occupied territory before being moved to Russia. And even if the Russian forces were not quite at the point where they could exercise the requisite occupation authority, the "Pictet theory" could apply. It holds that during the invasion phase of hostilities, certain occupation law protections attach once enemy forces exercise effective control over individuals, even if not yet over territory.[49] The approach has not been universally embraced, but in the context of deportation, it comports with the rule's object and purpose.

Second, purported annexation has no legal bearing on an area's status as occupied; the rule prohibiting deportation continues to apply. As I have explained elsewhere, Russia's so-called annexations of Ukrainian territory are categorically without legal effect.[50] This is because international law does not recognize territorial acquisition resulting from an unlawful use of force. Thus, despite the purported annexation, the individuals concerned qualify as being moved from occupied territory into that of the occupying power.

A further nuance of the rule deals with the permanency of the deportation. Although framed in the context of international criminal law rather than international humanitarian law, the International Criminal Tribunal for the former Yugoslavia (ICTY) Appeals Chamber, in its *Stakić* judgment, found that deportation need not be, nor be intended to be, permanent.[51] No rationale exists for

47. 1907 Hague Regulations, *supra* note 18, art. 42.

48. *See* discussion at Geneva Academy, *Military Occupation of Ukraine by Russia*, RULAC, https://www.rulac.org/browse/conflicts/military-occupation-of-ukraine#collapse1accord (last visited Oct. 22, 2023).

49. *See* discussion in ICRC, Expert Meeting: Occupation and Other Forms of Administration of Foreign Territory 24–26 (2012).

50. Michael N. Schmitt, *Territorial Acquisition and Armed Conflict*, Articles of War (Aug. 29, 2023), https://lieber.westpoint.edu/territorial-acquisition-armed-conflict/.

51. Prosecutor v. Stakić, Case. No. IT-97-24-A, Appeal Judgment, ¶¶ 278, 307 (Int'l Crim. Trib. for the former Yugoslavia Mar. 22, 2006).

suggesting that the international humanitarian law prohibition, which involves the issue of whether there has been an internationally wrongful act rather than individual criminal responsibility, would be more limited. On the contrary, State responsibility standards are typically easier to breach than criminal law is to violate. Therefore, the fact that some deportees may have returned from Russia is of no consequence to the unlawfulness of their original deportation.

Also noteworthy is the question of voluntariness.[52] Article 49 textually prohibits "forcible" transfers. Since deportation is usually involuntary by nature, there was no need to add that adjective in Article 49. This begs the question of how coercive the deportation must be to violate the rule. In *Stakić*, the ICTY's Appeals Chamber found the threshold of coerciveness to be relatively low: "The term 'forced,' when used in reference to the crime of deportation, is not to be limited to physical force but includes the threat of force or coercion, such as that caused by fear of violence, duress, detention, psychological oppression or abuse of power against such person or persons or another person, or by taking advantage of a coercive environment."[53] There is no reason not to apply its international criminal law explication to the offense's international humanitarian law counterpart.

An interesting aspect of deportation is whether it can occur indirectly, so-called "constructive" deportation. Both the Iran-U.S. Claims Tribunal and the Eritrea-Ethiopia Claims Commission have dealt with the issue of constructive expulsion. The latter, citing the former, notes that there is a "high threshold" for constructive expulsion, one in which "those who leave a country must have experienced dire or threatening conditions so extreme as to leave no realistic alternative to departure." Further, "[t]hese conditions must result from actions or policies of the host government, or be clearly attributable to that government. . . . [T]he government's actions must have been taken with the intention of causing the aliens to depart."[54]

This seems a sensible approach that can be applied by analogy to deportation in violation of Article 49. For example, the violation could occur when an occupying power starves the population, intending to force it to move from occupied territory into another country. However, open questions remain. For instance, what of a case where residents of an occupied area flee across a border, but the occupying power refuses to allow them to return? In my view, this too would amount to wrongful deportation.[55]

52. Note that Article 48 of GC IV, *supra* note 24, allows protected persons who are not nationals of the State whose territory is occupied to leave, although the departure can be prevented if contrary to the interests of the occupying power. *See also* Dinstein, *Belligerent Occupation*, *supra* note 32, at 174.

53. *Stakić*, *supra* note 51, at ¶ 281.

54. Partial Award: Civilians Claims, Ethiopia's Claim 5 (Eth.-Erit.), ¶ 126, 44 I.L.M. 630 (2004).

55. *See, e.g.*, Prosecutor v. Prlić et al., Case No. IT-04-74, Appeals Chamber Judgment, ¶ 493 (Int'l Crim. Trib. for the former Yugoslavia Nov. 29, 2017), finding forcible transfer where the houses of individuals were burned to keep them from returning. *See also* Prosecutor v. Mladić,

Considering, inter alia, the filtration camps practice and a child's lack of legal capacity, it is self-evident that most of the deportations from occupied Ukraine were nonconsensual. That said, recall Russia's claims that the civilians in question requested transportation to Russia. If true for any of them, or if children were sent to Russia at the request of their families, their movement to Russia would not qualify as unlawful deportation.

2.2 The Exceptions

Article 49(1) prohibits deportations "regardless of their motives." However, it also provides in Paragraph 2 that "the Occupying Power may undertake total or partial evacuation of a given area if the security of the population or imperative military reasons so demand." Thus, the rule has two exceptions, both of which may result in evacuation, a measure taken in the interest of the protected persons themselves.

The first applies when the movement of the individuals is for their own good. The ICRC's 1958 Commentary to Article 49 explains, "If therefore an area is in danger as a result of military operations or is liable to be subjected to intense bombing, the Occupying Power has the right and . . . the duty of evacuating it partially or wholly, by placing the inhabitants in places of refuge."[56] The security of the population refers to the security of those individuals who are to be evacuated, not others.

The second exception is based on the existence of "imperative military necessity."[57] The Commentary to the article offers the example of "the presence of protected persons in an area hamper[ing] military operations."[58] For instance, civilians in the vicinity of a force's critical maneuver might need to be moved. It must be cautioned that the adjective "imperative" sets a high standard. Mere

57. *See generally* Emma Brandon, *Grave Breaches and Justifications: The War Crime of Forcible Transfer or Deportation of Civilians and the Exception for Evacuations for Imperative Military Reasons*, 6 OSLO LAW REVIEW 107 (2019).

58. 1958 Geneva Convention IV Commentary, *supra* note 19, at 280. An interesting case in this regard came before the U.S. Military Tribunal at Nuremberg in 1948. General Lothar Rendulic was accused of violating Article 23(g) of the 1907 Hague Regulations, *supra* note 18, which prohibits the destruction or seizure of enemy property "unless such destruction or seizure be imperatively demanded by the necessities of war." As German forces were retreating in Norway, he engaged in scorched earth tactics. These tactics included the involuntary evacuation of Indigenous people in the north of the country. The tribunal found that the decision was justified by his conclusion that there was an "urgent military necessity" to do so, even though he was mistaken. U.S. Military Tribunal at Nuremberg, *In re List* (Hostages Trial), at 69–70, *available at* https://www.legal-tools.org/doc/b62664/pdf.

Case No. IT-09-92, Trial Chamber Judgment, ¶¶ 3167–70 (Int'l Crim. Trib. for the former Yugoslavia Nov. 22, 2017).

56. 1958 Geneva Convention IV Commentary, *supra* note 19, at 280.

military convenience or even good sense does not suffice. Imperative military necessity means that an operation may fail, or forces be at risk, if the action is not taken. It is hard to imagine how Russia could justify the deportation of Ukrainian nationals on this basis.

Imperative military necessity does not encompass security threats. Article 78 deals with that situation: "If the Occupying Power considers it necessary, for imperative reasons of security, to take safety measures concerning protected persons, it may, at the most, subject them to assigned residence or to internment."[59] As explained in the 1958 Commentary to the article, "Article 78 relates to people who have not been guilty of any infringement of the penal provisions enacted by the Occupying Power, but that Power may, for reasons of its own, consider them dangerous to its security and is consequently entitled to restrict their freedom of action."[60] There being no general security exception in Article 49, Article 78 actions may not involve movement from occupied territory into other countries.

A further question is whether the occupying power may deport individuals who are in the occupied territory unlawfully (e.g., illegal aliens), enter it clandestinely following occupation, or whose visas have expired. There are two views. By the first, the "regardless of their motive" text in Article 49(1) is categorical. Even though Article 64 of Geneva Convention IV requires an occupying power to keep the penal laws of the occupied territory in force, an exception applies when doing so would be an "obstacle to the application of the present Convention."[61] Thus, Article 49 remains in effect despite Article 64. Proponents would also point to Article 4's definition of "protected persons" as those who "find themselves" in the hands of a party to the conflict "at a given moment and in any manner whatsoever" as supportive of a broad application of Article 49.

In my opinion, those who unlawfully entered the area prior to occupation and qualify as protected persons enjoy the full protection of Article 49. Those who entered clandestinely after the commencement of occupation do not if their activities are inconsistent with the maintenance of order, a legal obligation, by the occupying power. Yoram Dinstein offers the compelling example of infiltrators. He points out that "their non-entitlement to protection is of particular significance in the context of an occupied territory like Iraq, where the ranks of local saboteurs were swollen by foreigners who had infiltrated Iraq unlawfully in order to take part in a *jihad* against infidel Occupying Powers."[62] And, as noted later, the war crime of deportation only encompasses deporting those who are lawfully present in occupied territory.[63] Nevertheless, in my view, the mere unlawfulness

59. GC IV, *supra* note 24, art. 78.

60. 1958 Geneva Convention IV Commentary, *supra* note 19, at 368.

61. GC IV, *supra* note 19, art. 64. *See also* 1907 Hague Regulations, *supra* note 18, art. 43.

62. Dinstein, *Belligerent Occupation*, *supra* note 32, at 181.

63. International Criminal Court, Elements of Crimes, Article 7(1)(d)4 (2013), *available at* https://www.icc-cpi.int/sites/default/files/Publications/Elements-of-Crimes.pdf.

of presence under the applicable domestic law governing the occupied territory, as in the case of civilians fleeing violence elsewhere or those overstaying a visa, should not, standing alone, take them beyond the reach of Article 49.

As noted, evacuation is a possible response to the situations addressed in the exceptions. In this regard, it is essential to caution that even when evacuations are for the safety of the individuals concerned or conducted for reasons of imperative military necessity, Article 49(2) provides that "[s]uch evacuations may not involve the displacement of protected persons outside the bounds of the occupied territory except when for material reasons it is impossible to avoid such displacement."[64] Unfortunately, the Commentary to the article does not explain what is meant by "material." The term suggests an impossibility to do otherwise. Article 49(2) also requires those who have been evacuated to "be transferred back to their homes as soon as hostilities in the area in question have ceased."

In the event of evacuation, Article 49(3) requires that the occupying power "to the greatest practicable extent," ensure that "proper accommodation is provided to receive the protected persons, that the removals are effected in satisfactory conditions of hygiene, health, safety and nutrition, and that members of the same family are not separated." It must also inform the protecting power "of any transfers and evacuations as soon as they have taken place."[65]

Finally, Article 49(5) prohibits those affected from being detained "in an area particularly exposed to the dangers of war unless the security of the population or imperative military reasons so demand." According to the 1958 Commentary, the term "detention" refers to restrictions on protected persons' movement and was included to account for certain situations in World War II.[66]

Given the scale and scope of the displacement, the Russian control of large areas of Ukraine and the fact that many of those affected have not been returned to Ukrainian territory, the only reasonable conclusion is that the deportations from occupied Ukrainian territory, except for Russian nationals or nationals of States maintaining diplomatic ties to Russia, were, and remain, unlawful.

2.3 The Case of Children

The deportation of children raises additional international humanitarian law concerns. It has been reported that Russian authorities have separated children from their parents, abducted children from Ukrainian orphanages and hospitals, and put some children up for adoption in Russia. Indeed, Russia modified its law to ease the adoption process and facilitate the children's acquisition of Russian

64. *Id.*, art. 49(2).

65. *Id.*, art. 49(4). *See also* DoD Law of War Manual, *supra* note 29, § 11.12.3.1; Army and Marine Corps Commander's Handbook on the Law of Land Warfare, *supra* note 37, ¶¶ 6-72, 6-73; U.K. Manual on the Law of Armed Conflict, *supra* note 38, at ¶ 11.55.

66. 1958 Geneva Convention Commentary, *supra* note 19, at 282–83.

nationality.[67] Of course, any consent to the removal of children by parents or legal guardians would have to be consensual. Such consent must be knowing. For instance, the Russian practice of taking Ukrainian children to a "summer camp" that turns out to be a re-education camp is nonconsensual. It would be subject to the prohibitions described later.[68]

Children, like other civilians in occupied territory, are protected persons. Thus, the same prohibitions and restrictions outlined in the preceding apply to them. However, they enjoy additional protections under international humanitarian law and international criminal law. In this regard, the 1974 UN Declaration on the Protection of Women and Children in Emergency and Armed Conflict observes, "[a]ll forms of repression and cruel and inhuman treatment of women and children, including . . . forcible eviction, committed by belligerents in the course of military operations or in occupied territories shall be considered criminal."[69]

As noted, though, evacuation to another country from occupied territory is, in exceptional circumstances, permissible. In such cases, and as noted previously, Article 49 requires the occupying power undertaking the evacuation to ensure "that members of the same family are not separated."[70] The theme of family unity is reflected throughout Geneva Convention IV and in Additional Protocol I.[71]

Nevertheless, the sad reality is that war often results in children being orphaned or otherwise separated from their parents. International humanitarian law accounts for this circumstance. Article 24 of Geneva Convention IV provides that parties to the conflict must "take the necessary measures to ensure that children under 15, who are orphaned or are separated from their families as a result of war, are not left to their own resources, and that their maintenance, the exercise of their religion and their education are facilitated in all circumstances."[72] In such cases, the parties "shall facilitate the reception of such children in a *neutral* country for the duration of the conflict with the consent of the Protecting Power,

67. Agence France-Presse in Kyiv, *Kyiv Accuses Moscow of Mass Abduction of Ukrainian Children*, The Guardian (Aug. 23, 2022);Michael Schnell, *Ukraine: Deported Children Facing Threat of "Illegal Adoption" in Russia*, The Hill (Apr. 14, 2022); Carlotta Gall, Oleksandr Chubko, & Cora Engelbrecht, *"Stolen" Children in Ukraine, Putin's Decree Authorizing Adoption*, N.Y. Times (May 31, 2022), https://www.nytimes.com/2024/06/02/world/europe/ukraine-children-russia-war.html.

68. Edith M. Lederer, *US Sanctions 11 Russians and 2 Re-education Facilities Involved in Forced Transfer of Ukrainian Kids*, Associated Press (Aug. 24, 2023), https://apnews.com/article/russia-ukraine-children-deported-us-sanctions-de8114daaba07690d88a6f8444716376.

69. Declaration on the Protection of Women and Children in Emergency and Armed Conflict, ¶ 5, G.A. Res. 3318, U.N. Doc. A/9631 (Dec. 14, 1974).

70. GC IV, *supra* note 24, art. 49.

71. *Id.*, arts. 25, 26, 27, and 82; AP I, *supra* note 28, art. 78.

72. GC IV, *supra* note 24, art. 24.

if any." There is no authority to take such children to the occupying power's territory, and certainly none allowing them to be put up for adoption there, as Russia has done.

To further protect children, Article 50 of the instrument also provides that an occupying power shall not change children's "personal status." The ICRC's 1958 Commentary on the article confirms this applies to changes in nationality.[73] Thus, granting Russian nationality to any child unlawfully taken from occupied Ukraine is, on its face, a clear violation.

Article 78(1) of Additional Protocol I to the 1949 Geneva Conventions, to which Russia and Ukraine are parties, provides an additional ground for characterizing Russia's deportation of children as unlawful:

> No Party to the conflict shall arrange for the evacuation of children, other than its own nationals, to a foreign country except for a temporary evacuation where compelling reasons of the health or medical treatment of the children or, except in occupied territory, their safety, so require. Where the parents or legal guardians can be found, their written consent to such evacuation is required. If these persons cannot be found, the written consent to such evacuation of the persons who by law or custom are primarily responsible for the care of the children is required. Any such evacuation shall be supervised by the Protecting Power in agreement with the Parties concerned, namely, the Party arranging for the evacuation, the Party receiving the children and any Parties whose nationals are being evacuated.[74]

Note that the need for medical care or other treatment related to a child's health is the only situation allowing for the evacuation of children from occupied territory. The 1987 ICRC Commentary to the article emphasizes that children concerned still benefit from Geneva Convention IV, Article 49. It also explains that "the limitation to evacuation for compelling reasons of health or medical treatment [and *not* for reasons of safety] where the evacuation is to be from occupied territory reflects a deep-seated concern among many representatives in the Committee that the dangers of Occupying Powers abusing their discretion are greater than the dangers of prohibiting evácuation for reasons of safety."[75] That Russia has violated Article 87 is apparent because it did not deport the children for health reasons. Even if it had, Russian authorities did not secure the requisite permissions.

73. 1958 Geneva Convention Commentary, *supra* note 19, at 288.

74. AP I, *supra* note 28, art. 78(1).

75. Commentary on the Additional Protocols of 8 June 1977 to the Geneva Conventions of 12 August 1949, ¶ 3227 (Yves Sandoz, Christophe Swinarski, & Bruno Zimmermann eds., 1987).

2.4 Other Internationally Wrongful Acts

Finally, Russia has committed internationally wrongful acts other than international humanitarian law violations, especially with respect to its obligation to respect human rights. As an occupying power, Russia owes human rights obligations to residents of occupied Ukraine due to its "effective control" over the area and its residents. For instance, concerning deportation in general, Protocol 4 to the European Convention on Human Rights provides that "[n]o one shall be expelled, by means either of an individual or of a collective measure, from the territory of the State of which he is a national."[76] The fact that Russia has been expelled from the Council of Europe and the European Court of Human Rights has accordingly resulted in the suspension of the Court's examination of petitions against Russia for acts or omissions occurring after September 16, 2022, an unfortunate obstacle to the instrument's enforcement.[77] The UN Convention on the Rights of the Child, to which Russia is party, also bears on Russia's malevolent conduct.[78]

3. INTERNATIONAL CRIMINAL LAW

Russia's actions breach a *State*'s obligation to refrain from deportation. They are internationally wrongful acts. However, those involved may also bear *individual* responsibility under international criminal law for deportation,[79] which has the same meaning as in international humanitarian law.[80]

Geneva Convention IV, Article 147, confirms that "unlawful deportation or transfer . . . of a protected person" is a grave breach of the Convention and thus subject to universal jurisdiction.[81] Article 85(4)(a) of the 1977 Additional

76. Protocol 4 to the European Convention for the Protection of Human Rights and Fundamental Freedoms, Securing Certain Rights and Freedoms Other than Those Already Included in the Convention and the First Protocol Thereto, art. 3, E.T.S. No. 46 (Sept. 16, 1963). *See also* American Convention on Human Rights, art. 22(5); African Union Convention for the Protection and Assistance of Internally Displaced Persons in Africa, arts. 3(1)(a), 4(4)(b), (c), (h).

77. Council of Europe, *Russia Ceases to Be a Party to the European Convention on Human* Rights (Sept. 16, 2022), *available at* https://www.coe.int/en/web/portal/-/russia-ceases-to-be-party-to-the-european-convention-on-human-rights.

78. Convention on the Rights of the Child, G.A. Res. 44/25 (1989). *See also* Alison Bisset, *Russia's Forcible Transfer of Children*, Articles of War (Oct. 5, 2022).

79. *See also* Vincent Chetail, *Is There Any Blood on My Hands: Deportation as a Crime of International Law*, 29 Leiden Journal of International Law 917 (2016).

80. *See, e.g.*, Prosecutor v. Krstić, Case No. IT-98-33, Judgment, ¶ 521 (Int'l Crim. Trib. for the former Yugoslavia Aug. 2, 2001).

81. GC IV, *supra* note 24, art. 147.

Protocol I to the 1949 Geneva Conventions restates that characterization.[82] As a grave breach, States party to the Geneva Conventions must enact legislation to punish the offenses, search for those who have allegedly committed them, and bring offenders before their courts or extradite them.[83] The obligations extend to all States. Of particular significance is that, as a crime of universal jurisdiction, any State may prosecute deportation, even absent any nexus to the offense.

Numerous international criminal tribunals have exercised subject matter jurisdiction over deportation. Following World War II, Article 6(b) of the 1945 Charter of the International Military Tribunal at Nuremberg included "deportation to slave labour or for any other purpose of civilian population of or in occupied territory" in its list of war crimes, while Article 6(c) recognized deportation as a crime against humanity whether "before or during the war."[84] Similarly, the Charter of the International Military Tribunal for the Far East characterized deportation as a crime against humanity,[85] and Allied Control Council Law No. 10 included the offense as a war crime and a crime against humanity.[86] In its judgment, the International Military Tribunal at Nuremberg noted that "[w]hole populations were deported to Germany for the purposes of slave labor on defence works, armament production and similar tasks connected with the war effort."[87] The tribunal convicted multiple defendants of war crimes or crimes against humanity based partly on their participation in deportation. For example, Hans Frank, the Governor General of Occupied Poland, was responsible for the deportation of nearly a million Poles. For this and other crimes, such as the extermination of over three million Jews, the tribunal convicted him of war crimes and crimes against humanity.[88] And it convicted Baldur von Schirach of crimes against humanity for his participation in the deportation of "tens of thousands

82. AP I, *supra* note 28, art. 85(4). *See also* DoD LAW OF WAR MANUAL, *supra* note 29, § 11.12.3.

83. Geneva Convention IV, *supra* note 24, art. 146; Additional Protocol I, *supra* note 28, art. 85(1).

84. Charter of the International Military Tribunal for Germany, annexed to the London Agreement, arts. 6(b) and 6(c) (Aug. 8, 1945), *available at* https://www.un.org/en/genocideprevention/documents/atrocity-crimes/Doc.2_Charter%20of%20IMT%201945.pdf.

85. Charter of the International Military Tribunal for the Far East, approved by an Executive Order, General Douglas MacArthur, Supreme Commander for the Allied Powers in Japan, art. 5(c) (Jan. 19, 1946), *available at* https://www.un.org/en/genocideprevention/documents/atrocity-crimes/Doc.3_1946%20Tokyo%20Charter.pdf.

86. Allied Control Council Law No. 10, Punishment of Persons Guilty of War Crimes, Crimes against Peace and against Humanity, enacted by the Allied Control Council of Germany, art. II (Dec. 20, 1945), *available at* https://www.legal-tools.org/doc/ffda62/pdf/.

87. The Trial of German Major War Criminals at Nuremberg, Judgment of Oct. 1, 1946, 1, 450, *available at* https://crimeofaggression.info/documents/6/1946_Nuremberg_Judgement.pdf.

88. *Id.* at 116.

upon tens of thousands" of Jews from Vienna to free up housing and "contribute to European culture."[89]

Tribunals run by the individual occupying powers followed suit. In the case of *U.S. v. Milch* before the U.S. Military Tribunal, for instance, Field Marshall Milch, who was also a member of the Central Planning Board under Albert Speer, was charged, inter alia, with war crimes and crimes against humanity based on his involvement in the deportation of slave labor from countries occupied by German forces. He was found guilty and sentenced to life (later commuted to fifteen years).[90]

In the case, Judge Fitzroy Phillips' concurring opinion developed the notion of deportation. He observed: "International Law has enunciated certain conditions under which the fact of deportation of civilians from one nation to another during times of war becomes a crime." The conditions were satisfied when "the transfer is carried out without a legal title, as in the case where people are deported from a country occupied by an invader while the occupied enemy still has an army in the field and is still resisting . . . ." Judge Phillips explained, "[t]he rationale of this rule lies in the supposition that the occupying power has temporarily prevented the rightful sovereign from exercising its power over its citizens."[91] His characterization was subsequently cited with approval in the well-known *Krupp* case, which also dealt with the deportation for slave labor of persons from occupied territory.[92] Other U.S. Military Tribunal cases addressing deportation under Control Council Law No. 10 include *Krauch* (the I.G. Farben Trial), *List* (the Hostages Trial), and *Von Leeb* (the High Command Trial).[93]

Following on the heels of those trials, the International Law Commission confirmed in its 1950 Nuremberg Principles that "deportation to slave-labour or for any other purpose of civilian population of or in occupied territory" is a war crime and "deportation and other inhuman acts done against any civilian population" can amount to a crime against humanity.[94] The Commission returned to the matter in its 1996 Draft Code of Crimes against the Peace and Security

89. *Id.* at 513.

90. United States v. Milch, Judgement, 1946–1947, VII Law Reports of Trials of War Criminals 27, United Nations War Crimes Commission (1948).

91. *Id.* at 45, Concurring Opinion of Judge Phillips.

92. United States v. Krupp et al., Judgment, 1947–1948, X Law Reports of Trials of War Criminals 69, 144, United Nations War Crimes Commission (1949).

93. United States v. Krauch (the I.G. Farben Case), 8 Trials of War Criminals before the Nuremberg Military Tribunals Under Control Council Law No. 10 (1948); United States v. List et al. (the Hostage Case), 11 Trials of War Criminals before the Nuremberg Military Tribunals Under Control Council Law No. 10, at 759 (1950); United States v. von Leeb et al. (the High Command Case), 10 Trials of War Criminals before the Nuremberg Military Tribunals Under Control Council Law No. 10 (1951).

94. Principles of International Law Recognized in the Charter of the Nuremberg Tribunal and in the Judgment of the Tribunal, adopted by the International Law Commission, Principles VI(b) and (c), U.N. Doc. A/1316 (1950).

of Mankind, where it is noted that "deportation or transfer . . . of protected persons" is a war crime and "arbitrary deportation or forcible transfer of population" can qualify as a crime against humanity.[95] In its Commentary on the latter, the Commission explained that "[t]he term 'arbitrary' is used to exclude the acts when committed for legitimate reasons, such as public health or wellbeing, in a manner consistent with international law."[96]

Statutes of more recent international criminal tribunals likewise encompass deportation. As to the ICC, Article 7(1)(d) of the Rome Statute treats "[d]eportation or forcible transfer of the population" as a crime against humanity.[97] There are five elements to the offense:

1. The perpetrator deported or forcibly transferred, without grounds permitted under international law, one or more persons to another State or location, by expulsion or other coercive acts.
2. Such person or persons were lawfully present in the area from which they were so deported or transferred.
3. The perpetrator was aware of the factual circumstances that established the lawfulness of such presence.
4. The conduct was committed as part of a widespread or systematic attack directed against a civilian population.
5. The perpetrator knew that the conduct was part of or intended the conduct to be part of a widespread or systematic attack directed against a civilian population.[98]

The Statute lists deportation among war crimes on two bases. First, Article 8(2)(a)(vii) confirms that unlawful deportation is a "grave breach" of the Geneva Conventions and, thus, a war crime within its jurisdiction.[99] It then characterizes, in Article 8(2)(b)(viii), the "deportation or transfer of all or parts of the population of the occupied territory within or outside this territory" as among the "[o]ther serious violations of the laws and customs applicable in international

95. Draft Code of Crimes against the Peace and Security of Mankind, adopted by the International Law Commission, arts. 20(a)(vii) and 18(g), U.N. Doc. A/51/10 (1996). An earlier version labeled "deportation or transfer of the civilian population" as an "exceptionally serious war crime." Draft Code of Crimes against the Peace and Security of Mankind, adopted by the International Law Commission, art. 22(2)(a), U.N. Doc. A/46/10 (1991).

96. *Draft Code of Crimes against the Peace and Security of Mankind with Commentaries*, II Yearbook of the International Law Commission 49, *available at* https://legal.un.org/ilc/texts/instruments/english/commentaries/7_4_1996.pdf.

97. Rome Statute of the International Criminal Court art. 7(1)(d), July 17, 1998, 2187 U.N.T.S. 90.

98. International Criminal Court, Elements of Crimes, *supra* note 64, at 4.

99. Rome Statute, *supra* note 97, art. 8(2)(a)(vii).

armed conflict, within the established framework of international law," that is, as a violation of customary international law.[100]

In extreme cases, the forcible transfer of children from the group in question to another "committed with the intent to destroy, in whole or in part, a national . . . group" amounts to genocide, as defined by the Convention on the Punishment of the Crime of Genocide.[101] The offense appears in the Rome Statute's genocide provision, Article 6.[102] As one scholar has observed, "When considered against the backdrop of Russian rhetoric on the destruction of the Ukrainian people, the possibility of genocide must be considered."[103]

Other tribunals take the same general approach. For instance, the ICTY treats deportation as a war crime and, in qualifying circumstances, a crime against humanity.[104] Indeed, it is this international tribunal that has provided the most jurisprudence on deportation.

Perhaps best known is the trial of Slobodan Milošević, former President of the Federal Republic of Yugoslavia and of Serbia, who died during his trial. Although he escaped justice, the tribunal had examined the issue of deportation in its 2004 Decision on Motion for Judgment of Acquittal.[105] It stated that three elements must be satisfied to find deportation. First, the individual must be displaced across a border. Although this might appear limiting, the tribunal observed, "there is no detriment to a victim if the crime of deportation is confined to transfer across borders, because if it is established that he has not been so transferred, then he is protected by the prohibition against forcible transfer, which applies to involuntary movements within national borders."[106] Second, the movement must be involuntary. For the tribunal, "[t]he determination as to whether a transferred person had a 'real choice' has to be made in the context of all the relevant circumstances and on a case by case basis."[107] Third, for the offense to lie, "there must be evidence of

100. *Id.*, art. 8(2)(b)(viii). Article 8(2)(e)(viii) sets forth the offense in non-international armed conflict.

101. Convention on the Prevention and Punishment of the Crime of Genocide art. II, Dec. 9, 1948, U.N.T.S. 277.

102. Rome Statute, *supra* note 97, art. 6(e).

103. Bisset, *supra* note 78.

104. Statute of the International Criminal Tribunal for the former Yugoslavia arts. 2(g) and 5(d), S.C. Res. 827 (May 25, 1993). The International Criminal Tribunal for Rwanda's statute, provides that "deportation, when committed as part of a widespread and systematic attack against any civilian population on national, political, ethnic, racial or religious grounds, constitutes a crime against humanity." Statute of the International Criminal Tribunal for Rwanda art. 3(d), S.C. Res. 955 annex (Nov. 8, 1994).

105. Prosecutor v. Milošević, Case No. IT-02-54-T, Decision on Motion for Judgment of Acquittal (Int'l Crim. Trib. for the former Yugoslavia June 16, 2004).

106. *Id.* at ¶ 69.

107. *Id.* at ¶ 76.

an intent to transfer the victim from his home or community; it must be established that the perpetrator either directly intended that the victim would leave or that it was reasonably foreseeable that this would occur as a consequence of his action."[108]

Also of note is the ICTY's *Stakić* case mentioned earlier, which deconstructed deportation as a crime against humanity in its 2006 Appeals Chamber judgment. There, it held "that the actus reus (material element) of deportation is the forced displacement of persons by expulsion or other forms of coercion from the area in which they are lawfully present, across a de jure state border or, in certain circumstances, a de facto border, without grounds permitted under international law."[109] The finding as to a de facto border, which departed from that in *Milošević*, was unique in the tribunal's jurisprudence. And regarding mens rea, the chamber found that there need be no intention to move the individual or group out of occupied territory permanently.[110]

Perhaps of greatest significance with regard to potential Russian claims of being motivated by a desire to enhance the security of the deported individuals is its finding that "displacement for humanitarian reasons is justifiable in certain situations [but] the Appeals Chamber agrees with the Prosecution that it is not justifiable where the humanitarian crisis that caused the displacement is itself the result of the accused's own unlawful activity."[111] Given the nature, scale, and scope of the deportations into Russia from occupied Ukraine following its unlawful use of force, there is little doubt that numerous Russians, including President Vladimir Putin, have committed war crimes and crimes against humanity.

Finally, like many other countries, Russia and Ukraine have criminalized deportation in their domestic law. Russia's Criminal Code includes as offenses the "deportation of the civilian populations" and "forcible transfer of children" as part of a campaign of genocide.[112] In Ukraine, deportation of the civilian population for the purpose of forced labor violates its Criminal Code. Like Russia, Ukraine also criminalizes the transfer of children as an act of genocide.[113] The Russians involved are subject to the domestic jurisdiction of both countries for their actions.

108. *Id.* at ¶ 78.

109. *Stakić*, *supra* note 51, at ¶ 278.

110. *Id.* This was confirmed by an ICTY Trial Chamber in *Krajišnik*, which also emphasized that displacement of civilians during armed conflict is allowed only based on their security or for imperative military reasons. According to the tribunal, in such cases "the displacement is temporary and must be carried out in such a manner as to ensure that displaced persons are returned to their homes as soon as the situation allows." Prosecutor v. Krajišnik, Case No. IT-00-39-T, ICTY, Judgment, ¶ 725 (Int'l Crim. Trib. for the former Yugoslavia Sept. 27, 2006).

111. *Stakić*, *supra* note 51, ¶ 287.

112. Russian Federation, Criminal Code, arts. 356(1) and 357 (1996), *available at* https://ihl-databases.icrc.org/en/customary-ihl/v2/rule129.

113. Ukraine, Criminal Code, arts. 438(1) and 442 (2001), *available at* https://ihl-databases.icrc.org/en/customary-ihl/v2/rule129.

4. CONCLUDING THOUGHTS

The legal reality addressed in this chapter is not complicated. An occupying power is prohibited under treaty and customary international humanitarian law from deporting protected persons residing in occupied territory into another country. If it does, it has committed an "internationally wrongful act" for which it is responsible. Moreover, depending on their role, those who participated in the actions may have committed a war crime and, in certain circumstances, a crime against humanity. The condemnable actions of Russia will hopefully lead to the enforcement of its State responsibility for the harm caused and the prosecution of those involved in international and domestic courts.

10

The Law and Modern Challenges Related to the Prohibition Against Forced Conscription

W. CASEY BIGGERSTAFF*

1. INTRODUCTION

Russia has systematically engaged in campaigns to recruit male residents into its armed forces since its occupation of Crimea in 2014.[1] According to UN and other reports, Russian efforts have resulted in the enlistment of up to 24,000 Crimean men.[2] Similar drives have been documented in the self-declared republics in

* Lieutenant Colonel W. Casey Biggerstaff is an Academy Professor in the Department of Law and Philosophy at the United States Military Academy. The thoughts and opinions expressed are his and not necessarily those of the U.S. government or its agencies.

1. Office of the United Nations High Commissioner for Human Rights, Report on the Human Rights Situation in Ukraine: 16 May to 15 August 2019, at 24 (2019) [hereinafter 2019 OHCHR Report], https://www.ohchr.org/en/documents/country-reports/report-human-rights-situation-ukraine-16-november-2019-15-february-2020; Office of the United Nations High Commissioner for Human Rights, Report on the Human Rights Situation in Ukraine: 1 February to 31 May 2022, at 25 (2022) [hereinafter 2022 OHCHR Report], https://www.ohchr.org/en/documents/country-reports/report-human-rights-situation-ukraine-1-february-31-july-2022; James S. Gilmore III, U.S. Ambassador to the Organization for Security and Cooperation in Europe, Remarks Before the Permanent Council: Russia's Illegal Conscription in Crimea in Violation of the Norms of International Law (May 21, 2020) (transcript available at https://osce.usmission.gov/on-illegal-conscription-in-crimea-in-violation-of-international-law/).

2. 2019 OHCHR Report, *supra* note 1, at 24; Gilmore, *supra* note 1.

W. Casey Biggerstaff, *The Law and Modern Challenges Related to the Prohibition Against Forced Conscription*
In: *Civilian Protection in Armed Conflict*. Edited by: Jelena Pejic and Captain Margaret Kotlik,
Oxford University Press. © W. Casey Biggerstaff 2025. DOI: 10.1093/oso/9780197793176.003.0010

Luhansk and Donetsk in the wake of Russia's renewed invasion of Ukraine in 2022.[3] The Ukrainian government alleges that approximately 55,000 to 60,000 residents from territories occupied by Russia have been inducted into Russia's armed forces over the past two years.[4]

Some Ukrainians have enlisted willingly.[5] The majority, however, have only done so due to coercive Russian tactics. In one media report, for example, officials forcibly dragged a Ukrainian passport holder from the Donbas to a local enlistment office.[6] Similar incidents have led many Ukrainian men of military age to attempt to flee or go into hiding. Russian soldiers have reportedly also prevented men between the ages of 18 and 35 from leaving occupied territories.[7] Those caught evading Russian draft orders are subject to criminal penalties, including confinement for up to two years in a Russian prison.[8]

Russia's recruiting methods beg the question of whether, and if so how, they violate international humanitarian law's prohibition against forced conscription.[9] The UN Office of the High Commissioner for Human Rights (OHCHR), for example, has admonished that "[a]s an occupying Power, the Russian Federation must comply with international humanitarian law prohibiting the compulsion of protected persons to serve in its armed or auxiliary forces."[10] Human Rights Watch has similarly claimed that "[i]nternational humanitarian law

3. 2022 OHCHR Report, *supra* note 1, at 25; *Crimea: Conscription Violates International Law*, Human Rights Watch (Nov. 1, 2019), https://www.hrw.org/news/2019/11/01/crimea-conscription-violates-international-law.

4. *HUR Reports Forcible Mobilization of 60,000 Residents of the Occupied Territories into Russian Army*, Kyiv Post (Aug. 1, 2023), https://www.kyivpost.com/post/20091.

5. Igor Burdyga & Regina Gimalova, *Ukraine Separatists Draft Anyone They Can*, Deutsche Welle (Apr. 27, 2022), https://www.dw.com/en/how-ukraine-separatists-are-mass-conscripting-anyone-of-fighting-age/a-61608760.

6. Peter Beaumont & Artem Mazhulin, *"They Hunt Us Like Stray Cats": Pro-Russia Separatists Step Up Forced Conscription as Losses Mount*, The Guardian (July 20, 2022), https://www.theguardian.com/world/2022/jul/20/pro-russian-separatists-step-up-forced-conscription-as-losses-mount.

7. Isobel Koshiw, *Conscription Fears as Young Ukrainian Men Stopped from Leaving Occupied Areas*, The Guardian (Sept. 27, 2022), https://www.theguardian.com/world/2022/sep/27/conscription-fears-young-ukrainian-men-stopped-leaving-occupied-areas-russian-soldiers-crossing-point; Burdyga & Gimalova, *supra* note 5.

8. 2019 OHCHR Report, *supra* note 1, at 24. As of 2019, at least 29 male residents of Crimea had been found guilty of draft evasion, most of whom received fines. *Id.* at 24–25; Human Rights Watch, *supra* note 1.

9. Depending on the context, conscription, enlistment, and recruitment may have distinct meanings. As used in this chapter, conscription refers to compulsory military service. Unless the text specifies otherwise, enlistment and recruitment refer generally to the voluntary or involuntary enrollment of an individual into the armed forces.

10. 2019 OHCHR Report, *supra* note 1, at 25.

explicitly forbids Russia from compelling Crimean residents to serve in its armed forces."[11] And the United States has gone as far as explicitly accusing Russia before the Permanent Council of the Organization for Security and Cooperation in Europe (OSCE) of committing a grave breach of the 1949 Geneva Conventions, taking care to specify that the judicial enforcement of Russian conscription laws constitutes the prohibited force or coercion at issue.[12]

Russia's actions are not a new occurrence in armed conflict. During World War II, for instance, the Third Reich conscripted thousands of foreign nationals into the Waffen Schutzstaffel (SS).[13] Throughout the same conflict, prisoners of war, likely seeking better treatment and conditions, filled the ranks of both German and Soviet units.[14] More recently, following Iraq's invasion and occupation of Kuwait, Iraq compelled Kuwaiti and other foreign nationals to serve in its armed forces.[15] Russia's violations are, in sum, simply the latest example in the prohibition's lengthy history.

This chapter outlines the prohibition against forced conscription and how it protects persons during international armed conflict, keeping in mind the context of the Russia-Ukraine war. It begins by surveying the relevant treaty provisions that comprise the prohibition and outlining their respective scopes. Discussion then turns to several challenges concerning the interpretation of various provisions within the overall prohibition that have persistently clouded the law's clarity. Although a detailed analysis of these and similar ambiguities is beyond the scope of this chapter, the analysis briefly highlights how they can frustrate the law's application.

The chapter is limited to examining the relevant prohibitions applicable to the parties to an international armed conflict. Whether the same or similar restrictions apply within the context of non-international armed conflicts is, accordingly, beyond the scope of the article. Analysis is further confined to addressing forced *conscription*—not other forms of labor that, depending on the circumstances, may or may not be prohibited by the same or similar rules. Nor does it address other rules that may indirectly or incidentally prohibit conscription, such as those requiring humane treatment. Finally, the chapter's discussion does not touch

11. Human Rights Watch, *supra* note 1.

12. Gilmore, *supra* note 1.

13. United States v. Ernst von Weizsäcker et al. (the Ministries Case), 15 Trial of War Criminals Before the Nuremberg Military Tribunals Under Control Council Law No. 10, at 548; *see also* Commentary to Geneva Convention III Relative to the Treatment of Prisoners of War 292–93 (Jean Pictet ed., 1960) [hereinafter 1960 Commentary to Geneva Convention III].

14. Howard S. Levie, *Prisoners of War in International Armed Conflict*, 59 International Law Studies 1, 362 n. 79 (1977).

15. U.S. Department of Defense, Conduct of the Persian Gulf War: Final Report to Congress, Appendix O: The Role of the Law of War 608, 623 (1992) [hereinafter Final Report to Congress].

upon the distinct international legal protections specifically applicable to children in armed conflict.

Before turning to the relevant international law, it is essential to clarify that compulsory military service is governed predominantly by domestic law. It should be noted that, subject to limited conditions,[16] States are generally free to prescribe who may, or with respect to their citizens, must join the armed forces as an exercise of their sovereignty. International humanitarian law does not prohibit States from drafting or otherwise conscripting their own nationals to serve in the armed forces.[17] This observation recognizes the long-established general principle that international law rules are not meant to intrude upon the domestic affairs of States.[18] Indeed, international law has long recognized that "[a]s every citizen or subject is bound to serve the state, the sovereign has a right to enlist whom he pleases."[19] Thus, in the context of international armed conflict, several international humanitarian law rules restrict whether, and if so how, a State may recruit individuals who do not share its nationality into its armed forces.

2. THE TREATY PROHIBITIONS

The various components comprising the prohibition against forced conscription are found in the Regulations annexed to the 1907 Hague Convention (IV) Respecting the Laws and Customs of War on Land (1907 Hague Regulations), the 1949 Geneva Convention Relative to the Treatment of Prisoners of War (Geneva Convention III), and the 1949 Geneva Convention Relative to the Treatment of

16. For example, international law imposes an absolute prohibition on the enlistment (compulsory or voluntary) of children under the age of fifteen into a State's armed forces. *See, e.g.*, Convention on the Rights of the Child art. 38(3), Nov. 20, 1989, 1577 U.N.T.S. 3; Protocol Additional to the Geneva Conventions of 12 August 1949, and Relating to the Protection of Victims of International Armed Conflicts art. 77(2), June 8, 1977, 1125 U.N.T.S. 3; Rome Statute of the International Criminal Court art. 8(2)(b)(xxvi) [hereinafter Rome Statute]. International human rights law may also restrict a State's right to conscript its adult nationals. Some argue, for instance, that certain human rights treaties imply obligations or limitations on States with respect to the compulsory military service of conscientious objectors. *See, e.g.*, International Covenant on Civil and Political Rights art. 18, Dec. 16, 1966, 999 U.N.T.S. 171; G.A. Res. 217 (III) A, Universal Declaration of Human Rights art. 18 (Dec. 10, 1948).

17. Office of the General Counsel, U.S. Department of Defense, Law of War Manual § 5.27.2 (rev. ed., July 2023) [hereinafter U.S. Law of War Manual] ("States are not prohibited by the law of war from compelling their nationals to serve in the armed forces.").

18. *See, e.g.*, UN Charter art. 2(7); Oscar M. Uhler et al., Commentary to Geneva Convention IV Relative to the Protection of Civilian Persons in Time of War 46 (1958) [hereinafter 1958 Commentary to Geneva Convention IV].

19. Emer de Vattel, The Law of Nations, bk. III, ch. II, § 9 (1758).

Civilian Persons in War (Geneva Convention IV).[20] In addition to being widely or, in the case of the two latter instruments, universally ratified, they are generally considered to reflect customary international law.[21]

The 1907 Hague Regulations set forth the cardinal proscription, violation of which is a war crime.[22] In relevant part, Article 23(h) provides that "[a] belligerent is [] forbidden to compel the nationals of the hostile party to take part in the operations of war directed against their own country, even if they were in the belligerent's service before the commencement of the war."[23] Jean Pictet observed in his 1958 *Commentary to Geneva Convention IV* that the rule fortifies "a basic principle, universally recognized in the law of war, [that] strictly prohibits belligerents from forcing enemy subjects to take up arms against their own country."[24] That this principle prohibits, among other forms of compelled labor, the conscription of an adversary's nationals to engage in war against their fellow countrymen is self-evident. Following World War II, for instance, the Nuremberg Military Tribunal reasoned that "[i]f, as has been often held, it is a crime to conscript foreign nationals to slave labor, it is a crime of equal rank to conscript them into the army to fight, bleed, and die."[25] As will be explained in section 3, however, considering the provision's limitation to "operations of war directed against their own country," the extent to which it prohibits conscription *as such* is unsettled.[26]

The Hague Regulations' Article 23(h) is unique in that it applies regardless of whether the national in question qualifies for a particular protected status. By contrast, the scope of similar provisions in other treaties with which Article 23(h)'s

20. Regulations Respecting the Laws and Customs of War on Land, annexed to Convention No. IV Respecting the Laws and Customs of War on Land, Oct. 18, 1907, 36 Stat. 2227, T.S. No. 539 [hereinafter 1907 Hague Regulations]; Convention (III) Relative to the Treatment of Prisoners of War art. 4, Aug. 12, 1949, 6 U.S.T. 3316, 75 U.N.T.S. 135 [hereinafter Geneva Convention III]; Geneva Convention (IV) Relative to the Protection of Civilian Persons in Time of War, Aug. 12, 1949, 6 U.S.T. 3516, 75 U.N.T.S. 287 [hereinafter Geneva Convention IV].

21. Legality of the Threat or Use of Nuclear Weapons, Advisory Opinion, 1996 I.C.J. Rep. 226, ¶¶ 79–82 (July 8); Report of the Secretary-General Pursuant to Paragraph 2 of Security Council Resolution 808, U.N. Doc. S/25704 (May 3, 1993) (introducing the Statute of the International Criminal Tribunal for the former Yugoslavia).

22. *See, e.g.*, Rome Statute, *supra* note 16, art. 8(2)(b)(xv).

23. 1907 Hague Regulations, *supra* note 20, art. 23(h).

24. 1958 Commentary to Geneva Convention IV, *supra* note 18, at 292; *see also* U.S. Law of War Manual, *supra* note 17, § 5.27 ("Underlying this prohibition is the principle that States must not compel foreign nationals to commit treason or otherwise to violate their allegiance to their country.").

25. *Ministries*, *supra* note 13, at 548–49.

26. *See, e.g.*, Marten Zwanenburg, *Forced Conscription in the Self-Declared Republics*, Articles of War (Aug. 8, 2022), https://lieber.westpoint.edu/forced-conscription-self-declared-republics/.

protection overlaps, depends on whether a national qualifies as a prisoner of war or a civilian entitled to protection.[27]

2.1 Prisoners of War

Article 6 of the 1907 Hague Regulations provides, among others, that "[t]he [Detaining] State may utilize the labour of prisoners of war according to their rank and aptitude, officers excepted. The tasks shall not be excessive and shall have no connection with the operations of the war."[28] It echoes comparable restrictions set forth in the 1874 Brussels Declaration and the 1880 Oxford Manual.[29] While limited to prisoners of war, the provision's scope is broader than that of the Hague Regulations' Article 23(h) by not being restricted to operations of war "directed against their own country." Utilizing prisoners of war in operations of war directed against, for example, their allies or other nations fighting alongside their own is therefore also prohibited.

Navigating the rule proved particularly problematic for belligerents during World War I, albeit not solely in the conscription context. Taking into account the considerable breadth of the phrase "operations of war," it was thought that it amounted to a near-universal prohibition on the employment of prisoners of

27. This distinction is likely of little consequence in practice, considering that only nationals who qualify for one or the other status would be at any appreciable risk of conscription by a detaining or occupying State.

28. 1907 Hague Regulations, *supra* note 20, art. 6 (emphasis added); *see also* LASSA OPPENHEIM, INTERNATIONAL LAW: A TREATISE, vol. II, § 126 (2018). An identical provision is contained in Article 6 of its predecessor, the 1899 Hague Regulations. Regulations annexed to the Convention No. II with Respect to the Laws and Customs of War on Land art. 6, July 29, 1899, 32 Stat. 1803, T.S. No. 403.

29. Project of an International Declaration concerning the Laws and Customs of War art. 26, Brussels, Aug. 27, 1874 [hereinafter 1874 Brussels Declaration], *reprinted in* THE LAWS OF ARMED CONFLICTS 23 (Dietrich Schindler & Jiri Toman eds., 4th ed. 2004) ("Prisoners of war cannot be compelled in any way to take any part whatever in carrying on the operations of the war."); Institute of International Law, The Laws of War on Land art. 70 (1880) [hereinafter 1880 Oxford Manual], *reprinted in* THE LAWS OF ARMED CONFLICTS 29 (Dietrich Schindler & Jiri Toman eds., 4th ed. 2004) ("Prisoners cannot be compelled in any manner to take any part whatever in the operations of war, nor compelled to give information about their country or their army."); *see also* 1874 Brussels Declaration art. 25 ("Prisoners of war may be employed on certain public works which have no direct connection with the operations in the theatre of war and which are not excessive or humiliating to their military rank, if they belong to the army, or to their official or social position, if they do not belong to it."); 1880 Oxford Manual art. 71 ("[Prisoners] may be employed on public works which have no direct connection with the operations in the theatre of war, which are not excessive and are not humiliating either to their military rank, if they belong to the army, or to their official or social position, if they do not form part thereof.").

war.[30] The Diplomatic Conference that produced the 1929 Geneva Convention Relative to the Treatment of Prisoners of War attempted to remedy this problem by slightly narrowing the nexus required to trigger the prohibition: "Work done by prisoners of war shall have no *direct* connection with the operations of the war. In particular, it is forbidden to employ prisoners in the manufacture or transport of arms or munitions of any kind, or on the transport of material destined for combatant units."[31] The added qualifier implied that any form of labor, conscription included, with a remote or indirect nexus to the war effort would not be prohibited. This led to more interpretive and practical challenges, however, such as delineating between direct and indirect connections with operations of war.[32]

Faced with this dilemma, the Diplomatic Conference that developed the 1949 Geneva Conventions ultimately adopted an alternative approach whereby the provisions pertaining to prisoners of war specifically describe the types of labor permitted rather than listing those proscribed.[33] Article 50 of Geneva Convention III, therefore, contains no explicit prohibition against conscripting prisoners of war.[34] But considering the Convention's approach, there is little question that conscription is implicitly prohibited because it is not expressly authorized.

Lest there be any doubt, Geneva Convention III's Article 130 unambiguously specifies that "compelling a prisoner of war to serve in the forces of the hostile Power" is a grave breach.[35] As the International Committee of the Red Cross (ICRC) explains in its 2020 *Commentary on Geneva Convention III*, "The prohibition on compelling a prisoner of war to serve in the forces of the hostile Power is not found *per se* in any particular article of the Third Convention, but reflects a well-established principle that a Detaining Power may not oblige protected

30. 1960 Commentary to Geneva Convention III, *supra* note 13, at 264.

31. Convention Relative to the Treatment of Prisoners of War art. 31, July 27, 1929, 47 Stat. 2021, 118 L.N.T.S. 343 (emphasis added).

32. 1960 Commentary to Geneva Convention III, *supra* note 13, at 264 ("How is one to interpret a provision such as this? What constitutes direct connection with the operations of the war? When is it indirect? What does the term 'combatant units' cover? Does it refer only to units engaged in the fighting, or does it also include those which for the time being are not taking part in the fighting, while remaining in the front-line area?").

33. *Id.* at 265; International Committee of the Red Cross, Commentary on the Third Geneva Convention: Convention (III) Relative to the Treatment of Prisoners of War ¶ 2706 (2020) [hereinafter 2020 Commentary on Geneva Convention III]; Sean Watts, The West Point Companion to the ICRC Commentary on the Third Geneva Convention 291–92 (2023).

34. Geneva Convention III, *supra* note 20, art. 50.

35. *Id.*, art. 130; *see* 2020 Commentary on Geneva Convention III, *supra* note 33, at ¶ 5272 ("This grave breach is indirectly linked to Article 50, which provides an exhaustive list of categories of labour in which prisoners of war may be employed, such as public utility services or public works and building operations which have no military character or purpose.").

persons to take up arms against the Power on which they depend."[36] Of note, in contrast to Article 23(h), the grave breach prohibits conscription regardless of its intended purpose or ultimate use, so long as the protected person is compelled to join forces hostile to their State of nationality.[37]

2.2 Civilians

Aside from prisoners of war, specific prohibitions relating to conscription apply to civilians protected by Geneva Convention IV, defined as those "who, at a given moment and in any manner whatsoever, find themselves, in case of a conflict or occupation, in the hands of a Party to the conflict or Occupying Power of which they are not nationals."[38] With respect to their presence in the territory of a party to the conflict, Article 40 of Geneva Convention IV, adopting the approach taken by the 1929 prisoner of war convention, prohibits them from being compelled to perform work "directly related to the conduct of military operations."[39] Pictet observed in his 1958 *Commentary to Geneva Convention IV* that, consistent with Article 23(h) of the 1907 Hague Regulations, the treaty rule is "based on an idea expressed in several other Articles of the Geneva Conventions, namely that an enemy subject who has fallen into the hands of the Opposing Power must not be forced to participate in warlike measures directed against his home country."[40]

Recall that Article 40 would not apply to the nationals of neutral or co-belligerent States that have normal diplomatic representation with the conscripting State.[41] As will be further explained in section 3, however, the customary international law rule exempting foreign nationals residing within a State from compulsory military service undoubtedly would.[42] Capturing the customary rule in his 1905 treatise *International Law*, Lassa Oppenheim observed, for example, that "an alien does not fall under the supremacy of the local State; therefore he cannot be made to serve in its army or navy, and cannot, like a citizen,

36. 2020 Commentary on Geneva Convention III, *supra* note 33, at ¶ 5271.

37. *See id.* at ¶ 5276; *see also* International Criminal Court, Elements of Crimes art. 8(2)(a)(v) (2011); Knut Dörmann, Elements of War Crimes Under the Rome Statute of the International Criminal Court 97 (2003) ("Some delegations wanted a clear indication that the crime is not limited to compelling a protected person to act against his/her country or forces, but also against other countries or forces, in particular allied countries and forces. In the end, the PrepCom felt that this particular case would be covered by 'otherwise serve in the forces of a hostile power' ").

38. Geneva Convention IV, *supra* note 20, art. 4.

39. *Id.*, art. 40.

40. 1958 Commentary to Geneva Convention IV, *supra* note 18, at 253–54, 292.

41. Geneva Convention IV, *supra* note 20, art. 4(2).

42. *See infra* notes 60–61 and accompanying text.

be treated according to discretion," which was recognized by his contemporaries as the "universally accepted opinion of the relation of aliens to military service."[43]

As for civilian protected persons residing in occupied territory, Article 51 of Geneva Convention IV sets forth their relevant protections. It mirrors earlier iterations of the long-standing rule embodied in the 1874 Brussels Declaration and the 1880 Oxford Manual by providing that "[p]rotected persons may not be compelled [by the occupying power] to undertake any work which would involve them in the obligation of taking part in military operations."[44] It further specifies, however, that "[t]he Occupying Power may not compel protected persons to serve in its armed or auxiliary forces. No pressure or propaganda which aims at securing voluntary enlistment is permitted."[45] The provision is reinforced by Article 147, which states that, like its prisoner of war counterpart, "compelling a protected person to serve in the forces of a hostile Power" is a grave breach, regardless of the nexus to military operations or whether it occurs in occupied territory or the territory of a party to the conflict.[46]

3. MODERN CHALLENGES IN TREATY INTERPRETATION AND APPLICATION

3.1 The Scope of "Operations of War"

The contrast between the approach taken in Article 51 of Geneva Convention IV and the grave breach clauses, which expressly reference conscription, and the approach utilized in Articles 6 and 23(h) of the 1907 Hague Regulations, the applicability of which depends on a State party engaging protected persons in "operations of war," begs the question of the extent to which the varying components of the prohibition overlap. With respect to the latter, there is little doubt that conscripting a protected person to engage in combat or other military operations in support thereof are encompassed within the notion of "operations of war." Concern lies instead in those scenarios in which a protected person is compelled into the armed forces but does not engage in activities intimately associated with

43. Oppenheim, *supra* note 28, at vol. I, § 317; Sterling E. Edmunds, *Aliens and the Draft*, 5 St. Louis Law Review 23, 24 (1920).

44. Geneva Convention IV, *supra* note 20, art. 51(2); 1874 Brussels Declaration, *supra* note 29, art. 36 ("The population of occupied territory cannot be forced to take part in military operations against its own country."); 1880 Oxford Manual art. 48 ("The inhabitants of an occupied territory who do not submit to the orders of the occupant maybe compelled to do so. The occupant, however, cannot compel the inhabitants to assist him in his works of attack or defense, or to take part in military operations against their own country.").

45. Geneva Convention IV, *supra* note 20, art. 51(1).

46. *Id.*, art. 147; Geneva Convention III, *supra* note 20, art. 130; *see* Rome Statute, *supra* note 16, art. 8(2)(a)(v); Dörmann, *supra* note 37, at 97.

combat or its supporting operations.[47] In other words, it is unclear whether mere military service, even if compelled, qualifies automatically as the requisite participation in operations of war contemplated by the Hague Regulations.

For example, reports indicate that Russia is currently stationing many of its Ukrainian conscripts at military bases inside its borders. They are not being deployed along operational fronts inside Ukraine. As such, one could argue that, due to their indirect nexus to the conflict, they are not engaging in "operations of war." Notably, U.S. accusations that Russia is violating the prohibition against forced conscription have only referenced the Geneva Conventions—not the Hague Regulations.[48] One scholarly observer has similarly suggested, albeit cautiously, that a Ukrainian conscript "who is still receiving military training away from the front would not seem to be taking part in the operations of war."[49]

Considering the term's ordinary meaning, such interpretations are not unreasonable.[50] After all, the approach taken by Article 23(h) and other provisions that utilize the term is that conscription is a subset of labor generally, the wrongfulness of which depends on its nexus to the war. If a restrictive interpretation of "operations of war" is indeed correct as a matter of law, Russia's conscription campaigns within occupied Ukrainian territory would violate Geneva Convention IV's Article 51 and constitute a grave breach of that convention, but whether they violate Article 23(h) of the Hague Regulations is less clear.

On the other hand, however, several scholars contend that pertinent "operations of war" include *any* compelled military service, regardless of how or where a conscript is employed. René-Jean Wilhelm, for instance, a senior ICRC legal adviser when the Conventions were adopted, asserted that "[a] belligerent is prohibited by international customary law from forcing nationals of the adverse party to take part in war operations directed against their own country. This principle, expressly laid down by the Hague Regulations, therefore prohibits *all* compulsion on the part of the Detaining Power in order to obtain the enrolment of prisoners of war."[51] Moreover, as Pictet's 1958 *Commentary to Geneva Convention IV* further observed, Article 51 was meant to "reaffirm" rather than to expand the prohibition set forth in the Hague Regulations.[52] Despite the omission of an explicit reference

47. *See, e.g.*, Human Rights Watch, *supra* note 1.

48. *See* Gilmore, *supra* note 1. The import of the omission is unclear. Similar U.S. accusations against Iraq following the First Gulf War also did not reference seemingly relevant 1907 Hague Regulation provisions. *See* Final Report to Congress, *supra* note 15, at 623.

49. Zwanenburg, *supra* note 26.

50. Vienna Convention on the Law of Treaties art. 31(1), May 23, 1969, 1155 U.N.T.S. 331 [hereinafter Vienna Convention].

51. René-Jean Wilhelm, *Can the Status of Prisoners of War Be Altered?*, 35 Revue Internationale de la Croix-Rouge 1, 22 (July & Sept. 1953) (emphasis added) (original in French, English reprint *available at* https://tile.loc.gov/storage-services/service/ll/llmlp/RC-Can-status-POWs-be-altered/RC-Can-status-POWs-be-altered.pdf) (emphasis added).

52. 1958 Commentary to Geneva Convention IV, *supra* note 18, at 293.

to conscription in Articles 6 and 23(h) of the Hague Regulations, it is therefore a reasonable interpretation considering the treaty's object and purpose.[53]

A broad interpretation of "operations of war" also accords with the *opinio juris* of States at the time the instruments utilizing the phrase were adopted, according to which resident foreign nationals are exempt from compulsory service in a State's armed forces regardless of where or how they would be utilized.[54]

Throughout the Napoleonic Wars, for example, the United States accused the British of violating international law by impressing American sailors into naval service to support Britain's war against France. In a letter to James Monroe, at the time the U.S. Minister to Britain, then-Secretary of State James Madison explained that "[c]itizens or subjects of one country residing in another . . . can never be rightfully forced into military service, particularly external service . . . . The law of nations protects them against both . . . ."[55] Continuation of the infamous practice by the British became a contributing cause of the War of 1812.[56]

Decades later, Secretary of State William Seward similarly admonished the governor of Indiana during the American Civil War that conscripting British citizens into the Union's armed forces was prohibited by international law. "There is no principle more distinctly and clearly settled in the law of nations, than the rule that resident aliens not naturalized are not liable to perform military service. We have uniformly claimed and insisted upon it in our intercourse with foreign nations."[57] Seward's caution was prompted, in part, by diplomatic threats from Britain that, "if enforced enlistments of British subjects for the war were persisted in, the [British] Government would be obliged to concert with other neutral powers for the protection of their respective subjects."[58] France likewise claimed that its nationals were exempt from compulsory military service during the war.[59] Tellingly, the United States promulgated the 1863 Lieber Code a year later, which provided in relevant part that "[i]t is no longer considered lawful—on the

53. Vienna Convention, *supra* note 50, art. 31(1).

54. Along with a treaty's context, interpretation shall consider "any relevant rules of international law applicable in the relations between the parties." *Id.*, art. 31(3)(c).

55. Letter from Sec. Madison to Mr. Monroe (Jan. 5, 1804), *in* John Bassett Moore, A Digest of International Law, vol. IV, 52 (1906); *see also* Letter from Mr. Blaine to Mr. Morgan (Mar. 14, 1881), *in* Moore, *supra*, at 61 ("It is notorious that the impressment of American seamen into the naval service of a foreign power was at one time a serious grievance, not to be acquiesced in, and raised a question upon which all parties in this country were unanimous in regarding as one of international character.").

56. Edmunds, *supra* note 43, at 25.

57. Mr. Seward to Gov. Morton (Sept. 5, 1862), *in* Moore, *supra* note 55, at 53; *see also* Atty. Gen. Cushing to Sec. Davis (May 30, 1854), *in* Joseph L. Delaney, *The Alien Enemy and the Draft*, 12 Brooklyn Law Review 91, 96 (1943).

58. Henry W. Halleck, International Law 558, vol. I, ch. XVIII (3d ed. 1893).

59. *Id.* at ch. XII, at 419.

contrary, it is held to be a serious breach of the law of war—to force the subjects of the enemy into the service of the victorious government."[60]

During World War I, in the midst a diplomatic plea from Sweden, the Judge Advocate General of the U.S. Army officially opined within the War Department that, according to international law, "alien enemies" and "alien [friends] whose presence is temporary" residing in the United States "are exempt from [compulsory] military service."[61] He further clarified that "[a]n alien enemy cannot be compelled to serve, for otherwise he would be compelled to fight against his own country," whereas, by contrast, "[a]n alien friend . . . cannot be compelled to serve . . . for otherwise commercial intercourse would be clogged and a person might be compelled to aid the mere ambitions of a country in which he is a stranger."[62] The former statement could arguably imply that only compelled service resulting in an alien enemy fighting against his own country is prohibited, but such a nuanced approach to the rule is absent from the general's opinion—as it was from Madison's and Seward's restatements decades before. Instead, without noting any conditions or exceptions, he plainly reiterated that "[a]n alien enemy is exempt from draft. This is recognized by international law and also by the statutes of the United States."[63]

In sum, although some components of the international legal prohibition against forced conscription make no express reference to conscription as such, it is reasonable to interpret the phrase "operations of war" to necessarily include acts of conscription regardless of their context. After all, considering that those formally integrated into the armed forces are combatants, it stands to reason that *any* conscription of a foreign national should be intimately associated with "operations of war," regardless of their location or function. To date, however, States have yet to engage in any meaningful discourse pertaining to how they interpret the term's scope. Accordingly, the question of how well treaty provisions utilizing that operative phrase overlap with Article 51 and the relevant grave breaches proscribed by the Geneva Conventions unfortunately remains.

60. U.S. Department of War, Instructions for the Government of Armies of the United States in the Field, General Orders No. 100, art. 33, Apr. 24, 1863.

61. U.S. Department of War, Opinions of the Judge Advocate General of the Army 347, vol. II (1918) [hereinafter 1918 JAG Opinions]. The Selective Service Act of 1917 provided that "all male citizens and male persons residing in the United States, not alien enemies, who have declared their intention to become citizens," were required to register for potential draft. 40 Stat. 77, 885, 955, 54 Stat. 1173, 50 USC App. § 202 (1918, 1940).

62. 1918 JAG Opinions, *supra* note 61, at 347.

63. *Id.* at 348; *see also* Johnson v. Eisentrager, 339 U.S. 763, 773 (1950) ("Thus the alien enemy status carries important immunities as well as disadvantages. The United States does not ask him to violate his allegiance or to commit treason toward his own country for the sake of ours. This also is the doctrine and the practice of other states comprising our Western Civilization."); Harisiades v. Shaughnessy, 342 U.S. 580, 585–86 (1952).

3.2 Compulsory Versus Voluntary Military Service

Another issue raised by the prohibition of forced conscription is what it means to *compel* military service. It is well settled that prohibited behavior must be forceful or otherwise coercive in nature. In the Nuremberg Military Tribunal's *Ministries* judgment, for example, the tribunal held that compulsion must be "brought about by force, threats, or duress."[64] Similarly, the International Criminal Court and the ICRC both take the position that the applicable war crime should include an "act or threat" of force.[65] And as the United States' remarks before the Permanent Council of the OSCE demonstrate with respect to Russia's conscription of Ukrainian nationals, coercion includes actual or threatened judicial enforcement of domestic conscription laws.[66] On these points there is broad agreement.

The requirement of compulsion, however, begs the corollary question of the extent to which a protected person can *voluntarily* enlist in the forces of a hostile power. With respect to civilians, there is little question that they may do so.[67] This is subject, of course, to the related rule applicable in occupied territory that no "pressure or propaganda" be used to procure their enlistment.[68] But that caveat prohibiting certain recruitment efforts must be distinguished from forced conscription itself. In other words, although pressure or propaganda in occupied territory violate one of Article 51's provisions, such actions would not implicate the prohibition against forced conscription nor the grave breach and associated war crime unless they are, in fact, coercive in nature.[69] The U.S. Department of Defense helpfully explains in its 2023 *Law of War Manual* that "[the] prohibition applies to attempts to compel enemy nationals, rather than measures short of compulsion, such as bribing enemy nationals or seeking to influence them through

64. *Ministries*, *supra* note 13, at 668 (explaining compulsion in the context of the 1907 Hague Regulations).

65. International Criminal Court, *supra* note 37; 2020 Commentary on Geneva Convention III, *supra* note 33, at ¶ 5273.

66. Gilmore, *supra* note 1.

67. *Ministries*, *supra* note 13, at 549 ("We hold that it is not illegal to recruit prisoners of war who volunteer to fight against their own country, but pressure or coercion to compel such persons to enter into the armed services obviously violates international law."); Moore, *supra* note 55, at 50 ("The voluntary enlistment of an alien in the military service raises in itself no international question."); Henry Wheaton, Elements of International Law 755, vol. II; U.S. Department of State, *Military Service*, *8* Digest of International Law 540, 561–62, 570 (1967) (citing Oppenheim's International Law, vol. II, § 207 (H. Lauterpacht ed., 6th ed.)). On the debate over whether propaganda was rightly included in the provision, *see* International Committee of the Red Cross, Final Record of the Diplomatic Conference of Geneva of 1949, vol. II-A, at 665, 776; 1958 Commentary to Geneva Convention IV, *supra* note 18, at 293.

68. Geneva Convention IV, *supra* note 20, art. 51(1).

69. *Id*., art. 147; Rome Statute, *supra* note 16, art. 8(2)(a)(v); *see Ministries*, *supra* note 13, at 668; D°rmann, *supra* note 37, at 98.

propaganda. However, it is specifically prohibited for an Occupying Power to use propaganda that aims at securing voluntary enlistment of protected persons in its armed or auxiliary forces."[70]

The issue is less straightforward as it pertains to prisoners of war. The Nuremberg Military Tribunal confronted the issue of whether the prohibition of forced conscription itself applies to prisoners' voluntary actions in its *Ministries* judgment. The prosecution argued that even the voluntary employment of prisoners of war against their own country violates the prohibition.[71] But the tribunal squarely rejected that contention:

> Ordinarily a national of a country, whether or not he is in military service, who gives aid or comfort to the enemy, is a traitor to his country. But we have never before heard it suggested that the enemy who takes advantage of his treason is guilty of a breach of international law. We hold that the cited prohibitions of the Hague Convention prohibit the use of prisoners of war in connection with war operations, and apply only when such use is brought about by force, threats, or duress, and not when the person renders the services voluntarily.[72]

This restatement pertaining to the 1907 Hague Regulations is consistent with how other provisions prohibiting compulsory service (like Article 51, as discussed previously) are understood.[73]

Still, the more critical inquiry with respect to prisoners of war is whether voluntary enlistment—or, more specifically, the hostile power's acceptance thereof—would amount to an impermissible renunciation of a prisoner of war's rights in violation of Article 7 of Geneva Convention III. The article provides that "[p]risoners of war may in no circumstances renounce in part or in entirety the rights secured to them by the present Convention, and by the special agreements referred to in the foregoing Article, if such there be."[74] A concern underlying the rule is that the purported voluntariness of the renunciation of a vulnerable person such as a prisoner of war is often a challenging question of fact.

Despite the rule's absolute and inalienable nature, some observers have queried whether Article 7 prevents a detaining power from accepting the enlistment of a prisoner of war if the decision to enlist is impartially confirmed to be

70. U.S. Law of War Manual, *supra* note 17, at § 5.27.1.

71. *Ministries*, *supra* note 13, at 667.

72. *Id.* at 667–68.

73. *See, e.g.*, 2020 Commentary on Geneva Convention III, *supra* note 33, at ¶ 5273 ("It is not illegal for the hostile power to recruit prisoners who volunteer to join its forces, but it is prohibited to use force or the threat of force for this purpose."); *see also* 1960 Commentary to Geneva Convention III, *supra* note 13, at 88–90.

74. Geneva Convention III, *supra* note 20, art. 7.

voluntary.[75] A number of other commentators and States maintain that it does. In 1953, for instance, Wilhelm argued that Article 7 categorically prohibits prisoners of war from renouncing their rights by enlisting in the detaining power's armed forces.[76] Pictet asserted the same in his 1960 *Commentary to Geneva Convention III*.[77] And Howard Levie, widely respected as an expert on the treatment of prisoners of war, stated in 1977 that the article bars accepting the voluntary enlistment of a prisoner of war even though the Convention does not expressly prohibit it. "Any holding to the contrary," he argued, "would, in effect, nullify [the grave breach in Article 130], as a Detaining Power so inclined would certainly contend that the challenged enlistments were all voluntary, and would certainly have documentary and other evidence to establish the voluntariness of the recruitment of the prisoners of war into its armed forces."[78]

Crucially, their interpretations align with those of States. The United States, for example, follows a similar position that reiterates many of the same concerns:

> POWs may in no circumstances renounce, in part or in entirety, the rights secured to them by the GPW, ...
>
> This rule is intended to prevent States from evading their obligations by coercing enemy nationals in their power to waive their rights. The prohibition on the non-renunciation of rights is based on a recognition that: (1) POWs are in a vulnerable position; (2) it would be difficult to establish whether a POW had voluntarily renounced his or her rights; and (3) an absolute prohibition would best serve the interests of the majority of POWs.
>
> *The non-renunciation of rights, in particular, prevents a POW from being compelled to serve in the armed forces of the Detaining Power.*[79]

Thus, though the prohibition against forced conscription itself may not strictly apply to the voluntary enlistments of prisoners of war, the weight of authority counsels in favor of interpreting Article 7 (reasonably, in my view) to preclude detaining powers from accepting such enlistments nonetheless.

75. *See, e.g.*, 2020 Commentary on Geneva Convention III, *supra* note 33, ¶ 1177; Watts, *supra* note 33, at 128.

76. Wilhelm, *supra* note 51, at 22–23.

77. 1960 Commentary to Geneva Convention III, *supra* note 13, at 88–89.

78. Levie, *supra* note 14, at 362.

79. U.S. Law of War Manual, *supra* note 17, § 9.3.7 (emphasis added); *see also* United Kingdom Ministry of Defence, The Manual of The Law of Armed Conflict ¶¶ 8.1, 8.24 (2004); Australian Defence Headquarters, ADDP 06.4, Law of Armed Conflict ¶ 10.18 (2006). The ICRC's commentary to Article 7 articulates many of the same concerns. 2020 Commentary on Geneva Convention III, *supra* note 33, ¶ 1177; *see also* Watts, *supra* note 33, at 128.

3.3 The Scope of Applicable "Forces"

Another pertinent question is whether some of the prohibition's treaty components only apply to conscripting protected persons into service in particular categories of forces.[80] Article 51 of Geneva Convention IV refers to "armed or auxiliary forces."[81] There is a general consensus that the forces meant are those outlined in Article 1 of the 1907 Hague Convention and Article 4A of Geneva Convention III, an interpretation which the Convention's *travaux préparatoires* confirm. Whereas the draft text produced by the International Conference of the Red Cross in Stockholm referenced "combatant or auxiliary" forces, the Diplomatic Conference deliberately amended the final text to conform with the language used in the 1907 Hague Regulations' Article 1 and Geneva Convention III's Article 4A.[82]

The matter is less clear with respect to the grave breach clauses outlined in Articles 130 and 147 of Geneva Conventions III and IV. Oddly, the English text does not qualify the type(s) of forces covered by the provisions, whereas the equally authoritative French text specifies that it applies to "armed"—without mentioning auxiliary—forces.[83] Interpretations, therefore, vary. At the 1956 Conference of the Commission of Experts convened to examine grave breaches, for example, the question was never conclusively resolved:

> One member of the Commission of Experts felt that the word "auxiliary" was intentionally omitted from the grave-breaches Article of the Convention so that compelling service in the hostile force would not be a grave breach unless the prisoner of war was compelled to take part in combat against his own country; other members of the Commission felt that the question should be left for determination by the judges trying cases which raise the problem; while still others were of the opinion that the categories of organizations mentioned in Article 1 of the 1907 Hague Regulations and in Article 4 of the 1949 Convention should govern.[84]

80. For an interpretation of "service," *see* 2020 COMMENTARY ON GENEVA CONVENTION III, *supra* note 33, ¶ 5274 ("It is submitted that the word 'serving' in relation to armed forces implies that a formal integration or enlistment is required. The formulation 'to take part in the operations of war' used in the Hague Regulations refers to participation in military operations without the person necessarily being integrated into the forces carrying them out.").

81. Geneva Convention IV, *supra* note 20, art. 51.

82. International Committee of the Red Cross, Final Record of the Diplomatic Conference of Geneva of 1949, vol. II-A, at 665, 776; *see also* 2020 COMMENTARY ON GENEVA CONVENTION III, *supra* note 33, ¶ 5277.

83. 2020 COMMENTARY ON GENEVA CONVENTION III, *supra* note 33, ¶ 5277 ("Les infractions graves visées à l'article précédent sont celles qui comportent l'un ou l'autre des actes suivants, . . . le fait de contraindre un prisonnier de guerre à servir dans les forces armées de la Puissance ennemie . . . .") According to the ICRC, "A review of the preparatory work of the Convention does not shed any light on the reason for this discrepancy." *Id.*

84. Levie, *supra* note 14, at 363.

The interpretations of scholars and other commentators are similarly mixed. Consistent with the first view, renowned war crimes expert Knut Dörmann maintains that the phrase "serve in the forces of a hostile power" implies that conscription "encompasses taking part in military operations," but would not include organized forces that, for example, engage in other forms of labor permitted under the Conventions.[85] In line with the second, Levie regretfully lamented that the "question will, of necessity, have to be decided by the tribunals which may be called upon to sit on cases of alleged violations."[86]

With respect to the third, the ICRC suggests in its 2020 *Commentary to Geneva Convention III* that the grave breaches imply that "formal integration or enlistment" in the "armed forces of the hostile Power, as defined in Article 4 of the Convention" is required—a reasonable interpretation considering the French text refers to *armed* forces.[87] The ICRC's view is also consistent with the customary, if historical, distinction between service of a military rather than a civil law enforcement character. For instance, while foreign nationals could not be forced to enroll in their host State's armed forces, they were traditionally liable to compelled service, subject to conditions, in local police or militia units.[88]

To date, however, States have provided little guidance on how to resolve this question. Nor has an applicable grave breach ever been prosecuted by an international tribunal. Thus, there is no persuasive authority in the form of case law with which to inform the analysis. As a practical matter, however, there is little doubt that conscription into other-than-armed forces in many cases would, depending on the circumstances, *likely* violate the prohibition's other treaty components, such as Article 23(h) of the 1907 Hague Regulations, and still constitute a war crime.[89]

85. Dörmann, *supra* note 37, at 98; *see also* 2020 Commentary on Geneva Convention III, *supra* note 33, ¶ 5275 ("The list of permissible work contained in Article 50 is excluded from these activities."). Note, Dörmann was analyzing the war crime set forth in the Rome State, but its legal bases are Articles 130 and 147.

86. Levie, *supra* note 14, at 363.

87. 2020 Commentary on Geneva Convention III, *supra* note 33, ¶¶ 5274, 5277.

88. *See, e.g.*, Oppenheim, *supra* note 28, at vol. I, § 317; Sec. Bayard to Mr. Bell (Feb. 3, 1888), *in* Moore, *supra* note 55, at 58, 62; Asst. Sec. Davis to Mr. Faxon (Feb. 17, 1870); William Edward Hall, A Treatise on International Law 218 (7th ed. 1917); JAG Opinions, *supra* note 61, at 348; Albert H. Washburn, *Obstacles in the Way of Drafting Aliens*, 207 The North American Review 671, 677–78 (1918).

89. Rome Statute, *supra* note 16, arts. 8(2)(a)(v), 8(2)(b)(xv); *see* Knut Dörmann, *War Crimes Under the Rome Statute of the International Criminal Court, With a Special Emphasis on the Negotiations on the Elements of Crimes*, 7 Max Planck Yearbook of United Nations Law 341, 374 (2003).

3.4 Nationality

While the concept of "nationality" is poorly settled in other international humanitarian law contexts and bodies of international law, it has historically proven to be especially problematic as it pertains to forced conscription.[90] Issues often arise, for example, in the context of aliens permanently residing in the territory of a party to the conflict who have established substantial connections to the conscripting State.

Throughout the American Civil War, for example, the Enrollment Act of 1863 (commonly referred to as the Conscription Act) was a significant point of contention between the United States and other States. Section 1 of the Act provided "[t]hat all able-bodies male citizens of the United States, *and persons of foreign birth who shall have declared on oath their intention to become citizens under and in pursuance of the laws thereof*, between the ages of twenty and forty-five years, except as hereinafter excepted, are hereby declared to constitute the national forces, and shall be liable to perform military duty in the service of the United States when called out by the President for that purpose."[91]

For the first time in U.S. history, therefore, so-called "declarant aliens," though not yet citizens, were subject to draft.[92] But according to British ministers, the statute conflicted with their domestic laws under which a "British subject owes allegiance to the British government until he has *completely* effected his naturalization in the United States and under the laws of Congress."[93] French diplomats similarly complained that French émigrés who had voted in the United States "had not forfeited their French nationality, or their right as aliens to be exempt from compulsory military service."[94] In the absence of any clear resolution as a matter of international law, President Abraham Lincoln ordered declarant aliens who had not yet exercised political rights (e.g., voting, holding office, etc.) exempt from the draft, so long as they withdrew their citizenship declarations and vacated the country within sixty-five days.[95]

Similar diplomatic protests characterized the two world wars. Prior to its entry into the Second World War, the United States continued the policy of subjecting

90. For a discussion of the issue in the context of prisoner of war status, for example, *see* W. Casey Biggerstaff & Michael N. Schmitt, *Prisoner of War Status and Nationals of the Detaining Power*, 100 International Law Studies 513, 536–39 (2023).

91. Conscription Act of 1863, § 1, 37th Cong, 3d Session, Ch. 74, 75, 3 Mar 1863 (emphasis added), *available at* https://glc.yale.edu/act-enrolling-and-calling-out-national-forces.

92. John Houck, *Aliens–Naturalization–Neutral Aliens Who Sought Relief from Military Service Barred from Becoming United States Citizens*, 52 Michigan Law Review 265, 266 (1953).

93. Letter from Sec. Seward to Gov. Morton (Sept. 5, 1862) (emphasis added), *in* Edmunds, *supra* note 43, at 26; *see also* Asst. Sec. Davis to Mr. Faxon (Feb. 17, 1870), *in* Moore, *supra* note 55, at 57.

94. Henry W. Halleck, International Law 365, vol. I, ch. XII (1878).

95. Houck, *supra* note 92, at 266.

declarant aliens to potential draft despite its recognition that "declarations of intention to become citizens do not have the effect of changing the nationality status of the declarants."[96] Thereafter, even those resident aliens who had not declared their intention of becoming a citizen were required to register for the draft.[97] These policies were highly controversial and caused the U.S. government to be "besieged" throughout the two conflicts with diplomatic complaints from States, including Sweden, Chile, Spain, Switzerland, and Mexico, claiming in chorus that "resident nationals of foreign countries are generally exempted from compulsory military service in international conflicts."[98]

The issue of determining nationality in the context of forced conscription has been, therefore, a persistent challenge. The character of the armed conflict and the composition of the States party to it can similarly complicate nationality assessments. In the Russia-Ukraine conflict, for instance, considering the history and demographics of the former Soviet Socialist Republics, and the consequences of Russia's illegitimate annexation of Crimea in 2014 and subsequently of other Ukrainian territories, both States may claim the residents of territories occupied by Russian forces are their respective nationals. For example, Russia has attempted to assimilate Ukrainians in occupied territories by, among others, compelling them into accepting Russian passports.[99] While there is a consensus that such coercive efforts are highly suspect, if not plainly in violation of international law,[100] claims that Ukrainian nationals have voluntarily accepted passports offered by Russia are more difficult to parse.

96. 40 Stat. 77, 885, 955, 54 Stat. 1173, 50 USC App. § 202 (1918, 1940); Act. Sec. Welles to Pres. Roosevelt (Mar. 18, 1941), https://history.state.gov/historicaldocuments/frus1941v01/d560.

97. In U.S. practice, the requirement to register for the draft must be distinguished from the act of being drafted—that is, conscripted—itself. Historically, following the registration of applicable persons, local draft boards adjudicated exemptions and decided who would actually be drafted into the armed forces.

98. Letter from Sec. Lansing to Pres. Wilson (Feb. 7, 1918), https://history.state.gov/historicaldocuments/frus1914-20v02/d136; Letter from Sec. Lansing to Mr. Shea (Dec. 22, 1917), https://history.state.gov/historicaldocuments/frus1914-20v02/d135; JAG Opinions, *supra* note 61, at 346–52; Letter from Mr. Boström to Sec. Hull (Jan. 27, 1942), https://history.state.gov/historicaldocuments/frus1942v01/d418; Telegram from Sec. Lansing to Amb. of Mexico (May 16, 1917), https://history.state.gov/historicaldocuments/frus1914-20v02/d128; Letter from Sec. Lansing to Pres. Wilson (Aug. 20, 1917), https://history.state.gov/historicaldocuments/frus1914-20v02/d130; Letter from Sec. Lansing to Pres. Wilson (Aug. 27, 1917), https://history.state.gov/historicaldocuments/frus1914-20v02/d131; Swiss Minister to Sec. State (June 5, 1942), https://history.state.gov/historicaldocuments/frus1942v01/d427.

99. *See, e.g.*, Vitaly Shevchenko, *Ukraine War: Locals Forced to Take Russian Passports, Report Says*, BBC.com (Nov. 16, 2023), https://www.bbc.com/news/world-europe-67427840.

100. *See, e.g.*, Anne Peters, *Passportization: Risks For International Law and Stability—Part I*, EJIL: Talk! (May 9, 2019), https://www.ejiltalk.org/passportisation-risks-for-international-law-and-stability-part-one/; Elia Bescotti et al., *Passportization: Russia's "Humanitarian" Tool*

Despite pervasive reference to nationality in treaty law, the relevant instruments do little to clarify the term's scope. With respect to the relevant prohibitions in Geneva Convention IV, for example, none of its provisions, including the definition of who is protected by the Convention in Article 4, clarify who is or should be included within a State's nationals. In his 1958 Commentary, Pictet observed that "[t]he problem [of nationality] presents so many varied aspects that it was difficult to deal with it fully in the Convention," further suggesting that "it will be for the Power in whose hands they are to decide whether the persons concerned should or should not be regarded as citizens of the country from which they have fled."[101] Under this view, nationality is a matter to be determined chiefly by domestic law.[102]

Other interpretations imply that, depending on the character of a conflict, protections may not be strictly conditioned on one's de jure nationality. In the *Tadic* case, for example, the Appeals Chamber of the International Criminal Tribunal for the former Yugoslavia interpreted Geneva Convention IV's Article 4 to include those "who, while having the nationality of the Party to the conflict in whose hands they find themselves, are refugees and thus no longer owe allegiance to this Party and no longer enjoy its diplomatic protection (...)."[103] In the tribunal's view, "not only the text and the drafting history of the Convention but also, and more importantly, the Convention's object and purpose suggest that allegiance to a Party to the conflict and, correspondingly, control by this Party over persons in a given territory, may be regarded as the crucial test."[104] To the extent it is correct as a matter of law, this so-called allegiance test is best understood as applying within limited contexts, for instance, when geopolitical conditions are such that ethnic or other groups may not receive their State of nationality's protection. Yet there is little consensus or definitive guidance on when and, if so, under which precise conditions and criteria States should interpret Article 4 in that manner. As these interpretations illustrate, the matter of assessing nationality is not well settled.

Within the historical context of forced conscription, the challenge has often been resolved by treaty or other special agreement.[105] Thus, the 1930 Protocol Relating to Military Obligations in Certain Cases of Double Nationality, which

102. *See* International Law Commission, *Draft Articles on Diplomatic Protection, with Commentaries*, art. 4, U.N. GAOR Supp. No. 10, U.N. Doc. A/61/10 (2006), *reprinted in* 2006 YEARBOOK OF THE INTERNATIONAL LAW COMMISSION, vol. II, pt. 2, at 24 [hereinafter *Draft Articles on Diplomatic Protection*].

103. Prosecutor v. Tadić, No. IT-94-1-A, Appeals Chamber Judgment, ¶ 164 (Int'l Crim. Trib. for the former Yugoslavia July 15, 1999) (emphasis added).

104. *Id.* at ¶ 166.

105. *See* Geneva Convention III, *supra* note 20, art. 6; Geneva Convention IV, *supra* note 20, art. 7.

for Foreign Policy, Extra-Territorial Governance, and Military Intervention, VERFASSUNGSBLOG (Mar. 23, 2022), https://verfassungsblog.de/passportization/; Zwanenburg, *supra* note 26.

101. 1958 COMMENTARY TO GENEVA CONVENTION IV, *supra* note 18, at 47.

entered into force in 1937 (but has not been widely ratified), provides that "[a] person possessing two or more nationalities who habitually resides in one of the countries whose nationality he possesses, and who is in fact most closely connected with that country, shall be exempt from all military obligations in the other country or countries."[106] Bilateral agreements are another vehicle available for dealing with the challenges of dual nationality in times of armed conflict. During World War II, for example, many States concluded such agreements with the United States outlining procedures concerning the compulsory military service of their respective nationals.[107]

In the absence of a relevant treaty or special agreement, references in Pictet's 1958 *Commentary to Geneva Convention IV* and the *Tadic* appeal judgment suggest that States may also resort to the law of diplomatic protection.[108] But determinations of nationality under that body of law are not well settled either. The International Court of Justice, for instance, has articulated a rigid, highly fact-dependent standard whereby nationality "may be said to constitute the juridical expression of the fact that the individual upon whom it is conferred, either directly by the law or as the result of an act of the authorities, is in fact more closely connected with the population of the State conferring nationality than with that of any other State."[109] It implies that international law should recognize only one nationality to the exclusion of all others.

Conversely, the International Law Commission suggests in its 2006 *Draft Articles on Diplomatic Protection* that it is possible for individuals to possess multiple nationalities under international law.[110] In such cases, the person's "predominant" nationality should prevail. In making that assessment, and while noting there are no authoritative criteria, the Commission suggests considering, among others, an individual's

> habitual residence, the amount of time spent in each country of nationality, date of naturalization (i.e., the length of the period spent as a national of the protecting State before the claim arose); place, curricula and language

106. Protocol Relating to Military Obligations in Certain Cases of Double Nationality art. 1, Apr. 12, 1935, League of Nations, Treaty Series, vol. 178, at 227, No. 4117.

107. *See* U.S. Department of State, *Military Service*, 8 Digest of International Law 540, 561–62, 570 (1967).

108. *See, e.g.*, 1958 Commentary to Geneva Convention IV, *supra* note 18, at 264; *Prosecutor v. Tadić*, *supra* note 103, ¶¶ 164–65.

109. Nottebohm (Liech. v. Guat.) Second Phase, Judgment, 1955 I.C.J. 4, 23 (Apr. 6).

110. *Draft Articles on Diplomatic Protection*, *supra* note 102, art. 4. Determining nationality is the province of each individual State, and the conditions listed are not exhaustive but instead illustrative of linkages that a State may find helpful in determining who qualifies for its nationality. *See id.* commentary to Draft Article 4, ¶¶ 1–4. If this is correct as a matter of law, it begs the question of how to handle conflicts between nationalities in light of the principle of sovereign equality of States.

> of education, employment and financial interests; place of family life; family ties in each country; participation in social and public life; use of language; taxation, bank account, social security insurance; visits to the other State of nationality, possession and use of passport of the other State; and military service.[111]

This alternative standard closely resembles that expressed in the 1930 Protocol, according to which only those who "in fact" are closely related to another State are exempt from compulsory military obligations. In the conscription context, protected persons would therefore only be exempt from compulsory service if their cumulative ties to the conscripting State were outweighed by a preponderance of those with another State.

While the determination of an individual's nationality would, in most cases, likely be the same under either standard, the Russia-Ukraine conflict highlights a scenario in which weighing the various factors could prove challenging. This is especially true because many of the legal questions at issue in the forced conscription context depend on the voluntariness of an individual's accumulation of ties to a conscripting State and the subjectivity of that State's judgment. Indeed, there are few, if any, international safeguards in place to ensure that States' nationality determinations are neither arbitrary nor fraudulent.

Other questions remain. For example, if nationality is contextual, should the particular international humanitarian law prohibition at issue—in this case, forced conscription—serve as a relevant consideration in assessing a person's nationality? In other words, could one argue that the rule's object and purpose should weigh in favor of determining that the nonconscripting State is the predominant nationality as a matter of law? Answers to these and similar queries could mitigate the risk of victims slipping through the prohibition's cracks but are beyond the scope of the present chapter.

4. CONCLUDING THOUGHTS

The prohibition against forced conscription is a fundamental rule of international humanitarian law. Its treaty components have been in force for decades, while the customary international law they reflect has existed for well over two centuries. Together they provide robust and overlapping safeguards that proscribe States from compelling foreign nationals into their armed forces.

Despite the prohibition's significance, however, the extent to which its components overlap remains uncertain due to ambiguities in their interpretation. Unresolved questions such as the scope of the phrase "operations of war" or the notion of hostile "forces" inject a lack of clarity into the law, providing opportunities for circumventing its protections. In addition, conflicts such as those

111. *Id.* at commentary to Draft Article 7, ¶ 5.

in the former Yugoslavia and more recently in Ukraine demonstrate that the issue of how to determine a protected person's nationality is hardly academic. The fact that there is broad international agreement that Russia is unlawfully conscripting Ukrainian nationals into its armed forces is reassuring. Public condemnations from the OHCHR, the United States, and others are extremely commendable. Accountability, however, will be the true litmus test for whether the prohibition, with all its lingering uncertainties, nevertheless effectively protects victims of war.

Civilian Data Protection in War

RUSSELL BUCHAN*

1. INTRODUCTION

Effective military strategy requires parties to armed conflicts to collect information on their opponents and better understand their capabilities and intentions.[1] International humanitarian law (IHL) has long permitted belligerents to collect information during international and non-international armed conflicts. During international armed conflict (IAC), Article 24 of the Hague Regulations 1907 states that "the employment of measures necessary for obtaining information about the enemy and the country . . . [is] considered permissible,"[2] and this provision reflects customary international law (CIL).[3] CIL also permits belligerents to collect information during times of non-international armed conflict (NIAC).[4] In fact, certain rules of IHL *require* parties to armed conflicts to establish effective regimes for the collection, processing, and evaluation of information. For example, the principles of distinction, proportionality, and precautions in attack

* Professor of International Law, University of Reading, United Kingdom.

1. "The obtaining of intelligence about the enemy is an important military activity." United Kingdom Ministry of Defence, The Manual of the Law of Armed Conflict ¶ 4.9.3 (2004) [hereinafter UK Law of War Manual].

2. Regulations Respecting the Laws and Customs of War on Land, annexed to Convention No. IV Respecting the Laws and Customs of War on Land art. 24, Oct. 18, 1907, 36 Stat. 2227, T.S. No. 539 [hereinafter 1907 Hague Regulations].

3. Heather Harrison Dinniss, *The Status and Treatment of Captured Spies under the Law of War*, *in* Research Handbook on Intelligence and International Law (Russell Buchan & Iñaki Navarrete eds., forthcoming).

4. *Id.*

Russell Buchan, *Civilian Data Protection in War* In: *Civilian Protection in Armed Conflict*. Edited by: Jelena Pejic and Captain Margaret Kotlik, Oxford University Press. © Russell Buchan 2025.
DOI: 10.1093/oso/9780197793176.003.0011

require commanders' targeting decisions to be informed by accurate and reliable information.[5]

Nowadays, information tends to be compiled, stored, and transmitted as electronic data. Cyberspace is thus a resource-rich environment for belligerents to target and acquire information on their opponents. The U.S. Department of Defense (DoD) "treats information as a strategic asset"[6] and sees it as the "currency of future warfare."[7] The DoD recognizes that it is in a "high stakes race to harness the power of data"[8] and is working to create a "culture of data-centric decision-making."[9] Parties to armed conflicts pursue data dominance by employing a range of new and emerging technologies, such as unmanned surveillance vehicles, facial and voice recognition technologies, and AI-powered computer software.

Collecting "big data" creates the challenge of how to effectively process it and separate out what is useful from what is not. As with data collection, militaries are increasingly using new and emerging technologies to process data, including AI-powered algorithms that can comb through massive amounts of data at speed, identify trends by correlating large and complex datasets, and share data with third parties autonomously.

Along with military necessity, humanity is a bedrock principle of IHL. The collection and processing of data creates a paradox insofar as it pulls the principle of humanity in different directions: on the one hand, collecting and processing data enables parties to armed conflicts to direct their operations against military objectives and spare the civilian population from the horrors of war, yet, on the other, it risks breaching the privacy and data protection rights of individuals caught up in armed conflict, such as civilians.

The aim of this chapter is to analyze the extent to which belligerents must respect the rights to privacy and data protection, including while collecting and processing civilian data. In doing so, this chapter provides militaries with a basis for reflection on how to protect civilian data during hostilities and streamline their conduct in accordance with international law. In pursuit of this objective, the

5. Office of the Prosecutor, International Criminal Tribunal for the former Yugoslavia, Final Report to the Prosecutor by the Committee Established to Review the NATO Bombing Campaign Against the Federal Republic of Yugoslavia, ¶¶ 28, 29 International Legal Materials 1257 (June 13, 2000), http://www.icty.org/x/file/Press/nato061300.pdf.

6. United States Department of Defense, *Digital Modernization Strategy* (July 12, 2019), https://media.defense.gov/2019/Jul/12/2002156622/-1/-1/1/DOD-DIGITAL-MODERNIZATION-STRATEGY-2019.PDF.

7. Tech. Sgt. Robert Barnett, *Goldfein Describes the Future of the Air Force*, Secretary of the Air Force Public Affairs (July 2, 2020), https://www.af.mil/News/Article-Display/Article/2245441/goldfein-describes-the-future-of-the-air-force/.

8. Admiral Bill Moran, *It's Time to Make Data Strategic for our Navy*, Defense One (Apr. 2, 2019), https://www.defenseone.com/ideas/2019/04/its-time-make-data-strategic-our-navy/156020/.

9. Michael Conlin, Defense Department's Chief Data Officer, *quoted in DoD Overcoming Culture Challenges to Turn Data "Snapshot" into Predictive Analytics*, Federal News Network (Nov.

chapter is structured as follows: Section 2 assesses the status, content, and scope of the right to privacy under international law, and section 3 pursues the same objective in relation to the right to data protection. Section 4 examines whether international law requires parties to armed conflicts to respect civilians' rights to privacy and data protection during hostilities. The final section offers conclusions.

Before moving on, three caveats are necessary. First, and in line with the theme of this book, this chapter focuses on the protection of *civilian* data. How international law protects combatant data is only considered incidentally in order to draw comparisons with how it protects civilian data. Second, the chapter examines the protection afforded by international law to civilian data during active military operations and does not consider the extent to which the rights to privacy and data protection must be respected when civilians are detained by a party to the armed conflict. Third, it focuses on military operations involving the collection and processing of data rather than on those that damage or modify data. The collection and processing of data does not constitute an "attack" within the meaning of IHL and thus the law of attack is not considered.[10]

2. THE RIGHT TO PRIVACY

The right to privacy is protected by multiple international and regional human rights treaties. Most notably, the right to privacy is guaranteed by Article 17 of the International Covenant on Civil and Political Rights (ICCPR) 1966, which provides: "No one shall be subjected to arbitrary or unlawful interference with his privacy, family, home or correspondence, nor to unlawful attacks on his honour and reputation."[11]

Given the widespread ratification of treaties protecting the right to privacy, some commentators claim that it has crystalized into a fundamental human right under CIL.[12]

The contours of the right to privacy have been extensively debated by human rights bodies. These bodies have not formulated an exhaustive definition of the right to privacy, instead preferring to interpret it on a case-by-case basis. That said, their jurisprudence supports a broad definition of the right, encompassing not just a negative right for persons to be "let alone"[13] but also a positive entitlement

21, 2019), https://federalnewsnetwork.com/big-data/2019/11/dod-overcoming-culture-challenge-to-turn-data-snapshot-into-predictive-analytics/.

10. *See* Protocol Additional to the Geneva Conventions of 12 August 1949, and Relating to the Protection of Victims of International Armed Conflicts arts. 48 and 52, June 8, 1977, 1125 U.N.T.S. 3 [hereinafter AP I].

11. The International Covenant on Civil and Political Rights, Dec. 16, 1966, 999 U.N.T.S. 171 [hereinafter ICCPR].

12. Alexandra Rengel, Privacy in the 21st Century 108 (2013).

13. Daniel Solove, Understanding Privacy 13 (2009).

to "establish details of their identity as individual human beings"[14] and "develop relationships with other human beings and the outside world."[15] Defined in this way, the right to privacy recognizes that individuals are entitled to an "area of autonomous development, interaction and liberty free from State intervention."[16] Information enabling individuals to establish and maintain a personal and professional life is therefore protected from interference,[17] including publicly available information such as a person's image.[18]

Today, "the same rights that people have offline must also be protected online,"[19] and States must "respect and protect the right to privacy, including in the context of digital communication."[20] An important question is whether the right to privacy is breached by the mere collection of data or, as the United States maintains,[21] only where the data is read and analyzed by a human (and not, for example, by a computer algorithm). The U.S. approach represents a narrow interpretation of the right to privacy and runs counter to the views of the UN Human Rights Committee and the European Court of Human Rights (ECtHR),[22] who regard the collection of data on its own as interfering with the right to privacy because it undermines personal autonomy and prevents individuals from forging meaningful relationships with others.

The U.S. also appears to take the position that the right to privacy does not protect metadata but only content data.[23] This approach is unpersuasive given that access to metadata can reveal important details about a person's identity and

14. Mikulic v. Croatia, App. No. 53176/99 (2002) (ECtHR).

15. Pretty v. United Kingdom, App. No. 2346/02 (2002) (ECtHR).

16. U.N. Human Rights Comm., *Report of The Special Rapporteur on the Promotion and Protection of Human Rights and Fundamental Freedoms while Countering Terrorism* ¶ 28, U.N. Doc. A/HRC/25/59 (Mar. 11, 2014).

17. Shimovolos v. Russia, App. No. 30194/09 (2011) (ECtHR). *See also* U.N. Human Rights Comm., *CCPR General Comment No. 16: Article 17 (Right to Privacy), The Right to Respect of Privacy, Family, Home and Correspondence, and Protection of Honour and Reputation*, U.N. Doc. CRC/C/GC/16 (Apr. 8, 1988).

18. Reklos and Davourlis v. Greece, App. No. 1234/05, ¶ 40 (2009) (ECtHR).

19. Human Rights Council, *The Promotion, Protection and Enjoyment of Human Rights on the Internet*, ¶ 1, U.N. Doc. A/HRC/20/L.13 (June 29, 2012).

20. U.N. Human Rights Council, *The Right to Privacy in the Digital Age*, ¶ 4(e), U.N. Doc. A/C.3/68/L.45/Rev.1 (Nov. 20, 2013).

21. U.S. Department of Defense, *Procedures Governing the Activities of DOD Intelligence Components that Affect United States Persons*, DOD 5240 1-R C2.2.1 (1982).

22. General Comment No. 16, *supra* note 17, at ¶ 8; *Shimovolos*, *supra* note 17, at ¶ 65.

23. *See, e.g.*, the statements by Senators Dianne Feinstein and Saxby Chambliss while they were the Co-Chairs of the US Senate Intelligence Committee: *Transcript: Dianne Feinstein, Saxby Chambliss Explain, Defend NSA Phone Records Program*, THE WASHINGTON POST (June 6,

behavior, and, especially when aggregated in significant amounts and correlated, it can be as revealing as content data. It is for this reason that human rights bodies have held that the right to privacy protects metadata such as the times, dates, contacts, language, and lengths of voice and video calls.[24]

Critically, privacy is not an absolute right and can be lawfully restricted where it is necessary to meet a legitimate aim. Synthesizing the jurisprudence of various human rights bodies, three key requirements must be met before a State can lawfully restrict the right to privacy:

1. *Legality*: interferences must be conducted in accordance with laws that are public, accessible, clear, precise, and nondiscriminatory;
2. *Legitimate aim*: interferences must pursue a legitimate aim, that is, they must be deployed in the interests of national security, public safety, or the economic well-being of the country; for the prevention of disorder or crime; or for the protection of health, morals, or the rights and freedoms of others; and
3. *Necessity*: interferences must be necessary to protect the legitimate aim they serve. The necessity principle also requires a proportionality assessment, namely, that the impugned measure is the least intrusive means available to achieve the legitimate aim. A key requirement of the proportionality principle is that adequate safeguards are put in place to protect the right to privacy.

With the emergence of big data and the concomitant development of powerful technologies to collect it, human rights bodies have had to address the legality of *bulk* digital surveillance. In its earlier jurisprudence, the ECtHR required surveillance operations to be targeted against specific individuals who were reasonably suspected of being engaged in illicit activities and expressed "serious concern" over the "strategic, large-scale interception" of communications.[25] However, the Court has taken a more permissive approach in recent years, holding that bulk digital surveillance is a "valuable" tool of "vital importance" to the security of States and not per se disproportionate and unlawful.[26] That said, the Court laid down a strict eight-part test which provides that bulk surveillance is lawful only where the State's domestic regulatory framework stipulates:

2013), https://www.washingtonpost.com/news/post-politics/wp/2013/06/06/transcript-dianne-feinstein-saxby-chambliss-explain-defend-nsa-phone-records-program/.

24. Kennedy v. United Kingdom, App. No. 26839/05, ¶ 118 (2010) (ECtHR); Case of Big Brother Watch and Others v. United Kingdom, App. Nos. 58170/13, 62322/14, and 24960/15, at ¶¶ 342, 363–64 (2021) (ECtHR).

25. Szabo and Vissy v. Hungary, App. No. 37138/14/4, ¶¶ 69–71 (2016) (ECtHR).

26. *Big Brother Watch*, *supra* note 24, at ¶¶ 323, 424; Centrum för Rättvisa v. Sweden, App. No. 35252/08, ¶ 373 (2021) (ECtHR).

1. the grounds on which bulk surveillance can be authorized;
2. the circumstances in which communications can be intercepted;
3. the procedures to be followed for granting authorization;
4. the procedures to be followed for selecting, examining, and using intercepted material;
5. the precautions to be taken when communicating the material to other parties;
6. the limits on the duration of the interception, the storage of the intercepted material, and the circumstances in which it must be erased or destroyed;
7. the procedures and modalities for supervision by an independent authority of compliance with the above safeguards and its powers to address non-compliance; and
8. the procedures for independent ex post facto review of such compliance and the powers vested in the competent body in addressing instances of non-compliance.[27]

The ECtHR's "normalization of mass surveillance"[28] has met with significant criticism.[29] Importantly, other human rights bodies have consistently held that bulk surveillance cannot be reconciled with the right to privacy.[30] Even in the aftermath of the ECtHR's recent jurisprudence, a report of the Office of the UN High Commissioner for Human Rights (adopted by the Human Rights Council) described bulk surveillance as a "deeply troubling practice"[31] that remains a "serious problem" for the protection of human rights including, specifically, the right to privacy.[32]

27. *Big Brother Watch*, *supra* note 24, at ¶ 361.

28. Marko Milanovic, *The Grand Normalization of Mass Surveillance: ECtHR Grand Chamber Judgments in Big Brother Watch and Centrum för Rättvisa*, EJIL: Talk! (May 26, 2021), https://www.ejiltalk.org/the-grand-normalization-of-mass-surveillance-ecthr-grand-chamber-judgments-in-big-brother-watch-and-centrum-for-rattvisa/.

29. *See, e.g.*, Eliza Watt, *Much Ado about Mass Surveillance—The ECtHR Grand Chamber "Opens the Gates of an Electronic 'Big Brother' in Europe" in Big Brother Watch v UK*, Strasbourg Observers (June 28, 2021), https://strasbourgobservers.com/2021/06/28/much-ado-about-mass-surveillance-the-ecthr-grand-chamber-opens-the-gates-of-an-electronic-big-brother-in-europe-in-big-brother-watch-v-uk/.

30. U.N. Human Rights Council, *The Right to Privacy in the Digital Age*, ¶ 25, U.N. Doc. A/HRC/27/37 (June 30, 2014); U.N. Human Rights Council, *The Right to Privacy in the Digital Age*, ¶ 17, U.N. Doc. A/HRC/39/29 (Aug. 3, 2016).

31. Human Rights Council, *The Right to Privacy in the Digital Age*, ¶ 29, U.N. Doc. A/HRC/51/17 (Aug. 4, 2022).

32. *Id.* at ¶ 53.

Human rights treaties permit States parties to derogate from their human rights obligations in cases of public emergency that threaten the life of the nation,[33] although in practice derogations are rare. Derogating from human rights obligations requires a number of strict procedural and substantive conditions to be met. Procedurally, an authorized government official must proclaim the existence of a state of emergency, and the State must notify other parties to the treaty of the derogation and explain which provisions are being derogated from and why.[34] Substantively, a derogating State must show there is a threat to the life of the nation.[35] Importantly, derogations do not operate on a blanket basis but are limited to "the extent strictly required by the exigencies of the situation."[36] As such, any derogation must be necessary and proportionate in the circumstances, which places strict limits on their geographical, material, and temporal scope of application.[37]

The onset of war is a recognized ground for derogation from human rights obligations.[38] The occurrence of an *external* armed conflict—that is, where a State is fighting an armed conflict on the territory of another State but no fighting takes place within its own territory—can constitute a basis for derogation, although it falls on the State to demonstrate that the external conflict threatens the life of the nation and that the derogation is necessary and proportionate in the circumstances.[39]

3. THE RIGHT TO DATA PROTECTION

Data protection laws are designed to limit the processing of personally identifiable data (PID). At the time of writing, 137 States have adopted such laws.[40] Data protection laws have also been developed at the regional level, with the European Union's General Data Protection Regulation (GDPR) being the most well known.[41]

33. *See, e.g.*, ICCPR, *supra* note 11, art. 4(1); Convention for the Protection of Human Rights and Fundamental Freedoms art. 15(1), Nov. 4, 1950, 213 U.N.T.S. 222 [hereinafter ECHR].

34. ICCPR, *supra* note 11, art. 4(3); ECHR, *supra* note 33, art. 15(3).

35. U.N. Human Rights Council, *General Comment No. 29: Article 4 (Derogations during a State of Emergency)*, ¶ 3, U.N. Doc. CCPR/C/21/Rev 1/Add 11 (Aug. 31, 2001).

36. ICCPR, *supra* note 11, art. 4(1); ECHR, *supra* note 33, art. 15(1).

37. *U.N. Human Rights Council*, General Comment No. 29, *supra* note 35.

38. ECHR, *supra* note 36 ("In time of war . . .").

39. Marko Milanovic, *Extraterritorial Derogations from Human Rights Treaties in Armed Conflict*, *in* The Frontiers of Human Rights (Nehal Bhuta ed., 2016).

40. U.N. Trade and Development (UNCTAD), *Data Protection and Privacy Legislation Worldwide* (Aug. 30, 2023), https://unctad.org/page/data-protection-and-privacy-legislation-worldwide.

41. Regulation (EU) 2016/679 of the European Parliament and of the Council of 27 April 2016 on the protection of natural persons with regard to the processing of personal data and on

Significantly, the GDPR imposes obligations on all data controllers and processers who process the PID of data subjects located in the European Union regardless of whether they operate beyond the European Union. The economic incentive of accessing the European Union's market means the GDPR has become a powerful driver in developing data protection practices, policies, and laws across the world, a phenomenon known as the "Brussels effect."[42] The GDPR has thus emerged as a gold-standard regime for data protection.

An important question is whether the right to data protection has emerged as a fundamental human entitlement under CIL. As we know, the threshold for the development of CIL is high: putative rules must be supported by a general practice accepted as law.[43] Many commentators doubt whether the right to data protection has achieved sufficient consensus among States to crystalize as CIL.[44] But it has been said that "personal data protection as a fundamental right is gaining wider acceptance around the world,"[45] and, referencing the GDPR, some commentators claim that "international law now includes human rights protections for personal data."[46] At a minimum, there appears to be a clear trajectory toward recognizing data protection as a human right under CIL (bar persistent objectors), which means that developing a better understanding of how it applies to the collection and processing of data by parties to armed conflicts is a worthwhile exercise. This chapter proceeds on the basis that data protection is, or will soon be, a legally protected right under international human rights law (IHRL).

The right to privacy is the handmaiden of the right to data protection, and they are closely related. In fact, given how broadly human rights bodies have interpreted the right to privacy, many aspects of the right to data protection are already covered

the free movement of such data, and repealing Directive 95/46/EC (General Data Protection Regulation) [hereinafter GDPR]. The Council of Europe's "Convention 108+" on the Protection of Individuals with regard to the Processing of Personal Data, which revises the Council's "Convention 108" and brings it into line with the GDPR, is also an important international convention on the protection of personal data.

42. Anu Bradford, *The Brussels Effect*, 107 Northwestern University Law Review 1 (2012).

43. Statute of the International Court of Justice art. 38(1)(b), June 26, 1945, 59 Stat. 1055, 33 U.N.T.S. 993.

44. Asaf Lubin, *The Rights to Privacy and Data Protection under International Humanitarian Law and Human Rights Law*, *in* Research Handbook on Human Rights and Humanitarian Law: Further Reflections and Perspectives (Robert Kolb, Gloria Gaggioli, & Pavle Kilibarda eds., 2022).

45. International Committee of the Red Cross, *Handbook on Data Protection in Humanitarian Action* 24 (2020), https://www.icrc.org/en/data-protection-humanitarian-action-handbook.

46. Mary Ellen O'Connell, *Data Privacy Rights: The Same in War and Peace*, *in* The Rights to Privacy and Data Protection in Times of Armed Conflict 17 (Russell Buchan & Asaf Lubin eds., 2022).

by the right to privacy. This often means that debates on data protection are subsumed under the right to privacy. For example, while the right to data protection covers the collection of PID, debates as to the legality of this activity are often discussed in the context of the right to privacy. That said, the right to data protection possesses its own legal identity and is "broader than the scope of [the right to] privacy," tending to have greatest purchase in relation to the processing of PID *after* it has been collected.[47] For instance, the right to privacy may not permit data subjects to correct inaccurate data or challenge the length of time for which it is stored, yet as we shall see these are core entitlements of the right to data protection.

The right to data protection must be respected by data controllers (those who determine the purposes and means of processing PID) and data processors (those who process PID on behalf of controllers), with both categories applying to State and non-State actors alike. This right applies to the "processing" of data, which covers the collection, recording, storage, transmission, disclosure, modification, and erasure of PID. PID is defined as:

> [A]ny information relating to an identified or identifiable natural person . . . one which can be identified, directly or indirectly, in particular by reference to an identifier such as a name, an identification number, location data, an online identifier or to one or more factors specific to the physical, physiological, genetic, mental, economic, cultural or social identity of that natural person.[48]

PID excludes aggregate or statistical datasets, although if there is a risk that PID can be extracted from them the data should be anonymized or pseudonymized or, if there is still a risk of identification, the datasets should not be released.[49] Sensitive data, such as data relating to racial or ethnic origin or religious, political, and philosophical beliefs, requires augmented protection procedures.[50]

While there are variations in data protection regimes, a survey of national laws and policies, the European Union's GDPR, the work of the International Law Commission (ILC),[51] and of the International Committee of the Red Cross (ICRC)[52] indicates that seven key principles underpin the right to data protection:

47. Juliane Kokott & Christoph Sobotta, *The Distinction between Privacy and Data Protection in the Jurisprudence of the CJEU and the ECtHR*, 3 International Data Privacy Law 222, 225 (2013).

48. GDPR, *supra* note 41, art. 4.

49. *Id.* at Recital 162.

50. GDPR, *supra* note 41, art. 9.

51. Report of the International Law Commission on the Work of its Fifty-Eighth Session, Annex IV: *Protection of Personal Data in Transborder Flow of Information*, U.N. Doc. Supplement No. 10 (A/61/10) (2006) [hereinafter ILC Report].

52. *Handbook on Data Protection in Humanitarian Action*, *supra* note 45.

1. The principle of *legality* and *fairness* requires the processing of data to be lawful and fair. There are several grounds for the lawful processing of PID: (i) consent of the data subject; if it is (ii) permitted by contract; (iii) required by law; (iv) necessary to protect someone's vital interests; (v) undertaken pursuant to an official public function; or (vi) necessary to protect the legitimate interests of the data controller or processor or a third party. To be "fair," data must be processed in the best interests of the data subject or at least consistent with wider public interests. Within the bounds of security and logistical considerations, "fairness" also requires that data subjects have a right to know what data of theirs is being processed, how it is being processed, and why;
2. The principle of *purpose limitation* means the data should be collected only for specific, explicit, and legitimate purposes and not further processed in a manner that is incompatible with them;
3. The principle of *data minimization* stipulates that the minimum amount of data should be collected and processed to meet the purpose of the operation. If the purpose can be met by anonymizing or pseudonymizing the data, this should be done. Data can be shared with third parties where pursuant to a lawful purpose, but again the amount of data shared must be the minimum necessary to achieve the relevant aim;
4. The principle of *data quality* requires data controllers and processors to ensure that data is accurate and up to date;
5. The principle of *storage limitation* means that data must be kept for no longer than is necessary for the purpose for which it is processed, unless longer periods of storage are in the public interest;
6. The principle of *data security* means that data controllers and processors must take reasonable measures to protect PID from unauthorized access, modification, erasure, or use; and
7. The principle of *accountability* requires data controllers and processors to implement systems that ensure the preceding principles are respected.

Data protection regimes invariably recognize a range of grounds on which data controllers and processors can derogate from some or all of their data protection obligations. For example, they are exempt from complying with data protection laws where necessary to protect national security, State sovereignty, and public order or for law enforcement purposes.[53] The national security exemption covers situations of armed conflict.[54]

Critically, derogations can be invoked only where necessary and proportionate in the circumstances, and these conditions are strictly applied by human rights bodies.[55] This means, for example, that the national security exemption does not

53. *See, e.g.*, GDPR, *supra* note 41, art. 23.

54. Robin Geiss & Henning Lahmann, *Protection of Data in Armed Conflict*, 97 INTERNATIONAL LAW STUDIES 556 (2021).

55. Tietosuojavaltuutettu v. Satakunnan Markkinapörssi Oy and Satamedia Oy, ¶ 56, Case C-73/07, ECLI:EU:C:2008: 727 (Dec. 16, 2008); *see also* ILC Report, *supra* note 51, at 224–25.

apply to situations of armed conflict en bloc. Rather, belligerents must demonstrate that their invocation of the national security exemption is necessary and proportionate whenever they seek to release themselves from their data protection obligations.

4. THE RIGHTS TO PRIVACY AND DATA PROTECTION DURING ARMED CONFLICT

At the outset, it is important to recognize that many information operations undertaken during armed conflict do not implicate the rights to privacy and data protection; for example, operations that track troop movements, intercept military communications, and map battlefield terrain. Yet information operations can involve the collection and processing of data that is covered by the rights to privacy and data protection, and this raises the question as to whether and to what extent these rights must be respected by belligerents.

Historically, international law was bifurcated into the law of peace and the law of war. The onset of armed conflict meant the latter displaced the former as the applicable legal framework. Today, it is well accepted that the law of peace and the law of war apply concurrently.[56]

IHRL is a body of international law that continues to apply during armed conflict.[57] An important question concerns the geographical scope of application of IHRL because States may conduct military operations on the territories of their opponents. Human rights treaties usually require States to protect human rights within their jurisdictions, which, at a minimum, means protecting the human rights of persons located within their territories. The International Court of Justice (ICJ) has gone further and held that a State's jurisdiction extends to territory (and people therein) over which it exercises effective control, for example, occupied territory.[58] Human rights courts[59] and bodies[60] have developed a broader approach, maintaining that individuals fall within a State's jurisdiction wherever it exercises physical authority and control over them. Recently, these human rights

56. *See, e.g.*, Legality of the Threat or Use of Nuclear Weapons, Advisory Opinion, 1996 I.C.J. Rep. 226, ¶ 25 (July 8); Legal Consequences of the Construction of a Wall in the Occupied Palestinian Territory, Advisory Opinion, I.C.J. Rep. 2004, 136, ¶ 106 (July 9); and Armed Activities on the Territory of the Congo (Democratic Republic of the Congo v. Uganda), Judgment, I.C.J. Rep. 2005, 168 ¶¶ 215–20 (Dec. 19).

57. *See, e.g.*, Case of Ukraine and the Netherlands v. Russia, App. Nos. 8019/16, 43800/14 and 28525/20, at ¶ 558 (2022) (ECtHR).

58. *Wall* case, *supra* note 56, at ¶ 112.

59. Alejandro Jimenez Blanco v. Cuba, Case No. 11.589, Inter-Amer. Comm'n. H.R., Report No. 86/99, ¶ 23 (1999); *Case of Ukraine and the Netherlands*, *supra* note 57, at ¶¶ 558, 571.

60. U.N. Human Rights Committee, *General Comment No. 31: The Nature of the General Legal Obligation Imposed on States Parties to the Covenant*, ¶ 10, U.N. Doc. CCPR/C/21/Rev.1/Add. 13 (May 26, 2004).

entities have gone further and established jurisdiction where States exercise authority and control over individuals through the medium of cyberspace.[61] This expanded approach has gained traction because it accords with the ethos of human rights law.[62] By their very nature, human rights are indivisible, inalienable, and universal.[63] Consequently, a State's duty to respect human rights should not depend on where individuals are geographically located but, instead, on whether it exercises authority and control over them and regardless of whether such authority and control is exercised by physical or virtual means.

The concurrent application of IHRL and IHL, along with the extraterritorial application of IHRL, raises the question as to how these regimes interact when they both contain rules that apply to the same activity or situation but require different conduct from States. This seems to be the case with information operations because, as explained previously, IHL permits (and sometimes requires) parties to armed conflicts to set up regimes for the collection and processing of information, while IHRL limits such operations by requiring parties to armed conflicts to observe the rights to privacy and data protection.

An important caveat is that, even if an armed conflict is occurring, IHL only applies to conduct that has a *nexus* to the conflict. If a nexus cannot be established, IHL does not apply and other international law regimes will be controlling, such as IHRL. According to the International Criminal Tribunal for the former Yugoslavia (ICTY), a nexus between impugned conduct and an armed conflict exists where the conflict "play[s] a substantial part in the perpetrator's ability to commit it, his decision to commit it, the manner in which it was committed or the purpose for which it was committed."[64] The key issue is that the conduct is "closely related to the armed conflict" or, to be more exact, "the perpetrator acted in furtherance of or under the guise of the armed conflict."[65]

To illustrate, if States A and B are parties to an IAC and a law enforcement agency from State A conducts an information collection operation against individuals located in State B because they are suspected of being involved in criminal activities in State A, IHL does not apply because the connection between

61. *Right to Privacy in the Digital Age*, *supra* note 30, at ¶¶ 33–34; Human Rights Committee, *Concluding Observations on the Fourth Periodic Report of the United States of America*, U.N. Doc. CCPR/C/USA/CO/4 (Apr. 23, 2014); *Big Brother Watch*, *supra* note 22.

62. Some States, such as the United States, reject the extraterritorial application of IHRL. Office of the General Counsel, U.S. Department of Defense, Law of War Manual, § 1.6.3.3. (rev. ed., Dec. 2016) [hereinafter DoD Law of War Manual].

63. G.A. Res. 217 (III) A, Universal Declaration of Human Rights Preamble (Dec. 10, 1948).

64. Prosecutor v. Kunarac, Appeals Judgment, Case Nos. IT-96-23 and IT-96-23/1-A, ¶ 58 (Int'l Crim. Trib. for the former Yugoslavia June 12, 2002). The Trial Chamber in the *Ntaganda* case confirmed this test: Prosecutor v. Bosco Ntaganda, Case No. ICC-01/04-02/06, Trial Chamber, ¶ 732 (July 8, 2019).

65. *Kunarac*, *supra* note 64, at ¶ 58.

the conduct and the armed conflict is too attenuated. Instead, other international legal regimes will apply, such as IHRL. By contrast, if State A's military launches a cyber surveillance operation against people located in the territory of State B to help identify and locate combatants, IHL applies (along with, potentially, other international law regimes) because the surveillance operation is undertaken in furtherance of hostilities. If the processing of data reveals that civilian data has been collected but does not serve a combat-related purpose, IHL ceases to apply, and other international law regimes (such as IHRL) will be operative. Unless such data serves another lawful purpose (for example, it relates to criminal activities and is therefore needed for law enforcement purposes), IHRL requires its processing to be terminated and the data deleted. Similarly, if a belligerent collects large amounts of data relating to a combatant but it transpires that certain data are not combat-relevant, IHRL applies. Admittedly, during armed conflict there may be very little data about a combatant that is not combat-relevant.

Relatedly, IHL ceases to apply "on the general close of military operations."[66] At this point, IHRL governs the processing of data collected during hostilities, such as its retention, storage, and sharing with third parties.[67] As we have seen, data protection regimes require data to be deleted once the purpose for its collection has been fulfilled or otherwise expires. States may be reluctant to delete data belonging to former enemy combatants even though the conflict has ended. If they continue to pose a threat to national security (e.g., because of their links to international terrorism), there remains a lawful basis to retain the data. But if States cannot demonstrate that such a threat exists, the data must be deleted. In other words, States cannot retain data collected during armed conflict indefinitely simply because they think it may be useful at some point in the future.

The focus of this chapter is on parties to armed conflicts who collect and process data in order to advance combat, which means that such operations occur during armed conflict and have a sufficiently close connection with the conflict for IHL to apply. This brings us back to the question raised earlier as to how IHRL and IHL interact when both regimes regulate the same conduct but pull in different directions.

International courts, human rights bodies, and commentators have developed various approaches to explain the interaction between IHRL and IHL.[68] It is not necessary to recapitulate these well-trodden debates because, in my view,

66. Convention (IV) Relative to the Protection of Civilian Persons in Time of War art 6, Aug. 12, 1949, 6 U.S.T. 3516, 75 U.N.T.S. 287 [hereinafter GC IV]. *See also* Prosecutor v. Gotovina, Case No. IT-06-90-T, Judgment, ¶ 1694 (Int'l Crim. Trib. for the former Yugoslavia Apr. 15, 2011) (IHL ceases to apply where there is "a general close of military operations and a general conclusion of peace").

67. That said, Convention (III) Relative to the Treatment of Prisoners of War art. 5, Aug. 12, 1949, 6 U.S.T. 3316, 75 U.N.T.S. 135 [hereinafter GC III], explains that IHL continues to protect prisoners of war "until their final release and repatriation."

68. *See* Yuval Shany, *Co-application and Harmonization of IHL and IHRL: Are Rumours About the Death of Lex Specialis Premature?*, *in* Kolb, Gaggioli & Kilibarda, *supra* note 44.

the complementary approach is the most defensible and has gained ascendancy in recent years.[69] At the heart of the complementary approach is the recognition that the "common underlying purpose of international humanitarian law and international human rights law is the protection of the life, health and dignity of human beings."[70] This common normative basis means that, in many instances, IHRL and IHL can be interpreted and applied consistently with each other,[71] and this is particularly the case where IHL rules are cast in broad and general terms and thus susceptible to interpretation and adaption. Importantly, this interpretive process leads to the harmonization and convergence of IHRL and IHL; in short, they fuse together and prescribe the same conduct. As such, IHRL and IHL are "complementary" rather than "mutually exclusive."[72] It is only in those rare instances where IHRL and IHL cannot be reconciled that a decision has to be taken as to which regime takes precedence. Here, the *lex specialis* principle comes into play and the applicable rule (whether IHRL or IHL) is the one that more specifically and directly regulates the conduct in question.[73]

As already noted, treaty and customary IHL permit belligerents to obtain information about their enemy and the country with which they are in conflict. Moreover, IHL does not *explicitly* require parties to armed conflicts to protect the rights to privacy and data protection. This is unsurprising given that, at least when IHL's core rules were formulated in 1949 and 1977, its central concern was to protect individuals from physical harm. If we adopt the complementary approach outlined earlier, the immediate question is whether there are any preexisting rules of IHL that can be interpreted and applied in conjunction with IHRL to require parties to armed conflicts to respect the rights to privacy and data protection while conducting information operations.

69. Marco Sassòli, International Humanitarian Law: Rules, Controversies, and Solutions to Problems Arising in Warfare 439 (2019). Support for the complementary approach is also found in Vienna Convention on the Law of Treaties art. 31(3)(c), May 23, 1969, 1155 U.N.T.S. 331.

70. Jakob Kellenberger, *International Humanitarian Law and Other Legal Regimes: Interplay in Situations of Violence*, ICRC (Sept. 4, 2003).

71. Helen Duffy, *Trials and Tribulations: Co-Applicability of IHL and Human Rights in an Age of Adjudication*, *in* Law Applicable to Armed Conflict 73 (Ziv Bohrer, Janina Dill, & Helen Duffy eds., 2020).

72. U.N. Human Rights Council, *General Comment 31: The Nature of the General Legal Obligation Imposed on States Parties to the Covenant*, ¶ 11, U.N. Doc. CCPR/C/21/Rev.1/Add.13 (May 26, 2004).

73. DoD Law of War Manual, *supra* note 62, at §1.6.3.1.

4.1 Article 24 of the Hague Regulations

To reiterate, Article 24 of the Hague Regulations permits "the employment of measures necessary for obtaining information about the enemy and the country."[74] While this is a broad and general provision, when applied in context it can be read to give belligerents precise and specific authority to carry out information operations against *combatants*. Significantly, this interpretation of IHL precludes normative space for IHRL to operate. IHL will prevail over IHRL as the *lex specialis*, and enemy combatants cannot raise the rights to privacy and data protection under the latter body of law to prevent the adversary from collecting their information. Put differently, parties to armed conflicts can gather information on enemy combatants without having to demonstrate that such operations are necessary to meet a legitimate aim within the meaning of IHRL. This interpretation of Article 24 is supported by the logic of IHL insofar as parties to armed conflicts can conduct lethal attacks against combatants without having to conduct an IHRL analysis. Applying the maxim *in eo quod plus sit semper inest et minus* (translated as: in the greater is always included the lesser), if belligerents can carry out lethal attacks against combatants without having to demonstrate that this conduct complies with IHRL standards, the same rationale must apply to information operations. Moreover, there is little (if any) evidence of State practice to suggest that parties to armed conflicts must respect the privacy and data protection rights of combatants.

The situation is different where parties to armed conflicts launch military operations involving the collection of *civilian* data. In this context, IHL does not provide belligerents with an unfettered right to collect such information even if their operations are undertaken in furtherance of hostilities. Applying the complementary approach, where belligerents conduct operations to obtain combat-relevant information and are reasonably aware that civilian data will be caught up in the process, IHRL influences the interpretation and application of IHL, and these regimes combine to require belligerents to respect the privacy and data protection rights of civilians. But critically, we have seen that the rights to privacy and data protection are not absolute and that their enjoyment can be restricted where necessary to meet a legitimate aim, such as the protection of national security. Thus, through the systemic integration of IHRL and IHL, belligerents can carry out military operations involving the collection of civilian data where such data is necessary to protect national security, for example, because it is necessary to fight the conflict and overcome the enemy. Information operations that are necessary to meet a legitimate aim are compliant with IHRL and IHL, whereas operations that do not satisfy this test constitute a breach of both IHRL and IHL.

Whether restrictions on human rights are necessary during times of hostilities requires a close assessment of the prevailing circumstances and must take into account the exigencies of armed conflict. In her work, Leah West suggests that

74. 1907 Hague Regulations, *supra* note 2, art. 24.

two factors are critical when assessing the legality of restrictions on the rights to privacy and data protection of civilians during armed conflict: the level of control that belligerents exercise over territory or people and the intensity of the violence, both of which can vary in time and place.[75]

To give an example, consider the situation where State A invades State B. During the early stages of an invasion there may be heavy fighting between the opposing forces, which permits State A to conduct extensive surveillance operations throughout the territory of State B in order to identify military objectives. If over time State A gains the upper hand and exercises effective control over parts of State B's territory, it becomes an occupying power under the law of occupation. If hostilities subside in the occupied territory, IHL still permits State A to collect information to meet its operational needs, but the change in the nature and intensity of the armed conflict means that the test for whether such operations are necessary is more demanding. In these circumstances, State A may be required to undertake more targeted surveillance operations and use less intrusive means and methods to carry them out. To use cyber surveillance as an example, commanders should put in place mitigation strategies to minimize the collection of civilian data, such as system-fencing (which prevents surveillance software executing itself unless there is a match with the target system), geo-fencing (which limits the operation of surveillance software to a specific IP range), and kill-switches (which allows the surveillance software to be disabled once the objective is achieved).[76] That said, in those parts of State B's territory where State A is not an occupying power and fighting remains heavy and protracted, the necessity assessment will need to be recalibrated accordingly.

Once collected, parties to armed conflicts process data and decide whether to retain, store, or share it with third parties. As already explained, civilian data must be deleted unless it serves a lawful purpose (e.g., law enforcement), and combatant data must be deleted once the conflict comes to an end unless its longer-term retention serves a lawful purpose (e.g., to counter terrorism). Data sharing is particularly important in the contemporary era given that States often prosecute armed conflicts by forming multilateral coalitions (where all members of the coalition are parties to the conflict).[77] As the wars in Iraq and Afghanistan demonstrate, coalition members regularly share individuals' PID (e.g., biometric data) in order to help identify combatants and track their movements, locations, and activities.

75. Leah West, *Face Value: Precaution versus Privacy in Armed Conflict*, *in* Buchan & Lubin, *supra* note 46, at 151–55.

76. ICRC Expert Meeting, *Avoiding Civilian Harm from Military Cyber Operations during Armed Conflicts* (Jan. 21–22, 2020), https://library.icrc.org/library/docs/DOC/icrc-4539-002.pdf.

77. Deborah A. Housen-Couriel, *Managing Data Privacy Rights in Multilateral Coalition Operations' Information Sharing Platforms: A "Legal Interoperability" Approach*, *in* Buchan & Lubin, *supra* note 46.

The right to data protection puts limits on the sharing of civilian PID with third parties. As we have seen, while data can be shared where there is a lawful purpose to do so, data controllers and processors must minimize the amount of data shared to that which is necessary to achieve the stated purpose. If data is collected during armed conflict and, while being processed, it transpires that civilian data has been obtained, that data can be shared with other parties to the armed conflict if it is combat-relevant, for example, because it enables the receiving party to protect civilians or civilian objects during targeting operations. But even then, the principle of data minimization requires parties to armed conflicts to limit the sharing of civilian data to that which is necessary for combat-related purposes. In other words, belligerents cannot indiscriminately share civilian data with their partners. The data must first be assessed to determine its relevance to the fighting.

Moreover, parties to armed conflicts must ensure that they only share civilian data with third parties where they are confident that those parties will respect the data subject's right to data protection. In *Schrems I*[78] and *Schrems II*,[79] the Court of Justice of the European Union (CJEU) examined two data sharing agreements concluded between the European Union and United States that allowed for the free flow of data between EU and U.S. organizations. The CJEU invalided these agreements because U.S. law did not put in place sufficient safeguards to ensure that U.S. national intelligence agencies would process PID in compliance with the GDPR. In short, the Court criticized U.S. law on the basis that it grants national intelligence agencies extensive powers to collect and use data, namely, powers that go beyond what is necessary to meet national security objectives.[80]

In the context of data sharing during armed conflict, the national security exemption looms large. The formation of multilateral coalitions is a complex process that depends on a plethora of highly sensitive factors. This means that, to effectively fight an armed conflict, States may need to form coalitions with States and share data with them even though their domestic laws are not compliant with the right to data protection. Refusing to share data with another State because of inadequacies in its data protection laws may hinder their ability to prosecute the armed conflict and even undermine the effective working of the coalition. Here, States can invoke the national security exemption to justify the sharing of data, although they must demonstrate that the exemption is necessary and proportionate in the circumstances.

78. Maximillian Schrems v. Data Protection Commissioner (joined by Digital Rights Ireland Ltd), Case C-363/14, Grand Chamber (Oct. 6, 2015) (CJEU).

79. Data Protection Commissioner v. Facebook Ireland Ltd, Case C-311/18, Grand Chamber (July 16, 2020) (CJEU).

80. *Id.* at ¶¶ 168–92.

4.2 Article 27 GC IV: Humane Treatment of Protected Persons

Overlapping protection for the privacy and data protection rights of civilians is found in Article 27 of the Geneva Convention (IV) Relative to the Protection of Civilian Persons in Time of War,[81] which is reflective of CIL.[82] It explains:

> Protected persons are entitled, in all circumstances, to respect for their persons, their honour, their family rights, their religious convictions and practices, and their manners and customs. They shall at all times be humanely treated, and shall be protected especially against all acts of violence or threats thereof and against insults and public curiosity. . . . However, the Parties to the conflict may take such measures of control and security in regard to protected persons as may be necessary as a result of war.[83]

In its official commentary, the ICRC encourages a broad reading of Article 27:

> [Article 27] must be understood in its widest sense: it covers all the rights of the individual, that is, the rights and qualities which are inseparable from the human being by the very fact of his existence and his mental and physical powers; it includes, in particular, the right to physical, moral and intellectual integrity—an essential attribute of the human person.[84]

The commentary further explains that Article 27 requires the "private lives" of protected persons to be respected,[85] which begs the question of whether this provision can be interpreted to require parties to armed conflicts to protect the privacy and data protection rights of such persons. Evidently, Article 27 is framed in broad and general terms. If IHRL is used to flesh out the meaning and content of Article 27 as the complementary approach requires, IHRL and IHL can be applied in conjunction with each other to require parties to armed conflicts to respect the privacy and data protection rights of protected persons while collecting and processing information.

Importantly, Article 27 permits belligerents to "take such measures of control and security in regard to protected persons as may be necessary as a result of war." As discussed, the rights to privacy and data protection can also be restricted where necessary to meet a legitimate aim such as national security, which brings IHRL

81. GC IV, *supra* note 66.

82. West, *supra* note 75, at 146.

83. Similarly, Article 75 of AP I, *supra* note 10, requires parties to armed conflicts to respect "the person, honour, convictions and religious practices" of all people in their power.

84. Oscar Uhler & Henri Coursier, Commentary to Geneva Convention (IV) Relative to the Protection of Civilian Persons in Time of War 201 (1958).

85. *Id.*

and IHL into alignment.[86] As explained, any assessment of whether restrictions on the rights to privacy and data protection of civilians are necessary during armed conflict must take into account the operational needs of belligerents, which may be more or less extensive at any given moment depending on the level of control they exercise over territory or people and the intensity of hostilities.

4.3 Article 57(1) AP I: The Duty of Constant Care

Article 57(1) of Additional Protocol I to the Geneva Conventions can also be leveraged to require parties to armed conflicts to respect civilians' rights to privacy and data protection. According to this provision:

> In the conduct of military operations, constant care shall be taken to spare the civilian population, civilians and civilian objects.[87]

Article 57(1)'s use of the imperative "shall" indicates that it imposes a legally binding obligation on States parties and, as such, it is a stand-alone rule of IHL.[88]

Article 57 is titled "precautions in attack," and Article 57(2) identifies the various precautions that commanders must take when launching "attacks." The concept of "attack" is a term of art in IHL that refers to acts of violence against the adversary whether in offense or defense.[89] Given Article 57's title (precautions in *attack*), it could be said that Article 57 in its totality (including Article 57(1)) applies only to attacks. If this interpretation is correct, Article 57(1) is of limited utility in the context of this chapter given that its focus is on military operations involving the collection and processing of data (that do not qualify as attacks).

This narrow interpretation of Article 57(1) is unconvincing. While Article 57(1) refers to "military operations," other provisions in Article 57 refer to "attacks." Given the fundamental difference between the concepts of "military operations" and "attack" under IHL, it can be assumed that the drafters of the Additional Protocol must have deliberately and purposely preferred the concept of "military operations" over "attack" when formulating the duty of constant care in Article

86. Ramin Mahnad, *In the Hands of Belligerents: Status and Protection under the Geneva Conventions*, Humanitarian Law and Policy (May 19, 2022), https://blogs.icrc.org/law-and-policy/2022/05/19/belligerents-status-protection-geneva-conventions/.

87. This provision reflects CIL: 2 Customary International Humanitarian Law r. 15 (Jean-Marie Henckaerts & Louise Doswald-Beck eds., 2005). *See also* Prosecutor v. Kupreskic, Case No. IT-95-16-T. Ch. II, Judgment, ¶ 524 (Int'l Crim. Trib. for the former Yugoslavia Jan. 14, 2000).

88. International Law Association Study Group, *The Conduct of Hostilities and International Humanitarian Law: Challenges of 21st Century Warfare* 43 (June 25, 2017).

89. AP I, *supra* note 10, art. 49(1).

57(1).[90] State practice supports this broader interpretation of Article 57(1).[91] Thus, Article 57(1) may be said to lay down a general duty to spare civilians from the deleterious effects of military operations, while Article 57(2) sets out more specific duties in relation to attacks.[92]

The next question is what constitutes a "military operation." The ICRC's commentary defines military operations as "any movements, manoeuvres and other activities whatsoever carried out by the armed forces with the view to combat."[93] An operation possesses a military character where it is designed to advance combat. As explained, IHL applies only where there is a nexus between impugned conduct and the advancement of hostilities. If this nexus is established as part of the first-order assessment to determine whether IHL applies, the conduct can be ipso facto considered a military operation for the purpose of Article 57(1).[94]

Consider, for example, the IAC between Russia and Ukraine, which began in 2014 with the invasion of Crimea and escalated dramatically in 2022. Western States (which are not party to the conflict) have been supplying Ukraine with significant amounts of information on Russia's military operations.[95] Ukraine's processing of that data (such as its evaluation and storage) constitutes a military operation to the extent that it supports its military activities, and should be covered by Article 57(1).

As noted, the provision states that constant care must be exercised to spare civilians during the planning and execution of military operations. This raises the question: Spare them from what? Article 57(1) certainly requires commanders to protect civilians from physical harm, but does it require them to protect civilians' rights to privacy and data protection?

As with the obligation contained in Article 27 of Geneva Convention IV, Article 57(1) is cast in broad and general terms and, it is submitted, must be interpreted and applied in conjunction with IHRL. Combining IHRL and IHL, Article 57(1) would require commanders to respect the privacy and data protection rights of

90. Eric Talbot Jensen, *Cyber Attacks: Proportionality and Precautions in Attack*, 89 International Law Studies 198, 202 (2013).

91. UK Law of War Manual, *supra* note 1, at ¶ 5.32.1.

92. *Id.*

93. Commentary on the Additional Protocols of 8 June 1977 to the Geneva Conventions of 12 August 1949, ¶ 2191 (Yves Sandoz, Christophe Swinarski, & Bruno Zimmermann eds., 1987).

94. Asaf Lubin, *The Duty of Constant Care and Data Protection in War*, *in* Big Data and Armed Conflict: Legal Issues Above and Below the Armed Conflict Threshold 11 (Laura A. Dickinson & Edward Berg eds., 2022).

95. *How One US Intelligence Agency Is Supporting Ukraine*, C4ISRNET (Apr. 10, 2023), https://www.c4isrnet.com/intel-geoint/2022/04/25/how-one-us-intelligence-agency-is-supporting-ukraine/.

civilians while conducting military operations involving the collection and processing of data.[96]

The duty of constant care is not absolute. Rather, it is relative insofar as commanders are only required to take reasonable steps to eliminate or at least minimize the deleterious effects of military operations on the civilian population.[97] What constitutes reasonable steps will depend on the prevailing circumstances, such as the degree of control exercised by the party to the armed conflict over the population or territory and the intensity of hostilities.[98] As the *U.K. Law of War Manual* explains, when applying Article 57(1) relevant factors include "the importance of the target and the urgency of the situation[;] what weapons are available and their range, accuracy, and radius of effect[; and] factors affecting incidental loss or damage, such as the proximity of civilians or civilian objects in the vicinity of the target."[99]

In order to fully understand the risks that military operations pose to the civilian population, Article 57(1) requires commanders to have "situational awareness at all times,"[100] which requires them to establish effective regimes for the collection and processing of information. It means, for example, that operators of cyber surveillance software must familiarize themselves with the technology and understand how it will operate once deployed and what in-built safety mechanisms can be leveraged to minimize its impact on civilian computer networks, systems, and data.

4.4 Specific Protections

IHL also confers specific protections on certain types of infrastructure. For instance, Article 19 of Geneva Convention I states that "units of the Medical Service may in no circumstances be attacked, but shall at all times be respected and protected by the Parties to the conflict,"[101] and Article 12 of Additional Protocol

96. Eliza Watt, *The Principle of Constant Care, Prolonged Drone Surveillance and the Right to Privacy of Non-Combatants in Armed Conflicts*, *in* Buchan & Lubin, *supra* note 46, at 117. *See also* Lubin, *supra* note 94; and West, *supra* note 75.

97. UK Law of War Manual, *supra* note 1, at ¶ 5.32.1;Tallinn Manual 2.0 on the International Law Applicable to Cyber Operations, r.114, ¶ 4 (Michael N. Schmitt ed., 2017).

98. West, *supra* note 75, at 151–55.

99. UK Law of War Manual, *supra* note 1, at ¶ 5.32.5.

100. Tallinn Manual 2.0, *supra* note 97, r. 115, at ¶ 5.

101. Convention (I) for the Amelioration of the Condition of the Wounded and Sick in Armed Forces in the Field art. 19, Aug. 12, 1949, 75 U.N.T.S. 31; Convention (II) for the Amelioration of the Condition of Wounded, Sick and Shipwrecked Members of Armed Forces at Sea art. 12, Aug. 12, 1949, 75 U.N.T.S. 85; GC IV, *supra* note 66, art. 18; AP I, *supra* note 10, art. 12; and Protocol Additional to the Geneva Conventions of August 12, 1949, and Relating to the

I extends this protection to civilian as well as military medical units. This rule is established in CIL.[102]

The obligation to "respect and protect" medical units indicates that parties to armed conflicts must refrain from engaging in any conduct "interfering with their work."[103] This interpretation is supported by State practice.[104] Importantly, the obligation requires parties to armed conflicts to respect and protect *data* held by medical units where it relates to the performance of their functions.[105] Protected medical data includes patient medical records irrespective of whether they are compiled in paper or electronic format. As Costa Rica has explained, the specific protection afforded to medical units by IHL "encompasses a prohibition against deleting or tampering with medical data (a category that includes data necessary for the proper use of medical equipment, tracking medical supplies, and personal medical data required for patient treatment)."[106] Consequently, parties to armed conflicts are prohibited from collecting and processing data belonging to medical units, thereby protecting the privacy and data protection rights of civilians to whom the data relates.

5. CONCLUSION

IHL permits (and sometimes requires) parties to armed conflicts to establish effective regimes for the collection and processing of information. This chapter has examined whether international law imposes any limits on information operations undertaken during times of armed conflict given the breadth and permissiveness of that rule. The question is important because protecting the rights

103. International Committee of the Red Cross, Commentary on the First Geneva Convention: Convention (I) for the Amelioration of the Condition of the Wounded and Sick in the Armed Forces in the Field ¶ 1799 (2016), https://ihl-databases.icrc.org/en/ihl-treaties/gci-1949/article-19/commentary/2016?activeTab=undefined.

104. DoD Law of War Manual, *supra* note 62, at § 7.8.2.

105. Tallinn Manual 2.0, *supra* note 97, at r. 132, at ¶ 3; Geiss & Lahmann, *supra* note 54, at 564.

106. *Costa Rica's Position on the Application of International Law in Cyberspace*, Costa Rica 17 (2023), *available at* https://docs-library.unoda.org/Open-Ended_Working_Group_on_Information_and_Communication_Technologies_-_(2021)/Costa_Rica_-_Position_Paper_-_International_Law_in_Cyberspace.pdf; International Committee of the Red Cross, Position Paper, *International Humanitarian Law and Cyber Operations during Armed Conflicts* 8 (Nov. 2019), https://www.icrc.org/en/document/international-humanitarian-law-and-cyber-operations-during-armed-conflicts.

Protection of Victims of Non-international Armed Conflicts art. 11, June 8, 1977, 1125 U.N.T.S. 609. *See also* S.C. Res. 2286 (May 3, 2016).

102. Customary IHL Study, *supra* note 87, rr. 25, 28, and 29.

to privacy and data protection is critical to maintaining personal autonomy and human dignity in the contemporary era.

IHL permits belligerents to collect and process information on battlefield combatants notwithstanding their rights to privacy and data protection under IHRL; it is the price they pay for participating in the armed conflict. However, where belligerents collect and process civilian data, IHL must be interpreted and applied harmoniously with IHRL. As shown, there are various rules of IHL that can be applied in conjunction with IHRL to require belligerents to protect the privacy and data protection rights of civilians. First, the rule permitting belligerents to engage in information operations under Article 24 of the Hague Regulations may nowadays be said to be circumscribed by the restriction that civilian data can be collected and processed only to the extent that it is necessary to meet the legitimate operational needs of the parties to the conflict. Second, Article 27 GC IV can be read to require parties to armed conflicts to respect the privacy and data protection rights of protected persons, although this obligation will likewise be subject to the legitimate operational needs of belligerents. Third, Article 57(1) AP I should be deemed to require commanders to take all reasonable steps to protect the human rights of civilians while undertaking military operations involving the collection and processing of data.

This chapter has also shown that IHL confers specific protection on medical units. In particular, parties to armed conflicts must respect and protect the work of military and civilian medical units, which imposes an obligation on belligerents to respect the confidentiality and integrity of medical data.

12

The Effect of Extraterritorial Data Migration on the Protection of Civilians and Civilian Objects

LEAH WEST*

1. INTRODUCTION

Russia's invasion of Ukraine in February 2022 did not begin with artillery fire or rolling tanks; it started with cyberattacks against Ukrainian cyberinfrastructure.[1] This opening salvo included attacks against Ukraine's broadband internet service provider Viasat[2] and nineteen government and critical infrastructure entities nationwide.[3] The attacks were not unanticipated.[4] Russian military

* Dr. Leah West is an Associate Professor of International Affairs at the Norman Paterson School of International Affairs at Carleton University where she teaches public international law, national security law, and counterterrorism.

1. Cynthia Brumfield, *Russia-linked Cyberattacks on Ukraine: A Timeline*, CSO (Aug. 24, 2022), https://www.csoonline.com/article/571865/a-timeline-of-russian-linked-cyberattacks-on-ukraine.html; Ariel (Eli) Levite, *Integrating Cyber into Warfighting: Some Early Takeaways from the Ukraine Conflict*, Carnegie Endowment for International Peace (Apr. 18, 2023) [hereinafter *Microsoft Report*].

2. Kristen E. Eichensehr, *Ukraine, Cyberattacks, and the Lessons for International Law*, 116 AJIL Unbound (2022).

3. *Microsoft Report*, *supra* note 1, at 7.

4. *U.S. Sends Top Security Official to Help NATO Brace for Russian Cyberattacks*, New York Times (Feb. 1, 2022), https://www.nytimes.com/2022/02/01/us/politics/russia-ukraine-cybersecurity-nato.html.

Leah West, *The Effect of Extraterritorial Data Migration on the Protection of Civilians and Civilian Objects* In: *Civilian Protection in Armed Conflict*. Edited by: Jelena Pejic and Captain Margaret Kotlik, Oxford University Press.
 DOI: 10.1093/oso/9780197793176.003.0012

strategy has incorporated preemptive cyberattacks since it invaded Georgia in 2008.[5]

This strategy is sound. Like artillery and aerial bombardments, cyberattacks can prepare the battlespace for ground troops by degrading, disrupting, or destroying key military objectives. However, unlike traditional fires, cyberattacks give users even greater "operational reach and the opportunity to compromise the integrity of critical infrastructures in direct and indirect ways without a physical presence,"[6] limiting the immediate risk to personnel or material. Deploying cyberattacks before using kinetic force also provides a level of deniability. Attributing cyberattacks to a State with sufficient confidence and verifiability to hold it accountable can be lengthy and resource-intensive.[7] Until other States can confirm enemy responsibility for an attack, they may be unwilling to respond with force in order to comply with international law or out of fear of condemnation by the international community. This delay creates a strategic advantage for the attacker.[8]

In anticipation of Russia's attacks, the government of Ukraine took unprecedented steps to defend its data and virtual cyberinfrastructure. On February 17, 2022, a week before Russia initiated its aerial and ground assault, Ukraine's parliament amended its data protection law which had long prohibited government authorities from processing and storing data in public clouds.[9] As a result of that law, the country ran its civil (meaning government, but nonmilitary) and military digital infrastructure on segregated servers physically located in government facilities within Ukraine's borders. This law also applied to select private sector data.[10] Parliament amended the law to authorize what Microsoft called an "evacuation" of Ukraine's critical government data.[11] Over the next ten weeks, government information officers and staff, with the assistance of (at least) Microsoft and Amazon, migrated Ukraine's most important digital operations and data onto a public cloud hosted on private sector servers across Europe.

5. Ronald J. Deibert, Rafal Rohozinski, & Masashi Crete-Nishihata, *Cyclones in Cyberspace: Information Shaping and Denial in the 2008 Russia–Georgia War*, 43 Security Dialogue 1, 3–24 (2012).

6. Chairman, Joint Chiefs of Staff, Joint Publication 3-12, Cyberspace Operations, i–ii (2018).

7. *Id.*

8. Following the ground invasion, Russia has continued to deploy cyberattacks in advance of launching attacks on the same target with conventional weapons. *See, e.g., Microsoft Report*, *supra* note 1, at 7.

9. *Id.* at 5.

10. About Amazon Team, *Safeguarding Ukraine's Data to Preserve Its Present and Build Its Future*, About Amazon Europe (June 9, 2022), https://www.aboutamazon.eu/news/aws/safeguarding-ukraines-data-to-preserve-its-present-and-build-its-future [hereinafter Amazon article].

11. *Id.*

Consequently, Microsoft reported that Russian cyber and kinetic attacks against Ukrainian government data centers and computer networks had limited operational impact.[12] As the conflict continued, additional data belonging to government entities, private sector companies like Ukraine's largest bank, and Ukraine's universities also migrated into the cloud, as did Ukraine's largest remote-learning primary and secondary school serving displaced children.[13] "The key to a country's digital resilience in wartime," touted Microsoft, "is the ability to quickly move data outside the country while still connecting to and relying on it for a government's digital operations."[14] While this may prove to be true, it is less clear whether such a strategy is consistent with international humanitarian law (IHL).

State parties have legal obligations to defend civilians and civilian objects from the effects of cyberattacks that initiate or arise during an armed conflict. Unlike some other norms of the law of armed conflict (LOAC), the rules governing precautions against attacks do not simply proscribe certain conduct during hostilities, rather, they create positive obligations on States to do one of two things: (1) segregate civilians and civilian objects from military objectives, or (2) where segregation is not possible, take other necessary precautions to protect them.[15]

To date, the literature interpreting how these rules apply to cyber operations has been largely theoretical. Scholars have conjured hypothetical examples to assess how States party to a conflict might comply with their obligations given the complex interdependence of military information and communications technology (ICT) on civilian networks and infrastructure.[16] Most of the literature argues that the best way to ensure compliance is to build entirely separate military and civilian networks or, at the very least, ensure that civilian digital infrastructure is marked and easily identifiable.[17] Others have argued that States should enhance their authority and capacity to defend private industry from cyberattacks.[18]

12. *Id.*

13. *Id.*

14. *Id.*

15. Eric Talbot Jensen, *Cyber Warfare and Precautions Against the Effects of Attacks*, 88 Texas Law Review 7, 1549 (2010).

16. *Id.*; Simon McKenzie & Eve Massingham, *Taking Care Against the Computer: Precautions Against Military Operations on Digital Infrastructure*, 12 Journal of International Humanitarian Legal Studies 2.

17. McKenzie & Massingham, *supra* note 16, at 246. *See also* Adam Segal, *Cyberspace Governance: The Next Step*, Council on Foreign Relations (Mar. 16, 2011), https://www.cfr.org/report/cyberspace-governance-next-step; Eric Jensen, *Ukraine and The Defender's Obligations*, Articles of War (Mar. 2, 2022), https://lieber.westpoint.edu/ukraine-defenders-obligations/.

18. Jensen, *supra* note 15, at 1564.

However, in the Ukrainian conflict, the exact opposite occurred. Ukraine interspersed its government data with private data to protect its critical government operations, both civil and military. The country has ceased relying on isolated government infrastructure in favor of civilian networks that it has no authority, and seemingly no capacity, to defend from attack. In a sense, Ukraine is using private European data and digital infrastructure to shield itself from attack. So far, these precautionary measures have proven effective, but are they lawful?

This chapter examines whether Ukraine's data migration and continued reliance on a foreign-based cloud to support its cyberinfrastructure are consistent with IHL's rules regarding precautions against the effects of attacks. In so doing, it explores the key debates arising from applying the relevant rules to cyber operations. It first describes the rules regarding precautions against the effects of attack in Article 58 of Additional Protocol I to the Geneva Conventions (AP I) and related precautionary obligations to identify and segregate protected objects and installations from military ones under a State's control. It then looks closer at the text of Article 58, setting out the current debates about how three key terms, "attack," "object," and "control," are interpreted in the cyber context. Considering the various approaches to interpreting these terms, it then assesses the precautionary measures taken by Ukraine to defend its civil and military cyberinfrastructure from Russian attacks. The chapter concludes that Ukraine's actions comply with the letter of Article 58, if not the spirit of IHL. Ultimately, this case study exemplifies how applying existing IHL rules in the cyber context can lead to uncomfortable outcomes.

2. PRECAUTIONS AGAINST THE EFFECTS OF ATTACKS

IHL, or LOAC, regulates the conduct of hostilities and the protection of persons in enemy hands. It comprises both customary rules and treaties, including the Hague Regulations of 1907 and, most significantly, the four Geneva Conventions of 1949 and their Additional Protocols of 1977. The former focus on protecting the victims of war, while Additional Protocol I, which will be referred to later, sets out rules on the means and methods of warfare.

A core principle of IHL in the conduct of hostilities is distinction, which requires that military operations be directed at "military objectives."[19] Under customary international law, military objectives include: (1) "objects which by their nature, location, purpose or use make an effective contribution to military action"; and (2) "whose total or partial destruction, capture or neutralization, in

19. Protocol Additional to the Geneva Conventions of 12 August 1949, and Relating to the Protection of Victims of International Armed Conflicts, June 8, 1977, 1125 U.N.T.S. 3, art. 48 [hereinafter AP I].

the circumstances ruling at the time, offers a definite military advantage."[20] Both elements of this two-part test must be satisfied for an object to qualify as a military objective. Civilian objects are defined in the negative; they are objects which are not military objectives.[21] Civilian objects may not be the subject of attack; however, they do not enjoy absolute protection against damage or destruction.[22]

What about civilian objects used for military purposes or simultaneously used for both military and civilian purposes (often referred to as dual-use)? In such circumstances, one must return to the definition of military objective and ask: (1) by virtue of an object's nature, location, purpose or use, does it make an effective contribution to military action, and (2) does its destruction, capture, or neutralization in the circumstances offer a definite military advantage. If the answer to both inquiries is yes, it is targetable. If there is any doubt about whether a civilian object makes an effective contribution to military action, the presumption is that it does not.[23]

IHL also prohibits indiscriminate attacks, meaning that attacks not specifically directed at a precise military objective are unlawful. The same is true for attacks that employ a method or means of combat that cannot be directed at, or whose effects cannot be limited to, a military objective or combatants.[24] In other words, any attack must be narrowly tailored to the military objective. Despite these requirements, IHL accepts that harm and damage may be caused to civilians and civilian objects ("collateral damage"). Civilians may only be incidentally killed or injured and civilian objects may be damaged in an attack on a military objective if the impact is not excessive in relation to the concrete and direct military advantage anticipated.[25] This rule of proportionality "establishes a link between the concepts of military necessity and humanity."[26]

Tied to proportionality and distinction is the precautionary principle. This customary rule is codified in Articles 57 and 58 of API. Article 57 sets out the obligations of the attacking party. It stipulates that "[i]n the conduct of military operations, constant care shall be taken to spare the civilian population, civilians and civilian objects," and that concerning attacks, "those who plan or decide upon

20. *Id.*, art. 52(2); International Committee Of The Red Cross, Customary International Humanitarian Law Database, ch. 2 r. 8, https://ihl-databases.icrc.org/en/customary-ihl/v1 [hereinafter Customary IHL].

21. AP I, *supra* note 19, art. 52.

22. *Id.*, art. 57.2(iii).

23. *Id.*, art. 52.3.

24. *Id.*, art. 51(4).

25. Customary IHL, *supra* note 20, at ch. 2, r. 14.

26. Canada, Office of the Judge Advocate General, Departmental catalogue number B-GJ-005-104/FP-02, Law of Armed Conflict Manual: At the Operational and Tactical Levels, 2-2 (2001).

an attack shall do everything feasible to verify that the objectives to be attacked are neither civilians nor civilian objects."[27]

Conversely, Article 58 codifies the defending party's obligations to protect civilians and civilian objects from the dangers of potential attacks by enemy forces.[28] The positive obligations set out in Article 58 are titled "Precautions against the effects of attack" and read:

> The Parties to the conflict shall, to the maximum extent feasible:
> (a) without prejudice to Article 49 of the Fourth Convention, endeavour to remove the civilian population, individual civilians and civilian objects under their control from the vicinity of military objectives;
> (b) avoid locating military objectives within or near densely populated areas;
> (c) take the other necessary precautions to protect the civilian population, individual civilians and civilian objects under their control against the dangers resulting from military operations.[29]

The International Committee of the Red Cross (ICRC) Commentary of 1987 on AP I explains that this article is concerned "with measures which every Power must take in its own territory in favour of its nationals, or in territory under its control."[30] As Eric Talbot Jensen succinctly explains, parties can comply with this clause in one of two ways: "[E]ither protect the civilians under your control or segregate them from areas where they are endangered."[31] The ICRC Commentary also notes that some of these measures must "be taken already in peacetime, even though, strictly speaking, the article is only addressed to Parties to a conflict."[32] The International Criminal Tribunal for the former Yugoslavia found that the

27. AP I, *supra* note 19, art. 57.

28. *Id.*, art. 58.

29. Article 58 takes its roots from the 1863 Lieber Code, which required specific civilian objects be "secured against all avoidable injury." U.S. Department of War, Instructions for the Government of Armies of the United States in the Field, General Orders No. 100, Apr. 24, 1863. This positive obligation on States was then clarified in the 1907 Hague Convention IV, which imposed obligations on "the besieged" to mark specific civilian objects with "distinctive and visible signs." *See generally* FRANCIS LIEBER, THE MISCELLANEOUS WRITINGS OF FRANCIS LIEBER: CONTRIBUTIONS TO POLITICAL SCIENCE 245, 254 (Daniel Coit Gilman ed., 1881); Regulations Respecting the Laws and Customs of War on Land, annexed to Convention No. IV Respecting the Laws and Customs of War on Land art. 27, Oct. 18, 1907, 36 Stat. 2227 [hereinafter 1907 Hague Regulations].

30. COMMENTARY ON THE ADDITIONAL PROTOCOLS OF 8 JUNE 1977 TO THE GENEVA CONVENTIONS OF 12 AUGUST 1949 692, 692 (Yves Sandoz, Christophe Swinarski, & Bruno Zimmermann eds., 1987) [hereinafter ICRC COMMENTARY].

31. Jensen, *supra* note 15, at 1549.

32. ICRC COMMENTARY, *supra* note 30, at 680–82.

clauses of Article 58 are customary principles of international law "not contested by any State."[33]

Importantly, this article is subject to the qualifier "to the maximum extent feasible." This phrase is similar to language in Article 57, which requires States to "do everything feasible." According to the ICRC Commentary on Article 57, the phrase "everything feasible" was discussed at length before the provision was adopted.[34] Some delegations, including the United Kingdom, understood the words to mean "everything that was practicable or practically possible, taking into account all the circumstances at the time of the attack, including those relevant to the success of military operations."[35] The Commentary suggests this last requirement is too broad as it could give the success of the mission precedence over humanitarian obligations. Instead, what is required is that necessary identifications must be carried out in a timely manner to spare the civilian population to the furthest extent possible.[36] As Jean-François Quéguiner explains, "when taking precautions in attack, armed forces cannot be required to do the objectively impossible, nor can they be content with merely doing what is possible."[37]

Article 58 did not give rise to as much discussion as Article 57. However, regarding the question of "feasibility" the ICRC Commentary notes, "it is clear that precautions should not go beyond the point where the life of the population would become difficult or even impossible."[38] Article 58 also does not restrict States from organizing their military installations on their territory as they see fit.[39] During the final debate on this point, several delegations stipulated that "this article should in no way affect the freedom of a State Party to the Protocol to organize its national defence to the best of its ability and in the most effective way."[40]

Apart from Article 58, AP I sets out several specific tasks parties must take to defend civilians and civilian objects from attack. Article 56 states that parties "shall endeavour to avoid locating any military objectives in the vicinity of" works and installations containing dangerous forces (damns, dykes, and nuclear electrical generating stations), and to facilitate the identification of such objects, parties "may mark them with a special sign." Additionally, Article 18 states that parties "shall endeavour to ensure that medical and religious personnel and medical

33. Prosecutor v. Kupresic, Case No. IT-95-16-T, Judgment, ¶ 524 (Int'l Crim. Trib. for the former Yugoslavia Jan. 14, 2000).

34. ICRC Commentary, *supra* note 30, at 680–82.

35. *Id.* at 680.

36. *Id.*

37. Jean-François Quéguiner, Precautions *Under the Law Governing the Conduct of Hostilities*, 88 International Review of the Red Cross 864, 809–10 (2006).

38. ICRC Commentary, *supra* note 30, at 692.

39. *Id.*

40. *Id.*

units are identifiable." Other treaties, like the *1954 Convention on the Protection of Cultural Property in the Event of Armed Conflict*, place positive obligations on States to identify, segregate, and "take all appropriate preparatory measures in time of peace to protect cultural property against foreseeable effects of armed conflict."[41]

In all cases, the precautionary rules set out in these treaties require parties to take proactive measures to defend their civilian population in anticipation of and throughout an armed conflict.

3. PRECAUTION DEBATES IN THE CYBER CONTEXT

A State party's obligations to civilians and civilian objects under Article 58 are relatively straightforward in conventional warfighting: segregate or protect. Like many things, however, applying this rule in the cyber context is more complicated. This section looks at the debates over how the terms "attack," "object," and "control" in the text of Article 58 ought to be interpreted and the impact of those positions on the scope of a party's obligations.

3.1 Attack

The international group of experts responsible for the *Tallinn Manual* considered the application of Article 58 in the context of cyber operations. They reframed the rule to read: "[P]arties to an armed conflict shall, to the maximum extent feasible, take necessary precautions to protect the civilian population, individual civilians, and civilian objects under their control against the dangers resulting from cyberattacks."[42]

Crucially, the rule's application is limited to dangers resulting from "attacks" and not military operations more broadly.[43] The majority of experts argued that Article 58 only applies to attacks, evidenced by its title in AP I. They also pointed to the lack of support for the idea that customary international law extended the precautionary principle to all military operations. This author agrees with that position; however, under Article 58, the party's duty is not simply to defend civilians and civilian objects from attacks but to defend them from the *effects* of attacks.[44]

41. Convention on the Protection of Cultural Property in the Event of Armed Conflict art. 3, May 14, 1954, 249 U.N.T.S. 240.

42. TALLINN MANUAL 2.0 ON THE INTERNATIONAL LAW APPLICABLE TO CYBER WARFARE, at 488 (Michael N. Schmitt ed., 2017) [hereinafter TALLINN MANUAL 2.0].

43. *Id.*

44. McKenzie & Massingham, *supra* note 16, at 243.

Nevertheless, what amounts to an "attack" under IHL in or via cyberspace is unsettled. Article 49 of AP I defines attacks as "acts of violence against the adversary, whether in offence or in defence." Building from this, the *Tallinn Manual* defines a cyberattack as a "cyber operation, whether offensive or defensive, that is reasonably expected to cause injury or death to persons or destruction to objects."[45] Any operation with these results qualifies as an attack regardless of whether they are the direct or indirect target of a cyber operation.[46]

What was unclear for the *Tallinn Manual* was what "destruction to objects" entails. For the majority of experts, interfering with the functionality of a system would amount to destruction if its restoration required the replacement of physical components. Others would extend it to situations requiring reinstalling an operating system or data. Few believed that any loss of usability of cyberinfrastructure constituted an attack, a position supported by the ICRC.[47] Amongst international law scholars, there is also debate as to whether cyber operations that are disruptive without being destructive qualify as a cyberattack.[48]

Few States have enunciated their position on the meaning of attack in the cyber context. Of those who have, some, like the Netherlands, simply reaffirm the application of Article 49,[49] while others, like the United States and Norway, posit that whether a cyber operation amounts to an attack depends on the nature and scope of its effects.[50]

Some States take the narrow view that a cyber operation amounts to an attack when it produces effects similar to those of a kinetic attack, in other words, where a cyber operation can be reasonably expected to cause injury, death, or physical

45. Tallinn Manual 2.0, *supra* note 42, at 415.

46. *Id.* at 419.

47. Position paper by the International Committee of the Red Cross submitted to the United Nations Open-Ended Working Group on Developments in the Field of Information and Telecommunications in the Context of International Security and the United Nations Group of Governmental Experts on Advancing Responsible State Behaviour in Cyberspace in the Context of International Security, International Humanitarian Law and Cyber Operations during Armed Conflicts, at 7 (Nov. 2019) [hereinafter ICRC Position Paper].

48. *See, e.g.*, Ido Kilovatry, *Virtual Violence—Disruptive Cyberspace Operations as "Attacks" Under International Humanitarian Law*, 23 Michigan Telecommunications and Technology Law Review 1 (2016).

49. Official compendium of voluntary national contributions on the subject of how international law applies to the use of information and communications technologies by States submitted by participating governmental experts in the Group of Governmental Experts on Advancing Responsible State Behaviour in Cyberspace in the Context of International Security established pursuant to General Assembly resolution 73/266, U.N. Doc. A/76/136 (July 13, 2021) [hereinafter U.N. Doc. A/76/136].

50. *Id.*; Brian J. Egan, *International Law and Stability in Cyberspace*, 35 Berkeley Journal of International Law 1 (2017).

damage to individuals or objects. This is the position of Denmark,[51] the United Kingdom,[52] and Australia.[53] Canada,[54] Sweden,[55] and Switzerland[56] agree that an attack includes "at least" such operations.

Israel takes the view that if physical damage impedes a computer system's functionality, or when an act causing the loss of functionality is a link in a chain of the expected physical damage, that act may amount to an attack.[57] New Zealand[58] and Ireland[59] go a step further, stating that damage includes loss of functionality. Italy's view is similar, applying the term to "an act of violence resulting in more than minimal physical damage of property or disruption in the functioning of critical infrastructure, or human injury and loss of life."[60] Japan does not provide a definition but offers examples that mirror this position, asserting that "cyber operations

51. Jeppe Mejer Kjelgaard & Ulf Melgaard, *Denmark's Position Paper on the Application of International Law in Cyberspace*, NORDIC JOURNAL OF INTERNATIONAL LAW (2023).

52. Application of International Law to States' Conduct in Cyberspace: UK Statement, UNITED KINGDOM FOREIGN, COMMONWEALTH & DEVELOPMENT OFFICE (June 3, 2021), https://www.gov.uk/government/publications/application-of-international-law-to-states-conduct-in-cyberspace-uk-statement/application-of-international-law-to-states-conduct-in-cyberspace-uk-statement.

53. 2021 International Cyber and Critical Technology Engagement Strategy, Annex B: Australia's Position on How International Law Applies to State Conduct in Cyberspace, AUSTRALIAN GOVERNMENT (2021), *available at* https://www.internationalcybertech.gov.au/our-work/annexes/annex-b.

54. International Law Applicable in Cyberspace, GOVERNMENT OF CANADA, ¶¶ 38–40 (Apr. 22, 2022).

55. Position Paper on the Application of International Law in Cyberspace, GOVERNMENT OFFICES OF SWEDEN (July 1, 2022), *available at* https://www.government.se/contentassets/3c2cb6febd0e4ab0bd542f653283b140/swedens-position-paper-on-the-application-of-international-law-in-cyberspace.pdf.

56. Switzerland's Position Paper on the Application of International Law in Cyberspace, SWISS FEDERAL DEPARTMENT OF FOREIGN AFFAIRS (May 2021), *available at* https://www.eda.admin.ch/dam/eda/en/documents/aussenpolitik/voelkerrecht/20210527-Schweiz-Annex-UN-GGE-Cybersecurity-2019-2021_EN.pdf.

57. Roy Schöndorf, *Israel's Perspective on Key Legal and Practical Issues Concerning the Application of International Law to Cyber Operations*, 97 INTERNATIONAL LAW STUDIES 395.

58. The Application of International Law to State Activity in Cyberspace, NEW ZEALAND MINISTRY OF FOREIGN AFFAIRS & TRADE (Dec. 1, 2020), *available at* https://www.dpmc.govt.nz/sites/default/files/2020-12/The%20Application%20of%20International%20Law%20to%20State%20Activity%20in%20Cyberspace.pdf.

59. Position Paper on the Application of International Law in Cyberspace, GOVERNMENT OF IRELAND DEPARTMENT OF FOREIGN AFFAIRS (July 2023), *available at* https://www.dfa.ie/media/dfa/ourrolepolicies/internationallaw/Ireland---National-Position-Paper.pdf.

60. Italian Position Paper on "International Law and Cyberspace" GOVERNMENT OF ITALY (2021), https://www.esteri.it/mae/resource/doc/2021/11/italian_position_paper_on_international_law_and_cyberspace.pdf.

during armed conflict that cause physical damage or loss of functionality to medical institutions" may amount to attacks that would violate IHL.[61]

Germany and France take an even more expansive view, explicitly rejecting the need for physical or material harm. Germany defines a cyberattack in the context of IHL as an act or action initiated in or through cyberspace to cause harmful effects on communication, information, or other electronic systems, on the information that is stored, processed, or transmitted on these systems or on physical objects or persons.[62] The French classify a cyber operation as an attack "where the targeted equipment or systems no longer provide the service for which they were implemented, whether temporarily or permanently, reversibly or not."[63]

Finally, Pakistan offers an outlying position that cyber operations are attacks if they cause financial loss at a mass scale or undermine "the confidentiality, integrity, and the availability of a critical civilian infrastructure," and include attempts to "delete, destroy and manipulate the data essential for the smooth functioning of the critical civilian infrastructure and may impair its operations."[64] According to Pakistan, the same is true for operations that spread fear and chaos through disinformation.

Taking all of the preceding into consideration, it is submitted that parties seeking to comply with their precautionary obligations should take all feasible measures to defend their civilian population and civilian objects from the effects of cyber operations that directly or indirectly result in (1) physical harm to persons; (2) more than a de minimus harm to objects; and (3) more than a de minimus loss of functionality of a system or network.

3.2 Civilian Objects

A second key term in Article 58 is "object." Article 52 of AP I defines civilian objects as "all objects which are not military objectives." As noted previously, military objectives are objects which, by their nature, location, purpose, or use make

61. Basic Position of the Government of Japan on International Law Applicable to Cyber Operations, MINISTRY OF FOREIGN AFFAIRS OF JAPAN (May 28, 2021), https://www.mofa.go.jp/files/100200935.pdf.

62. On the Application of International Law in Cyberspace, GERMAN FEDERAL FOREIGN OFFICE AND THE GERMAN FEDERAL MINISTRY OF DEFENCE (Mar. 2021), https://www.auswaertigesamt.de/blob/2446304/32e7b2498e10b74fb17204c54665bdf0/on-the-application-of-international-law-in-cyberspace-data.pdf.

63. Droit International Appliqué aux Opérations Dans Le Cyberespace, MINISTᵉRE DES ARMᵉES DE LA RᵉPUBLIQUE FRANçAISE (2019), *available at* https://www.justsecurity.org/wp-content/uploads/2019/09/droit-internat-appliqu%C3%A9-aux-op%C3%A9rations-cyberespace-france.pdf.

64. Letter from the Permanent Mission of Pakistan to the United Nations in New York, Regarding Pakistan's Position on the Application of International Law in Cyberspace (Mar. 3, 2023), https://docs-library.unoda.org/Open-Ended_Working_Group_on_Information_and_Communication_Technologies_-_(2021)/UNODA.pdf.

an effective contribution to military action and whose total or partial destruction, capture, or neutralization, in the circumstances at the time, offer a definite military advantage.

The *Tallinn Manual* was unequivocal that cyberinfrastructure may qualify as a military objective,[65] defined as "the communications, storage, and computing devices upon which information systems are built and operate."[66] Disagreement arose over whether the term "object" includes data. The majority was unconvinced that it does as data is neither visible nor tangible, which, according to their reading of the ICRC Commentary, are defining characteristics of objects.[67]

If data is not an object, operations that delete or corrupt data and do not otherwise meet the definition of "attack" are not subject to targeting rules. This means there is no prohibition on deletion or corruption of critical civilian records stored electronically, including tax records, social security information, and banking information. However, the specific protection regimes regulating operations against medical facilities or objects indispensable to a civilian population's survival would likely extend to data essential to their operation.[68]

A minority of the *Tallinn Manual* disagreed with the majority's interpretation, arguing that certain data should qualify as an object for the purposes of targeting. Their position is that, at a minimum, data essential to the well-being of the civilian population ought to benefit from the protections afforded civilian objects.[69] The ICRC agrees, stressing that deleting and tampering with such essential civilian data could cause more harm to civilians than the destruction of physical objects. The ICRC finds the assertion that such operations are not "prohibited by IHL in today's data-reliant world seems difficult to reconcile with the object and purpose of IHL."[70] As Mike Schmitt points out, this view has visceral appeal but relies on normative logic to justify defining a single thing (data) differently depending on the outcome of an attack against it.[71]

Legal scholars offer alternative positions. Like the ICRC, Kubo Mačák appeals to the purpose of IHL, arguing that a modern interpretation of the term in light

65. Tallinn Manual 2.0, *supra* note 42, at 463.

66. *Id.* at 564.

67. *Id.* at 437. Others reject this interpretation, noting that this commentary was meant to distinguish "objects" from such concepts as "aim" or "purpose," and is not meant to suggest that objects could only amount to tangible goods. *See, e.g.*, Laurent Gisel, Tilman Rodenhäuser, & Knut Dörmann, *Twenty Years On: International Humanitarian Law and the Protection of Civilians Against the Effects of Cyber Operations During Armed Conflicts*, 102 International Review of the Red Cross 913, 318 (2020).

68. Gisel, Rodenhäuser, & Dörmann, *supra* note 67, at 318.

69. Tallinn Manual 2.0, *supra* note 42, at 437.

70. ICRC Position Paper, *supra* note 47, at 8.

71. Michael N. Schmitt, *Wired Warfare 3.0: Protecting the Civilian Population During Cyber Operations*, 101 International Review of the Red Cross 910, 342 (2019).

of the broader normative context and the object and purpose of AP I supports a finding that all data qualifies as an object.[72] The result of this position is that all cyber operations that alter civilian data during an armed conflict, regardless of consequence or purpose (espionage, information operations, psychological operations, etc.), are prohibited.[73]

Alternatively, Heather Harrison Dinnis argues that whether data is an object should depend on whether it is operational data (code) or content data.[74] The basis for her position is that the destruction of operational-level data will result in the loss of functionality of a system, while attacks on content data have more limited effects.[75] However, as Schmitt explains, if the proper interpretation of "attack" includes cyber operations that impact the functionality of a system, IHL already prohibits attacks on civilian operational data.[76] If the proper definition of attack is more restrictive and only captures operations that cause injury, death, or physical destruction, operations that merely affect an operating system's code are not prohibited, regardless of whether or not data is a civilian object. Thus, there is no basis for qualifying only operational data as an object.

Few States have commented directly on this question. Denmark adopts the view advanced by the majority of the *Tallinn Manual* that data is generally not an object under IHL, but where operations against data lead to effects that would otherwise qualify as an attack, data may be considered an object of attack.[77] France takes the opposite view of Dinnis, asserting that "[g]iven the current state of digital dependence, content data (such as civilian, bank or medical data, etc.) are protected under the principle of distinction."[78] Romania, like Mačák, takes "the preliminary view that cyber operations against data do trigger the application of IHL."[79] For its part, Finland simply asserts that "[c]onstant care shall be taken to ensure the protection of civilians and civilian objects, including essential civilian infrastructure,

72. Kubo Mačák, *Military Objectives 2.0: The Case for Interpreting Computer Data as Objects under International Humanitarian Law*, 48 Israel Law Review 1 (2015).

73. Schmitt, *supra* note 71.

74. Heather A. Harrison Dinniss, *The Nature of Objects: Targeting Networks and the Challenge of Defining Cyber Military Objectives*, 48 Israel Law Review 39 (2015).

75. *Id.* at 42.

76. Michael N. Schmitt, *The Notion of "Objects" During Cyber Operations: A Riposte in Defence of Interpretive and Applicative Precision*, 48 Israel Law Review 1, 102 (2015).

77. Kjelgaard & Melgaard, *supra* note 51.

78. Communication from France to the United Nations Open-ended Working Group on Security of and in the Use of Information and Communications Technologies 2021 ¶ 2025, Regarding International Law Applied to Operations in Cyberspace, 14 (Dec. 2021), *available at* https://documents.unoda.org/wp-content/uploads/2021/12/French-position-on-international-law-applied-to-cyberspace.pdf.

79. U.N. Doc. A/76/136, *supra* note 49, at 78.

civilian services and civilian data."[80] Some State's domestic courts have also found that data constitutes property, which supports the argument that it may be an object. In 2017, New Zealand's Supreme Court found that digital information is property,[81] and in Italy there is a line of cases that affirm data as objects,[82] albeit never in the context of interpreting IHL.

Resolving the legal status of data under IHL is not necessary for the purpose of this discussion. Rather, we can proceed by asking what are the implications in either case for a defending party's precautionary obligations.[83]

If data is not an object, parties are not required to endeavor to segregate civilian data from military data/objectives to the maximum extent feasible. However, as mentioned previously, a cyber operation targeting civilian data that rises to the level of an attack (i.e., produces effects similar to a kinetic attack) is still an attack under IHL. A defending party is obligated to take necessary precautions to protect the civilian population from dangers arising from an attack that results in the physical destruction, deletion, or corruption of civilian data. Dangers, which the ICRC points out, could "bring government services and private business to a complete standstill."[84] Consequently, defending States must take measures to protect civilian data from attack. One obvious way to minimize the potential effects is to not store civilian data with data that effectively contributes to military action or on infrastructure that qualifies as a military objective. In other words, segregation.

On the other hand, if data is an object, parties have a positive obligation to endeavor to segregate civilian data from data, networks, servers, buildings, and so forth that are military objectives. Parties should also avoid housing data that is a military objective on civilian cyberinfrastructure, as doing so makes that infrastructure a military objective which may be targeted virtually and kinetically. Where data amounts to a military objective, it may be lawfully targeted so long as the incidental loss of civilian life or damage to civilian objects is not excessive in relation to the concrete and direct military advantage anticipated by the attack. Thus, compliance with Article 58, inter alia, requires defending States to avoid storing data that may be a military objective on servers within or near densely populated areas.[85] Finally, where segregation is not possible, parties must take

80. Finnish Ministry for Foreign Affairs, International Law and Cyberspace: Finland's National Positions (Oct. 15, 2020), *available at* https://um.fi/documents/35732/0/KyberkannatPDF_EN.pdf/12bbbbde-623b-9f86-b254-07d5af3c6d85?t=1603097522727.

81. Jonathan Dixon v. The Queen (Dixon v. R), SC 82/2014 (New Zealand), *reprinted in* 2015 NZSC 147.

82. David Giovannelli, *Customary International Law, National Law, and Considering Data as Objects*, Articles of war (Nov. 15, 2023), https://lieber.westpoint.edu/customary-international-law-national-law-considering-data-objects/.

83. At the time of writing, this author is unaware of any commentary on that question. The remaining analysis thus extrapolates from the debate about data and precautions in attack.

84. ICRC Position Paper, *supra* note 47, at 8.

85. AP I, *supra* note 19, art. 58(b).

other necessary precautions to protect civilian data from the effects of an attack. The *Tallinn Manual* offer a number of examples, including: "[D]istributing protective software products, monitoring networks and systems, maintaining a strategic cyber reserve of bandwidth and cyber capability, and developing response capabilities that prevent bleed over into the civilian system."[86] Another method may be the use of digital emblems or markings to identify specially protected civilian objects like medical and health records, cultural property, and data and systems tied to the operation of dams, dykes, and nuclear plants.[87]

Before moving on, it is worth mentioning that there is a separate debate over how broadly parties can conceive of military objectives given the interconnectedness of cyberspace and how extensively the dual-use rule could apply to cyberinfrastructure.[88] Although beyond the scope of this chapter, the question is important for States contemplating the extent to which they would need to segregate civilian objects from military objectives (data or otherwise) to protect them from attack.

3.3 Control

A third concept that raises questions in the context of cyber operations is control. Per Article 58, the precautionary obligations of defending States only extend to civilians and civilian objects "under their control."

There is very little scholarship or national commentary on the issue of control. The ICRC Commentary on Article 58 begins with this statement:

> This article is a corollary to the numerous articles contained in the Protocol for the benefit of the population of enemy countries. It is not concerned with laying down rules for the conduct to be observed in attacks on territory under the control of the adversary, but with measures which every Power must take in its own territory in favour of its nationals, or in territory under its control.[89]

In other words, a State party does not have defensive precautionary obligations for civilians and objects in enemy territory. On this basis, the *Tallinn Manual* concluded that the concept of control in Article 58 was thought of in territorial terms. However, the experts were divided on how to apply it in the cyber context.

86. Tallinn Manual 2.0, *supra* note 42, at 491.

87. Tilman Rodenhäuser & Mauro Vignati, *How Can a "Digital Emblem" Help Protect Medical Facilities Against Cyber Operations?*, Lawfare (Jan. 27, 2023), https://www.lawfaremedia.org/article/how-can-a-digital-emblem-help-protect-medical-facilities-against-cyber-operations.

88. *See, e.g.*, Gisel, Rodenhäuser & Dörmann, *supra* note 67, at 320–22; Harrison Dinniss, *supra* note 74, at 50–54.

89. ICRC Commentary, *supra* note 30, at 692.

The majority determined that all civilian cyberinfrastructure and activities in a party's territory—including unoccupied and occupied enemy territory—would be subject to its precautionary obligations.[90] The minority disagreed, "asserting that the prohibition [i.e., the concept of control] should not necessarily be conceived of territorially. For them, not every computer system within territory controlled by a party is within its control for the purpose of the Rule."[91] They suggested that even within a party's territory, military communications could travel across civilian cyber networks and infrastructure over which it has no de facto control.[92] The text makes no mention of how the minority would apply the rule to computer systems, data, and so forth subject to a party's control but not within its territory. Accordingly, it may be more appropriate to describe the minority's view as holding that an object's presence within a party's territory is a necessary but not sufficient factor: control requires that the object be present within the party's territory and subject to its de facto control.

In the record of the conference that produced the Additional Protocols, the original language in the proposed article was "civilian objects under their authority."[93] The term "authority" was changed to "control" to expand a State's obligations, not narrow them. The Canadian Judge Advocate General who introduced the amendment "said that the use of the word 'control' would impose obligations on the parties which would not necessarily be implied by the use of the word 'authority.'" It referred to the de facto as opposed to the de jure situation.[94] The Egyptian representative agreed, expressing that "authority was not the correct word to use in connexion with the activities of an occupying Power."[95] This supports the majority position reflected in the *Tallinn Manual* that the issue is not whether a party is itself in control of a computer system or even whether it has the legal authority to do so but whether it can physically exercise control over it on the basis of it being within its territory. In any event, the two sides were of the view that this disagreement would have little practical effect because of the caveat that a State should act to the "maximum extent feasible."[96]

90. Tallinn Manual 2.0, *supra* note 42, at 489.

91. *Id.* It's notable that in this instance, this rule is framed as a *prohibition*.

92. *Id.*

93. Official Records of the Diplomatic Conference on the Reaffirmation and Development of International Humanitarian Law Applicable in Armed Conflicts, Geneva 3, 17 (1974–1977) (Switzerland Federal Council Political Department eds., 1978).

94. Official Records of the Diplomatic Conference on the Reaffirmation and Development of International Humanitarian Law Applicable in Armed Conflicts, Geneva (1974–1977) 198, 199 (Switzerland Federal Council Political Department ed., 1978) (emphasis in original).

95. *Id.* at 199.

96. Tallinn Manual 2.0, *supra* note 42, at 489.

Curiously, the *Tallinn Manual* concludes on this point by noting that "[a]ll the Experts agreed that if the party *can dictate the operations* of a civilian computer system, it is under the control of that party."[97] Given the realities of cloud computing technology, this view seems to be at odds with the majority and minority stances outlined previously, both of which found presence within a party's territory to be a necessary condition for control over an object.[98] This consensus position is, however, more reflective of the modern cyber context.

For example, a State party may, in practice, compel a civilian entity within its territory to provide communication or technical assistance to its military efforts and that entity could comply by leveraging civilian computer systems in other States. Parties can also create, access, alter, manipulate, analyze, and delete data and digital cyberinfrastructure hosted by civilian computer systems outside their territory. In the latter example, the party has de facto control over data and operating systems even though they are hosted on infrastructure beyond its borders. Moreover, it may exercise that control from within *its own territory in favor of its nationals*.

A comparison may be drawn to the *Tallinn Manual*'s description of when a party acquires control over a weapon by cyber means. In that context, the notion of control "implies that the Party using cyber means exercises sufficient control over the system to employ it as if it were its own."[99] Once a party acquires cyber control over a weapon system, it must comply with the IHL rules governing its use. In the context of precautions, if a State party exercises a comparable level of control via cyber means over civilian objects, it should conceivably have to comply with IHL rules governing their defense and use. Other evidence of control could be limits imposed on access to the civilian data by the State party, State party-controlled encryption and firewalls, and cyber security measures undertaken by the party.

It is arguably in keeping with the purpose of Article 58 to require parties to segregate civilian objects and military objectives over which they exercise control by cyber means or, where segregation is impossible, to take necessary precautions to defend civilian objects. The ICRC commentary makes clear that the distinguishing feature of Article 58 from the many other provisions regulating the conduct of hostilities is that it creates obligations on parties to take "all possible precautions for the benefit of their own population as is in any case in their own interest."[100] The fact that a party chooses to store civilian data or run virtual operating systems that serve civilian functions on servers outside its territory should not negate its precautionary obligations.

The flip side, of course, is that a State has no authority to take measures to defend civilian data, operating systems, and so forth stored on foreign servers from a

97. *Id.*

98. Unless the term "dictate" is used to mean exercise enforcement jurisdiction.

99. TALLINN MANUAL 2.0, *supra* note 42, at 451–52.

100. ICRC COMMENTARY, *supra* note 30, at 692.

kinetic attack or cyberattacks against the hardware. Nevertheless, given the "maximum extent feasible" caveat, this limitation should not be a barrier to applying precautionary obligations to objects under a party's virtual control.

4. ANALYZING UKRAINE'S COMPLIANCE WITH ARTICLE 58

Now that it has been established that a party's precautionary obligations extend to the cyber domain and some of the key debates about the application of Article 58 have been outlined, the question remains: Was Ukraine's migration of government data, both civil and military, to a European-based cloud compliant with these obligations? Furthermore, is Ukraine's continued reliance on the cloud to host data, government applications, and software consistent with Article 58?

First, if data is an object, Ukraine must endeavor to remove civilian data from the vicinity of military objectives to the maximum extent feasible. It unquestionably met this criterion by migrating it off government hardware inside Ukraine, which was the target of both cyber and kinetic strikes by Russia in the early days of the war. If data is not an object, Ukraine's actions nevertheless protected the civilian population from the effects of Russia's attacks.

Reports are sparse on details about what kind of data was migrated, but it is known that the early migration included data from 42 government entities. Reporting also indicates that the first migration prioritized critical government data.[101] It is reasonable to assume that at least some of this data, based on its nature, purpose, or use, makes an effective contribution to military action, and whose destruction, capture, or neutralization would offer a definite military advantage. Such data could include military personnel records, organization charts, code words, maps, blueprints, or records about power plants, airports, and bridges, or about the location and condition of military weapons, ammunition, material, and outposts. It is also likely that much of the migrated data does not make an effective military contribution, such as land and title records, social security and passport numbers, and records related to the provision of social services. Thus, if data is an object, it is likely that the migration included civilian objects and military objectives.

Reporting indicates Ukrainian migrated all of its data onto the same cloud.[102] This likely means that civilian and military data is stored on the same or networked cyberinfrastructure. Rather than segregating data that qualifies as a military objective from civilian objects, Ukraine is using the public and dispersed nature of the cloud to shield it from attack. The presence of data that qualifies as a military objective on the public cloud renders the cloud, and (to some degree) the physical infrastructure supporting it, a military objective that may be targeted by Russia

101. Amazon article, *supra* note 10.

102. *Id.*

under IHL.[103] *The same is true even if data is not an object.* What remains unknown is whether any servers on which the data is stored are in built-up areas, which could run afoul of Article 58(2). Given that Microsoft's cloud is supported by data centers in London, Frankfurt, Geneva, and Zurich, and Amazon AWS has centers in Paris, Madrid, Amsterdam, Berlin, Dublin, and Milan, this seems likely.

Leaving aside lawfulness under other bodies of international law, would this move be lawful under IHL if the objects at issue were weapons or ammunition and not data? Would Ukraine be permitted to hide firearms and bullets in private gun shops or shooting ranges across Europe? In other words, can a party to an international armed conflict comply with Article 58 and the obligation to defend its civilian population from the effects of attack by putting the civilian objects and population of States nonparties at risk? Even if the answer is yes, such actions are at odds with the more general obligation in Article 51 of AP I that "the civilian population and individual civilians enjoy general protection against dangers arising from military operations."

What is more, despite the assertions of Microsoft that this move secures Ukraine's governmental functions, there is little to suggest that Russia will avoid targeting Ukrainian data or the infrastructure supporting it because it is outside of Ukraine or hosted in NATO countries. While it is true that Russia is exponentially less likely to launch kinetic attacks on European data centers than it did in Ukraine, Russia has launched numerous cyber operations against government and private entities in NATO States since the outbreak of the war. "If nothing else," writes James A. Lewis, Ukraine's data migration "complicated and constrained Russian planning."[104] It has also placed Europe's data and cyberinfrastructure in the line of fire.

Second, if data is an object, do Ukrainian data, applications, operating systems, or virtual machines stored on European servers fall within Ukraine's control such that Ukraine has a continuing obligation to protect it? Accepting the *Tallinn Manual* territorial-based interpretation of control, the answer is no: Ukraine has no obligation to segregate or take additional measures to protect civilian data and other digital assets hosted abroad from Russian attacks. This finding remains true even if that data and virtual systems and networks are critical to the functioning of the Ukrainian government and key private sector entities. This too, seems at odds with the object and purpose of Article 58. As Jensen points out, "it is certainly not in keeping with the spirit of the law of armed conflict for government action to bring civilians and civilian companies within the scope of lawful attacks and then allow those same governments to leave the civilian and civilian companies completely alone to defend themselves."[105] If, however, one takes a less restrictive

103. Of course, any operation by Russia, virtual or kinetic, that amounts to an attack against a target in a State not party to the conflict would be governed by *jus ad bellum*.

104. James A. Lewis, *Cyber War and Ukraine*, CENTER FOR STRATEGIC AND INTERNATIONAL STUDIES 8 (June 16, 2022), https://csis.org/analysis/cyber-war-and-ukraine.

105. Jensen, *supra* note 15, at 1552.

view of the term and accepts that States have precautionary obligations over civilian objects that fall within its control by cyber means, Ukraine has continuing obligations to protect, to the maximum extent feasible, Ukraine's civilian data, virtual operating systems, and so forth from the effects of a Russian attack.

To reiterate, adopting the position of the majority of the *Tallinn Manual*, Ukraine's actions are consistent with Article 58. Moving the data off government servers in Ukraine protects civilians from the effects of Russian cyber and kinetic attacks on government installations. Upon migration to the European-based cloud, the data no longer falls within Ukraine's control. Thus, Ukraine is not obligated to segregate or protect civilian data or the virtual operating systems upon which the State's civil and private institutions rely.

The conclusion is the same if the *Tallinn Manual* minority positions on data and control are accepted. Ukraine is taking measures to protect essential civilian data by migrating it off government servers in Ukraine. Once the data is stored in Europe, it is beyond Ukraine's control and no longer benefits from Ukraine's precautionary obligations. Thus, we need not assess Ukraine's actions to protect or segregate civilian data once it has migrated to the cloud. In either case, Ukraine's strategy is consistent with Article 58.

This finding raises two subsequent issues for the State, or States, hosting Ukrainian data and remote operating systems. First, it raises concerns about the host State's compliance with its own precautionary obligations under Article 58 already in peacetime. The servers upon which Ukraine is storing its data are potential military objectives. Under IHL, the host State, therefore, has an obligation to proactively segregate or otherwise protect its civilian population from the effects of attack on those servers and avoid locating them within or near densely populated areas. Second, hosting Ukrainian data and remote cyber infrastructure could violate a host State's obligations under the law of neutrality. As interpreted by the *Tallinn Manual*, the law of neutrality stipulates that "a neutral state may not knowingly allow the exercise of belligerent rights by the parties to a conflict from the cyber infrastructure located in its territory."[106] Should the neutral State fail to terminate the exercise of belligerent rights on its territory, it is susceptible to countermeasures by the opposing party to the conflict.[107]

5. CONCLUSION

Ukraine's efforts to protect its military and civil cyber systems from the effects of attack fly in the face of the conventional understanding of compliance with

106. Tallinn Manual 2.0, *supra* note 42, at 558. *See also* Jaqueline Van De Velde, *From Telegraphs to Terabytes: The Implications of the Law of Neutrality for Data Protection by "Third" States and the Corporations Within Them*, *in* The Rights to Privacy and Data Protection in Times of Armed Conflict 67 (Russell Buchan & Asaf Lubin eds., 2022).

107. Tallinn Manual 2.0, *supra* note 42, at 560.

Article 58 in the cyber context. Not only has Ukraine's strategy proven effective but also, as this chapter establishes, it may be consistent with the State's precautionary obligations under Article 58 of AP I. Nothing in IHL prohibits a party to an international armed conflict from migrating its civilian cyberinfrastructure to nonparty States to shield its civil and military data from attack, even if doing so may make that infrastructure a military objective. Moreover, no State practice supports the extension of a defender's (in the present case, Ukraine's) precautionary obligations to objects located in foreign States that it maintains control over by cyber means. This could, admittedly, change should Russian attacks on Ukrainian data in the public cloud have significant incidental effects on Europe's population, economy, or institutions. The conclusion that Ukraine's obligations to protect data stop at its border may be deeply unsatisfying as a matter of IHL, but points to the need for further reflection on the possible practical and legal consequences of extraterritorial data migration in armed conflict. While IHL must be the starting point for such an examination, other relevant bodies of law will need to be analyzed as well.

PART THREE

Interfaces

Civilian Protection, Gender, and GC IV: Has Interpretation Filled the Gaps?

VALERIE OOSTERVELD*

1. INTRODUCTION

A significant amount of attention has been devoted to gender issues in international humanitarian law (IHL) in recent years. The wide range of topics addressed has included the gendered effects of conflict,[1] gender and disability,[2] gender and environmental destruction,[3] gender and AI in the conduct of hostilities,[4] gender

* Valerie Oosterveld is a Professor at Western University's Faculty of Law, Canada, and the Western Research Chair in International Criminal Justice.

1. International Committee of the Red Cross, Gendered Impacts of Armed Conflict and Implications for the Application of International Humanitarian Law (2022) [hereinafter ICRC, Gendered Impacts].

2. Sara La Vecchia, *The Protection of Women and Girls with Disabilities in Armed Conflict: Adopting a Gender-, Age- and Disability-inclusive Approach to Select IHL Provisions*, 992 International Review of the Red Cross 105, 161 (2023).

3. Catherine O'Rourke & Ana Martin, *Gender, Conflict and the Environment: Surfacing Connections in International Humanitarian Law*, 924 International Review of the Red Cross 105, 1600 (2023).

4. Noel Sharkey, *The Impact of Gender and Race Bias in AI*, ICRC Humanitarian Law and Policy Blog (Aug. 28, 2018), https://blogs.icrc.org/law-and-policy/2018/08/28/impact-gender-race-bias-ai/; Andrea Farrés Jiménez, *Embedding Gender in International Humanitarian Law: Is Artificial Intelligence Up to the Task?*, Just Security (Aug. 27, 2021), https://www.justsecurity.org/77970/embedding-gender-in-international-humanitarian-law-is-artificial-intelligence-up-to-the-task/.

Valerie Oosterveld, *Civilian Protection, Gender, and GC IV: Has Interpretation Filled the Gaps?* In: *Civilian Protection in Armed Conflict*. Edited by: Jelena Pejic and Captain Margaret Kotlik, Oxford University Press.
 DOI: 10.1093/oso/9780197793176.003.0013

and firearms,[5] and gender and protracted urban warfare,[6] to name only some.[7] This attention is both needed and warranted: as a recent ICRC report notes, "gender inequalities embedded in contexts where hostilities occur are a factor that influences civilian harm," gendered assumptions and expectations shape the experiences of everyone in the conduct of hostilities, and the high-intensity context of military decision-making can enhance gender biases.[8] In sum, gender-related concerns may be found at all stages of conflict and in all contexts of war.

Given that attention to gender issues began, in a sense, with the drafting of the Geneva Conventions, especially Geneva Convention IV (GC IV),[9] it is fitting to focus on the gender-related developments prompted by this treaty's adoption. This chapter will begin by briefly outlining the gender-related provisions of GC IV, to provide a sense of their focus and breadth. It will then turn to two GC IV provisions that have been the subject of significant feminist commentary and debate, as well as legislative and jurisprudential development: Article 27(2) (on international armed conflicts, or IACs) and Common Article 3 (on non-international armed conflicts, or NIACs). Consideration of these articles provides an excellent illustration of how the interpretation of IHL has evolved since 1949 to account for certain gender-related gaps in the original language. This chapter concludes that the interpretive evolution of these articles has filled much of the lacunae identified by feminist scholars. However, it has not done so entirely.

2. GENDER-RELATED PROVISIONS IN GC IV

When GC IV was drafted, issues of gender were considered solely through provisions focusing on women and on nondiscrimination on the basis of sex. There was no consideration of, for example, LGBTQI+ individuals,[10] even though

5. Hana Salama, *Sexual Violence in Conflict and Weapons: Unpacking the Links for Better Prevention*, ICRC Humanitarian Law and Policy Blog (Sept. 28, 2023), https://blogs.icrc.org/law-and-policy/2023/09/28/sexual-violence-in-conflict-weapons-unpacking-the-links-for-better-prevention/.

6. Helen Durham & Laura Green, *Contemporary Armed Conflict and Gender*, *in* Gender and International Criminal Law 371, 372–75 (Indira Rosenthal, Valerie Oosterveld, & Susana SáCouto eds., 2021).

7. *Id.* at 375–85, discussing gender and explosive weapons in populated areas, shifting parties to conflict, new technology, and terrorism/counterterrorism.

8. ICRC, Gendered Impacts, *supra* note 1, at 12–13. This report also mentions that there is a data gap on the gendered impacts of the conduct of hostilities.

9. Tuba Inal, Looting and Rape in Wartime: Law and Change in International Relations 92 (2013). Convention (IV) Relative to the Protection of Civilian Persons in Time of War, Aug. 12, 1949, 6 U.S.T. 3516, 75 U.N.T.S. 287 [hereinafter GC IV].

10. Marco Sassòli states: IHL "assumes that all persons are heterosexual and that their gender identity corresponds to their sex assigned at birth. Thus, IHL neglects lesbian, gay, transgender,

gay men were targeted for persecution and death during the Holocaust, and the specific needs of girls were not separated from those of boy children. Noëlle Quénivet, Judith Gardam, Michelle Jarvis, Orly Maya Stern, and others have noted that "[t]he Geneva Conventions proceed from the premise that whilst the men are fighting, women are in charge of the children and the household."[11] This assumption, based on gender norms in place in many societies in 1949, underlies several of the provisions in GC IV, which is why there is a focus on women's roles (such as women as child-bearers and child-carers).[12] Quénivet groups these provisions into interrelated categories: those relating to personal safety and women's caretaking functions, and those covering women detainees/internees.[13]

The provisions relating to the personal safety and caretaking functions of certain categories of women include Articles 14, 16, 17, 18, 21, 22, 38, and 50. Article 14 allows expectant mothers and mothers of children under seven years of age to take refuge in hospital and safety zones so as to be protected from the indirect and direct effects of war.[14] This is matched with Articles 18, 21, and 22, which indicate that civilian hospitals organized to provide care to "maternity cases," that is, women during labor and those recovering a short time after birth,[15] "may in no circumstances be the object of attack," nor may "convoys of vehicles or hospital trains" on land or sea or aircraft employed to remove maternity cases. Article 16 indicates that expectant mothers (classed with the wounded, sick, and infirm) "shall be the object of particular protection and respect," while Article 17 allows for the conclusion of local agreements for the evacuation of groups, including maternity cases. Finally, Articles 38 and 50 indicate that occupying powers must not hinder the application of preferential treatment to expectant mothers and mothers of children under seven years to food, medical care, and protection against the effects of war, and that aliens in the territory of a party at conflict may access similar care as nationals.

The provisions on women detainees/internees are crafted to protect their reproductive health and sexual integrity.[16] Women in pretrial detention and internees

bisexual, intersex, queer and other (LGTBIQ+) persons." Marco Sassòli, International Humanitarian Law: Rules, Controversies, and Solutions to Problems Arising in Warfare, ¶ 10.175 (2d ed. 2024).

11. Noëlle Quénivet, *Special Rules on Women*, *in* The 1949 Geneva Conventions: A Commentary 1271, ¶ 17 (Andrew Clapham, Paola Gaeta, & Marco Sassòli eds., 2015); Judith Gardam & Michelle Jarvis, Women, Armed Conflict, and International Law 93, 93–97 (2001); Orly Maya Stern, Gender, Conflict and International Humanitarian Law: A Critique of the "Principle of Distinction" 89, 90–100 (2018).

12. Stern, *supra* note 11, at 103.

13. Quénivet, *supra* note 11, at §§ II and III.

14. *Id.* at ¶ 20, describes direct effects as stemming from bombardment, aerial attacks, and similar situations, while indirect effects include "health, sanitation, housing, shelter, heating, etc."

15. Quénivet, *supra* note 11, at ¶ 19.

16. *Id.*, at ¶ 29.

subjected to disciplinary punishment are meant to be protected through women-only separate quarters "under the direct supervision of women" under Articles 76 and 124. Article 86 provides for adequate accommodation, with sex considered in the determination of what is "sufficient." The accommodation shall include "separate sleeping quarters" for women internees "who are not members of a family unit," as well as hygiene, including "sanitary conveniences." Female internees are only to be searched by women, under Article 97. Article 89 provides that internees who are expectant and nursing mothers shall be given an appropriate amount of additional food, while Article 91 stipulates that maternity cases must be admitted to institutions "where adequate treatment can be given." Also relating to internees, Article 132 requires parties to the conflict to endeavor to conclude agreements for the release of interned pregnant women and mothers with infants and young children. Finally, Article 127, on transfer of detainees, indicates that maternity cases shall not be transferred unless it can be done safely or unless the women would be exposed to greater risks by not being transferred.

This summary of female-specific provisions in GC IV provides a sense of how civilian women's experiences in armed conflict was envisaged and provided for by the drafters of that treaty: as individuals needing protection from fellow male detainees/internees, as pregnant individuals, as mothers who are giving birth or have recently done so, as nursing mothers, and as mothers of young children. Catherine O'Rourke correctly observes that this definition of women's rights in conflict, while "clearly valuable," has "narrow boundaries."[17] Stern also expresses concern that, while there is merit in these gender-related protections, other gender-related risks are left unaddressed:

> While women are subject to specific types of dangers in conflict, men are at a higher risk of being intentionally harmed or killed—in large part due to stereotypes about men being violent and to perceptions that all men are combatants, or at least potential combatants.[18]

Her concern is that "[g]ender stereotypes [including in GC IV] affect compliance with the principle of distinction, ultimately putting both men and women's safety at risk."[19]

Keeping in mind Stern's warning about gendered risk, the remainder of the chapter will focus on two specific articles nested within these gender-related GC IV provisions—Article 27(2) and Common Article 3—in order to illustrate how IHL has evolved in the area of protection of sexual integrity in particular.

17. Catherine O'Rourke, Women's Rights in Armed Conflict under International Law 60–61 (2020).

18. Stern, *supra* note 11, at 89.

19. *Id.*

3. ARTICLE 27(2) OF GENEVA CONVENTION IV

Article 27, a cornerstone of GC IV,[20] focuses on the humane treatment of protected persons in the context of an international armed conflict. Article 27(1) provides the overarching requirement that protected persons "are entitled . . . to respect for their persons, their honour, their family rights, their religious convictions and practices, and their manners and customs." It also goes on to require that protected persons must be humanely treated and protected from violence. Article 27(3) contains a no-adverse distinction (nondiscrimination) requirement, except where more favorable treatment is already indicated in GC IV. These two clauses surround and inform Article 27(2), which is explored in some detail in this section. Article 27 protections are additional to gender-neutral safeguards in GC IV.[21]

Article 27(2) of the Fourth Geneva Convention states: "Women shall be especially protected against any attack on their honour, in particular against rape, enforced prostitution, or any form of indecent assault." This provision represented the "first express conventional reference to rape and other forms of sexual mistreatment,"[22] and therefore was a step forward at the time for IHL.[23] It is the only article in the Geneva Conventions to refer explicitly to, and require protection from, sexual violence.[24] That said, this provision also reflected the era in which it was drafted.

3.1 "Attack on their Honour"

Article 27(2) indicates that the special protection provided for women in this subarticle is against "an attack on their honour."[25] The Pictet Commentary indicates that, at the time of drafting, "honour" was understood as "a moral and social quality," and that its use with respect to women was understood to be linked to modesty.[26] Two civil society

20. Quénivet, *supra* note 11, at ¶ 6, referring to Oscar M. Uhler et al., Commentary to Geneva Convention IV Relative to the Protection of Civilian Persons in Time of War 199–200 (1958) [hereinafter ICRC Commentary].

21. Quénivet, *supra* note 11, at ¶ 6; ICRC Commentary, *supra* note 20, at 205.

22. Articles 37(1), 44, and 47 of the 1863 Lieber Code contained a provision for the specific protection of women and listed rape as a serious violation of war, punishable by death. This, however, was not a treaty. It was U.S. military law. U.S. Department of War, Instructions for the Government of Armies of the United States in the Field, General Orders No. 100, Apr. 24, 1863.

23. Gardam & Jarvis, *supra* note 11, at 64. This article was based on a proposal from the International Women's Congress and the International Federation of Abolitionists. ICRC Commentary, *supra* note 20, at 205.

24. Patricia Viseur Sellers & Indira Rosenthal, *Rape and Other Sexual Violence*, *in* The 1949 Geneva Conventions: A Commentary, *supra* note 11, at 343, ¶ 7.

25. *Id.* at ¶ 20.

26. ICRC Commentary, *supra* note 20, at 202 and 206.

groups[27] were involved in pressing for the protection of women to be directly mentioned in the drafting of GC IV.[28] The International Alliance of Women/International Women's Congress in particular, one of the leading women's organizations at the time, had been heavily involved in the drafting of the UN Charter and Universal Declaration of Human Rights immediately prior and had much experience trying to influence international organizations by not being "too radical."[29] Thus, it supported language referencing rape as an attack on honor, "since it was likely that states would not accept it any other way."[30] Thus, conflict-related sexual violence was intentionally linked to the honor of women.[31]

This framing has several negative effects. It imported a number of inaccurate understandings of rape prevalent at the time, in particular that rape targets women's chastity and modesty and therefore the value of women to their men.[32] O'Rourke points out that the notion of honor deflects from a focus on bodily integrity or autonomy,[33] and Maria Eriksson states that it "implies that the harm [of sexual violence] is itself a violation of property."[34] Patricia Viseur Sellers and Indira Rosenthal state that the reference to honor "is based on a mischaracterization of the harm" caused by sexual violence, as it turns the focus to protecting honor rather than protecting people.[35] In Stern's view, this is "a view that IHL should not be perpetuating."[36]

On the other hand, Quénivet argues that this is not the inevitable or current understanding of the reference to honor. She points out that the term "honour" is also used in Article 27(1) covering all protected persons, and that the Article

27. Tuba Inal names them as the International Alliance of Women (*Alliance Internationale des Femmes*) and the International Abolitionist Federation (*Fédération Abolitionniste Internationale*). Inal, *supra* note 9, at 106. Pictet lists them slightly differently as the "International Women's Congress and the International Federation of Abolitionists." ICRC Commentary, *supra* note 20, at 205.

28. Their proposal was likely adapted from Article 46 of the 1899 and 1907 Hague Regulations, which states that "family honour and rights . . . must be respected." Anna Crowe, *All the Regard Due to their Sex: Women in the Geneva Conventions of 1949*, Harvard Research Working Paper Series, Harvard Human Rights Program 7–8 (2016); Regulations Respecting the Laws and Customs of War on Land, annexed to Convention No. IV Respecting the Laws and Customs of War on Land, Oct. 18, 1907, 36 Stat. 2227, T.S. No. 539.

29. Inal, *supra* note 9, at 98, 106.

30. *Id.* at 97.

31. Gardam & Jarvis, *supra* note 11, at 64; *see also* ICRC Commentary, *supra* note 20, at 206.

32. Gardam & Jarvis, *supra* note 11, at 97, 110.

33. O'Rourke, *supra* note 17, at 60.

34. Maria Eriksson, Defining Rape: Emerging Obligations for States under International Law 350 (2011).

35. Sellers & Rosenthal, *supra* note 24, at ¶ 21.

36. Stern, *supra* note 11, at 103.

27(2) reference should be interpreted in exactly the same way: "[P]reserving their moral integrity and avoiding shame and humiliation."[37] She contends that to read the word "honour" in Article 27(2) as referring to a socially constructed norm "sustained by male ideas about women's chastity, modesty, and associated frailty and dependence" is inappropriate.[38] This is because the concept has evolved over time in three complementary ways. First, Article 75(2)(b) of Additional Protocol I (AP I) understands attacks on honor as comprising outrages upon personal dignity, while Article 76 does not use the word "honour."[39] This reflects a change: IHL "has thus distanced itself from a concept of honour that used to be defined not by the nature of the act but rather by the wider community, and now tends to view these acts as violent attacks upon women's physical [and mental] integrity."[40] In the same vein, Sellers and Rosenthal indicate that the word "honour" in relation to sexual violence committed against women is found nowhere else in IHL (or in international human rights law) and that the gender-neutral concept of dignity in both IACs and NIACs is now the reigning approach in IHL.[41]

Second, the jurisprudence of the International Criminal Tribunal for the former Yugoslavia (ICTY) views honor as reflecting human dignity.[42] Third, international human rights law interprets attacks on honor as physical and psychological attacks on women and girls,[43] rather than reputational attacks.[44] Sellers and Rosenthal agree with Quénivet about this reading of "honour" and posit that this evolution is important, as it moves away from a stereotype of women as inherently weak and susceptible to sexual violence to a recognition that the disproportionate targeting of women for sexual violence in conflict is due to widespread, global gender inequality.[45]

37. Quénivet, *supra* note 11, at ¶ 12.

38. *Id.*

39. Protocol Additional to the Geneva Conventions of 12 August 1949, and Relating to the Protection of Victims of International Armed Conflicts art. 75(2)(b), June 8, 1977, 1125 U.N.T.S. 3 [hereinafter AP I]; Quénivet, *supra* note 11, at ¶ 13.

40. Quénivet, *supra* note 11, at ¶ 13.

41. Sellers & Rosenthal, *supra* note 24, at ¶ 18. They point to AP I Articles 75(2)(b) and 76, *supra* note 9, and AP II Article 4(2)(e). Protocol Additional to the Geneva Conventions of August 12, 1949, and Relating to the Protection of Victims of Non-international Armed Conflicts art. 4(2)(e), June 8, 1977, 1125 U.N.T.S. 609 [hereinafter AP II].

42. Prosecutor v. Furundžija, Case No. IT-95-17/1-T, Judgment, ¶ 183 (Int'l Crim. Trib. for the former Yugoslavia Dec. 10, 1998). The ICTY Trial Chamber stated that it "interprets 'honour' [in Article 27(2)] in the sense of 'dignity,' without thereby detracting from its view that these are violent crimes." Prosecutor v. Kunarac et al., Case No. IT-IT-96-23-T& IT-96-23/1-T, Judgment, ¶ 187 fn. 1299 (Int'l Crim. Trib. for the former Yugoslavia Feb. 22, 2001).

43. Quénivet, *supra* note 11, at n. 33.

44. *Id.*, at ¶ 13.

45. Sellers & Rosenthal, *supra* note 24, at ¶¶ 19–20.

At the same time, Sellers and Rosenthal recognize that honor is a concept that resonates in certain cultures and situations and thus the provision as written may have helpful deterrent effect.[46] As Charlotte Lindsay notes, "the concept of honour is much more complex than merely a 'value' term"—"honour is a code by which many men and women are raised, and by which they define and lead their lives."[47] Thus, even though the term as understood in 1949 is dated and promotes stereotypes, the concept of honor as understood today may be useful in certain circumstances in promoting compliance.

3.2 "Especially Protected"

The reference to sexual violence is preceded by a recognition that women are to be "especially protected against any attack on their honour." The word "especially" in Article 27(2) indicates an additional level of protection: "This means that women benefit from the general protections and respect stated in paragraph 1 *and* those listed in paragraph 2."[48] This can be seen as positive, insofar as women and girls are very often targeted for sexual violence in conflicts. At the same time, the qualifier "especially" fails to recognize that men and boys are also targeted for sexual violence, such as torture, mutilation of genitals, rape, forced nudity, and forced witnessing of sexual violence.[49]

The concept of protection of specific groups is a central and overarching aim of IHL, and thus the terms "protect" and "protection," occur throughout the Geneva Conventions. For example, Article 13 of Geneva Convention III (GCIII) states that "prisoners of war must at all times be protected, particularly against acts of violence or intimidation and against insults and public curiosity."[50] The 2020 GCIII Commentary to this article states that "[t]o protect someone means to stand up for them, to give them assistance and support and to defend or guard them from injury or danger . . . The obligation to protect is an obligation of conduct."[51] Thus,

46. *Id.* at ¶ 21.

47. Charlotte Lindsey, *The Impact of Armed Conflict on Women*, *in* Listening to the Silences: Women and War 21, 33 (Helen Durham & Tracey Gurd eds., 2005).

48. Quénivet, *supra* note 11, at ¶ 11.

49. ICRC and Norwegian Red Cross, *"That Never Happens Here" Sexual and Gender-Based Violence against Men, Boys and/including LGBTIQ + Persons in Humanitarian Settings* 27 (Feb. 3, 2022), https://www.icrc.org/en/document/sexual-gender-violence-against-men-boys-lgbtiq.

50. Geneva Convention Relative to the Treatment of Prisoners of War art. 13, Aug. 12, 1949, 6 U.S.T. 3316, 75 U.N.T.S. 135 [hereinafter GC III].

51. International Committee of the Red Cross, Convention (III) Relative to the Treatment of Prisoners of War, Geneva, 12 August 1949 ¶ 1611 (2020), https://ihl-databases.icrc.org/en/ihl-treaties/gciii-1949 [hereinafter ICRC 2020 GC III Commentary]. The Commentary also notes at ¶ 1613 that "the obligation to protect could be interpreted as requiring the use of protective measures against other dangers arising in the context of an armed

under this understanding, the term "protected" in Article 27(2) has a similar meaning, with the result that the humane treatment of women in armed conflict is to be supported and defended.

On the other hand, the term "protected" has also been critiqued. Even if its use in Article 27(2) is meant to improve the situation of female civilians in conflict in line with the goals of IHL, it also exists in a context. The first context is temporal, as the term was deployed in this article at a time of substantial and global gender inequality and discrimination. Rather than directly *prohibiting* particular acts, as other GC IV articles do (see, for example, Article 33: "Pillage is prohibited. Reprisals against protected persons are prohibited"), this article *protects*.[52] The language of safeguarding rather than prohibiting is reflective of "the male perception [in 1949] of not only what it is to be a woman, but also what it is about a woman that warrants protection," which does not reflect the complex realities of women's lives in war.[53] It is for this reason that some view the term, as used in this specific article, linked to women, as de jure about giving assistance and de facto about reinforcing a paternalistic understanding of women's needs.[54] At the same time, the current recognition of civilian women's lived experiences of armed conflict weighs in favor of a more modern (and nondiscriminatory) interpretation of "protected."[55] The second context is exclusionary. All those vulnerable to sexual violence require protection and only women are protected under this clause.[56] (Though Sellers and Rosenthal respond that males are protected from sexual violence under Article 27(1)).[57]

The protection wording of Article 27(2) has led to some discussion about its effect: Does it prohibit conflict-related sexual violence, or not? There are varying views. Boyd van Dijk argues that Article 27(2) "stigmatize[d]" sexual violence, but "neither prohibited nor powerfully deterred rape."[58] Christine Chinkin states that Article 27(2) does "not impose a blanket prohibition against sexual abuse, but rather oblige[s] States to offer women protection against attacks on their

conflict, such as from ongoing hostilities, from natural hazards or from explosive remnants of war."

52. Article 33 is also found in GC IV Part III, Section I. GC IV, *supra* note 9. *See also* Boyd van Dijk, *Gendering the Geneva Conventions*, 44 Human Rights Quarterly 286, 297 (2022).

53. Gardam & Jarvis, *supra* note 11, at 10–11.

54. *See, e.g.*, Judith Gardam, *A Feminist Analysis of Certain Aspects of International Humanitarian Law*, 12 Australian Yearbook of International Law 265, 266, 277 (1992); O'Rourke, *supra* note 17, at 36–43.

55. *See*, inter alia, ICRC, Gendered Impacts, *supra* note 1, for this current recognition.

56. Stern, *supra* note 11, at 103–04.

57. Sellers & Rosenthal, *supra* note 24, at ¶ 8.

58. Van Dijk, *supra* note 52, at 297.

honour."[59] On the other hand, others interpret Article 27(2) as a clear prohibition of rape.[60] For example, Theodor Meron stated in 1993, prompted by the atrocities of the conflict in the former Yugoslavia, that Article 27(2) "explicitly and categorically prohibit[s] rape."[61] Rhonda Copelon took the same view.[62] Jean Pictet is clear in the GC IV Commentary that (despite the language of Article 27(2)), "[t]hese acts [rape, etc.] are and remain prohibited in all places and in all circumstances."[63] Rule 93 in the ICRC Customary IHL Database makes the same point,[64] as did the ICTY[65] and Special Court for Sierra Leone (SCSL).[66]

Even if there is agreement that Article 27(2) prohibits sexual violence, does this mean rape, enforced prostitution, and indecent assault are war crimes? Gardam writes: "Although nowadays regarded by most commentators as designating rape as a war crime for which there is individual responsibility, on its face it does no such thing and was not regarded as doing so at the time it was adopted."[67] The reality may have been more complex. The original language of Article 27(2) was included in response to widespread reports of sexual violence against women committed by combatants in World War II, particularly in occupied areas,[68] which prompted two civil society

59. Christine Chinkin, *Rape and Sexual Abuse of Women under International Humanitarian Law*, 5 European Journal of International Law 326, 332 (1994).

60. *See, e.g.*, La Vecchia, *supra* note 2, at 182, n. 110; Judith Gardam, *The Law of Armed Conflict: A Gendered Regime*, 171 Studies in Transnational Legal Policy 171, 195 (1993).

61. Theodor Meron, *Rape as a Crime under International Humanitarian Law*, 87 American Journal of International Law 424, 426 (1993). He added that rape is also prohibited through the grave breaches provisions: "As early as 1958, the ICRC Commentary on the fourth Geneva Convention recognized that the grave breach of 'inhuman treatment' (Art. 147) should be interpreted in the context of Article 27, which also prohibits rape."

62. Rhonda Copelon, *Surfacing Gender: Reengraving Crimes Against Women in Humanitarian Law*, *in* Women and War in the Twentieth Century: Enlisted With or Without Consent 245, 248 (Nicole Dombrowski ed., 1998).

63. ICRC Commentary, *supra* note 20, at 206.

64. International Committee of the Red Cross, *Customary International Humanitarian Law Database*, https://ihl-databases.icrc.org/en/customary-ihl/v1/rule93 [hereinafter ICRC IHL Database].

65. Prosecutor v. Delalić et al., Case No. IT-96-21-T, Judgment, ¶ 476 (Int'l Crim. Trib. for the former Yugoslavia Nov. 16, 1998).

66. Prosecutor v. Sesay et al., Case No. SCSL-04-15-T, Judgment, ¶ 144, n. 278 (Mar. 2, 2009).

67. Judith Gardam, *Women and the Law of Armed Conflict: Why the Silence?*, 46(1) International and Comparative Law Quarterly 455, 474 (1997).

68. ICRC Commentary, *supra* note 20, at 205. On this, van Dijk writes: "[T]his ICRC report noted how countless women of all ages, and even small girls were the victims of the most abominable outrages during the war. In occupied territories, very many cases of rape occurred, and unheard-of brutalities were perpetrated, sometimes accompanied by mutilations and indecent

groups[69] to press for the protection of women[70] to be directly mentioned in the drafting of GC IV.[71] While the suggestion was ultimately included, some have commented that a number of the drafters were reluctant to discuss the fact of rape in war or to go any further than requiring protection of women from sexual violence: both Tuba Inal and van Dijk argue that "some drafters appeared to believe that rape was a natural consequence of warfare" and others believed that brothels were a necessary part of "containing" male sexual urges while serving as combatants.[72] While this may be true, it is not dispositive of the question of whether rape, enforced prostitution, and indecent assault were considered to be war crimes. As the ICRC Customary IHL database indicates, at the time of drafting and in the years immediately afterward, rape and other forms of sexual violence were seen as war crimes in certain national case law, and since then in legislation and military manuals.[73]

Some point to the lack of explicit inclusion of sexual violence in the list of grave breaches as confirmation that Article 27(2) was not intended to create war crimes.[74] However, as Anna Crowe explains: "The explanation for this absence probably lies in general indifference and neglect, rather than deliberate omission: the picture that emerges from the 1949 diplomatic conference and the meetings that preceded it is one in which rape was a marginal issue to the participants."[75] Indeed, rape in particular has since been interpreted to fall within certain grave breaches.[76]

The use of the term "especially protected" originated in a time when the social expectation was that men's role in armed conflict was one of protector and women's as protected, but it has evolved to encapsulate a more complex and gender-equal meaning today. As well, potentially at the time and undeniably

assault upon women and young girls. Wherever troops have passed or been stationed venereal diseases have increased to an alarming degree," van Dijk, *supra* note 52, at n. 69.

69. Tuba Inal explains that the International Alliance of Women (also known as the International Women's Congress) was one of the leading women's organizations at the time and had been heavily involved in the drafting of the Universal Declaration of Human Rights the year prior. Inal, *supra* note 9, at 106.

70. Patricia Sellers and Indira Rosenthal write that these groups were "probably lacking awareness of the extent to which males are also targeted for sexual and gender-based violence." Sellers & Rosenthal, *supra* note 24, at ¶ 8.

71. *See, e.g.*, ICRC Commentary, and Crowe, *supra* notes 20 and 28.

72. Van Dijk, *supra* note 52, at 299; Inal, *supra* note 9, at 107–08.

73. ICRC IHL Database, *supra* note 64, at r. 93.

74. Gardam, *supra* note 67, at 75.

75. Crowe, *supra* note 28, at 11.

76. Hilary Charlesworth & Christine Chinkin, The Boundaries of International Law: A Feminist Analysis 316 (2000). As Stern notes, in 2013, the G8 specifically recognized rape in armed conflict as a grave breach. *See* Quénivet, *supra* note 11, at 104, *citing* G8 Declaration on Preventing Sexual Violence in Conflict ¶ 4 (Apr. 11, 2013).

today as a result of subsequent legal practice, it is interpreted as creating a prohibition and as identifying a war crime.

3.3 "In Particular Against Rape, Enforced Prostitution, or Any Form of Indecent Assault"

The interpretation of Article 27(2) has been shaped by, inter alia, the 1977 Additional Protocols, the statutes of international criminal courts, and the jurisprudence of the International Criminal Tribunals for the former Yugoslavia and Rwanda (the latter, ICTR), the Special Court for Sierra Leone, and the International Criminal Court (ICC), among others.[77] For example, Article 27(2) was "updated"[78] in Additional Protocol II, which prohibits, in a gender-neutral manner, "outrages upon personal dignity, in particular humiliating and degrading treatment, rape, enforced prostitution and any form of indecent assault in Art 4(2)(e)."[79] The Rome Statute of the ICC criminalizes "[r]ape, sexual slavery, enforced prostitution, forced pregnancy, enforced sterilization, or any other form of sexual violence" as war crimes and crimes against humanity.[80] Note, however, that no international criminal tribunal cases have been anchored in Article 27(2) of GC IV (and the notion of "honour") because this article is viewed as being superseded by the 1977 Additional Protocols.[81] Additionally, rape, enforced prostitution, and other forms of indecent assault have been explicitly and directly recognized as war crimes in both IAC and NIAC over the past thirty years by international courts.

77. *See also* the jurisprudence of the Extraordinary Chambers in the Courts of Cambodia and the Extraordinary African Chambers in Senegal (particularly, the *Hissène Habré* case). Prosecutor v. Hissène Habré et al., Case No. 002/PCC/SG/001, Decision on the Unconstitutionality Raised by the Victims of Crimes and Political Repression on the Criminal Case opened against the agents of the DDS of Hissène Habré (Constitutional Court, Chad, Apr. 6, 2001).

78. Helen Durham & Katie O'Byrne, *The Dialogue of Difference: Gender Perspectives on International Humanitarian Law*, 92(877) INTERNATIONAL REVIEW OF THE RED CROSS 31, 47 (2010).

79. *See also* AP I, *supra* note 39, art. 76, which expands the scope of women who are covered by the provision to all women in the territory of the parties involved in the conflict. It also eliminates the language of "honour": Women "shall be the object of special respect and shall be protected in particular against rape, forced prostitution and any other form of indecent assault."

80. Rome Statute of the International Criminal Court arts. 7(1)(g); 8(2)(b)(xii); and 8(2)(e)(vi), July 17, 1998, 2187 U.N.T.S. 90 [hereinafter ICC Statute]. Note that the crime against humanity provision adds "of comparable gravity" at the end of this list, while the war crime in IAC ends with "also constituting a grave breach of the Geneva Conventions," and the war crime in NIAC ends in "also constituting a serious violation of article 3 common to the four Geneva Conventions."

81. Sellers & Rosenthal, *supra* note 24, at ¶ 24.

Rape has been prosecuted and convicted as a war crime in the ICTY,[82] the Special Court for Sierra Leone,[83] and the ICC.[84] Since GC IV, the APs, and the ICRC Commentaries thereto do not define rape, the case law of international criminal tribunals has done so.[85] The ICC's definition of rape was subject to diplomatic negotiation and was set out in its Elements of Crimes document.[86] These definitions do not differentiate between IACs and NIACs, and all contain a gender-neutral recognition of rape as a violation of personal and sexual autonomy. As Cordula Droege and Eirini Giorgou conclude, "[a]s a result of these developments, it is now unquestionable that . . . sexual violence is prohibited not by requirements related to gendered notions of honour, but by prohibitions of violence to person, and that it is prohibited against everyone regardless of gender."[87]

Enforced prostitution was included in Article 27(2) because drafters were aware that thousands of women were forced into military brothels against their will in World War II, especially in the Japanese "comfort women" system of institutionalized enslavement.[88] This act was not elaborated in GC IV, though Pictet defines it as "the forcing of a woman into immorality by violence or threats."[89] While

82. *See, e.g.*, *Furundžija*, *supra* note 42; *Kunarac*, *supra* note 42; and *Delalić*, *supra* note 65.

83. *See Sesay*, *supra* note 66; Prosecutor v. Brima et al., Case No. SCSL-2004-16-A, Judgment (Feb. 22, 2008); Prosecutor v. Charles Taylor, Case No. SCSL-03-01-T, Judgment (May 18, 2012).

84. Prosecutor v. Ntaganda, Case No. ICC-01/04-02/06, Judgment (July 8, 2019); Prosecutor v. Ongwen, Case No. ICC-02/04-01/15, Judgment (Feb. 4, 2021).

85. *See, e.g.*, Prosecutor v. Kunarac et al., Case No. IT-96-23 & IT-96-23/1-A, Judgment, ¶ 128 (Int'l Crim. Trib. for the former Yugoslavia June 12, 2002); *Taylor*, *supra* note 83, at ¶ 415. Even though Article 27(2) addresses IACs, case law stemming from NIACs defining terms such as "rape" is useful. The qualification of an act as rape, for example, does not differ depending on the classification of the conflict.

86. The ICC's Elements of Crime document defines rape in this way:

1. The perpetrator invaded the body of a person by conduct resulting in penetration, however slight, of any part of the body of the victim or of the perpetrator with a sexual organ, or of the anal or genital opening of the victim with any object or any other part of the body.
2. The invasion was committed by force, or by threat of force or coercion, such as that caused by fear of violence, duress, detention, psychological oppression or abuse of power, against such person or another person, or by taking advantage of a coercive environment, or the invasion was committed against a person incapable of giving genuine consent.

(The term "invaded" contains a footnote stating: "The concept of 'invasion' is intended to be broad enough to be gender-neutral.") Official Records of the Assembly of States Parties to the Rome Statute of the International Criminal Court, First session, New York, U.N. Doc. E.03.V.2 (Sept. 3–10, 2002).

87. Cordula Droege & Eirini Giorgou, *How International Humanitarian Law Develops*, 104(920–921) International Review of the Red Cross 1798, 1819 (2022).

88. ICRC Commentary, *supra* note 20, at 205.

89. *Id.* at 206.

enforced prostitution has not been litigated at the international level,[90] it was included in the war crimes provisions of the Statutes of the ICTR, Special Court for Sierra Leone, and ICC.[91] It has been defined in the ICC's Elements of Crimes as well.[92] The wording of this provision prompted the addition of the crime against humanity and war crime of sexual slavery in the Rome Statute, as a more accurate label for what happened to the "comfort women."[93] Despite this, the Rome Statute drafters retained enforced prostitution both for its historical significance[94] and to capture situations falling short of enslavement.[95]

The term "indecent assault" is not defined in GC IV, though the term is used in AP I and AP II.[96] It is also included in the ICTR and Special Court for Sierra Leone Statutes.[97] The ICRC Study on Customary International Law indicates that this term includes "any form of sexual violence."[98] This was confirmed by the ICTY.[99] "Any form of indecent assault" is a residual category and "covers any form

90. It was litigated in the aftermath of World War II: the Dutch Temporary Court Martial in Batavia convicted a number of Japanese military individuals of this crime for forcing 35 Dutch nationals to be "comfort women." Sellers & Rosenthal, *supra* note 24, at ¶ 31, *citing* Judge-Advocate v. X et al., Netherlands Temporary Court Martial in Batavia, Case No. 72/1947, Verdict 231 (1948).

91. Statute of the International Criminal Tribunal for Rwanda art. 4(e), S.C. Res. 955 annex (Nov. 8, 1994), *reprinted in* 33 INTERNATIONAL LEGAL MATERIALS 1598 (1994) [hereinafter ICTR Statute]; Statute of the Special Court for Sierra Leone, art. 3(e), Jan. 16, 2002, 2178 U.N.T.S. 145 [hereinafter SCSL Statute] (also as a crime against humanity in Article 2(g)); ICC Statute, *supra* note 80 (also a crime against humanity in Article 7(2)(g)).

92. The ICC Statute, *supra* note 80, in its Elements of Crime document, *supra* note 86, defines enforced prostitution:

1. The perpetrator caused one or more persons to engage in one or more acts of a sexual nature by force, or by threat of force or coercion, such as that caused by fear of violence, duress, detention, psychological oppression or abuse of power, against such person or persons or another person, or by taking advantage of a coercive environment or such person's or persons' incapacity to give genuine consent.
2. The perpetrator or another person obtained or expected to obtain pecuniary or other advantage in exchange for or in connection with the acts of a sexual nature.

93. Valerie Oosterveld, *Sexual Slavery and the International Criminal Court: Advancing International Law*, 25(3) MICHIGAN JOURNAL OF INTERNATIONAL LAW 605, 615, 649 (2004).

94. Sellers & Rosenthal, *supra* note 24, at ¶ 36.

95. Oosterveld, *supra* note 93, at 622.

96. *See* Articles 75(2)(b), 76(1), and 77(1) of AP I, *supra* note 39, and Article 4(e) of AP II, *supra* note 41.

97. ICTR Statute, *supra* note 91, art. 4; SCSL Statute, *supra* note 91, art. 3.

98. ICRC IHL Database, *supra* note 64, at r. 93.

99. The ICTY has significant case law on sexual assault as a cognizable violation. *See, e.g.*, the discussion in Prosecutor v. Milutinović et al., Case No. IT-05-87-T, Judgment, Vol. 1, ¶¶ 183–201 (Int'l Crim. Trib. for the former Yugoslavia Feb. 26, 2009).

of sexualized conduct that contravenes humane treatment and is not expressly listed."[100]

In sum, each of the three named violations in Article 27(2) have since been recognized as war crimes in IACs and NIACs and have been interpreted and defined, giving them legal substance. It is for this reason that there is no logical debate in 2024 about whether these acts are prohibited and criminalized.

3.4 Conclusions on Article 27(2) and Remaining Gaps

Given all of this legislative, jurisprudential, and interpretive development, Eriksson points out that the question has been raised as to whether GC IV is superfluous.[101] She correctly answers "no": "[F]or victims in states not subject to the jurisdiction of the ICC or any [other international court], the main recourse will be the possible adjudication in national courts, based on IHL regulations."[102] For example, many countries have national legislation designating rape, enforced prostitution, and indecent assault as war crimes, and some have jurisprudence saying the same.[103] As well, GC IV is important in and of itself, especially given its universal ratification.[104]

What is missing from Article 27(2), even with this evolution? First, Article 27(2) does not cover conflict-related sexual violence against men, boys, and nonbinary individuals, although such acts are implicitly prohibited under Article 27(1) and are included under the gender-neutral sexual violence provisions in the Additional Protocols, under customary IHL, and under international criminal law.[105] Second, Article 27(2) does not directly address how women's other intersecting identities (for example, as disabled,[106] lesbian or

100. Sellers & Rosenthal, *supra* note 24, at ¶ 4. *See also* the ICRC IHL Database, *supra* note 64, at r. 93. For a list of potential forms of indecent assault, *see* Sellers & Rosenthal, *supra* note 24, at n. 86.

101. Eriksson, *supra* note 34, at 353.

102. *Id.*

103. ICRC IHL Database, *supra* note 64, at r. 93.

104. As of April 14, 2024, GC IV, *supra* note 9, has been ratified by 196 States.

105. It does, however, protect girls today. *See* ICRC 2020 GC III Commentary, *supra* note 51, at ¶ 772. Sexual violence directed against girls was raised at the time of drafting. Crowe, *supra* note 28, n. 39. Girls are often at serious risk of sexual violence in armed conflict. *See, e.g.*, Miriam Denov, *Wartime Sexual Violence: Assessing a Human Security Response to War-Affected Girls in Sierra Leone*, 37(3) Security Dialogue 275 (2006).

106. "Women and girls with disabilities are, for example, exposed to a heightened risk of sexual violence when compared to other groups of people." La Vecchia, *supra* note 2, at 167.

trans,[107] or Indigenous persons) heighten the risk of sexual violence.[108] Third, Article 27(2) does not take into account the fact that women may be vulnerable to sexual violence in armed conflict because they exist in a context of widespread, pervasive, and structural gender-based discrimination in countries around the world.[109] Fourth, while Article 27(2) covers a wide array of sexual violence crimes, it does not protect women from gendered violations that do not amount to sexual violence. Finally, while there is disagreement as to whether or not this is a gap in IAC, it should be noted that Article 27(2) "does not protect individuals from the activities of the States of which they are a national"[110] and therefore does not provide protection for women raped by combatants from their own country's armed forces.[111] Given its wording, it is unlikely that the understanding of Article 27(2) could ever evolve to cover all of these gaps, but Article 27(1) could potentially be interpreted to address at least some of these aspects to reflect the full experience of civilians vulnerable to gender-based violence in armed conflict.

4. COMMON ARTICLE 3

Common Article 3 provides, in part, that persons taking no active part in NIAC hostilities "shall in all circumstances be treated humanely, without any adverse distinction founded on . . . sex . . . , or any other similar criteria." It then prohibits "at any time and in any place whatsoever" four categories of acts against these individuals, including these two:

(a) violence to life and person, in particular murder of all kinds, mutilation, cruel treatment and torture; . . .
(c) outrages upon personal dignity, in particular humiliating and degrading treatment.

This article represents the "minimum standard of humane treatment to be given to persons taking no active part in hostilities."[112] The obligation falls on all parties,

107. *See* Sassòli, *supra* note 10, at ¶ 10.175, for a discussion of the silence of IHL in this regard.

108. This, however, is recognized by the ICRC. ICRC, Gendered Impacts, *supra* note 1, at 7.

109. *Id.*; CEDAW Committee, *General Recommendation No. 35 on Gender-based Violence against Women Updating General Recommendation No. 19*, U.N. Doc. CEDAW/G/GC/35, ¶¶ 12, 14 (July 26, 2017).

110. Gardam & Jarvis, *supra* note 11, at 64.

111. Acts of rape and sexual slavery committed by members of a militia group against others within their own group were prosecuted and convicted as war crimes in a NIAC in *Ntaganda* (see discussion at notes 121–26, *infra*), and by the Colombian Constitutional Court in the case of *Helena*, Judgment SU 599 (Dec. 11, 2019). However, these cases do not answer the questions of whether such an argument could be made in an IAC.

112. Sellers & Rosenthal, *supra* note 24, at ¶ 54.

with no exceptions.[113] The categories of prohibited acts do not directly specify sexual violence, but sexual violence falls under categories (a) and (c) mentioned previously, with (c) being the most often utilized. This is clear from the case law of international criminal tribunals.

The ICTY *Furundžija* trial judgment indicated that Common Article 3, which was incorporated into the ICTY Statute through Article 3,[114] implicitly prohibits both rape and "other sexual assaults."[115] The Trial Chamber observed: "[T]he ripening of the fundamental prohibition of 'outrages upon personal dignity' laid down in common article 3 into customary international law, has contributed to the evolution of universally accepted norms of international law prohibiting rape as well as serious sexual assault."[116] Additionally, Article 4(e) of the ICTR Statute and Article 3(e) of the Statute of the Special Court for Sierra Leone specifically list "[o]utrages upon personal dignity, in particular humiliating and degrading treatment, rape, enforced prostitution and any form of indecent assault" as a violation of Common Article 3. The ICC Statute goes one step further and lists "rape, sexual slavery, enforced prostitution, forced pregnancy, . . . enforced sterilization, or any other form of sexual violence" as war crimes in IAC and NIAC, thereby explicitly recognizing violations that had previously been implicitly recognized particularly through "outrages upon personal dignity" in Common Article 3.

Common Article 3 (coupled with AP II) has formed the basis of several prosecutions for rape and other forms of sexual violence at the ICTY and SCSL. For example, in the ICTY's *Kunarac* case, the Trial Chamber found that forcing women and girls to dance naked on tables amounted to an outrage upon personal dignity under Common Article 3: one of the accused was found to have known that "having to stand naked on a table, while the accused watched them, was a painful and humiliating experience for the three women involved, even more so because of their young age."[117] As well, the Special Court for Sierra Leone's prosecutions of rape were conducted through Common Article 3 and AP II as

113. ICRC Commentary, *supra* note 20, at 37.

114. In the *Tadić* case, the judges stated:

> Article 3 thus confers on the International Tribunal jurisdiction over any serious offence against international humanitarian law not covered by Article 2, 4 or 5. Article 3 is a fundamental provision laying down that any "serious violation of international humanitarian law" must be prosecuted by the International Tribunal. In other words, Article 3 functions as a residual clause designed to ensure that no serious violation of international humanitarian law is taken away from the jurisdiction of the International Tribunal. Article 3 aims to make such jurisdiction watertight and inescapable.

Prosecutor v. Tadić, Case No. IT-94-1, Decision on the Defence Motion for Interlocutory Appeal on Jurisdiction, ¶ 91 (Int'l Crim. Trib. for the former Yugoslavia Oct. 2, 1995).

115. *Furundžija*, *supra* note 42, at ¶¶ 165–66 and related footnotes.

116. *Id.* at ¶ 168.

117. *Kunarac*, *supra* note 42, at ¶ 773.

outrages upon personal dignity. In *Sesay*, *Kallon*, and *Gbao*, the Trial Chamber noted that "[i]t is well established that the offence of outrages upon personal dignity exists under customary international law and entails individual criminal responsibility."[118]

Importantly, ICTY case law has drawn connections between the Common Article 3 violations of torture and rape. In the *Furundžija* case, the Trial Chamber noted that "[r]ape is resorted to either by the interrogator himself or by other persons associated with the interrogation of a detainee, as a means of punishing, intimidating, coercing or humiliating the victim, or obtaining information, or a confession, from the victim or a third person."[119]

Rather than focus on charges stemming from Article 8(2)(c) and Common Article 3 language, the ICC Prosecutor has made use of a different NIAC article because of its specificity. In *Ntaganda*, the prosecution charged the sexual violation of girl soldiers by male members of their own armed group under Article 8(2)(e), "other serious violations of the laws and customs applicable in armed conflict," not under Article 8(2)(c). This allowed for the specific labeling of these acts as rape and sexual slavery, both of which are expressly included under Article 8(2)(e)(vi).[120] The defense argued that this charging is not permitted because the victim must be a protected person under Common Article 3 and fellow armed group members are not protected persons.[121] The prosecution argued that, under Article 8(2)(e), the victim need not be a protected person under Common Article 3, and even if this was required, the victims could be treated as not taking active part in hostilities at the time of their sexual assault.[122] The Pre-Trial Chamber agreed with this latter argument, while the Trial Chamber agreed with the former argument.[123] The Trial Chamber stated that an armed group cannot forcibly recruit children in violation of IHL and then rely upon that violation to claim that sexual violence against those children is not a war crime.[124] The Appeals Chamber took an

118. *Sesay*, *supra* note 66, at ¶ 174.

119. *Furundžija*, *supra* note 42, at ¶ 163.

120. This helps to fulfill the principle of legality, which requires fair labeling of crimes. On this, *see* Hilmi Zawati, Fair Labelling and the Dilemma of Prosecuting Gender-based Crimes at the International Criminal Tribunals (2014).

121. *Ntaganda*, *supra* note 84, at ¶ 40.

122. Prosecutor v. Ntaganda, Case No. ICC-01/04-02/06-1278, Prosecution's Response to Mr Ntaganda's "Consolidated Submissions Challenging Jurisdiction" Regarding Counts 6 and 9, ¶¶ 58–94 (Apr. 14, 2016).

123. Prosecutor v. Ntaganda, Case No. ICC-01/04-02/06-309, Decision Pursuant to Article 61(7)(a) and (b) of the Rome Statute on the Charges of the Prosecutor Against Bosco Ntaganda, ¶¶ 79–80 (June 9, 2017); Prosecutor v. Ntaganda, Case No. ICC-01/04-02/06-1707, Second Decision on the Defence's Challenge to the Jurisdiction of the Court in Respect of Counts 6 and 9, ¶¶ 46–54 (Jan. 4, 2017) (hereinafter *Ntaganda*, Second Decision).

124. *Ntaganda*, Second Decision, *supra* note 123, at ¶ 53.

approach similar to the Trial Chamber.[125] The Appeals Chamber also concluded that, even though there is no requirement that the victim be a protected person under Common Article 3, there must be a nexus between the sexual violence and the armed conflict: "[I]t is this nexus requirement, and not the purported Status Requirement, that sufficiently and appropriately delineates war crimes from ordinary crimes."[126] As in *Ntaganda*, the sexual violence war crimes charges in *Ongwen* were brought under Article 8(2)(e) for specificity purposes.[127]

The case law of the international criminal tribunals has provided significant substance to Common Article 3. This is to be celebrated, as it helps to operationalize the application of IHL in NIACs. The use of Common Article 3 to prosecute war crimes of sexual violence was especially important for the ICTY and ICTR. Under the ICC, it is less important due to the presence of a separate provision, Article 8(2)(e)(vi), explicitly listing a range of sexual and gender-based violence crimes. However, the previous case law of the ICTY and ICTR on rape and sexual assault crimes is regularly cited by the ICC under this provision. As Ingeborg de Koningh notes, "the international criminal tribunals have strongly contributed to putting flesh on the bones of the prohibition of sexual violence under IHL."[128]

Considering this "flesh on the bones," is there any development still needed in considering Common Article 3's coverage of sexual violence? As mentioned previously, it would be helpful for further recognition that sexual violence directed at men and boys also falls under (a) and (c), just as sexual violence directed against women and girls has been recognized to do so. While there has been some helpful case law in this respect,[129] more would assist. And, on a similar theme as mentioned earlier, more recognition could be provided, when applying IHL in international criminal law, to the interlinkages between sex discrimination and sexual violence, particularly when women and girls are targeted by combatants because they are perceived to transgress gender norms. While there is a substantive

125. Prosecutor v. Ntaganda, Case No. ICC-01/04-02/06-1962, Judgment on the Appeal of Mr Ntaganda against the "Second Decision on the Defence's Challenge to the Jurisdiction of the Court in Respect of Counts 6 and 9," ¶¶ 46–51 (June 15, 2017).

126. *Id.* at ¶ 68.

127. *Ongwen*, *supra* note 84, at ¶¶ 35–36 and associated notes.

128. Ingeborg de Koningh, *Consolidating International Humanitarian Law and International Human Rights Law: Protection from Gender-Based Violence Against Women in Non-International Armed Conflict*, 70 Netherlands International Law Review 87, 95 (2023).

129. *See, e.g.*, Prosecutor v. Češić, Case No. IT-95-10/1-S, Sentencing Judgment, ¶¶ 13–14, 33 (Int'l Crim. Trib. for the former Yugoslavia Mar. 11, 2004); Prosecutor v. Todorovic, Case No. IT-95-9/1-S, Sentencing Judgment, ¶¶ 39–40 (Int'l Crim. Trib. for the former Yugoslavia July 31, 2001); Prosecutor v. Simić, Case No. IT-95-9-T, Judgment, ¶ 728 (Int'l Crim. Trib. for the former Yugoslavia, Oct. 17, 2003), at ¶ 728. *See also* Valerie Oosterveld, *Sexual Violence Directed Against Men and Boys in Armed Conflict and Mass Atrocity: Addressing a Gendered Harm in International Criminal Tribunals*, 10(1) Journal of International Law and International Relations 107 (2014).

conversation on this with respect to the crime against humanity of persecution on gender grounds,[130] there is less attention paid with respect to war crimes. Finally, certain forms of sexual violence, like forced nudity, which is a significant concern stemming from Russian forces' treatment of Ukrainian civilians,[131] as well as a host of other forms of sexual violence recognized in the updated Commentary to Common Article 3 in Geneva Convention III,[132] could benefit from more substantive consideration in prosecutions under Common Article 3.

5. CONCLUSION

Feminist discussion and international criminal tribunal jurisprudence around Article 27(2) and Common Article 3 over the past 30 years have made a significant impact on how sexual violence crimes in IAC and NIAC are defined and applied. As Eriksson notes, it has led to the "redefinition of the harm of rape, for example, from being treated as a violation of a woman's honour in the 1949 Geneva Conventions, to the harm being viewed as a transgression against the person's sexual autonomy."[133] This thinking and consideration of GC IV has prompted wider discussions, as shown, for example, in the ICC Prosecutor recognizing that there may be gender dimensions to other war crimes, such as the intentional targeting of civilians.[134] The progress achieved should be celebrated, as it has filled many gaps inherent in the original terminology of Articles 27(2) and Common Article 3 and taken off the table many of the critiques raised by feminist scholars regarding GC IV. This evolutive development will hopefully be captured in the release of the updated commentary to the Fourth Geneva Convention.[135] At the same time, there is still a way to go to reflect the full range of sexual and gendered violence directed against civilians in armed conflict.

130. *See, e.g.*, ICC Office of the Prosecutor, *Policy on the Crime of Gender Persecution* (2022), https://www.icc-cpi.int/sites/default/files/2022-12/2022-12-07-Policy-on-the-Crime-of-Gender-Persecution.pdf.

131. Independent International Commission of Inquiry on Ukraine, Conference Room Paper of the Independent International Commission of Inquiry on Ukraine, U.N. Doc. A/HRC/52/CRP.4, ¶¶ 562, 565, 567, 569, 574, 592, 615–623 (Aug. 29, 2023).

132. ICRC 2020 GC III COMMENTARY, *supra* note 51, at ¶ 734 (forced stripping, mutilation of sexual organs, forced marriage, forced inspections for virginity, sexual exploitation such as obtaining sexual services in return for food or protection, forced abortions, and trafficking for sexual exploitation).

133. ERIKSSON, *supra* note 34, at 498.

134. ICC Office of the Prosecutor, *Policy on Gender-Based Crimes: Crimes Involving Sexual, Reproductive and other Gender-based Violence* ¶. 67 (2023), https://www.icc-cpi.int/sites/default/files/2023-12/2023-policy-gender-en-web.pdf.

135. Just as sexual violence is clearly recognized in ICRC 2020 GC III COMMENTARY, *supra* note 51, at ¶¶ 732–43.

14

Environmental Protection as Civilian Protection

LAKMINI SENEVIRATNE AND KOSUKE ONISHI*

1. INTRODUCTION

There was a time when one could be forgiven for overlooking the effects of armed conflict on the natural environment given the fatalities, injuries, and ruin caused by wars to humans. Thankfully, technological advancements have allowed for a better understanding of the impact of armed conflict on the environment.[1] Due also to the efforts of a range of organizations and individuals, as well as State practice over the past three decades, the moniker of the natural environment as a "silent victim" of armed conflict is no longer fitting.[2]

* At the time of writing, Lakmini Seneviratne was the Legal Adviser and Head of the Legal Department at the ICRC Regional Delegation for the United States & Canada, and Kosuke Onishi was a Legal Adviser at the same delegation. This article was written in their personal capacities.

1. *See generally* Doug Weir, Dan McQuillan, & Robert A. Francis, *Civilian Science: The Potential of Participatory Environmental Monitoring in Areas Affected by Armed Conflicts*, 191 Environmental Monitoring and Assessment 619 (2019); Wim Zwijnenburg et al., *Solving the Jigsaw of Conflict-Related Environmental Damage: Utilizing Open-Source Analysis to Improve Research inter Environmental Health Risks*, 42 Journal Of Public Health 352 (2020); Wim Zwijnenburg & Ollie Ballinger, *Leveraging Emerging Technologies to Enable Environmental Monitoring and Accountability in Conflict Zones*, 105 International Review of the Red Cross 1497 (2023).

2. *See, e.g.*, the military manuals of Australia, Belgium, Burundi, Chad, Côte d'Ivoire, Italy, Mexico, the Netherlands, Switzerland, the United Kingdom, and the United States. These manuals, as well as other categories of relevant State practice from these and other countries, are sourced from the ICRC Customary IHL Database, *Practice relating to Rule 43, Application*

Lakmini Seneviratne and Kosuke Onishi, *Environmental Protection as Civilian Protection* In: *Civilian Protection in Armed Conflict*. Edited by: Jelena Pejic and Captain Margaret Kotlik, Oxford University Press.
 DOI: 10.1093/oso/9780197793176.003.0014

This chapter seeks to examine the protection of the natural environment under international humanitarian law (IHL), especially in light of recent initiatives and developments in the field. In 2020, the International Committee of the Red Cross (ICRC) published its *Guidelines on the Protection of the Natural Environment in Armed Conflict* (*ICRC Guidelines*),[3] an update to its 1994 *Guidelines* covering the same topic.[4] This was followed in 2022 by the UN International Law Commission's (ILC) *Principles on Protection of the Environment in Relation to Armed Conflicts* (*PERAC Principles*), which were annexed to UN General Assembly Resolution 77/104.[5]

These two complementary products aim to clarify and foster greater respect for a range of preexisting IHL rules (although the *PERAC Principles* are broader temporally and in the bodies of law covered). In addition to instruments that specifically deal with select facets of environmental damage in armed conflict,[6] the First Additional Protocol (AP I) to the Geneva Conventions and customary IHL contain specific rules that aim to protect the natural environment from the effects of armed conflict.[7] Moreover, there are protections that extend to all parts of the natural environment as civilian objects under IHL, unless a part of it meets

of General Principles on the Conduct of Hostilities to the Natural Environment, https://ihl-databases.icrc.org/en/customary-ihl/v2/rule43 (last accessed June 13, 2024).

3. International Committee of the Red Cross, Guidelines on the Protection of the Natural Environment in Armed Conflict: Rules and Recommendations Relating to the Protection of the Natural Environment Under International Humanitarian Law (2020), *available at* https://www.icrc.org/en/download/file/141079/guidelines_on_the_protection_of_the_natural_environment_in_armed_conflict_advance-copy.pdf [hereinafter ICRC Guidelines].

4. International Committee of the Red Cross, Guidelines for Military Manuals and Instructions on the Protection of the Environment in Times of Armed Conflict (1994), in U.N. Doc. A/49/323, annex (Aug. 19, 1994).

5. United Nations International Law Commission, *Principles on the Protection of the Environment in Relation to Armed Conflicts*, in G.A. Res. 77/104, Protection of the Environment in Relation to Armed Conflicts, annex (Dec. 7, 2022) [hereinafter *PERAC Principles*].

6. Convention on the Prohibition of Military or Any Other Hostile Use of Environmental Modification Techniques, May 18, 1977, 1108 U.N.T.S. 151; Treaty on the Prohibition of Nuclear Weapons art. 6(2), July 10, 2017, 3379 U.N.T.S.; Rome Statute of the International Criminal Court art. 8(2)(b)(iv), July 17, 1998, 2187 U.N.T.S. 90.

7. *See* Protocol Additional to the Geneva Conventions of 12 August 1949, and Relating to the Protection of Victims of International Armed Conflicts, arts. 35(3) and 55, June 8, 1977, 1125 U.N.T.S. 3 [hereinafter AP I]; 1 Customary International Humanitarian rr. 43–45 (Jean-Marie Henckaerts & Louise Doswald-Beck eds., 2005) [hereinafter *CIHL Study*]; Convention No. IV Respecting the Laws and Customs of War on Land art. 23(g), Oct. 18, 1907, 36 Stat. 2227, T.S. No. 539 also extends to the natural environment in as much as it prohibits the destruction or seizure "of the enemy's property, unless such destruction or seizure be imperatively demanded by the necessities of war." There are also discussions on the establishment of demilitarized zones and their utility in protecting the natural environment, but they fall outside the scope of this chapter.

the definition of a military objective under the relevant rules on the conduct of hostilities.

The focus of the discussion in this chapter is on the civilian character of the natural environment. However, the protections afforded to it as a civilian object under IHL cannot be fully appreciated without at least touching upon key IHL rules specifically protecting the environment. These protections posit, among other things, an absolute limit on damage reaching the threshold of "widespread, long-term and severe." The rules and principles that protect civilian objects thus play a crucial role in protecting the environment, including from damage that falls below that notoriously high threshold. As we argue, adherence to IHL norms that protect the natural environment based on its civilian character are likely to generate positive outcomes for both the natural environment and the humans that inevitably depend on it.[8] Demonstrating how these norms can be applied in practice, this chapter draws on examples from the discussion at the State Expert Meeting on IHL and the Protection of the Environment co-organized by Switzerland and the ICRC in 2023.[9]

The substantive examination in the chapter commences with a definition of the natural environment followed, in section 2, by an overview of IHL rules protecting it. Included are the aforementioned provisions prohibiting "widespread, long-term, and severe" damage to the environment and those that generally protect civilians and civilian objects in the conduct of hostilities under IHL. Section 3 focuses on challenges and good practices in implementing the relevant IHL protections by States and non-State armed groups (NSAGs). Section 4 argues that any supposed bifurcation between environmental damage that results in harm to humans, and that which does not, is untenable. Scientific understandings today affirm that such a distinction is artificial given the environmental and climate crisis threatening humanity's survival.[10]

Two preliminary caveats are in order. First, this contribution does not seek to provide a comprehensive overview of all the potentially relevant IHL rules or other

8. Helen Obregón Gieseken & Vanessa Murphy, *The Protection of the Natural Environment under International Humanitarian Law: ICRC's 2020 Guidelines*, 105 International Review of the Red Cross 924 (2023); *Climate Change 2022: Impacts, Adaptation, and Vulnerability, Contribution of Working Group II to the Sixth Assessment Report of the Intergovernmental Panel on Climate Change, Summary for Policymakers*, Intergovernmental Panel on Climate Change (IPPC) 12, 32 (June 29, 2023).

9. These discussions have been summarized in *State Expert Meeting on International Humanitarian Law: Protecting the Environment in Armed Conflicts: Chair's Summary* (Aug. 8, 2023), *available at* https://www.icrc.org/en/document/chairs-summary-report-state-expert-meeting-ihl-protecting-natural-environment-armed [hereinafter *Chair's Summary*].

10. Notably, the preamble of the *PERAC Principles*, *supra* note 5, begins by "[r]ecognizing that environmental consequences of armed conflicts may be severe and have the potential to exacerbate global environmental challenges, such as climate change and biodiversity loss," and likewise asserts "[a]ware[ness] of the importance of the environment for livelihoods, food and water security, maintenance of traditions and cultures, and the enjoyment of human rights."

bodies of international law.[11] Rather, the focus is primarily on the rules governing civilian protection and the complementary prohibition of widespread, long-term, and severe damage to the natural environment. IHL rules related to weaponry or those specific to situations of occupation, among others, are omitted from the discussion. Secondly, the substantive content of applicable IHL rules draws heavily on the *ICRC Guidelines* without reproducing, amending, or developing them.

2. HOW PROTECTING THE ENVIRONMENT DURING ARMED CONFLICT IS ESSENTIAL FOR CIVILIAN PROTECTION

2.1 Definition of the Natural Environment

The 1987 ICRC Commentary to Article 55 of AP I[12] states:

> The concept of the natural environment should be understood in the widest sense to cover the biological environment in which a population is living. It does not consist merely of the objects indispensable to survival mentioned in Article 54 "(Protection of objects indispensable to the survival of the civilian population)"—foodstuffs, agricultural areas, drinking water, livestock—but also includes forests and other vegetation mentioned in the Convention of 10 October 1980 on Prohibitions or Restrictions on the Use of Certain Conventional Weapons, . . . as well as fauna, flora and other biological or climatic elements.

The Commentary further clarifies in relation to Article 35(3) of API:[13]

> . . . [T]he term "natural environment" in the Protocol does refer to this system of inextricable interrelations between living organisms and their inanimate environment. This is a kind of permanent or transient equilibrium depending on the situation, though always relatively fragile, of forces which keep each other in balance and condition the life of biological groups.

11. For discussions on the applicability and relevance of international environmental law, human rights law, and the law of the sea, *see* ICRC Guidelines, *supra* note 3, at ¶¶ 25–41. While the *ICRC Guidelines* focus primarily on IHL, the *PERAC Principles* more comprehensively address the relevance and applicability of international human rights and international environmental law.

12. Commentary on the Additional Protocols of 8 June 1977 to the Geneva Conventions of 12 August 1949 ¶ 2126 (Yves Sandoz, Christophe Swinarski, & Bruno Zimmermann eds., 1987) [hereinafter ICRC Commentary to the APs].

13. *Id.* at ¶ 1451.

Relying on this foundation, the *ICRC Guidelines* state:

> [T]he notion of the natural environment under IHL includes everything that exists or occurs naturally, such as the general hydrosphere, biosphere, geosphere and atmosphere (including fauna, flora, oceans and other bodies of water, soil and rocks). The natural environment moreover includes natural elements that are or may be the product of human intervention, such as foodstuffs, agricultural areas, drinking water and livestock.

The *ICRC Guidelines* further note that a broad definition ". . . accords with the fact that the notion of the 'natural environment' may evolve over time, as knowledge about it increases and as the environment itself is constantly changing."[14] This approach is supported by the ILC.[15]

The natural environment is an interdependent system that—particularly due to the interconnected nature of its composite parts—can be damaged in a variety of long-lasting ways,[16] including as a consequence of war.[17] The effect of burning oil fields in the 1991 Gulf War on the atmosphere, land, waterways, and animals is a stark example.[18] Experience has shown that damage to the natural environment in times of armed conflict has often been a combination of incidental damage and deliberate attacks, with consequences far beyond the immediate.[19] Moreover, according to reports, during the 15-year civil war in Mozambique, the Gorongosa National Park lost more than 90 percent of its animals. The elephant population declined from 2,000 to 200, as elephant meat was used to feed soldiers and ivory was sold to finance the purchase of weapons, ammunition, and supplies.[20] The

14. ICRC Guidelines, *supra* note 3, at ¶¶ 16 and 17.

15. *Second Report on Protection of the Environment in Relation to Armed Conflicts by Marja Lehto, Special Rapporteur*, ILC, U.N. Doc. A/CN.4/728, ¶ 192 (Mar. 27, 2019); *PERAC Principles*, *supra* note 5, commentary accompanying Draft Principle 14.

16. International Committee of the Red Cross, When Rain Turns to Dust: Understanding and Responding to the Combined Impact of Armed Conflicts and the Environment and Climate Crisis on People's Lives (2020), *available at* https://www.icrc.org/sites/default/files/topic/file_plus_list/rain_turns_to_dust_climate_change_conflict.pdf [hereinafter *When Rain Turns to Dust*].

17. *Witnessing the Environmental Impacts of War: Environmental Case Studies from Conflict Zones Around the World*, International Law and Policy Institute (Nov. 29, 2020), *available at* https://paxforpeace.nl/publications/witnessing-the-environmental-impacts-of-war/.

18. Adam Roberts, *Environmental Destruction in the 1991 Gulf War*, 32 International Review of the Red Cross 538 (1992).

19. International Committee of the Red Cross, Bled Dry: How War in the Middle East Is Bringing the Region's Water Supplies to Breaking Point (2014), *available at* https://www.icrc.org/en/download/file/5508/full_report-water-middle-east-icrc.pdf.

20. Rachel Nuwer, *War's Other Victims: Animals*, New York Times (Jan. 12, 2018), https://www.nytimes.com/2018/01/12/science/africa-war-animals-conservation.html.

natural environment is also not spared the harmful effects of the breakdown of environmental governance structures and surges in practices such as poaching,[21] including during armed conflict, which do not necessarily fall within the material scope of IHL.

2.2 Protection of the Natural Environment Under International Humanitarian Law

IHL contains a handful of rules that *specifically* protect the natural environment. This subsection briefly introduces the prohibition of "widespread, long-term, and severe" damage to the natural environment as a backdrop to the subsequent discussion of the general protections extended to it as a civilian object.

The prohibition of "widespread, long-term, and severe" damage to the natural environment

IHL prohibits the use of means or methods of warfare that are "intended, or may be expected," to cause "widespread, long-term, and severe" damage to the natural environment[22] in Articles 35(3) and 55(1) of AP I. In the ICRC's view the prohibitions constitute a norm of customary IHL.[23] Adopted in the wake of the Vietnam War, these provisions in AP I marked a historic step toward protecting the natural environment during armed conflict.

The "widespread, long-term, and severe" threshold has so far been difficult to substantiate. The criteria are cumulative, meaning that all three must be satisfied for it to be fulfilled.[24] Moreover, even though the terms "widespread, long-term, and severe" are not defined in AP I, discussions of their interpretation have revealed that each represents a relatively rigorous standard.[25] Drawing on the drafting history of AP I and examples of environmental damage in conflict, the

21. Governance, Natural Resources, and Post-Conflict Peacebuilding (Carl Bruch, Carroll Muffett, & Sandra S. Nichols eds., 2016); U.N. Environment Programme, *Environmental Rule of Law: First Global Report*, 19, at 231–32 (Jan. 2019), https://www.unep.org/resources/assessment/environmental-rule-law-first-global-report.

22. For further detail on this, *see* ICRC Guidelines, *supra* note 3, at r. 2.

23. *CIHL Study*, *supra* note 7, r. 45 and State practice thereto. The ICRC Guidelines, *supra* note 3, take note of persistent objectors to this rule. *See id.* at ¶ 48.

24. ICRC Guidelines, *supra* note 3, at ¶ 50. This is in contrast to the Convention on the Prohibition of Military or Any Other Hostile Use of Environmental Modification Techniques (ENMOD), which prohibits environmental modification techniques that satisfy any one of these criteria. Convention on the Prohibition of Military or Any Hostile Use of Environmental Modification Techniques, May 18, 1977, 31 U.S.T. 333, 1108 U.N.T.S. 151.

25. Richard Desgagné, *The Prevention of Environmental Damage in Time of Armed Conflict: Proportionality and Precautionary Measures*, 3 Yearbook of International Humanitarian Law 109, 113 (2000).

ICRC understands the term "widespread" as denoting damage covering "several hundred square kilometres";[26] "long-term" as referring to damage with impacts in the range of years (potentially a scale of ten to thirty years);[27] and "severe" as amounting to "the disruption or damage to an ecosystem or harm to the health or survival of the population on a large scale."[28] The ICRC acknowledges that there could be a range of other interpretations; more detail related to its interpretation is set out in the *ICRC Guidelines*.[29]

Damage to the natural environment arising out of normal troop movement or artillery bombardment will fall short of the required threshold,[30] which is understandable given the function and express terms of the rule. But it should be noted that the prohibition of widespread, long-term, and severe damage is absolute. Unlike the principle of proportionality applicable to civilians and civilian objects more generally,[31] damage meeting the threshold is prohibited regardless of the anticipated military advantage.[32] The same holds true even if the relevant part of the natural environment satisfies the definition of a military objective under Article 52(2) of AP I. In other words, it is an "absolute ceiling of permissible destruction,"[33] and care must be taken to avoid erroneously disregarding the importance and utility of the prohibition due to the high "widespread, long-term, and severe" threshold. It should be borne in mind that the damage referred to is not limited to the direct effects of a given means or method of warfare, but also includes indirect or reverberating effects provided it is intended or expected.[34] Moreover, as technological advances and knowledge in accounting for environmental damage to the natural environment increase, so too does the possibility of

26. ICRC Guidelines, *supra* note 3, at ¶ 60.

27. *Id.* at ¶¶ 63, 66.

28. *Id.* at ¶ 72.

29. For a more comprehensive discussion, including the interpretive methods to arrive at these definitions, *see id.* at ¶¶ 50–72.

30. *Id.* at ¶ 63; Official Records of the Diplomatic Conference of Geneva of 1974–1977, vol. XV, CDDH/215/Rev. I, ¶ 27; Report of the Chairman of the Group "Biotope," March 11, 1975, CDDH/III/GT/35, ¶ 5; ICRC Commentary to the APs, *supra* note 12, ¶ 1454.

31. *See* subsection 2.2, *infra*.

32. Desgagné, *supra* note 25, at 111. Separately, within the field of international criminal law, Article 8(2)(b)(iv) of the Rome Statute, *supra* note 6, introduces a proportionality consideration on top of the requirement of "widespread, long-term, and severe." The text of the Statute provides: "Intentionally launching an attack in the knowledge that such an attack will cause incidental loss of life or injury to civilians or damage to civilian objects or widespread, long-term and severe damage to the natural environment which would be clearly excessive in relation to the concrete and direct overall military advantage anticipated."

33. ICRC Guidelines, *supra* note 3, at ¶ 49.

34. This applies to all three of the terms "widespread," "long-term," and "severe." ICRC Guidelines, *supra* note 3, at ¶ 70.

finding that a particular means or method of warfare will meet the threshold of "widespread, long-term, and severe."

Some historical precedent may be recalled. For instance, the burning of oil wells during the 1990–1991 Gulf War may have fulfilled at least two of the criteria.[35] Conversely, a committee that in 2000 reviewed the NATO bombing campaign against the Federal Republic of Yugoslavia did not determine that the "widespread, long-term, and severe" threshold had been met despite serious pollution at several sites which reportedly posed a "threat to human health."[36]

Customary IHL posits that "[m]eans and methods of warfare must be employed with due regard to the protection and preservation of the natural environment."[37] The *ICRC Guidelines* explain that this obligation requires:[38]

> [P]arties to conflict to take steps to avoid or minimize environmental damage. For example, those participating in military operations must take into account the possible negative implications for the natural environment arising from, among other things, the weapons employed, and the type of target selected. They consequently must consider the specificities of the battlefield terrain in which they are operating.

The obligation of "due regard" is particularly, albeit not exclusively, relevant for operational planning.[39] It exists as a matter of customary law applicable specifically to the natural environment, but, as will be elaborated in the subsequent section, it is operationalized through the rules applicable to civilian objects, notably those flowing from the principle of precautions.

35. *Id.* at ¶¶ 57, 70 regarding "widespread" and "severe" respectively, *citing* United Kingdom Ministry of Defence, the Manual of the Law of Armed Conflict ¶ 5.29.2, fn. 153 (2004).

36. Office of the Prosecutor, International Criminal Tribunal for the former Yugoslavia, Final Report to the Prosecutor by the Committee Established to Review the NATO Bombing Campaign Against the Federal Republic of Yugoslavia, ¶¶ 16 and 17, 39 International Legal Materials 1257 (June 13, 2000), https://www.icty.org/x/file/Press/nato061300.pdf. The finding was due to numerous factors, including insufficient access to relevant information, difficulty in attributing environmental damage to NATO, and insufficient time to fully comprehend the degree and kind of damage caused to the environment.

37. *CIHL Study*, *supra* note 7, r. 44.

38. ICRC Guidelines, *supra* note 3, at ¶ 44.

39. *Id.*; Lakmini Seneviratne, Abby Zeith, & Kosuke Onishi, *Reducing the Human Cost of Large-Scale Military Operations*, Articles of War (July 3, 2023), https://lieber.westpoint.edu/category/large-scale-combat-operations-symposium/.

2.3 Protection of the Natural Environment by Virtue of Its Civilian Character

The natural environment is civilian in character as a matter of IHL. Its composite parts are civilian objects and enjoy protection as such. This understanding is reflected in the recent work of the ICRC[40] and ILC[41] and is based on decades of State practice;[42] it is also consistent with the dicta of international tribunals[43] and opinions of legal scholars.[44]

As is well known, IHL takes a binary approach to objects; everything that is not a military objective is a civilian object by default.[45] There is no legal space between the two types of objects. This does not mean that parts of the natural environment cannot become military objectives. Both customary IHL and Article 52(2) of AP I define military objectives as follows:

> . . . In so far as objects are concerned, military objectives are limited to those objects which by their nature, location, purpose or use make an effective contribution to military action and whose total or partial destruction, capture or neutralization, in the circumstances ruling at the time, offers a definite military advantage.

Failing this, all parts of the natural environment are civilian objects under IHL and enjoy protection as such. The most salient of these protections are provided under

40. ICRC Guidelines, *supra* note 3, at ¶¶ 18–21.

41. *PERAC Principles*, *supra* note 5, Principles 13(3) and 14. The *PERAC Principles* underwent State consultations and regular discussion among States in the UN Sixth Committee.

42. *CIHL Study*, *supra* note 7, r. 43, at 266. *See, e.g.*, Department of the Navy & Department of Homeland Security, NWP 1-14M/MCTP 11- 10-B/COMDTPUB P5800.7A, The Commander's Handbook on the Law of Naval Operations, ¶ 8.4 (2022); Australian Defence Headquarters, ADDP 06.4, Law of Armed Conflict, ¶ 5.50 (2006), http://www.defence.gov.au/adfwc/Documents/DoctrineLibrary/ADDP/ADDP06.4-LawofArmedConflict.pdf; EU Military Committee, European Union Military Concept on Environmental Protection and Energy Efficiency for EU-Led Military Operations, ¶ 11(g) (2012); for a comprehensive appraisal of State practice, *see* ICRC Guidelines, *supra* note 3, footnote 33.

43. Legality of the Threat or Use of Nuclear Weapons, Advisory Opinion, 1996 I.C.J. Rep. 226, ¶¶ 30, 32 (July 8).

44. *See, e.g.*, Michael Bothe et al., *International Law Protecting the Environment during Armed Conflict: Gaps and Opportunities*, 92 International Review of the Red Cross 569, 576 (2010); Yoram Dinstein, *Protection of the Environment in International Armed Conflict*, 5 Max Planck Yearbook of United Nations Law 523, 533–34 (2001); Cordula Droege & Marie-Louise Tougas, *The Protection of the Natural Environment in Armed Conflict—Existing Rules and Need for Further Legal Protection*, 82 Nordic Journal of International Law 21, 24 (2013). For a full list, *see* the ICRC Guidelines, *supra* note 3, at footnote 35.

45. AP I, *supra* note 7, art. 52(1); *CIHL Study*, *supra* note 7, at r. 9; ICRC Guidelines, *supra* note 3, at ¶ 18.

the principles of distinction, proportionality, and precaution. Without attempting to reproduce the text of the *ICRC Guidelines*, the following subsections will strive to introduce these principles as they apply to the natural environment.

The principle of distinction applied to the natural environment

The principle of distinction has been described by the International Court of Justice as one of the "cardinal principles" of IHL.[46] It is codified in Articles 48, 51, and 52 of AP I and is unequivocally part of customary law applicable in both international armed conflicts (IACs) and non-international armed conflicts (NIACs).[47] Put simply, under the principle of distinction, the natural environment may not be attacked unless it has become a military objective pursuant to the aforementioned definition. Crucially, however, the definition of a military objective can only be fulfilled by distinct parts of the natural environment (such as a hill or mountain pass), not by nature as a whole. While the natural environment is an interrelated system, that system is composed of parts; it would be absurd for the entirety of the natural environment worldwide to be lawfully targetable if one hill, for example, has become a military objective.

The test for whether something is a military objective is a two-pronged. First, a part of the natural environment in question must make an effective contribution to military action. Second, its total or partial destruction, capture, or neutralization must offer a definite military advantage in the circumstances ruling at the time of an attack. With respect to the first prong, the natural environment cannot be deemed to make an effective contribution to military action due to its *nature*.[48] Nature in this sense means "intrinsic character," and, as explained earlier, the intrinsic character of the natural environment is civilian.[49] The natural environment can, however, make an effective contribution to military action through its location, purpose, or use. As for the second prong, total or partial destruction, capture, or neutralization of "a distinct part or specific object belonging to the natural environment"[50] would need to offer a definite—in other words, a concrete and foreseeable—military advantage. Parts of the environment that fulfill these two criteria will qualify as military objectives and will not be afforded the protection granted to civilian objects.

There are, however, a number of common practices by which militaries direct fire or release ordinance on parts of the natural environment that do not

46. *Nuclear Weapons Opinion*, *supra* note 43, at ¶ 78.

47. *CIHL Study*, *supra* note 7, at r. 1.

48. ICRC Guidelines, *supra* note 3, at ¶ 101.

49. *Id.*; Droege & Tougas, *supra* note 44, at 27; Emanuela-Chiara Gillard, *Proportionality in the Conduct of Hostilities: The Incidental Harm Side of the Assessment*, Chatham House: Royal Institute of International Affairs 37, ¶ 136 (2018) (in particular fn. 110, noting that "[n]o element of the environment will be a military objective by its 'nature,' i.e. its intrinsic character").

50. ICRC Guidelines, *supra* note 3, at ¶ 103.

necessarily fulfill the definition of military objective.[51] Such practices include calibrating artillery by firing a shell at empty open ground or a group of trees in order to improve accuracy, or fighter jets jettisoning unused pieces of ordnance in the ocean before returning to aircraft carriers in order to reduce the risk of accidents upon landing.[52] Among such common practices, some would not necessarily amount to an attack under IHL and would therefore not be governed by the prohibition to direct attacks against civilian objects and other rules within the conduct of hostilities regime specific to attacks. Additionally, the damage they cause might also be understood to be minimal, and the ICRC observes that these practices have therefore not risen to the forefront of legal debates on the application of IHL rules to the natural environment.[53] Even if such conduct amounts to an attack, extensive and uncontroversial State practice in situations where the damage is minimal and is not the object of the operation, but occurs during activities meant to avoid greater incidental civilian harm or for different (lawful) purposes, should be understood as carving out an exception to the general rules providing protection to the natural environment as a civilian object.[54] Hence, the ICRC does not view States' affirmation of the civilian character of the natural environment as intending to outlaw these standard practices. At the same time, the ICRC does not consider that these limited practices prejudice the rule that the environment enjoys the general protection afforded to civilian objects and may not be attacked, unless a specific part of it becomes a military objective.[55]

In addition to prohibiting direct attacks against the natural environment, AP I includes specific rules prohibiting indiscriminate attacks in Article 51(4). These are reflected in Rule 6 of the *ICRC Guidelines* as attacks which are "of a nature to strike military objectives and civilians or civilian objects, including the natural environment, without distinction" as a consequence of the fact that they:

- are not directed at a specific military objective; or
- employ a method or means of combat which cannot be directed at a specific military objective; or
- employ a method or means of combat the effects of which cannot be limited as required by international humanitarian law.

The first modality listed here needs little explanation, although it should be noted that the issue at hand is not the choice of weaponry but how it is

51. *Id.* at ¶ 105.

52. Other examples are addressed in Vanessa Murphy et al., *The Civilian Character of the Natural Environment: A Response to Keinan and Rosenthal*, International Review of the Red Cross (forthcoming).

53. ICRC Guidelines, *supra* note 3, at ¶ 105.

54. *Id.*

55. For an in-depth discussion on these points, *see* Murphy et al., *supra* note 52.

used.[56] For instance, targeting an entire forest for the purpose of an attack on an adversary's military camp without efforts to locate or direct the attack at the camp itself would be a violation of this rule.[57] The second and third modalities regulate the weapons and weapon systems (means of warfare) in addition to the way in which they are used (methods of warfare).[58] For example, the third modality prohibits the employment of methods or means whose effects may be expected to escape in time or space from the control of those who employ them in the circumstances ruling at the time. This includes—depending on how they are used—the use of water or fire.[59] The difficulty of directing water, and its potential indiscriminate effects, is illustrated by the Allied bombing of Germany's Möhne and Eder dams in 1943. The bombing released water in such force and volume that it could not be directed at specific weapons-industry targets downstream, but rather caused extensive flooding that killed 1,300 people, damaged 3,000 hectares of cultivated land, and killed 6,500 head of livestock.

The principle of proportionality applied to the natural environment

The principle of proportionality is codified under Article 51(5)(b) of AP I and is likewise a rule of customary IHL applicable in both IACs and NIACs.[60] The *CIHL Study* articulates the application of this principle to the natural environment, as do the *ICRC Guidelines*:[61]

> Any part of the natural environment that is not a military objective must be protected not only against *direct* attack, but also against "incidental damage", which must not be excessive—alone or in combination with other incidental civilian harm—in relation to the concrete and direct military advantage from an attack against a military objective [*emphasis added*].

The practicalities of how the principle of proportionality applies to protect the environment has long been a subject of concern among scholars and practitioners.[62] The *ICRC Guidelines* seek to provide some guidance. What is clear is that the

56. ICRC Guidelines, *supra* note 3, at ¶ 107.

57. *Id.*

58. Under IHL, weapons and weapon systems in their widest sense denote "means of warfare," while the way in which weapons are used is a "method of warfare." In this sense these two rules are distinct form the first modality of indiscriminate attacks.

59. For further discussion, *see* ICRC Guidelines, *supra* note 3, at ¶¶ 112–13.

60. *CIHL Study*, *supra* note 7, at r. 14.

61. *Id.* at r. 43(c); ICRC Guidelines, *supra* note 3, at ¶¶ 114–15.

62. Michael N. Schmitt, *Green War: An Assessment of the Environmental Law of International Armed Conflict*, 22 Yale Journal of International Law 1, 55–61 (1997); Bothe et al., *supra* note 44, at 577–78.

application of the principle of proportionality requires a highly fact-dependent assessment and a value-laden balancing act between the concrete and direct military advantage anticipated and incidental harm to the environment, among other civilian objects, and civilians themselves.[63] Indeed, there is no exact formula for the calculation.[64] Bearing in mind the highly context-dependent nature of any assessment, the burning of oil fields and deliberate spilling of millions of gallons of oil into the sea during the 1990–1991 Gulf War has been considered to be an example of disproportionate incidental damage to the natural environment, to the extent that these effects constituted damage incidental to an attack under the rule of proportionality.[65] Other rules of IHL may also be of relevance in assessing operations designed or expected to result in the burning of oil wells, including the rules on unlawful destruction of property and the prohibition of widespread, long-term, and severe damage.

A question that arises is how far down the causal chain parties must go when anticipating incidental harm to the natural environment from their attacks. Put simply, whether and to what degree "reverberating effects" such as long-term risks to the disruption of ecosystems[66] must be considered depends on whether such harm is reasonably foreseeable. This includes information garnered from past practice and empirical data.[67] As the wealth of knowledge and ability to identify and comprehend damage to the environment advances, so too does the ability, and therefore obligation, to foresee incidental harm to the natural environment and weigh it against the concrete and direct military advantage anticipated from an attack. On this point, the ICRC has produced in-depth research on the reverberating effects[68] of attacks on critical infrastructure that in turn have a knock-on effect on contaminating water sources, rendering arable land unusable, polluting the air, and unsettling food chains which in turn destabilize human life.[69]

63. ICRC GUIDELINES, *supra* note 3, at ¶ 121.

64. *Id.*

65. *Id.* at ¶ 122.

66. *Id.* at ¶ 118.

67. *Id.*

68. INTERNATIONAL COMMITTEE OF THE RED CROSS, EXPLOSIVE WEAPONS WITH WIDE AREA EFFECTS: A DEADLY CHOICE IN POPULATED AREAS (2022), *available at* https://www.icrc.org/en/download/file/229018/ewipa_explosive_weapons_with_wide_area_effect_final.pdf; Isabel Robinson & Ellen Nohle, *Proportionality and Precautions in Attack: The Reverberating Effects of Using Explosive Weapons in Populated Areas*, 98 INTERNATIONAL REVIEW OF THE RED CROSS 107 (2016); Michael Talhami & Mark Zeitoun, *The Impact of Attacks on Urban Services II: Reverberating Effects of Damage to Water and Wastewater Systems on Infectious Disease*, 102 INTERNATIONAL REVIEW OF THE RED CROSS 1293 (2021).

69. Michael Talhami & Mark Zeitoun, *Armed Conflicts Spread Contaminated Water and Disease: Here's How to Better Protect Civilians*, JUST SECURITY (Mar. 17 2023), https://www.justsecurity.org/85514/armed-conflicts-spread-contaminated-water-and-disease-heres-how-to-better-protect-civilians/ .

However, not all foreseeable damage to the natural environment will carry the same weight when contrasted against military advantage (which is the case for all civilian objects). For instance, water that is relied upon by humans should be "valued" more in a proportionality assessment than the natural environment in the middle of an uninhabited desert.[70]

The principle of precautions applied to the natural environment

Owing to its civilian character, the natural environment also enjoys the protections stemming from the principle of precautions. Like distinction and proportionality, this principle is found in AP I,[71] as well as in customary IHL applicable in both IACs and NIACs.[72] The *ICRC Guidelines* reflect it in Rule 8:[73]

> In the conduct of military operations, constant care must be taken to spare the civilian population, civilians and civilian objects, including the natural environment. All feasible precautions must be taken to avoid, and in any event minimize, incidental loss of civilian life, injury to civilians and damage to civilian objects, including the natural environment.

Military operations denote "any movements, maneuvers and other activities whatsoever carried out by the armed forces with a view to combat."[74] As stipulated in Rule 8, persons involved in military operations must continuously bear in mind their effects on the natural environment, reduce them as much as possible, and avoid them when they are unnecessary.[75] This is important because such operations can have a significant adverse impact on the natural environment.[76]

Merely taking some precautions will not suffice. The requirement is that "*all* those precautions that are feasible in the circumstances are taken."[77] This will, among other things, oblige parties to actively seek out reasonably available information, including that which is relevant to assessing the harm anticipated to the natural environment.[78] Relevant considerations include the "area expected to be affected and the scope of those effects, the fragility or vulnerability of the natural

70. ICRC Guidelines, *supra* note 3, at ¶ 121.

71. AP I, *supra* note 7, art. 57.

72. *CIHL Study*, *supra* note 7, at r. 44.

73. ICRC Guidelines, *supra* note 3, at r. 8.

74. *Id.* at footnote 316, *citing* ICRC Commentary to the APs, *supra* note 12, at ¶ 2191.

75. ICRC Guidelines, *supra* note 3, at ¶ 127.

76. *Id.* at ¶ 126.

77. *Id.* at ¶ 130.

78. *Id.* at ¶ 130.

environment in that area," as well as the expected severity and duration of potential harm.[79]

With respect to military operations that qualify as attacks, the *ICRC Guidelines* draw on Article 57 of AP I to describe the specific obligations of parties to a conflict as follows:[80]

- Do everything feasible to verify that targets are military objectives, including that any part of the natural environment has become a military objective before it is attacked;
- Take feasible precautions in the choice of means and methods of warfare with a view to avoiding, and in any event to minimizing damage to any part of the natural environment that is not a military objective;
- Do everything feasible to assess whether the attack may be expected to cause damage to the natural environment that would be disproportionate, alone or in combination with loss of civilian life, injury to civilians, and damage to other civilian objects;
- Do everything feasible to cancel or suspend an attack if it becomes apparent that the target, including when it is a part of the natural environment, is not a military objective or that the attack may be expected to cause loss of civilian life, injury to civilians, damage to civilian objects, including the natural environment, that would be disproportionate;
- Unless circumstances do not permit, effective advance warning of attacks that may affect the natural environment should be given to allow for measures to safeguard it;
- When a choice is possible between several military objectives for obtaining a similar military advantage, the objective to be selected must be that the attack on which may be expected to cause the least danger to civilian lives and to civilian objects, including any part of the natural environment that is not a military objective.

One of the challenges linked to the protection of the environment in armed conflict, and during peacetime for that matter, is the potential uncertainty about the degree and kinds of damage anticipated from particular activities. It is important to note that "there is practice to the effect that lack of scientific certainty as to the effects on the environment of certain military operations does not absolve parties to a conflict from taking proper precautionary measures to prevent undue damage."[81] This reflects the precautionary principle of international environmental law.

79. *Id.* at ¶ 129.

80. For the exact wording, *see id.* at ¶¶ 132–37.

81. *Id.* at ¶ 124, *citing CIHL Study*, *supra* note 7, at commentary on r. 44.

2.4 Relevance to Non-International Armed Conflict

The updated *ICRC Guidelines* are meant to be a tool for all parties to armed conflict, including NSAGs.[82] Of the 32 rules and recommendations contained therein, 22 unquestionably apply to NIACs,[83] and an additional three (Rules 1, 2, and 3.A) arguably do as well.[84] Principles emanating from the civilian character of the natural environment such as distinction, proportionality, and precautions, unequivocally bind States and NSAGs alike due to their customary character.[85]

As is the case with States, the integration of these IHL principles into the doctrine, training, and compliance mechanisms of NSAGs boosts the likelihood of adherence.[86] In 2023, the ICRC released an operational handbook for NSAGs that included specific guidance on accounting for likely immediate and long-term harm to the natural environment resulting from attacks, as well as advice on how to collect relevant information when planning military operations.[87] Other tools to promote compliance, such as Geneva Call's new deed of commitment on starvation and food insecurity designed to be signed by NSAGs to indicate their commitment to respecting the law, includes a preamble that recognizes IHL's protection of the natural environment.[88]

Informal norms can also play a critical role in influencing the behavior of parties to armed conflict, including NSAGs.[89] Because they are value-based or passed down generations, resulting in practice among communities over a long period of time, linking the law to such local norms and values is likely to have traction. As Helen Obregón Gieseken and Vanessa Murphy emphasize, exclusive reliance on the *ICRC Guidelines* may be less effective if removed from the values

82. *Id.* at ¶ 11.

83. *Id.* at rr. 5, 6, 7, 8, 9, 10, 11, 12,13, 14, 16, 19, 20, 21, 22, 23, 24, 26, 28, and 29; Recommendations 17 and 18.

84. Obregón Gieseken & Murphy, *supra* note 8, at 1201.

85. *Id.*

86. *Id.* at 1202.

87. International Committee of the Red Cross, Reducing Civilian Harm in Urban Warfare: A Handbook for Armed Groups 13, 15, 16, 23 (2023), *available at* https://www.icrc.org/en/publication/4682-reducing-civilian-harm-urban-warfare-handbook-armed-groups.

88. *Geneva Call's New Deed of Commitment on the Prevention of Starvation and Addressing Conflict-Related Food Insecurity*, Geneva Call, https://www.genevacall.org/news/geneva-calls-new-deed-of-commitment-on-the-prevention-of-starvation-and-addressing-conflict-related-food-insecurity/.

89. Obregón Gieseken & Murphy, *supra* note 8, at 1202, *citing* International Committee of the Red Cross, the Roots of Restraint in War (2018), https://www.icrc.org/en/publication/4352-roots-restraint-war.

that underpin its norms.[90] As is the case with IHL in general, linking rules that protect the natural environment to local, often informal, values, customs, and norms may foster greater restraint in armed conflict.[91]

3. ACCOUNTING FOR THE UNIQUE ATTRIBUTES OF THE NATURAL ENVIRONMENT

This section seeks to take stock of recent discussions on the identification of good practices in applying IHL rules to the natural environment. As the climate and environmental crises deepen and States' rhetoric on large-scale military operations looms, ensuring civilian protection in armed conflict will require accelerated progress on the practical measures that militaries take to minimize environmental damage.[92]

The section draws primarily on discussions that took place at the "State Expert Meeting on International Humanitarian Law: Protecting the Environment in Armed Conflict" organized by Switzerland and the ICRC in early 2023. Experts from over 120 countries, drawn from ministries of defense, environment, and foreign affairs, were in attendance. Representatives of United Nations Environment Programme (UNEP), the ILC, and the International Union for Conservation of Nature also attended select sessions to provide expertise on technical questions and support the exchanges.

The objective of the meeting was to "contribute to achieving realistic and pragmatic progress on the national implementation"[93] of IHL relating to the protection of the natural environment. States collectively identified challenges and good practices related to three topics: (1) IHL dissemination, training, and integration at the national level, including proactively in peacetime; (2) assessing the effects of military operations on the natural environment and implications for operations; and (3) identifying and designating areas of particular environmental importance or fragility as demilitarized zones and how they might be better protected in armed conflict beyond demilitarization measures. Given the scope of the present chapter, analysis is limited to the second topic.

The unique challenges relating to assessing the effects of military operations on the natural environment were summarized as follows by the Chairs of the State Expert Meeting:[94]

90. Obregón Gieseken & Murphy, *supra* note 8, at 1203.

91. Ahmed Al-Dawoody & Sarah Gale, *Protecting the Environment During Armed Conflict: IHL and Islamic Law*, Humanitarian Law & Policy (June 3, 2021), https://blogs.icrc.org/law-and-policy/2021/06/03/protecting-environment-armed-conflict-ihl-islamic-law/.

92. The most important challenge to IHL continues to be lack of compliance with its rules, and accordingly the concrete implementation of the law is one of the focuses of the ICRC's work.

93. *Chair's Summary*, *supra* note 9, at 2.

94. *Id.* at 8.

> First, damage to the environment may not be immediately apparent to the eye in the manner that loss of civilian life, injury or building destruction can be. Instead, the effects can take time to be felt or require technical expertise to assess, though this does not mean they are not grave. Second, environmental damage may flow from a chain of events—or a combination of factors—rather than a single act, and this can be a challenge to commanders who must consider damage that is reasonably foreseeable in the application of relevant IHL, such as the rules implementing proportionality and precautions in attack. Third, assessing environmental damage in peacetime would typically depart from a baseline study against which environmental change is measured. This baseline tends to be less available in conduct of hostility scenarios, so damage often needs to be estimated via recourse to other sources of information. Fourth, some delegations mentioned that determining the parts of the natural environment to take into account when planning military operations—in a manner that is realistic for commanders—is difficult.

With a view to addressing these challenges, the participating delegations shared what they considered to be good practices, some of which are succinctly laid out in the following.

Several States underscored the importance of incorporating assessments of environmental aspects, including an analysis of the risk of environmental harm, at the outset of military operational planning and throughout the operational cycle.[95] Collecting environmental data on the relevant area prior to deployment was identified as an important step.[96] This could include, among other things, identifying locations prone to environmental hazards, as well as fragile and protected ecosystems.[97] Such data should be included in operational orders to allow the actors involved to be aware of the environmental issues and risks at hand and to take measures to protect and preserve the area from harm.

Tools to collect relevant data were also highlighted by States as being essential to adequately taking environmental factors into account when planning military operations. The use of dedicated databases and data sheets that track the impact of military activities on the environment was cited as being useful, including when shared across different parts of the defense sector and its partners.[98] Advanced technologies used to conduct geospatial analysis, such as in disaster relief operations by armed forces, could be used to better understand the natural environment in which the parties to the armed conflict plan to operate.[99] Coordination

95. *Id.* at 9.

96. *Id.*

97. *Id.*; *see also PERAC Principles*, *supra* note 5, at Commentary on Principle 4; ICRC Guidelines, *supra* note 3, ¶ 208.

98. *Chair's Summary*, *supra* note 9, at 10.

99. *Id.*

and information sharing across governments, particularly with national bodies mandated with environment responsibilities such as water and forest agencies was also deemed important.[100] Reference was also made to the importance of coordination between armed or other security forces and conservation actors in identifying protected areas, and the value of involving local communities in identifying environmentally fragile areas. Given the technical nature of understanding and mitigating effects on the natural environment, sharing expertise between governments was deemed valuable as well.[101] Some States highlighted practices undertaken in their legal reviews of new weapons and means and methods of warfare an obligation for states party to AP I.[102]

Regarding challenges, States emphasized the lack of expertise within their forces—that is, personnel with the requisite awareness, knowledge, and training to understand and apply IHL protecting the natural environment.[103] Particularly with respect to assessing the impact of military operations on the natural environment, specialized staff, or lack thereof, was seen by many States as a salient challenge in assessing and reducing the impact of military operations on the environment.[104] More generally, States emphasized the importance of integrating IHL rules protecting the environment into military doctrine and of providing effective education, training, and exercises for the armed forces,[105] noting the potential cost-effectiveness of such preventive measures compared with compensating for damage caused.

A noteworthy example in this regard is U.S. Joint Publication 3-60, which inter alia recognizes the commander's responsibility in relation to the environment as follows:

> . . . [T]he commander has an affirmative obligation to avoid unnecessary damage to the environment to the extent that it is practical to do so consistent with mission accomplishment. To that end, and as far as military requirements dictate, methods and means of attack should be employed with due regard to the protection and preservation of the natural environment. Destruction of the environment not required by military necessity and carried out wantonly is prohibited.[106]

100. *Id.* at 11.

101. *Id.* at 11–12.

102. *Id.* at 12.

103. This theme ran through all three topics discussed. *Id.* at 4, 8, and 13.

104. *Id.* at 8–9.

105. *Id.* at 5–6.

106. Chairman, Joint Chiefs of Staff, Publication 3-60, Joint Targeting, Appendix A—Legal Considerations, ¶ 8(b), Chapter II-30, ¶ 4.g, and Chapter III-11, ¶ 6 (2018).

A suggestion was made at the State Expert Meeting to explore the idea of "involving experts in the decision-making chain to systematically integrate environmental considerations during military operations, including to advise against certain attacks.[107] For example, such a function could be integrated into the work of so-called "red card holders,"[108] whose responsibility could be to effectively "veto" an attack if environmental considerations were insufficiently taken into account or would otherwise violate IHL rules protecting the natural environment. The idea is particularly noteworthy in the U.S. context, where the Department of Defense's (DoD's) CHMR-AP[109] refers to the concept of red teaming as part of "deliberate and systemic measures to mitigate the risks of target misidentification"[110] and allocates specific resources for training and developing best practices.[111] As the DoD prepares to implement the CHMR-AP across different combatant commands, it would be opportune to include considerations on unlawful damage to the natural environment in armed conflict within the remit of these red teams.

State experts also discussed the extent to which practices adopted to prevent and mitigate environmental damage in peacetime are feasible in armed conflict situations. While this question requires reflection based on specific contexts and measures, some States affirmed that peacetime measures influence how they conduct their military operations in armed conflict abroad.[112] An example was expertise gained during peacetime for protecting the environment by minimizing the contamination of water supplies during military training through appropriate waste management procedures, which could also limit inadvertent contamination of water by military operations in wartime, despite the constraints of hostilities.[113]

107. *Chair's Summary*, *supra* note 9, at 11.

108. "Red card holder" is a term usually used in the context of coalition or partnered operations. The function of the "red card holder" could include advising against or vetoing military operations that violate IHL, insufficiently take civilian harm into consideration, or go against national caveats. Marten Zwanenburg, *International Humanitarian Law Interoperability in Multinational Operations*, 95 International Review of the Red Cross 681, 686 (2014).

109. U.S. Department Of Defense, Civilian Harm Mitigation and Response Action Plan (CHMR-AP) (Aug. 25, 2022), https://media.defense.gov/2022/Aug/25/2003064740/-1/-1/1/civilian-harm-mitigation-and-response-action-plan.pdf.

110. *Id.* at Objective 5.

111. *Id.* at Action 5(j).

112. *Chair's Summary*, *supra* note 9, at 3.

113. *Id.* at 11.

4. PROTECTING THE NATURAL ENVIRONMENT: WHAT'S IN IT FOR CIVILIANS

The IHL rules protecting the natural environment are likely to become more relevant to practitioners concerned with the protection of civilians in the years to come, as the climate and environmental crises deepen and the interlinkage between human health and the environment is more acutely felt. This is all the more the case in conflict-affected contexts, which are simultaneously on the frontlines of climate change.[114] While a minority view posits that the environment is not civilian by default—rather, that its parts are only protected by the rules governing the conduct of hostilities if damage to them will prejudice the "health or survival of the civilian population" as per Article 55 of AP I[115]—such a distinction is rendered moot by scientific evidence of the interlinkage between planetary and human health.

War does not occur in a vacuum. Today, it is known that biodiversity and ecosystems are crucial to sustaining human life and supporting human adaptation to climate change: in 2022, a working group of the Intergovernmental Panel on Climate Change found, with high confidence, that human and ecosystem vulnerability are interdependent and, with very high confidence, that safeguarding biodiversity and ecosystems is fundamental to climate-resilient development.[116] As ecosystems are damaged—including by hostilities—climate adaptation becomes more difficult, searing conflict-affected communities that are already the most exposed.[117] In other words, armed conflicts have direct and indirect impacts on the natural environment, and climate risks magnify this harm for dependent communities.

The UN Secretary General has referred to climate change as an "existential threat" to humanity.[118] The ICRC too is quite clear on the stakes, declaring in its Climate Charter that today's climate and environmental crises threaten the survival of humanity, that all dimensions of our lives are affected, from our physical and mental health to our food, water, and economic security, and that our ability to protect the lives and the rights of present and future generations depends on whether we

114. *See generally* International Committee of the Red Cross, Weathering the Storm: Reducing the Impact of Climate Risks and Environmental Degradation on People Enduring Armed Conflicts (2023), *available at* https://www.icrc.org/en/publication/4742-weathering-storm-reducing-impact-climate-risks-and-environmental-degradation-people.

115. *See* Israel's comments in International Law Commission, *Protection of the Environment in Relation to Armed Conflicts: Comments and Observations Received from Governments, International Organizations and Others*, U.N. Doc. A/CN.4/749 (Jan. 17, 2022).

116. *IPPC*, *supra* note 8, at 12, 32.

117. *When Rain Turns to Dust*, *supra* note 16, at 17.

118. *Climate Change: An "Existential Threat" to Humanity, UN Chief Warns Global Summit*, UN News (May 15, 2018), https://news.un.org/en/story/2018/05/1009782.

make the right choices now.[119] The ICRC has documented the interdependence of populations and the environment in conflict-affected contexts: in places like Fao, south of Basra, for example, people attribute their water and farming problems to the cutting of emblematic date palms for military purposes during the Iran-Iraq war.[120] Beyond dramatic and direct health impacts, water scarcity and environmental problems have likewise pushed agricultural productivity down and, along with macroeconomic and political factors, have resulted in food and economic insecurity. In other contexts, the pollution and contamination of air, surface and groundwater, and soil by the targeting of industrial and petrochemical facilities have contributed to respiratory and other diseases.[121]

Practitioners concerned with protection of civilians during contemporary armed conflict should presume that the effects of a damaged environment are holistic and interlinked. As the environment becomes less capable of absorbing the shocks of combat damage, greater respect for IHL obligations protecting it can reduce the harm to which conflict-affected communities are exposed.[122]

5. CONCLUSION

Humankind needs to move beyond a debate on whether there is a link between the survival of the natural environment and its own. The challenge, now, is to slow biodiversity decline and climate change so that a harmonious balance between protection of the environment and humankind's survival can be reached. The direct and indirect ways in which the conduct of States and NSAGs causes damage to the natural environment in war has become increasingly foreseeable. Accordingly, efforts to underscore the symbiotic relationship between environmental protection and civilian protection under IHL must be an important goal going forward. It is crucial for the success of this endeavor to harness and share knowledge and good practices, while devoting and directing resources and tools toward measures to reduce risks to the natural environment in war. The pressing question is not whether we do so, but how.

119. Climate Charter, *The Climate and Environment Charter for Humanitarian Organizations: Sign the Charter*, https://www.climate-charter.org/#sign-the-charter.

120. *When Rain Turns to Dust*, *supra* note 16, at 30–32.

121. International Committee of the Red Cross, Making Adaptation Work: Addressing the Compounding Impacts of Climate Change, Environmental Degradation and Conflict in the Near and Middle East 22 (2023), https://www.icrc.org/en/publication/maw-making-adaptation-work.

122. *See* the ICRC's related call to parties to armed conflict *in* Peter Maurer, *Protecting the Environment in Armed Conflict: An ICRC View*, Environmental Policy and Law (Feb. 23, 2021), https://environmentalpolicyandlaw.com/news-blog/protecting-natural-environment-armed-conflicts-icrc-view.

15

The Contribution of Forensic Science to Managing the Dead and Preventing the Missing in Armed Conflict

MORRIS TIDBALL-BINZ*

1. INTRODUCTION

"For a long time, I had realized that this uncertainty was the greatest agony of all."[1]

This quotation is the testimony of Dr. Marcel Junod, a delegate of the International Committee of the Red Cross (ICRC) during the Spanish Civil War,[2] referring to the suffering of the relatives of persons missing[3] in that armed conflict. This

* Dr. Morris Tidball-Binz is the UN Special Rapporteur on Extrajudicial, Summary or Arbitrary Executions.

1. Marcel Junod, Warrior Without Weapons 114–15 (1951).

2. Iñaki Anasagasti, Marcel Junod (2007).

3. "Missing person" is a person whose whereabouts are unknown to his/her relatives and/or who, on the basis of reliable information, has been reported missing in connection with an international armed conflict (IAC) or non-international armed conflict (NIAC), a situation of internal violence or of disturbances, natural disasters, or any other situation that may require the

Morris Tidball-Binz, *The Contribution of Forensic Science to Managing the Dead and Preventing the Missing in Armed Conflict* In: *Civilian Protection in Armed Conflict*. Edited by: Jelena Pejic and Captain Margaret Kotlik, Oxford University Press. © Morris Tidball-Binz 2025. DOI: 10.1093/oso/9780197793176.003.0015

understanding succinctly anticipates the reasons for today's universal recognition, in various branches of international law, of the enduring pain suffered by those who have lost loved ones in war or other catastrophic events and do not know their whereabouts. As elaborated by the Inter-American Court of Human Rights in the *Blake* case several decades later:

> The forced disappearance of Mr. Nicholas Blake (a U.S. citizen) caused his parents and brothers suffering, intense anguish, and frustration in the face of the Guatemalan authorities' failure to investigate and cover up of what occurred. The suffering of the family members, in violation of Article 5 of the American Convention on Human Rights [prohibition of torture and ill-treatment], cannot be disassociated from the situation created by the forced disappearance of Mr. Nicholas Blake that lasted until 1992 when his mortal remains were located. The Court, in conclusion, holds that the grave moral damage suffered by the four family members of Mr. Nicholas Blake is completely proved.[4]

To help prevent the enduring pain caused to families by the disappearance of a loved one in armed conflict, the four Geneva Conventions of 1949 (GC I–IV)[5] and their Additional Protocols I and II (AP I and AP II) of 1977,[6] as well as customary

intervention of a competent State authority. This broad category of victims includes the victims of enforced disappearance, a crime defined under the 2006 International Convention for the Protection of All Persons from Enforced Disappearance, G.A. Res. 61/177 (Jan. 12, 2007), as:

> [T]he arrest, detention, abduction or any other form of deprivation of liberty by agents of the State or by persons or groups of persons acting with the authorization, support or acquiescence of the State, followed by a refusal to acknowledge the deprivation of liberty or by concealment of the fate or whereabouts of the disappeared person, which place such a person outside the protection of the law.

4. Blake v. Guatemala, Case No. 57, Inter-Amer. Comm'n H.R., Report No. 48 (1999) (discussing art. 63[1] of the American Convention on Human Rights).

5. Convention (I) for the Amelioration of the Conditions of the Wounded and Sick in the Armed forces in the Field, 12 August 1949, 75 U.N.T.S. 31 [hereinafter GC I]; Convention (II) for the Amelioration of the Condition of the Wounded, Sick and Shipwrecked Members of the Armed Forces at Sea, 12 August 1949, 75 U.N.T.S. 85 [hereinafter GC II]; Convention (III) relative to the Treatment of Prisoners of War, 12 August 1949, 75 U.N.T.S. 135 [hereinafter GC III]; Convention (IV) relative to the Protection of Civilian Persons in Time of War, 12 August 1949, 75 U.N.T.S. 287 [hereinafter GC IV].

6. Protocol Additional to the Geneva Conventions of 12 August 1949, and relating to the Protection of Victims of International Armed Conflicts, 8 June 1977, 1125 U.N.T.S. 3 [hereinafter AP I]; Protocol Additional to the Geneva Conventions of 12 August 1949, and relating to the Protection of Victims of Non-International Armed Conflicts, 8 June 1977, 1125 U.N.T.S. 609 [hereinafter AP II]. A Third Additional Protocol to the Geneva Conventions, which entered into force in 2007, adopted the Red Crystal.

international humanitarian law[7] (IHL), contain various provisions dealing with the dead, mortal remains, gravesites, and the missing in armed conflict.[8] The relevant norms require the warring parties to search for, recover, and identify the dead, ensure the proper and dignified management of the remains of the deceased, and to respect every family's right to know the fate and whereabouts of their missing loved one. As is well known, the Geneva Conventions are binding international treaties that enjoy universal ratification, while the two Additional Protocols thereto have been ratified by a great majority of States, albeit not by some with extensive experience in armed conflict.[9]

After briefly recalling the importance of the issue of the dead and missing in armed conflict, this chapter outlines IHL norms on the search, recovery, identification, and respect of the dead, and on the search for missing persons. It then addresses the role of the forensic sciences and provides some real-life examples of best practice. It draws attention to the need for forensic capacity by armed forces, before providing very brief concluding remarks.

2. THE IMPORTANCE OF THE DEAD AND MISSING IN ARMED CONFLICT

Respect and deference for the dead and missing as a result of armed conflict are universally accepted values which have always been a subject of cultural and religious concern.[10,11] This is often symbolically represented in the form of special cemeteries, memorials, and monuments dedicated to the war dead and those missing in action.[12] For the same reasons, handling the remains of those killed in armed conflict is often a highly sensitive issue, and their desecration, which is strictly prohibited under IHL, is regarded as shameful and deeply offensive.

7. International Committee of the Red Cross, *Customary International Humanitarian Law Database* (2005), http://www.icrc.org/customary-ihl/eng/docs/home.

8. International humanitarian law is different from, albeit complementary to, international human rights law, which is mainly focused on protecting individuals and groups from violations by the State. The principles behind the duty to help resolve and prevent the tragedy of the missing and ensure the proper and dignified management of the dead are also applicable to situations other than armed conflicts, including natural disasters.

9. 196 States have ratified the Geneva Conventions. For a full list, *see, e.g.*, the ICRC database, *available at* https://ihl-databases.icrc.org/public/refdocs/IHL_and_other_related_Treaties.pdf.

10. Protection of the Dead - Report of the Special Rapporteur on Extrajudicial, Summary or Arbitrary Executions; U.N. Document: A/HRC/56/56, April 2024.

11. Nikolai Münch, Johannes Müller-Salo, & Clara-Sophie Schwarz, *How to Conceive the Dignity of the Dead? A Disposition Account*, 138 International Journal of Legal Medicine 177–86 (2024).

12. Anna Petrig, *The War and Their Gravesites*, 91 International Review of the Red Cross, No. 874, 341–69 (June 2009).

The image of dead American soldiers mutilated and dragged through the streets of Mogadishu, Somalia, in October 1993, to give an example, caused international uproar and contributed to the withdrawal of U.S. forces from that country. Similarly, the removal in 2007 of a Second World War monument in Tallinn, Estonia, marking the graves and honoring Red Army soldiers killed in that conflict sparked popular protests which caused the death of one person and the wounding of several others, and almost led to the severing of diplomatic relations between Estonia and Russia.[13] The images of U.S. Marines urinating on dead Taliban fighters, posted on social media in January 2012, caused mass protests and risked derailing peace talks ongoing in Afghanistan at the time.[14]

Nations go to great lengths to recover, identify, and honor their war dead, for which forensic sciences are increasingly regarded as a necessary tool. For example, the activities and achievements of the Joint Missing in Action, Prisoner of War Accounting Command (JPAC) and, after 2015, the new Defense POW/MIA Accounting Agency (DPAA) of the U.S. Department of Defense,[15] to search, recover, identify, and help honor their service members killed and or missing in action in armed conflicts anywhere in the world stand as a remarkable example of such efforts and of the central role that forensic sciences play in these activities today. The JPAC's forensic anthropology laboratory was the world's first to be fully accredited to international standards and currently represents a model of best practice in forensic sciences as applied to the DPAA's own humanitarian endeavor of naming the dead, bringing answers to the bereaved, and helping them mourn their loved ones.[16]

The search and recovery of the missing may span events which occurred many decades ago, but in relation to which families are still searching for their loved ones. Thus, ongoing efforts to recover and identify the victims of the Spanish Civil War respond to the long-enduring needs of families to know and honor their dead and missing in that conflict from the 1930s.[17] In 2011, the Spanish Congress adopted *Protocols for the exhumation of victims of the Spanish Civil War*, which outline forensic best practices applicable to forensic recovery and identification procedures for victims of the conflict.[18] These constitute an important official

13. Ivo Juurvee & Mariita Mattiisen, *The Bronze Soldier Crisis of 2007: Revisiting an Early Case of Hybrid Conflict*, International Centre for Defence and Security, Estonia (Aug. 2020).

14. *See, e.g.*, *US to Probe Taliban Corpses Desecration*, Pakistan Today (Jan. 13, 2012), https://archive.pakistantoday.com.pk/2012/01/13/us-to-probe-taliban-corpses-desecration/.

15. Defense POW/MIA Accounting Agency, Department of Defense, https://www.dpaa.mil/.

16. Matthew C. Go et al., *The Korean War Identification Project: 30 Years of Expanding Scope and Complexity in the Accounting of American War Dead*, 5 Wiley Interdisciplinary Reviews: Forensic Science 4 (2023).

17. Layla Renshaw, Exhuming Loss, Memory, Materiality and Mass Graves of the Spanish Civil War (2011).

18. *See Boletín Oficial del Estado, Núm. 310*, jueves 27 de diciembre de 2007, Pág. 53410–53416 http://www.boe.es/boe/dias/2007/12/27/pdfs/A53410-53416.pdf.

recognition of the need to recover and identify the dead and to follow forensic best practices to help resolve the fate of the missing.

3. THE PROTECTION OF THE WAR DEAD

IHL contains detailed provisions for the protection of those killed in armed conflict, including on the search, recovery, documentation, identification, notification, protection, and respectful treatment of the dead. These duties, enshrined in the four Geneva Conventions and Additional Protocols I and II applicable in IAC and NIAC, respectively, are summarized here:[19]

> Whenever circumstances permit, and particularly after an engagement, all possible measures must be taken, without delay, to search for and collect the dead, without adverse distinction.[20]
> Each party to the conflict must treat the dead with respect and dignity and prevent their being despoiled.[21]
> Each party to the conflict must take measures to identify the dead before disposing of their remains.[22]
> The dead must be disposed of in a respectful manner and their graves respected.[23]
> Burial should be in individual graves unless unavoidable circumstances require the use of collective graves. All graves must be marked.[24]
> At the commencement of hostilities, the parties to the conflict must establish an official Graves Registration Service to see to the dead, including burials, and to record the particulars for identification of graves and those there interred.[25]

19. ICRC Legal Factsheet, *Humanity After Life: Respecting and Protecting the Dead* (Apr. 2020), https://www.icrc.org/en/document/humanity-after-life-respect-and-protection-dead.

20. GC I, *supra* note 5, art. 15; GC II, *supra* note 5, art. 18; GC IV, *supra* note 5, art. 16; AP I, *supra* note 6, art. 33; AP II, *supra* note 6, art. 8.

21. GC I, *supra* note 5, art. 15; GC II, *supra* note 5, art. 18; GC IV, *supra* note 5, art. 16; AP I, *supra* note 6, art. 34; AP II, *supra* note 6, art. 8.

22. GC I, *supra* note 5, arts. 16, 17; GC II, *supra* note 5, arts. 19, 20; GC III, *supra* note 5, arts. 120, 121; GC IV, *supra* note 5, arts. 129, 131.

23. GC I, *supra* note 5, art. 17; GC II, *supra* note 5, art. 20; GC III, *supra* note 5, art. 120; GC IV, *supra* note 5, art. 130; AP I, *supra* note 6, art. 34(1); AP II, *supra* note 6, art. 8.

24. GC I, *supra* note 5, art. 17; GC II, *supra* note 5, art. 20; GC III, *supra* note 5, art. 120; GC IV, *supra* note 5, art. 130; AP I, *supra* note 6, art. 34.

25. GC I, *supra* note 5, art. 17(3); GC II, *supra* note 5, art. 20(2); GC III, *supra* note 5, art. 120(6); GC IV, *supra* note 5, art. 130(3).

Each party to the conflict must take all possible measures to provide information to the appropriate authorities or to the family of the deceased regarding the deceased's identity, location, and cause of death.[26]

Upon the outbreak of a conflict and in all cases of occupation, each party to the conflict must establish an official Information Bureau. This bureau will centralize, without adverse distinction, all information on the wounded, sick, shipwrecked, dead, protected persons deprived of their liberty, children whose identity is in doubt, and persons who have been reported missing and to provide this information to the appropriate authorities, through the intermediary of the Protecting Powers and likewise to the ICRC Central Tracing Agency;[27]

The bureau will also be responsible for replying to all enquiries concerning protected persons and for making any enquiries necessary to obtain information which is asked for if this is not in its possession.[28]

Finally, the bureau will act as an intermediary for the free transport of materials, including correspondence, sent to and by protected persons (and whenever requested through the ICRC Central Tracing Agency).[29]

Information recorded on protected persons deprived of their liberty or on deceased persons must be of such a character as to make it possible to identify the person exactly and to advise the next of kin quickly.[30]

Within the shortest possible period, each of the parties to the conflict must transmit to the Information Bureau the following information, when available, on each wounded, sick, shipwrecked, or dead person:[31]

- full name;
- army, regimental, personal, or serial number;
- date of birth;
- any other particulars figuring on the identity card or disc;

26. GC I, *supra* note 5, arts. 16, 17; GC II, *supra* note 5, art. 19; GC III, *supra* note 5, art. 120; GC IV, *supra* note 5, art. 130; AP I, *supra* note 6, art. 33.

27. GC I, *supra* note 5, arts. 16, 17(4). GC II, *supra* note 5, arts. 19(2), 20; GC III, *supra* note 5, arts. 120, 122, 123; GC IV, *supra* note 5, arts. 130, 136–38, 140; AP I, *supra* note 6, art. 33(3); Hague Regulations Respecting the Laws and Customs of War on Land, annexed to Convention No. IV Respecting the Laws and Customs of War on Land arts. 14, 16, Oct. 18, 1907, 36 Stat. 2227, T.S. No. 539 [hereinafter Hague Regulations].

28. GC III, *supra* note 5, art. 122(7); GC IV, *supra* note 5, art. 137(1); AP I, *supra* note 5, art. 33(3).

29. GC III, *supra* note 5, art. 74; GC IV, *supra* note 5, art. 110; Hague Regulations, *supra* note 26, art. 14.

30. GC I, *supra* note 5, art. 16; GC II, *supra* note 5, art. 19; GC III, *supra* note 5, arts. 120, 122; GC IV, *supra* note 5, arts. 129, 138(1), 139; AP I, *supra* note 6, art. 34.

31. GC I, *supra* note 5, art. 16; GC II, *supra* note 5, art. 19.

- date and place of capture or death;
- particulars concerning wounds or illnesses, or cause of death.

In case of death, the following must be collected and transmitted to the Information Bureau with:[32]

- date and place of (capture and) death;
- particulars concerning wounds/illnesses or cause of death;
- all other personal effects;
- date and place of burial with particulars to identify the grave,
- when applicable, half of the identity disc must remain with the body and the other half transmitted.

Each party to the conflict must endeavor to facilitate the return of the deceased's remains and personal effects to the home country at its request or at the request of the next of kin.[33]

Many of the preceding provisions also represent customary IHL[34] applicable to the management of the dead and human remains. Of particular importance in this regard are Rules 112 to 116 identified by the ICRC in its 2005 Study of Customary IHL, which deal with the collection, treatment, identification, disposal, and return of the remains of the dead.

Rule 112 states: "Whenever circumstances permit, and particularly after an engagement, each party to the conflict must, without delay, take all possible measures to search for, collect and evacuate the dead without adverse distinction."[35] The rule is applicable in both IAC and NIAC.

The ICRC recalls that the obligation to search for and collect the dead is an obligation of means. Each party to the conflict must take "all possible measures" to search for and collect the dead. This rule applies to all the dead without distinction, regardless of the party to which they belong and whether they have taken a direct part in hostilities.

Rule 113 states: "Each party to the conflict must take all possible measures to prevent the dead from being despoiled. Mutilation of dead bodies is prohibited."[36] The rule is applicable in both IAC and NIAC. It applies to all the dead without distinction, regardless of the party to which they belong and whether they have taken a direct part in hostilities.

32. GC I, *supra* note 5, arts. 16, 17, 40(2); GC II, *supra* note 5, arts. 19, 20, 42(2); GC III, *supra* note 5, art. 120; GC IV, *supra* note 5, arts. 129, 130, 139; Hague Regulations, *supra* note 26, arts. 14, 19; AP I, *supra* note 6, art. 34.

33. AP I, *supra* note 6, art. 34(2)(c).

34. 2 Customary International Humanitarian Law (Jean-Marie Henckaerts & Louise Doswald-Beck eds., 2005) [hereinafter CIHL Study].

35. *Id.* at r. 112.

36. CIHL Study, *supra* note 33, at r. 113.

Rule 114 states: "Parties to the conflict must endeavour to facilitate the return of the remains of the deceased upon request of the party to which they belong. They must return their personal effects to them."[37] The rule is only applicable in IAC. It applies to all the dead without distinction, regardless of the party to which they belong and whether they have taken a direct part in hostilities.

Rule 115 states: "The dead must be disposed of in a respectful manner and their graves respected and properly maintained."[38] It is applicable in both IAC and NIAC.

The Geneva Conventions specify that the dead must be buried, if possible, according to the rites of the religion to which they belonged. This rule applies to all the dead without distinction, regardless of the party to which they belong and whether they have taken a direct part in hostilities.

Rule 116 prescribes: "With a view to the identification of the dead, each party to the conflict must record all available information prior to disposal and mark the location of the graves."[39] The rule is applicable in both IAC and NIAC. It applies to all the dead without distinction, regardless of the party to which they belong and whether they have taken a direct part in hostilities.

4. THE MISSING IN WAR AND THE RIGHTS OF THEIR FAMILIES

IHL requires parties to an armed conflict to clarify the fate of persons reported missing. The main obligations in this regard are contained in Article 33 of Additional Protocol I. It requires each party to an armed conflict to search for all those reported missing by an adverse party as soon as circumstances permit, and at the latest from the end of active hostilities. With a view to facilitating searches, the adverse party must transmit all relevant information concerning such persons to the requested party.[40] Article 33 also establishes obligations of the parties to an IAC to gather, record, and, if necessary, search for information related to missing persons and to transmit such information or requests for information to the adverse party directly or through the ICRC's Central Tracing Agency.[41] In case information is channeled through National Red Cross and Red Crescent Societies, each party to an IAC must ensure that it is supplied to the ICRC's Central Tracing Agency.[42]

37. *Id.* at r. 114.

38. *Id.* at r. 115.

39. *Id.* at r. 116.

40. AP I, *supra* note 6, art. 33, ¶ 1.

41. *Id.* at ¶ 2.

42. *Id.* at ¶ 3.

With regards to the actual search for missing persons, Article 33 calls on the parties to an IAC to make arrangements "for teams to search for, identify and recover the dead from battlefield areas, including arrangements, if appropriate, for such teams to be accompanied by personnel of the adverse Party while carrying out these missions in areas controlled by the adverse Party. Personnel of such teams shall be respected and protected while exclusively carrying out these duties."[43]

IHL also protects the rights of families of those reported missing in armed conflict to know the whereabouts of their loved ones. This right is specifically protected under Article 32 of AP I, which requires that "the activities of the High Contracting Parties, of the Parties to the conflict and of the international humanitarian organizations mentioned in the Conventions and in this Protocol shall be prompted mainly by the right of families to know the fate of their relatives."[44]

Customary IHL (CIHL) Rules 98 and 117 apply equally in IAC and NIAC. Rule 117 provides that "each party to the conflict must take all feasible measures to account for persons reported missing as a result of armed conflict and must provide their family members with any information it has on their fate." Rule 98, from which the obligation to account for missing persons is also derived, affirms that enforced disappearance is prohibited, in both IAC and NIAC.

5. THE ROLE OF FORENSIC SCIENCE

Forensic science is increasingly relied upon throughout the world to help fulfill humanitarian obligations toward the dead and the missing. This has especially been the case since the emergence of a new discipline called Humanitarian Forensic Action (HFA).[45] This term was first used in 2012 and is defined as "the application of forensic science to humanitarian activities."[46]

The effective and scientifically reliable search, recovery, and identification of those who die in armed conflict, as well as of those missing in war (whether presumed dead or alive) are essential steps for fulfilling the obligations under IHL described previously. This is nowadays made possible by HFA, which uses a variety of specialized procedures and methods from different fields of forensic science, in particular: forensic archaeology and anthropology; forensic radiology,

43. AP I, *supra* note 6, art. 33 at ¶ 4.

44. AP I, *supra* note 6, art. 32.

45. 1–2 Forensic Science and Humanitarian Action: Interacting with the Dead and the Living 738 (Roberto Parra, Sara ZAP Ico & Douglas Ubelaker eds. 2020).

46. Morris Tidball-Binz, keynote speech at the biennial Graeme Schofield Victorian Institute of Forensic Medicine Oration: For Whom the Bell Tolls: The Development of Humanitarian Forensic Action (June 2012), *available at* https://www.monash.edu/news/articles/forensic-science-to-be-examined-in-melbourne.

including CT scanning; forensic genetics, including high-throughput DNA analysis; and forensic pathology and medicine.

The field of HFA was developed in 2004 by the ICRC and initially focused on the prevention and resolution of the phenomenon of persons missing as a result of armed conflicts, other situations of violence, major natural disasters, and migratory phenomena. Over the last 20 years, HFA has rapidly developed. Its scope has expanded to include the proper and dignified management and scientifically reliable identification of the deceased; the documentation of torture and ill-treatment,[47] including sexual violence and other violations in contexts of armed conflict;[48] and the protection of vulnerable populations and groups, including migrants and children,[49] and, where appropriate, to help ensure accountability for violations of IHL.[50]

The ICRC has had a particular role to play in offering assistance, advisory services, and guidance for the proper management, identification, and protection of the dead and searching for the missing in armed conflicts and natural disasters. It established a forensic unit,[51] which currently employs more than 100 forensic specialists from all regions who work around the world in support of a variety of stakeholders, including armed forces, forensic services, National Red Cross and Red Crescent Societies, and first responders.[52]

This rapidly evolving and evidence-based discipline has already given rise to special editions of prestigious forensic publications,[53] as well as dedicated manuals,[54] and has been included in some of the most important forensic congresses in the world such as the International Association of Forensic Sciences,

47. Michael Pollanen, *The Pathology of Torture*, 284 Forensic Science International 85–96 (2018).

48. David Wells, *Sexual Violence Interventions: Considerations for Humanitarian Settings*, 276 Forensic Science International 1–4 (2017).

49. Zarah Obertova & Cristina Cattaneo, *Child Trafficking and the European Migration Crisis: The Role of Forensic Practitioners*, 282 Forensic Science International 46–59 (2018).

50. Anjli Perrin, *"How Did They Die?": Bridging Humanitarian and Criminal Justice Objectives in Forensic Science to Advance the Rights of Families of the Missing under International Humanitarian Law*, 105 (923) International Review of the Red Cross 1047–70 (2023).

51. *See* International Committee of the Red Cross, *Protection of the Deceased through Forensic Action*, https://www.icrc.org/en/what-we-do/forensic-action (last accessed June 3, 2024).

52. *See, e.g.*, International Committee of the Red Cross, Operational Best Practices Regarding the Management of Human Remains and information on the Dead by Non-Specialists (2004).

53. Morris Tidball-Binz et al., *A Special Edition on Humanitarian Forensic Science*, 285 Forensic Science International 65–228 (2018).

54. 1– 2 Forensic Science and Humanitarian Action: Interacting with the Dead and the Living 738 (Roberto Parra, Sara Zapico, & Douglas Ubelaker eds., 2020).

the International Academy of Legal Medicine, and the American Academy of Forensic Sciences. In 2014, the latter launched its Humanitarian and Human Rights Resource Center to promote the application of contemporary forensic science and forensic medicine principles in humanitarian and/or human rights projects worldwide.[55] The discipline is also a matter of interest, research, and teaching in academic centers. In June 2018, for example, the Gujarat Forensic Sciences University of India inaugurated an International Centre for Humanitarian Forensics;[56] in November 2019 ,the University of Coimbra, Portugal, inaugurated its *Centro de Investigação e Formação Forense em Direitos Humanos e Ação Humanitária* (Coimbra University Centre for Humanitarian and Human Rights Forensic Research and Training),[57] dedicated to the development and promotion of this new discipline, and in 2021, Monash University and the Victoria Institute of Forensic Medicine launched the Global Research Initiative on Forensic Medicine and Human Rights, focusing on research into the interaction of forensic medicine, human rights, and humanitarian action.[58]

6. EXAMPLES OF BEST PRACTICE

6.1 The Committee on Missing Persons in Cyprus

The Committee on Missing Persons (CMP) was established in 1981 in Cyprus pursuant to UN General Assembly Resolutions to search for persons who had disappeared during the 1974 armed conflict in that country in order to fulfill IHL requirements pertaining to the dead and missing.[59] For the next two decades, however, the CMP lacked forensic capacity and thus failed to resolve any cases. In 2004, the CMP requested the assistance of the ICRC's forensic services to develop its own forensic search and identification capacity. The ICRC provided the

55. *See* American Academy of Forensic Sciences, Humanitarian and Human Rights Resources, https://www.aafs.org/HHRRC (last accessed June 3, 2024).

56. *See PG Diploma Humanitarian Forensics (in association with ICRC)*, National Forensic Sciences University, https://www.nfsu.ac.in/international-centre-for-humanitarian-forensics (last accessed June 13, 2024).

57. *See Faculdade de Medicina da Universidade de Coimbra promove Curso Prático de Formação em Exame de Vítimas de Agressão Sexual em São Tomé e Príncipe*, Universidade d Coimbra (Jan. 13, 2023), https://www.uc.pt/fmuc/noticias-fmuc/faculdade-de-medicina-da-universidade-de-coimbra-promove-curso-pratico-de-formacao-em-exame-de-vitimas-de-agressao-sexual-e/.

58. *See Public Health and Preventive Medicine Home, About Us*, Monash University, https://www.aph.gov.au/DocumentStore.ashx?id=ae8f713a-d9b1-4827-b291 623886e56a22&subId=728216 (last accessed June13, 2024).

59. *See Who We Are*, Committee on Missing Persons in Cyprus, https://www.cmp-cyprus.org/ (last accessed June 3, 2024).

requested support mainly through advice to and training of a sustainable local group of scientists, composed of Greek and Turkish Cypriots, which was the first bi-communal team of its kind. In addition to advising on the construction of a purpose-built mortuary and training the scientists, the ICRC's forensic services also rallied forensic experts from different countries (e.g., Argentina, the United States, Colombia, and the United Kingdom) to assist in building the capacity of the CMP's new forensic group.

As a result, the CMP developed its own fully Cypriot forensic team able to apply an exemplary integrated approach to the forensic search, recovery, and identification of those dead and missing in the armed conflict. To date, the CMP has managed to recover, identify, and return to their families a total of 1,033 previously disappeared persons, thus becoming a model of good practice in the field of humanitarian forensic action.[60]

The CMP has also proven to be a successful example of cooperation, local integration, and peacebuilding. Its multidisciplinary team of talented forensic experts made up of young Cypriots from both communities on the island worked harmoniously together for the sake of a shared humanitarian objective: to find the disappeared[61] and thereby overcome the wounds of the past.[62]

6.2 The Falkland Islands (Malvinas) Humanitarian Project Plan

The 2017 Humanitarian Project Plan (HPP) carried out by an ICRC forensic team at the request of the governments of Argentina and the United Kingdom was an unprecedented humanitarian operation for the identification of soldiers killed in military action. The operation resulted in the identification, to date, of 115 of the 122 soldiers who were initially buried without identification in the Argentine military cemetery of Darwin, a hamlet on the Falkland (Malvinas)[63] Islands, after the end of the 1982 IAC between these two countries. As a result, the tombstones that used to read "Argentine soldier known only to God" now bear the proper name of the resting soldier, fulfilling their family's fundamental right to know the fate and resting place of their loved one.

60. *Id.* at Statistics reported May 31, 2024, https://www.cmp-cyprus.org/statistics/.

61. *Forensic Identification of Human Remains in Cyprus* (CMP), *in* 2 Forensic Science and Humanitarian Action: Interacting with the Dead and the Living 609–24 (Roberto Parra, Sara ZAP Ico, & Douglas Ubelaker eds., 2020).

62. Maria Mikellide, *Recovery and Identification of Human Remains in Post-Conflict Environments: A Comparative Study of the Humanitarian Forensic Programs in Cyprus And Kosovo*, 279 Forensic Science International 33–40 (2017).

63. Denomination of the islands follows UN usage. *See, e.g.*, The United Nations and Decolonization, *Falkland Islands (Malvinas)*, https://www.un.org/dppa/decolonization/en/content/falkland-islands-malvinas.

The project was originally called for by relatives of unidentified soldiers and certain veterans of the 1982 war in the South Atlantic and was eventually supported by both States. The HPP first required extensive humanitarian diplomacy by the ICRC to broker the necessary agreement between the two formerly belligerent parties. This was followed by a complex and unprecedented forensic operation of exhumation, analysis, documentation, and re-interment of each of the bodies that had been buried without a name for more than three decades, in order to ensure their reliable identification using methods and processes expressly developed for the operation.

Although the unidentified soldiers were formally considered missing in action, it was known for certain that they had died on the battlefield. Their bodies had been collected and respectfully and honorably buried after the war in a specially built military cemetery near the hamlet of Darwin, although without identification due to technical limitations that made it impossible at the time. All stakeholders agreed that the identity of the fallen soldiers deserved to be recovered. It was essential, in particular, that relatives should be able to identify their loved ones and be able to honor them by visiting their respective graves.

This forensic operation serves as a model for the new discipline of humanitarian forensic action still today. It overcame important logistical difficulties, such as those related to the establishment of a high-tech mortuary with the required equipment despite the geographic isolation and extreme climatic conditions prevailing on the location. Complex forensic issues, including those inherent in an integrated, large-scale identification process with short and tight deadlines, needed to be resolved. Throughout the work, meticulous quality control was applied and maximum respect for the dignity of the dead was maintained, to the satisfaction of the families and the parties concerned, while complying with multiple and demanding legal and diplomatic requirements arising from the operation.

Background of the HPP

Immediately after the end of the armed conflict between Argentina and the United Kingdom over the Falkland (Malvinas) Islands in June 1982, the British side recovered Argentine soldiers who had died in combat from the battlefield. All the bodies were duly buried in a purpose-built Argentine military cemetery near the islands' hamlet of Darwin.

Despite efforts at the time to identify all the fallen, a certain number could not be identified and were therefore buried without a name, with the inscription "Known unto God," as used worldwide by the Commonwealth War Grave Commission (CWGC) for the graves of unknown soldiers.[64] This phrase was devised by Rudyard Kipling, the British writer who had worked for the CWGC during the First World War. In the reconstruction of the Argentine military cemetery of Darwin, carried out in 2001 by the Commission of Relatives of the Fallen in Malvinas and Islas del Atlántico Sur with the support of an Argentine private

64. *See* Commonwealth War Graves, Caring for the Fallen, https://www.cwgc.org/.

company (*Aeropuertos Argentina 2000 SA*), those same graves came to bear the Spanish epitaph "*Soldado argentino solo conocido por Dios*" (Argentine soldier known only to God).

In April 2012, the ICRC received an official request from the Argentine government to assist in the identification of all the soldiers buried without a name in the Darwin military cemetery. The ICRC accepted Argentina's request, focusing strictly on its humanitarian role, and based on the needs and interests of the families.

What followed was intense diplomatic work in Geneva, Buenos Aires, and London to set up and sustain negotiations between the two sides and prepare for the complex mission envisaged, with the full agreement of all concerned. From 2014 onward the ICRC also worked closely with the Argentine authorities involved in the collection of information and samples from participating families required for identification purposes, with the latter's informed consent. An interdisciplinary group including forensic scientists, psychologists, social workers, and lawyers was created by the Argentine government for this purpose, which continued with the interviews following commonly agreed protocols.

A fundamental step in designing the project was a preliminary visit carried out to the islands in mid-2016 by an ICRC delegation. The visit confirmed that an identification process was possible and provided the evidence-based information required for designing and preparing the forensic operation. It resulted, among other things, in a feasibility study based on a collection and analysis of soil samples, a determination of the special infrastructure and equipment that would be required for the task given the extreme isolation and weather conditions on site, as well as the logistics necessary to meet those needs. The logistical challenge of ensuring the installation and proper functioning of everything that was materially and technically needed for the operation required months of preparatory work. It should be noted that the HPP could not have been carried out without the support of the local population, who were motivated by the humanitarian objective of the task.

The forensic operation of the HPP

At the end of 2016, high diplomatic representatives of Argentina and the United Kingdom were invited by the ICRC to its headquarters in Geneva to finalize the terms of the project. On December 20 of that year both states and the ICRC signed an agreement setting up the HPP.[65] It defined the objectives, roles, responsibilities, and deadlines for the execution of the operation, as well as the forensic process required in accordance with the ICRC's proposal.

After a lengthy consultation process conducted by the Argentine authorities, by early 2017 a total of 107 families from around the country had come forward

65. *See* International Committee of the Red Cross, *Diplomacy in the Service of Humanitarian Objectives: Falkland/Malvinas Islands* (Nov. 22, 2018), https://www.icrc.org/en/document/diplomacy-service-humanitarian-objectives-lessons-learned-humanitarian-project-plan.

to participate in the process. It was then decided to continue efforts to reach out to all remaining families in order to inform them about the project and to offer to collect from those who so wished the information and the biological/DNA samples required for the identification of their loved ones.

Between December 2016 and May 2017, the ICRC finalized its own preparations for the forensic operation. This required defining the standard operating procedures, protocols, and forms required for each stage of the humanitarian forensic operation, including the exhumation, analysis, sampling, and documentation of the remains recovered, as well as the reburial of the bodies. This documentary framework aimed to ensure, guide, and facilitate the systematic collection of the necessary information and samples; ensure adequate and reliable documentation of all findings, including as required for the integrated identification of the bodies, quality control of all the procedures used, and surety of the investigation throughout; ensure the drafting of protocolized reports—in English and Spanish—for every step in each individual case; and ensure the utmost respect for the dignity of the remains and the cemetery site throughout the entire process.

All forensic activities followed predefined plans, flow charts, and schedules, prepared in advance for the operation. A specially equipped temporary mortuary and forensic laboratory were designed and installed at the Darwin military cemetery. It was decided to furnish them with state-of-the-art equipment and technology, including for the systematic radiography of all the bodies and body parts analyzed. As required by the HPP, the site included a surveyed security perimeter with strict access protocols.

Given that no forensic genetics services are available in the islands, the HPP transferred samples collected for DNA analysis to laboratories in Argentina, the United Kingdom, and Spain. The matching process was carried out by the same Argentine forensic genetics' laboratory that had profiled samples from relatives, while laboratories in Spain and the United Kingdom carried out the required quality control of tests. The latter laboratories unanimously confirmed the reliability of the analysis and results obtained in Argentina. The format of the forensic genetics' reports, as well as the prior and posterior probabilities required for matching calculations and the identification threshold, were defined jointly with the participating laboratories beforehand.

An elaborate computer support system was designed for the operation, which allowed the management and safeguarding of all the data and information produced in real time and in total security. To this was added a forensic database specially designed by the ICRC for large-scale identification processes.

Between late May and the end of August 2017, a carefully selected ICRC forensic team moved to the islands to carry out the field and laboratory tasks necessary to complete the project. It was composed of fourteen specialists experienced in HFA from Argentina, Australia, Chile, Spain, Mexico, and the United Kingdom, representing different forensic disciplines. Between June and August 2017, the forensic team proceeded to exhume, analyze, obtain samples, and document each of the bodies that were buried in the 121 graves in the cemetery marked with the legend "Argentine soldier known only to God." The work was intensive, carried out from dawn to dusk six days a week in order to meet the deadlines set for the operation. The team operated in a truly multidisciplinary and interdisciplinary manner to help ensure the daily completion of pre-assigned tasks, the necessary reporting, and quality assurance and control procedures.

The exhumation of each body, using adapted archaeological methods and procedures, was systematically followed by a meticulous analysis of the forensic team (including full radiology and photography), documentation, and the taking of samples for subsequent genetic analysis. After completing the analysis, documentation, and sampling required for each body, the experts would place the body in a new coffin for same-day burial in the original grave, with full respect for the dignity of the deceased. Same-day recovery, analysis, and reburial of the bodies was a requirement under the HPP, which the forensic team had to honor while simultaneously ensuring the highest scientific standards. Reports on each case were prepared on the same day as the analysis, in Spanish and English, ready for completion once the genetic results were made available, several weeks later.

A small number of personal objects of special emotional and/or identification value were found with some of the bodies, such as identification cards and wedding rings. The exhaustive forensic examination, including the use of state-of-the-art radiological equipment, helped find these objects among the several layers of clothing worn by the soldiers. They had been understandably overlooked by non-forensic service personnel at the time of recovery from the battlefield. Given the IHL obligation to return such objects to the families of the fallen, the objects found were preserved and handed over to the Argentine authorities at the end of the HPP. They were duly presented to concerned families together with the reports about their cases. At the completion of the fieldwork, the military cemetery and its facilities were restored to their original condition, as required under the HPP. In the weeks that followed, new grass was planted at the site.

After the forensic field operation, the team of specialists met again in Geneva. They integrated the results of the forensic studies carried out on the islands with the results of the genetic analyses in order to finalize the identification reports, in English and in Spanish, and to also adequately prepare the personal items recovered for delivery to families. Reports were prepared for all families who submitted samples, including those whose loved one had not been identified.

On December 1, 2017, the date scheduled for presenting the reports, the results of the HPP process were submitted to the delegations of Argentina and the United Kingdom at ICRC headquarters in Geneva. The diplomatic meeting convened on this occasion underlined the quality of the process, the commitment and support of all those who collaborated in the operation, and the results achieved.[66]

66. *See* Relief Web, *Falkland/Malvinas Islands: ICRC Presents Argentina and the United Kingdom with Results of Humanitarian Forensic Identification Project*, Relief Web (Dec. 1, 2017), https://reliefweb.int/report/falkland-islands-malvinas/falklandmalvinas-islands-icrc-presents-argentina-and-united-kingdom.

At the time of delivery of the results in Geneva, the ICRC forensic team had identified 88 soldiers and collected information and processed samples necessary to make it possible to identify all the 34 remaining bodies, provided that the necessary information and samples be made available by concerned families. In the days following the delivery of the reports to the governments, the Argentine authorities proceeded to inform all the participating families, personally and confidentially, about the results of the operation and to deliver the corresponding reports and personal belongings recovered. This highly sensitive process followed good practices in the matter, shared in advance by the ICRC to the intervening teams, who also received training in this respect from the organization's experts.

In March 2018 and 2019, the families of the soldiers identified as a result of the HPP were able to visit their loved ones' graves, with their names newly engraved on the tombstones.[67] The visits were organized jointly by the British and Argentine authorities, with logistical support provided for two flights to the islands by a private Argentine company (Aeropuertos Argentina 2000 SA).[68]

The touching and profoundly humanitarian ceremonies held on both occasions in the islands' military cemetery were made possible by an unprecedented combination of diplomacy in the service of humanitarian principles and the innovative use of forensic science to make them a reality. They also fostered a renewed dialogue and cooperation between former foes, aimed at the opening of new commercial flights between Argentina and the islands, helping overcome their isolation and contributing to a peacebuilding process between those affected by war.

As of August 2023, a total of 115 soldiers, out of 122 originally buried without a name, have been positively identified, and their families have been thus able to honor their dead as envisaged under IHL. The fact that some of the war dead have no living relatives left to provide information and biological reference samples required for their identification helps explain why the remaining seven have not yet been identified.

The forensic operation carried out on the islands also paved the way for a follow-up of the HPP, to help individualize the bodies of six Argentine service members who died together in a helicopter crash during the conflict and whose fragmented and commingled remains were buried together in Darwin military cemetery. Because their names were known and listed on the common grave, this group was not included in the original HPP. However, based on the success of the latter, concerned families requested another humanitarian forensic operation to help identify the remains of each of their loved ones separately. The agreement between the ICRC and the two governments was signed on March 18, 2021,[69] and

67. *See* Commonwealth War Graves, *supra* note 63.

68. *Id.*

69. *See* International Committee of the Red Cross, *Joint Statement from the ICRC, The Government of Argentina and the Government of the United Kingdom* (Mar. 18, 2021), *available at* https://www.icrc.org/en/document/falkland-islands-islas-malvinas-humanitarian-plan-identify-argentine-soldiers-buried-darwin.

the operation was carried out that same year following the model developed for the HPP forensic operation. It helped identify and reliably individualize the remains of the six victims who had perished in the helicopter crash.[70]

The HPP continues to stand as a model of humanitarian forensic action's contribution to the successful fulfillment of IHL obligations, in this case long after the facts.[71] As such, and beyond the success of the HPP forensic operation, it provides a practical and valuable model for other contexts around the world.[72]

7. ARMED FORCES AND FORENSIC CAPACITY

Despite the many obligations contained in IHL with respect to the dead and missing and the obvious contribution that today's forensic science offers for fulfilling these duties—both in past and current armed conflicts—not all armed forces in the world have permanent mortuary services with their own forensic capacity. Where they exist, such services have largely proven their added value and importance, in times of war and in peace, including for responding to natural disasters and other catastrophic events.

In the United States, the DPAA is charged with the search, recovery, and identification of the fallen from past conflicts, as mentioned previously.[73] The U.S. Armed Forces Medical Examiner System, including its Air Force Mortuary Affairs Operation, based at the Dover Air Force Base, Delaware, cares for the dead from current conflicts. In addition to the task for which these agencies were primarily established, they are also called upon, where necessary, to assist in the forensic recovery and identification of victims of catastrophic events in the United States and occasionally in other countries within the framework of international cooperation. Such was the case after the 2005 tsunami that devastated Southeast Asia.

In order to best fulfill IHL duties toward the dead and missing in armed conflicts, the best option for armed forces is to set up their own mortuary services with specialized forensic capacity, ideally in the form of permanent units ready to operate at short notice and according to standards of best practice. These services could also be called upon in times of peace, to assist in the response to major

70. The International Committee of the Red Cross presented its final report on forensic work to identify the remains of Argentine soldiers in the Falkland Islands (Malvinas) (Nov. 8, 2021), *available at* https://www.icrc.org/en/document/falkland-islands-malvinas-icrc-presents-final-report-six-argentine-soldiers-identified.

71. *See* Comision por Memoria, *Identificación*, https://www.comisionporlamemoria.org/memoriamalvinas/identificacion/ (last accessed June 3, 2024).

72. International Committee of the Red Cross, *Diplomacy in the Service of Humanitarian Objectives: Falkland/Malvinas Islands* (Nov. 22, 2018), https://www.icrc.org/en/document/diplomacy-service-humanitarian-objectives-lessons-learned-humanitarian-project-plan.

73. *See* Defense POW/MIA Accounting Agency, *supra* note 14.

disasters and other catastrophic events involving large numbers of fatalities, such as pandemics.

8. CONCLUSION

The proper care of the dead and the search for the missing in armed conflicts is not an option but an obligation under IHL.[74] The remarkable development of HFA is a measure of its proven practical value as a useful tool for fulfilling humanitarian obligations and responding to needs arising from humanitarian emergencies, past and present.

HFA is the result of cross-fertilization between evolving forensic science knowledge, techniques and tools, on one hand, and IHL and humanitarian practice on the other, especially in relation to the care of the dead and the search for missing persons.[75] Close attention will be required to ensure that this valuable synergy continues to be guided by the highest ethical and professional values and the necessary quality standards, as well as by applicable international law, and that the perspectives, the needs and the rights of victims of humanitarian tragedies are respected throughout.

Armed forces should make use of the skills and tools offered by HFA to help fulfill their duties toward the dead and the missing in armed conflicts. Ideally, they would have a dedicated mortuary service with specialized forensic capacity able to operate at short notice and to the highest standards of forensic humanitarian action.

74. *See, e.g.*, International Committee for the Red Cross, Guiding Principles for Dignified Management of the Dead in Humanitarian Emergencies and to Prevent Them Becoming Missing Persons, Publication No. 4586 (2020).

75. Mass Graves, Truth and Justice: Interdisciplinary Perspectives on the Investigation of Mass Graves (Ellie Smith & Melanie Klinker eds., 2023).

PART FOUR

Accountability

Unlawful Confinement as a War Crime in Armed Conflict

MARCO SASSÒLI*

1. INTRODUCTION

Unlawful confinement, along with unlawful killing, constitutes one of the most frequent and typical violations of international humanitarian law (IHL) endured by victims of armed conflict. It has been recognized as a war crime[1] in international armed conflict (IAC), but individuals have only rarely been charged with it. Beyond the usual difficulties encountered in defining the elements of a war crime, unlawful confinement faces particular challenges, an examination of which is the focus of this chapter. First, the substantive rules of IHL determining when a confinement is unlawful are controversial, especially in non-international armed conflicts (NIACs). Second, the person physically hindering the victim of the crime from leaving a certain location is only rarely the person causing the unlawfulness of the confinement, which raises several problems for establishing the *mens rea*, participation in the offense and concurrence with other offenses. All

* Marco Sassòli is a Professor of International Law at the University of Geneva, Switzerland.
I would like to thank Ms. Eugénie Duss, PhD, Geneva, and Ms. Vanessa Bliecke, PhD Student and Research Associate at the Ruhr-Universität Bochum, Germany, for their thorough research on which this contribution is based. I also thank my colleague, Prof. Paola Gaeta, for her critical remarks about an earlier version of this text.

1. Rome Statute of the International Criminal Court art. 8(2)(a)(vii), July 17, 1998, 2187 U.N.T.S. 90 [hereinafter ICC Statute]; Convention (IV) Relative to the Protection of Civilian Persons in Time of War art. 4, Aug. 12, 1949, 6 U.S.T. 3516, 75 U.N.T.S. 287 [hereinafter Geneva Convention IV or GC IV]. GC IV art. 147 lists unlawful confinement of a protected civilian as a grave breach of the Convention.

Marco Sassòli, *Unlawful Confinement as a War Crime in Armed Conflict* In: *Civilian Protection in Armed Conflict*. Edited by: Jelena Pejic and Captain Margaret Kotlik, Oxford University Press. © Marco Sassòli 2025.
DOI: 10.1093/oso/9780197793176.003.0016

this raises wider issues of IHL, which will only be summarized in this chapter, as well as of the relationship between IHL and war crimes law, in particular the issues of whether an accused must be acquitted if the substantive IHL violated is too controversial and vague, and how much of the substantive law an accused must (be able to) know to commit the war crime.

In this chapter I will move from the most stable to the most shaky grounds. First the actus reus of the war crime of unlawful confinement of civilians in IACs will be discussed, focusing on the factors that may make a confinement "unlawful." Next, I will explore whether the actus reus also covers the confinement of civilians resulting from an unfair trial, certain cases of confinement of prisoners of war and, for both civilians and prisoners of war, unlawfulness due to how the detainee is treated. I will then move on to the much less charted waters of NIACs, to discuss the same questions, after dealing with the fundamental controversy of whether the crime of unlawful confinement exists at all in such conflicts. Following this I will discuss the *mens rea*, who can commit the crime and whether a person may be sentenced for multiple offenses related or connected to unlawful confinement, in particular if the unlawfulness of the confinement results from a denial of fair trial.

2. THE ACTUS REUS: WHEN IS THE CONFINEMENT "UNLAWFUL"?

2.1 In International Armed Conflict

Security or administrative detention of civilians

The most typical case of unlawful confinement, for which several persons have been tried, is that of internment for security reasons of protected civilians without respect for the limitations foreseen in Articles 42 and 43 of Geneva Convention IV for a party's own territory and Article 78 for an occupied territory. Such confinement may violate substantive IHL for several reasons.

Absence of sufficient reasons

First, internment in a party's own territory is unlawful if the security of the detaining power does not make it absolutely necessary[2] or if an occupying power does not consider it to be necessary for imperative security reasons.[3] Such wording leaves States large discretion in deciding whether internment is justified.[4] The

2. GC IV, *supra* note 1, art. 42.

3. *Id.*, art. 78.

4. Oscar M. Uhler et al., Commentary to Geneva Convention IV Relative to the Protection of Civilian Persons in Time of War (1958) [hereinafter Commentary GC IV]. *See also* Prosecutor v. Delalić et al., Case No. IT-96-21-T, Trial Judgment, ¶ 574 (Int'l Crim. Trib.

International Criminal Tribunal for the former Yugoslavia (ICTY) has nevertheless held that there must be "serious and legitimate reasons to think that [persons] may seriously prejudice [State] security by means such as sabotage or espionage."[5] As internment can only be ordered on a case-by-case basis,[6] the fact that a civilian belongs to a certain category of persons based on their nationality, ethnicity, (military) age, and/or gender does not constitute a sufficient security reason.[7] Even mere alignment with the enemy is insufficient.[8] I agree with the ICTY that a party must have "good reason to think that the person concerned, by his activities, knowledge or qualifications, represents a real threat to its present or future security."[9] I must nevertheless mention that the Eritrea-Ethiopia Claims Commission accepted as lawful the internment of Eritrean men by Ethiopia just because they were of military age.[10] I would also accept internment on the basis of organizational affiliation, provided that it equally considers the individual threat emanating from the person concerned,[11] but it must be recognized that States have expressed differing views on this question in relation to NIACs.[12] Despite the vagueness and uncertainty of the substantive law, the ICTY has considered that it is possible to convict a person for unlawful confinement if they placed a civilian in internment without reasonable grounds for believing that the civilian constituted a security risk.[13] In the IAC between Cambodia and Vietnam, the Extraordinary Chambers of the Courts of Cambodia (ECCC) actually convicted a defendant for interning Vietnamese civilians "in the absence of factors indicating that the security of Cambodia required their internment."[14] The absence pertained to all detainees, and the case decided by the ECCC was related to the internment of a number of them.

for the former Yugoslavia Nov. 16, 1998), UK MINISTRY OF DEFENCE, THE MANUAL OF THE LAW OF ARMED CONFLICT ¶ 9.31 (2004).

5. Delalić Trial Judgment, *supra* note 4, at ¶ 576; Prosecutor v. Delalić et al., Case No. IT-96-21-A, Appeals Judgment, ¶ 322 (Int'l Crim. Trib. for the former Yugoslavia Feb. 20, 2001).

6. Delalić Trial Judgment, *supra* note 5, at ¶ 578.

7. *Id.* at ¶ 577; UK MANUAL, *supra* note 4, at ¶ 9.31.

8. Delalić Appeals Judgment, *supra* note 5, at ¶ 327.

9. Delalić Trial Judgment, *supra* note 4, at ¶ 577.

10. Civilians Claims, Eritrea's Claims 15, 16, 23 & 27–32, Between the State of Eritrea and the Federal Democratic Republic of Ethiopia, Partial Award, ¶ 117 (Eritrea-Ethiopia Claims Commission Dec. 17, 2004).

11. COMMENTARY GC IV, *supra* note 4, at 258.

12. *See* INTERNATIONAL COMMITTEE OF THE RED CROSS, STRENGTHENING INTERNATIONAL HUMANITARIAN LAW PROTECTING PERSONS DEPRIVED OF THEIR LIBERTY, CONCLUDING REPORT, 32nd International Conference of the Red Cross and Red Crescent 28 (2015) [hereinafter ICRC, STRENGTHENING IHL].

13. Delalić Appeals Judgment, *supra* note 5, at ¶¶ 322, 330, and 377.

14. Prosecutor v. KAING Guek Eav, alias Duch, Case File/Dossier No. 001/18-07-2007/ECCC/TC, Judgment ¶ 469 (July 26, 2010) (Extraordinary Chambers in the Courts of Cambodia).

Absence of a sufficient procedure

Second, internment can only be ordered after a regular procedure, on an individual basis. The ICTY has held that "an initially lawful internment clearly becomes unlawful if the detaining party does not respect the basic procedural rights of the detained persons and does not establish an appropriate court or administrative board."[15] It convicted a prison administrator, Zdravko Mucić, for detaining protected civilians without a proper procedure.[16] The ECCC did the same with the infamous Khmer Rouge leader Duch, in relation to the confinement of Vietnamese civilians.[17] However, in the latter case there had been absolutely no procedure, while in the former case Mucić was convicted because he had not released detainees at a point in time when he knew that they had not been afforded the procedural rights to which they were entitled (an internal commission had already noted in a critical tone that certain internees "stayed in detention even after it had been established that they had been detained for no reason"[18]).

Internment decisions in occupied territory[19] must be made according to a regular procedure prescribed by the occupying power. This procedure must include "a right of appeal." IHL specifies that in a State's own territory the competent body to hear the appeal may be "an appropriate court or administrative board designated by the Detaining Power for that purpose."[20] An administrative board is also sufficient to hear appeals in occupied territory. The admissibility of the internment must also be periodically reviewed at least every six months to determine whether its maintenance is justifiable.[21] Admittedly, in occupied territory this periodicity must only be respected if it is "possible." Nevertheless, it may be argued that an internment will become unlawful after a certain time in the absence of any periodic review.

Neither the procedure resulting in the initial internment of a protected civilian, nor the subsequent review, amount to a criminal trial. As both are administrative in nature, international human rights law (IHRL) fair trial guarantees, including the requirements of the full independence and impartiality of a tribunal that may convict a person, do not apply. Nevertheless, the relevant court or administrative board must have the necessary power to make a final decision on release.[22] Taking IHL into account, the Inter-American Commission on Human Rights has held that a "quasi-judicial body" is sufficient even under IHRL in the case of internees

15. Delalić Appeals Judgment, *supra* note 5, at ¶ 320.

16. Delalić Trial Judgment, *supra* note 4, ¶ 1145; Delalić Appeals Judgment, *supra* note 5, at ¶ 377.

17. *Duch* case, *supra* note 14.

18. Delalić Trial Judgment, *supra* note 4, at ¶ 1138.

19. GC IV, *supra* note 1, art. 78(2).

20. *Id.*, art. 43(1).

21. *Id.*, arts. 43(1) and 78(2).

22. Delalić Trial Judgment, *supra* note 4, at ¶ 1137.

in IAC.[23] The European Court of Human Rights held in the *Hassan* case[24] that "the first review should take place shortly after the person is taken into detention, with subsequent reviews at frequent intervals, to ensure that any person who does not fall into one of the categories subject to internment under international humanitarian law is released without undue delay." It recognized that the constraints inherent in military operations during an IAC might render it impractical for States to use independent "courts" to determine the legality of an internment, but it also held that the IHL requirement that such internment is reviewed periodically by a "competent body" must be read in accordance with IHRL obligations. In its view, "the 'competent body' should provide sufficient guarantees of impartiality and fair procedure to protect against arbitrariness."[25]

The UN Working Group on Arbitrary Detention has gone further by providing that internees should have prompt access to habeas corpus given that such access is non-derogable under IHRL.[26] With regard to the nature of the review body, it requires "[a] court . . . [that] shall be established by law and [that] bear[s] the full characteristics of a competent, independent and impartial judicial authority capable of exercising recognizable judicial powers, including the power to order immediate release if the detention is arbitrary or unlawful."[27] In its view, this requirement applies to any "[r]econsideration, appeal or periodic review of decisions to intern or place in assigned residence alien civilians in the territory of a party to an international armed conflict, or civilians in an occupied territory."[28] However, this interpretation has been met by stiff resistance from some States.[29]

All this raises the fascinating question of whether the unlawfulness of a confinement constituting the actus reus of the war crime must take IHRL into account where it constitutes the *lex specialis* for certain issues, such as arguably the procedure in which the legality of an internment is upheld on appeal. I would answer affirmatively because what counts under the text of the grave breaches provision of the Fourth Geneva Convention and the Statute of the International

23. *See* Coard et al. v. United States, Case 10.951, Inter-Am Comm'n H.R., Report No. 109/99, OEA Ser.L/V/II.106 Doc. 6 rev., ¶ 58 (1999).

24. Hassan v. UK, App. No. 55721/07, Eur.Ct. H.R., ¶ 106 (2011).

25. *Id.*

26. U.N. Working Group on Arbitrary Detention, *United Nations Basic Principles and Guidelines on Remedies and Procedures on the Right of Anyone Deprived of Their Liberty to Bring Proceedings Before a Court*, as annexed to U.N. General Assembly, *Report of the Working Group on Arbitrary Detention*, U.N. Doc A/HRC/30/37 (July 6, 2015), Principles 4 and 16 and Guideline 3, ¶¶ 4–5, 27–8, and 50, respectively.

27. *Id.* at ¶ 9, Principle 6.

28. *Id.* at ¶¶ 9 and 29, Principles 6 and 16. *But see id.* at ¶ 94, Guideline 17.

29. *See, e.g.*, Comments by the Government of Canada, ¶ 6 (Apr. 28, 2015), https://www.ohchr.org/en/calls-for-input/report-basic-principles-and-guidelines-remedies-and-procedures-right-anyone.

Criminal Court (ICC) is that the confinement is unlawful under international law. Contrary to the grave breach of violating fair trial guarantees, which explicitly refers to those "prescribed in the present Convention,"[30] there is no indication that the unlawfulness of confinement must result from a violation of the Convention.

Nevertheless, I argue later that controversies and uncertainties about the procedural requirements for the lawfulness of an administrative detention law must chalked up to the benefit of a person accused of the war crime regardless of what the correct interpretation of the procedural obligations of States is believed to be. Therefore, even though a combination of IHL and IHRL can generate requirements for the procedure to be followed, the existing procedural uncertainties would not suffice for a conviction for the war crime of unlawful confinement. Only one of the following circumstances, known to the accused, would do so: the absence of any procedure, the absence of any information to the internee of the reasons for internment, internment decisions taken by the same person who initially deprived a person of liberty, review of an appeal by that person's commander, the absence of any hearing of the internee in presence, or the impossibility for him or her to make arguments against the existence of imperative security reasons.

Missing legal basis?

Third, in order not to be arbitrary and to therefore to be lawful, IHRL and an alleged rule of customary IHL require a legal basis for any deprivation of liberty.[31] The question arises whether the aforementioned articles of Geneva Convention IV (42, 43, and 78) constitute a sufficient legal basis. At least in occupied territory, one may express doubts because IHL requires a "regular procedure *to be prescribed* by the Occupying Power"[32] and one cannot imagine how an occupying power can prescribe a procedure without also mentioning the reasons for which a person may be detained in it. Israel has indeed adopted military orders prescribing the reasons and procedure for the internment of civilians.[33] In the *Hassan* case, the European Court of Human Rights opined, however, that the internment of the applicant "was consistent with the powers available to the United Kingdom under the . . . Fourth Geneva Convention"[34] and specifically mentioned that Article 78 "provided a legitimate ground for capture and detention."[35] On the other hand, the UN Working Group on Arbitrary Detention mentions particular procedural

30. GC IV, *supra* note 1, art. 147.

31. *See* 1 Customary International Humanitarian Law 348–49 (Jean-Marie Henckaerts & Louise Doswald-Beck eds., 2005).

32. GC IV, *supra* note 1, art. 78 (emphasis added).

33. Israel Defense Forces, Order No. 1651 Regarding Security Directives arts. 272–76 (Consolidated Version) (Judea and Samaria) (2009), http://www.militarycourtwatch.org/files/server/military_order_1651.pdf.

34. Hassan, *supra* note 24, at ¶ 111.

35. *Id.* at ¶ 110.

guarantees for civilians detained in an IAC,[36] but does not specifically refer to the requirement of a legal basis in national law.[37] It would nevertheless be prudent if States were to adopt a national legal basis for the internment of protected civilians in an IAC. However, for reasons that will be discussed in relation to the *mens rea*, I do not think that internment exclusively based upon Convention IV could lead to a conviction for the war crime of unlawful confinement (if all other conditions discussed previously are respected). Admittedly, the ECCC convicted an accused for unlawful confinement, noting that all "detainees were intentionally and arbitrarily imprisoned without legal basis."[38] This, however, was only one of the cumulative reasons for the judgment, and the case was obvious.

Criminal detention of civilians?

If a protected person is accused of a crime, but is not brought to trial or is tried without benefiting from the judicial guarantees (fair trial rights) prescribed by Geneva Convention IV in occupied territory, and is then confined, such confinement is obviously unlawful. In my view, a cumulative conviction with that of willfully depriving a protected person of the rights of a fair and regular trial is possible in such a scenario because the protected interests are different: on the one hand, personal liberty, and on the other, the right to a fair trial (which exists, e.g., even if someone is not confined). But it is important for another reason to keep in mind that a denial of fundamental judicial guarantees will lead to unlawful confinement. This is because a person involved in a confinement may know that a detainee was deprived of a fair trial (and is therefore unlawfully detained) but cannot be accused of the former crime because they were not involved in the trial. Such person could therefore only be tried for unlawful confinement.

Unlawful confinement of POWs?

Under the Geneva Conventions, the grave breach of unlawful confinement can only be committed against a protected civilian.[39] This is understandable because prisoners of war (POWs) may be interned without further justification until the end of active hostilities.[40] POWs may nevertheless be considered unlawfully confined if they are not repatriated, as required by Article 118 of Geneva

36. United Nations Basic Principles, *supra* note 26, at ¶ 96.

37. *Id.* at ¶¶ 48–49.

38. *Duch* case, *supra* note 14, at ¶ 468.

39. GC IV, *supra* note 1, art. 147.

40. Convention (III) Relative to the Treatment of Prisoners of War, arts. 21 and 118, Aug. 12, 1949, 6 U.S.T. 3316, 75 U.N.T.S. 135 [hereinafter GC III].

Convention III, at the end of active hostilities, which is a separate grave breach under Additional Protocol I.[41]

Under the ICC Statute, the grave breach of unlawful confinement may be committed against any "persons . . . protected under the provisions of the relevant Geneva Convention,"[42] which seems to also cover persons protected by Conventions I, II, and III. Commentators on the ICC Statute's elements of the crime of unlawful confinement equally list under its legal basis the provisions of Conventions I, II, and III on the modalities of confinement of protected persons, and Article 118 of Convention III on the repatriation of POWs.[43] The German government likewise considers that the crime of unlawful confinement may concern POWs.[44] The German International Criminal Code combines this crime with unjustifiable delay in the repatriation of protected persons, which clearly focuses on POWs.[45]

However, the chapeau of Article 8(2)(a) of the ICC Statute clearly incriminates only "grave breaches of the Geneva Conventions." These are defined in the Conventions and cannot be extended to other acts prohibited in them. In addition, unlawful confinement is criminalized in the ICC Statute together with unlawful deportation or transfer, indicating that it relates only to conduct in respect of civilians.[46] As is well known, forced transfers of protected civilians in and out of occupied territories will often be unlawful as such,[47] while POWs may be held everywhere on Earth as long as it is on land, and their transfer can only be unlawful because of the conditions of transfer, which are covered by other war crimes.

Violations related to Convention III other than nonrelease and nonrepatriation, such as depriving a person of POW status without the involvement of a tribunal prescribed by Article 5, or holding a person who is not a POW in the POW regime, will result in the application of the provisions discussed previously concerning the confinement of civilians under Convention IV. Indeed, a person who is not a POW is nearly always a protected civilian based on the operation of Convention IV.[48] A perpetrator who denies a person POW status without the involvement of

41. Protocol Additional to the Geneva Conventions of 12 August 1949, and Relating to the Protection of Victims of International Armed Conflicts art. 85(4)(b), June 8, 1977, 1125 U.N.T.S. 3 [hereinafter AP I]. The ICC Statute, *supra* note 1, does not incriminate this war crime.

42. ICC Statute, *supra* note 1, art. 8(2)(a).

43. Knut D°rmann, Elements of War Crimes under the Rome Statute of the International Criminal Court 118–23 (2002).

44. Deutscher Bundestag, 14 Wahlperiode, Drucksache 14/8524, 13 March 2002, Gesetzentwurf der Bundesregierung, Entwurf eines Gesetzes zur Einführung des Völkerstrafgesetzbuches, 29.

45. V°lkerstrafgesetzbuch [VStGB] [German Code of Crimes against International Law (CCAIL)] June 26, 2002, Federal Law Gazette I, 2254, art. 8(3)(1) (Ger.).

46. ICC Statute, *supra* note 1, art. 8(2)(a)(vii).

47. GC IV, *supra* note 1, art. 49.

48. *Id.*, arts. 4(1) and (4).

an Article 5 tribunal must classify him or her a civilian. If the perpetrator then detains such a person without respecting the procedural guarantees civilians benefit from, he or she commits the war crime of unlawful confinement.

Finally, those following the U.S. theory that some enemies in an IAC are neither POWs nor protected civilians but "unlawful combatants," "unprivileged belligerents," or "enemy combatants,"[49] could be committing the war crime of unlawful confinement if the victims are correctly classified as protected civilians. I will discuss the impact of a mistake in law later in the chapter. In any case, the U.S. approach does not, to my understanding, imply that a person who captured an "unlawful combatant" may determine on their own whether the captured person fulfills the conditions for unlawful combatancy. In U.S. practice, it is the commander of the person who captured an "unlawful combatant" who reviews the legality of the detention and may thus be potentially responsible for the war crime. Under the requirements I suggested previously, application of the relevant procedure[50] and membership in an enemy armed group would suffice to avoid an accusation of committing the war crime of unlawful confinement.

Unlawfulness of the treatment of protected persons?

The ICC Statute incriminates "imprisonment or other severe deprivation of physical liberty in violation of fundamental rules of international law" as a *crime against humanity*.[51] This is believed by some to comprise not only unjustified confinement and violations of procedural guarantees but also any detention in which the fundamental rules of humane treatment have been violated.[52] Thus, one may wonder whether the *war crime* of unlawful confinement too may, on its own, result from the inhumane treatment of a confined person. The formulation of the two crimes in the ICC Statute cited previously is different, but this does not really solve the issue. It is interesting to note that commentators on the ICC Statute's elements of the crime of unlawful confinement list under its legal basis, as already mentioned, provisions on the treatment of protected persons but, astonishingly, only those of Conventions I, II, and III, while on protected civilians, only provisions related to the admissibility of their internment and the applicable procedural guarantees.[53]

49. For a discussion, *see* Marco Sassòli, International Humanitarian Law: Rules, Controversies, and Solutions to Problems Arising in Warfare ¶¶ 8.116–8.120 (2d ed. 2024).

50. Office of the General Counsel, U.S. Department of Defense, Law of War Manual § 8.14.2. (rev. ed., Dec. 2016).

51. ICC Statute, *supra* note 1, art. 7(1)(e).

52. For details, jurisprudence, and scholarly opinions, *see* Philippe Currat, Les crimes contre l'humanité dans le Statut de la Cour pénale internationale 288–97 (2006).

53. Dörmann, *supra* note 44, at 118–23.

In my view, ill-treatment of detainees is covered by other war crimes, such as torture or inhuman or degrading treatment, including biological experiments, willfully causing great suffering, or serious injury to body or health, or acts of sexual and gender-based violence.[54] By contrast, crimes against humanity that are linked to the treatment of detainees are expressly limited to torture and sexual violence,[55] while "other inhumane acts of a similar character intentionally causing great suffering, or serious injury to body or to mental or physical health"[56] are only a subsidiary case, if no other crime against humanity is committed.[57] This militates against the possibility that the war crime of unlawful confinement also covers cases of inhumane treatment (by means other than the denial of procedural guarantees). In any case, the specific war crimes relating to the treatment of detainees constitute the *lex specialis* and an accused could not be sentenced based on the same conduct for unlawful confinement (if it included, contrary to my interpretation, the treatment of the person confined). The crime of unlawful confinement would have no materially distinct element from the specific treatment crimes, in other words, an element that would require proof of a fact not already required by the other specific incriminations.[58]

2.2 Extension to Non-International Armed Conflict?

The ICC Statute does not incriminate unlawful confinement as a war crime in NIAC. The ICTY, which had a general tendency to consider that war crimes under customary law are the same in IAC and NIAC, made only two exceptions, one of which was the unlawful confinement of civilians.[59]

More recently, however, both a Pre-Trial Judge and a Panel of the Court of Appeals Chamber of the Kosovo Specialist Chambers opined that arbitrary detention constituted a serious violation of IHL in NIAC and was criminalized by customary international law.[60] The same Panel confirmed its decision in a later

54. ICC Statute, *supra* note 1, arts. 8(2)(a)(ii) and (iii) as well as (b)(x), (xxi), and (xxii).

55. *Id.*, arts. 7(1)(f) and (g).

56. *Id.*, art. 7(1)(k).

57. Currat, *supra* note 52, at 572.

58. Delalić Appeals Judgment, *supra* note 5, at ¶ 412.

59. Delalić Trial Judgment, *supra* note 4, at ¶ 317.

60. Prosecutor v. Hashim Thaçi, Kedri Veseli, Rexhep Selimi, and Jakup Krasniqi, Case No. KSC-BC-2020-06, Decision on Motions Challenging the Jurisdiction of the Specialist Chambers ¶¶ 143–66 (Kosovo Specialist Chambers, Pre-Trial Judge, July 22, 2021) [hereinafter Thaçi, Pre-Trial Judge]; Prosecutor v. Hashim Thaçi, Kedri Veseli, Rexhep Selimi, and Jakup Krasniqi, Case No. KSC-BC-2020-06, Decision on Appeals Against Decision on Motions Challenging the Jurisdiction of the Specialist Chambers ¶¶ 85–111 (Kosovo Specialist Chambers, A Panel of the Court of Appeals Chamber, Dec. 23, 2021) [hereinafter Thaçi, Appeals Chamber].

Appeals Judgment.[61] The Pre-Trial Judge went as far as to consider that any detention by a non-State armed group was arbitrary because it lacked a legal basis (without excluding the possibility that an armed group could create such a basis).[62] The Panel of the Court of Appeals Chamber left open whether this conclusion was correct, but held that the Pre-Trial Judge's alternative justification was correct, that is, that any detention that did not comply with basic procedural guarantees was inhumane and a serious violation of Article 3 common to the Geneva Conventions and thus constituted a war crime.[63] On the facts of another case, the ICTY had earlier rejected the idea that prolonged unlawful detention could constitute cruel treatment.[64] The idea that unlawful confinement in a NIAC could be subsumed under the war crime of "cruel treatment" prohibited by Common Article 3 had, admittedly, been put forward in a 2004 academic article, but without a single sentence explaining the legality of detention in NIAC as such.[65] The Pre-Trial Judge and the Panel of the Kosovo Chambers also did not do so. As will be explained later, the main argument against an extension of the war crime of unlawful confinement to NIAC is that it remains highly controversial in IHL in which circumstances confinement outside a criminal procedure in NIAC is lawful or unlawful.

The Pre-Trial Judge mentioned another problem arising from such an extension, which relates to when confinement by an armed group is lawful under IHL. He wrote that an armed group must enforce

> where practically feasible . . . basic guarantees [that] include (i) the obligation to inform a person who is arrested of the reasons for arrest; (ii) the obligation to bring a person arrested on a criminal charge promptly before a judge or other competent authority; and (iii) the obligation to provide a

61. Prosecutor v. Salih Mustafa, Case No. KSC-CA-2023-02, Appeal Judgment ¶ 430-1 (Kosovo Specialist Chambers, A Panel of the Court of Appeals Chamber, Dec. 23, 2021).

62. Thaçi, Pre-Trial Judge, *supra* note 60, at ¶ 152.

63. Thaçi, Appeals Chamber, *supra* note 60, at ¶ 109; Customary International Humanitarian Law, *supra* note 31, at 306, 344; International Committee of the Red Cross, Convention (III) Relative to the Treatment of Prisoners of War, Geneva, 12 August 1949 ¶¶ 588–89 and 765 (2020), https://ihl-databases.icrc.org/en/ihl-treaties/gciii-1949 [hereinafter ICRC 2020 GC III Commentary]; Commentary on the Additional Protocols of 8 June 1977 to the Geneva Conventions of 12 August 1949 ¶¶ 4565–70 (Yves Sandoz, Christophe Swinarski, & Bruno Zimmermann eds., 1987); Prosecutor v. Zlatko Aleksovski, Case No. IT-95-14/1-T, Trial Judgment, ¶ 49 (Int'l Crim. Trib. for the former Yugoslavia June 25, 1999).

64. Prosecutor v. Limaj, Case No. IT-03-66-T, Judgment, ¶ 232 (Int'l Crim. Trib. for the former Yugoslavia Nov. 30, 2005).

65. Joanna Dingwall, *Unlawful Confinement as a War Crime: The Jurisprudence of the Yugoslav Tribunal and the Common Core of International Humanitarian Law Applicable to Contemporary Armed Conflicts*, 9 Journal of Conflict & Security Law 133–79 (2004).

person deprived of liberty with an opportunity to challenge the lawfulness of detention.[66]

To justify their rather revolutionary finding, both the Pre-Trial Judge and subsequently the Appeals Chamber relied on the commentary to Rule 99 of the International Committee of the Red Cross's (ICRC's) Customary IHL Study and the practice identified in its database,[67] neither of which deals specifically with detention by armed groups, nor distinguishes between the IHL and IHRL practice of States. Moreover, in the eighteen cases of State legislation criminalizing unlawful detention included in the Study—on which both the Pre-Trial Judge and the Appeals Chamber heavily relied in discussing the theoretically distinct question of whether customary IHL *criminalizes* unlawful detention in NIACs[68]—the ICRC considered such legislation to apply to NIAC if it did not state or imply the contrary (by referring to "grave breaches").[69] I simply note here that the German International Criminal Code, which normally applies grave breaches in NIACs, makes an exception for unlawful confinement.[70] The government justified this exception in its report to parliament based on the fact that the incrimination of such conduct under customary international law is not sufficiently certain.[71] The Swiss Criminal Code foresees application of the grave breaches incriminations, including unlawful confinement, to NIAC "unless the nature of the offence requires otherwise."[72] Scholarly opinion is divided on whether unlawful confinement may be considered a war crime in NIAC. Those in favor simply invoke the seriousness and widespread character of practices violative of the customary prohibition of arbitrary detention in NIACs.[73] Those who object mention, in my view correctly,

66. Thaçi, Pre-Trial Judge, *supra* note 60, at ¶ 154.

67. *Id.* at ¶¶ 151, 155; Thaçi, Appeals Chamber, *supra* note 60, at ¶ 99.

68. Thaçi, Pre-Trial Judge, *supra* note 60, at ¶ 159; Thaçi, Appeals Chamber, *supra* note 60, at ¶ 106.

69. *See* Customary International Humanitarian Law, *supra* note 32, at r. 99, ¶¶ 2554, 2562, 2563, 2565, 2572, 2576, 2579, 2598, 2605, 2606, 2607, 2608, 2611, 2613, 2615, 2616, 2623, 2624.

70. German Code, *supra* note 45, art. 8(3)(1).

71. Deutscher Bundestag, *supra* note 45, at 28, approving 9 Münchener Kommentar zum Strafgesetzbuch: StGB, Nebenstrafrecht III, Völkerstrafgesetzbuch (4th ed. 2022); Robin Geiss and Andreas Zimmermann, ¶ 230 at § 8 of the International Criminal Code, and Lars Berster, *Entscheidungsbesprechung: Leichenschändung als Kriegsverbrechen—BGH, Beschl. v. 8.9.2016 – StB 27/16*, 5 Zeitschrift für Internationale Strafrechtsdogmatik 264, at 265 (2017).

72. Schwizerisches Strafgesetzbuch [StGB] [Criminal Code] Dec. 21, 1937, 311.0., Art. 264b (Status as of 1 January 2015) (Federal law, Classified compilation) (Switz.).

73. Tornike Keshelava & Bruno Zehnder, *Art. 264c*, *in* Basler Kommentar, Strafrecht at 4746, ¶ 79 (Marcel Alexander Niggli & Hans Wiprächtiger eds., 4th ed. 2019).

the vague and controversial character of the criteria that make confinement in a NIAC unlawful.[74]

The Pre-Trial Judge and the Appeals Chamber[75] also refer to ICRC Guidelines,[76] which, in addition to IHL, draw on IHRL soft law instruments and jurisprudence that "should as a matter of policy and good practice be applied with respect to internment/administrative detention."[77]

The Appeals Chamber admitted that the number of national criminal codes which criminalize (I would add: could be possibly interpreted as criminalizing) unlawful detention in NIAC was limited.[78] However, it relied on a number of UN Security Council, UN General Assembly, and (former) UN Human Rights Commission resolutions. It conceded "that such resolutions do not expressly mention the criminalisation of arbitrary detention as a distinct crime in non-international armed conflicts." It considered, however, that they show that in 1998 "arbitrary or unlawful detention was already widely condemned and recognised as constituting a serious violation of IHL, including in non-international armed conflicts, and that such violation could trigger consequences in terms of criminal responsibility."[79] I would simply note that the latter part of the conclusion is based merely on the fact that a condemnation of practices of arbitrary detention was mentioned in these instruments. They were adopted in relation to the armed conflicts in the former Yugoslavia, whose classification as IAC or NIAC was always controversial, and included references to individual criminal responsibility without explicitly linking it to arbitrary detention.

If the crime of unlawful confinement is considered to apply in NIACs, one would first have to clarify whether the offense can be committed only against civilians, as is the case in IAC for the relevant grave breach of Geneva Convention IV and, as also explained previously, in the corresponding war crime under the ICC Statute.[80] If so, the problem is that civilians are not defined in the IHL of

74. Raphaël Jakob & Hikmat Maleh, *Art. 264c*, *in* Commentaire romand, Code Pénal II 1541, ¶ 80 (Alain Macaluso, Laurent Moreillon, & Nicolas Queloz eds., 2017).

75. Thaçi, Pre-Trial Judge, *supra* note 60, at ¶ 154; Thaçi, Appeals Chamber, *supra* note 60, at ¶¶ 96 and 99.

76. Jelena Pejic, *Procedural Principles and Safeguards for Internment/Administrative Detention in Armed Conflict and Other Situations of Violence*, 87 International Review of the Red Cross 375 (2005). In 2007, the ICRC adopted these principles and safeguards as its institutional position. *See* Procedural Principles and Safeguards for Internment/Administrative Detention in Armed Conflict and Other Situations of Violence, annexed as Annex 1 to ICRC, International Humanitarian Law and the Challenges of Contemporary Armed Conflicts (Report prepared by the ICRC for the 30th International Conference of the Red Cross and Red Crescent), U.N. Doc. No. 30IC/07/8.4 (2007).

77. *Id.* at 379.

78. Thaçi, Appeals Chamber, *supra* note 60, at ¶ 106.

79. *Id.* at ¶ 108.

80. This is what the first author suggesting the extension of the war crime of unlawful confinement, Dingwall, *supra* note 65, suggested without one sentence about who is a civilian in a NIAC.

NIAC; there are no combatants in NIAC, and civilians are a category in contradistinction to combatants in IACs. The ICRC has certainly tried to clarify who is *not* a civilian for targeting purposes, that is, who may only be attacked if and for such time as they directly participate in hostilities.[81] It has stressed, however, that such exclusion of members of an armed group with a continuous combat function does not apply when a person is in the power of a party to the conflict.[82] Indeed, nowhere does the IHL of NIAC use the term, or limit its protection to, "civilians" in terms of safeguards for detainees, who, by definition are persons no longer directly participating in hostilities.

Much more importantly, and in particular if one does not limit the offense to civilians, the difficulty is that the conditions under which confinement may be unlawful under the substantive IHL of NIAC are much more controversial than in IACs. The ICRC made an unsuccessful attempt to get States to clarify this question.[83] It is unsettled whether IHL offers a legal basis for interning enemies in NIAC, whether and what procedural guarantees must be respected in internment, and whether the answers to those questions for States also apply to armed groups.[84] Their members could obviously commit the crime of unlawful confinement if it is a deemed to be a war crime in NIAC, but every detention by an armed group in a NIAC, although unlawful under domestic law, cannot possibly constitute a war crime. In my view, members of armed groups cannot even be held to the same standards, influenced by IHRL, as those discussed hereafter for States.[85]

The treaty rules of IHL do not clarify when confinement in a NIAC is unlawful as neither Common Article 3 to the four Geneva Conventions, nor Additional Protocol II[86] mention when, on what grounds, and following what procedure a person may be interned (while providing anyone interned fundamental guarantees of humane treatment and anyone to be sentenced for a crime judicial guarantees).

According to the ICRC's Customary Law Study, which, as already mentioned, arguably cannot be divided into State practice under IHL and IHRL, customary law prohibits the arbitrary deprivation of liberty in both IACs and NIACs.[87] This rule is thus interpreted using significant references to IHRL. The study states that

81. International Committee of the Red Cross, Interpretive Guidance on the Notion of Direct Participation in Hostilities under International Humanitarian Law 27–36 (2009).

82. *Id.* at 12, notes 5 and 22, notes 15 and 17.

83. ICRC, Strengthening IHL, *supra* note 12.

84. For a discussion, *see* Sassòli, *supra* note 49, at ¶¶ 10.341–10.367.

85. *Id.* at ¶¶ 10.360–10.361.

86. Protocol Additional to the Geneva Conventions of 12 August 1949, and Relating to the Protection of Victims of Non-International Armed Conflicts, June 8, 1977, 1125 U.N.T.S. 609 [hereinafter Protocol II].

87. Customary International Humanitarian Law, *supra* note 31, at 344–52.

laws must previously establish the legal basis for internment and that there is an "obligation to provide a person deprived of liberty with an opportunity to challenge the lawfulness of detention."[88]

Given that States, and I would add non-State armed groups, regularly intern enemies in NIAC without trying them, the ICRC and many others, including the United States and the United Kingdom, argue that the customary law of NIACs provides an inherent legal basis for internment.[89] However, this alleged customary rule neither clarifies the admissible reasons for internment, nor the procedural guarantees benefiting those who may be interned. Therefore, the ICRC concedes that "a valid domestic and/or international legal source (depending on the type of NIAC involved), setting out the grounds and process for internment, must exist or be adopted in order to satisfy the principle of legality."[90] In my opinion, if the State must anyway legislate, there is no practical relevance in affirming that an inherent legal basis exists in customary law. Furthermore, a number of States confronted with an internal NIAC have adopted specific legislation authorizing the internment of fighters. Many of them also systematically consider captured rebels as criminals.[91] The fact that they often do not respect their fair trial guarantees is irrelevant for our discussion. Both internment based on security legislation and the detention of fighters as criminals demonstrate that no general practice and *opinio juris* exist according to which IHL alone would provide a sufficient legal basis.[92] Even a majority of States involved in extraterritorial NIACs took the view that they could not intern fighters beyond a limited period of time.[93]

Without clearly distinguishing it from customary law, some States and many scholars have reasoned by analogy to transpose the rules on internment governing in IAC to NIAC. Some have suggested applying the POW regime, including its

88. *Id.* at 348–51.

89. For the ICRC, *see* Jelena Pejic, *The Protective Scope of Common Article 3: More Than Meets the Eye*, 93 International Review of the Red Cross 189, 207 (2011). For the United States, *see* District Court for the District of Columbia, In Re: Guantánamo Bay Detainee Litigation, Respondents' Memorandum Regarding the Government's Authority Relative to Detainees Held at Guantánamo Bay, Misc. No. 08-442 TFH (2009), *available at* http://www.usdoj.gov/opa/documents/memo-re-det-auth.pdf. For the United Kingdom, *see* Serdar Mohammed & Others v. Secretary of State for Defence [2015] EWCA Civ. 843, Case Nos. A2/2014/1862; A2/2014/4084; A2/2014/4086, In the Court of Appeal (Civil Division), ¶ 174.

90. Pejic, *supra* note 89, at 207.

91. Jelena Plamenac, Unravelling Unlawful Confinement in Contemporary Armed Conflicts: Belligerents' Detention Practices in Afghanistan, Syria and Ukraine 81–145 (2022).

92. *See also* Els Debuf, Captured in War: Lawful Internment in Armed Conflict 469–72 (2013).

93. Sassòli, *supra* note 49, at ¶ 10.020.

absence of procedure for interning POWs.[94] Others, including the ICRC, have suggested that imperative reasons of security and an individual (administrative) procedure are required, as is the case for civilian internees in IAC.[95]

Even if it was clear with what rules of IAC the analogy must be drawn, the objection may be made that because of the principle of legality and the requirement of *nullum crimen sine lege*, a reasoning by analogy would not be permitted as a matter of international criminal law.[96] Under some domestic criminal laws, however, the prohibition of analogies covers only incriminations and not reasoning by analogy outside criminal law by means of which the criminalization of certain conduct could be extended (as is the case here).[97]

Regardless of the admissibility (or not) of analogies for war crimes incriminations, it is highly controversial whether the internment of members of an armed group by a government, and of government soldiers by an armed group, must be based on individual imperative security reasons to render it lawful, whether IHL suffices as a legal basis for such confinement, and whether and which procedures are necessary to decide upon possible confinement. Treaty law is silent. While some argue that a more flexible approach must be taken when assessing customary law in the field of IHL and even international criminal law,[98] State practice, both in words and deeds, on these questions is so divergent that one cannot claim that customary law provides the answers. I will discuss later the impact of such controversies on the possibility of convicting a person for violating these controversial rules. I will add here for the sake of completeness that the arguments made previously for IAC also negate the idea

94. This was the initial position of the United States during the George W. Bush administration. Marco Sassòli, *The International Legal Framework for Fighting Terrorists According to the Bush and Obama Administrations: Same or Different, Correct or Incorrect?*, 104 Proceedings of the Annual Meeting of the American Society of International Law 277 (2011). Until today, the United States asserts that it can detain (for example, in Guantánamo) individuals who are a part of or who provide substantial support to Al-Qaeda, the Taliban, and their "associated forces" in the same manner as POWs in an IAC without giving them the corresponding rights as they are by definition "unprivileged" combatants (as, indeed, no combatant privilege exists in NIACs). *See* Respondent's Memorandum, *supra* note 89.

95. *See* Pejic, *supra* note 76; 2020 GC III Commentary, *supra* note 63, at ¶ 761; Marco Sassòli & Laura Olson, *The Relationship Between International Humanitarian and Human Rights Law Where It Matters: Admissible Killing and Internment of Fighters in Non-International Armed Conflicts*, 90 International Review of the Red Cross 599, 624–27 (2008).

96. Silja Vöneky, *Analogy in International Law (2008), in* 1 Max-Planck Encyclopedia of Public International Law 374, ¶ 22 (Rüdiger Wolfrum ed., 2012); ICC Statute, *supra* note 1, art. 22(2).

97. For German law, *see* Stefanie Bock, *Das Völkerstrafgesetzbuch im Lichte des Grundgesetzes, in* Alternativen zur Freiheitsstrafe - 36. Strafverteidigertag Hannover 117, 133–34 (Strafverteidigervereinigungen ed., 2013).

98. *See* Dingwall, *supra* note 65, at 136–38.

that conditions of detention could, on their own, render a confinement unlawful in NIAC.[99]

3. *MENS REA*: WHAT MUST THE ACCUSED KNOW ABOUT THE "UNLAWFULNESS" OF THE CONFINEMENT?.

As with all crimes, to be convicted of the crime of unlawful confinement the accused must not only have engaged in the unlawful conduct but must also have done so with the necessary *mens rea*. Given that war crimes cannot be committed by negligence, this requires knowledge and intent. In particular, in view of the aforementioned controversies about when confinement in an armed conflict is lawful (under IHL and in light of its relationship with IHRL), this raises the question of when an accused may be said to know that the confinement he or she may be involved in is unlawful. I would not suggest that anyone with a different interpretation from mine regarding when confinement is lawful under IHL is a "criminal." However, it should be possible to convict perpetrators in obvious cases even if a prosecutor does not succeed in proving that the accused knew that the confinement he or she was involved in was unlawful, but deprived the victims of their liberty. There are several ways, discussed hereafter, out of this conundrum, none of which covers all the situations it should, but which could be combined and, in any case, cannot be "clinically" separated.

3.1 Mistake of Law?

When an accused does not know that a confinement in which they are involved is unlawful, this appears prima facie and at least in common language to be a mistake of law. International criminal law (and Anglo-American law generally) is very reluctant to recognize mistakes of law as a defense. In view of the abhorrence of the conduct criminalized, a reluctance to admit that a person could not know of the prohibition is understandable. The ICC Statute considers that mistakes of law are irrelevant whether or not they were avoidable,[100] except if they lead to the absence of the mental element (and even in that case they *may*, but will not always, exclude criminal responsibility).[101]

99. For the specific war crimes covering the treatment of detainees in NIACs, *see* ICC Statute, *supra* note 1, arts. 8(2)(c)(i) and (ii), as well as (e)(vi) and (xi).

100. Albin Eser, *Mental Elements—Mistake of Fact and Mistake of Law*, *in* The Rome Statute of the International Criminal Court 889, 942 (Antonio Cassese, Paola Gaeta, & John R.W.D. Jones eds., 2002).

101. ICC Statute, *supra* note 1, art. 32(2).

One should nevertheless recognize, despite the wording of the ICC Statute, that unavoidable mistakes of law operate to exclude criminal responsibility in this and similar cases.[102] Domestic courts take them into account by applying the general rules on mistakes of law provided for in their criminal law.[103] Even Anglo-American courts, generally reluctant to admit mistakes of law, make an exception if the perpetrator relied on an official statement or interpretation.[104] In the context of international criminal law such exclusion would, of course, only be admissible if the relevant interpretation was not manifestly unlawful. Having this in mind, it is submitted that even the ICC should recognize mistakes of law regardless of the wording of its Statute.[105] A perpetrator is obviously not obliged be an international law expert. It is sufficient that he or she was aware of the existence of legal requirements for the lawfulness of a confinement, and that his or her acts had a violative impact on respect for those norms.[106] International and domestic courts should, in view of the controversies discussed, adopt a broad understanding of when a mistake concerning the unlawfulness of a confinement is unavoidable: an accused cannot be expected to act as a judge and be capable of determining which of several interpretations of IHL defended by States and in scholarly writings is correct.

3.2 Mistake of Facts?

Contrary to what was aimed at in the *travaux préparatoires*,[107] the wording of Article 32(2) of the ICC Statute seems to consider a mistake of law relevant if it leads to the absence of the mental element. This means it will constitute a mistake of facts if it does not result from ignorance that an act is prohibited by the ICC Statute, but from a lack of knowledge of rules outside the ICC Statute, called "normative facts" (e.g., that an object is someone else's property).[108] Such a mistake on a noncriminal law (or a non-ICC Statute) rule should, in my view, be recognized as exonerating a person from criminal responsibility. This would be in

102. There is skepticism as to whether this corresponds to the *lex lata*. Nevertheless, Antonio Coco suggests this *de lege ferenda*. *See* Antonio Coco, The Defence of Mistake of Law in International Criminal Law 161–64 (2022).

103. *Id.* at 59–74.

104. For an overview of domestic practice, *see id.* at 86–92. Specifically for the United States, *see* American Law Institute, Model Penal Code and Commentaries, Part I: General Provisions, 1985, 274–76, concerning § 2.04 (3)(b).

105. Eser, *supra* note 100, at 944–46.

106. *Id.* at 927, referring to 924.

107. Coco, *supra* note 102, at 128–34.

108. Kai Ambos, Der Allgemeine Teil des Vᵒlkerstrafrechts, Ansᵃtze einer Dogmatisierung 814 (2002).

line with the common law approach under which (only) ignorance of a prohibition constitutes an irrelevant mistake of law.[109]

If the perpetrator is unaware of the normative element which makes the confinement he or she is accused of unlawful, this should be considered as excluding the *mens rea* under Article 32(2) of the ICC Statute because it leads to the absence of the mental element. The unlawfulness of the confinement could be qualified as a "legal material element" of the offense,[110] and not as part of the prohibition. A "legal material element" must be distinguished from a "factual normative element," such as "inhumane" (treatment), which only requires that the perpetrator understands the social significance of the relevant facts. Such a "legal material element" rather constitutes a genuine "legal element." If the perpetrator lacks knowledge of such an element, he or she lacks the necessary *mens rea*.[111] Indeed, in the *Delalic* case, the ICTY Appeals Chamber inferred from the evidence that the accused, Mucić, had or should have had knowledge of the prisoners' rights,[112] without which he would not have had the necessary *mens rea* and would have been acquitted.[113]

3.3 Violation of the Principle of Legality

A dynamic reference (i.e., a reference in a criminal law rule that adapts itself to the regulation of another branch) to controversial and developing rules of IHL on when a confinement is "unlawful" is equally problematic under the principle of legality,[114] which comprises the requirement that ambiguities be resolved in favor of the accused.[115] The principle is, however, less strict in international criminal law than in domestic law, and is difficult, if not impossible, to distinguish from the defense of a mistake of law in international law.[116] The ICTY has stated that "the principle *nullum crimen sine lege* does not prevent a court from interpreting and clarifying the elements of a particular crime."[117] This loosening of the principle

109. Kevin Jon Heller, *Mistake of Legal Element, the Common Law, and Article 32 of the Rome Statute: A Critical Analysis*, 6 Journal of International Criminal Justice 419, 427–29 (2008).

110. Coco, *supra* note 102, at 183.

111. *Id.* at 137–39; Otto Triffterer & Jens Ohlin, *Article 32— Mistake of Fact or Mistake of Law*, *in* Rome Statute of the International Criminal Court 1382, 1390 (Kai Ambos ed., 4th ed. 2022).

112. Delalić Appeals Judgment, *supra* note 5, at ¶ 380-6.

113. Coco, *supra* note 102, at 120.

114. For the difference between mistake of law and violation of the principle of legality, *see id.* at 54–55.

115. Bruce Broomhall, *Art. 22*, *in* Rome Statute, *supra* note 111, at 1149, 1164.

116. Coco, *supra* note 102, at 56–57.

117. Delalić Appeals Judgment, *supra* note 5, at ¶ 173.

of legality has been justified by one author based on the fact that IHL is "expert law."[118] Such reasoning has, in my view correctly, been criticized.[119] As regards the crime being discussed, one cannot expect that every soldier or camp commander must have been briefed about the circumstances in which an internment decision by an authority competent under domestic law must be deemed unlawful. In this context, it also bears recalling that both the ICTY and the International Criminal Tribunal for Rwanda (ICTR) have held that the offense of "violence to life and person" in violation of Common Article 3, contrary to the specific acts that follow in the text, lacks the necessary clarity on which to base a criminal conviction.[120] If this is so for a NIAC violation that is less controversial than the requirement of unlawfulness of confinement, it must be even more so in that case.

3.4 *In Dubio Pro Reo*

A criminal court can, in light of the preceding discussion, also have a legitimate doubt about the correct interpretation of the substantive law. Both in international and domestic criminal law opinions differ about whether the principle *in dubio pro reo* only concerns the facts or the interpretation of the substantive law as well.[121] Article 22 of the ICC Statute, for example, explicitly requires that "[i]n case of ambiguity, the definition [of a crime] shall be interpreted in favour of the person being investigated, prosecuted or convicted." It is true that this rule applies only to the ICC and only with respect to the definition of a crime.[122] However, the rules of international law defining when a confinement is unlawful are, in my view, part of the definition of the crime of unlawful confinement.

118. Gerhard Werle, *Völkerstrafrecht und Deutsches Völkerstrafgesetzbuch*, 67(8) JURISTENZEITUNG 373, 376 (2012).

119. Florian Schmidt, *Das Völkerstrafrecht als Herausforderung für das Gesetzlichkeitsprinzip? Untersuchungen zur Frage der Verletzung von Art. 103 Abs. 2 GG im Gewand der völkerstrafrechtsfreundlichen Auslegung*, 7–8 ZEITSCHRIFT FÜR INTERNATIONALE STRAFRECHTSDOGMATIK 349, 359 (2020).

120. Prosecutor v. Vasilljević, Case No. IT-98-32, Trial Chamber Judgment, ¶ 203 (Int'l Crim. Trib. for the former Yugoslavia Nov. 29, 2002); Prosecutor v. Ntakirutimana, Case No. ICTR-96-10 and 96-17-T, Trial Chamber Judgment, ¶ 861 (Int'l Crim. Trib. for Rwanda, Feb. 21, 2003), concerning Protocol II, *supra* note 85, art. 4(2).

121. Fabian Raimundo, *In Dubio Pro Reo*, *in* MAX PLANCK ENCYCLOPEDIA OF INTERNATIONAL PROCEDURAL LAW ¶¶ 17 and 37 (Hélène Ruiz-Fabri ed., 2020).

122. Broomhall, *supra* note 115, at 1163; Susan Lamb, *Nullum Crimen, nulla poena sine lege in International Criminal Law*, *in* THE ROME STATUTE, *supra* note 100, at 753.

3.5 Superior Orders

Finally, most of the differing State interpretations about when confinement in armed conflict is lawful have a link to the issue of superior orders. It remains controversial whether a defense of superior orders is acceptable in war crimes cases. The Charter of the Nuremberg Tribunal explicitly ruled it out as a defense, but allowed it to be considered a mitigating circumstance.[123] However, the Nuremberg Tribunal itself refused to take superior orders into account during sentencing. The ICTY and ICTR Statutes accepted superior orders as a mitigating circumstance only "if justice so requires."[124] In contrast, the ICC Statute accepts superior orders, including the orders of a government as a defense, if the following cumulative conditions are fulfilled: the subordinate was under a legal obligation to obey the order; they "did not know that the order was unlawful"; and the order was not manifestly unlawful.[125] We may assume that in many cases of confinement the person acting will not be following their own legal judgment, but will be doing so because they were instructed by a superior, by a legal adviser empowered under domestic law to give legal advice, or by domestic legislation.[126] In addition, it is only in rare circumstances that a confinement ordered by a competent authority in conformity with domestic law will be manifestly unlawful. As Yoram Dinstein has noted, "one should take into account the relative uncertainty of laws of war and other branches of international law."[127] This result also corresponds to the exception, already mentioned previously, which Anglo-American law makes in relation to its reluctance to recognize mistakes of law as relevant: such a mistake may be acceptable when the perpetrator relied on an official statement or interpretation.[128]

123. Charter of the International Military Tribunal art. 8, Aug. 8, 1945, 82 U.N.T.S. 284.

124. Statute of the International Criminal Tribunal for the former Yugoslavia art. 7(4), S.C. Res. 827 (May 25, 1993), adopting The Secretary-General Report Pursuant to Paragraph 2 of Security Council Resolution 808 Statute of the International Criminal Tribunal for Rwanda art. 6(3), S.C. Res. 955 annex (Nov. 8, 1994), *reprinted in* 33 INTERNATIONAL LEGAL MATERIALS 1598 (1994).

125. ICC Statute, *supra* note 1, art. 33(1).

126. The title of art. 33 of the ICC Statute, *supra* note 1, explicitly refers to "superior orders and prescription of law."

127. YORAM DINSTEIN, THE DEFENCE OF OBEDIENCE TO SUPERIOR ORDERS IN INTERNATIONAL LAW 33 (1965).

128. *See* American Law Institute, Model Penal Code, *supra* note 104.

4. PARTICIPATION

This is not the place to elaborate on the distinction between the perpetration of and aiding and assisting in a crime. Under the ICC Statute, both lead to criminal responsibility for the crime. A perpetrator is one who commits his or her own crime, that is, has control over its execution, while an aider and abettor contributes to someone else's crime. In the case of unlawful confinement, however, it has been held that a perpetrator is not only a person who decided to confine another but also someone who had the authority to release a detainee and failed to exercise that power.[129] This demonstrates that unlawful confinement constitutes a continuing crime, linked to the fact of the ICTY's acceptance of the concept of commission by omission,[130] but considerably reduces the possibility of aiding or abetting. Indeed, the ICTY has held that "even in relation to aiding and abetting, it must be established that the accused's assistance to the principal must have a substantial effect on the commission of the crime."[131] The tribunal rejected the idea "that any prison guard who is aware that there are detainees within the camp who were detained without reasonable grounds to suspect that they were a security risk is, without more, responsible for the crime of unlawful confinement."[132] It has opined that the crime can be committed only by

> those who are responsible for the detention in a more direct or complete sense, such as those who actually place an accused in detention . . . ; or who, having some powers over the place of detention, accept a civilian into detention . . . ; or who, having power or authority to release detainees, fail to do so despite knowledge that no reasonable grounds for their detention exist, or that any such reasons have ceased to exist.[133]

5. CONCURRENCE WITH OTHER OFFENSES

The ICTY has held, in my view correctly, that "multiple criminal convictions entered under different statutory provisions but based on the same conduct are permissible only if each statutory provision involved has a materially distinct element not contained in the other. An element is materially distinct from another if it requires proof of a fact not required by the other."[134] A defendant may therefore

129. Delalić Appeals Judgment, *supra* note 5, at ¶ 378.

130. Lars C. Berster, L.C., *"Duty to Act" and "Commission by Omission" in International Criminal Law*, 10(5) INTERNATIONAL CRIMINAL LAW REVIEW, 619–46 (2010).

131. Delalić Appeals Judgment, *supra* note 5, at ¶ 364.

132. *Id.*

133. *Id.* at ¶ 342.

134. *Id.* at ¶ 412.

be sentenced for the crime of unlawful confinement and for any of the specific war crimes related to the treatment of persons, including detainees. The crime of hostage-taking will,[135] however, prevail over that of unlawful confinement because it necessarily involves such confinement, but comprises further elements. As regards the crimes of unfair trial in IAC or (if the crime of unlawful confinement exists in NIAC) sentencing without a fair trial in NIAC,[136] both presuppose that a trial has occurred or at least that a "sentence" has been pronounced. As explained previously, the frequently resulting unlawfulness of confinement may, in my view, be charged cumulatively, as the interests protected by the respective crimes (fair trial rights and personal freedom) are different. One could, conversely, claim that if an accused did nothing more than sentence a civilian to imprisonment after an unfair trial, he or she may only be convicted for the denial of fair trial rights, which constitutes the *lex specialis*.[137] I would nevertheless point out that an unfair trial could also result in a fine or a death sentence. In the latter case, an additional element appears and a cumulative conviction for murder is in my view possible. I then fail to see why the unlawful confinement itself could not be considered an additional element separate from the act of unlawful sentencing.

6. CONCLUSION

The war crime of unlawful confinement raises particular interpretative difficulties. Not only are the underlying IHL rules on the requirements of lawful confinement controversial, particularly in NIAC, but unresolved questions of a purely international criminal law nature also arise: Who can be a perpetrator and who an aider and abettor of the crime? Can the principle of legality be respected in light of the controversies over the substantive IHL? Should the errors of an accused related to the unlawfulness of a given confinement exclude criminal responsibility or at least mitigate punishment? If so, should such errors be deemed a mistake of facts or of law, the latter of which is not normally recognized in international criminal law? Can a person be cumulatively convicted for the crime of unlawful confinement and a denial of fair trial rights leading to the confinement (provided criminal punishment can even fall under the war crime of unlawful confinement, as has been argued previously)? While expressing clear opinions on the answers to the underlying IHL controversies, I have nevertheless suggested a very restrictive and cautious approach to identifying the legal elements of the war crime. This is not in line with current tendencies in the jurisprudence and scholarship of either IHL or international criminal law, which are frequently conflated. My approach results from a desire to reserve the classification of "war crime" (a category

135. *See* ICC Statute, *supra* note 1, arts. 8(2)(a)(viii) and (c)(iii).

136. *Id.*, arts. 8(2)(a)(vi) and (c)(iv), respectively.

137. Jakob & Maleh, *supra* note 74, at ¶ 58.

that remains shockingly underprosecuted) for the most egregious violations of IHL. Unfortunately, it is clear that, even if one accepts a cautious approach, there have been numerous cases of the crime of "unlawful confinement" in IAC, ones in which the lawfulness of the underlying conduct simply cannot be argued as matter of IHL. As for NIACs, I will confess that my approach leaves lacunas in the criminalization of undoubtedly shocking conduct, but I believe that States should first agree on the IHL rules justifying internment in this type of conflict before criminal courts can try their violation.

17

Armed Forces' Investigations of IHL Violations Against Civilians

JENNIFER MADDOCKS* ■

1. INTRODUCTION

Armed forces face frequent criticism regarding their investigations into potential international humanitarian law (IHL) violations involving harm to civilians.[1] Such critiques are unsurprising. The conduct of investigations in situations of armed conflict is an inherently challenging task. This chapter explores that challenge, examining the difficult balance that armed forces must strike between military necessity, which may preclude a detailed and impartial investigation, and the principle of humanity from which the investigatory duty stems.[2] Considerations of humanity, including accountability, justice for victims, and learning lessons to mitigate future incidents of civilian harm, call for higher investigatory standards. These considerations, however, must be weighed against the steps that States' armed forces can feasibly take in an ongoing armed conflict.

* Jennifer Maddocks is an Assistant Professor in the Department of Law and Philosophy at the United States Military Academy.

1. *See, e.g.*, Susannah George, *As U.S. Air War in Afghanistan Surged, Investigations into Civilian Harm Plunged*, WASHINGTON POST (Sept. 4, 2020), https://www.washingtonpost.com/world/2020/09/04/afghanistan-civilian-casualties-us-airstrikes/; Azmat Khan et al., *Documents Reveal Basic Flaws in Pentagon Dismissals of Civilian Casualty Claims*, NEW YORK TIMES (Dec. 31, 2021), https://www.nytimes.com/2021/12/31/us/pentagon-airstrikes-syria-iraq.html.

2. Regarding the balance between military necessity and humanity in IHL, *see generally* Michael N. Schmitt, *Military Necessity and Humanity in International Humanitarian Law: Preserving the Delicate Balance*, 50 VIRGINIA JOURNAL OF INTERNATIONAL LAW 795 (2010).

Jennifer Maddocks, *Armed Forces' Investigations of IHL Violations Against Civilians* In: *Civilian Protection in Armed Conflict*. Edited by: Jelena Pejic and Captain Margaret Kotlik, Oxford University Press.
 DOI: 10.1093/oso/9780197793176.003.0017

Allegations of civilian harm often relate to incidents during warfighting, for example, because the State caused civilian casualties when conducting attacks. Alternatively, they might relate to a State's security operations, for instance, if the State fails to treat civilians in occupied territory in accordance with the provisions of the Fourth Geneva Convention.[3] Whatever the context surrounding the allegations, the armed forces must decide whether, and if so how, to investigate.

These determinations are not straightforward. Any investigation necessarily takes valuable resources away from other military missions. It might also face significant hurdles due to the ongoing armed conflict. For instance, the location of the incident might be behind enemy lines, witnesses might have fled or be unwilling to cooperate, and the armed forces might lack the requisite manpower or the expertise to conduct an effective investigation.

Further complexity stems from the character of IHL and the balance it seeks between humanity and military necessity.[4] Reflecting this balance, not every allegation of civilian harm involves a possible IHL violation requiring investigation. For example, a commander might have reasonable grounds to conclude that the civilians concerned had forfeited their protection from attack by directly participating in hostilities.[5] In situations such as this, the armed forces' investigatory obligations, if any, may be far from clear.

This chapter considers when and how States must investigate allegations of IHL violations against civilians, assessing not only States' obligations under IHL but also those arising under international human rights law (IHRL) and the Rome Statute of the International Criminal Court (ICC). In practice, it is these latter bodies of law that impose the highest investigatory burden on States. The chapter then considers the challenges States might face in meeting those investigative obligations. Finally, it assesses how States might balance compliance with the requisite investigatory standards against military considerations, including the necessity to accomplish the mission.

2. WHEN TO INITIATE AN INVESTIGATION

When States become aware of potential IHL violations against civilians, either from internal reports or external sources, they must assess the allegation and decide whether to launch an investigation. A first consideration is whether the

3. Convention (IV) Relative to the Protection of Civilian Persons in Time of War, Aug. 12, 1949, 6 U.S.T. 3516, 75 U.N.T.S. 287 [hereinafter GC IV].

4. Schmitt, *supra* note 2.

5. Protocol Additional to the Geneva Conventions of 12 August 1949, and Relating to the Protection of Victims of International Armed Conflicts art. 51(3), June 8, 1977, 1125 U.N.T.S. 3 [hereinafter AP I].

allegation is credible. If it is not, no investigation is required.[6] The armed forces' records might indicate, for instance, that none of its units were present in the area where the alleged violation took place.

This section examines when international law places a legal obligation on States to investigate, focusing first on IHL before turning to IHRL and the ICC Statute. It also assesses the practical or policy imperatives in favor of investigating, even in the absence of any duty imposed by law.

2.1 The Duty to Investigate Under IHL

The obligation on States to investigate IHL violations derives from the four Geneva Conventions and their Additional Protocol I (AP I),[7] as well as from customary international law.[8] The 1949 Geneva Conventions introduced the concept of "grave breaches," meaning war crimes of such seriousness as to admit universal jurisdiction.[9] While the Conventions do not refer explicitly to any duty to investigate grave breaches, this is an essential element of the obligation to "search for" potential offenders.[10]

The duty to investigate extends beyond grave breaches to encompass all war crimes.[11] This categorization includes all serious violations of the laws and

6. Michael N. Schmitt, *Investigating Violations of International Law in Armed Conflict*, 2 Harvard National Security Journal 31, 39 (2011).

7. Convention (I) for the Amelioration of the Condition of the Wounded and Sick in the Armed Forces in the Field art. 49, Aug. 12, 1949, 6 U.S.T. 3114, 75 U.N.T.S. 31 [hereinafter GC I]; Convention (II) for the Amelioration of the Condition of the Wounded, Sick, and Shipwrecked Members of Armed Forces at Sea art. 50, Aug. 12, 1949, 6 U.S.T. 3217, 75 U.N.T.S. 85 [hereinafter GC II]; Convention (III) Relative to the Treatment of Prisoners of War art. 129, Aug. 12, 1949, 6 U.S.T. 3316, 75 U.N.T.S. 135 [hereinafter GC III]; GC IV, *supra* note 3, art. 146; AP I, *supra* note 5, art. 87.

8. 1 Customary International Humanitarian Law, r. 158 (Jean-Marie Henckaerts & Louise Doswald-Beck eds., 2005) [hereinafter Customary IHL]. *See also* Schmitt, *supra* note 6, at 44–46.

9. International Committee of the Red Cross, Commentary on the First Geneva Convention: Convention (I) for the Amelioration of the Condition of the Wounded and Sick in the Armed Forces in the Field ¶¶ 2863–65 (2016), https://ihl-databases.icrc.org/en/ihl-treaties/gci-1949/article-49/commentary/2016?activeTab=undefined [hereinafter 2016 Commentary to GC I]. The grave breaches are articulated in other articles of the conventions. *See* GC I, *supra* note 7, art. 50; GC II, *supra* note 7, art. 51; GC III, *supra* note 7, art. 130; GC IV, *supra* note 3, art. 147.

10. Schmitt, *supra* note 6, at 38. *See also* 2016 Commentary to GC I, *supra* note 9, ¶¶ 2860, 2891, 2859.

11. Customary IHL, *supra* note 8, at r. 158, *citing* the military manuals of Australia, Cameroon, Canada, Colombia, Ecuador, Germany, Netherlands, Switzerland, United Kingdom, United States, and Yugoslavia. *See id.* at n. 212.

customs of war that give rise to individual criminal responsibility.[12] In its study of customary IHL, the International Committee of the Red Cross (ICRC) concluded that, in practice, IHL violations are treated as serious, and therefore as war crimes, if they endanger protected persons or objects or if they breach important values.[13] As such, the majority of allegations involving harm to civilians are likely to constitute war crimes, if proven, and give rise to a clear duty to investigate in both international and non-international armed conflict.[14]

Not all IHL violations, however, amount to war crimes. For instance, IHL imposes an obligation on States to take feasible precautions in attack,[15] but a failure to do so does not lead to individual criminal responsibility. Legal scholars increasingly argue that even if the alleged conduct does not amount to a war crime, an investigative duty arises.[16] This argument stems from the obligation articulated in the Geneva Conventions and AP I to "suppress" IHL violations.[17] While States must "repress" grave breaches,[18] meaning they must take measures to include criminal prosecutions, the term "suppress" denotes a wider range of steps that States may take to ensure that other IHL violations cease and do not reoccur.[19] To fulfill this obligation, States must ascertain whether their armed forces violated

12. Customary IHL, *supra* note 8, at r. 156. *See also* Rome Statute of the International Criminal Court art. 8, July 17, 1998, 2187 U.N.T.S. 90 [hereinafter Rome Statute].

13. Customary IHL, *supra* note 8, r. 156.

14. *Id.* at r. 158; Schmitt, *supra* note 6, at 47–48. *See also* Geneva Academy of International Humanitarian Law and Human Rights, International Committee of the Red Cross, Guidelines on Investigating Violations of International Humanitarian Law: Law, Policy, and Good Practice ¶ 13 (Sept. 2019) [hereinafter Guidelines].

15. AP I, *supra* note 5, art. 57.

16. *See, e.g.*, Amichai Cohen & Yuval Shany, *Beyond the Grave Breaches Regime: The Duty to Investigate Alleged Violations of International Law Governing Armed Conflicts*, *in* Yearbook of International Humanitarian Law 2011 (Michael N. Schmitt & Louise Arimatsu eds., 2011); Amy M.L. Tan, *The Duty to Investigate Alleged Violations of International Humanitarian Law: Outdated Deference to an Intentional Accountability Problem*, 49 International Law and Politics 181 (2016); Alon Margalit, *The Duty to Investigate Civilian Casualties During Armed Conflict and its Implementation in Practice*, *in* 2013 Yearbook of International Humanitarian Law 161–62 (Terry Gill et al., eds., 2013); Mark Lattimer, *The Duty in International Law to Investigate Civilian Deaths in Armed Conflict*, *in* The Grey Zone: Civilian Protection Between Human Rights and the Laws of War (Mark Lattimer & Philippe Sands eds., 2018).

17. GC I, *supra* note 7, art. 49; GC II, *supra* note 7, art. 50; GC III, *supra* note 7, art. 129; GC IV, *supra* note 3, art. 146; AP I, *supra* note 5, art. 86.

18. AP I, *supra* note 5, art. 86.

19. New Rules for Victims of Armed Conflicts: Commentary on the Two 1977 Protocols Additional to the Geneva Conventions of 1949, at 594–95 (2d ed. revision by Michael Bothe, 2013); Guidelines, *supra* note 14, 5, ¶ 16.

IHL and, if they did, why the breach occurred and how similar breaches can be prevented in future. By necessity, this requires some form of investigation.[20]

Consistent with this approach, the 2019 *Guidelines on Investigating Violations of International Humanitarian Law*, formulated by the ICRC and the Geneva Academy of IHL and Human Rights, do not make any distinction between the investigative requirements applicable to war crimes and those relevant to other IHL violations.[21] This broader stance regarding the duty to investigate aligns with States' more general obligations under IHL, including the duty to "respect and to ensure respect" for IHL and to take "constant care" to spare the civilian population.[22] Whether States accept that the legal duty to investigate applies to all alleged IHL violations, or only potential war crimes, however, remains unclear.[23]

In certain scenarios, IHL imposes specific obligations on States to investigate civilian harm even when there is no suggestion of any IHL violation. The first arises when interned civilians are killed, seriously injured, or die due to unknown causes.[24] In these circumstances, IHL requires the detaining power to launch "an official enquiry" and, if this indicates someone was at fault, to "take all necessary steps to ensure the prosecution of the person or persons responsible."[25]

Second, States party to a conflict must "search for the persons who have been reported missing by an adverse party."[26] This duty applies "as soon as circumstances permit, and at the latest from the end of active hostilities"[27] and requires some form of investigation to determine the individuals' whereabouts.[28]

20. 2 Jacob Turkel et al., The Public Commission to Examine the Maritime Incident of 31 May 2010, at 99 (2011), https://www.gov.il/en/departments/general/turkel_committee [hereinafter Turkel Commission Second Report]. Regarding the differences between criminal and administrative investigations, *see infra* section 3.4.

21. Guidelines, *supra* note 14, at 11, ¶ 47.

22. GC I, *supra* note 7, art. 1; AP I, *supra* note 5, arts. 1, 57. *See also* Margalit, *supra* note 16, at 161; Cohen & Shany, *supra* note 16, at 47–48; Tan, *supra* note 16, at 204–05.

23. States' military manuals take different approaches to the issue. *See, e.g.*, Office of the General Counsel, U.S. Department of Defense, Law of War Manual § 18.13.1 (rev. ed., Dec. 2016) [hereinafter DoD Law of War Manual]; Ministère des Armées, Manuel de Droit des Opérations Militaires 98–99, 324 (2022) (Fr.), https://www.defense.gouv.fr/sga/droit-defense/droit-conflits-armes. The United States' manual refers to "duties to investigate reports of alleged violations of the laws of war," whereas the French manual focuses on the narrower duty to investigate war crimes.

24. GC IV, *supra* note 3, art. 131. An equivalent investigative obligation arises in respect of prisoners of war. *See* GC III, *supra* note 7, art. 121.

25. GC IV, *supra* note 3, art. 131.

26. AP I, *supra* note 5, art. 33. *See also* Customary IHL, *supra* note 8, r. 117.

27. AP I, *supra* note 5, art. 33.

28. Commentary on the Additional Protocols of 8 June 1977 to the Geneva Conventions of 12 August 1949, ¶ 1224 (Yves Sandoz, Christophe Swinarski, & Bruno Zimmermann eds., 1987).

2.2 The Impact of Other Bodies of International Law

The duty to investigate allegations of civilian harm derives not only from IHL but also from other bodies of international law. In particular, the Rome Statute of the ICC requires States party to investigate allegations that could amount to genocide, war crimes, or crimes against humanity.[29] If a State fails to properly investigate, it runs the risk that the ICC could initiate its own investigations and prosecutions and that a member of its own armed forces could be convicted of international crimes by the ICC.

This provides a clear incentive to States that are party to the Rome Statute to ensure their armed forces effectively investigate potential international law violations. Otherwise, the State could face a lengthy and detailed investigation by the ICC's Office of the Prosecutor (OTP), as occurred in respect of the United Kingdom's operations in Iraq.[30] While the OTP ultimately closed its preliminary examination, this happened only after the United Kingdom had established an independent investigatory body, at considerable public expense, to investigate the allegations.[31]

The impact of IHRL is even greater. This body of law can require States to initiate an investigation into allegations of civilian harm, even when there is no suggestion of any international law violation. While the United States maintains that IHRL has no extraterritorial application and therefore does not operate in armed conflicts occurring outside its territory,[32] human rights bodies have taken a different view.[33] Notably, the European Court of Human Rights (ECtHR) has developed extensive jurisprudence regarding the duty to investigate during armed conflict.[34] However, the circumstances in which IHRL imposes investigatory obligations on States depends on several factors, including the human rights treaties to which the State is a party and the context in which the incident occurs.

Regarding the latter criterion, the Turkel Commission, which examined Israel's investigative obligations, differentiated between incidents occurring during active hostilities and those arising during law enforcement activities, such as policing operations in occupied territory.[35] Whereas deaths or injuries caused to civilians

29. Rome Statute, *supra* note 12, art. 17.

30. International Criminal Court Office of the Prosecutor, Situation in Iraq/UK Final Report (Dec. 9, 2020), https://www.icc-cpi.int/sites/default/files/itemsDocuments/201209-otp-final-report-iraq-uk-eng.pdf [hereinafter ICC Iraq/UK Final Report].

31. *Id. See also infra* section 3.1.

32. Turkel Commission Second Report, *supra* note 20, at 494–96.

33. *See, e.g.*, U.N. Human Rights Comm., *General Comment No. 36: Article 6: Right to Life*, ¶¶ 63–64, U.N. Doc. CCPR/C/CG/36 (Sept. 3, 2019) [hereinafter General Comment 36].

34. *See, e.g.*, Al-Skeini and Others v. United Kingdom, App. No. 55721/07 (2011) (ECtHR), http://hudoc.echr.coe.int/eng?i=001-105606; Georgia v. Russia (II), App. No. 38263/08 (2021) (ECtHR); Hanan v. Germany, App. No. 4871/16 (2021) (ECtHR).

35. Turkel Commission Second Report, *supra* note 20, at 100–06.

in the conduct of hostilities are governed by the *lex specialis* of IHL, those arising as a result of law enforcement activities are governed by the *lex generalis* of IHRL.[36] Relying on this distinction, the commission concluded that when IHRL applies, the mere occurrence of civilian casualties leads to an automatic duty to investigate even in the absence of any allegation of wrongdoing. Conversely, during active hostilities, the investigative duty arises only when there is a credible allegation of IHL violations.[37]

The UN Human Rights Committee, which interprets and monitors States' compliance with the International Covenant on Civil and Political Rights (ICCPR), takes a similar approach. In its General Comment 36 relating to the right to life, the committee asserts that States party to the ICCPR must investigate "lethal incidents and other life-threatening incidents" involving "law enforcement officials, including soldiers charged with law enforcement missions."[38] However, in situations of armed conflicts, "[u]se of lethal force consistent with [IHL] and other applicable international law norms is, in general, not arbitrary."[39] Such uses of force, therefore, do not violate the right to life and do not require investigation unless there is evidence of conduct unlawful under IHL.[40]

This binary distinction between warfighting and law enforcement operations is appealing, yet potentially problematic for States' armed forces. As the United Kingdom's Henriques Review[41] observed, the catch-all reference to law enforcement or "security operations" can encompass a wide range of military activities, from mounting patrols and vehicle checkpoints, to containing violent demonstrations, through to "hard knock" operations to detain those suspected of involvement in attacks on coalition forces.[42] Depending on the circumstances, it

36. *Id.*

37. *Id.*

38. General Comment 36, *supra* note 33, ¶ 13.

39. *Id.* at ¶ 64.

40. *Id.* The Minnesota Protocol, which General Comment 36 cites in this context, asserts that "[w]here, during the conduct of hostilities, it appears that casualties have resulted from an attack, a post-operation assessment should be conducted to establish the facts." A full investigation if required only when there is evidence of unlawful conduct. General Comment 36, *supra* note 33, at ¶ 64, n. 261, *citing* U.N. Human Rights Office of the High Commissioner, *The Minnesota Protocol on the Investigation of Potentially Unlawful Death*, ¶ 22 (2016), https://www.ohchr.org/sites/default/files/Documents/Publications/MinnesotaProtocol.pdf.

41. The U.K. Defence Secretary commissioned this review to consider the framework, processes, and skills that the United Kingdom's service justice system requires when addressing allegations of wrongdoing against U.K. forces on overseas operations. *See* Report of the Henriques Review into the Framework, Processes and Skills that the Service Justice System Required for Overseas Operations (Oct. 21, 2021), https://www.gov.uk/government/publications/sir-richard-henriques-review-report-on-strengthening-the-service-justice-system [hereinafter Henriques Review].

42. *Id.* at 22.

may be far from easy to categorize an incident as "warfighting" rather than "law enforcement" and therefore conclude, in the absence of any suggestion that IHL was violated, that no investigation is required.

Moreover, not all human rights bodies follow this binary approach. The ECtHR has ruled that the duty to investigate "continues to apply in difficult security conditions, including in the context of armed conflict."[43] For the ECtHR, the existence of an investigatory duty does not depend upon any distinction between law enforcement and warfighting but rather on whether the incident to be investigated falls under the State's jurisdiction.[44] When a State operates outside its own territory, its extraterritorial jurisdiction normally arises in two circumstances: first, when the State exerts control over the area concerned; and second, when the State's agents exercise authority and control over the victims of the alleged violation.[45]

In the "context of chaos" associated with active hostilities, a State is unlikely to exercise effective control over the combat area, meaning that the events do not fall within its jurisdiction, and it is not subject to the substantive obligation to respect and protect individuals' right to life.[46] Yet the ECtHR has formulated a looser jurisdictional test regarding the separate procedural element of the right to life, from which the duty to investigate arises. A jurisdictional link for investigatory purposes can be established due to "special features" of the case that are not linked to the State's exercise of control.[47] Such "special features" might include the fact that the State has exclusive criminal law jurisdiction over the armed forces personnel involved in the incident or that the territorial State is unable to investigate effectively.[48]

For States party to the European Convention on Human Rights (ECHR), "special features" such as these will often be present whenever their armed forces cause civilian harm during armed conflict.[49] Alternatively, if they are not and the State declines to investigate, there is always the possibility that the ECtHR might identify new "special features," given the Court's failure to list these definitively.[50]

43. *Al-Skeini*, *supra* note 34, ¶ 164.

44. *See, e.g.*, *id.* at ¶¶ 130–50.

45. For a summary of cases addressing extraterritorial jurisdiction under the ECHR, *see, e.g.*, ECtHR Press Unit, *Extra-Territorial Jurisdiction of States Parties to the European Convention on Human Rights* (July 2018), https://www.echr.coe.int/documents/d/echr/fs_extra-territorial_jurisdiction_eng#.

46. *Georgia v. Russia (II)*, *supra* note 34, at ¶¶ 126, 137–38.

47. *Id.* at ¶¶ 330–31; *Hanan v. Germany*, *supra* note 34, at ¶¶ 137–39.

48. *See, e.g.*, *Georgia v. Russia (II)*, *supra* note 34, at ¶¶ 137–38; *Hanan v. Germany*, *supra* note 34, at ¶¶ 137–39.

49. *See* Floris Tan & Marten Zwanenburg, *One Step Forward, Two Steps Back? Georgia v Russia (II), European Court of Human Rights Appl No 38263/08*, 22 Melbourne Journal of International Law 136 (2021).

50. *See Hanan v. Germany*, *supra* note 34, ¶ 136.

In the *Georgia v. Russia (II)* case, the ECtHR concluded that although events occurring during the active phase of hostilities fell outside Russia's jurisdiction, the State was nevertheless under a duty to investigate those same events due to "special features" of the case.[51] The Court's jurisprudence on this issue leads to a lack of legal certainty and means that in practice, European States would be well advised to initiate an investigation whenever they become aware of credible allegations of civilian deaths or other serious forms of harm involving their armed forces, even in the absence of any suggestion of wrongdoing.[52]

In a similar manner, the American Convention on Human Rights (ACHR) imposes clear investigative duties on States party that continue to apply during armed conflict.[53] Compliance with these obligations is particularly important for those States that have accepted the contentious jurisdiction of the Inter-American Court (IACtHR). Once States become aware of a potential violation of the ACHR, they must immediately initiate "a genuine, impartial and effective investigation . . . ."[54] If they fail to do so, the IACtHR may order that a full investigation is conducted, even years after the event, as a reparative measure.[55]

Due to the strength of their enforcement mechanisms, the ECHR, the ACHR, and the ICC Statute place far greater investigative pressure on States party to those treaties than IHL. The same impact is not felt by States party to the ICCPR or the African Charter on Human and Peoples' Rights due to the weakness of the respective enforcement mechanisms.[56] Yet it is not only a sense of legal obligation that leads States to initiate investigations into civilian harm. Practical or policy considerations may additionally cause States to investigate, often in broader circumstances than the law strictly requires.

51. *Georgia v. Russia (II)*, *supra* note 34, ¶¶ 329–332. *See also* Marko Milanović, *Georgia v. Russia No. 2: The European Court's Resurrection of Bankovic in the Contexts of Chaos*, EJIL: Talk! (Jan. 25, 2021), https://www.ejiltalk.org/georgia-v-russia-no-2-the-european-courts-resurrection-of-bankovic-in-the-contexts-of-chaos/.

52. *See Al-Skeini*, *supra* note 34, ¶ 163. For a critique of the "special features" test, *see Hanan v. Germany*, *supra* note 34, Joint Partly Dissenting Opinion of Judges Grozev, Ranzoni and Eicke.

53. *See generally* Giovanna Maria Frisso, *The Duty to Investigate Violations of the Right to Life in Armed Conflicts in the Jurisprudence of the Inter-American Court of Human Rights*, 51(2) Israel Law Review 169 (2018).

54. Ituango Massacres v. Colombia, Inter-Amer Comm'n H.R., Report No. 148 (ser. C), ¶ 296 (2006).

55. Frisso, *supra* note 53, at 174, 189.

56. *See generally* European Commission for Democracy Through Law (Venice Commission), Report on the Implementation of International Human Rights Treaties in Domestic Law (2014) [hereinafter Venice Commission]; Martin Faix & Ayyoub Jamali, *Is the African Court on Human and Peoples' Rights in an Existential Crisis?*, 40 Netherlands Quarterly of Human Rights 3 (2022); Lilian Chenwi, *Successes of African Human Rights Court Undermined by Resistance from States*, The Conversation (Aug. 31, 2021), https://thec

2.3 Policy Considerations

There are good reasons for States to investigate allegations of civilian harm even if they are under no strict legal obligation to do so. Not only can this enhance a State's military effectiveness by assisting in the identification of good practice and lessons learned; it is also an essential element of military discipline.[57] To maintain effective command and control, soldiers must know that any incidents of concern will be promptly and appropriately investigated.

Investigating incidents of civilian harm can have the additional benefit of increasing trust in the military, both within its own population and in the territory where it is operating.[58] More broadly, demonstrating IHL compliance is crucial to maintaining international legitimacy and the support of allies. This is apparent from the conflict in Ukraine, where the United States closely tracked alleged IHL violations involving Ukrainian troops, emphasizing that "all parties to the conflict must abide by international law or face the consequences."[59] The considerable materiel and other support provided to Ukraine was thus contingent, at least to some extent, on the State's IHL compliance, including its investigation of potential violations. Meanwhile, Russia's seeming disregard for international law, together with its failure to investigate and prosecute those responsible for the many alleged IHL violations, served to cement the pro-Ukraine alliance.[60]

Initiating timely investigations can help ensure that States are well placed to address any future allegations that may arise. It may not be evident at the time an incident occurs that there was any breach of IHL. This might become apparent only later when an external organization raises an allegation. However, if the armed forces did not collect and retain evidence at the time of the incident, the State might not be able to prove that its personnel acted in accordance with IHL. Thus, the conclusions of the Dutch civil court in 2022 regarding the Netherlands' military operations in Afghanistan serve as a stark warning to States: if they do not

onversation.com/successes-of-african-human-rights-court-undermined-by-resistance-from-states-166454.

57. GUIDELINES, *supra* note 14, at 8, ¶ 26.

58. *Id.* at 8, ¶ 27. *See also* Mark Kersten, *It's in Ukraine's Interest to Prosecute Its Own Alleged Crimes*, AL JAZEERA (June 10, 2022), https://www.aljazeera.com/opinions/2022/6/10/its-in-kyivs-interest-to-investigate-war-crimes-by-ukrainians.

59. Simon Lewis & Humeyra Pamuk, *U.S. Monitoring Alleged Executions in Ukraine, Says War Crimes Envoy*, REUTERS (Nov. 21, 2022), https://www.reuters.com/world/europe/us-monitoring-alleged-executions-ukraine-says-war-crimes-envoy-2022-11-21/.

60. Michael N. Schmitt, *Year Ahead—Does International Law Still Matter in Ukraine?*, ARTICLES OF WAR (Jan. 3, 2023), https://lieber.westpoint.edu/does-international-law-still-matter-in-ukraine/.

have the evidence to prove that they complied with IHL, a court might conclude otherwise.[61]

Considerations such as these help explain why armed forces often initiate investigations in circumstances when they may not be legally obliged to do so. New Zealand's policy, for instance, requires that all "possibly credible" allegations of "critical civilian harm" must be investigated, "regardless of whether it is the result of lawful or unlawful military activity." The impact of this policy is extended through its broad definition of "critical civilian harm," which encompasses not only civilian deaths or injuries but also "any significant degradation of quality of life imposed on a community, including that caused through residual effects."[62]

Each State has its own policy regarding the initiation of investigations.[63] In the counterinsurgency fights of recent decades, however, a common theme has emerged whereby States often investigate allegations of civilian harm even if there is no suggestion that war crimes were committed.[64] Initiating investigations in a broad range of circumstances makes sense, due to both legal and policy considerations. Yet it places a heavy burden on States' armed forces, which may be particularly difficult to bear during large-scale combat operations involving high numbers of civilian casualties.[65] The precise weight of this burden depends on the surrounding circumstances, as well as the investigatory standards the State is required to meet.

3. INVESTIGATORY STANDARDS

Once States decide to initiate an investigation, they face further choices regarding the scope of the investigation, the investigative steps they should take, and who should carry them out. Again, it is not only IHL that impacts this decision-making process. While IHL allows States a considerable discretion in fulfilling their investigatory duties, IHRL and the ICC Statute are far more prescriptive regarding the investigative standards that States must satisfy. The type of investigation also

61. Marten Zwanenburg, *Dutch Judgment on IHL Compliance in Chora District, Afghanistan*, Articles of War (Dec. 19, 2022), https://lieber.westpoint.edu/dutch-judgment-ihl-compliance-chora-district-afghanistan/; Marieke de Hoon, *Dutch Court, Applying IHL, Delivers Civil Judgment for Victims of 2007 Afghanistan Attack*, Just Security (Feb. 27, 2023), https://www.justsecurity.org/85223/dutch-court-applying-ihl-delivers-civil-judgment-for-victims-of-2007-afghanistan-attack/.

62. Chief of Defence Force, Defence Force Order 35, New Zealand Defence Force Response to Civilian Harm 3-3 ¶ 3.02(3) (Jan. 21, 2021), https://www.nzdf.mil.nz/assets/Uploads/DocumentLibrary/dfo_35.pdf.

63. *See, e.g.*, *id.*; DoD Law of War Manual, *supra* note 23, §§ 18.13.1–18.13.2 (rev. ed., Dec. 2016).

64. Lattimer, *supra* note 16, at 59–60.

65. Margalit, *supra* note 16, at 172.

influences the requisite investigative steps, particularly depending on whether it is criminal or administrative in nature.

3.1 Standards Under IHL

IHL does not stipulate the standards that investigations into potential violations must meet, either in treaty texts or in customary international law. Nevertheless, certain conclusions can be drawn by implication. First, investigations must be effective in the sense that they must be capable of enabling a determination of whether IHL has been violated and, if so, the causes of that violation.[66] Second, the specific steps that it is appropriate for the State to take are context dependent. These vary according to the complexity of the matter and its seriousness as well as the surrounding circumstances.[67]

Regarding the effectiveness requirement, as Amichai Cohen and Yuval Shany observe, "[i]t is difficult, if not impossible, to conceive of an effective and legitimate manner in which the duty to investigate can be carried which lacks good faith, independence and impartiality or reasonable promptness."[68] The ICRC and Geneva Academy *Guidelines on Investigating Violations of International Humanitarian Law* similarly draw on the internationally recognized principles of independence, impartiality, thoroughness, and promptness.[69] They additionally deem a fifth principle of transparency to be applicable to investigations in armed conflict, albeit in modified form.[70]

With the possible exception of transparency, States largely accept that when conducting criminal investigations, they are bound by these investigatory principles as matter of IHL.[71] What the requirements mean in practice, however, depends on the context. Investigative obligations in armed conflict are subject to a feasibility standard that takes into account all relevant circumstances, including the severity of the allegations, the situation on the ground, and the available resources. Factors such as ongoing hostilities, the availability of witnesses, and the number of incidents to investigate will influence the depth of the investigation the State is able to undertake, as well as its robustness.[72] From a pure IHL perspective,

66. GUIDELINES, *supra* note 14, at 8–9, ¶¶ 30–32. *See also* INTERNATIONAL COMMITTEE OF THE RED CROSS, COMMENTARY ON THE THIRD GENEVA CONVENTION: CONVENTION (III) RELATIVE TO THE TREATMENT OF PRISONERS OF WAR ¶ 4661 (2020), https://ihl-databases.icrc.org/en/ihl-treaties/gciii-1949/article-121/commentary/2020?activeTab=undefined.

67. Schmitt, *supra* note 6, at 80.

68. Cohen & Shany, *supra* note 16, at 58. *See also* Schmitt, *supra* note 6, at 55.

69. GUIDELINES, *supra* note 14, at 9, ¶ 32.

70. *Id.*

71. Schmitt, *supra* note 6, at 55.

72. *Id.* at 80.

a State will comply with its investigative obligations provided it acts reasonably and with due diligence, in light of the circumstances ruling at the time.[73] Thus, a more detailed investigation may be required regarding grave allegations, when the armed forces are in control of the relevant location, than in respect of less serious allegations arising in the context of active hostilities.[74]

Regarding the requirements of independence and impartiality, IHL imposes no requirement on States for investigations to be conducted outside the chain of command. AP I stipulates that it is the commander who bears the primary responsibility to initiate an investigation and, if appropriate, to take action against the perpetrators and report the matter to the competent authorities.[75] The investigative obligation is thus a component of normal military command and discipline.[76] IHL recognizes that it is military commanders who are best placed to initiate investigations regarding potential war crimes. Military commanders are familiar with the operational context, they have access to the relevant witness and other evidence, and they have unit assets available to them to conduct initial enquiries into the incident of concern.[77] Once an investigation is underway, IHL does not dictate who should have final say in terms of decision-making or punishment.[78] In disciplinary cases, these decisions will commonly remain within the chain of command, whereas more serious criminal cases may be referred to an external authority.

3.2 Standards Under IHRL

When it applies to a situation of armed conflict, IHRL prescribes far more demanding investigative standards. This is because IHRL applies mainly in peacetime, where there is a presumption of stability and fully functioning State institutions, which is not the case in the turmoil of armed conflict. All the investigative principles outlined in the preceding analysis have their roots in this body of law. Thus, according to the Human Rights Committee, "Investigations into allegations of violations of [the right to life] must always be independent, impartial, prompt, thorough, effective, credible and transparent."[79]

73. Cohen & Shany, *supra* note 16, at 60; Margalit, *supra* note 16, at 176.

74. Margalit, *supra* note 16, at 176.

75. AP I, *supra* note 5, art. 87.

76. Commentary on the Additional Protocols, *supra* note 28, ¶ 3550; New Rules for Victims of Armed Conflicts, *supra* note 19, at 599.

77. Commentary on the Additional Protocols, *supra* note 28, ¶ 3560; Margalit, *supra* note 16, at 179.

78. AP I, *supra* note 5, art. 87(3).

79. General Comment 36, *supra* note 33, ¶¶ 28, 64. *See also* U.N. Human Rights Comm., *General Comment No. 31: The Nature of the General Legal Obligation Imposed on States Parties to the Covenant*, ¶ 15, U.N. Doc. CCPR/C/21/Rev.1/Add. 13 (May 26, 2004).

Although the Human Rights Committee's views should influence the investigative standards employed by States party to the ICCPR,[80] in practice, it is regional human rights courts, with the power to issue binding judgments, that have a greater influence on armed forces' investigations. For States party to the ECHR and States that have accepted the contentious jurisdiction of the IACtHR, these courts' judgments regarding the requisite investigatory standards are likely to be of greater practical significance than their obligations under IHL.

The difference between the standards that IHRL imposes, as compared to IHL, is particularly striking when considering the principles of independence and impartiality. The IACtHR has ruled consistently that military authorities are not competent to investigate or prosecute cases involving alleged violations of human rights.[81] This is the case even if military personnel are involved in the incident or it occurred during armed conflict.[82] The Court's strict stance on the issue is linked to the history of Latin America, where authoritarian regimes have frequently used military justice as a tool of repression.[83] Despite the Court's jurisprudence, however, States in the region continue to pass domestic laws providing for broad military jurisdiction.[84]

The ECtHR has taken a more nuanced approach, finding that military authorities can investigate, but that the investigating authority must be operationally independent from those implicated in the events.[85] In the *Al-Skeini* case, for instance, the Court found that the United Kingdom failed to satisfy its ECHR obligations with respect to those investigations that remained entirely within the military chain of command.[86] Regarding those investigations conducted by the military police, these only lacked the requisite degree of independence and impartiality because the police were not operationally independent from the military chain of command. Decisions whether to report cases to the police or to the Army Prosecuting Authority, as well as those relating to the continuation of investigations, remained with the commanding officer.[87] Therefore, it was the

80. Venice Commission, *supra* note 56, at 21–22.

81. Sebastian Abad Jara & Daniel Pereira Campos, *Military Courts and Human Rights Violations in Brazil from the Perspective of the Inter-American Human Rights System*, EJIL: Talk! (June 23, 2023), https://www.ejiltalk.org/military-courts-and-human-rights-violations-in-brazil-from-the-perspective-of-the-inter-american-human-rights-system/.

82. *Id.*, *citing* Case of Herzog et al. v. Brazil, Inter-Amer. Comm'n H.R., Report No. 353 (ser. C), ¶ 247 (2018); Frisso, *supra* note 53, at 189, *citing* Massacres of El Mozote and Nearby Places v. El Salvador, Inter-Amer. Comm'n H.R, Report No. 252 (ser. C) (2012); Cruz Sánchez and Others v. Peru, Inter-Amer. Comm'n H.R., Report No. 292 (ser. C) (2015).

83. *See, e.g.*, Andrew G. Reiter & Brett J. Kyle, *Latin America's Re-Militarization*, Jacobin (Nov. 10, 2018), https://jacobin.com/2018/11/latin-america-courts-military-democracy.

84. *Id.*

85. *Al-Skeini*, *supra* note 34, ¶ 167.

86. *Id.* at ¶ 171.

87. *Id.* at ¶ 172.

involvement of the chain of command in the decision-making process rather than role of the military police or the Army Prosecuting Authority that violated the ECHR. Findings such as these, combined with due process concerns, have led European States to implement changes to their military justice systems to remove any command influence from military police investigations and subsequent prosecutions.[88]

Regarding the other investigatory principles, the ECtHR and IACtHR have highlighted the necessity for investigations to be completed in a timely manner.[89] This is "essential in maintaining public confidence in [the State's] adherence to the rule of law and in preventing any appearance of collusion in or tolerance of unlawful acts."[90] For similar reasons, the ECtHR has also emphasized the need for transparency. While the degree of public scrutiny may vary, in every case "the victim's next of kin must be involved in the procedure to the extent necessary to safeguard his or her legitimate interests."[91]

Human rights bodies, however, are not blind to the impacts of armed conflict on States' abilities to investigate. Both the ECtHR and the IACtHR claim to recognize that the investigative obligation is one of means, not results, even if their judgments do not always reflect this.[92] Thus, a State's ability to adhere to all the investigative principles, including thoroughness, should always depend on the context. As the United Kingdom's Henriques Review concluded, "investigators must do their realistic best, but are fully entitled to take into account the dangers, logistical difficulties and other realities in deciding what steps can practically be pursued."[93]

This is illustrated most clearly in the *Hanan* case. Here, the ECtHR concluded that although Germany's investigation into a use of force resulting in civilian deaths was far from perfect, the State did not violate its investigatory obligations due to the difficult circumstances in which it was operating.[94] In other words, the

88. *See, e.g.*, Henriques Review, *supra* note 41, at 29–32; H.H.J. Jeff & Darren Reed, *The Effect of the European Convention on Human Rights on the Services Justice System*, *in* Rant on the Court Martial and Service Law (Jeff Blackett & Darren Reed eds., 4th ed. 2022); Cohen & Shany, *supra* note 16, at 66, 69–70.

89. *Al-Skeini*, *supra* note 34, ¶ 167; El Mozote v. El Salvador, *supra* note 82, ¶¶ 247, 299.

90. *Al-Skeini*, *supra* note 34, ¶ 167.

91. *Id. See also* General Comment 36, *supra* note 33, ¶ 28.

92. *See, e.g.*, *Cruz Sánchez and Others v. Peru*, *supra* note 80, ¶ 350; Jaloud v. The Netherlands, App. No. 47708/08, ¶ 226; *Al-Skeini*, *supra* note 34, ¶ 166; *Hanan v. Germany*, *supra* note 34, ¶ 202; Afro-Descendant Communities Displaced from the Cacarica River Basin (Operation Genesis) v. Columbia, Inter-Amer. Comm'n H.R Report No. 270, ¶ 371 (ser. C) (2013). For a critique of the ECtHR majority's failure to take proper account of operational considerations in its ruling regarding the Netherlands' investigative obligations, *see Jaloud*, *supra*, Joint Concurring Opinion of Judges Cadadevall, Berro-Lefevre, Šikuta, Hirvelä, López Guerra, Sajó and Silvis.

93. Henriques Review, *supra* note 41, at 106. *See also* Cohen & Shany *supra* note 16, at 61.

94. *Hanan v. Germany*, *supra* note 34, ¶¶ 200, 211–36.

fact that the deaths occurred during active hostilities meant that the State was afforded a degree of latitude in terms of its investigative obligations.[95] This judgment can be contrasted with *Al-Skeini* and *Jaloud*, in which the ECtHR concluded that the United Kingdom and the Netherlands' investigations did not comply with their respective ECHR obligations, notwithstanding the difficult circumstances in which both States were operating in Iraq.[96] Thus, it can be difficult for States party to the ECHR to know at the time of an investigation whether the steps they are taking are sufficient. In the words of the U.K. Henriques Review, "with the legal landscape still so changeable the only safe assumption must be that any Service police investigation should come as close to the Human Rights standards applied to civilian investigations as is possible given the operational context. Where there are legitimate reasons for not meeting the standard, these should be meticulously documented."[97]

This is sound advice for States party to the ECHR. Yet the impact of IHRL on States' investigations into civilian harm varies considerably. Whereas the U.S. armed forces can choose to disregard the enhanced investigative obligations IHRL imposes,[98] the same is not true of European countries, or States that have accepted the contentious jurisdiction of the IACtHR. These latter States have little option but to consider their IHRL obligations when conducting investigations, even if the incident concerned occurred during active hostilities.

3.3 The Impact of the International Criminal Court

Under the principle of complementarity, the ICC Statute recognizes that States have the first responsibility to prosecute international crimes.[99] The ICC can only exercise jurisdiction in cases where national legal systems are unwilling or unable to do so.[100] When assessing a State's unwillingness to investigate, echoes of the IHRL investigatory principles emerge. The OTP considers whether there has

95. *Id. See also* Marko Milanović, *Extraterritorial Investigations in Hanan v. Germany; Extraterritorial Assassinations in New Interstate Claim Filed by Ukraine Against Russia*, EJIL: TALK! (Feb. 26, 2021), https://www.ejiltalk.org/extraterritorial-investigations-in-hanan-v-germany-extraterritorial-assassinations-in-new-interstate-claim-filed-by-ukraine-against-russia/.

96. *Al-Skeini*, *supra* note 34, ¶¶ 171–74; *Jaloud*, *supra* note 92.

97. HENRIQUES REVIEW, *supra* note 41, at 12.

98. TURKEL COMMISSION SECOND REPORT, *supra* note 20, at 494–96; Sean Watts, *Domestic Investigation of Suspected Law of Armed Conflict Violations: United States Procedures, Policies, and Practices*, *in* YEARBOOK OF INTERNATIONAL LAW (2013).

99. Rome Statute, *supra* note 12, art. 1.

100. *See generally* INTERNATIONAL CRIMINAL COURT OFFICE OF THE PROSECUTOR, INFORMAL EXPERT PAPER: THE PRINCIPLE OF COMPLEMENTARITY IN PRACTICE (2003), https://www.

been an unjustified delay in the proceedings, whether they were not conducted independently or impartially, and whether the manner of the proceedings was inconsistent with an intent to bring the person concerned to justice.[101] Intent to shield a perpetrator from criminal responsibility may be assessed in light of such indicators as a "lack of resources allocated to the proceedings," "flawed forensic examination," and "manifestly insufficient steps in investigation."[102]

If a State party to the Rome Statute does not effectively investigate alleged IHL violations, there is a risk that the ICC could open its own investigation into the case. This occurred regarding the United Kingdom's operations in Iraq after 2003.[103] Following a factual and legal assessment, the OTP concluded that there were reasonable grounds to believe that members of the U.K. armed forces committed war crimes within the ICC's jurisdiction against detained Iraqi civilians.[104] Regarding the United Kingdom's investigation into those allegations, the OTP found:

> [T]he initial measures taken by the British army to investigate and prosecute alleged crimes in the midst and immediate aftermath of the armed conflict fell short of the standards set out in article 17(1)(a)–(b) and article 17(2) of the [Rome] Statute, both in terms of inaction and unwillingness to genuinely carry out the relevant investigations.[105]

However, in view of the United Kingdom's later steps to establish an independent investigative body to examine historical allegations, the OTP could not conclude that the U.K. authorities had been unwilling genuinely to carry out relevant investigative inquiries and/or prosecutions.[106] Therefore, it closed the preliminary examination.[107]

The United Kingdom's experience illustrates the stringent investigative standards that States party to the Rome Statute must satisfy to avoid the ICC's jurisdiction. The OTP closely scrutinized the United Kingdom's investigative decision-making and despite its ultimate conclusion criticized various aspects of the process, including the unjustified delay and the lack of independence and

icc-cpi.int/sites/default/files/NR/rdonlyres/20BB4494-70F9-4698-8E30-907F631453ED/281984/complementarity.pdf.

101. International Criminal Court Office of the Prosecutor, Policy Paper on Preliminary Examinations 13, ¶ 50 (Nov. 2013), https://www.icc-cpi.int/sites/default/files/iccdocs/otp/OTP-Policy_Paper_Preliminary_Examinations_2013-ENG.pdf.

102. *Id.* at ¶ 51.

103. ICC Iraq/UK Final Report, *supra* note 30.

104. *Id.* at ¶¶ 1, 493.

105. ICC Iraq/UK Final Report, *supra* note 30, at ¶ 494.

106. *Id.* at ¶¶ 495–502.

107. *Id.* at ¶ 503.

impartiality.[108] Thus, although IHL does not mandate professionalized and independent investigative processes outside the chain of command, a desire to avoid ICC investigations and prosecutions may lead States party to the Rome Statute toward this course.

3.4 Administrative Versus Criminal Investigations

States' investigations into allegations of civilian harm will often be criminal in nature. This type of investigation is necessary when the evidence suggests that a war crime or other criminal offense has been committed.[109] In addition, some human rights bodies take the view that a criminal investigation is required when the harm caused to civilians potentially violates the right to life. For instance, the Human Rights Committee asserts that "[g]iven the importance of the right to life, States parties [to the ICCPR] must generally refrain from addressing violations of article 6 merely through administrative or disciplinary measures . . . ."[110]

Yet the majority of investigations States' armed forces undertake are administrative rather than criminal in nature.[111] Many allegations of civilian harm involve no suggestion of any IHL violations. For example, the serviceperson concerned might have honestly believed that the civilian victims had forfeited their protection from attack by directly participating in hostilities.[112] If that belief proves to be incorrect, it is important for the armed forces to learn lessons from the mistake made, notwithstanding the absence of any breach of IHL. An administrative investigation into such an incident can have numerous benefits. It can increase transparency and provide an acknowledgment to the victims' families of the harm caused and perhaps lead to some form of remedy.[113] From a military perspective, it can help maintain discipline within the unit and provide tactical insights to prevent the occurrence of similar incidents.[114]

Unlike criminal investigations, which are highly regulated by law and policy, administrative investigations allow the armed forces a greater degree of latitude

108. *Id.* at ¶¶ 413–91.

109. GC I, *supra* note 7, art. 49; GC II, *supra* note 7, art. 50; GC III, *supra* note 7, art. 129; GC IV, *supra* note 3, art. 146. *See also* Guidelines, *supra* note 14, at 12, ¶¶ 55, 56.

110. General Comment 36, *supra* note 33, ¶ 27.

111. Center for Civilians in Conflict, In Search of Answers: U.S. Military Investigations and Civilian Harm 8 (2020), https://civiliansinconflict.org/wp-content/uploads/2020/02/PDF-Report-for-Website.pdf [hereinafter In Search of Answers].

112. AP I, *supra* note 5, art. 51(3). *See also* Dan Mahanty, *In Search of Answers: U.S. Military Investigations and Civilian Harm*, War on the Rocks (Feb. 20, 2020), https://warontherocks.com/2020/02/in-search-of-answers-u-s-military-investigations-and-civilian-harm/.

113. Mahanty, *supra* note 112.

114. *Id.*

regarding the form of the inquiry and the standards with which it must comply.[115] This greater degree of flexibility can enhance an investigation's effectiveness in establishing the facts of what happened, the causes of any civilian harm, and in learning lessons for the future. Administrative investigations can be particularly useful when there is evidence of systemic issues, such as concerns regarding targeting guidelines or the treatment of civilian internees. Although they do not lead to criminal prosecutions, this form of investigation can result in disciplinary or administrative sanctions for the armed forces personnel concerned. These measures, such as sending a soldier home from deployment, or the loss of rank or seniority, can play a critical role in both maintaining military discipline and ensuring adherence to IHL.

For many incidents involving civilian harm, including potential violations of IHL, administrative investigations may be the most effective means by which to establish the truth of what happened.[116] Often the available evidence will not support a criminal prosecution. Armed forces personnel are judged based upon what they knew and the reasonableness of their decisions at the time they acted, not upon the consequences of their actions.[117] As such, proving guilt beyond reasonable doubt often presents a considerable challenge. Moreover, as armed forces act collectively, it might not be possible to pin the blame for an incident on one or more individuals.[118]

In view of such difficulties, overreliance on criminal investigations can fail to effectively address allegations of civilian harm. To illustrate, the United Kingdom has faced criticism for prioritizing lengthy criminal investigations, which focused mainly on junior personnel and led to very few prosecutions, rather than taking a more flexible investigative approach that might have led to the swift correction of mistakes and enhanced civilian protection.[119]

However, the flexibility inherent in administrative investigations can lead to inconsistencies in the processes followed. Studies relating to the U.S. armed forces found a high degree of variation in the administrative investigations conducted, particularly in terms of their thoroughness and depth.[120] This lack of consistency

115. In Search of Answers, *supra* note 111, at 8; Schmitt, *supra* note 6, at 81.

116. Cohen & Shany, *supra* note 16, at 75–78.

117. *See generally* Honest Errors? Combat Decision-Making 75 Years After the Hostage Case (Nobuo Hayashi & Carola Lingaas eds., 2023).

118. Cohen & Shany, *supra* note 16, at 76; Henriques Review, *supra* note 41, at 13–14.

119. Henriques Review, *supra* note 41, at 48; Mark Lattimer, *The Duty to Investigate Civilian Deaths in Armed Conflict: Looking Beyond Criminal Investigations*, EJIL: Talk! (Oct. 22, 2018), https://www.ejiltalk.org/the-duty-to-investigate-civilian-deaths-in-armed-conflict-looking-beyond-criminal-investigations/.

120. Michael J. McNerney et al., *U.S. Department of Defense Civilian Casualty Policies and Procedures*, Rand Corporation, at ix (2022), https://www.rand.org/pubs/research_reports/RRA418-1.html [hereinafter Rand]; In Search of Answers, *supra* note 111, at 22.

can diminish the effectiveness of administrative investigations, leading to missed opportunities to learn lessons from past mistakes.[121] To address this concern, States should establish clear procedures that all administrative investigations should follow, while still allowing sufficient flexibility to account for operational circumstances. Moreover, it may be wise for like-minded States, particularly when working in a coalition, to agree to basic investigative guidelines to ensure a consistent approach.

Putting such guidelines in place should assist States to determine what type of investigation is most appropriate in the circumstances. Immediately following an incident, the priority will be to gather sufficient facts and evidence to complete an initial assessment of the situation. It might become apparent then, or later, that there is, or is not, evidence of criminal wrongdoing. If the evidence points toward the potential commission of a war crime, the State must commence a criminal investigation. However, it may be appropriate to also conduct an administrative investigation in parallel, for example, to address operational or disciplinary issues linked to the incident.[122] Alternatively, if a criminal investigation commences but reveals insufficient evidence to proceed with a prosecution, it may be pertinent at that time to change the form of the investigation so that it becomes administrative in nature.

To enhance armed forces' investigations, therefore, it is advisable for States to maintain a degree of flexibility regarding the form those investigations take. The priority, whether the investigation is criminal or administrative in character, is effectiveness, namely, ensuring that the proceedings are sufficiently thorough to enable a determination whether IHL was violated and identify the cause of that violation, as well as any necessary remedial measures.[123] In situations of armed conflict, however, this can present a considerable challenge.

4. CHALLENGES TO THE EFFECTIVENESS OF MILITARY INVESTIGATIONS

Investigations into allegations of civilian harm during armed conflict are time-consuming and resource intensive and divert the armed forces' attention away from the military mission. While IHL rightly places the commander at the heart of the investigative process, as an element of normal military command and discipline,[124] this may hinder the independence and impartiality of the process. Meanwhile, the realities of armed conflict often raise numerous practical

121. In Search of Answers, *supra* note 111, at 22.

122. Guidelines, *supra* note 14, at 13, ¶ 59.

123. *Id.* at 34, ¶ 162.

124. AP I, *supra* note 5, art. 87. *See also* Commentary on the Additional Protocols, *supra* note 28, ¶ 3550; New Rules for Victims of Armed Conflicts, *supra* note 19, at 599.

difficulties that impede the thoroughness and timeliness of any investigation. This section outlines some of the challenges to armed forces' investigations and considers their impact on States' adherence to the investigatory principles outlined in the preceding analysis.

4.1 The Realities of Armed Conflict

The frictions, uncertainties, and complexities of combat pose huge challenges to armed forces faced with an obligation to investigate allegations of civilian harm. Practical hurdles, such as an inability to interview witnesses located behind enemy lines, significantly impacted armed forces' conduct of investigations in recent decades. Frequently, investigations have taken place in unsecured environments where investigators faced the risk of attack, evidence was destroyed, and local customs prohibited forensic examinations.[125]

Large-scale combat operations of the future may further exacerbate such difficulties.[126] These might involve higher intensity conflict, greater numbers of civilian casualties, proportionally fewer military lawyers, and a requirement for units to continually disperse and relocate.[127] In such circumstances, the feasibility of conducting many investigative steps may be limited and the military imperative to devote precious resources to the ongoing fight, rather than to investigating civilian harm, may be overwhelming.

Even today, resource constraints can seriously impede the effectiveness of armed forces' investigations. New Zealand's inquiry into its defense forces' conduct during Operation Burnham in Afghanistan highlighted the significant impact that a lack of resources had on its forces' ability to investigate allegations of civilian casualties.[128] Similarly, the United Kingdom's Henriques Review noted the substantial manpower required to provide force protection for investigators to get to the scene of an incident, alongside the time and other restraints that limit the steps investigators can realistically take.[129]

125. Henriques Review, *supra* note 41, at 23–28.

126. Rand, *supra* note 120, at 26–27.

127. Nate Bankson & Keoni Medici, *The Place of Judge Advocates on the Next Battlefield*, Articles of War (May 19, 2023), https://lieber.westpoint.edu/place-judge-advocates-next-battlefield/.

128. Report of the Government Inquiry into Operation Burnham and Related Matters 378 (2020), https://operationburnham.inquiry.govt.nz/inquiry-report/ [hereinafter Op Burnham Report].

129. Henriques Review, *supra* note 41, at 12. *See also* In Search of Answers, *supra* note 111, at 45.

Such constraints mean that an investigation during armed conflict might look very different, in terms of its scope and thoroughness, from one conducted during peacetime. Visiting the site of the incident and conducting witness interviews is often impracticable. Instead, security concerns combined with resource limitations may mean that the only feasible way to assess potential civilian harm following an attack is via air assets. Yet studies have shown that aerial video has significant blind spots and can lead to underestimates of civilian casualties.[130]

Resource constraints may also manifest in terms of manpower. While it is true that military personnel are often best placed to investigate due to their understanding of the operational realities surrounding an incident,[131] commanders do not always have the luxury of choosing an investigating officer with the most appropriate skills to undertake the task. The nominated individual might simply be the next available person in the chain of command.[132] Moreover, that individual might lack training in investigative techniques as well as the necessary language skills.[133]

The very real difficulties that armed forces experience when seeking to satisfy their investigative obligations can lead to a perception within the military that investigations are overly onerous and detract from the mission. The Brereton Report relating to the operations of Australian special forces in Afghanistan, for instance, observed a desire on the part of commanders "to protect subordinates from what was seen as over-enthusiastic scrutiny."[134] Meanwhile, the officers tasked with initial assessments of any allegations of civilian harm "generally approached their task as being to collect evidence to refute a complaint, rather than to present a fair and balanced assessment of the evidence."[135] It is unsurprising, therefore, that questions arise regarding the chain of command's key role in the investigative process.

4.2 The Involvement of the Chain of Command

A particular challenge for States' armed forces when investigating allegations of civilian harm is the apparent conflict between the principles of independence and

130. Open Society Foundation, The Strategic Costs of Civilian Harm 54 (2016), https://www.opensocietyfoundations.org/publications/strategic-costs-civilian-harm; In Search of Answers, *supra* note 111, at 29.

131. Schmitt, *supra* note 6, at 84.

132. In Search of Answers, *supra* note 111, at 49–50.

133. *Id.* at 4, 50.

134. Inspector-General of the Australian Defence Force, Afghanistan Inquiry Report, at 34, ¶ 41 (2020), https://www.defence.gov.au/about/reviews-inquiries/afghanistan-inquiry [hereinafter Brereton Report].

135. *Id.* at 35, ¶ 44.

impartiality and the position of the commander at the heart of States' investigative procedures. As AP I acknowledges, commanders bear the initial responsibility to respond to potential IHL violations involving troops under their command, as a component of military discipline.[136] From a practical viewpoint the commander is best placed to investigate due to presence at the scene and the necessary expertise and information regarding the matter under investigation.[137] Moreover, from a legal perspective, it is the armed forces that normally have jurisdiction over the personnel involved in the events at issue. It might only be the military that can deal with the relevant offenses, particularly if these are administrative rather than criminal in nature.[138]

However, as many inquiries have recognized, the involvement of the chain of command can have a deleterious impact on investigations' effectiveness. The Brereton Report noted commanders' natural inclination to support their subordinates and give them the benefit of the doubt, particularly given the difficult conditions in which they operate.[139] It is equally natural that commanders should prioritize military readiness, which could be compromised if service members are implicated in an investigation.[140] But these inherent elements of command can lead to partiality in the investigative process, including a tendency to discount potentially credible allegations as insurgent propaganda or motivated by compensation.[141] Commanders' role in the investigative process can thus result in potentially credible allegations not being investigated, or to unbalanced investigations that favor the versions of events of the military personnel involved.

While IHL imposes no requirement for investigations to take place outside the chain of command,[142] concerns such as these have led human rights bodies to rule either that military authorities are not competent to investigate[143] or that military investigating authorities must be operationally independent from those

136. AP I, *supra* note 5, art. 87.

137. Claire Simmons, *Whose Perception of Justice? Real and Perceived Challenges to Military Investigations in Armed Conflict*, 102 International Review of the Red Cross 807, 811 (2020).

138. *Id.*

139. Brereton Report, *supra* note 134, at 497, ¶ 75.

140. Silvaine Wong, *Investigating Civilian Casualties in Armed Conflict: Comparing U.S. Military Investigations with Alternatives under International Humanitarian and Human Rights Law*, 64 Naval Law Review 111, 135–36 (2015).

141. Brereton Report, *supra* note 134, at 359. *See also* Op Burnham Report, *supra* note 128, at 280, ¶ 156.

142. Schmitt, *supra* note 6, at 80.

143. *See, e.g.*, Jara & Campos, *supra* note 81.

implicated in the events.[144] In many States, particularly in Europe, this has led toward a civilianization of military justice.[145]

Even in those States where reforms have taken place, the commander often retains some involvement in the investigatory process. For instance, the commander might have the authority to decide how to deal with incidents when they first occur, including whether to refer matters to an independent investigator.[146] In the United States, meanwhile, command influence pervades the entire investigative process.[147] As one study into U.S. military investigations observed, "[w]here commanders do not actively encourage effective investigations, they are far less likely to take place."[148] Ensuring that commanders retain their role at the heart of military discipline yet do not negatively influence investigations into potential IHL violations requires a delicate balancing act that may vary considerably from State to State. The following section addresses that balance.

5. BALANCING INVESTIGATORY STANDARDS AGAINST MILITARY EFFECTIVENESS

As already mentioned, IHL represents a delicate balance between military necessity and humanity.[149] While developments in the law have progressively prioritized humanitarian considerations, States must maintain the freedom to effectively conduct their military operations.[150] A similar requirement for balance is evident when considering armed forces' investigations into alleged IHL violations against civilians. In recent years, IHRL and the ICC Statute have placed an increasingly heavy investigative burden on some States. Even for those States that are not party to regional human rights treaties or the ICC Statute, the modern information environment means that effective and transparent investigations into allegations of civilian harm have become a strategic imperative.[151]

144. *See, e.g.*, *Al-Skeini*, *supra* note 34, ¶ 167.

145. *See generally* Victor Hansen, *The Impact of Military Justice Reforms on the Law of Armed Conflict: How to Avoid Unintended Consequences*, 21 MICHIGAN STATE INTERNATIONAL LAW REVIEW 229 (2013); Finabel, *The Role of Military Courts Across Europe: A Comparative Understanding of Military Justice Systems* (2021) https://finabel.org/wp-content/uploads/2021/06/20.-The-role-of-Military-Courts-across-Europ.pdf.

146. HENRIQUES REVIEW, *supra* note 41, at 168–69; Finabel, *supra* note 145, at 8–9.

147. Watts, *supra* note 98.

148. IN SEARCH OF ANSWERS, *supra* note 111, at 2.

149. Schmitt, *supra* note 2.

150. *Id.* at 837.

151. *See, e.g.*, Dan Stigall, *Future Conflicts, Civilian Harm, and the CHMR-AP—Part I*, ARTICLES OF WAR (May 3, 2020), https://lieber.westpoint.edu/future-conflicts-civilian-harm-chmr-ap-part-i/.

Yet the investigative standards that armed forces are required to satisfy must be balanced against the military necessity to accomplish the mission. They must take account of the very real challenges of conducting investigations in situations of armed conflict. This section considers each of the investigative principles in turn, examining how States, in their criminal and administrative investigations, can strike a proper balance between legal and policy requirements and the military necessity to achieve the mission. In each case, it is important to note that the recommended approach represents a suggestion of best practice rather than charting legal obligations with which all States must comply.

5.1 Thoroughness

The thoroughness of an investigation relates to its effectiveness in achieving its intended purpose. A thorough and effective investigation should uncover the facts of what happened by collecting, analyzing, and preserving relevant evidence.[152] The precise requirements of the investigatory process vary according to whether it is criminal or administrative in nature, with the former needing to comply with standards of evidence for a criminal trial.[153] For both types of investigation, however, the assessment of thoroughness depends heavily upon the context in which it takes place.

The same degree of thoroughness should therefore not be expected of every investigation. Several factors will influence the appropriate investigatory standards, in addition to its criminal or administrative character. The first is the operational context, including the degree of control the State has over the situation. It is not feasible for States to investigate an incident during ongoing active hostilities to the same level of depth as it might achieve if the incident occurred in a rear area such as at a detention facility. If the site of the incident is controlled by the enemy or in a contested location, this is likely to limit the investigatory steps the State can feasibly take. Numerous considerations may need to be weighed in the balance, including the security of investigative personnel, the location of witnesses, and the attitude of the local population.[154]

A second key factor is the severity of the allegation.[155] If the incident is serious, involving the suspected commission of a war crime or high numbers of unanticipated civilian casualties, for example, the State might be required to go to greater lengths to overcome investigatory hurdles. For instance, if security concerns mean that it is not possible to conduct a site visit, it might nevertheless be feasible for

152. Guidelines, *supra* note 14, at 28–29; Turkel Commission Second Report, *supra* note 20, at 131.

153. Guidelines, *supra* note 14, at 28, ¶ 136.

154. *Id.* at 28, ¶ 138.

155. *Id.* at 34, ¶ 162; Schmitt, *supra* note 6, at 80.

the State to engage with third parties, such as a partner force, to collect evidence or interview witnesses.[156]

Third, to ensure that mission success is properly weighed in the balance, the wider circumstances are relevant, including the operational environment, the number of ongoing investigations, and the resources available to the unit concerned. Taking these factors into account, a degree of prioritization may be necessary so that the armed forces can allocate scarce resources to the most important tasks, and to those investigative steps that are most likely to prove fruitful.[157]

Whatever the surrounding circumstances, the thoroughness of States' investigations during armed conflict is likely to be enhanced through effective prior planning.[158] States' ability to plead a lack of feasibility might be limited if, as part of the planning process, they have not anticipated the requirement to address allegations of civilian harm. This should ensure that adequate numbers of military police and other personnel are deployed forward to support the armed forces' investigations.[159] Other early steps might also enhance armed forces' investigations such as instructing troops on basic investigative techniques as part of their training so that they know how to preserve or photograph evidence at the scene of an incident.[160]

Effective operational record keeping from the occurrence of a potential violation and throughout the investigative process is also key. While the realities of conflict might make recording difficult, particularly due to the high volumes of information and frequent turnovers of personnel, this is something that States should prioritize.[161] If they do not, detrimental outcomes could ensue, as illustrated by the 2022 Dutch civil court case, in which the Netherlands was found to have violated IHL because it did not have the requisite evidence to prove otherwise.[162] Prior to engaging in any conflict, therefore, States should take all feasible steps to ensure that service members are trained and resourced to record and maintain comprehensive operational records, relating both to their actions and the reasoning behind their decisions, to support potential investigations and demonstrate IHL compliance.

156. In Search of Answers, *supra* note 111, at 4.

157. Guidelines, *supra* note 14, at 29, ¶ 140.

158. RAND, *supra* note 120, at 26.

159. Henriques Review, *supra* note 41, at 25–26;

160. *Id.* at 84.

161. Guidelines, *supra* note 14, at 16–17; Op Burnham Report, *supra* note 128, at 28, 33; Henriques Review, *supra* note 41, at 175.

162. Zwanenburg, *supra* note 61; de Hoon, *supra* note 61.

5.2 Independence and Impartiality

IHL envisions the commander at the heart of military discipline.[163] To comply with their duties to "prevent and suppress breaches" of IHL,[164] commanders play a critical role in investigating potential offenders. This also makes sense from an operational perspective. When incidents first occur, it is commanders who are best placed to assess the facts due to their access to the relevant intelligence and operational records and to the military personnel involved, as well as their knowledge of the operational context. When allegations arise during armed conflict, it will often be impracticable for anyone other than the commander to take the initial investigative steps.

It does not necessarily follow, however, that the commander is best placed to conduct the ensuing investigation. This depends on the facts, including the severity of the allegation, the criminal or administrative nature of the investigation, the security situation in the location concerned, and the availability of investigators outside the chain of command.[165] In circumstances where there is no suggestion that war crimes have been committed, the incident occurred during active hostilities, or security threats limit the investigative steps that can feasibly be taken, it may be most appropriate for the unit to investigate. But where the allegation is more serious and the circumstances allow, a commander would be well advised to refer the matter to an external and independent investigative body.[166] This might be necessary not only to ensure compliance with the State's obligations under IHRL and the ICC Statute, but also to enhance the legitimacy of the investigation and perceptions of fairness.

Rather than a "one-size-fits-all" approach, therefore, a flexible policy that allows commanders to investigate when appropriate but for independent investigators to step in as and when it is necessary and feasible to do so, would better balance States' investigative obligations against mission accomplishment.[167] This would allow commanders to take swift action in combat environments to address minor misconduct or systemic issues that impact civilians, such as concerns regarding the rules of engagement, via administrative investigations.

But equally, when security conditions and resources permit, commanders would be wise to ensure that investigators outside the chain of command address more serious allegations, particularly those involving potential criminality. This would minimize legal risk as well as the reputational harm that can result from seemingly biased or unfair investigative processes. As the Henriques Review put it, "Demonstrable independence and impartiality, in which not only the public

163. AP I, *supra* note 5, art. 87.

164. *Id.*

165. Guidelines, *supra* note 14, at 23.

166. *Id.* at 26–28.

167. Hansen, *supra* note 145, at 264–65.

but investigators themselves can have confidence, is the best safeguard against cover up, and the best safeguard against any perception of it."[168]

5.3 Promptness

If operational conditions permit, investigations into potential IHL violations against civilians should commence as soon as practicable after the incident occurred. In any investigation, the passage of time has detrimental impacts: "[A] crime scene will change, evidence may disappear, memories fade, witnesses can be threatened, suspects may collude."[169] In the complexities of armed conflict, these effects may only accelerate. Thus, the prompt investigation of alleged IHL violations complements the principles of effectiveness and thoroughness and contributes to perceptions that justice is being done.[170]

When planning for military operations, armed forces should prepare for likely investigative requirements, for example, by ensuring that investigators can surge forward to respond quickly to events.[171] Effective planning should help ensure that investigations can commence promptly and maintain momentum. Yet operational realities may inevitably lead to delays. The location of the incident might be too dangerous to visit, for instance, or military witnesses might have deployed elsewhere. The reasonableness of any delays must therefore be assessed in light of the operational context,[172] and records should be made of the reasons in case justification is later necessary.

It is notable that there is no statute of limitations on the prosecution of war crimes.[173] As such, it is inappropriate to impose strict time limits on investigations, especially if they involve potential criminal wrongdoing. Sometimes, allegations of IHL violations will not come to light until long after the event. In such circumstances, or when operational constraints cause delay, the investigation should commence as soon as it is practicable to do so, and progress as quickly as is feasible in all the circumstances.

168. Henriques Review, *supra* note 41, at 119.

169. Guidelines, *supra* note 14, at 30.

170. Turkel Commission Second Report, *supra* note 20, at 132.

171. Henriques Review, *supra* note 41, at 109.

172. Turkel Commission Second Report, *supra* note 20, at 144.

173. Customary IHL, *supra* note 8, r. 160; Rome Statute, *supra* note 12, art. 29.

5.4 Transparency

IHL does not impose any obligation on States to inform the public regarding their armed forces' investigations, or to notify victims or their families of the outcome.[174] The only reference to a notion of transparency appears in AP I, which refers to "the right of families to know the fate of their relatives."[175] Yet, unlike IHRL,[176] this provision does not impose a positive obligation on the armed forces to disseminate information regarding their investigations.[177] Indeed, there may be strong operational reasons for not releasing information, such as the sensitivity of the relevant intelligence or operational tactics, or the possibility of putting witnesses at risk.[178] There can be an enormous operational cost if a State publicly exposes sensitive information such as where and when its armed forces were operating, their capabilities, or the intelligence they were acting on.

Nonetheless, a failure to keep victims and the public informed regarding investigations into alleged IHL violations against civilians can lead to reputational harm, impacting the State's legitimacy and public perceptions of its procedures and IHL compliance.[179] In the modern information environment, it may be unwise for the armed forces to simply refuse to engage with victims or with the wider public regarding their investigations. Civilian casualties are no longer nameless to the wider public; their photographs are published online, and their relatives heard. Thus, refusing to engage with the media or with the bereaved can now impose strategic costs, leading to reduced public confidence in the armed forces and their mission.[180]

States' armed forces should, therefore, seek to engage with victims and the public regarding their investigations when it is feasible to do so. While some information will necessarily remain classified, militaries would be well advised to consider carefully what they can release without harming national security or negatively impacting individuals.[181] This is important not only for those States

174. Schmitt, *supra* note 6, at 81.

175. AP I, *supra* note 5, art. 32.

176. *See supra* section 3.2.

177. Commentary on the Additional Protocols, *supra* note 28, ¶ 1212; New Rules for Victims of Armed Conflicts, *supra* note 19, at 196.

178. Schmitt, *supra* note 6, at 81, n. 210; Cohen & Shany, *supra* note 16, at 64.

179. Turkel Commission Second Report, *supra* note 20, at 134–36, 145; Henriques Review, *supra* note 41, at 13–14, 44; Simmons, *supra* note 137, at 820.

180. Dan E. Stigall, *Future Conflicts, Civilian Harm, and the CHMR-AP—Part II*, Articles of War (May 5, 2023), https://lieber.westpoint.edu/future-conflicts-civilian-harm-chmr-ap-part-ii/.

181. Guidelines, *supra* note 14, at 30–32; Henriques Review, *supra* note 41, at 109.

that are subject to human rights obligations during armed conflict but for any State wishing to maintain legitimacy in its military operations.

Internal transparency within the State's own armed forces is also essential, particularly with respect to administrative investigations. One of the most important reasons for investigating an incident is to learn lessons, to make sure the same mistakes are not repeated. Yet one study related to U.S. civilian casualty procedures found that lessons learned from strikes that caused civilian harm were not shared across the relevant Department of Defense organizations in a way that meaningfully mitigated future civilian casualties.[182] Armed forces have little excuse for this type of failing; it cannot easily be justified on grounds of feasibility or classification. For reasons both of military necessity and of investigative effectiveness, therefore, States should ensure that the findings of prior investigations are properly disseminated and stored in an accessible way so that lessons can be learned and future harm to civilians can be minimized.

6. CONCLUSION

The wars of the future, like those of the past, will continue to be fought among the civilian population and to cause civilian harm. In some cases, that harm might indicate a potential violation of IHL. In others, it may not. But whether or not a breach of international law is alleged, States' armed forces will need to determine whether to investigate the allegations and, if so, how those investigations should be conducted.

Such decisions are not straightforward. While legal obligations combined with considerations of legitimacy and accountability call for thorough investigations, the realities of combat might preclude many investigative steps. A balance must therefore be struck. States' armed forces must weigh the imperative to defeat the enemy and devote only those resources they can feasibly spare to investigations of potential civilian harm against the requirements of humanity, which demand effective investigations and answerability for injuries caused.

The choices made will vary from State to State. They will clearly be influenced by the State's treaty obligations, particularly if it is party to the ICC Statute or a regional human rights treaty. The State's domestic laws, operational concerns, and distinct military culture will additionally guide its choices.[183] Yet whatever a State's individual circumstances, a strategic imperative to investigate is clear. As the United Kingdom's *Manual on the Law of Armed Conflict* observes, a State's failure to investigate and, if appropriate, punish offenders "can contribute to the loss of public and world support, leading to isolation for the state involved."[184] This

182. RAND, *supra* note 120, at viii, 31. *See also* HENRIQUES REVIEW, *supra* note 41, at 79–80.

183. TURKEL COMMISSION SECOND REPORT, *supra* note 20, at 264;

184. UNITED KINGDOM MINISTRY OF DEFENCE, THE MANUAL OF THE LAW OF ARMED CONFLICT ¶ 413 (2004).

reality, together with a recognition that States must acknowledge and learn from past mistakes, is evident in the many enquiries States have undertaken regarding their armed forces' investigations,[185] as well as the United States' adoption, in August 2022, of the Civilian Harm Mitigation and Response Action Plan.[186]

Whatever their strict legal obligations, States must investigate credible allegations of serious civilian harm. This is critical not only to maintain legitimacy but also to address indiscipline, identify lessons that can be learned, and thereby support the military mission. That said, it is entirely inappropriate to dictate either the investigatory steps States must take, or who should investigate. States must retain discretion in this respect so that they can make investigatory decisions that take into account the operational context and the seriousness of the allegations, as well as wider military concerns.

To assist in the difficult decision-making process following an incident involving civilian harm, like-minded States would be well advised to come together to agree to certain basic guidelines to steer their investigative processes. These would assist in filling the gaps left by IHL while ensuring that any investigatory standards imported from IHRL properly take account of operational realities and feasibility concerns. Feasibility is key to all investigative procedures that States' armed forces may conduct. Whether imposed by policy or law, investigatory standards that ignore feasibility and operational realities would prove unacceptable to States and ultimately detrimental to a proper balance between humanity and military necessity.

185. *See, e.g.*, Turkel Commission Second Report, *supra* note 20; Brereton Report, *supra* note 134; Op Burnham Report, *supra* note 128; Henriques Review, *supra* note 41.

186. U.S. Department of Defense, *Civilian Harm Mitigation and Response Action Plan, Objective 7* (Aug. 25, 2022), https://media.defense.gov/2022/Aug/25/2003064740/-1/-1/1/CIVILIAN-HARM-MITIGATION-AND-RESPONSE-ACTION-PLAN.PDF.

18

Redressing Civilian Harm

TOM DANNENBAUM*

1. SCOPE AND ARGUMENT

This chapter outlines key areas of consensus and dissensus regarding reparation for civilian harm under international humanitarian law (IHL).[1] It argues that the legal case for civilian reparative rights in both international and non-international armed conflicts (IACs and NIACs) is stronger than often recognized, particularly given the interpretive significance of international human rights law (IHRL).

2. CONSENSUS ON STATES' REPARATIVE OBLIGATION

Four points of consensus provide the foundation. First, States have a general duty under international law to repair harms caused by their internationally wrongful acts. Second, IHL affirms this obligation. Third, when applicable, IHRL provides for individual rights (1) to reparation for harms arising from rights violations, and (2) to access to justice in that regard. Finally, ex gratia payments to civilians for wartime harms are external to legal reparation.

* Associate Professor of International Law at the Fletcher School of Law & Diplomacy, where he is also Co-Director of the Center for International Law & Governance.

1. Unless specifically referring to collective reparations, this chapter uses the singular "reparation." Although applicable in principle to all forms of reparation, the analysis takes compensation as its paradigmatic case.

Tom Dannenbaum, *Redressing Civilian Harm* In: *Civilian Protection in Armed Conflict*. Edited by: Jelena Pejic and Captain Margaret Kotlik, Oxford University Press. © Tom Dannenbaum 2025.
DOI: 10.1093/oso/9780197793176.003.0018

2.1 The General Reparative Obligation

In *Factory at Chorzów*, the Permanent Court of International Justice held "it is a principle of international law, and even a general conception of law, that any breach of an engagement involves an obligation to make reparation."[2] This principle is now reflected in Article 31 of the International Law Commission's (ILC's) Articles on Responsibility of States for Internationally Wrongful Acts, which provides, "[t]he responsible State is under an obligation to make full reparation for the injury caused by the internationally wrongful act" and specifies that such "[i]njury includes any damage, whether material or moral, caused by the internationally wrongful act of a State."[3] As a general principle, the rule has a legal authority independent from treaty or custom.[4]

Unlike criminal accountability, the function of reparation is not to punish or to deter. Rather, "reparation must, as far as possible, wipe out all the consequences of the illegal act and reestablish the situation which would, in all probability, have existed if that act had not been committed."[5] This animating objective applies equally to armed conflict.[6] Thus understood, awarding reparation is not about imposing a new cost on the violator; it is about transferring an existing cost because it was imposed illegally on those bearing it.

The framework developed in the ILC Articles is focused on inter-State reparations. However, this is "without prejudice to any right, arising from the international responsibility of a State, which may accrue directly to any person or entity other than a State."[7] Individual rights along those lines are "a matter for the particular primary rule."[8]

2.2 Reparation and IHL

In principle, States can supplant any nonperemptory rule of general international law in a specific regime. They have not availed themselves of that prerogative as it relates to reparation for IHL violations.

2. Factory at Chorzów (Ger. v. Pol.), 1928 P.C.I.J. (ser. A) No. 9, at 29 (Sept. 13).

3. International Law Commission, Report on the Work of its Fifty-Third Session, U.N. Doc. A/56/10, at 43 (2001), *reprinted in* [2001] 2 Yearbook of the International Law Commission 32, U.N. Doc. A/CN.4/SER.A/2001/Add.1 (Part 2) [hereinafter ARSIWA].

4. *Chorzów*, *supra* note 2, at 29, 47 (framing it as a principle of law); Statute of the International Court of Justice art. 38, June 26, 1945, 59 Stat. 1055, 33 U.N.T.S. 993.

5. *Chorzów*, *supra* note 2, at 47.

6. Final Award: Ethiopia's Damages Claims (Eri. v. Eth.), 26 R.I.A.A. 631 ¶¶ 26–27 (Eri.-Eth. Claims Comm'n 2009); Armed Activities on the Territory of the Congo (Dem. Rep. Congo v. Uganda), Reparations, 2022 I.C.J. Rep.13 ¶ 102 (Feb. 9).

7. ARSIWA, *supra* note 3, art. 33(2).

8. *Id.* at 95 (art. 33 commentary, ¶ 4).

In IACs, Article 3 of Hague Convention IV of 1907 provides that a State that violates the Hague Regulations "shall, if the case demands, be liable to pay compensation" on the basis of its "responsib[ility] for all acts committed by persons forming part of its armed forces."[9] Seven decades later, this formulation was reiterated in Article 91 of Protocol Additional to the Geneva Conventions (AP I).[10] It is widely understood to reflect customary IHL.[11] The universally ratified Geneva Conventions of 1949 further provide that "[n]o High Contracting Party shall be allowed to absolve itself or any other High Contracting Party of any liability incurred by itself or by another High Contracting Party in respect of [grave] breaches" of the Conventions.[12] If anything, precluding the absolution of *other* States indicates an IHL-specific strengthening of the general reparative obligation, at least with respect to grave breaches.[13]

Non-international armed conflict IHL is less developed than its IAC counterpart and lacks parallel reparation provisions in treaty law. However, absent contrary codification, the general principle articulated in *Factory at Chorzów* presumptively applies.[14] Moreover, leading analyses of customary IHL indicate that this principle is indeed applicable in NIACs—a proposition that is buttressed by both "verbal" practice and significant reparative programming across multiple States.[15]

9. Regulations Respecting the Laws and Customs of War on Land, annexed to Convention No. IV Respecting the Laws and Customs of War on Land, art. 3, Oct. 18, 1907, 36 Stat. 2277, T.S. No. 539 [hereinafter Hague IV].

10. Protocol Additional to the Geneva Conventions of 12 August 1949, and Relating to the Protection of Victims of International Armed Conflicts art. 91, June 8, 1977, 1125 U.N.T.S. 3 [hereinafter AP I].

11. *See* Customary International Humanitarian Law Database r. 150, International Committee of the Red Cross, https://ihl-databases.icrc.org/en/customary-ihl (last accessed June 14, 2024); Office of the General Counsel, U.S. Dept. of Defense, Law of War Manual § 18.16 (rev. ed. 2023) [hereinafter DoD LoWM].

12. Geneva Convention for the Amelioration of the Condition of the Wounded and Sick in Armed Forces in the Field art. 51, Aug. 12, 1949, 75 U.N.T.S. 31 [hereinafter GC I]; Geneva Convention for the Amelioration of the Condition of Wounded, Sick and Shipwrecked Members of Armed Forces at Sea art. 52, Aug. 12, 1949, 75 U.N.T.S. 85 [hereinafter GC II]; Geneva Convention Relative to the Treatment of Prisoners of War art. 131, Aug. 12, 1949, 75 U.N.T.S. 135 [hereinafter GC III]; Geneva Convention Relative to the Protection of Civilian Persons in Time of War art. 148, Aug. 12, 1949, 75 U.N.T.S. 287 [hereinafter GC IV] (emphasis added). *See also* S.C. Res. 670, U.N. Doc. S/RES/670 ¶ 13 (1990).

13. *See infra* note 114.

14. *Chorzów*, *supra* note 2.

15. ICRC, *supra* note 11, r. 150; Elizabeth Salmón & Juan-Pablo Pérez-León-Acevedo, *Reparation for Victims of Serious Violations of International Humanitarian Law*, 919 International Review of the Red Cross pt. II (2022). *See also infra* notes 19, 50–51.

2.3 Reparation and Human Rights Law

Despite decades of jurisprudence and practice, the relationship between IHRL and IHL remains contested, as does the extraterritorial reach of human rights obligations.[16] However, when IHRL *is* applicable, individuals have a clear right to reparation for human rights violations and to the access to justice necessary to vindicate it. At the global level, this is reflected in Article 8 of the Universal Declaration and Articles 2, 9(5), and 14(6) of the International Covenant on Civil and Political Rights.[17] Regionally, this individual right is codified in the American, African, and European human rights frameworks.[18] The case law of the Inter-American Court of Human Rights offers a particularly useful jurisprudential resource.[19]

2.4 Ex Gratia Payments

Some States offer ex gratia payments to select individuals harmed by their military operations.[20] These payments recognize neither wrongful causation nor any reparative obligation. Rather, as the name indicates, they are charitable (and thus

16. *See infra* notes 97–127.

17. G.A. Res. 217 (III) A, Universal Declaration of Human Rights art. 8 (Dec. 10, 1948); International Covenant on Civil and Political Rights arts. 2, 9(5), 14(6), Dec. 16, 1966, 999 U.N.T.S. 171 [hereinafter ICCPR]; U.N. Human Rights Comm., *General Comment No. 31: The Nature of the General Legal Obligation Imposed on States Parties to the Covenant*, ¶ 16, U.N. Doc. CCPR/C/21/Rev.1/Add. 13 (May 26, 2004).

18. European Convention for the Protection of Human Rights and Fundamental Freedoms, arts. 5(5), 13, 41, Nov. 4, 1950, 213 U.N.T.S. 221 [hereinafter ECHR]; American Convention on Human Rights arts. 7, 25, 63, Nov. 22, 1969, 1144 U.N.T.S. 123 [hereinafter ACHR]; African Charter on Human and Peoples' Rights arts. 50, 56, Oct. 21, 1986, 1520 U.N.T.S. 217 [hereinafter ACHPR].

19. Inter-American Commission on Human Rights, Truth, Justice and Reparation in Transitional Justice: The Inter-American Standards 109–20 (2021); Salmón & Pérez-León-Acevedo, *supra* note 15, pt. II; Abella v. Argentina, Case 11.137, Inter-Amer. Comm'n H.R., Rep. No. 55/97, OEA/Ser.L/V/II.95, Doc. 7 rev., ¶ 161 (1997). *See also infra* note 119.

20. Amsterdam International Law Clinic, Monetary Payments for Civilian Harm in International and National Practice (2013); Center for Civilians in Conflict, Making Amends (Jan. 7, 2023); Center for Civilians in Conflict, Monetary Payments for Civilian Harm in International and National Practice (2013); Steven van de Put, *Ex Gratia Payments and Reparations*, 14 Journal of International Humanitarian Legal Studies 131 (2023); U.S. Under Secretary of Defense, *Interim Regulations for Condolence or Sympathy Payments to Friendly Civilians for Injury or Loss that is Incident to Military Operations* (June 22, 2020); Scott T. Paul, *The Duty to Make Amends to Victims of Armed Conflict*, 22 Tulane Journal of International and Comparative Law 87, 101–04 (2013).

discretionary) gestures.[21] As such, these payments are orthogonal to IHL and to the associated reparation framework. And yet they may be the only compensation that most victims can obtain from the responsible State and many ex gratia offers are contingent on the recipient waiving future claims.[22] Such payments function in part to shield the donor State from the accountability that is a key component of true reparation.

2.5 Contested Issues

Notwithstanding the consensus just outlined, several points remain contested.[23] The focus here is on two. First, although States have a clear duty to repair harms arising from their IHL violations, some dispute that civilian victims hold a right to such reparation. Second, even assuming they hold that right, civilians' procedural standing to claim said reparation has also been questioned.

These two issues are often conflated.[24] However, an individual can hold a reparative right and yet lack the procedural capacity to vindicate it.[25] That person's dependence on another agent to issue the reparative claim neither diminishes the reality of the individual right, nor indicates its contingency.[26] Analogously, the forum for the resolution of disputes under the Genocide Convention is the International Court of Justice (ICJ)—a forum before which only States have

21. *See* p. 3, n.1 & Action 8.c, Civilian Harm Mitigation and Response Action Plan (CHMR-AP), U.S. Department of Defense (Aug. 25, 2022), https://media.defense.gov/2022/Aug/25/2003064740/-1/-1/1/CIVILIAN-HARM-MITIGATION-AND-RESPONSE-ACTION-PLAN.PDF; DoD LoWM, *supra* note 11, § 18.6.3. On their rarity, *see* Joanna Naples-Mitchell, *Under the Pentagon's New Civilian Harm Action Plan, Addressing Credible Cases Is a Moral Imperative*, Just Security (Jan. 4, 2023), https://www.justsecurity.org/84563/under-pentagons-civilian-harm-plan-addressing-credible-cases-moral-imperative/; Annie Shiel & Priyanka Motaparthy, *Pentagon Investigation into Syria Strike*, Just Security (June 23, 2023), https://www.justsecurity.org/87020/pentagon-investigation-into-syria-strike-a-litmus-test-for-civilian-harm-response/.

22. Mwatana & Lowenstein Clinic, The Case for Reparations to Civilians in Yemen 96 (June 2022); Emily Gilbert, *The Gift of War*, 46 Security Dialogue 403, 413 (2015) *But see* Steven van de Put, *The Dutch Chora Judgment*, Articles of War (Apr. 10, 2023), https://lieber.westpoint.edu/dutch-chora-judgment-ex-gratia-payments-compensation/.

23. The civil liability of non-State actors is debated, for example. ICRC, *supra* note 11, r. 150; Emanuela-Chiara Gillard, *Reparation for Violations of IHL*, 85 International Review of the Red Cross 529, 535 (2003). Luke Moffett, Reparations and War ch. 7 (2023).

24. Tokyo Chiho Saibansho [Tokyo Dist. Ct.] Dec. 7, 1963 (Shimoda et al. v. State), *reprinted in* 32 International Law Reports 626, 636 (Japan).

25. Reparation for Victims of Armed Conflict, International Law Association, 14 (2010), https://www.ila-hq.org/en_GB/documents/conference-report-the-hague-2010-10; ARSIWA, *supra* note 3, at 95; Liesbeth Zegveld, *Remedies for Victims of Violations of Humanitarian Law*, 85 International Review of the Red Cross 497, 506 (2003).

26. Zegveld, *supra* note 25, at 505-06.; ARSIWA, *supra* note 3, at 91.

standing. And yet, plainly, the substantive rights-holders in such a context (with respect to both violation and reparation) are the communities and individuals targeted with genocide. It would be absurd to suggest that The Gambia holds the substantive right to reparation vis-à-vis the alleged genocide of the Rohingya simply because it is The Gambia that had standing, brought the case, and issued the claim. Appropriately, The Gambia's request is instead for the Court to require various forms of reparation to Rohingya victims of genocidal acts.[27]

3. THE SUBSTANTIVE REPARATIVE RIGHT

Having drawn this distinction, consider first the substantive right to reparation. Various States and authorities have insisted that only States hold reparative rights under IHL (at least in IACs) and that IHRL is either inapplicable or overridden on this. Whether or not that was true historically, a strong case can now be made that individuals hold substantive reparative rights vis-à-vis IHL violations.

3.1 Substantive Reparative Rights Under IHL

Articulating the putatively traditional view, the U.S. Department of Defense *Law of War Manual* denies any "private right to compensation" under IHL, asserting that States' general reparative responsibility is "owed to other States" and that no IHL treaty or custom "provide[s] a private right for individuals to claim compensation directly from a State."[28] The Manual cites the Geneva Conventions' ICRC Commentary, which reasons, "it is inconceivable, at least as the law stands today, that claimants should be able to bring a direct action for damages against the State in whose service the person committing the breach was working."[29] Here, already, is a conflation of who holds the reparative right and who has the legal capability to claim it.

On the former, the traditional view reflects the following structure: IHL's protection of individuals in IACs is the consequence of States' imposition of symmetrical rights and obligations upon one another in their mutual interest. Thus, despite protecting human beings, the rules of IHL do not manifest the protected

27. Application of the Convention on the Prevention and Punishment of the Crime of Genocide (Gam. v. Myan.), The Gambia's Application Instituting Proceedings and Request for Provisional Measures, 2019 I.C.J. Rep. 178, ¶ 112 (Nov. 11).

28. DoD LoWM, *supra* note 11, at § 18.16.4; Tel-Oren v. Libyan Arab Republic, 726 F.2d 774 (D.C. Cir. 1984); Goldstar et al. v. United States, 967 F.2d 965 (4th Cir. 1992); Princz v. Federal Republic of Germany, 26 F.3d 116 (D.C. Cir. 1994).

29. Oscar M. Uhler et al., Commentary to Geneva Convention IV Relative to the Protection of Civilian Persons in Time of War 603 (1958).

individuals' *rights*.[30] When those rules are violated, "it is, from a legal point of view, the individual's country of origin that is injured" and therefore owed compensation.[31] The State, when it claims reparation, "asserts its *own right*, namely the right to ensure in the person of its nationals respect for the rules of international law."[32]

This perspective is reflected in German and Japanese court decisions rejecting individual claims on the grounds that the law during World War II (as articulated in Article 3 of Hague Convention IV) included no individual right to compensation.[33] Germany also advanced this view at the ICJ.[34] It is a position its courts have reaffirmed in litigation on NATO's bombing of Varvarin Bridge in Serbia in 1999[35] and on a 2009 airstrike in Kunduz, Afghanistan,[36] although some of the reasoning is focused more on denying an individual procedural right than on the substantive reparative right.[37] The fact of States' mutual waiving of reparation claims after IACs is also invoked as evidence that States hold the substantive right to those reparations.[38] From this perspective, creating individual claims mechanisms is an

30. Ren^é Provost, International Human Rights and Humanitarian Law 16 (2002); Cordula Droege, *Elective Affinities?*, 90 International Review of the Red Cross 501, 503 (2008); Louise Doswald-Beck & Sylvain Vité, *International Humanitarian Law and Human Rights Law*, 33 International Review of the Red Cross 94, 101 (1993); Markovic and Others v. Italy, App. No. 1398/03, ¶ 109 (2006) (ECtHR), https://hudoc.echr.coe.int/eng-press?i=003-1868477-1961993.

31. Marco Sass^òli, International Humanitarian Law 92 (1st ed. 2019).

32. Bundesgerichtshof [BGH] [Federal Supreme Court of Germany] June 26, 2003, III ZR 245/98 (Ger.) (Greek Citizens v. Germany), *reprinted in* 42 International Legal Materials 1030, 1037 (emphasis added).

33. Tōkyō Kōtō Saibansho [Tokyo High Court] Aug. 7, 1996 (Japan) (X. et al. v. Japan); Saikō Saibansho [Sup. Ct.] Apr. 27, 2007 (X. v. Y.) (Japan); *Shimoda*, *supra* note 24; *Greek Citizens v. Germany*, *supra* note 32; Bundesverfassungsgericht [BVerfG] [Federal Constitutional Court of Germany] Feb. 15, 2006, 2 BVerfGE 1476/03 (Ger.) (Greek Citizens v. Germany), *reprinted in* 135 International Law Reports 186 (2009).

34. Jurisdictional Immunities of the State (Ger. v. It.), Reply of Germany, 2010 I.C.J. Rep. 143 ¶ 39 (Oct. 5).

35. Bundesverfassungsgericht [BVerfG] [Federal Constitutional Court of Germany] Aug. 13, 2013, 2 BVerfGE 2660/06, 2 BVerfGE 487/07 (Ger.) (Vavarin case).

36. Bundesgerichtshof [BGH] [Federal Court of Justice] Oct. 6, 2016, III ZR 140/15 (Ger.) (Kunduz case).

37. Vavarin case, *supra* note 35, at 14 (acknowledging that Hague IV Article 3's history shows it was "indirectly also intended to protect individual rights"); Gillard, *supra* note 23, at 538. *But see Shimoda*, *supra* note 24, at 638.

38. Gillard, *supra* note 23, at 537–38; Bundesverfassungsgericht [BVerfG] [Federal Constitutional Court of Germany] Oct. 26, 2004, 2 BVerfGE 955/00-1038/01, ¶ 114 (Ger.) (East German Expropriation case). Nonetheless, postwar practice included significant individual reparative programming. Gillard, *supra* note 23, at 543 notes 34–35.

act of State or UN Security Council discretion, rather than a response to legal obligation.

The traditional credentials of this position are less clear-cut than is often presumed. When confronted with the issue in *Jurisdictional Immunities*, the ICJ avoided it, holding that Germany's immunity before foreign courts rendered the issue moot.[39] Relying in part on human rights law, Judge Cançado Trindade reasoned that there was an individual reparative right,[40] while Judges Keith and Koroma rejected the notion, with Koroma reasoning, "a provision requiring state payments to individuals would have been inconceivable in 1907, when the Hague Convention IV was concluded."[41] But Koroma's framing may rest on a faulty assumption. Hill-Cawthorne has shown that the Convention's *travaux* "strongly suggested a general acceptance among the [Hague Peace Conference] delegates that the draft article endowed the individual victims of violations with the right to compensation."[42] It was only later in the 20th century that State practice moved toward an inter-State reparative model in IHL, a shift that Hill-Cawthorne contends has since reversed.[43] The "traditional" approach might not be quite so traditional after all.

Moreover, a striking feature of the case law invoked in arguments against an individual right is that, with rare exceptions,[44] the legal analysis is focused on the IHL of World War II.[45] Regardless of how one understands the purpose of Article 3 of Hague Convention IV, the law of armed conflict of that period was generally structured as a framework of obligations owed by States to one another. This is manifest not only in the regime's exclusion of NIACs and wars of colonial domination but also in the scope of codified human protection in the wars to which the regime *did* apply, which served primarily to benefit persons associated with a belligerent party. Civilians were protected in a relatively limited manner, subject to flexible assessments of military necessity in a regime that bore little resemblance to a framework of rights.[46] Even as IHL expanded to include more comprehensive and codified civilian protections in Geneva Convention IV, most of those protections were applicable exclusively to civilians who were nationals of

39. Jurisdictional Immunities of the State (Ger. v. It.), Judgment, 2012 I.C.J. 99, ¶ 108 (Feb. 3).

40. *Id.* at ¶ 70 (Cançado Trindade, J. dissenting).

41. *Id.* at ¶ 9 (Koroma, J. sep. op.); *see also id.* at ¶¶ 18–19 (Keith, J. sep. op.).

42. Lawrence Hill-Cawthorne, *Rights under International Humanitarian Law*, 28 European Journal of International Law 1187, 1197 (2017).

43. *Id.* at 1195–1211.

44. Vavarin case, *supra* note 35, at 18. This was predicated questionably on the inapplicability of human rights law. *See* Vavarin case, *supra* note 35, at 3. *Cf. infra* notes 99–100, 120–27.

45. *See, e.g.*, *Greek Citizens v. Germany*, *supra* note 32, at 1036–37. *See also supra* notes 35–36. At the ICJ, Germany relied on this to dismiss contrary trends. *See* Reply of Germany, *supra* note 34, ¶ 41.

46. John Fabian Witt, Lincoln's Code 183 (2012).

an enemy State.[47] Consequently, the violation of even protected civilians could be understood as a violation of the State of which they were citizens.

Even at that stage, however, it would be too simplistic to characterize this as a regime of exclusively inter-State rights and obligations. Individual rights are referenced at various points in the Geneva Conventions, including in Common Article 6/6/6/7, which prohibits States making special agreements with one another that would "restrict the [individual] rights" of protected persons.[48] The ban on States relieving one another of reparative duties vis-à-vis grave breaches might be considered in that same vein.[49] The extension of a limited range of IHL protections to NIACs in Common Article 3 further complicates a purely inter-State characterization of the 1949 Conventions.

The critical developments would occur three decades later. The regulation of NIACs was expanded with the Protocol Additional to the Geneva Conventions (AP II) in 1977 and has developed further with the significant convergence of customary IAC and NIAC law, including on reparative obligations. In theory, States might owe reparation *erga omnes* or to their NIAC adversaries. However, given both the law's internal logic and consistency across NIAC practice (informed also by human rights law and related domestic law principles), the far stronger interpretation is that reparation is owed to the individual victims.[50] This presumption is bolstered by the clearly complementary relationship between human rights law and IHL in NIACs.[51]

If civilians harmed by IHL violations in IACs were to lack such a substantive reparative claim, this would be a notable deviation from the relative strength of IHL protections in IACs, as compared to NIACs.[52] However, establishing an individual reparative right in IACs does not depend on teleological harmonization across conflict classifications.[53] AP I eschewed Convention IV's focus on civilian nationality, instead defining the protected category as including all who are not

47. GC IV, *supra* note 12, art. 4.

48. GC I, *supra* note 12, art. 6; GC II, *supra* note 12, art. 6; GC III, *supra* note 12, art. 6; GC IV, *supra* note 12, art. 7. *See also* GC I, *supra* note 12, art. 7; GC II, *supra* note 12, art. 7; GC III, *supra* note 12, art. 7; GC IV, *supra* note 12, art. 8.

49. *See supra* note 12 and *infra* notes 113–14.

50. ICRC, *supra* note 11, r. 150; Salmón & Pérez-León-Acevedo, *supra* note 19, pt. II.

51. Protocol Additional to the Geneva Conventions of 12 August 1949, and Relating to the Protection of Victims of Non-International Armed Conflicts pmbl., June 8, 1977, 1125 U.N.T.S. 609 [hereinafter AP II] ("human rights offer a basic protection"). IHRL extraterritoriality (*infra* notes 96–97 and 120–27) poses less of an obstacle in NIACs.

52. *See also* AP I, *supra* note 10, art. 54(5), and AP II, *supra* note 51, art. 14.

53. *Cf.* Prosecutor v. Tadić, Case No. IT-94-1-AR-72, Decision on Defence Motion for Interlocutory Appeal on Jurisdiction, ¶ 119 (Int'l Crim. Trib. for the former Yugoslavia Oct. 2, 1995).

members of the armed forces or associated armed groups.[54] The Commentary emphasizes that "the important aspect is not so much their nationality as the inoffensive character of the persons to be spared and the situation in which they find themselves."[55] As such, in regulating the conduct of hostilities, AP I treats civilians as protected from their own State and its allies as much as they are from the enemy.[56]

Most obviously, a State's nationals are typically the primary victims of its use of human shields or failure to exercise passive precautions.[57] Providing that one party's use of human shields does not relieve its adversary of obligations toward the affected civilians, AP I shifted the normative gravitational force of these rules.[58] Understanding the primary victims of the first violation to be the endangered civilians, rather than the State whose operational choice-set is limited by its adversary's violation, clarifies why it would be incoherent to compound the endangerment of the former by loosening their legal protection vis-à-vis the latter. A similar observation can be made regarding the elimination of lawful reprisals in the context of human protection rules.[59]

The point, however, is not limited to human shields or reprisals. Article 49(2) of AP I specifies that the rules governing attacks "apply to all attacks in whatever territory conducted, including the national territory belonging to a Party to the conflict but under the control of an adverse Party."[60] The AP I Commentary confirms the intent to protect "the civilian population of the Party concerned."[61] Applying this concretely, with the overwhelming majority of Ukraine's current military activity against Russian forces occurring in Ukraine,[62] any Ukrainian breach of conduct-of-hostilities rules to the detriment of the civilian population would include as its primary victims the State's own nationals.[63]

54. AP I, *supra* note 10, art. 50. *See also* AP I, *supra* note 10, art. 75. *Cf.* GC IV, *supra* note 12, art. 4.

55. Commentary on the Additional Protocols of 8 June 1977 to the Geneva Conventions of 12 August 1949 (Yves Sandoz, Christophe Swinarski, & Bruno Zimmermann eds., 1987) [hereinafter AP Commentary].

56. Exceptionally, *see* excerpts from AP I and AP II, *supra* note 52.

57. AP I, *supra* note 10, arts. 51(7), 56(5), 58.

58. AP I, *supra* note 10, art. 51(8). *Cf.* GC IV, *supra* note 12, art. 28.

59. AP I, *supra* note 10, art. 51(6); Prosecutor v. Kupreškić, IT-95-16-T, Judgment, ¶¶ 527–36 (Int'l Crim. Trib. For the former Yugoslavia Jan. 14, 2000).

60. AP I, *supra* note 10, art. 49(2).

61. AP Commentary, *supra* note 55, at ¶ 1877.

62. *Ukraine's Counteroffensive against Russia in Maps*, Fin. Times (Jan. 9, 2024), https://www.ft.com/content/4351d5b0-0888-4b47-9368-6bc4dfbccbf5.

63. OSCE Office for Democratic Institutions and Human Rights (ODIHR), *Interim Report on Reported Violations* ¶¶ 50–51 (July 20, 2022); ODIHR, *Second Interim Report on Reported*

For parties to AP I, the IAC classification of wars of national liberation (such as the Polisario Front's conflict with Morocco) provides another context in which universal civilian protection is critical.[64] Analogously, when the ICJ determined that Israel was engaged in a Common Article 2 belligerent occupation of Palestinian territory in 2004, without taking a position on Palestinian statehood,[65] it did not hesitate in identifying the reparative rights-holders:

> [G]iven that the construction of the wall in the Occupied Palestinian Territory has, inter alia, entailed the requisition and destruction of homes, businesses and agricultural holdings, the Court finds further that Israel has the obligation to make reparation for the damage caused to all the natural or legal persons concerned [and the] obligation to compensate, in accordance with the applicable rules of international law, all natural or legal persons having suffered any form of material damage as a result of the wall's construction.[66]

Today, it is difficult to take seriously the notion that the harm arising from any of the violations previously described would not "demand" compensation.[67] The imperative to return things to their likely state absent the violation would be no less potent for the fact of the victims' and perpetrators' shared nationality. Per the AP I Commentary, "demand" indicates that for the obligation to attach, the violation must have caused "loss or damage which in most cases will be of a material or personal nature."[68] Particularly given the NIAC parallel, the natural conclusion is that the substantive reparative rights are held by the affected individuals.

On point, the AP I Commentary specifies, "persons with a foreign nationality who have been wronged by the unlawful conduct of a Party to the conflict should address themselves to their own government, which will submit *their* complaints" to the responsible party.[69] Parsing this, several implications arise. First, when States make reparative claims regarding civilian harm, they do so on behalf of the persons harmed. Second, the constituency of those seeking reparation is broader than "persons with a foreign nationality." Third, nationals of the violating State should make claims directly. Even the exhortation to foreign nationals to seek

Violations ¶¶ 47–48 (Dec. 14, 2022); ODIHR, *Fourth Interim Report on Reported Violations* ¶ 25 (Dec. 12, 2023).

64. Kubo Mačák, *Wars of National Liberation II*, OUP Blog (July 30, 2018) https://blog.oup.com/2018/07/wars-national-liberation-unusual-rule-part-2/.

65. Legal Consequences of the Construction of a Wall in the Occupied Palestinian Territory, Advisory Opinion, 2004 I.C.J. Rep. 136, ¶¶ 90–101 (July 9).

66. *Id.* at ¶¶ 152–53.

67. AP I, *supra* note 10, art. 91; Hague IV, *supra* note 9, art. 3.

68. AP Commentary, *supra* note 55, ¶ 3655.

69. *Id.* at ¶ 3657 (emphasis added).

reparative relief through their State specifies that they may avoid doing so in "exceptional cases."[70] Ultimately, the AP I Commentary notes that "since 1945 a tendency has emerged to recognize the exercise of rights by individuals" regardless of nationality.[71]

In other areas of international law, the notion that individual reparative rights may coexist with a procedural reliance on States is clearly established. For example, building on the ILC's Draft Articles on Diplomatic Protection,[72] the ICJ in *Diallo* described Guinea as exercising "its diplomatic protection *on behalf* of Mr. Diallo in respect of the DRC's alleged violation of *his rights*."[73] The Court noted that Guinea sought "compensation for the injury caused *to him*" and that the analysis would therefore focus on "injury resulting from the breach of Mr. Diallo's *rights as an individual*."[74] Following the award, the Court emphasized that "the sum awarded to Guinea in the exercise of diplomatic protection of Mr. Diallo is intended to provide reparation for the *latter's* injury."[75] Precisely this is also the right way to think about inter-State human rights litigation. Thus, in *Cyprus v. Turkey*, the European Court of Human Rights (ECtHR) held:

> [A]ccording to the very nature of the Convention, it is the individual, and not the State, who is directly or indirectly harmed and primarily "injured" by a violation of one or several Convention rights. Therefore, if just satisfaction is afforded in an inter-State case, it should always be done for the benefit of individual victims.[76]

The ILC specifies that States engaged in diplomatic protection should "transfer *to the injured person* any compensation obtained . . . subject to any reasonable deductions."[77]

Exemplifying the applicability of this concept in IHL, the ICJ's 2022 reparations judgment in *Armed Activities* held that the "reparation awarded to the DRC . . . for damage to persons and to property reflects the harm suffered by individuals and communities" and "welcome[d] the undertaking given by the Agent of the DRC

70. *Id.*

71. *Id.*

72. International Law Commission, Draft Articles on Diplomatic Protection art. 1 (2006), 61 U.N. GAOR Supp. No. 10, U.N. Doc. A/61/10 (2006); Ahmadou Sadio Diallo (Guinea v. Dem. Rep. Congo), Preliminary Objections, 2007 I.C.J. 582, ¶ 39 (May 24). *Cf.* Final Award, *supra* note 6, ¶ 25.

73. Diallo, Preliminary Objections, *supra* note 72, ¶ 40 (emphasis added).

74. Ahmadou Sadio Diallo (Guinea v. DRC), Compensation, 2012 I.C.J. 324, ¶¶ 13, 17 (June 19).

75. *Id.* at ¶ 344.

76. Cyprus v. Turkey, App. No. 25781/94, ¶ 46 (ECtHR) (2014), https://hudoc.echr.coe.int/fre?i=001-144151. *See also id.* at ¶¶ 39–47; ARSIWA, *supra* note 3, at 95, 128.

77. Articles on Diplomatic Protection, *supra* note 72, art. 19.

during the oral proceedings regarding the fund that has been established by the Government of the DRC, according to which the compensation to be paid by Uganda will be fairly and effectively distributed to victims of the harm."[78]

Opinio juris supports recognizing individuals as the reparative rights-holders. In 2005, the UN General Assembly affirmed by consensus the Basic Principles and Guidelines on the Right to a Remedy and Reparation for Victims of Gross Violations of International Human Rights Law and Serious Violations of International Humanitarian Law.[79] Articulating "existing legal obligations"[80] in IACs and NIACs, the document defines "victims" as "persons who individually or collectively suffered harm, including physical or mental injury, emotional suffering, economic loss or substantial impairment of their fundamental rights, through acts or omissions that constitute . . . serious violations of international humanitarian law."[81] It expresses States' obligation to "provide effective remedies to victims, including reparation"[82] and affirms victims' corresponding right to "adequate, effective and prompt reparation"[83] that is "proportional to the gravity of the violations and the harms suffered."[84] The International Law Association (ILA) has taken a similar approach.[85] These positions are frequently reiterated by investigative bodies, special procedures, and other components of the UN human rights system.[86]

Despite IACs' relative contemporary infrequency, there is State practice matching this *opinio juris*.[87] Notwithstanding its primary focus on compensating

78. Armed Activities, Reparations, *supra* note 6, ¶¶ 407–08. *See also id.* at ¶ 102; Final Award, *supra* note 6, ¶ 82. *But see* Armed Activities, Reparations, *supra* note 6, at ¶¶ 25, 110, 209.

79. Basic Principles and Guidelines on the Right to a Remedy and Reparation for Victims of Gross Violations of International Human Rights Law and Serious Violations of International Humanitarian Law, G.A. Res. 60/147, U.N. Doc. A/RES/60/147 (Dec. 15, 2005).

80. *Id.* at pmbl.

81. *Id.*, art. 8.

82. *Id.*, art. 3(d).

83. *Id.*, art. 11(b).

84. *Id.*, art. 15.

85. International Law Association, *Declaration of International Law Principles on Reparation for Victims of Armed Conflict* (Res. 2/2010), *in* International Law Association Report of the 76th Conference arts. 4(1), 5, 6 (2010).

86. *See, e.g.*, Detailed Report of the Group of Eminent Int'l and Reg'l Experts on Yemen, ¶¶ 403–05, U.N. Doc. A/HRC/45/CRP.7 (Sept. 29, 2020); UN High Commissioner for Human Rights, *Situation of human rights in Yemen* ¶ 79, U.N. Doc. A/HRC/36/33 (Sept. 13, 2017); Report of the International Commission of Inquiry on Darfur to the United Nations Secretary-General, Pursuant to Security Council Resolution 1564 of 18 September 2004, ¶ 597 (Jan. 25, 2005); Letter dated 12 October 2000 from the President of the ICTY to the U.N. Secretary-General, U.N. Doc. S/2000/1063 ¶¶ 20–22 (Nov. 3, 2000).

87. Similarly, most war crimes are never investigated. Sassòli, *supra* note 31, at 77–78, 97–98.

harms arising from Iraq's *jus ad bellum* violation in invading Kuwait in 1990, the UN Compensation Commission recognized the individual claim eligibility of prisoners of war who suffered "loss or injury [that] resulted from mistreatment in violation of international humanitarian law."[88] In creating the Register of Damage Caused by the Construction of the Wall in the Occupied Palestinian Territory, the General Assembly in 2007 reiterated the ICJ's 2004 analysis and identified the Register's function as recording "the damage caused to all *natural* and legal persons."[89] In 2022, the Assembly replicated that language and drew on the Basic Principles in recommending the creation of a register for harms arising from Russia's unlawful acts in and against Ukraine.[90] The following year, the Council of Europe took up that call on those terms.[91]

Given the connection between the International Criminal Court's (ICC's) war crimes framework and customary IHL as understood by its States Parties,[92] the Court's approach to reparation is also instructive. Thus far, almost all of those recognized as war crimes victims and awarded reparation at the ICC have been natural persons. In *Al-Mahdi*, which involved the destruction of cultural heritage, the Court supplemented the primary reparation award to the people of Timbuktu with a symbolic award to Mali.[93] The availability of that option clarifies that the general absence of States from ICC reparation orders is because, with rare exceptions, they are not the primary reparative rights-holders vis-à-vis serious violations of IHL.

3.2 IHRL, Armed Conflict, and Reparation

Human rights law complements this analysis.[94] The key question with respect to IHRL is not whether individuals are reparative rights holders (which is

88. U.N. Compensation Commission [UNCC], Governing Council, Decision 11, U.N. Doc. S/AC.216/1992/11 (June 26, 1992); UNCC, Governing Council, Decision 3, U.N. Doc. S/AC.26/1991/3 (Oct. 18, 1992). *See* Walter Kälin, Report on the Situation of Human Rights in Occupied Kuwait, U.N. Doc. E/CN/1992/26 ¶¶ 259–62 (Jan. 16, 1992); U.N. Commission on Human Rights, Res. 2003/34, ¶ 1 (Apr. 23, 2003).

89. Establishment of the United Nations Register of Damage Caused by the Construction of the Wall in the Occupied Palestinian Territory, pmbl & ¶ 3(a), U.N. Doc. A/RES/ES-10/17 (Jan. 24, 2007).

90. Furtherance of Remedy and Reparation for Aggression against Ukraine, pmbl & ¶¶ 2, 4, U.N. Doc. A/ES-11/L.6 (Nov. 7, 2022).

91. Council of Europe Comm. of Ministers, CM/Res(2023)3 (May 12, 2023).

92. Rome Statute of the International Criminal Court art. 8(2)(b, e), July 17, 1998, 2187 U.N.T.S. 90; Tom Dannenbaum, *Criminalizing Starvation in an Age of Mass Deprivation in War*, 55 VANDERBILT JOURNAL OF TRANSNATIONAL LAW 682, 701–09 (2022).

93. Prosecutor v. Al Mahdi, Case No. ICC-01/12-01/15-236, Reparations, ¶¶ 51–56, 106–07 (Aug. 17, 2017).

94. SASSÒLI, *supra* note 31, at 91–93.

clear),[95] but whether and how this should inform reparation in IHL. Historically, the putative obstacles to IHRL applicability in armed conflict have been twofold.[96] First, some have argued that when IHL applies, this precludes IHRL applicability altogether. Second, it has been argued that States' human rights obligations do not apply extraterritorially.

Both issues have been debated at length. Suffice it to say that absolutist positions regarding either the blanket inapplicability of human rights in armed conflict or their blanket inapplicability outside of the impugned State's territory have become increasingly untenable, with key legal authorities repeatedly rejecting such positions.[97] Having long been one of the leading advocates of those absolutist positions, the United States began to soften its stance a decade and a half ago and regularly operates in coalition with partners for whom the extraterritorial applicability of human rights obligations in armed conflict is an institutional reality.[98] It is now relatively uncontroversial that human rights law is not precluded as a framework in armed conflict and that it applies extraterritorially in at least certain circumstances. Ongoing debates relate instead to the details of IHRL's applicability.

One approach to the interaction between human rights and IHL is to apply the regimes cumulatively. Here, a difficulty arises only if the regimes *require* contradictory things. Their *permitting* different things does not preclude holding States to the more demanding standard, because there is no obligation to act to the limit of one's permissions. This has sometimes been framed as the *lex protector* or *pro homine* approach.[99] In the reparative context the individual human right

95. *See* Declaration of Human Rights, ICCPR, General Comment 31, ECHR, ACHR, ACHPR, and Inter-American Standards, *supra* notes 17–19, respectively.

96. *See, e.g.*, Michael Dennis, *ICJ Advisory Opinion on Construction of a Wall in the Occupied Palestinian Territory*, 99 American Journal of International Law 119 (2005). On challenges at the intersection, *see* Naz Modirzadeh, *The Dark Sides of Convergence*, 86 International Legal Studies 349 (2010).

97. IHRL in conflict: Legality of the Threat or Use of Nuclear Weapons, Advisory Opinion, 1996 I.C.J. 226 ¶ 25 (July 8); General Comment 31, *supra* note 17, at ¶ 11; Wall Advisory Opinion, *supra* note 65, at ¶¶ 111–14, 130; Armed Activities on the Territory of the Congo (Dem. Rep. Congo v. Uganda), Merits, 2005 I.C.J. 168, ¶ 216 (Dec. 19); Human Rights Committee, *General Comment 36: Right to Life*, ¶ 64, U.N. Doc. CCPR/C/GC/36 (Oct. 30, 2018). On IHRL extraterritoriality, *see* Armed Activities, Merits, *supra*, at ¶¶ 178–80; U.N. Human Rights Comm., *López Burgos v. Uruguay*, ¶¶ 12.1–12.3, U.N. Doc. CCPR/C/OP/1 (July 29, 1981); Carter v. Russia, App. No. 20914/07, ¶¶ 125–30 (2021) (ECtHR), https://hudoc.echr.coe.int/fre?i=001-211972; Jaloud v. the Netherlands, App. No. 47708/08, ¶¶ 139–53 (2014) (ECtHR), https://hudoc.echr.coe.int/fre?i=001-148367; Marko Milanovic, Extraterritorial Application of Human Rights Treaties (2011).

98. Fourth Periodic Report of the United States to the Human Rights Committee ¶¶ 502–09 (2011), https://2009-2017.state.gov/j/drl/rls/179781.htm.

99. Alonso Gurmendi Dunkelberg, *There and Back Again*, 56 Military Law & Law of War Review 1 (2017–2018). *See also* Al-Jedda v. United Kingdom, App. No. 27021/08, ¶¶ 98–110 (2011) (ECtHR), http://hudoc.echr.coe.int/eng?i=001-105612.

to reparation would apply alongside the IHL duty to provide compensation.[100] Ultimately, however, even those authorities that have taken this approach have either retreated from it or applied it only in narrow contexts.

A second, coordinated interpretation approach, draws on Article 31(3)(c) of the Vienna Convention on the Law of Treaties, which requires that treaty interpretation take account of "any relevant rules of international law applicable in the relations between the parties."[101] In *Hassan v. UK*, the ECtHR invoked this concept to find a mutual accommodation between the European Convention protection of the right to liberty and the admittedly not "congruent" IHL detention authorizations under Geneva Conventions III and IV.[102] The upshot was a controversial interpretation of the European Convention pursuant to which the IHL grounds for detention were to be "accommodated as far as possible" into the noncongruent right to liberty under the ECHR, but with procedural safeguards informed by a combination of Geneva and European Convention requirements.[103]

On this second approach, the case for individuals as reparative rights-holders in armed conflict is overwhelming. First, given the unambiguous individual right to reparation in IHRL, the viability of an IHL interpretation recognizing such a right, and the imperative to reach a harmonious interpretation under Article 31(3)(c) of the Vienna Convention, the basis for coordinating around an individual reparative right is clear.[104] Second, given that reparations are ordinarily applied after the general close of military operations, IHL's relative situational aptness as compared to IHRL is far less compelling than it is during active hostilities. Arguably, then, the IHRL rule ought to be "accommodated as far as possible" in IHL interpretation, rather than vice versa. Third, as exemplified in *Hassan*, even during ongoing hostilities IHRL may play an elevated interpretive role on aspects removed from fighting, such as those relating to claims, process, and review.[105]

Emphasizing IHL's tailoring to armed conflict, a final approach identifies IHL as *lex specialis* to IHRL's *lex generalis*. Although sometimes invoked to support the preclusion of human rights as a framework, *lex specialis* is understood most commonly to entail that IHRL applies in armed conflict, but that, on points of divergence, IHRL rules are reinterpreted to conform to the corollary IHL

100. *Al-Jedda*, *supra* note 99, at ¶¶ 111–18.

101. Vienna Convention on the Law of Treaties, art. 31(3)(c), May 23, 1969, 1155 U.N.T.S. 331 [hereinafter VCLT].

102. Hassan v. United Kingdom, App. 29750/09, ¶¶ 96–107 (2004) (ECtHR), https://hudoc.echr.coe.int/fre?i=001-146501. *See also* General Comment 36, *supra* note 97, at ¶ 64.

103. *Hassan*, The Gambia note 102, at ¶ 104.

104. International Committee of the Red Cross (Jean-Marie Henckaerts et al. eds.), Commentary on the First Geneva Convention: Convention (I) for the Amelioration of the Condition of the Wounded and Sick in the Armed Forces in the Field ¶ 3025 (2016) (on the IHL rule's openness to interpretation).

105. *Hassan*, *supra* note 102, at ¶ 106.

rules.[106] The theory is on its strongest footing as applied to questions such as who may be targeted or detained in armed conflict and on what grounds, given the tensions between the regimes on those points and IHL rules' specific responsiveness to the exigencies of war. IHRL rules that are *not* in tension with IHL are thought to apply without modification.[107]

Given the decline of the notion that IHRL is precluded as a framework in armed conflict, something like this version of *lex specialis* is the currently viable model of regime interaction that is most deferential to IHL. Yet, even here, a strong argument can be made for individual reparative rights. After all, the central claim of this approach is that IHL protections define the scope of, and therefore implicate, individual human rights in armed conflict. IHL's interpretive dominance in this dynamic has significant implications for the *scope* of individuals' IHRL protections. But that substantive interpretive dominance does not affect the characterization of those protections in terms of individual rights. Plausibly, the latter characterization leads directly to the applicability of the IHRL right to reparation.

The contrary argument would be that *lex specialis* demands reinterpreting the IHRL reparation rules to accommodate the "traditional" inter-State interpretation of IHL. However, this presumes that all IHL rules are necessarily *lex specialis* in relation to all corollary IHRL rules, regardless of content or context.[108] And yet, given its failure to specify a rights-holder, the best case for the inter-State framing of the IHL reparation rule is that it channels the general inter-State obligation to compensate for internationally wrongful acts, and is thus simply a manifestation of *lex generalis*. In contrast, the individual right to reparation under IHRL is specially tailored to the reparative imperative vis-à-vis violations the primary victims of which are human beings.[109] Per the preceding reasoning, that framing is apt not only to human rights violations but also to the corollary violations of IHL. Here, too, the argument for IHRL's interpretive dominance on a *lex specialis* model is strengthened by the fact that reparation awards ordinarily occur after the general close of military operations or at a remove from hostilities.[110]

Given this, the strongest case for IHL as the enduring *lex specialis* on this point would need to emphasize not the exigencies of armed conflict but the challenges of peace-making. Three points might be invoked to that end. First, given the depletion of State resources after armed conflict and the difficulty of credibly processing large numbers of claims in contexts of low trust and evidentiary obstacles, the notion that war victims could bring individual claims against belligerents may seem procedurally impractical.[111] Second, centralized control over reparative

106. *See, e.g.*, Nuclear Weapons Advisory Opinion, *supra* note 97, at ¶ 25.

107. Wall Advisory Opinion, *supra* note 65, at ¶¶ 104–06.

108. *Cf.* General Comment 36, *supra* note 97, at ¶¶ 64, 70. VCLT, *supra* note 101, art. 31(3)(c).

109. ARSIWA, *supra* note 3, at 95.

110. Compare *supra* notes 101–05 and text. *See also* Paul, *supra* note 20, at 99.

111. Jurisdictional Immunities, *supra* note 39, at ¶¶ 18–19 (Keith, J. sep. op.).

claims can empower States to smooth the path to peace with a comprehensive settlement. The diffusion of control across individual claimants would fragment that capability, narrowing the space for productive trust-building. Third, the harms of war are such that the animating reparative goal of wiping out the consequences of illegal conduct is utopian. Under such conditions, the fragmentation of rights claims risks inequity and chaos, privileging those with resource and procedural advantages. A centralized authority would be more capable of balancing competing equities.

In response, it is first worth clarifying a point on costs. Clearly, the scale of the *transaction* costs introduced by a particular approach to reparation ought to inform its viability. The fragmentation of claims is likely to exacerbate those costs. However, the scale of the *substantive* reparative cost cannot plausibly be invoked as a reason to eschew reparation, or to endow States with the authority mutually to do so. In the absence of reparation, that substantive cost is not eliminated; it is borne by the victims. The question of reparation is whether that *existing* cost is to be transferred to those who illegally imposed it.[112]

That aside, arguments in favor of a centralized process have merit. However, they imply the State's multifaceted value as the primary *procedural* vessel through which to pursue reparation, not as the reparative rights-holder. Two final points are worth emphasizing on that.

First, even within IHL, Common Article 51/52/131/148 of Geneva Conventions I–IV prohibits States from absolving themselves, *or one another* from reparative obligations vis-à-vis grave breaches.[113] There is no exception permitting adversaries to grant such absolution. Indeed, the provision was intended to limit the capacity of a victor to extract waivers from the vanquished (albeit with primary focus on criminal amnesty).[114]

Second, the individual human right to reparation does not preclude centralized negotiation and distribution. Rather, it requires such processes to be subject to human rights scrutiny. As such, there would need to be legitimate reasons for the rights limitation—peace would have a robust claim to this status[115]—and any agreed concessions would need to be (1) necessary and proportionate to realizing those legitimate aims, and (2) compatible with preserving the essence of the right.[116] Recognizing individuals as the reparative rights-holders would mean

112. *See Chorzów*, *supra* note 2, at 47; Final Award, *supra* note 6; DRC v. Ugan., Reparations, *supra* note 6.

113. GC I-IV, *supra* note 12.

114. ICRC Commentary (Henckaerts et al. eds.), *supra* note 104, at ¶ 3022.

115. Jenna Sapiano, *Peace Settlements and Human Rights*, *in* International Law and Peace Settlements 655 (Marc Weller, Mark Retter, & Andrea Varga eds., 2021). *See also* VCLT, *supra* note 101, at pmbl; Eri. v. Eth., Final Award, *supra* note 6, at ¶ 315.

116. Suichi Furuya, *The Right to Reparation for Victims of Armed Conflicts*, *in* Reparation for Victims of Armed Conflict 16, 70–71 (Cristián Correa, Shuichi Furuya, & Clara Sandoval

recognizing their rights claims on their State to meet those standards when it acts on their behalf.[117] This would not privilege absolutist reparative demands. Per the ECtHR:

> [I]t is not [the Court's] role under Article 41 to function akin to a domestic tort mechanism court in apportioning fault and compensatory damages between civil parties. Its guiding principle is equity, which above all involves flexibility and an objective consideration of what is just, fair and reasonable in all the circumstances of the case, including not only the position of the applicant but the overall context in which the breach occurred.[118]

Human rights jurisprudence on the right to reparation in contexts of mass violation and societal transition has identified mechanisms by which to reduce transaction costs, simplify proceedings, adjust burdens of proof, and tailor overall reparative burdens to context.[119] These systems could be applied equally by a State distributing a collective award to its own people or by the responsible State granting direct claims to individuals. Here, again, a strong case can be made that human rights law is better tailored to balancing the equities than is IHL.

Of course, the relevance of human rights law depends not only on its interpretive relationship with IHL but also on its territorial reach. In many contexts, this should not have a significant impact on the preceding analysis. As Marko Milanovic has argued persuasively, the cause-effect approach to the extraterritorial application of negative human rights obligations (favored by many human rights authorities) is ultimately the only normatively sustainable approach.[120] Some jurisdictions, however, have relied on State control (whether over foreign territory, as in an occupation, or individuals, as in contexts of detention) as the condition predicate to extraterritorial application. Within this category, the ECtHR has long stood out for its tortuous jurisprudential trajectory.

eds., 2020); Clara Sandoval, *International Human Rights Adjudication, Subsidiarity, and Reparation for Victims of Armed Conflict*, *in id.* at 179.

117. Sassòli, *supra* note 31, at 97; Hill-Cawthorne, *supra* note 42, at 1193–94; Jurisdictional Immunities of the State (Ger. v. It.) Counter-Memorial of Italy, 2009 I.C.J. Rep. 143, ¶¶ 5.47–5.52 (Dec. 22); Jurisdictional Immunities, *supra* note 39, ¶ 71 (Cançado Trindade J., dissenting). *But see Shimoda*, *supra* note 24, at 640. On human rights and adversary negotiation, *see* Ilaşcu v. Moldova and Russia, 2004-VII Eur. Ct. H.R. 179, ¶¶ 336–52, 386–94, 488–94. *But see Greek Citizens v. Germany*, *supra* note 32, at 1037.

118. *Al-Jedda*, *supra* note 99, at ¶ 114.

119. Cristián Correa, *Operationalising the Right of Victims of War to Reparation*, *in* Correa, Furuya & Sandoval, *supra* note 116, at 126, § III(A); Furuya, *supra* note 116, at 46; Salmón & Pérez-León-Acevedo, *supra* note 15, pt. II. *Cf.* International Law Commission, Draft articles on Prevention and Punishment of Crimes Against Humanity, art. 12(3), U.N. Doc. A/74/10 (2019).

120. Milanovic, *supra* note 97.

Two recent decisions are notable both for reversing what had seemed to be halting progress toward cause-effect jurisdiction and for conflating territorial jurisdiction and IHL/IHRL interaction. In *Georgia v. Russia (II)*, the Court reasoned that the "context of chaos" associated with "armed confrontation and fighting between enemy military forces" precluded the extraterritorial application of human rights obligations to Russia's actions in Georgia during the period of fighting in 2008.[121] Although framing the issue in terms of territorial jurisdiction, the Court invoked IHL's applicability to allay concerns of a legal vacuum.[122] Puzzlingly, given the applicability of war crimes law, the Court also reasoned that such contexts are too complex for judicial review.[123] In *Shavlokhova v. Georgia*, the Court held that Georgia lacked human rights obligations on its *own* territory when the chaos of armed conflict precluded its normal exercise of jurisdiction.[124]

Arguably, given the reference to IHL, these cases revived atrophied aspects of the framework preclusion approach to IHL/IHRL interaction.[125] However, their precedential durability is questionable. They have been roundly criticized and aspects of the *ratio decidendi* have already been walked back in subsequent cases.[126] Litigation relating to the Russia-Ukraine conflict will test the Court's commitment to this approach.[127]

4. PROCEDURAL RIGHTS

Notwithstanding individuals' substantive right to reparation for harm arising from IHL violations, key components of existing doctrine and practice might be

121. Georgia v. Russia (II), App. No. 38263/08, ¶¶ 126, 137 (2021) (ECtHR), https://hudoc.echr.coe.int/fre?i=001-207757.

122. *Id.* at ¶ 141.

123. *Id.* at ¶¶ 140–41, 143.

124. Shavlokhova v. Georgia, App. No. 45431/09, ¶¶ 27–35 (2021) (ECtHR), https://hudoc.echr.coe.int/eng?i=002-13446.

125. *See* Dennis, Modirzadeh, General Comment 36, *supra* notes 96–97, respectively, and text.

126. *See, e.g.*, Marko Milanovic, *Georgia v. Russia No. 2*, EJIL: Talk! (Jan. 25, 2021), https://www.ejiltalk.org/georgia-v-russia-no-2-the-european-courts-resurrection-of-bankovic-in-the-contexts-of-chaos/; Anastasiia Moiseieva, *The ECtHR in Georgia v. Russia—A Farewell to Arms?*, EJIL: Talk! (Feb. 24, 2021), https://www.ejiltalk.org/the-ecthr-in-georgia-v-russia-a-farewell-to-arms-the-effects-of-the-courts-judgment-on-the-conflict-in-eastern-ukraine/; Kanstantsin Dzehtsiar, *Georgia v. Russia (II)*, 115 American Journal of International Law 288 (2021).

127. Ukraine and the Netherlands v. Russia, App. Nos. 8019/16, 43800/14, 28525/20 (2022) (ECtHR), https://hudoc.echr.coe.int/fre?i=001-222889; Marko Milanovic, *The European Court's Admissibility Decision in Ukraine and the Netherlands v Russia—Part II*, EJIL: Talk! (Jan. 26, 2023), https://www.ejiltalk.org/the-european-courts-admissibility-decision-in-ukraine-and-the-netherlands-v-russia-the-good-the-bad-and-the-ugly-part-ii/.

invoked to deny their right to the procedural capacity to bring a claim against the reparative duty-bearer.

First, whereas the Geneva Conventions and AP I provide the basis for "present-in" universal criminal jurisdiction over grave breaches, no equivalent basis is provided for civil jurisdiction of any kind, whether domestic or international.[128] States often exclude their armed forces' acts of war from domestic tort litigation.[129] Moreover, in contrast to official immunity from criminal prosecution, the sovereign immunity of States from suit in foreign domestic courts lacks a recognized *jus cogens* or international crime exception.[130]

Second, States' long-standing control over negotiating, waiving, or transferring and distributing reparations contradicts the notion that individuals have the right to a process through which to vindicate their substantive reparative claim. Indeed, key jurisprudence, particularly in Germany and Japan, has rejected direct individual standing under international law.[131]

However, contrary developments provide at least the foundations for an individual procedural right, albeit one that can be adjusted for the exigencies of conflict and its aftermath.[132] In IACs, such adjustments may entail limiting reparative standing to States as the vessels for aggregate claims. Nonetheless, recognizing the underlying individual right would structure the framework within which such adjustments must be justified. It would also bolster arguments for a standing international individual complaints body for IHL harms.[133] Consider the following five points in support of an individual procedural right.

First, twenty years ago, in the most comprehensive study of customary IHL to date, Jean-Marie Henckaerts and Louise Doswald-Beck observed "an increasing trend" toward "enabling" individual victims of IHL violations "to seek reparation directly from the responsible State."[134] Reparative practice and jurisprudence in the context of NIACs and the transitions from them remains supportive of

128. GC I, *supra* note 12, art. 49; GC II, *supra* note 12, art. 50; GC III, *supra* note 12, art. 129; AP I, *supra* note 86, art. 85.

129. *See, e.g.*, 28 U.S. Code § 2680 (2006); Civil Wrongs (Liability of the State) Law, No. 5712-1952 art. 5 (Isr.); Crown Proceeding Act 1947, c. 44, § 10 (UK). *But see* Marieke de Hoon, *Dutch Court, Applying IHL, Delivers Civil Judgment for Victims of 2007 Afghanistan Attack*, Just Security (Feb. 27, 2023), https://www.justsecurity.org/85223/dutch-court-applying-ihl-delivers-civil-judgment-for-victims-of-2007-afghanistan-attack/.

130. Jurisdictional Immunities, *supra* note 39, at ¶¶ 81–97; Al-Adsani v. U.K., App. No. 35763/97, ¶¶ 52–67 (2001) (ECtHR), https://hudoc.echr.coe.int/fre?i=001-59885.

131. *See X. et al. v. Japan*, *X. v. Y.*, *Shimoda*, *Greek Citizens v. Germany*, *supra* note 33.

132. *See infra* notes 152–54.

133. Jann K. Kleffner & Lisbeth Zegveld, *Establishing an Individual Complaints Procedure for Violations of International Humanitarian Law*, 3 Yearbook of International Humanitarian Law 384 (2000).

134. 1 Jean-Marie Henckaerts & Louise Doswald-Beck, I Customary International Humanitarian Law 541 (2005). More equivocally, *see* Gillard, *supra* note 23, at 536, 549.

that assessment.[135] Meanwhile, the practice establishing and sustaining the UN Compensation Commission in the aftermath of Iraq's 1990 invasion of Kuwait and the multilateral nature, legal rootedness, and rights-based framing of the registers for individual damage relating in part to IHL violations in Palestine and Ukraine reflect a parallel right in IACs.[136] In the latter context, States are mobilizing toward creating a compensation commission despite lacking Russian consent or Security Council authorization.[137] Sovereign immunity, not the individualization of reparation channels, has been the crux of debates regarding whether Russian assets could be seized to fund such reparations.[138]

Second, the Greek and Italian cases (as well as Dutch cases)[139] that predated the ICJ's *Jurisdictional Immunities* case contradict the Japanese and German case law rejecting individual claims. Rather than resolving that contradiction in State practice, the ICJ relied on sovereign immunity to find in Germany's favor.[140] Since a forum State's duty to uphold sovereign immunity obtains even when it blocks a valid individual right to access justice, the Court's decision left open whether there is an individual procedural right.[141] Recent cases in South Korea and the Netherlands affirm such a right.[142]

Third, war crimes victims have procedural rights in ICC cases.[143] To be sure, their claims against convicted individuals are distinct from their rights vis-à-vis

135. Correa, *supra* note 119, at 126, § III(A); Mapiripán Massacre v. Colombia, Inter-Amer. Ct. H.R., No. 134 (ser. C) ¶ 335.12–335.17 (2005); Merchants v. Colombia, Inter-Amer. Ct. H.R. No. 109 (ser. C) ¶¶ 283–84 (2005); *Jaloud v. Netherlands*, *supra* note 97, at ¶¶ 139–53; *Al-Jedda*, *supra* note 99, at ¶¶ 112–18 (2011); Bhandari et al. v. Prime Minister et al., Nepal Supreme Court, Division Bench, Writ. 0863 (2009), *reprinted in* National Judicial Academy Law Journal 261, 270 (2010).

136. Establishment of U.N. Register, *supra* note 89, pmbl & ¶ 3; Furtherance of remedy and reparation, *supra* note 90, pmbl. & ¶ 2; CM/Res(2023)3, *supra* note 91, pmbl, arts. 1.1, 2.3, 3.4. *See also* Пошкоджене маЙно [Damaged Property], Дія [Diia (Ukrainian e-governance app)], https://diia.gov.ua/services/poshkodzhene-majno.

137. CM/Res (2023) 3, *supra* note 91, art. 2.5.

138. Oona A. Hathaway, Maggie Mills, & Thomas M. Poston, *War Reparations*, 76 Stanford Law Review pts. II–III (2024).

139. Gerechtshof Amsterdan [Amsterdam Court of Appeal] July 6, 2000 (Dedovic et al. v. W. Kok et al.), *reprinted in* 35 Netherlands Yearbook of International Law 508, 521–22 (2004); Hoge Raad [Netherlands Supreme Court] Nov. 29, 2002 (Danikovic et al. v. Netherlands), *reprinted in* 35 Netherlands Yearbook of International Law 522 (2004).

140. Jurisdictional Immunities, *supra* note 39, at ¶ 108.

141. *Id.* at ¶ 94; *Al-Adsani*, *supra* note 130, at ¶¶ 52–67.

142. Jingwen Liu, *South Korea Appellate Court Orders Japan to Compensate Former Victims of Japanese Occupation Sexual Slavery*, Jurist (Nov. 24, 2023); van de Put, *supra* note 22; de Hoon, *supra* note 129.

143. Rome Statute, *supra* note 92, arts. 68, 75; Claude Jorda & Jerome de Hemptinne, *The Status and Role of the Victim*, *in* The Rome Statute of the International Criminal Court 1387

States, and, at the ICC, even the former rights depend on the Prosecutor initiating the relevant case. Nonetheless, States may not waive or block individuals' procedural rights to participate and to claim reparation at the Court. This has customary law significance. The legality of the Rome Statute's retroactive application to the nationals of non-parties acting on non-party territory, whether pursuant to an Article 12(3) declaration or a Security Council referral under Article 13(b), depends on the customary law status of the underlying crimes included in the treaty.[144] As such, those and other features of the Statute that can be applied retroactively on this basis (such as the reparation framework) manifest an important component of the practice and *opinio juris* of the 124 States Parties.[145] This matches many of those States' understanding.[146]

Fourth, underpinning these features of State practice, the *opinio juris* articulated in the UN Basic Principles specifies not only that there is an individual right to reparation but also that victims have a right to the procedural information and access necessary to vindicate it.[147] The ILA has similarly identified State obligations to enable individual access to reparation[148] and specified victims' "right to access an effective mechanism to claim reparation" for IHL violations, including "adequate rules for collecting, registering and processing claims."[149]

Fifth, as with the substantive reparative right, the applicability of IHRL offers a robust basis for individuals' right to access systems of reparative justice for IHL violations.[150] Specifically, human rights conventions often *require* individual

(Antonio Cassese, Paola Gaeta, & John R.W.D. Jones eds., 2d ed. 2002); David Donat Cattin, *Article 68*, *in* Rome Statute of the International Criminal Court 2001 (Kai Ambos ed., 4th ed. 2022); David Donat Cattin, *Article 75*, in *id.* at 2240.

144. The use of the term "retroactive" here refers to the capacity of an Article 12(3) declaration or an Article 13(b) referral to authorize the ICC to exercise jurisdiction over cases involving conduct that occurred prior to the Rome Statute's jurisdictional applicability to the impugned conduct (albeit not prior to the general entry into force of the Statute in 2002). Talita de Souza Dias, *The Retroactive Application of the Rome Statute in Cases of Security Council Referrals and Ad Hoc Declarations*, 16 Journal of International Criminal Justice 65 (2018).

145. Dannenbaum, *supra* note 92, at 701–10.

146. Leila Nadya Sadat, *Custom, Codification and Some Thoughts About the Relationship Between the Two*, 49 DePaul Law Review 909, 919–20 (2000); Prosecutor v. Abd-Al-Rahman, Case No. ICC-02/05-01/20 OA8, Judgment on the Appeal of Mr. Abd-Al-Rahman against the Pre-Trial Chamber II's "Decision on the Defence 'Exception d'incompétence' (ICC-02/05-01/20-302)" ¶ 89 (Nov. 1, 2021).

147. Basic Principles, *supra* note 79, arts. 11(a), 11(c).

148. International Law Association, Resolution 2/2010, arts. 11(2), 13 (Aug. 2010).

149. ILA, Resolution 1/2014, principles 1, 6 (Apr. 2014).

150. Yoram Dinstein, The Conduct of Hostilities under the Law of International Armed Conflict 40 (2022). *See also supra* note 135.

access to justice at the domestic level (even while providing for it only on an opt-in basis if the State consents at the international level).[151]

Affirming an individual procedural right on these grounds does not preclude centralizing reparation negotiations and claims through a State representing those harmed by IHL violations.[152] Rather, the implication is that such processes must be evaluated through the lens of victims' procedural and substantive reparative rights, in accordance with the contextual flexibility of human rights law.[153]

Existing jurisprudence is instructive on how to accommodate the logistical and evidentiary difficulties associated with assessing reparation claims after war while respecting these rights. Adjustments may include: joining claims, providing stripped-down administrative processing, lowering the evidentiary threshold for individual claim eligibility (as distinct from establishing a violation), reducing awards together with burdens of proof to reflect uncertainty regarding eligibility, applying presumptions regarding issues on which noncooperative States have unique access to information, and adjusting reparation awards to account for economic conditions and related human rights implications in the responsible State.[154] It is also worth emphasizing that precisely these contexts can be the focus of (more evidentiarily demanding) criminal investigation and prosecution. Additionally, feasibility must be considered in light of developments in the practice and technology of open-source investigation.

5. BEYOND IHL REPARATION

Notwithstanding their importance, reparation awards are inevitably inadequate. Most of the harm inflicted in war is irreparable and the practicalities of compensation in its aftermath are fraught with difficulty. There is no real prospect of restoring victims to their situation ex ante.[155] Moreover, even assuming a perfectly

151. *See supra* notes 17–19.

152. Jurisdictional Immunities, *supra* note 39, at ¶¶ 16–20 (Yusuf J., dissenting).

153. Compare the analysis of the relationship between immunities and the right to access justice, *supra* note 141. On proportionality in human and constitutional rights law, *see, e.g.*, Proportionality and the Rule of Law (Grant Huscroft, Bradley W. Miller, & Grégoire Webber eds., 2014); Robert Alexy, A Theory of Constitutional Rights (2002). On flexibility, *see* Al-Jedda v. UK, App. No. 27021/08 Eur. Ct. H.R. ¶ 114 (2011).

154. *See supra* note 119; Afro-Descendant Communities Displaced from the Cacarica River Basin (Operation Genesis) v. Colombia, IACtHR (ser. C) No. 270 ¶ 470 (Nov. 20, 2013); Redressing Injustices Through Mass Claims Processes (Permanent Court of Arbitration ed., 2006); Final Award, *supra* note 6, at ¶¶ 10–11, 19–22, 38, 313; Armed Activities, Reparations, *supra* note 6, at ¶¶ 107–08, 114, 120, 124–26, 157–62, 166, 179, 181, 193, 206, 225, 258, 407; de Hoon, *supra* note 129; Velásquez Rodríguez case, IACtHR (ser. C) No. 4, ¶ 135 (July 29, 1988); Godínez Cruz case, IACtHR (ser. C) No. 5 ¶ 141 (Jan. 20, 1989).

155. *Cf. Chorzów*, *supra* note 2, at 47; Eri. v. Eth., *supra* note 6; DRC v. Ugan., *supra* note 6.

functioning reparative system, gaps would remain regarding harms inflicted in compliance with IHL. Space precludes addressing these gaps in detail here. However, three points are worthy of brief note.

First, the reasoning of both the Human Rights Committee and the ICJ indicate growing recognition that, in an aggressive war, even IHL-compliant killing violates the right to life.[156] Logically, this can be extended to other rights.[157] Full implementation of this interpretation would close one of the most glaring gaps in war reparations.[158]

Second, it has long been argued that civilians killed or maimed in IHL-proportionate collateral damage are no less worthy of compensation than those in collateral damage that was excessive to the anticipated military advantage.[159] This has led some to argue for a system of war torts that would require States to internalize the costs of their military actions, legal or not.[160] Such proposals demand consideration.

Third, given the procedural, evidentiary, and financial challenges associated with pursuing IHL reparation, ex gratia payments offer what might appear to be an efficient, simplified, timely, and potentially wide-ranging alternative. Thus far, ex gratia programs have fallen far short of that potential. Bureaucratic obstacles, transparency issues, and limited implementation undermine the efficiency and simplicity that ought to be their key advantages.[161] Moreover, they are often oriented toward objectives orthogonal to repair, such as obtaining and maintaining friendly, or at least functional, relations with local populations in counterinsurgency operations.[162] Finally, given that they lack any expression of fault, ex gratia offers that are contingent on reparation waivers sacrifice accountability in the

156. General Comment 36, *supra* note 97, at ¶ 70; Armed Activities, Reparations, *supra* note 6, at ¶ 145.

157. Armed Activities, Reparations, *supra* note 6, at ¶ 173, at 214.

158. Tom Dannenbaum, The Crime of Aggression, Humanity, and the Soldier (2018).

159. W. Michael Reisman, *The Lessons of Qana*, 22 Yale Journal of International Law 381, 398 (1997); Gillard, *supra* note 23, at 551; Paul, *supra* note 20, at 100–01, 106–15.

160. Haim Abraham, *Tort Liability for Belligerent Wrongs*, 38 Oxford Journal of Legal Studies 808 (2019); Rebecca Crootof, *War Torts*, 97 New York University Law Review 1063 (2022).

161. Naples-Mitchell, *supra* note 21; Annie Shiel, *DoD's New Ex Gratia Policy*, Just Security (July 10, 2020), https://www.justsecurity.org/71332/dods-new-ex-gratia-policy-whats-right-whats-wrong-and-whats-next/; Daphne Eviatar, *Toward a Consistent and Coherent Ex Gratia Policy for Civilian Casualties*, Just Security (July 10, 2020), https://www.justsecurity.org/71248/toward-a-consistent-and-coherent-ex-gratia-policy-for-civilian-casualties/; Mwatana & Lowenstein, *supra* note 22, at 10–15, 83–85, 92–96.

162. 10 U.S.C. § 2734(a) (2012); U.S. CHMR-AP, *supra* note 21; 4 The Handbook of International Humanitarian Law 735 (Dieter Fleck ed., 2021).

service of facilitating compensation, thus failing to deliver on a key reparative value.[163]

Nonetheless, the enduring challenge of pursuing reparation, the inevitable gaps in IHL protection, and the low probability of a war torts regime all militate in favor of reforming rather than discarding ex gratia frameworks.[164] The starting point must be to root them not in strategic or political goals but in the worth of all civilians harmed in war and in the importance of taking responsibility for agency in the infliction of such harm.

6. CONCLUSION

Reparation awards are costly, logistically challenging, and potentially disruptive to peace. Nonetheless, they are a legal imperative and a right. Without them, the costs of repair are not eliminated; they are borne by the victims. To recognize their right to repair is not to assert the unchecked prevalence of that right over the demands of peace or the need to manage transaction costs amidst scarcity. It is, however, to hold that the pursuit of such objectives must be justified according to the underlying right. The legitimacy of States' lawful acts of war hinges in part on their willingness to accept responsibility for their violations, not only vis-à-vis one another but also with respect to the human beings that bear the burden of those wrongs.

163. And yet sometimes non-fault is used to deny claims. *See, e.g.*, Andrea Prascow, *Civilian Casualties*, Just Security (Jan. 6, 2020), https://www.justsecurity.org/67872/civilian-casualties-a-case-for-u-s-condolence-payments-in-syria/.

164. Annie Shiel, *How the FY23 NDAA Can Strengthen U.S. Efforts to Prevent and Respond to Civilian Harm* (Part I), Just Security (Aug. 25, 2022), https://www.justsecurity.org/82829/how-the-fy23-ndaa-can-strengthen-u-s-efforts-to-prevent-and-respond-to-civilian-harm-part-i/; Shiel & Motaparthy, *supra* note 21; Eviatar, *supra* note 161.

INDEX

For the benefit of digital users, indexed terms that span two pages (e.g., 52–53) may, on occasion, appear on only one of those pages.